Guides to Sources for British History
based on the National Register of Archives

9

Records of
BRITISH BUSINESS
AND INDUSTRY
1760-1914
Metal Processing and
Engineering

London   HMSO

© Crown copyright 1994
Applications for reproduction should be made to HMSO
First published 1994

British Library Cataloguing in Publication Data

A CIP catalogue record for this book is available from the British Library

ISBN 0 11 440232 9

PPR

HMSO publications are available from:

HMSO Publications Centre
(Mail, fax and telephone orders only)
PO Box 276, London, SW8 5DT
Telephone orders 071-873 9090
General enquiries 071-873 0011
(queuing system in operation for both numbers)
Fax orders 071-873 8200

HMSO Bookshops
49 High Holborn, London, WC1V 6HB
(counter service only)
071-873 0011 Fax 071-831 1326
258 Broad Street, Birmingham, B1 2HE
021-643 3740 Fax 021-643 6510
33 Wine Street, Bristol, BS1 2BQ
0272 264306 Fax 0272 294515
9–21 Princess Street, Manchester, M60 8AS
061-834 7201 Fax 061-833 0634
16 Arthur Street, Belfast, BT1 4GD
0232 238451 Fax 0232 235401
71 Lothian Road, Edinburgh, EH3 9AZ
031-228 4181 Fax 031-229 2734

HMSO's Accredited Agents
(see Yellow Pages)

and through good booksellers

Preface

This volume is the second to deal with business records in the series of *Guides to sources for British history based on the National Register of Archives*. A large amount of information concerning the key industrial sectors of metal processing and engineering was already present in the Register when research for the present guide began. Survey work, notably among the metalworking firms of Birmingham and the Black Country, at British Steel's records centres and in the field of electrical engineering, has considerably enriched the Register through the incorporation of many new reports on archival collections and the wealth of new entries added to its Business Index.

The Commission is grateful to all those owners and custodians of records who have contributed to the present enterprise by generously responding to requests for information or access. It acknowledges the assistance received from previous surveys, especially those mentioned in the editorial note, and from Mrs BMD Smith, formerly of Birmingham University, who first surveyed many of the collections of business records in the Birmingham area during 1963-4. Unfortunately, much of the material uncovered by earlier researchers has subsequently disappeared along with many of the firms which created it. The Commission hopes that those businesses which no longer have any need to retain their historical records for current or statutory purposes, or any interest in doing so, will continue to avail themselves of the facilities offered by the many local and specialist repositories which care for such records. Advice on these matters can always be sought from the Business Archives Council (The Clove Building, 4 Maguire Street, London SE1 2NQ) or from the Commission itself.

The investigatory work and the compilation of the guide were undertaken by Dr C Evans, Dr DA Leitch, Mr LA Ritchie (who compiled the shipbuilding entries) and Dr SG Roberts under the direction of Dr NW James.

CJ KITCHING
Secretary
15 April 1994

Quality House, Quality Court,
Chancery Lane, London WC2A 1HP

Contents

Introduction

The National Register of Archives, founded in 1945, soon came to include information about the existence, nature and availability for research of business records. In the last few years, the computerisation of the NRA's indexes has enabled scholars who have visited the Commission's offices to carry out searches according to a combination of chronological, sectoral and geographical criteria to identify the records of particular industries, or of firms in one region, or within specified dates if desired. This is in addition to searches for the records of individual, named, businesses. The present guide offers something more—a synopsis of the significant surviving records of two major industrial sectors, which systematically describes the different classes of records for each firm wherever such information is available. By drawing attention to similar material created by a number of different firms, it may encourage comparative studies of business and commercial behaviour.

The division in the present compilation between the processing of the metals and their subsequent use in a wide range of engineering is helpful for practical as well as for expository reasons, because the interests of those who use these records usually lie heavily in one section or in the other. The metal processors themselves fall into distinct groups determined by the metal they worked, with relatively little connection between each other. Workers in precious metals have had an influential position both in the economy and in society in general, but they operated on a small scale. Until the late eighteenth century the non-ferrous metals were of greater relative importance than subsequently and provide some of the most comprehensive collections listed, but by the beginning of the period covered by this survey the processing of the ferrous metals began the marked expansion which gave rise to a popular but erroneous view that they were the only metals with significant industrial uses. Their transformation was based on several technical innovations, ranging from the use of coke instead of charcoal, which emancipated the iron industry from the constraints of inadequate supplies of fuel, to those of the second half of the nineteenth century, from the Bessemer converter to the open-hearth furnace and the basic process, which led to the production of cheap steel and so removed the dependence of many industrial and engineering users on malleable or wrought iron made by the increasingly costly labour-intensive process of puddling.

Some of the major iron and steel firms which grew out of the technical changes were important, not only because of their individual size but because their semi-finished products, especially of cheap steel, encouraged the expansion of an enormously diversified range of mechanical engineering. The records show how and why they adopted new technologies, whether by moving from older processes or by being set up in the first place specifically to exploit the new. In this way the records cast a more general light on the vexed questions of the nature of technical change and its consequences. It has been common in recent years for many historians to suggest that the technical changes of the last two to three hundred years, especially, but not exclusively, those associated with the conventional industrial revolution, have been much less dramatic and radical in their impact then was formerly believed. A glance at the present guide alone is sufficient to cast doubt on some of the more extreme of the revised interpretations for it is easy to see how the firms listed can be linked to some significant technical change. Detailed examination of the evidence they have left will show if new technology was as attractive as it seems in retrospect to an age which sees it as the solution to so many problems, or if the old methods persisted because they were still profitable and so remained economically attractive, with the result that the comparative economic advantage of the new methods took time to become apparent.

Whatever the opportunities, taken or missed, a new industrial order was well established by 1914 and one central to British economic success in the later nineteenth century. By 1914 the older metal industries were stagnating. From the 1880s the copper mined in the United Kingdom was of no significance. In 1913 the output of metallic lead was only a shade over a quarter of what it had been in 1870. The output of white tin in 1913, though higher than it had been for twenty years, was still only half of what it had been at its peak in 1878. By contrast, pig iron production of about 10.25 million tons in 1913 was a record as was the 7.66 million tons of steel ingots and castings. Statistics of engineering output are less clear because of its diversity but one example, which is representative of the success of many others based on the use of the growing supplies of steel, was shipbuilding which launched a record of almost one million tons in 1913.

By 1914 the processing of non-ferrous metals had passed its zenith; the iron and steel industries had reached theirs; but developments in some aspects of scientific and electrical engineering were only beginning. Any peaks in their performance lay in the future. The early achievements of scientific engineering are evident in a large number of watch and clock makers, locksmiths and other specialists, as well as the makers of precision and optical instruments, many quite small, though including some of major international importance in their fields, among them Milners', the safemakers, and Barr and Stroud, the precision engineers. By then electrical engineering was making its mark as the foundations of great firms of the future, such as Marconi and Ferranti, were being laid.

The industrial achievements are usually associated with some of the visually most dramatic products of British industry at any time. It was the age of the great ships, of the passenger liners and dreadnoughts, of the giant steam locomotives, and of such constructional wonders as the Forth bridge. The records of their builders are well represented. Among them are those of Sir William Arrol and Company, the North British Locomotive Company, and an impressive range of shipbuilders. The guide also provides a salutary warning that preoccupation with the striking achievements of such firms should never detract from proper recognition of the plethora of other commodities made by the engineers, some well-known, others less so. Though the established non-ferrous industries were losing their position in the economy, they continued to make their special contributions, and their records carry on the story to recent times. Even firms whose output included famous products turned their hand to making less well-known goods. The shipyards which launched the passenger liners also built smaller vessels which plied the waterways of the world and the great steam locomotives were accompanied by the many smaller engines which gave sterling service for decades in the outposts of the empire and far-flung trading stations. A seemingly endless range of engineering products can be examined in the records of the firms surveyed, some of them very unexpected, from Savages' who manufactured fairground equipment at King's Lynn to Henry Maxwell, who made spurs in London in the 1820s. Sometimes the smaller firms have the best, or at least the more manageable collections, such as the Bowling Iron Company of Bradford, or some of the tin mining and smelting concerns, particularly Thomas Bolitho and Sons of Penzance whose records go back to 1703. These smaller and less well-known firms should not be ignored though inevitably most use will be made of such enormous archives as those of Boulton and Watt. Perhaps it would have pleased Adam Smith that some of the records of early industrial success are those of John English and Company, needle, pin and fish hook manufacturers of Feckenham in Worcestershire.

II

The bulk of the records listed are of more recent origin. Though 1914 has been chosen as the terminal date, it has been applied with discretion. Many series of records extend beyond it. Of course, firms which did not come into being before 1914, or whose pre-1914 records do not survive, are excluded, with the result that coverage of the nascent electrical engineering group is necessarily limited. Listing business records of more recent years gives rise to a practical difficulty. They contain much that will not be worthy of permanent preservation once its immediate commercial relevance has passed, or that would not have been open for consultation because of its confidentiality. To have listed them would have led to the inclusion of material which still calls for some difficult decisions on what should be, and is going to be, preserved.

Modern material survives in such bulk partly for the simple reason that there has been less time for it to be destroyed or lost, but also because commercial records are retained and preserved for reasons very different from those which determine the fate of family or estate records. Two in particular help explain the nature of many of those in the present survey. The first is the very simple one that the emergence and growth of many of the firms listed, especially the larger ones, followed the technological changes which have been mentioned. Bolckow Vaughan of Middlesbrough and Colvilles of Motherwell are but two examples of major concerns which were built on the success of modern steelmaking processes. It is not an exaggeration to hold that without these innovations which led to the availability of cheap steel a large part of the records in the volume would never have appeared. The second reason is less straightforward but lies behind the survival of many of them. Formal records, especially those which have some precise legal significance, and above all those which were compiled to meet statutory requirements, have usually to be held for a period of years at least, and that can lead to their permanent preservation, unless lack of space or some other extraneous cause decrees otherwise. They are put aside and are forgotten. Many other records, which may in practice be more pertinent to an understanding of the success or otherwise of a firm, are less likely to survive once their immediate commercial use has passed, and such relevance is often of quite short duration. They are less likely to be put aside and forgotten. The consequences of this bias come out in the guide. Until the Companies Acts of the second half of the nineteenth century, and especially the moves to incorporation at its end, few firms were other than private partnerships and so were not subject to comprehensive legal requirements. Many of the firms listed assumed their present form only under the Companies Acts, even if some—or parts of them—had existed earlier, and the difference is evident in their surviving records. Not many collections are as good before and after incorporation as that of the Kirkstall Forge Limited. Some of the more formal records provide information which may be obtained from other sources, especially from the records of the Registrar of Joint-Stock Companies, and so may prove less rewarding than less comprehensive collections, even some of those with only scrappy and apparently ephemeral material. Good solid runs of records are not the only ones which yield fruit to those who search diligently.

If survival of records is often a matter of chance through the passage of years, a more specific hazard of recent times, growing from the 1930s, has been the restructuring of British industry. Restructuring has not necessarily led to the destruction of records, but it has led to the relocation and sometimes to the merging of collections. Such changes can give rise to confusion in attempts to trace collections of some of the firms in a merger. Major examples of this problem are in the merger of electrical engineering companies in GEC and of the various firms which, after many changes, became part of British Steel plc. The guide makes the unravelling of such amalgamations much easier and ensures that absorbed firms are not lost. Outright liquidation, whether voluntary or forced, has been a greater threat as it can easily lead to the wholesale destruction of valuable collections. In recent years this would have been the fate of many records but for the timely intervention of alert archivists, often in local record offices. The combination of amalgamations and liquidations can lead to records appearing in unexpected locations or spread over several. Those of Alex Chaplin, crane manufacturer in Glasgow, are in Leicestershire Record Office and those of Nasmyth, Wilson and Company are in five repositories. The volume reveals such peculiarities which might easily be missed.

The sheer bulk of the records uncovered by this and the Commission's previous survey of the textile and leather industries is surprising, even daunting for those who would use them. Like official records, many of the collections listed will grow as the firms which produced them are still in business, though the bulk may be reduced by modern methods of storage. All cannot be retained, and the danger is that among so much the material which should be preserved is as likely to be jettisoned as the material which should go. If permanent retention is to be advanced as a reasonable policy, with proper cataloguing and storage to make the records fully available, some principles of selection must first be applied. The compilation of this survey, covering some major extant firms, shows the need for both archivists and historians to direct attention to such principles of selection, apart from the subsequent question of where, and by whom, the selected material is to be stored. Such selection is not a field where the commercial concerns which produced the records have any special skill. Even where they have a full system of records management in place, controlled perhaps by a professional archivist, quite properly their main concern is not with meeting the needs of posterity but with those of their customers and so of their own prosperity. However, it is good to see that some firms, a notable example being British Steel, are depositing in various record offices and libraries, those records which have ceased to be of commercial relevance and the continued preservation of which by the firm can only be an expensive activity. Another fruitful course of action, which others might follow, is to deposit records with a professional body such as the Institution of Electrical Engineers.

A notable feature of the policies of many commercial concerns in recent years has been their concern with their place in society. Their records deserve more attention than has often been shown to them for they are a valuable, though neglected part of the national heritage. It may come as a surprise to many firms to learn that their records should be valued in this way. For that reason a firm's contribution to posterity may call for more than simply ensuring that records no longer required are deposited in some record office; rather, care of today's records should be a continuous process, carried out in association with others, to ensure that nothing is lost that the future may value.

III

The immense quantity of business records may call for discrimination in their retention and use; it offers also promising prospects in the development of business history. The subject evolved from the histories of individual firms and many still think that this is the form it takes. The histories were almost invariably those of fairly large and long-established firms. One commendable aspect of the growth of business history has been a move, encouraged by the greater availablity of records, away from what were too often little more than attempts to highlight the virtues of the firms in question to more objective assessments, even though it must be admitted that detailed work on any firm usually encourages the adoption of a sympathetic approach. Even a quick perusal of the guide shows that there are still a number of firms whose individual histories are worth writing and where the records are available to do so. A difficulty in the past was that it was not easy to write the histories of firms which had failed. So often records evaporated as completely as the firm. Largely because of the rescue operations which have been launched to save the records of firms which have gone out of existence, their histories can now be written to offset the achievements of the more obviously successful survivors and so uncover reasons for failure as well as for success. A more balanced assessment of comparative achievements is possible.

It may be suggested, however, that, with some exceptions, the writing of the histories of individual firms is now experiencing diminishing returns. The need is to move from the particular to the general. Even the biographies of businessmen, on which distinguished work has been carried out in recent years, do not lead easily to generalisations on entrepreneurial behaviour. In the past it was difficult to make this transition because of the lack of available or readily located material. The present survey facilitates this move from the studies of individual firms to an examination of some of the main themes which interest business historians. Business records can be used in the work of a wider range of historians than those accustomed to them, and even of non-historians. Those who teach business administration and management spend much time simulating conditions of real life. Many do not realise how much relevant material is often available in the historical records, with the added advantage that the consequences of decisions made in the past are available to compare with any alternative strategy which may be suggested.

It is usually easy to distinguish in the entries in the guide those records which are unique to a particular firm, often the more formal ones such as board minutes, which are essential to the writing of the history of that firm, and those which deal with the same topic, though in different forms, for each business. A large part of the material listed is of this type and can usefully be classified in three main groups.

The first are accounting and financial records. It is not surprising that, since many of the records are modern, this group bulks large in the records of many firms. They may be deployed either to deal with the traditional approach, which aimed at revealing the profitability or otherwise of the firm, or to help analyse more general issues of financial management and control and of cost accountancy. The more fruitful prospects are in the latter because of the need for investigations behind the formal, final accounts which were often returned from limited liability companies and can often be a rather bare statement.

Accounting history has never appealed greatly to historians and few accountants are historically minded. Often insufficient material was available to enable comparative analyses to be made and so it was difficult to ensure that any wider conclusions drawn were not distorted by the domination of material from one firm. The entries in the guide show that this obstacle has been diminished, if not entirely removed, but there is still a warning to be taken to heart by those who seek to use the material. Few historians have any formal training in accounting techniques and even skilled modern accountants find themselves confused when they deal with material compiled in a different age and for different purposes. An investigation of even a small sample of the accounting records listed shows the variety and complexity of procedures adopted and how variable were the methods of dealing with knotty issues such as fixed costs and depreciation, though the variety can be used to uncover the evolution of accounting methods. The attraction of the accounting and financial records is that they provide a degree of precision which is attractive to a quantitatively-minded age, but these records should be used with the utmost care, especially in making comparisons between firms, or over time in one firm, as the methods used vary greatly.

Labour history is the second field where there is a large amount of material which offers the possibility of study beyond the traditional field and approaches of business history. As would be expected, much consists of wage records, but, as with accounting methods, they show the same variety and give rise to difficulties of comparison. Still, with careful selection it is possible to compile information on wage trends and even indices of wages and earnings. Particularly useful is the possibility of using regional wage material, which, when combined with costs of production from financial records, enables comparisons to be made, and so judgements reached, on wage rates and productivity and their effects on inter-regional competition. Material on wages and earnings is only one matter available to labour historians. There is information, though less extensive, on social conditions, such as housing, but little on negotiations over any form of industrial relations, perhaps not surprisingly because such matters were not thought worth recording, or retaining, until more recent years. Otherwise it is often only snippets which remain, though sometimes fascinating ones, such as the 'tommy' shop records of Newton, Chambers and Company for the first half of the nineteenth century. Labour records are yet another source of information which could prove useful to a wider range of historians than might be expected. Wage records enable individuals to be identified and the records of apprentices can prove helpful to the family historian. Those in the extensive collection of Harvey and Company of Hayle in Cornwall Record Office stretch fom 1823 to 1893.

The full potential for a variety of readers of the third voluminous category is only beginning to be realised by archivists and historians. It is the whole range of technical records, the various designs and specifications of all types found in order books and given visual expression in drawings, photographs and slides. These collections are sometimes very extensive as with the 10,000 or so negatives and lantern slides of Mavor and Coulson. Technical records appear in the lists with striking frequency. Some of the early order books, often now in the Science Museum, show an earlier tradition of technical records in precision engineering, which spread enormously and became increasingly visual in the later nineteenth century. The slides and photographs provide a popular record of an age of achievement but they are also essential aids to any serious study of the history of technology. They supplement and clarify the specifications in order books. They also enable a major question of industrial history to be probed more deeply and in parallel with the firm's economic performance. The achievements of the consultant engineer have been praised, and with justification, but the profession has also been criticised for failing to adapt to meet the needs of newer and lighter engineering. The records may show if economic success was sacrificed to technical success.

Each of these three groups of records shows directions in which this volume may direct historical enquiries, but, while they are of interest to specialists in each field, they—indeed all the records—contribute to an overall assessment of the British economy at a critical phase of its history. The achievements of the British economy, and of some regions in particular, reached their peak in the years before 1914, and strikingly so in the industries covered by the guide. In retrospect, it is possible to see that the achievements, and the sense of economic security which they engendered, may have been insecurely based. The records enable this phase of economic history to be examined through the experience of individual firms, many of them the giants of their day, to see in detail how securely based was their individual prosperity and whether it was being challenged, and the challenge met, before 1914. Not only is there material to study the old, established industries; the inclusion of the records of scientific and electrical engineering provides information on these industries in which it is often alleged that Britain was slow in developing, especially when compared with her continental rivals. There is evidence here for an examination of the nature of the Victorian transformation of the British economy to one with a heavy industrial component and also for an examination of the roots of the loss of international competitiveness which has persisted throughout the twentieth century. That loss is evident in the way in which so many of the firms in this survey exist no longer. Some have disappeared entirely; others have been absorbed in restructuring, sometimes successfully and sometimes not. Whatever has happened, the records provide many insights into an industrial structure very different from that of the present.

Study of the records will help unravel some of the great problems of the British economy and provide the material for international comparisons, but there is another use. Even a firm which did not have a leading role nationally may still have had a vital role in its local economy. Local historians should be able to identify such firms easily from a perusal of the guide.

One of the attractive features of any records is that they often produce the unusual and the unexpected. Business records are no exception. Those of the jewellers, goldsmiths and gunsmiths give insights into the customs and ways of select social groups. Garrard and Company have 'gentlemen's ledgers' from 1735. Visitors' books are worth examining to see if industrial achievement was more attractive to earlier generations than to today's tourists. Adam Smith took Edmund Burke to see the Carron ironworks as well as Loch Lomond. Or were the visitors mainly customers? There are even more unexpected sources, the scores of the cricket club and the details of a fishing club. Those inclined to think that business records hold nothing for them should think again.

Much of the material listed is to be found in local record offices throughout the country, the location usually determined by where the firm operated. There is some concentration, as of shipbuilding records in Glasgow, agricultural engineering records in Reading, records of early precision engineering in the Science Museum. With the records spread so widely, and some in unexpected places, this comprehensive survey will be received with gratitude by many who have known the frustrations of searching for elusive sources. They will now have the satisfaction of finding records they might otherwise have missed.

RH CAMPBELL

Access to privately owned papers

Privately owned collections of papers deposited on loan in libraries, record offices and other public institutions are normally available for research without restriction. Special conditions, however, may sometimes apply, particularly if a collection is as yet uncatalogued, and advice on access and related matters should be sought from the institutions concerned.

Permission to study papers that remain with a company or other private owner should be sought from the owner in writing, either direct or, where indicated, through an intermediary. Applicants are reminded that such papers can normally be made available only at considerable inconvenience to their owners, and that access for the purposes of research is a privilege and not a right. The conditions of access cited in the guide are those that prevailed in April 1994. Details of the present location of collections whose ownership or whereabouts is not specified in the guide may, where appropriate, be obtained from the Commission.[1]

Those wishing to study papers in private hands are also advised to consult catalogues or other finding aids available in the Commission's search room or elsewhere before approaching owners or custodians.

1. Enquiries to the Commission should be addressed to the Secretary, The Royal Commission on Historical Manuscripts, Quality House, Quality Court, Chancery Lane, London WC2A 1HP. Where indicated, enquiries about Scottish collections should be addressed to the Secretary, National Register of Archives (Scotland), West Register House, Charlotte Square, Edinburgh EH2 4DF. For addresses of repositories generally, see the Commission's *Record Repositories in Great Britain, a geographical directory*, HMSO, ninth edition, revised 1994.

Editorial note

Firms are assigned to sub-sections on the basis of their main business activity. The name of the firm given is that by which it was known for the longest period covered by the surviving records. The geographical location relates to the head office or the particular factories from which records emanate. The county names used for identification are those of the counties prior to local government reorganisation in 1974. Where a collection has been the subject of a large-scale printed survey, only a brief description of the records is given with a reference to the work. The records are normally described in the following order: partnership deeds, minutes and other corporate records, accounting, order, sales, production, staff, property and miscellaneous records.

The following abbreviations are used in the text.

BAC *Company Archives*   L Richmond and B Stockford, *Company archives: the survey of the records of 1,000 of the first registered companies in England and Wales*, Business Archives Council, 1986.

Business in Avon and Somerset   J Green, P Ollerenshaw, P Wardley, *Business in Avon and Somerset: a survey of archives*, 1991.

Lane   J Lane, *Register of business records of Coventry and related areas*, 1977.

NRA   Lists available for consultation in the National Register of Archives.

NRA(S)   Surveys produced or circulated by the National Register of Archives (Scotland).

Ritchie   LA Ritchie, *The shipbuilding industry: a guide to historical records*, 1992.

Records of British Business and Industry 1760-1914
Metal Processing and Engineering

METAL PROCESSING

[1] JOHN ABBOT & CO LTD, iron and brass founders and engineers, Gateshead, co Durham

Directors' minutes 1870, general meeting minutes 1865, work ledger 1871-92.
Gateshead Central Library (Accs 58/10, 71/14). NRA 13001.

[2] WILLIAM ADAM & CO, coppersmiths and brassfounders, Greenock, Renfrewshire

Records 1870-1925 incl letter books 1874-1922, business and family corresp.
In private possession. Enquiries to NRA (Scotland) (survey 545). NRA 14669.

[3] JOHN ADE, tinman, brazier and ironmonger, Lutterworth, Leics

General ledgers (2) 1863-74, day books (9) 1862-8, 1871-4.
Leicestershire RO (18 D 67/353-63). NRA 18795.

[4] ALBION IRON & WIRE WORK CO LTD, London

Certificates of incorporation and memorandum and articles of association 1885, 1949, 1951, register of members (1 vol) 1885–1943, share certificates and related papers (16 items) 1944–50, nd, ledgers, journals and cash books (13) 1921–72, estimate books (16) 1910-60, order books (46) 1912-59, invoice books (5) 1926-44, stock books (2) 1897-1943, pattern book 1967, wages, income tax and pension books (4) 1936-70, fire spotters' log book 1942-5, leases and related papers (31 items) 1937-56, photographs of products (6 items) nd.
Greater London RO (Acc 2169/1-114). NRA 34765.

[5] ALEXANDER, FERGUSSON & CO LTD, lead sheet and pipe, paint and varnish mfrs, Glasgow

Copartnery contracts (1 bundle) 1882-95, directors' minutes (6 vols) 1897-1964, agenda books (4) 1933-68, register of directors 1901-46, share ledgers (2) 1897-c1965, transfers and capital summary registers (2) 1918-83, balance sheets and accounts 1941-66, private ledgers (4) 1897-1974, journals (5) 1897-1983, private cash book 1914-32, special purchases book c1924-46, salaries book 1920-53, plans and photographs mainly of staff and works 1952-79, misc papers (6 files) 1983-8, printed company history and catalogues c1955-60.
Glasgow University Archives and Business Record Centre (UGD/258). NRA 33879.

Directors' reports (1 bundle, 11 files) 1930-41, balance sheets and accounts (1 bundle, 20 vols) 1929-40, publicity brochure c1930.
Tyne and Wear Archives Service (12717-48, 13181). NRA 32095.

[6] THOMAS ALLAN & SONS LTD, ironfounders and cast iron pipe mfrs, Thornaby-on-Tees, Yorks

Minutes (2 vols) 1935-c1953, annotated prospectus 1900, misc share records (3 bundles, 3 items) 1912-41, accounts 1872-3, corresp, agreements, etc with North Eastern Railway Co (1 bundle) 1901-7, patent licences and related corresp (1 bundle) 1933-5, daily record of moulders' production (1 vol) 1917-18, register of employees (1 vol) c1935-65, agreements, corresp, plans, etc rel to property (5 bundles, 5 items) 1897-1947.
Cleveland Archives (U/AL). NRA 34086.

[7] EDGAR ALLEN & CO LTD, iron and steel mfrs, Sheffield

Directors' letter books (3) 1883-1900, capital account 1918-30, journal 1924-30, invoice books (2) 1929-35, order books (38) 1898-1935, wages books (2) 1914-41, papers (3 boxes) rel to history of firm 19th-20th cent.
Sheffield Archives (MD 2296-2339, 3167-9, 3970-2). NRA 23246.

Memorandum and articles of association 1908-74, letter books (2) 1880, 1899-1904 and loose corresp 1889, 1907-14, annual reports and accounts (1 file) 1914-52, committee minutes, secretary's files, share records and accounting records 1936-78, trade mark register 1906-65, visitors' book 1936-71, personnel and salaries records 1910-69, valuations 1948-67.
Sheffield Archives (Aurora 513-77). NRA 26201.

Tramway order books (13) 1906-29, photographs (c3,000) of track manufactured and laid nd.
National Tramway Museum, Crich. NRA 33431.

[8] **THOMAS ALTHAM & SON LTD**, ironfounders, ironmongers and range mfrs, Penrith, Cumberland

Profit and loss account 1883, ledgers (2) 1849-76, 1933-4, day books (11) 1846-58, 1875-8, 1925-9, cash books (21) 1843-51, 1863-9, 1904-79, sales ledgers (9) 1914-67, sales day books (8) 1831-3, 1845-55, 1925-30, vouchers (1 vol, etc) 1840s, invoice and half-yearly order book 1849-60, 1872-8, other sales records (3 vols, 1 file) c1971-81, letters from suppliers (10 files, etc) 1927-1930s, registers of goods received (2 vols) 1932-4, foundry books (6) 1881-8, 1931-62, foundry day books (12) 1896-1906, 1925-9, castings register 1911-20, drawings (3 items) 1961-80, nd, account of hours worked 1888-97, wages books (3) 1860-79, 1914-56, publicity material (2 items) c1980, catalogues of other firms and misc papers c1938-81.
Cumbria RO, Carlisle (DB/97). NRA 35356.

[9] **ANDERSON, NEW & CO**, brass mfrs, Bristol

Draft minutes of weekly proprietors' meetings (37 folios) 1798-9.
London University Library (MS 725): see *Catalogue of additional manuscripts*.

[10] **ANDERSTON FOUNDRY CO LTD**, ironfounders and engineers, Glasgow and Port Clarence, co Durham

Memorandum and articles of association and related papers (14 files) 1884-8, minutes (5 vols) 1884-1959, share registers (4) 1884-1929, 1953-8, dividend payments (1 vol, 17 items) 1927-43, private letter books (2) 1885-1911, private out-letters (26 files) 1923-61, Glasgow head office out-letters (15 vols, 44 files) 1910-27, general corresp, etc (c1,300 files) 1927-61, annual returns, reports, balance sheets and financial statements, etc (4 vols, 40 files, 36 items) 19th-20th cent, ledgers (14) 1853-1960, journals (4) 1884-1952, cash books (2) 1953-9, sales day books (21) 1928-60, bolts and foundry order, estimate and quotation books (63) 1875-1960, memoranda books (8) 1876-1947, cost books (43) 1876-1958, accounts for commissions (4 vols) 1873-1941, pig iron (19 items) 1900-18 and transport (1 vol) 1924-52, foundry output books (3) 1928-31, 1945-7, patents and specifications (1 vol, 2 files, 10 items) 1884-1930, 1941-51, wages, income tax and holiday fund records (32 vols, 1 file) 1877-1961, notes on negotiations with trade unions (1 file) 1925-42, list of regulations for employees nd, valuation books (2) 1885, plans (3) 1925-7 and other records (3 files, 1 bundle, etc) rel to the Port Clarence and Glasgow works 1875-83, 1928-31, nd, photographs of Port Clarence Works and material supplied by the firm 1929, nd, history of the company 1796-1962, press cuttings, etc; corresp and papers rel to iron and steel producers' associations (10 files) 1910-15, 1921-4, 1938-53 and the switch and crossing syndicate (10 files) 1924-7.
Durham County RO (D/AF). NRA 32812.

[11] **THOMAS ANDREWS & CO LTD**, steel mfrs, Sheffield

Memorandum and articles of association 1908, letter book 1901-2, share certificate counterfoils 1908-35, annual reports and accounts 1954, 1958, nominal ledger 1915-40, sales ledger 1912-36, crucible purchase journal 1941-6, test records (1 vol, 1 file) 1907-32.
Sheffield Archives (MD 7058-67). NRA 34824.

Day book 1946-59.
Sheffield Archives (LD 1950). NRA 34866.

[12] **ANDREWS TOLEDO LTD** (formerly **JH ANDREW & CO LTD**), steel mfrs, Sheffield

Directors' minutes (2 vols) 1914-40, general meeting and shareholders' minutes (1 vol) 1898-1926, annual reports, balance sheets and other corporate and accounting records (21 vols and files) 1929-61, visitors' book 1895-1945, printed labels (1 vol) c1930, deeds and related papers (7 bundles) 1783-1946.
Sheffield Archives (Aurora 56-81, 490-6). NRA 26201.

[13] **APPLEBY-FRODINGHAM STEEL CO LTD** (formerly **APPLEBY IRON CO LTD** and **FRODINGHAM IRON & STEEL CO LTD**), iron and steel mfrs, Scunthorpe, Lincs

Appleby Iron Co Ltd memorandum and articles of association nd, board minutes (2 vols) 1874-1934, general meeting minutes (1 vol) 1874-1934, Renishaw foundry catalogue 1867; Frodingham Iron & Steel Co Ltd minutes 1904-34 and salaries books 1918-37; Appleby-Frodingham Steel Co Ltd memorandum and articles of association nd, minutes 1941-80, register of members (2 vols) 1946-80, nd, misc corporate records, plans, photographs, etc 1889, 1900, 1934-70.
British Steel East Midlands Regional Records Centre, Irthlingborough. NRA 35548.

[14] **ROBERT ARMOUR**, coppersmith and plumber, Campbeltown, Argyllshire

Account books 1811-17.
In private possession. A microfilm is in the Scottish Record Office (RH 4/42): see *Keeper's Report 1969*, p14.

[15] **ASKAM & MONZELL IRON CO LTD**, Askam, Lancs

Letter books (2) 1886-8, pig iron order book 1881-90, deeds (c30) of Sparkbridge estate 1756-1854.
Cumbria RO, Barrow: see *Report of the County Archivist* January 1980, p11.

[16] **ATKIN BROTHERS**, silversmiths and britannia metal mfrs, Sheffield

Letter book 1842-63, cash book 1826-41, orders 1872, wages book 1828-40, catalogues (2) 1840s.
Sheffield Archives (BR 305-9, 311). NRA 34862.

[17] **AUSTIN & DODSON LTD**, steel and file mfrs, Sheffield

General ledger 1888-1935 incl balance sheets, profit and loss, trading and salaries accounts, etc, letter books, accounting and sales records and stock book (8 vols, 1 file) 1936-c1970.
Sheffield Archives (HSM 34-43). NRA 34854.

[18] **AUTO MACHINERY CO LTD**, ball bearing, bolt and nut mfrs, Coventry

Directors' minutes from early 20th cent and other records.
Peugeot Talbot Motor Co Ltd. Enquiries to the Company Secretary.

Orders received and related papers (75 items) 1899-1901, 1906-11, memoranda rel to personnel matters (13 items) 1914-19, photographs (8 items) 1920s-1970s.
Coventry City RO (Acc 987). NRA 20069.

[19] **BACKBARROW CO**, ironmasters, Backbarrow, Lancs

Partnership agreements and papers (11 items) 1734-52, journal incl accounts for Backbarrow, Leighton and Cunsey furnaces (8 vols) 1731-44, furnace account book 1728-31, cast iron wares ledgers (2) 1737-42, bar iron ledgers (2) 1735-45, agreements and papers rel to timber and iron ore (167 items) 1714-54, papers rel to appointment and dismissal of staff (9 items) 1712-53, misc leases, agreements, legal papers, etc rel to partnership and premises (c30 items) 1711-53.
Lancashire RO (DDMc/30). NRA 18075.

Backbarrow and Pennybridge furnace accounts 1763-80.
Lancashire RO (DP 373): see *Guide to the Lancashire Record Office*, 1985, p167.

Deed of copartnership for Backbarrow and Pennybridge Co 1750, ledger 1713-18, journals (6) 1711-13, 1724-9, 1787-8, 1791-2, 1798-1801, cast iron wares journal 1746-53, Leighton furnace journal 1715-17 incl accounts 1725-8, Kendal warehouse accounts (2 vols) 1718-23, agreements rel to timber (3 items) 1761, 1781, misc agreements and legal papers rel to partnership and premises (8 items) 1748-1820, sale particulars 1852.
Cumbria RO, Barrow (Furness Collection). NRA 35515.

Journal 1713-15.
Newcastle upon Tyne University Library (Misc MS 32).

[20] **JAMES BAIN & CO**, iron mfrs and iron ore and coal mine proprietors, Harrington, Cumberland

Legal records (19 bundles) 1869-1914 incl papers rel to pig iron delivery (6 bundles) 1880-2 and deeds (8 items) 1898-1908.
Cumbria RO, Carlisle (D/BH/6). NRA 36543.

[21] **WILLIAM BAIRD & CO LTD** (afterwards **BAIRDS & SCOTTISH STEEL LTD**), iron and coal masters, Glasgow and Coatbridge, Lanarkshire

Directors' minutes, agendas, reports, etc (32 vols) 1893-1971, share records (9 vols) 1893-1949, general corresp (29 files) 1910-51, corresp and papers rel to modernisation and nationalisation (20 files) 1931-59, balance sheets, etc (1 vol) 1904-9, profit and loss accounts, etc (2 vols) 1912-19, annual returns (1 vol) 1936-42, ledgers and journals (14) 1867-92, 1915-39, other accounting records (6 vols and bundles) 1911-28, wages and salaries records (7 vols and bundles) 1914-19, deeds and leases (4 vols) 1895-1963, nd; diaries and notebooks, etc of Robert Baird (24 vols) 1824-53.
Glasgow University Archives and Business Record Centre (UGD/164). NRA 15635.

Manager's notebook from 1844, private ledgers (4) 1925-30, 1961-4, nd, general ledgers (21) 1921-66, ledgers (22) 1871-1957, private journals (2) 1912-26, 1952, general journals (8) 1921-64, cash books (62) 1845-6, 1923-65, balance sheets (6 vols, 1 bundle) 1934-50, 1951-65, capital transactions book 1904-61, other accounting records 1937-67, sales ledgers (3) 1940-56, other sales records 1912-67, purchase journals (2) 1919-65, ironwork abstracts 1879-1938, rails and plates book 1897, works register c1920-30 and other production records 1910-67, wages and pay books (98) 1884-1969, time books (32) 1928-67, workmen's terms of contract (1 vol) 1880-1914, compensation register and ledger 1913-17, accident reports (1 bundle) 1949, inventories (11 vols) 1906-66, rent books and rolls (8) 1907-62, property abstracts (5 vols) 1916-45, valuation returns (1 vol) 1917, plant book 1927-61.
Strathclyde University Archives. NRA (Scotland) (survey 430). NRA 15635.

[22] **BALDWIN, SON & CO LTD**, ironfounders, Stourport-on-Severn, Worcs

Private ledgers (2) 1863-86.
British Steel East Midlands Regional Records Centre, Irthlingborough. NRA 35552.

Bank book 1821-6, price lists (4 items) 1882-1907, leases and legal papers (1 bundle, 3 items) 1821, 1878-9, 1902-11.
Black Country Museum, Dudley (Kenrick Collection). NRA 33584.

Misc records incl copartnership and other deeds.
Hereford and Worcester RO, Worcester (705:775). NRA 17881.

[23] **BALDWINS LTD**, sheet iron, steel and tinplate mfrs, Stourport-on-Severn, Worcs and Swansea, Glam

EP & W Baldwin Ltd letter books (2) 1887-1901, share and debenture register 1893-1901, deeds of copartnership, letters, accounts, deeds, legal and other papers (c300 items) 1776-1928, wages book 1865-71, corresp and papers rel to wages (c60 items) 1869-78; Alfred Baldwin & Co Ltd memorandum and articles of association 1886, misc letters, accounts, etc (c30 items) 1878-95; Bowesfield Steel Co letters, minutes and papers (c40 items) 1896-7;

Baldwin family corresp, diaries and papers
1838-1947.
Hereford and Worcester RO, Worcester (705:775). NRA
17881.

EP & W Baldwin Ltd share certificate book
1898-1901, balance sheets and related accounts
1870-1, private ledgers (4) 1863-89, nominal ledger
1889-90, bank ledger 1890-6, cash books (6)
1864-95, sold day book 1886-90, stock and plant
inventories (3 vols) 1894-1901; Baldwins Ltd misc
corresp (1 file) 1919-21, private ledger 1912-15,
Stourport Works sales output 1906-7, boat book
1901-29, railway rates (1 vol, 1 file) 1913-58,
summary of production 1904-37, office finding aids
(2 vols) 1901-14, clerks' wages book 1912-18,
salaries book 1942, works plans and misc property
records 1879-1948, insurance policies 1922-31;
Richard Thomas & Baldwins Ltd purchase journals
(6) 1956-69, registers of contracts (5 files) 1953-67,
Swindon Works registers of fitness and accidents
(2 vols) 1938-62, legal department records (c160
boxes) 1906-72, estate reference books (30 boxes)
1877-1982.
*British Steel East Midlands Regional Records Centre,
Irthlingborough.* NRA 35552.

Records 19th-20th cent rel to South Wales works
incl capital expenditure journal 1925-39, trade
ledger 1938-40, trade marks register 1876-1957,
workmen's nominal roll ledgers (2) 1895-1930, staff
payroll records (4 boxes) 1900-30, copy leases
(1 vol) 1872-1900, leases index c1876-1944 and
inventory summaries (8 boxes) 1923-69; Robert B
Byass & Co Ltd minutes (1 vol) nd, copy documents
book 1829-93, schedules and valuations book
1858-88.
British Steel Records Centre, Shotton. NRA 36012.

See also Richard Thomas & Co Ltd.

[24] **ARTHUR BALFOUR & CO LTD**, steel
mfrs, Sheffield

Directors' meeting and weekly conference minutes
(4 vols) 1899-1936, general meeting minutes (1 vol)
1921-61, directors' meeting agendas and other
papers (5 bundles and files) 1955-66, register of
directors 1919-44, annual accounts, balance sheets
and taxation returns (3 bundles and files) 1955-66,
misc corporate records (2 parcels) 1902-26, foreign
ledgers (3), 1921-3, 1951-65 and Paris journal
1919-24, day books (71) 1869-75, 1879-1948, cash
books (4) 1900-43, memoranda book 1879-91 incl
analysis of foreign ledger 1882-98 and stock and
production 1884-1922, valuations of stock 1920-32,
misc financial records (2 files) 1946-62, steel
production records (13 vols, 2 packets) c1905,
1920-61, staff superannuation society records
(5 vols, 1 item) 1926-54 and papers rel to war
damage insurance (2 boxes) 1940s; records of
subsidiaries trading abroad 1902-58 incl Eagle &
Globe Steel Co minutes (2 vols) 1902-55 and
French subsidiary's ledgers, accounts, inventories,
etc 1907-28.
Sheffield Archives (BDR). NRA 15735.

Board and committee minutes (5 vols) 1936-68,
copies of minutes, etc (1 vol) 1920-9, board files

1969-71, reports and accounts 1950-73, day book
1865-8, cash book 1969-76, visitors' cards
1876-1912, nd, wages book 1920-5.
Sheffield Archives (Aurora 578-93). NRA 26201.

[25] **BALLYRONEY FOUNDRY**, Ballyroney, co
Down

Ledgers and day books (8) 1893-1922.
Public Record Office of Northern Ireland (D 2059).
Deputy Keeper's Report 1966-72, p45.

[26] **BARKER ELLIS SILVER CO LTD**,
silversmiths and electroplaters, Birmingham

Minutes (4 vols, 1 bundle) 1924-72, register of
directors' holdings 1950s, reports and accounts
(7 items) 1907-14, ledger 1898-1907, cost and order
books (10 vols) c1885-c1940, 'odds bought' book
(items to serve as patterns, etc) 1910-16, pattern
and design books (48) 19th cent-1963, specification
books (2) 1897, c1910, other technical records
(2 vols) 20th cent and drawings 19th-20th cent,
patents, deeds and other legal records (1 box) 1816,
1896-1964, list of employees and rates of pay (1 vol)
1920-7, scrapbooks (2) 1901-67, suggestions book
from 1904, photographs, catalogues and other
printed items (31 vols, 2 bundles) from 1900.
In private possession. Enquiries to the Historical
Manuscripts Commission. NRA 33996.

[27] **BARKER & WILKINSON**, lead miners and
smelters, Chesterfield, Derbys

Agreement between John Barker and Benjamin
Wyatt 1816, valuation of Barker's shares in lead
mines c1782, partnership accounts, cash books, etc
(10 vols and bundles) 1734-1857, accounts of ore
mined, bought, smelted and sold (15 vols)
1729-1859, papers rel to marketing of lead (4 vols
and bundles) 1773-1859, cupola accounts (11 vols)
1790-1861, record of coal and slag delivered (5 vols)
1772-3, 1830-58, list of shareholders and miners in
Ashford lordship 1832; business and other corresp of
the Barker and Wyatt families 1763-1858.
Sheffield Archives (Bagshawe Collection, parts IIID,
IVA). NRA 7871.

[28] **EDWARD BARNARD & SONS LTD**,
silversmiths, London

Register of members and share ledger 1910-17,
private ledgers (4) 1884-1924, 1934-44, private
journal 1881-1935, stocktaking and balance books
(5) 1864-1945, profit and loss ledger c1906-1912,
debit list 1937-41, customer accounts (7 vols)
1805-8, 1892-1937, order books (40) 1910-57,
orders day books (47) 1821-4, 1831-74, 1879-1944
and indexes (30 vols) 1867-99, customer letter
books (2) 1922-5, purchase books (10) 1922-53,
factory silver supply accounts (6 vols) 1912-50,
pattern, cost and estimate books, etc (29 vols)
c1808-1820, 1890-1951, stock books (57)
1828-1961, wages books (8) 1885-1940, glass
negatives of objects produced nd.
Victoria & Albert Museum, Archive of Art and Design
(AAD 5-1988, AAD 7-1989). NRA 34432.

[29] **BARNARDS LTD**, wire netting, chain link and wrought ironwork mfrs, Norwich, Norfolk

Deed of partnership 1846, memorandum and articles of association 1887-92, board minutes (3 vols) 1902-60, general meeting minutes (2 vols) 1908-c1963, debenture holders' minutes (1 vol) 1893-1902, annual returns (4 vols, 13 items) 1908-57, registers (7) of directors, shareholders, transfers, mortgages and debentures 1887-1973, other share records (2 vols, 1 file, 27 items) 1887-1963, managing director's reports (3 files) 1912-41 and other board papers (1 file, 17 items) 1886-1955, company secretary's papers (21 files) 1935-47, ledgers (5) 1838-87, private ledgers (2) 1907-56, nominal ledgers (3) 1925-68, private journal 1887-1959, cash books (6) 1860-71, 1891-1901, 1907-22, 1945-64, financial papers (5 files) 1940-55, order sheets (40 vols, 25 files) 1935-41, wage accounts (1 vol) 1887-91 and other staff records (6 vols, 3 files) 1925-77, plans, etc rel to premises (4 files, 6 items) 1907-76, catalogues, price lists and other printed papers 1850-1985, photographs (17 vols, 1 file) 1920s-1960s, papers rel to firm's history and the Barnard family 1843-1989; Wire Netting Association minutes, etc 1900-25, 1956-7.
Norfolk RO (BR 220). NRA 34910.

[30] **BARNES & PYE LTD**, general founders and mfrs of structural ironwork, Norwich, Norfolk

Ledgers (5) 1879-81, 1926-41, job book 1904-5, order book 1927-8, photograph 1895.
Norfolk RO (BR 101). NRA 27707.

[31] **SAMUEL BARRETT & CO**, tinplate mfrs, King's Bromley, Staffs

Letter book 1796-1803.
Staffordshire RO (D 872). NRA 12375.

[32] **BARROW HAEMATITE STEEL CO LTD**, iron masters, steel mfrs and mine owners, Barrow-in-Furness, Lancs

Board minutes (1 vol) 1926-53, general meeting minutes (1 vol) 1930-64, minutes (1 vol) of debenture stock trustees 1904-15 incl list of debenture stock 1895, register of mortgages 1895-1930, journal 1952-64, sales department memoranda book 1920s-1940s, plans of steel rails (10 items) 1893-1912, plans of premises (1 bundle, 1 item) 1868, c1890, misc papers 1890, 1937-8.
Cumbria RO, Barrow (BDB/8). NRA 35448.

Records 19th-20th cent.
Cumbria RO, Barrow (BDB/47).

Cost records 1914-19, production calculations and analysis (2 items) 1909, reports on processes and works incl some rel to other firms (13 items) from 1901, drawings and plans of machinery and plant (20 items) 1910-18, misc staff records 20th cent, misc papers 1911-19.
Cumbria RO, Barrow (BDB/9A). NRA 35447.

Records (3 boxes) 1853-1967 incl legal papers and plans of property.
Cumbria RO, Barrow (BD/HJ/161-3). NRA 32581.

Corresp 1934-65, estimate for casting pit 1942, accounting, development, technical and staff records (c10 boxes) 1934-75, inventory 1951.
British Steel East Midlands Regional Records Centre, Irthlingborough. NRA 35548.

Further records.
British Steel Records Centre, Shotton. NRA 35447.

[33] **JACOB BARTON**, nail maker, Halesowen, Worcs

Account book 1899-1900, raw materials bills (c70 items) 1897-8, rent books (14) 1895-7, 1922-33.
Hereford and Worcester RO, Worcester (705:732, 705:838). NRA 16430.

[34] **HENRY BATES & SONS**, ironfounders, Northwich, Cheshire

Daily account books (4) 1942-58, 1967-75, orders returned (1 vol) 1950-6, wages books (5) 1898-1904, 1914-20, 1930-5, 1944-51, misc plans, photographs, etc (20 items) 1887-1942, nd.
Cheshire RO (DDX 543). NRA 5236.

[35] **JAMES BATES & SONS**, ironfounders, Winsford, Cheshire

Payments book 1887-97.
Cheshire RO (D 3644). *Guide*, 1991, p126.

[36] **E BAYLIE & CO LTD**, chain mfrs, Stourbridge, Worcs

Board meeting minutes (1 vol) 1939-66, general meeting minutes (1 vol) 1899-1965, register of members, etc 1898-1925, annual summaries book 1929-32, ledgers and account books (5) 1947-65.
Dudley Archives and Local History Service (Acc 8264). NRA 25008.

[37] **BAYLISS, JONES & BAYLISS LTD**, iron fencing and railway fastening mfrs, Wolverhampton, Staffs

Records 19th-20th cent.
Wolverhampton Borough Archives: see Summary of collections, 5th edn 1989, p4.

[38] **WILLIAM BEAL LTD**, gas lamp and chandelier mfrs, Birmingham

Memorandum and articles of association nd, combined register nd, papers (6 bundles, 4 items) rel to liquidation 1911-14, misc trading accounts, share certificates, etc 1907-13, ledger nd, bank books (5) 1908-13, cheque book and credit counterfoils 1907-13, petty cash book c1909-10, receipts (1 bundle, 6 items) 1909-12, stock books (8) 1899, 1907-11, wages books (2) 1907-12.
Birmingham Central Library Archives Division (MS 146). NRA 29841.

[39] **WILLIAM BEARDMORE & CO LTD**, engineers, shipbuilders, steel and ordnance mfrs, Glasgow and Dalmuir, Dunbarton

Articles of association 1902, 1974, directors', general meeting and committee minutes (23 vols, etc) 1902-75, agenda books (3) 1903-29, directors' attendance books (3) 1914-40, lists of directors (1 file) 1901-56, reports for board, etc 1967-74, share registers (2) 1902-29, statements of account 1901-75, register of seals 1929, ledgers (23) 1922-76, journals (7) 1936-74, cash books (3) 1937-72, other financial records 1951-75, production records (5 vols) 1921-6, papers of James Mowat, technical director, 1899-1978 incl foundry specification book 1936-47, salaries books (5) 1902-37, other staff records 1963-75, registers of mortgages (2) 1880-7, 1904-29, records rel to property, plant and machinery 1904-71, visitors' books (5) 1914-50, catalogues 1910-38, press cuttings, etc 1928-56, photographs (7 albums, 1 bundle, etc) 1901-52, notes on company history and misc papers 1864-75.
Glasgow University Archives and Business Record Centre (UGD/100, 127, 137, 179). NRA 14667.

Directors' minutes 1957-71, annual reports and accounts, etc 1955-71, corresp and papers 1954-73, press cuttings 1957.
Sheffield Archives. BAC *Company Archives* no 372.

[40] **J BEARDSHAW & SON LTD**, steel converters and mfrs of files, saws and edge tools, Sheffield

Memorandum and articles of association 1953, minutes (6 vols) 1893-1967, register of seals 1965-75, register of members (4 vols) 1893-1971, share certificate books (3) 1951-71, dividend account books (2) 1946-68, papers rel to liquidation (2 vols, 1 file) 1966-76, salaries book 1970-4.
Sheffield Archives (MD 7081). NRA 34857.

Bill book 1855-1911.
Sheffield Archives (MD 6324). NRA 23246.

[41] **WT BEESLEY & CO LTD**, steel strip rollers, Sheffield

Memorandum and articles of association 1888, minutes (2 vols) 1888-1923, 1929-54, share certificate book 1923-51, report on the company's works and processes 1904.
Sheffield Archives (389/B/7). NRA 28062.

[42] **BELL BROTHERS LTD**, ironmasters, steel mfrs, colliery and quarry owners, Middlesbrough

Memorandum and articles of association, balance sheets, etc (2 vols) 1872-7, memorandum and articles of association 1899, directors' minutes (4 vols) 1873-1923, general meeting minutes (1 vol) 1899-1935, management-workforce disputes committee minutes (1 vol) 1895-1914, annual reports, accounts and general meeting proceedings 1900-21, seal books (2) 1896-1923, profit and loss accounts, balance sheets and auditors' reports (7 vols) 1864-1923, capital expenditure records (1 vol)

1903-7, private ledgers (10) 1864-1921, personal ledgers (8) 1899-1923, impersonal ledgers (7) 1902-23, private journals (4) 1864-1923, Clarence furnace working records (6 vols) 1908-30, deed books (6) 1863-1923, press cuttings, etc (1 vol) 1898-9.
British Steel Northern Regional Records Centre, Middlesbrough. NRA 35680.

Pay books (51) of Brancepeth Colliery and Clarence Ironworks 1863-1905.
British Library of Political and Economic Science (MISC COLL 3). NRA 28876.

[43] **DAVID BENNIE & SONS LTD**, steel mfrs and rollers, Glasgow

Minutes (5 vols) 1899-1964, share ledger 1951-67 and transfer forms (1 bundle) 1914-77, annual returns and accounts (2 vols, 4 envelopes) 1945-75, corporate corresp and papers (2 files) 1932-66, business diaries (9 vols) 1936-55, agreements, assignments and patents (2 bundles, 2 envelopes, 1 item) 1884, 1923-51, inventories and valuations, etc 1898, 1904-71.
In private possession. Enquiries to NRA (Scotland) (survey 3406). NRA 36859.

Minutes (1 vol) 1958-80, register of members 1899-1950, share certificate books (2) 1899-1977, annual returns 1962-78, accounts nd.
British Steel East Midlands Regional Records Centre, Irthlingborough. NRA 35555.

[44] **BETTS & CO LTD**, mfrs of tinfoil, metallic capsules and collapsible tubes, London

Records 19th-20th cent incl directors' minutes (2 vols) 1880-8, 1958-60, registers (4) of members and shareholdings 1880-1934, share transfers 1881-1934, mortgages 1880-1944 and seals 1904-49, balance sheets, profit and loss accounts, etc 1913-31, 1959-61, private ledger 1896-1903, and misc papers (1 envelope) rel to sales, stock and production 1852-1929.
Courtaulds plc, Coventry (BET). Enquiries to the Head of Archives. NRA 29343.

[45] **BIRMINGHAM BATTERY & METAL CO LTD**, mfrs of copper and brass battery ware, tubes, plates and stampings, Birmingham

Records 1796-1991 incl articles of copartnership 1836, certificate of company registration 1845, memorandum and articles of association, etc (1 vol, 1 bundle, 1 drawer) 1897-1967, board minute books (9 vols, 1 parcel) 1836-1990, general meeting minute books (3) 1930-91, committee minute book 1836-8, management board minute books (6) 1922-55, register of directors 1908-42, directors' salaries books (1 vol, 1 binder) 1968-76, share and dividend records (7 vols) 1897-1991, seal book 1944-91, annual returns, balance sheets, reports and accounts from c1897, monthly account book 1925-38, misc corresp and papers (1 sack) from c1905, private ledgers (11) c1836-1984, ledgers (2) 1836-49, 1897-1916, account books (3) 1860-84, cash books (16) 1836-1991, bills receivable (1 vol)

1884-1924, audit book 1872-83, stock and profit and loss accounts 1864-5, 1891-6, trading accounts (1 binder) 1957, order books (3) 1842-81, letter book rel to sales and orders 1892-7, customers' credit and business standing reference book c1870-1906, stock sheets 1841, 1873, tubes work books (2) 1853-62 and other production records (4 vols, 1 file, 1 bundle) 1915-67, technical drawings, plans, specifications and related papers 1839, 20th cent, nd (originals and microfilms), patent and trade mark records and related papers 1839-43, 1878-9, nd, wages, pension scheme and other staff records 1841-2, 1872 and from 1910, premises records incl deeds and legal papers 1796-1982, plans of Digbeth Works (2 items) 1836 and valuations and inventories of Selly Oak Works (4 vols, etc) 1896-1950s; corporate records, etc of subsidiaries 20th cent; corresp and papers rel to the Solid Drawn Tube Manufacturers Association (1 envelope) 1865-8, 1933 and Brass Tube Association expenses book 1879; Gibbins family papers, and papers, photographs, etc rel to company history 1811-1957, nd incl business corresp of Joseph Gibbins (3 bundles, 3 items) 1839-40.
Birmingham Central Library Archives Division (MS 1787). NRA 34477.

[46] BIRMINGHAM METAL & MUNITIONS CO LTD, Birmingham

Directors' minutes (5 vols) 1897-1915, general meeting minutes (1 vol) 1897-1910, share registers (2 vols) 1900-20.
Birmingham Central Library Archives Division (MS 1422). NRA 32859.

[47] BISSOE MINING & SMELTING CO, Bissoe, Cornwall

Cost book incl shareholders' minutes 1852-6.
Cornwall RO (X363/6). NRA 5235 (Summary of accessions Oct-Dec 1970).

[48] BISSOE TIN SMELTING & ARSENIC CO LTD, Bissoe, Cornwall

Letter book, petty cash book, sales and purchase books (3), order book, metal price book and wages book 1890-1.
Cornwall RO (X 642). *List of Accessions April 1981-March 1982*, p6.

[49] BLAENAVON CO LTD, iron and steel mfrs and colliery proprietors, Blaenavon, Mon

Memorandum and articles of association 1870, partnership and related agreements (4 items) 1870, 1879-80, minutes (15 vols) 1837-64, 1880-3, 1892-1948, general meeting proceedings 1910-40, register of directors (2 vols) 1901-31 and other board papers 1918-49, shareholders' attendance register 1881-1909, corresp and papers rel to debentures and share issues, etc 1874-20th cent, balance sheets and profit and loss accounts 1920-36, 1943-4, 1949, private ledgers (3) 1911-42, account books (2) 1904-18, journal 1881-1921, sales, purchase and nominal ledgers (24) 1911-57, misc

financial papers incl reports on subsidiaries 1892-1940, contracts and commercial agreements 19th-20th cent, papers rel to war production (3 files, 6 items) 1918, 1939-45, salaries books (2) 1887-1903, 1929-37 and related papers (5 files, etc) 1910-42, papers rel to staff appointments and pension schemes 1911-46, agreements rel to the construction of coke and tar works 1911-18 (c5 items), reports on premises, maps, mineral leases and deeds 18th-20th cent.
Gwent RO (D 480, D 591, D 751). NRA 10268.

Minutes (1 vol) 1870-8, corresp and board meeting papers 1877-8, reports and corresp rel to plant and production processes 1846, 1946-9, nd; misc colliery records 1877-20th cent.
Gwent RO (D 2133). NRA 14003.

Ledger incl capital accounts 1879-1912.
Gwent RO (Acc 2745).

Colliery records 19th-20th cent.
Gwent RO (D 2732). See also *Accessions to repositories 1991*, p54.

General meeting minutes (1 vol) 1880-1957, board minutes (2 vols) 1948-57, directors' private minutes (1 vol) 1920-50, other corporate records (4 vols, 3 files, etc) 1934-62, accounting and sales records (2 vols, etc) 1947-58, corresp, papers, stock inventories, plans, etc rel to the works and its demolition (6 files) 1947-57.
Sheffield Archives (TW 170-91). NRA 34879.

[50] D BLAKEMORE & SONS LTD, sheet metal workers, Coventry

Minute book 1916-84, corresp and papers rel to changes of directors 1973-83, share records 1916-74, annual returns 1951-83, accounts and taxation and liquidation records (2 vols, 22 files) 1906-10, 1916-85, general ledgers (2) 1915-21, 1963-82, day books (2) 1913-15, cash books and receipts (13 vols, 5 bundles) 1974-83, bank books (6) 1893-1909, 1920-2, 1982-4 and statements (3 bundles) nd, purchase, sales, invoice and stock records (11 vols, 13 bundles) c1942-1983, wages records (2 vols, 6 files, 3 items) 1922-5, 1976-83, photograph of employees c1945.
Coventry City RO (Acc 1151, 1282 and 1351). NRA 30531.

[51] BLOCHAIRN IRON CO, ironmasters, Glasgow

Partners' accounts, balance sheets and stock valuations (1 bundle) 1853-63, corresp and papers 1839-65 of Thomas Brownlie, partner in the company.
Strathclyde Regional Archives (TD 949). NRA 12501.

[52] THOMAS BLUNDELL, nail and pig-ring maker, Gloucester

Customer account book 1873-83 incl price lists of other firms.
Gloucestershire RO (D 5357). NRA 3514.

[53] **BOARDMAN, GLOSSOP & CO**,
silversmiths, Sheffield

Ledger 1908-11, description books (5) *c*1873-1921,
costings books (2) 1881-92, catalogues (2) *c*1890,
*c*1900.
Sheffield Archives (COBB 4). NRA 34872.

[54] **BODLEY BROS & CO LTD**, engineers and
ironfounders, Exeter, Devon

Articles of association 1922, corresp 1896-1934,
letter books (25) 1945-62, ledgers (3) 1862-6,
1941-51, ledger index nd, journals (16) 1861-1954,
cash books (4) 1929-57, order, quotation, estimate
and invoice records (6 boxes, 31 vols, 4 files)
1918-62, working drawings, blueprints, etc (3 vols,
2 bundles, 2,257 items) 1853-1963, production
records (9 vols) 1938-55, photographs (26) of
machinery 19th-20th cent, wages books (18)
1937-60 and staff roll of honour 1914-18, deeds
(11) and related papers 1767-1933, notes and
articles rel to history of firm 1913-69; misc Kingdon
family papers 19th-20th cent.
Devon RO (67/5). NRA 34803.

[55] **BOLCKOW VAUGHAN & CO LTD**,
ironmasters, steel mfrs and colliery owners,
Middlesbrough

Memorandum and articles of association 1864,
board and general meeting minutes (18 vols)
1864-1929, special minutes passed by board (2 vols)
1897-1929, reports and accounts (3 vols, etc)
1865-1929, comparative balances and profit and loss
accounts (6 vols) 1898-1922, papers rel to takeover
by Dorman Long (1 bundle) 1929, private ledgers
(2) 1914-29, private journal 1923-9, epitome book
of agreements and deeds 1878-96.
Cleveland Archives and *British Steel Northern Regional
Records Centre, Middlesbrough*. Enquiries to Cleveland
Archives. NRA 35680.

Auckland collieries wage accounts (2 vols) 1876-9,
1886-1900; deeds, plans and related papers (13 files,
2 items) 1878-1924, nd.
Durham County RO (NCB 1/X/4-5, NCB 13/1-15).
NRA 19490.

[56] **THOMAS BOLITHO & SONS**, tin miners,
smelters and merchants, Penzance, Cornwall

Records 18th-20th cent incl letter books, etc
(11 vols) 1798-1801, 1842-55, balance book
1867-87, tin ledgers (5) 1742-62, 1773-83,
1809-15, 1872-7, general ledgers (2) 1832-45,
1866-71, general accounts (8 vols) 1731-61,
1828-81, cash books (3) 1842-51, 1854-6, 1884-90,
bills receivable (2 vols) 1834-44, 1861-9, balances
due to the committee for the smelting of tin (1 vol)
1791-8, statistics of tin sales (1 vol) 1839-40, tin and
leather sales account (1 vol) 1857-66, purchase
records (14 vols) 1839-96, tin bills (7 vols) 1703-7,
1778-1805, 1815-37, contract book 1852-61,
London order book 1888-91, delivery books (3)
1703-6, 1713-24, import, export and despatch
records (9 vols) 1833-85, stock books (6)
1781-1806, 1826-31, 1840-3, 1850-6, coinage

accounts (23 vols) 1702-1827 and statistics (2 vols)
1805-38, smelting house ledger 1718-25, journal
1725-9, accounts (1 vol) 1798-1811 and invoice
books (2) 1803-13, 1885-90, blowing house
accounts (2 vols) 1771-1823 and general
memoranda books (3) 1814-35.
Cornwall RO (RG). NRA 627.

Business and estate records 18th-20th cent incl letter
books (4) 1837-8, 1850, balance book 1887-97, tin
ledgers (6) 1783-98, 1816-27, 1835-53, 1877-84,
sales accounts (1 vol) 1840-56, purchase accounts
(7 vols) 1817-51, 1857-66, weights of tin despatched
(2 vols) 1891-8, Birmingham stock accounts (1 vol)
1876-91, patent 1852, coinage accounts (2 vols)
1708-12, 1807-17, smelting house ledgers (2)
1842-80, journal 1813-18 and cash books (2)
1842-80, and black tin scale book 1862-4.
Cornwall RO (BL). NRA 35850.

Misc business and family papers 17th-20th cent incl
tin accounts 1746-1835 and notebook containing
coinage weights 1766-74.
Cornwall RO (X 104). NRA 2643.

See also Consolidated Tin Smelting Co Ltd.

[57] **THOMAS BOLTON & SONS LTD**, copper
and brass mfrs, Froghall, Staffs

Oakamoor mills wire strip rolling and slitting
accounts (1 vol) 1852-8, wages book 1844-65,
typescript notes rel to Thomas Bolton & Sons Ltd,
Cheadle Brass Wire Co, etc (1 folder) nd.
Staffordshire RO (D 1406). NRA 19772.

Oakamoor brassworks cash books, letters, charity
fund records and other papers 1907-8.
Staffordshire RO (D 239/M 2678-2703). NRA 5872.

Deeds rel to mines, etc and misc papers (44 bundles
and items) 1715-1932.
Staffordshire RO (D 953). NRA 19772.

Further deeds 19th-20th cent.
*National Museums and Galleries on Merseyside,
Merseyside Maritime Museum* (BICC archive).

[58] **JW BOND & CO**, horseshoe and shoe rivet
mfrs, Birmingham

Memorandum and articles of association 1888,
accounts (1 vol, 58 items) 1893-1957, share
certificates and debenture (4 items) 1899, 1919.
Birmingham Central Library Archives Division
(MS 180). NRA 29842.

[59] **BOOTH & BROOKES LTD**, ironfounders,
Burnham on Crouch, Essex

Deeds of partnership (2 items) 1899, 1902, articles
of association 1919, share registers (4) 1907-43,
balance sheets and profit and loss accounts, etc
(3 bundles, 3 items) 1900-8, 1913-14, 1921-80,
ledgers (2) 1913-21, journals (2) 1910-28, cash
books (3) 1900, 1907-25, sales and purchase ledgers
and journals (9) 1907-45, credit worthiness status
reports (1 vol) 1899-1920, stock books (2) 1911-37,
registers (2) of output, etc 1922-4, register of
castings *c*1910-25, works job book 1910-29,

specifications (2 vols) c1932, registers of drawings
(2 vols, 1 envelope) c1930, nd, patents (9 items)
1908, 1924-30, registers of wages (7) 1900-20, time
books (3) 1917-20, other employee records
(1 bundle, 2 items) c1920-42, corresp rel to
purchase of premises and equipment (1 bundle)
1899, photographs of ironworks, products, family,
employees, etc (c185 items) c1884-1970, misc
corresp and papers 1873-1980.
Essex RO, Chelmsford (D/F 42). NRA 25606.

[60] **BOTFIELD family**, coal and iron masters,
Dawley, Salop

Share transfer receipts c1790-1820, letter books (36)
1802-73, letters received (180 boxes) 1830-73,
agreements with suppliers and employees (1 vol)
1788-91, annual and monthly accounts (9 boxes)
1837-72, reckoning accounts (8 boxes, 8 vols, etc)
1841-73, other accounts (1 vol) 1839-40, account
books (4) 1807-71, ledgers (17) 1789-1873, ledgers
and inventories (3 vols) 1788-1801, journals (7)
1801-24, 1829-73, cash books, etc (7 vols, 1 file)
1795-1810, 1836-73, receipt books (10) 1790-1829,
1839-71, invoice book 1836-50, bill books (3)
1802-49, customer account books (2) 1812-18, sales
ledger 1801-44, sales journals (3) 1835-51, sales
cash book 1836-43, quotations book 1859-60,
record of goods ordered and received (1 vol)
1811-41, records of iron, ironstone and coal
deliveries (20 vols) 1824-73, production notebook
1871, wages accounts (14 boxes, 1 vol) 1832-54,
wages books (2) 1816-27, inventory of tools 1753,
deeds and other papers rel to property (2 boxes)
c1758-1848, valuations and inventory (4 vols)
1787-1859, papers rel to insurance (1 envelope)
1817-48, farm, yard and hay accounts (3 vols)
1836-56, rent books (4) 1805-56; account book
1832-9 of William Botfield, estate account book
1864 and bank book 1864-70 of Mrs Botfield.
John Rylands University Library of Manchester. NRA
35780.

[61] **JOSEPH BOWERBANK & SON**, iron and
brass founders and ironmongers, Penrith,
Cumberland

Letter book 1956-7, ledgers (8) 1894-1965, waste
books (7) 1912-49, day books (55) 1887-92,
1912-68, sales and sundries books (13) 1907-53,
wages book 1888-1901, photographs of kitchen
ranges (2 items) nd, price list 20th cent.
Cumbria RO, Carlisle (DB/49). NRA 35351.

[62] **BOWESFIELD STEEL CO LTD**, steel sheet
rollers, Stockton-on-Tees, co Durham

Articles of association 1939, directors' minutes
(10 vols) 1896-1969, share ledger, register of
transfers, etc (1 vol) 1896-1970, share transfers
(1 vol) 1939-70, seal book 1889-1967, annual
returns 1954-70, private ledgers 1913-70, journals
1933-49.
*British Steel Northern Regional Records Centre,
Middlesbrough.* NRA 35680.

[63] **BOWLING IRON CO LTD** (formerly **JOHN
STURGES & CO**), ironfounders, Bradford, Yorks

Lists of managers, trustees and proprietors,
appointments of managers and agreements
(c24 items) 1833-94, lists of shareholders, share
transfers, etc 1800-68, nd, legal papers (15 bundles
and items) 1807-1907, misc corresp (5 bundles)
1817-59, 1893-4, accounts, balance sheets, bills and
receipts (15 bundles) 1796-1876, valuations,
surveys, plans and misc property records 1790-1907,
deeds, schedules and related papers (479 items)
1701-1919, press cuttings and other printed papers
1814-1914.
West Yorkshire Archive Service, Bradford (BIC). NRA
34869.

Trust deed 1854, certificate of incorporation 1870,
conveyances (2) 1862, 1870, balance sheets (2)
1860, 1864, letters and dividend warrants 1863-70,
list of patterns of wheels 1846, company regulations
nd, deed book 1857-64, Sturges family papers 19th
cent.
Wakefield Libraries Department of Local Studies
(Goodchild Loan MSS: Iron MSS). NRA 23032.

Summary accounts ledger 1804-23.
Science Museum Library (MS 486).

[64] **JOHN BOWLING & CO LTD**, ironfounders,
Leeds

Ledger 1878-1910, general ledger 1886-95, balance
books (4) 1898-1951, bill book 1882-1901, financial
memoranda book 1887-96, sales ledgers (3)
1895-1920, sales day books (4) 1939-54, inwards
ledgers (3) 1926-39, wages books (3) 1886-92.
Brotherton Library, Leeds University (MS 170). NRA
34054.

[65] **FREDERICK BRABY & CO LTD**,
constructional engineers, hollow-ware and sheet
metal mfrs, London and Bristol

Memorandum and articles of association 1865,
directors' minutes (13 vols) 1865-1943 and indexes
(9 vols) 1882-1943, registers (2) of shareholders
1865-81, 1919-c1924, registers (3) of share transfers
1885-1928, reports and balance sheets, etc (4 vols)
1865-1920, ledgers (8) 1866-c1946, journals (9)
1866-1962, superannuation fund trustees' minutes
(1 vol) 1924-76, deeds and other records rel to
property in London and Bristol (3 bundles)
c1850-1931, photograph of London premises 1885.
Bristol RO (Acc 40033). NRA 30797.

Records incl prospectus 1864, certificate of
incorporation 1865, share records, chairman's
papers 20th cent, catalogues 1873-98, photographs
nd and printed papers rel to sports and social clubs
1889-1911.
Braby-Fuller Ltd. NRA 28631; BAC *Company
Archives* no 78.

[66] **THOMAS BRADBURY & SONS LTD**
(formerly **WATSON & BRADBURY**, formerly
MATTHEW FENTON & CO), silver and
electroplate mfrs, Sheffield

Balance sheets 1896-1942, letter books (2)
1787-1816, 1832-61, ledgers (4) 1776-1832, day
book 1777-95, cash books and journals (10)
1771-82, 1791-9, 1816-21, 1825-54, cost books (5)
1793-1812, nd, order books (16) 1793-4, 1828-9,
1923-37, corresp and orders (35 files) 1794-1801,
1817-53, invoices (20 files) 1815-50, vouchers
(1 box) 1802-1962, delivery book 1797-1804, notes
rel to shipments to America (2 vols) 1844, nd, stock
records (4 vols, 1 file) 1822-7, 1837, 1848-50, nd,
pattern books and catalogues (5) 1820, nd, number
books (4) 1849, 1879, 1909, nd, calculations for
candlesticks and teapots (2 vols) nd, notes rel to
assay 1817-28, misc corresp (3 files) 1805-1962,
London agency monthly accounts and stocktaking
records (140 items) 1818-60, misc papers rel to legal
affairs, staff and premises (3 files, 24 items)
1766-1882, nd, printed bills, notices, price lists, etc
1817-44; household and personal bills of Thomas
Bradbury 1841-6, papers mainly of Frederick
Bradbury rel to history of the Sheffield plate
industry 20th cent, pattern books and catalogues
1775-1846, nd collected by Frederick Bradbury, MS
account of the founders of the Sheffield silver and
plating industries by RM Hirst 1820-32.
Sheffield Archives (BR). NRA 34862.

[67] **BRADLEY & CO LTD**, hollow-ware mfrs,
Bilston, Staffs

Cost books (3) 1905-15, corresp, tenders, contracts,
etc, mainly for munitions and other war supplies,
c1905-19.
Wolverhampton Borough Archives (DB/6). NRA
21915.

[68] **JOHN BRADLEY & CO
(STOURBRIDGE) LTD**, ironfounders,
Stourbridge, Worcs

Records (22 boxes, c50 vols, 7 bundles) 1729-1982
incl articles of copartnership 1802, minutes and
other corporate records 1919-66, ledgers (5)
1907-61, journal 1888-1963, other accounting and
sales records 1916-c1965, deeds and legal papers
(11 boxes, 6 bundles) from 1729, and papers rel to
Midland Iron & Steel Wages Board and South
Staffordshire Iron & Steel Association (5 boxes)
1930s-1940s.
Dudley Archives and Local History Service (Accs 8435,
8439, 8441).

Letters mainly from customers (132 items) 1830.
London University Library (MS 798). NRA 15774.

Cash books (7) 1892-1932, 1941-6, castings book
1885-1913 incl cash accounts 1932-56, corresp,
output reports and accident book (1 vol, 2 bundles,
79 items) c1945-52, catalogues, etc (5 vols) 20th
cent.
Staffordshire RO (D 888/13-18). NRA 26673.

Papers of JU Rastrick 1800-55 incl diary 1820 and
misc letters as a partner in the firm.
London University Library (Rastrick Papers). NRA
12776.

Balance sheets (52 items) 1920-30, works committee
minute book 1929-45.
Staffordshire RO (3409). NRA 3505.

[69] **BRADLEY & TURTON LTD**, ironfounders
and press mfrs, Kidderminster, Worcs

Ledgers (4) 1903-30, private ledgers (2) 1922-43,
journals (3) 1919-23, 1937-44, sundries journals (4)
1902-29, 1941-4, purchase day books (2) 1944-9,
letters, accounts, memoranda, etc (1 vol) 1831-43.
Hereford and Worcester RO, Worcester (705:918). NRA
34884.

[70] **HENRY BRAMALL & SONS**, cast and shear
steel mfrs, Sheffield

Cash books (27) 1853-88, invoices and statements
(9 bundles) 1874-95, sales and purchase ledger
1856, 1865-8, corresp mainly rel to orders (4 vols,
21 bundles) 1866-95, 1910-32, orders (1 bundle)
1854-65 and order books (3) 1897-8, 1916-25,
delivery book 1892-3, receipts (1 vol, 13 bundles)
1856-1932 and notes 1896, 1901-5, travellers'
notebooks (2) 1880-1, 1907-14, wages records
1858, 1898-9, list of engineering, quarrying and
colliery firms 1894, misc printed material 19th-20th
cent.
Sheffield Archives (BRAM). NRA 10603.

Receipt book 1866-7, order books (34) 1891-1927,
delivery book 1905-10.
Kelham Island Industrial Museum, Sheffield. NRA
10603.

[71] **BRAMPTON BROTHERS LTD**, cycle
chain mfrs, Birmingham

Records from 1896 incl memorandum and articles
of association 1897, board and general meeting
minutes 1897-1936, misc financial papers 1922-31,
guard book 1931-6 and catalogues 1896-1922.
Manchester Central Library Local Studies Unit
(M501/BB). NRA 35782.

[72] **C BRANDAUER & CO LTD**, steel pen mfrs,
Birmingham

Partnership agreement 1897, balance sheets and
accounts 1898-1900, 1909-19, 1927, report 1927,
patent for improved steel pens 1871, catalogue,
photographs and misc publicity material
c1886-1900, nd.
The Company. Enquiries to the Business Archives
Council. NRA 24137.

[73] **BRASS BATTERY WIRE & COPPER CO**,
Bristol

General meeting minutes and abstract of balances
1779.
Somerset Archive and Record Service (DD/DN/238):
see *Business in Avon and Somerset.*

[74] **GEORGE BRAY & CO LTD**, gas burner and
electrical appliance mfrs, Leeds

Memorandum and articles of association 1903-73,
directors' minutes (8 vols) 1903-63, directors'

attendance books (3) 1903-42, 1964-70, legal papers (6 boxes, 4 bundles, etc) 1880-95, 1925, balance sheets 1880-1901, profit and loss summaries 1963, ledger 1882-1902, private ledger 1903-19, bill book 1897-1940, corresp and papers (20 vols, files, etc) rel to sales 1907-58, costings records (7 vols and bundles) 1908-20, quotations books and other records of orders (6 vols, 1 file) 1904-21, calculations and charts rel to output, sales, wages, etc 1906-16, production records (*c*18 vols, 9 files, 7 bundles, 6 items) incl experiment books (3) 1874-1906, instructions issued in works (1 vol) 1898-1950 and works manager's desk diaries (6) 1909, 1913-18, misc staff and wages records (5 vols, 1 file, 4 items) 1907-39, fire insurance policies (15) 1906-7, machinery maintenance ledger 1911, valuation of plant (3 vols) 1925, plans and photographs of works, etc 1874-*c*1975, history of firm 1943 and related papers 1948-*c*1975, catalogues, brochures, press cuttings and other printed papers 1876-*c*1970.
West Yorkshire Archive Service, Leeds (Acc 2742, 3036). NRA 33801.

[75] **BRETT'S STAMPING CO LTD**, drop forgers, Coventry

Memorandum and articles of association 1898, minutes 1964-8, registers (2) of directors *c*1900-61 and directors' holdings 1948-61, attendance book 1950-60, agenda book 1949-62, share registers and ledgers (5) 1897-1976, annual accounts 1956-75, inventory of fixtures, stock and fittings 1898, deeds (1 bundle) 1828-85, misc photographs (1 vol, 18 items) *c*1900-45.
In liquidator's custody. Enquiries to Coventry City RO. See also Lane.

Order book 20th cent.
Coventry City RO: see Annual Report 1987-8, p11.

[76] **BRIDGE IRON FOUNDRY**, Warrington, Lancs

General corresp 1802-30, accounts (6 vols, etc) 1806-30, cash books (2) 1812-18, bonds (4 items) 1798-1814 and promissory notes (18 items) 1788-1828, misc financial papers 1764-1830, stock valuations (8 items) 1810, 1819-29 and inventories (3 items) 1829-30, receipt for deeds 1807, insurance policies (6 items) 1808-29, misc papers (3 items) 1816-40.
Manchester Central Library Local Studies Unit (L24/5).

[77] **BRIDGENESS IRON WORKS**, Bridgeness, West Lothian

Cost book 1863-83.
National Library of Scotland (Acc 5381, box 12). NRA 29147.

[78] **BRIMSDOWN LEAD CO LTD** (formerly **BISCHOF WHITE LEAD CORPORATION (1900) LTD**), lead mfrs, Enfield, Middx

Articles of association 1900, directors' minutes (2 vols) 1911-39, balance sheets (1 vol) 1902-37.
Tyne and Wear Archives Service (Acc 1512/1005A-1008). NRA 32095.

[79] **BRITISH MACHINE MADE CABLE CO LTD**, Netherton, Worcs

Articles of association 1909, general meeting and directors' minutes 1946-59, register of directors 1911, board agenda papers (1 file) 1910-11, profit and loss accounts and balance sheets (3 items) 1911, cash book 1910-16, other financial papers (1 file, etc) 1909-17, licences (1 bundle) 1900-10, test house certificates, etc (1 file) 1908-11, corresp and papers (8 files, etc) *c*1900-1920s.
Dudley Archives and Local History Service (Acc 8264). NRA 25008.

[80] **BRITISH MANNESMANN TUBE CO LTD** (later **NEWPORT & SOUTH WALES TUBE CO LTD**), weldless steel tube mfrs, Swansea, Glam and Newport, Mon

Memorandum and articles of association 1917-28, directors' minutes (5 vols, etc) 1897-1940, shareholders' minutes 1900-40, register of directors 1901-30, registers of members and share transfers (8) 1919-21, share ledgers, register of members, register of probates, mortgage debentures, etc (3 boxes) nd, record of assets purchased 1899-1900, agreement with other tube manufacturers 1932, recommendations rel to policy and management 1936, trust deeds (2 items) 1918, 1924, ledger 1936-42, Board of Trade certificates 1929, patents and trade marks (1 box) nd, employment contracts (1 box) nd, list of staff at works and sales office 1936, leases, agreements and plant register rel to Landore Works 1870-1961.
British Steel East Midlands Regional Records Centre, Irthlingborough. NRA 35554.

See also Stewarts & Lloyds Ltd.

[81] **BRITISH PENS LTD** (formerly **GRAPHO LTD**), mfrs of steel pens, lead pencils and springs, London

Articles of association nd, minute books nd, annual accounts 1920-6, 1954, share certificates nd, cash books nd, work books (15) 1913-22, instructions to labellers 1949-68, trade marks *c*1900-40, wages books (8) 1907-9, 1912-16, 1921-32, catalogues 20th cent.
The Company. Enquiries to the Business Archives Council. NRA 26587.

[82] **BRITISH SCREW CO LTD**, screw mfrs, Leeds

Annual accounts (2 vols) 1898-1928.
Birmingham Central Library Archives Division (MS 298/45-6). NRA 30297.

[83] BRITISH STRUCTURAL STEEL CO LTD, Middlesbrough

Minutes (3 vols) from 1911, private ledger from 1911, ledger 1911-23, cost book 1921-3.
Cleveland Archives and *British Steel Northern Regional Records Centre, Middlesbrough*. Enquiries to Cleveland Archives. NRA 35680.

Memorandum and articles of association 1911, register of members 1911-80, register of directors 1948-60.
British Steel East Midlands Regional Records Centre, Irthlingborough. NRA 35550.

[84] BRITISH WELDING CO LTD, steel pipe mfrs, Motherwell, Lanarkshire

Minutes of agreement (2 items) 1900-8, 1910, agenda book 1908-21, registers of shareholders and directors 1909-30, register of transfers and annual returns 1909-30.
British Steel East Midlands Regional Records Centre, Irthlingborough. NRA 35554.

See also Stewarts & Lloyds Ltd.

[85] SS BRITTAIN & CO, tool mfrs, Sheffield

Invoice book 1845-67, leases of firm's premises 1857-75.
Sheffield Archives (LD 266, 314). *Catalogue of business and industrial records in Sheffield City Libraries*, p12.

Trading accounts 1917-60, invoices (6 boxes) for South American customers 1910-28, index of customers *c*1858, names and addresses of foreign customers (1 vol) nd, letters (5) 1832-46, lease 1904 and agreements 1914, 1918, account book of executors of Frederick Brittain 1917-18.
Sheffield Archives (Marsh 137-9, 145-6, 200, 229-31). NRA 4806.

Letters and circulars to Frederick Brittain (17 items) 1870-80.
Sheffield Archives (MD 1484). NRA 23246.

[86] BROOKFIELD FOUNDRY CO, St Helens, Lancs

Ledger 1886-1919.
St Helens Local History and Archives Library. NRA 24416.

[87] BROUGHTON COPPER CO LTD, copper smelters and roller and tube mfrs, Salford, Lancs

Memorandum and articles of association 1928, trust deed 1897 and appointment of trustee 1921, directors' minutes, etc (16 vols, 2 files) 1881-1942, general meeting minutes (1 vol) 1897-1920, annual reports (1 bundle) 1866-1932, register of documents sealed 1935-44, report on company accounts (1 vol) 1935, deeds (9 bundles) 1800-1928, Broughton works committee annual reports, etc (5 items) 1919-23.
Birmingham Central Library Archives Division (MS 1422). NRA 32859.

[88] ARCHIBALD BROWN & CO LTD, coppersmiths and brassfounders, Liverpool

Tally books (5) 1912-63, accounts 1964-71, cash book 1900-19, sales journal 1956-72, work books (3) 1910-19, 1940-60 and other production records (18 vols) 1947-76, wages books (106) 1927-70, Factory Act register 1921-38, national service register 1940, misc papers 1899-1952.
National Museums and Galleries on Merseyside, Merseyside Maritime Museum (B/AB). NRA 35595.

[89] BROWN BAYLEY'S STEEL WORKS LTD, steel mfrs, Sheffield

Board minutes (4 vols) 1888-1916, 1945-50, general meeting minutes (1 vol) 1951-73, register of directors' interests 1948-66, seal book 1965-73, summary of production and wages costs 1913-15.
Sheffield Archives (Hadfields records). NRA 34874.

[90] BROWN & ENGLEFIELD (formerly **T & H COMPTON**), pewterers, London

Letter book 1848-1901 incl details of bills received 1798-1807 and lists of tenders 19th cent, design notebooks (2) *c*1850, *c*1890, list of customers and products *c*1890, job book 1914-36, patent granted to WJ Englefield 1905, price lists *c*1845, *c*1932-40, catalogues of sales of machinery, plant and stock of Henry Compton & Co 1888-9, press cuttings and photographs 20th cent.
Englefields (London) Ltd. Enquiries to the Business Archives Council. NRA 26586.

[91] JOHN BROWN & CO LTD, mfrs of steel and ordnance and colliery owners, Sheffield

Directors' meeting minutes 1864-1962, debenture holders' meeting minutes 1924-51, general ledgers 1891-1950 and other accounting and property records 1921-51, nd.
John Brown plc. BAC *Company Archives* no 50.

Records incl annual reports and accounts 1898-1902, works committee meeting minutes 1919-23, nominal ledger 1894-*c*1923, journals (4) 1890-1935, production memoranda book 1885-92, property ledger 1902-25, plans of Atlas Works (1 vol) 1864-9, and deeds and related papers from 1850s.
Sheffield Archives. NRA 28631; BAC *Company Archives* no 372.

Colliery accounts, contracts, output books, accident report books, etc 1877-1955.
Sheffield Archives (NCB 406-58, 1276, 1608-11). NRA 14792.

See also John Brown & Co Ltd, shipbuilders and engineers, Clydebank.

[92] BROWN, LENOX & CO LTD, chain cable and anchor mfrs, Pontypridd, Glam

Articles of copartnership 1824, extraordinary resolution rel to the company's capital 1919, list of shareholders, directors and staff (2 items) 1930, corresp rel to management of the Newbridge Works

and the London agency (6 files, 1 item) 1902-10, other corresp (12 files) 1923-30, account 1819, ledger 1823-31, journal 1823-6, order book 1884-8, corresp and papers rel to contracts (c34 items) 1840-68, technical corresp and papers (2 files, 42 items) 1812-1929, report on cast steel cables (2 files) 1929, letters patent, etc (5 files, 20 items) 1815-75, 1914-29, lists of employees (3 items) 1855 and roll of honour c1918, rates of work book 1872-86, agreement book 1856-1901, property records 1813-1956 incl Newbridge Works buildings report (1 vol) 1885 and works plans (3 items) 1878-c1920, photographs of founder and products (26 items) c1824-1930, misc corresp (2 files, 13 items) 1844-1927 and printed papers 1745-1943.
Glamorgan Archive Service (D/DBL). NRA 5619.

'No 4 Hammer' account book 1883-8, foreman's account book 1887-91.
Glamorgan Archive Service (D/D Xab 2).

[93] **BRYMBO STEEL CO LTD**, Brymbo, Denbighs

Records incl memorandum and articles of association 1884, directors' minutes (1 vol) 1948-60, general meeting minutes, etc (2 vols) 1885-1911, 1957-69, directors' reports and balance sheets (1 bundle) 1898-1939, cost accounts (3 vols) 1907-31, salaries and wages books (2) 1919-42 and other wages records (10 files) 1940-72, drawings 20th cent.
Clwyd RO, Hawarden (AN 2827-30). NRA 35998.

Corresp and papers (28 bundles, etc) 1842-75, 1885-1924 incl mortgages, patents, licences and leases.
Clwyd RO, Hawarden (D/BC 2211-14, 2330-64). NRA 29391.

Accounts and balance sheets 1922-8, agreements (3 items) 1873-4, 1914, payment accounts (1 vol) 1936-48, leases (2 items) 1893-1906, plans of property (2 items) early 20th cent, misc corresp and papers 1913-35; letter books of Henry Robertson (20 vols) 1845-88 and Sir Henry Robertson (27 vols) 1891-1936 rel to business and other affairs.
Clwyd RO, Ruthin (DD/CH 71-90, 97-123, 303-48). NRA 19485.

[94] **BRYN WORKS LTD**, tinplate mfrs, Pontardawe, Glam

Board minutes (4 vols) 1901-39, general meeting minutes (1 vol) 1936-9, register of members, etc (1 vol) 1901-16, liquidator's book 1939.
British Steel Records Centre, Shotton. NRA 36012.

[95] **BULLIVANT & CO LTD**, wire rope and netting mfrs, London

Account of legal fees for dissolution of partnership 1876, cash book 1888-9, statements (2) of accounts owing 1889, bank book 1900-1, list of legal documents 1895, orders, drawings and corresp (33 items) 1885-1919, lease 1864, valuer's certificate 1923, catalogues, etc 20th cent.
Doncaster Archives Department (DY.BRI/6). NRA 21369.

[96] **WILLIAM BULLOCK & CO**, ironfounders, West Bromwich, Staffs

Bills, price lists and circulars (c500 items) 1860s-1870s.
Dudley Archives and Local History Service.

[97] **ALFRED BULLOWS & SONS LTD**, malleable ironfounders and buckle makers, Walsall, Staffs

Receipt book 1870-1900, inventory and valuation of works 1895.
Walsall Archives Service (Accs 595, 609).

[98] **BURGON & BALL LTD**, sheep and garden shears mfrs, Sheffield

Partnership agreements and related papers (3 bundles) 1865-83, memorandum and articles of association 1898, minutes (1 vol) 1898-1915, general meeting agenda 1903, share records (1 vol, 1 bundle) 1898-1929, letter books (3) 1895, 1899-1906, private ledgers (2) 1884-98, private ledger draft accounts (1 bundle) 1914, ledgers (2) in account with Daniel Doncaster & Sons 1888-98 incl abstracts of other ledgers 1921-56, petty cash book 1877-9, bank books (19) 1898-1934, corresp, accounts, etc rel to overseas trade mainly with Australia and South America 1867-1943, sales and order books, cost analyses and other sales and purchase records 1872-1940, patent, trade mark and misc legal papers 1865-1938 incl accounts, sales, stock and wages records, etc (2 files, c3 bundles) 1865-79; deeds and premises records (c4 bundles) 1865-99, insurance policies, etc 1884-1935, inventories and valuations with related corresp (7 vols, etc) 1898-1946, staff and wages records 1865-1939 incl wages book 1876-8, time books (6) c1895-1907, work completed register 1881-1939, papers rel to trade unions 1887-1908 and fishing club papers 1893-1903; price lists, catalogues and misc printed papers c1880-1940s, photographs (1 bundle, 9 items) c1893-1916; balance sheet 1869 and other papers rel to formation and liquidation of Burgon & Wilkinson Ltd 1895-9; misc papers of Frederick Burgon (2 bundles) 1893-7 and Benjamin Hind, managing director, 1898-1929, nd.
Sheffield Archives (B & B). NRA 18605.

Deeds (7 bundles) 1800-1940.
In private possession. Enquiries to Sheffield Archives. NRA 18605.

[99] **BURNELL & CO LTD**, galvanised iron mfrs, Ellesmere Port, Cheshire

Minutes (5 vols) 20th cent, register of directors' holdings nd, preference share ledgers (3) nd, registers of share transfers (6) 1900-41, dividend books nd, annual returns 1943-62, balance sheets and accounts 1956-69, Mersey Iron Works capital and special expenditure books 1904-53, private ledgers (7) 20th cent, ledger 1944-62, journal, cash book and bank books nd, misc accounting records 1950s-1960s, sales ledgers (2) and journals (3) nd, purchase journals 1950, nd, staff records incl wages books 1950-63, nd, income tax records 1964-6 and accident books (4) 1925-35.
British Steel Records Centre, Shotton. NRA 36011.

Memorandum and articles of association 1900, general meeting minutes (1 vol) 1940-80, register of directors 1918-80, ordinary share ledger 1956-63.
British Steel East Midlands Regional Records Centre, Irthlingborough. NRA 35555.

[100] **BURYS & CO LTD**, steel, edge tool and file mfrs, Sheffield

Board minutes incl annual reports and balance sheets (5 vols) 1865-79, 1890-1923, private ledgers (3) 1874-1903, 1915-23, nominal ledger 1938-51, private journal 1915-19, purchase journal 1940-9, stock books (2) 1926-51, inventory and valuation of works 1880.
Sheffield Archives (Osborn 138-49). NRA 21582.

Records 1864-c1970 incl memorandum and articles of association 1865, 1890, board minutes (1 vol) 1880-91, board and general meeting minutes (1 binder) 1922-59, agenda book 1881-90, directors' attendance book 1916-70, papers rel to company registration 1914-27, trading and profit and loss accounts and balance sheets from 1914, copy of judgement in case of Bury *v* Bedford 1864, agency agreements 1919-45, letters patent to WT Bury 1870, corresp and papers rel to trade marks 1870s-1960s and valuations, sale particulars, plans and other premises records c1870-95.
Sheffield Archives (Aurora III). NRA 26201.

[101] **BUTLER, SPRAGG & CO LTD**, screw, nut and bolt mfrs, Birmingham

Private ledger 1905-17.
Birmingham Central Library Archives Division (MS 298/44). NRA 30297.

[102] **THOMAS BUTLIN & CO LTD**, ironfounders, Wellingborough, Northants

Private ledger 1889-1908, United Steel Companies Ltd (Butlin branch) journals (2) 1935-47 and account book 1942-7, photographs and misc printed papers 1852-c1980.
Northamptonshire RO (ZB 266). NRA 4039.

[103] **CAERLEON TIN PLATE WORKS**, Caerleon, Mon

Ledger 1759-61, cash books (3) 1758-63, 1781-3, waste books (3) 1758-60, 1761-2, 1763-4, sales book 1756-65, stock book 1834-43.
Newport Central Library. NRA 36195.

[104] **DAVID CAIRD LTD**, ironfounders and engineers, Barrow-in-Furness, Lancs

Balance sheets and profit and loss accounts 1896-1935, letter books (2) 1882-4, 1907-10 and corresp (58 files and bundles) 1897-1920, reports on accounts 1894-1901, 1915-24, capital allowance and tax accounts 1916-21, account book 1968-76, ledgers (2) 1894-1973, day book nd, journals (2) 1946-60, cash book 1961-74, cash vouchers and receipts 1898-1911, orders for ingot moulds c1900-24, contract books (10) 1915-77 and notes

(2 files) 1902-7, record of work for customers (1 bundle) 1902, advice and delivery notes 1907-23, patterns and pattern shop notes 1900-19, work books (2) of pattern maker 1903-4, foundry records 1904-c1917, wages book 1957-9, medical certificates 1914-17, plant inventory (1 vol) 1916-58, misc corresp, papers and photographs 1887-1945.
Cumbria RO, Barrow (BDB/9). NRA 35447.

[105] **CALDER IRON CO**, iron smelters, Bradford, Yorks

Ledger 1807-15, cash books (5) 1806-18, waste book 1807-14, wages book 1812-15.
West Yorkshire Archive Service, Leeds (Kirkstall Forge records). NRA 6539.

Cash book 1803-5, daily accounts of metal made (2 vols) 1805-15, notebook 1812-15, wages book 1809-12, valuation of ironworks 1813, drawing for blast furnace nd.
GKN Axles Ltd, Leeds. Enquiries to West Yorkshire Archive Service, Leeds. NRA 6539.

[106] **CALDER IRONWORKS**, Calder Lanarkshire

Letter book 1821-4.
In private possession. Microfilm in Strathclyde Regional Archives (TD 433). NRA 12501.

[107] **CAMERON & ROBERTON LTD**, ironfounders, Kirkintilloch, Dunbarton

Minutes (1 vol) 1899-1917, balance sheets, profit and loss accounts, reports to shareholders 1901-18, price lists and catalogues (5) 1905-10, c1950, nd, apprenticeship indenture 1868.
In private possession. Enquiries to NRA (Scotland) (survey 641). NRA 15646.

[108] **CANNON INDUSTRIES LTD** (formerly **E SHELDON & CO**), cooking utensil and gas and electrical applicance mfrs, Coseley, Staffs

Records 18th-20th cent incl minutes (6 vols) from 1884, account of T Hartland with Smith, Sheldon & Co (1 vol) 1820-4, ledger of E & S Sheldon 1830-3, cash receipt book of Edward Sheldon 1852, account of John Bradley with E Sheldon & Co and related papers (1 envelope) 1856-79, corresp with accountants and related papers (1 bundle) 1894-6, ledgers, bank books and other accounting records (c20 vols) 20th cent, agreements, corresp, accounts, etc with agents and representatives (c90 envelopes and bundles) c1904-39, gas stove department memoranda book 1898-1909, output and delivery books (2) 1899-1923 and complaints book 1907-10, analysis of meter sales 1918-27, stock book 1891-5, pattern book c1896-c1933, blueprints and specifications (26 files) mainly 1960s-1970s, enamel recipe books nd, printed catalogues and price lists c1847-1980s, corresp and papers rel to patents and trade marks (191 files, 1 vol, 2 bundles, 3 envelopes, etc) 1857-1952, misc staff records (3 vols, 7 envelopes, 1 item) 1840-1958 incl papers (3 envelopes) rel to dismissal of works manager

1895, corresp, deeds, plans and legal papers rel to firm's estates 1787-1967, papers rel to company history 1850s-1970s incl albums (2) of memorabilia *c*1880-*c*1942 and photographs of premises, products and staff late 19th-20th cent.
Dudley Archives and Local History Service. NRA 34107.

[109] **CARGO FLEET IRON CO LTD**, iron and steel mfrs, Middlesbrough

Memorandum and articles of association 1883, trust deeds 1935, 1938, directors' minutes (10 vols) 1883-1969, committee minutes (3 vols) 1908-13, shareholders' minutes (1 vol) 1905-69, directors' attendance books (3) 1910-69, register of members (20 vols) 1883-1902 and from 1904, mortgage register 1874-1938, letter book 1936-7, report on company's position 1905, auditors' reports (4 vols) 1900-30, agreements records (4 vols) 1870-1905, 1911-27, abstracts of accounts (2 vols) 1907-43, private ledgers (5) 1883-1956, impersonal ledgers (4) 1895-1930, private journals (3) 1883-1954, capital expenditure journal 1916-23, journals (2) 1929-35, cash books (14) 1909-53, memoranda of payments (1 vol) 1906, cost sheets (1 vol) 1873-7, cost journals (5) 1905-68, private ledger costs (3 vols) 1905-50, summary of costs, selling prices and profits (3 vols) 1907-42, material stock books (2) 1907-13, manufacturing ledgers (3) 1905-21, make book 1906-52, misc contract, invoice and production records (8 vols) 1920-4, 1938-69, plant ledger 1905-15, mill plant accounts (1 vol) and corresp (1 bundle) 1904-6, copies of deeds (1 vol) 1865-94.
British Steel Northern Regional Records Centre, Middlesbrough. Enquiries to Cleveland Archives. NRA 35685.

[110] **CARLTON IRON CO LTD** (formerly **NORTH OF ENGLAND INDUSTRIAL IRON & COAL CO LTD**), pig iron mfrs, colliery and coke oven proprietors, Stockton-on-Tees, co Durham

Register of documents sealed 1920-35, private ledgers (2) 1887-1923.
British Steel Northern Regional Records Centre, Middlesbrough. NRA 35680.

[111] **JOHN & RILEY CARR**, file mfrs, Sheffield

Agreement book 1858-65, cost book *c*1912-15, sales ledgers (3) 1915-1950s, printed price list 1859.
Sheffield Archives (MD 4050-4). NRA 23246.

[112] **CARRINGTON & CO LTD**, jewellers, electroplaters and manufacturing silversmiths, London

Specifications and costings (1 vol) 1904-5, jewellery received for repair or safe deposit (1 vol) 1924-8.
Westminster City Archives, Victoria Library (Acc 1626). *Accessions to repositories 1991*, p37.

Accounts and designs (13 vols) *c*1870-*c*1930.
Untraced. Sold at Lawrence Fine Art of Crewkerne 14 Feb 1980, lots 10 and 11.

[113] **CARRON CO**, ironfounders, engineers, coal masters and shipowners, Carron, Stirlingshire

Articles of copartnery, charters, bye-laws, etc 1759-73, 1813-78, 1903-63, general court minutes (23 vols) 1755-1963, board minutes and papers 1964-9, committee minutes (56 vols) 1768-1813, 1874-1972 and papers 1949-64, record of securities (5 vols) 1751-1805, record books rel to pledged stock (3 vols) 1772-1962 and to stock transfers (9 vols) 1770-1964, stock sale certificates (1 vol) 1815-1921, share register 1903-28 and certificate books (3) 1903, 1962-78, notices to shareholders 1953-65, dividend book *c*1881-1933, directors' reports and accounts 1948-68, managers' half-yearly reports 1879-1961, quarterly reports 1962, monthly reports 1938-62, annual accounts 1870-1950 and half-yearly accounts 1874-1962, balance sheets (21 items) 1824, 1863-73, profit and loss accounts, etc 1952-72, balance books (20) 1770-1962, letter books (357) 1759-1965, litigation records 1768-1966, inventory of writs 18th-19th cent, review of company organisation, etc 1769, accounts with Roebuck & Garbett 1759-64, misc accounts 1852-74, 1912-47, financial estimates and budgets 1883-91, petty ledger 1769, current ledgers (37) 1786-95, 1813-29, 1838-1946, ledgers (11) 1908-42, journals (3) 1909-17, day books (8) 1764-9, 1779-81, 1794-7, 1802-16, cash books (11) 1760-95, 1829-33, invoice books (31) 1762-1813, bill books (2) 1827-99, transactions analysis 1880-3, corresp rel to supply of cannon to Spain (1 vol) 1769-79, orders for locomotives 1891-1951, engineering department order books (8) 1919-76, agency corresp and related papers 1897-1976, other sales records 1937-75, inventory of pig iron and goods 1768, stock books and ledgers (24) 1768-1839, 1848-60, 1897-1946, stock inventories (4 vols) 1783-1802, 1905-45, report book of warehouse keeper 1772, cost records (46 vols) 1881-95, 1919-46 and cost abstract books (10) 1880-4, ironstone record book 1770-1810, blast furnace reports, etc 1792-7, 1888-91, foundry department regulations *c*1881-5, weekly foundry reports 1882-3, foundry manager's half-yearly reports 1890, foundry department manufacturing expenses (3 vols) 1907-17 and corresp 1913-22, foundry and engineering department corresp and papers incl leases and licences *c*1897-1964, gun castings notebooks (2) 1823-5, 1829, statement rel to pig iron production costs 1885, product registers (60 photographic and woodcut albums) 19th cent-1960s, particulars of guns and carronades *c*1765-1850, proof of Carron guns 1796, particulars and drawings of guns supplied to the British and foreign governments (1 vol) *c*1779-97, specifications 1762, 1816, patent certificates (5 bundles) from *c*1855, letters patent from *c*1900, trade mark specimens 19th cent and certificates (3 packets) *c*1920-60, drawing and design books (5) 18th-19th cent, diagrams mainly of furnaces (6 items) 1857-75, nd, sketches and drawings of products (538 items) *c*1880-1930, nd, technical and production corresp and papers 1905-76, wages books (2) 1871-84, lists of staff and salaries (6 vols, etc) 1868, 1876, *c*1912-63, records of piecemens' wages 1884 and of foundry wage rates 1870-9,

papers rel to moulders' strike 1879, instructions, notices and memoranda to employees (1 vol) 1879-88, records of Carron Founders' Friendly Society 1829-58, Carron Victualling Society 1840-61 and Carron Hearse Association 1831-77, workers' loan book 1879-86, other staff records 1884-1971, valuations of works and plant 1894-1964, insurance records 1792-1850, c1930-74, chartularies, feu charters, lease books, etc (24 vols) c1711-1961, property writs 1478-1813, stipends ledgers (2) 1833-46, 1860-9, estates ledgers (5) 1881-1947, rent ledgers (4) 1885-1943, land valuation books (2) 1897-1910, deeds and legal papers mainly rel to property 1707-1899, plans mainly of works, mines and other company properties 1763-1979, other estate and property records 1889-1975, photographs of products, works, staff, etc (22 albums, etc) 19th cent-c1966, nd, price lists 1816, 1844-92, c1930-72 and product catalogues incl some of other firms c1880-1970, company magazines, newsletters and press cuttings (57 vols, 111 files) 1922-82, posters (4 items) 1779-82, c1970, corresp and papers rel to company history c1774-1963; minute book of Fifeshire Main Colleries Ltd 1891-5, colliery account book 1759-60, receipt book 1770-1, coal deliveries record 1859-79, Niddry Colliery weekly record of coal and salt 1760, and other coal mining records 1800-1952; ironstone accounts 1878-82, reports on ironstone works 1770-2, day book 1882-6, deliveries record 1880-2 and output books (8) 1852-82; timber book 1802-9, rules rel to Cadder coal and ironstone works c1873, reports, plans and papers rel to mineral fields 1887-90; shipping department records 1805, 1852-1953; account book of Charles Gascoigne 1757-64.
Scottish Record Office (GD 58, RHP 1619-24, 2953-63, 43568-70, 44351-44671, 16981-47000, 48604-17, 49756-986, 69892-70000, 72501-94). NRA 14654.

Misc records incl bills for work done at Hopetoun House (2 items) 1767, 1770, notebooks rel to pay and discharge of employees (2 vols) 1882-1910, memorial to employee 1919, plan of works 1887 and maps of properties 1860-80, visitors' book 1882-1950, catalogues and publicity material c1871-1975.
Falkirk Museum. NRA 18888.

Copies of royal charter, articles of copartnery and bye-laws, etc (1 vol, etc) 1759-1962, product catalogues 20th cent, press cuttings rel to royal visit (1 vol) 1932, printed maps and plans of company's works and estates (84 items) c1763-1967, newsletters, etc 1950-69, booklet rel to company history 1909, misc corresp and papers 1810-1965.
Central Regional Council Archives Department (CN, MP/CN). NRA 24511.

[114] RICHARD CARTER LTD, spade and shovel mfrs, Kirkburton, Yorks

Accounts and goods supplied (1 vol) 1810-33, accounts (9 vols) 1831-4, 1844-1909, ledgers (3) 1869-99, journals (3) 1831-83, record of goods supplied (2 vols) 1818-28, production and goods supplied (1 vol) 1857-61, notes (1 vol) rel to book-keeping 1836.
West Yorkshire Archive Service, Kirklees (B/RC/a). NRA 34066.

[115] JAMES CHADWICK (IRONFOUNDERS) LTD, Bolton, Lancs

Wages books (6) 1867-70, 1890-1908, 1913-23, leases, mortgages and plan of premises (10 items) 1866-1915.
Bolton Archive Service (ZZ/124). NRA 27568.

[116] CHAMPION, DRUCE & CO LTD, white lead mfrs, London

Records of predecessor companies 1828-71 incl partnership ledger 1847-51, memoranda rel to profits (3 items) 1837-56, stock books (2) 1847-57 and Hankey family and business papers (12 items) 1840-8; directors' minutes (2 vols) 1930-60, register of managers, shareholders and share transfers 1929-52, trust deeds and deed of amalgamation (2 vols, 12 items) 1930-8, journal 1930-52, plans and photographs of works (31 items) 1919-45, papers rel to company history (2 items) 1950.
Tyne and Wear Archives Service (Acc 1512/1009-86). NRA 32095.

[117] CHARLESTOWN TIN SMELTING CO, Charlestown, Cornwall

Black tin account book 1840-1.
Cornwall RO (X 363/4). NRA 5235 (Summary of accessions Oct-Dec 1970).

Account books (2) 1869-84.
Cornwall RO (RG 32, 35). NRA 627.

[118] CHEADLE BRASS WIRE CO, Cheadle, Staffs

Minutes (1 vol) 1788-1831, partnership accounts (1 vol) of Thomas Patten 1788-1805, accounts (1 vol) of Thomas Wilson with the company 1805-11, record of partners' investment in 3% consols 1812-23; ledgers (2) of predecessor partnerships 1761-6, 1769-72.
Thomas Bolton Ltd. Microfilm in Staffordshire RO (MF 58/2). NRA 22812.

[119] GEORGE CHRISTIE LTD, wire drawers and weavers, Glasgow

Minute book 1889-1910.
United Wire Group plc. Enquiries to NRA (Scotland) (survey 763). NRA 17522.

[120] DANIEL CLARK, ironfounders and sanitary engineers, Carlisle, Cumberland

Private ledger 1866-81, ledgers (7) 1899-1973, cash books (2) 1888-1908, 1971-4, bank book 1867-78, petrol account 1969-73, corresp rel to carriage of goods 1907-28, bills 1841-1932, steam boiler inspection reports 1902-6, licences and patents, etc

1864-1902, factory registers 1868-1938, employment returns 1901-4, notices rel to holidays and working hours 1908-15, stock valuation 1848, plans of premises *c*1914-78, advertisements and sketches late 19th cent-1939, machinery sale particulars 1884-1919, government pamphlets 1878-1928, notes rel to Carlisle iron foundries *c*1950-77, misc business and Clark family papers 1846-1960.
Cumbria RO, Carlisle (DB/85). NRA 35354; and see *Report of the County Archivist*, Oct 1982, p3.

[121] **ROBERT CLARK**, iron and brass founder, Clitheroe, Lancs

Ledgers (5) 1840-58, day books (4) 1847-57, cash books (3) 1842-59, waste books (2) 1849-54, order books (2) 1849-55, time and wages books (2) 1849-56, building book 1837-52, letter from John Browne, Liverpool 1851.
Lancashire RO (CYC 3/5-24). NRA 15239.

[122] **T & C CLARK & CO LTD**, ironfounders and hollow-ware mfrs, Wolverhampton, Staffs

Corresp mainly rel to liquidation of other companies 1920s, country ledger 1920-8, export ledgers (2) 1912-28, price books (14) 1850s-*c*1925, prices, specifications, addresses, etc (1 vol) 1860s, patents (2) 1855, 1876, pattern books (3) 1878, *c*1880, nd, record of waste casting 1943-52, report book and index (2 vols) 1922-8, conveyance 1836, plan of firm's foundry and adjoining premises 1886, printed catalogues, price lists and handbills 1880-1929.
Wolverhampton Borough Archives (DB/4). NRA 23034.

[123] **EDWARD CLAY**, goldbeater, Liverpool

Financial records 1901-69, business and family corresp and papers 1887-1970.
National Museums and Galleries on Merseyside, Merseyside Maritime Museum (B/C). NRA 35596.

[124] **CLAYTON TINPLATE CO LTD**, Pontardulais, Carms

Board minutes (2 vols) 1883-1953, general meeting minutes (2 vols) 1884-1954, directors' attendance book 1937-53, register of directors (3 vols) 1901-25, 1938-50, register of members, etc 1922-9, share ledger 1883-1936, register of transfers 1932-8, annual returns (1 vol, 1 file) 1936-55.
British Steel Records Centre, Shotton. NRA 36012.

[125] **CLEATOR FORGE**, Cleator, Cumberland

Share ledgers (3) 1804-38.
Cumbria RO, Carlisle (D/LIN). NRA 23772.

[126] **CLYDACH IRON CO**, iron smelters, Llanelly, Brecon

Partnership papers (7 items) 1803, 1822-37, papers rel to John and Walter Powell's holding in the company 1842-50, report on the management of the works 1810, corresp rel to the Clydach Ironworks

incl reports and summaries of weekly output (over 500 items) *c*1804-31, balance sheets and other misc accounting records (14 items) 1821-8, 1838-56, memoranda rel to financial state of works (8 items) 1829 and circular letter to company's creditors 1864, misc papers rel to iron ordered and supplied and coal received, stocked and consumed (4 items) 1823-5, nd, specification of new process for refining pig iron 1841, salaries statement *c*1830, printed papers rel to proposed sale of works 1813, 1817, 1829, misc mineral and building leases (6 items) 1808-33, nd.
National Library of Wales (Maybery MSS *passim*). NRA 23719.

[127] **CLYDE IRON WORKS**, iron smelters, Glasgow

Bills and vouchers (1 bundle) 1809.
Strathclyde Regional Archives (TD 465/20). NRA 22009.

Corresp and papers of the Cadell family rel to the ironworks (1 folder) 1787-1812, 1869.
National Library of Scotland (Acc 5381, box 39). NRA 29147.

[128] **CLYDESIDE TUBE CO LTD**, steel tube mfrs, Glasgow

Memorandum and articles of association (3 items) 1898-1916, certificate of incorporation 1898, minutes (4 vols) 1898-1940, notice of extraordinary meeting 1905, register of directors 1925-48, returns of directors 1948-68, registers of members (1 vol, etc) 1904-*c*1952, share agreements 1900-3 and transfers 1912-67, annual returns 1927-69, auditors' report 1900, corresp rel to acquisition by Lloyd & Lloyd Ltd 1901, works committee minutes 1901, private ledger 1911-34, record of business in various districts 1898-1902.
British Steel East Midlands Regional Records Centre, Irthlingborough. NRA 35554.

[129] **COALBROOKDALE CO LTD**, ironfounders and engineers, Coalbrookdale, Salop

Articles of agreement (7 items) 1707-73, papers rel to shares (18 items) 1718, 1796-9, 1858-96, memoranda (3) on the management of the works *c*1774, *c*1795-7, *c*1799, profit account 1739-45, corresp rel to reconstruction of the firm (27 items) 1880-1, draft accounts 1881, cash books (2) of Abraham Darby III 1769-81, 1784-9, stock and warehouse accounts 1792, inventory and list of debts due 1740, materials consumed and output 1799, 1820, calculations rel to iron needed for the Iron Bridge (1 item) 1775, analyses of ore and materials (5 items) 1837-8, cost calculations and notes of experiments rel to boat and engine building, etc (16 items) 1794-1810, descriptive account of Coalbrookdale Iron Works *c*1834-50, catalogue of pumping engines 1876; Darby family accounts with the company 1802, 1881-7.
Shropshire RO (SRO 1987/38-65). NRA 35748.

Minutes (1 vol) 1789-96, profit and loss accounts (1 vol) 1805-52, settling journal 1798-1808, stock

book 1728-38, petitions (2) from Shropshire ironmasters to House of Commons nd, misc letters, cheques, etc 18th-19th cent.
Ironbridge Gorge Museum (CBD). NRA 36642.

Misc records incl articles of partnership 1709, memorandum and articles of association 1881, partners' minutes 1790-4, 1801-14, draft minutes 1790-6, 1801-6, 1810-14, directors' minutes 1902-13, misc share records 1887, 1896, personal ledger of Abraham Darby III 1771-81, misc accounting records 1739-1908, loose pages from stock book 1727, 1738, iron production statistics 1816-20, papers rel to the Iron Bridge c1775-7, engineering notebook nd, notebooks of Joseph Picken nd, patent 1850, apprenticeship indentures (2) 1901, 1910, works notice 1786, plan 1756 and description c1899 of Coalbrookdale Works, and catalogues c1860-1920s.
Ironbridge Gorge Museum. NRA 36642.

Cash books (2) 1718-49, sales book 1679-1709 incl accounts 1708-9, stock book 1718-27; Horsehay Works account book 1754-62, journals (2) 1802-8, day book 1794-8, blast furnace weekly accounts 1798-1807, and wages and waste book 1767-74.
Shropshire Local Studies Library (MSS 328-37). NRA 19299.

Corresp, notebook, memoranda and notices (c105 items) 1796, 1803-30, nd, wages book 1774-81, Horsehay forges wages book 1796-8.
Shropshire RO (SRO 245). NRA 35795.

Letter book of Richard Ford 1732-7.
Ironbridge Gorge Museum (1992.11941). NRA 35856.

See also Horsehay Co Ltd.

[130] **COALBURN IRONWORKS**, Coalburn, Lanarkshire

Cash account 1855-6.
The Marquess of Bute. Enquiries to NRA (Scotland) (survey 631, bundle A/2119). NRA 15459.

[131] **COCHRANE & CO LTD**, iron smelters and cast iron pipe mfrs, Middlesbrough

Memorandum and articles of association 1926, register of directors 1927-33, staff committee minutes 1920, private ledger 1890-1920, private journal 1890-1921, summary of sales and orders 1935-40, catalogue of products 1909, cost book 1921-5, cost ledgers (7) 1934-45, materials ledgers (2) 1939-43, analysis of annual output 1908, summary of foundry output 1934-40, stock valuation (1 vol) 1919, valuation of spare parts (1 vol) 1954, staff committee minutes 1920, foundry wages summary books (11) 1928-33, register of male employees (2 vols) 1916.
Cleveland Archives and *British Steel Northern Regional Records Centre, Middlesbrough.* Enquiries to Cleveland Archives. NRA 35679.

Corresp (1 bundle) 1893-7, experiment reports, calculations and production memoranda (3 files) 1883-98, notes, plans and diagrams of furnaces, kilns and engines (14 bundles and items) 1883-97, misc papers rel to firm's history 20th cent incl copy of patent specification 1882.
Cleveland Archives (U/CO, U/S/27). NRA 34102.

[132] **COCKER BROS LTD**, spring mfrs, Sheffield

Records 1874-1974 incl minutes (2 vols) 1908-73, share records (2 vols, etc) 1875-1949, balance sheets and trading accounts 1882-1917, cost price book 1874-88, plant account book 1896-1974, and corresp (1 bundle) rel to trade marks 1888-1964.
In private possession. NRA 28631; BAC *Company Archives* no 221.

[133] **WH COLE & CO**, pin mfrs, Painswick, Glos

Records from c1880.
Gloucestershire RO (D 6892).

[134] **COLTNESS IRON CO LTD**, coal and iron masters, Newmains, Lanarkshire

Memorandum and articles of association 1899, 1951, special resolutions (5 items) 1900-34, share registers (8) c1907-61, transfers (14 boxes) 1953-61 and certificates (1 box) 1950s-1960s, dividend payments (8 bundles) 1950s-1960s, annual returns 1947-57, scheme for capital reduction (1 file) 1948-51, record of minerals, leases and agreements (16 vols) 1839-1948, title deeds, legal corresp and papers (18 boxes) c1832-20th cent, misc corresp and papers (4 boxes) 1920s-1950s.
Strathclyde Regional Archives (TD 1090). NRA 33980.

Profit and loss accounts (1 file) 1930-46, balance sheets (1 file) 1926-55, valuations and plans of collieries (12 files) 1930-50.
Glasgow University Archives and Business Record Centre (UGD/109). NRA 21082.

[135] **COLVILLES LTD** (formerly **DAVID COLVILLE & SONS LTD**), steel mfrs, Glasgow

Records 1845-1985 incl memorandum and articles of association 1895, 1930, 1954, certificates of incorporation 1895, 1973, minutes 1895-1978, board meeting papers 1925-47, 1961-70, agenda books and general meeting papers 1895-1934, registers of directors 1901-2, 1950-80, records of directors' interests (1 envelope) 1936-50, registers of shareholders 1885-1935, share ledger 1895-1902, share certificates 1895-1934, 1962, share transfer deeds book c1920-35, dividend account books (3) 1895-1936, letter books 1885-1916, trust dispositions and settlements, agreements, etc 1865-1932, register of documents 1871-1925, register of seals 1895-1938, 1959-73, corresp and agreements rel to acquisition of Clydebridge and Glengarnock works c1914-18, corresp and papers rel to amalgamations and the establishment of the Colviles group c1915-1930s, records rel to reorganisation of subsidiaries (3 files) 1954, record of profits, interest and directors' salaries 1899-1910, taxation papers 1899-1914, ledgers, journals and cash books (c26 vols) 1895-1976, Dalzell Works accounting records (3 vols) 1871-1902, 1908-14, contract book 1927-9, agent's commission book 1929, agency and patent agreements 1893-1922, Dalzell and Clydebridge works production records 1917-72, monthly returns 1922-35, technical and

production notebooks (*c*30 vols) 1900-60, papers rel
to the Ministry of Munitions 1916-25 and the
Ministry of Supply 1940-1, production and cost
charts 1927-36, specifications, drawings, drawing
registers, plans, maps, etc 1845-1985, salaries, wages
and bonus books (17) 1898-1961, registers of
employees at Dalzell and Victoria works (2 boxes)
1900-77, superannuation fund records (7 boxes, etc)
1920-71, Dalzell Works construction accounts
1879-1909, legal and property records rel to
Glengarnock Works 1886-1930, misc property
records *c*1904-35, 1970, Clyde Iron Works drawing
office photographs *c*1900-64, and press cuttings
books 1896-1921, 1936-9; Clydebridge Steel Co Ltd
private ledger *c*1901-15, journal 1901-15 and cash
book 1901-10.
Scottish Record Office and *British Steel East Midlands
Records Centre, Irthlingborough.* Enquiries to the
Scottish Record Office. NRA 35553.

Records 19th-20th cent incl directors' minutes
(7 vols) 1930-65, Clyde Iron Works production
notebook 1892-*c*1898 and other production and
misc records 1945-78, nd, Clydebridge Works job
books (2) 1893-1954 and acceptance books (7)
1899-1916; Glengarnock Works manager's records
(2 boxes) 1894-1972, other accounting and
production records (45 boxes) 1917-78, drawings,
etc *c*1845-1972 and drawing office memoranda
books (87) 1915-60, and industrial relations records,
etc (11 boxes) 1919-75.
British Steel Records Centre, Shotton. NRA 36006.

Corresp and papers of Sir Andrew McCance as
director (126 files, etc) 1909-64 and misc personal
and business corresp and papers of Sir John Craig,
chairman (14 bundles and files) 1916-66, wages
book 1921-31, Glengarnock and Ardeer works
inventory 1872.
Glasgow University Archives and Business Record Centre
(UGD/104). NRA 27344.

[136] WILLIAM COMYNS & SONS LTD,
silversmiths, London

Records 19th-20th cent incl memorandum and
articles of association 1930, 1968, board minutes
1982, directors' attendance book 1930-41, works
committee minutes 1956-83, share records 1930-67,
balance sheets 1937-58, annual reports and accounts
1949-83, other corporate corresp and papers 1896,
1921-1984, ledgers (2) 1947-57, day books (2)
1941-53, cash books (6) 1947-79, monthly accounts
(1 vol) 1910-53, sales agreement 1960, bought
ledger 1908-11, sales ledgers and day books
1952-80, special orders records (3 vols) 1904-28,
price codes (1 vol) 1902-7, nd, price notebook
*c*1955, price list of accessories *c*1933-55, invoices
1948-82, receipts 1946-*c*1981, export licences
1949-55, stock books (18) 1904-38, misc
production records *c*1945-84, trade mark
registration certificate 1909, wages records 1950-78,
time sheets 1986-7, apprenticeship indentures
(1 envelope) 1952-6, factory act registers (4)
1915-38, leases and other papers rel to premises
1923-84, inventory and valuation 1953, photographs

of silverware (1 envelope) nd, publicity material
1924-81, nd and misc papers from 1893.
Victoria & Albert Museum, Archive of Art and Design
(AAD3-1987). NRA 36794.

[137] CONSETT IRON CO LTD, iron and steel
mfrs, colliery and quarry proprietors, Consett, co
Durham

Records mainly 19th-20th cent, incl prospectus and
articles of association (1 bundle) 1886, 1900,
directors' minutes (40 vols) 1864-1947, general
meeting minutes (2 vols) 1864-1947, indexes to
board and general meeting minutes 1864-1919,
directors' attendance book 1865-1952, finance
committee minutes (12 vols) 1930-43, share
registers, ledgers, allotment books, transfer registers
and other share records (58 vols) 1864-1951, nd,
register of mortgages (2 vols) 1871-80, 1922-4 and
stockholders (2 vols) 1940s-1950s, list of loans
(2 vols) 1864-1901, interest payments on loans and
pre-paid calls (5 vols) 1864-1900, profit and loss
accounts (2 vols) 1871-93, 1898-1937, statements
book 1914-51, annual reports (11 vols) 1864-1967,
agreements and other legal papers 1868-1946,
private letter books (21) 1887-1903, general
manager's agenda books (11) 1905-12, 1921-40,
journal 1864, cash book 1864, selling price book
1937-42, cost records (16 vols) 1867-1940, stock
books (3) 1869-1919, manufacturing journals (3)
1864-1922, job ledgers (8) 1921-44, Smith's Forge
account book 1921-42, blast furnace records (2 vols)
1925-52, locomotive works repair registers (7)
1915-45, coke and tar works makes books (3)
1933-58, misc staff records 1888-1960s, deeds and
plans of machinery and buildings 1518-1950, nd,
valuations and inventories (7 vols) 1946-52, press
cuttings (1 vol) 1872-1940, visitors' books (2)
1929-51 and coal royalties, etc (5 vols) 1861-1947;
Shotley Bridge Iron Co board and general meeting
minutes (2 vols) 1863-6 and directors' reports
1864-6; records of other subsidiaries 1873-1956.
*British Steel Northern Regional Records Centre,
Middlesbrough.* NRA 35688.

Colliery records 1878-1947 incl agreements
1878-1929, staff records 1890-1947 and surveys
1900-42.
Durham County RO (NCB 2/5, 3/16-18, 13/19-56,
15/264-6, 19/2/4). NRA 19490.

[138] CONSOLIDATED TIN SMELTING CO
LTD, London

Minute book 1891-1912, register of members and
share ledger 1891-1908, list of shareholders 1891,
private ledger 1891-1912, private ledger entry book
1891-1912, tin accounts 1891-1912, order book
1901-12.
Cornwall RO (BL(1)38, BL(2)12-15, BL(5)28,
BL(9)1). NRA 35850.

Ledger 1902-12, accounts with Stenhouse & Co
1891-3, ticketing books (2) 1893-1904, stock and
despatch book 1888-91, stock book 1892-1903,
dispatch book 1892-5, delivery book 1892-1906.
Cornwall RO (RG 63-65, 89, 90, 113, 118, 246).
NRA 627.

[139] **WILLIAM COOK**, saw, file, plane and edge tool maker, Glasgow

Day book 1859-60.
Strathclyde Regional Archives (TD 998). *Annual Report 1986*, p9.

[140] **WILLIAM COOKE & CO LTD**, wire rope mfrs, Sheffield

Minutes (5 vols) 1873-1959, visitors' books (2) 1956-62.
Doncaster Archives Department (DY.BRI/7). NRA 21369.

[141] **COOKSON LEAD & ANTIMONY CO LTD**, lead mfrs, Newcastle upon Tyne

Partnership corresp and papers (1 vol, 10 files, etc) 1851, 1868-77, memorandum and articles of association (2 vols) 1904, 1924, board minutes (4 vols) 1904-52 and proxies (1 file, etc) 1944, directors' register 1924-31, share records (1 vol, 3 files, etc) 1917-48, seal book 1928-49, papers rel to take-over of Locke, Blackett & Co (4 files) 1937-9, auditors' reports and balance sheets (4 vols) 1905-34, departmental profit and loss accounts (46 vols, 2 bundles, 1 file) 1905-48, private ledgers (6) 1889-94, 1907-15, 1926-52, cash ledgers (9) 1913-55, accounts ledgers (5) 1874-82, 1909-10, 1922-38, stock books (21) 1870-1943, lead production memoranda (1 vol) 1880-1900, desilvering cost book 1900-14, Howdon Works production records (1 vol) 1892-8 and notes on manufacturing processes (1 vol) 1911-28, corresp, papers and production records rel to the Barton smelting process (13 vols, 10 files, several hundred items) 1899-1946, corresp and licences rel to patents (1 vol, 6 files, etc) 1875-1945, salaries records (7 vols, 4 files) 1875-1961, wages books (5) 1893-5, 1899-1941, Christmas bonus records (3 vols) 1874-84, 1892-5, income tax returns (2 vols) 1863-97, other staff records (10 vols, etc) 1919-73, deeds, agreements and papers rel to the Hayhole Works 1876-1951 incl records (38 files) rel to capital expenditure and plant maintenance 1912-51, deeds and papers rel to the Howdon Works 1810-1937; Cookson family papers 1850-1971 and papers rel to Cookson Glass Works 1744-1851.
Tyne and Wear Archives Service (Acc 1512/1087-6763). NRA 32095.

Memoranda and corresp rel to the partnership (26 items) 1868-76, letters rel to the Alkali Bill (3 items) 1904.
Durham University Library (Cookson MSS, box 3, 1-29). NRA 25679.

[142] **AT COOPER & CO**, ironworkers, Walsall, Staffs

Sales account book 1820-40, estimates book 1891-1926.
Walsall Archives Service (Acc 255). NRA 21950.

[143] **COOPER BROS & SONS LTD**, cutlery mfrs and silversmiths, Sheffield

Memorandum and articles of association 1895, letter book 1883-1912 and misc corresp 1880-1912, ledgers (3) 1866-1922, cash books (2) 1866-74, 1884-9, costings book nd, notebook rel to prices for various processes nd, stocktaking book 1866-71, agreements, details of designs and trade marks, notes rel to wages and working hours, etc (1 vol) 1913-64, wages books (2) 1850-1, 1866-79.
Sheffield Archives (499/B). NRA 26195.

Directors' minutes (1 vol) 1938-54, register of shareholders 1896-1947, annual report 1982, private ledger 1945-71, nominal ledgers (2) 1945-82, costings books (6) c1920-1934, 1971-82, working drawings 1960s.
Sheffield Archives (COBB 2). NRA 34872.

[144] **GEORGE COOPER**, tinsmith and brazier, Sheffield

Day books (2) 1849, 1853-4, product catalogues nd.
Sheffield Archives (MD 3527). NRA 23246.

[145] **CORDES (DOS WORKS) LTD**, nail mfrs, Newport, Mon

Partnership agreements and corresp rel to the running of the company (38 items) 1840-69, board and general meeting minutes (1 vol) 1883-99, letter book 1885-1908, agreements and papers rel to the liquidation and sale of the company (1 bundle, 6 items) 1903-4, book of works regulations 1848, misc leases and papers rel to premises (11 items) 1776-1900, plan of works 1884; Cordes family papers 1850-74 and corresp and printed papers rel to the history of the firm 1914, 1952-7.
Gwent RO (D 169, D 372). NRA 34979.

[146] **WILLIAM CORNTHWAITE & SONS**, steel mfrs, Sheffield

Sales and purchase ledger 1902-59.
Sheffield Archives (LD 1945). NRA 34866.

[147] **FW COTTERILL & CO LTD**, bolt and nut mfrs, Darlaston, Staffs

Memorandum and articles of association 1881, 1919, directors' minutes (1 vol) 1897-1919 and reports (1 vol) 1899-1919, share register c1887-1910 and resolution for share allotment 1899, dividend account book 1898-1913, annual summaries of shares (1 bundle) 1886-1918, balance sheets, etc (1 file, 1 item) 1910-25, register of seals 1923-5, papers rel to registration (1 bundle) 1918-25 and liquidation (1 file) 1925-6, private ledgers (3) 1897-1940, ledgers (6) 1880-2, 1890-1925, cash books (2) 1895-1922, bill (1 item) 1910-11, corresp and papers rel to sales and supplies (2 bundles) 1907-14, notes by GH Bayley rel to production and prices (1 vol) c1921-5, wages book 1873-1919, letter from employees rel to foreman 1893, printed report rel to new engines 1895.
Walsall Archives Service (Acc 265, 280, 313). NRA 23872.

[148] **COVENTRY CHAIN CO LTD**, chain mfrs, Coventry

Records 20th cent incl memorandum and articles of association from 1907, board and general meeting minutes 1902-35, private ledgers (4) 1910-31, product engineer's inventories c1907-34, guard book 1931-5 and misc papers and publications 1907-29.
Manchester Central Library Local Studies Unit (M501/CC). NRA 35782.

[149] **COVENTRY SWAGING CO LTD**, needle and screw mfrs, Coventry

Certificates (2) of incorporation 1899 and change of name 1953, minute book 1899-1948, bank books (5) 1903-52, misc financial papers 1943-50, technical drawings (22 bundles) 1899-1965, premises, insurance and legal records 1876-1954, printed catalogues and manuals c1930-8; American Supplies Co Ltd minute book 1899-1948, share transfer files 1899-1952, assignment of book debts 1930, etc.
Torrington Co Ltd: see Lane.

[150] **COX BROTHERS & CO (DERBY) LTD**, lead mfrs, Derby

Directors' meeting minutes (2 vols) 1914-63, register of directors (2 vols) 1917-62, register of seals 1953-64, annual returns 1959-64, statement of accounts (1 vol) 1823-6, private ledgers (4) 1882-1910, 1913-53, general ledgers (2) 1896-1913, stock and debtors' ledgers (3) 1819, 1828, 1830, misc corresp and papers mainly rel to firm's history (3 files, 50 items) c1806, 1857-1966.
Tyne and Wear Archives Service (Acc 1512/6764-6826). NRA 32095.

[151] **GEORGE COYTE**, silversmith, London

Memoranda and accounts (1 vol) 1771-7.
Victoria & Albert Museum, National Art Library: see Catalogue of English non-illuminated MSS. . . up to December 1973, p36.

[152] **JOSEPH CRAWHALL & SONS LTD**, wire rope mfrs, Gateshead, co Durham

Auditor's report and balance sheet 1893, agreement with other companies 1941, impersonal ledgers (5) 1916-51, South African ledger 1914-24, cash books (3) 1887-1905, 1941-62, sales ledgers (3) 1926-54, wire rope sales books (3) 1940-58, merchandise journal 1931-51, papers rel to trade with South Africa nd, corresp with Ministry of Munitions 1917, wages books (6) 1916-58, summary of capital and shares of the Hartlepool Ropery 1922, photographs (3 items) c1911-12.
Gateshead Central Library (69/3). NRA 35242.

Minutes (1 vol, 1 file) 1931-67, share corresp (1 file) 1931-64, private ledgers (2) 1887-1923.
Strathclyde Regional Archives (TD 914/13). NRA 30664.

[153] **CRAWSHAY BROTHERS (CYFARTHFA) LTD**, ironmasters and colliery proprietors, Merthyr Tydfil, Glam

Memorandum and articles of association c1890, London partnership and related legal papers, etc (98 items) 1823-43, 1854, letter book of William Crawshay I 1813-17, letter books of William Crawshay II (2) 1830-9, 1851-5 and Robert Thompson Crawshay (2) 1856-70, corresp, etc (174 bundles) 1786-1877, memoranda books (2) of William Crawshay II 1822-8, 1853-64, ledgers (3) 1826-55, London House private ledger 1839-52, journals (2) 1832-55, balance sheets of the London House (2 vols, etc) 1827-67 and balance sheets and accounts of the Cyfarthfa, Hirwaun, Treforest and Cinderford works (211 items) 1810-34, 1847-66, cash books (4) 1834-43, 1863-80, bank pass books (2) 1813-30 and transactions (3 vols) 1855-67, lists (9) of orders 1855, lists (23) of Cardiff stock 1847-58, deeds (15 bundles) 1706-1863 incl Hirwaun (1 bundle) 1822-58 and London premises (1 bundle) 1787-1863, sale papers 1873 (1 vol, 1 item) and other misc plans and papers mainly rel to Cyfarthfa Works 1805-85, plans of Cyfarthfa New Works and other properties 1901-2, other family and estate papers 19th cent.
National Library of Wales (Cyfarthfa Papers). NRA 31420; see also *Annual Report 1952-53*, p23.

Journal of Cyfarthfa Works manager 1766-7.
In private possession. Microfilm in Glamorgan RO.

Letter book of Richard Crawshay 1788-97.
Gwent RO (D2.162).

Cyfarthfa Works ledgers (3) 1791-8, 1802-6, 1817-46.
Glamorgan Archive Service (D/D Cy 1-3).

Directors' attendance book 1890-1906, letter books (8) 1897, 1905-19, legal case papers (1 box) 1884-92 and misc papers rel to ironworks and collieries (1 box) 1805, 1862-93.
Glamorgan Archive Service (D/DG). NRA 7863.

[154] **CRITCHLEY BROS LTD**, pin mfrs, Brimscombe, Glos

Certificate of incorporation 1909 and articles of association 1951-75, directors' minutes (2 vols) 1909-55, private ledgers (4) 1889-1955, nominal ledgers (2) 1932-46, cash books (3) 1939-56, order book 1908-32, orders from overseas (8 items) 1895-8, suppliers' ledgers (2) 1936-52, customers' accounts (3 vols) 1948-50, production record cards (2 bundles) 1946-78, printing department artwork (24 bundles, 2 folders, 15 items) c1945-1979, record (1 vol) of purchase of machinery, expenditure on buildings, etc 1904-32, visitors' book 1895-1916, salaries and wages books (9 vols, 1 bundle) 1891-5, 1909-22, 1937-60, registers of employees (2 vols) 1891-9, 1902-7, notices of fines for employees (3 items) c1890-1907, notes rel to FE and Henry Critchley 1949, price lists, photographs, press cuttings, etc 1883-1983.
Gloucestershire RO (D4331). NRA 25018.

[155] **F BURTON CROSBEE** (formerly **WILFRED C GRIFFITHS**), silversmiths and dram flask makers, Birmingham

Ledgers (2) 1880-95, 1921-8, cash book 1875-82, sales day books (3) 1875-85, 1953-61, purchases day book 1920-50, misc photographs and papers (4 items) early 20th cent.
Birmingham Central Library Archives Division (MS 1230). NRA 32220.

[156] **CROWTHER & GEE LTD** (formerly **R GEE & SON**), brassfounders, Huddersfield, Yorks

Memorandum and articles of association 1960, cash books (9) 1938-80, sales ledgers (6) 1904-83, day books (10) 1894-7, 1902-63 and cost books (2) 1869-1948, purchase ledgers (4) 1906-85 and day books (4) 1903-43, sales and purchase price lists c1935-55, foundry books (2) 1917-52, assessment of firm's casting production 1982, wages books (4) 1912-71.
West Yorkshire Archive Service, Kirklees (KC 259). NRA 16766.

Foundry costings book c1904-1917.
In private possession. Microfilm copies of this volume and some of those above are in Huddersfield Library Local Studies Department.

[157] **RICHARD CROWTHER & SONS**, whitesmiths and engineers, Elland, Yorks

Ledgers (2) 1895-1905, account books (2) 1873-81, 1886-92, cash book 1886-91, sales accounts (1 vol) 1914-32, misc accounts and receipts 1915-16.
West Yorkshire Archive Service, Calderdale (MISC:112). NRA 27644.

[158] **CRUIKSHANK & CO LTD**, ironfounders, Denny, Stirlingshire

Records c1899-1973 incl account books rel to orders for castings and pig iron used, and catalogues.
Falkirk Museum (A30). NRA 18888.

[159] **CUNINGHAMS & SIMPSON**, silver platers, Edinburgh

Order book 1810-11.
Scottish Record Office (CS 96/3854). *Court of Session Productions*, List & Index Society, special series vol 23, 1987, p208.

[160] **CWMFELIN STEEL & TINPLATE CO LTD**, Swansea, Glam

Board minutes (2 vols) 1897-1918, copy documents book 1889-1910.
British Steel Records Centre, Shotton. NRA 36012.

Share certificates 1897-9, company secretary's desk diary 1911, account book (expenditure and costings) 1886-7, creditors' and debtors' ledger 1900-4, indenture rel to works reservoir 1889, misc corresp

and papers 1905-19; Swansea Steel Co share certificates 1899-1902.
University College of Swansea Library (Paul Jenkins MSS). NRA 14358.

[161] **DALE family**, braziers, tinners and ironmongers, Stafford

Letter books (3) rel to fishing tackle and ironmongery 1914-29, misc business corresp c1890, ledgers (12) 1808-9, 1827-1916, day books (37) 1827-1922, fishing day book 1903-15, ironmongery day books (3) 1922-9, rough day book 1916-17, small debts books (7) 1840-50, 1880-1917, bills receivable (2 vols) 1865-82, cash books (3) 1843-73, 1921-4, order books (10) 1855-1919, memoranda of orders (1 vol, etc) 1891-2, 1905-6, wants books (2) 1891-1913, debit ledger of goods purchased 1837-64, workmen's time books (38) 1889-1932, inventories (3) 1829-40, price lists (6) 1822-c1921, misc records 1840-95, printed publicity material and catalogues of other firms 1826-84; family and election papers 19th-20th cent.
Staffordshire RO (D 256). NRA 23051.

[162] **DALLAM FORGE CO LTD**, iron mfrs, Warrington and Wigan, Lancs

Minutes (2 vols) 1865-74, agenda book nd, nominal register 1865, numerical register with bonds 1870.
British Steel Records Centre, Shotton. NRA 36007.

[163] **DARLINGTON FORGE LTD**, iron forgings and steel mfrs, Darlington, co Durham

Memorandum and articles of association 1873, 1908, 1919, minutes (7 vols) 1873-1976, register of directors (2 vols) 1901-6, 1918-33, directors' attendance book (2 files) 1933-69, directors' holdings and interests nd, notices of meetings 1934-70, register of mortgages and bonds 1887-1931, debenture transfer register (3 vols) 1894-1904, c1930, other papers rel to debentures (6 vols) 1927-32, nd, share registers (8) 1873-89, from 1926 and nd, share certificate books (4) 1873-1912, nd, other share records 1887-9, 1916-19, 1929-70, letter books (3) 1918-30, papers rel to reconstructions of company c1917-19, 1933-42, corresp rel to company finances (1 vol) 1924 and to the Carnforth Hematite Iron Co Ltd (1 vol) 1927-32, register of seals 1933-70, annual summaries (3 vols) 1874-1907, returns to Board of Trade and Registrar of Companies 1933-70, misc corporate records (1 box) 1874-1936, accounts 1930-9, private ledger 1913-19, private journal 1870-3, payments and receipts ledger 1866-1927, cheque book counterfoils (7 vols) 1904-33, trade ledgers (2) 1873-87, 1913-19, sales agreements 1933, agreements and corresp 1954-6, manufacturing cost accounts (1 vol) 1927-9, sports club committee minutes (1 vol) 1962-74, tithe rent charge purchases (1 vol) 1910-21, rent book c1925.
British Steel Northern Regional Records Centre, Middlesbrough. NRA 35681.

[164] **DARLINGTON WIRE MILLS LTD**,
Darlington, co Durham

Minutes (2 vols) 1904-60, Companies Act register
1904-32, private ledgers (2) 1904-38, ledger
1911-13.
Doncaster Archives Department (DY.BRI/10). NRA
21369.

[165] **DARWEN & MOSTYN IRON CO LTD**,
iron ore mine operators and iron mfrs, Mostyn,
Flints

Memorandum and articles of association 1887,
minutes (1 vol) 1887-1915, corresp rel to premises
(1 file) 1934-6, photographs of works, memorabilia,
etc 1906-60; corresp and papers rel to history of the
works (1 file) 1971-8 and personal papers of
JH Storey 1918-73.
Clwyd RO, Hawarden (D/DM/584). NRA 24328.

Private ledgers (4) 1877-1927.
Clwyd RO, Hawarden (D/DM/844). NRA 26883.

Tonnage account of coal delivered at the Mostyn
Ironworks (1 file) 1889-90.
University College of North Wales Library
(Lloyd-Mostyn MS 7170). NRA 22953.

[166] **DAVIES BROS & CO LTD**, galvanisers,
Wolverhampton, Staffs

Minutes (1 vol) 1885-1920 and draft minutes
1885-9, papers (c10 bundles and items) mainly rel to
formation of company 1885, re-formation 1908 and
the Companies Act 1929, share transfer register and
other share and debenture records (4 vols,
4 bundles, 30 items) 1885-1918, 1940-51, nd, letter
books (2) 1889-1918, misc corresp (3 bundles)
1887-1909, register of mortgages 1889-1922,
balance sheets 1893-1932, private ledgers (4)
1886-1951, royalties ledger and day book (2 vols)
1895-1904, bad debts ledgers (2) 1892-1965,
private cash books (5) 1885-1948, other accounting
records (8 vols) 1927-54, corresp and papers (1 vol,
1 bundle) mainly rel to orders 1890s-1920s,
customer address books (5) 1880s-1920s, corresp
and papers (c6 bundles) rel to patents and trade
marks 1877-1930s, output summaries 1937-58,
maintenance materials registers (2) 1939-56, deeds
1870-1952, registers (3) of buildings and plant
1920s-1940s, misc legal, property and insurance
records (c15 bundles and items) 1879-1930s,
catalogues, price lists and photographs 1890s-1963,
papers rel to Galvanised Iron Association 1904-7;
Ettingshall Ironworks journal nd, inventory 1887
and reports 1897.
Wolverhampton Borough Archives (DB/12). NRA
25556.

[167] **J DAVY & CO (ELSECAR) LTD**,
ironfounders, Elsecar, Yorks

Memorandum and articles of association 1908,
1914, directors' and general meeting minutes (1 vol)
1908-68, letter book 1909-10, private ledgers incl
balance sheets (3 vols) 1908-57, general ledgers (2)
1890-1908, day books (2) 1879-81, 1885-98, cash

books (2) 1869-77, 1890-7, trading accounts and
balance sheets (1 folder) 1945-71, lists of goods
made and supplied (3 vols) 1871-7, 1894-1921,
invoice book 1907-11, inventory of stock and
materials (2 vols) 1936-61, papers (3 folders) rel to
factory regulations 1870-1939, munitions work
1915-16 and production 1949-54, cottage rent
books (2) 1942-69, stationery, illustrations of
products, etc nd.
Sheffield Archives (309/B). NRA 24081.

[168] **NELSON & EDITH DAWSON**,
silversmiths and decorative artists, London

Corresp and papers 1884-1939 incl corresp mainly
with clients 1904-26, letter book 1912-18, cash
books (2) 1920-1, notebooks (2) recording silver,
iron and brass work c1900-23, sketches, watercolour
drawings, photographs, glass negatives and printed
items.
Victoria & Albert Museum, Archive of Art and Design
(AAD 7-1987, AAD 8-1988, AAD 9-1991). NRA
34446.

[169] **DEAKIN & FRANCIS LTD**, jewellery mfrs,
Birmingham

Papers (2 items) rel to purchase of the business
1848-50, articles of copartnership, agreement for
dissolution and related papers (5 items) 1864-1902,
directors' and general meeting minutes (4 vols) from
1920 and committee minutes (1 vol) 1919-35,
general corresp (1 vol, 3 bundles, etc) 1848-1902,
balance sheets, accounts, etc (1 envelope, 9 items)
1899, 1931-6, private ledgers (10) to 1973, ledgers
(4) from 1853, expenses ledger nd, private cash
book 1897-1900, cash books (2) 1848-53, nd, bank
books (2) 1848-53, 1927-36, misc accounts, etc
1853-1974, sales and profit and loss accounts
(1 envelope) 1887-90, sales analysis 1931-2, corresp
with customers, etc 1869-1950s, other customer
records (1 vol, 1 item) c1940, nd, pattern and design
records (18 vols, 1 box, etc) 19th-20th cent, job
record cards (3 boxes, 3 items) 20th cent, stock
book (gems) 1960s-1970s, patent records (6 bundles
and envelopes) 1910-14 and trade mark papers
(1 file) from 1931, corresp and memorandum rel to
salaries (2 files) 1912-14, works committee minute
book 1919-23, valuation and misc premises records
(4 items) 1849, 1901-6, nd, misc photographs,
publicity material, price lists and other printed items
1815-late 20th cent; misc Deakin and Francis family
papers 18th-20th cent.
The Company. Enquiries to the Chairman. NRA
34734.

[170] **DEIGHTON'S PATENT FLUE & TUBE
CO LTD**, boiler flue mfrs, Leeds

Balance sheets and accounts 1925-31, general ledger
1901-4, private ledgers (2) nd, cash books (4)
1928-35, flue department accounts (3 files)
1911-26, order books (35) 1897-1900, 1921-63,
corresp with customers (1 box) 1903-63, purchase,
sales and delivery records (13 vols, 3 parcels)
1917-53, surveyors' books (2) 1905-9, 1914-19 and
other inspection and test records 1920-60, reports

on welding costs, etc (1 file) 1922-4, time and wages records (2 vols, 1 parcel, 1 file) 1913-30, 1951-3, fire insurance policies (5) 1919, schedule of premises 1929, catalogues of other firms (2) 1909, nd, will of William Deighton and related papers 1918, 1927-8.
West Yorkshire Archive Service, Leeds (Acc 1240). NRA 34491.

[171] **DENNYSTOWN FORGE CO LTD**, iron forgers, Dumbarton

Partnership agreements and certificate of incorporation nd, minutes (2 vols) 1884-1961, letter books (2) 1854-8, 1886-90, corresp and papers from *c*1902, account book 1862-86, private ledgers and journals (9) 1881-1957, ledgers (9) 1854-66, 1952-76, cash book 1854-66, receipts (1 file) 1904, order book 1872-87, cost ledgers (21) 1959-71 and other production records (4 vols, 4 files) 1973-9, drawings and charts (5 bundles, etc) nd, wages book 1897-1905, staff register 1910-79, inventories and plans of premises 1934-78, nd.
Dumbarton Library. NRA (Scotland) (survey 2539). NRA 22906.

[172] **JOHN HENRY DICKINSON LTD**, cutlery forgers, Sheffield

Misc papers rel to annual meetings, accounts and balance sheets *c*1937-63, share certificate counterfoil book 1904-24, private ledgers (2) 1918-43, nd, general ledger 1889-1902, statements ledgers (3) 1945-72, stock book and balance ledger 1904-18, journal incl trading and profit and loss ledger 1904-61, cash books (2) 1882-95, day books (18) 1921-81, purchase, sales and order records (15 vols and bundles) 1919-77, wages books (2) 1878-1900, contracts of employment 1977, photographs (2) of workforce, plans and drawing of firm's premises, accounts rel to JH Dickinson deceased 1889-1904.
Sheffield Archives (JH Dickinson records). NRA 34843.

[173] **DICKSON & MANN LTD**, steelfounders and colliery engineers, Armadale, West Lothian

Directors' and general meeting minutes (3 vols) 1948-69, directors' agenda book 1892-1943, private ledgers (7) 1888-1952, register of members 1892-1965, share ledger 1892-1927, balance sheets (1 box) 1892-1950.
Scottish Record Office (GD 1/728). NRA 19370.

[174] **DIXON, CORBITT LTD**, wire and hemp rope mfrs, Gateshead, co Durham

General meeting minutes (2 vols) 1890-1963, register of directors or managers 1901-67, directors' attendance book 1946-63, Companies Act register 1941-6, annual returns and corresp (1 bundle) 1946-63, share records (4 vols) 1904-69, lease 1883, misc catalogues and printed papers 1854-1969.
Doncaster Archives Department (DY.BRI/11). NRA 21369.

[175] **JAMES DIXON & SONS LTD**, mfrs of silver and silver-plated goods, Sheffield

Records (over 800 vols, files, etc) 1806-1975 incl deeds of partnership, agreements, etc 1825-1932, letter books (6) 1809-26, 1835-44, memoranda books (4) 1823-31, 1844-1941, partnership accounts of James Dixon (2 vols) 1806-22, income tax receipts (1 bundle) 1871-4, ledgers (13) 1806-66, private ledgers (7) 1836-1920, nominal ledgers (9) 1889-97, 1921-55, clerks' ledgers (2) 1883-*c*1914, capital and investment accounts (1 vol) 1898-1911, day books (6) 1844-1975 and indexes (2) 19th cent, cash books (8) 1813-48, 1858-66, 1880-3, bill books (7) 1806-13, 1818-53, 1865-9, 1905-41, bank books (9) 1906-28, list of debts owing to firm 1814, sales ledgers (9) 1814-18, 1822-30, 1840-98, day books (2) 1817-26, 1873-80 and journal 1826-31, bought ledger 1822-8, purchase ledger 1898-1929, other sales and purchase records from *c*1908, receipt book 1854-7, estimates books (8) *c*1871-6, *c*1898-1920, order books (2) 1831, *c*1900, salesmen's order notebooks (27) 1813-39, *c*1896, 1916, 1950-60, journey ledgers (5) 1822-37, 1869-88, foreign trade corresp and order records (5 vols, 22 files and bundles) *c*1841-54, 1864-75, 1886, 1912, price books and prices lists (*c*40 vols) 1815, 1839 and from 1862, cost books (*c*38) *c*1836-1975 and indexes (4) 1907-8, nd, specifications book 1911, die books (2) 1875, 1909-15, pattern books (7) *c*1881-1904, *c*1910-14, nd, numbers index books (2) *c*1884-*c*1925, nd, hollow-ware deposit books (2) 1887, spoon and fork depot book *c*1900, alloys recipe book *c*1838-57, stock books (8) 1823, 1835-9, 1842-7, patents and related papers 1851-1911, calculation books (*c*75) 1858-62, 1870-1949, wages books (15) 1898-1957, insurance policies *c*1833-*c*1930, accounts for new buildings (1 bundle) 1857-9, photographs of products (1 vol) *c*1870, and Dixon family executors' and property records 1811-*c*1942.
Sheffield Archives (James Dixon records). NRA 34873.

Corresp, estimates, costs, orders, sketches, printed notices, etc (1 box) *c*1885-*c*1911.
Sheffield Archives (Aurora III). NRA 26201.

[176] **WILLIAM DIXON LTD**, coal and iron masters, Glasgow and Coatbridge, Lanarkshire

Prospectus 1906, memorandum and articles of association 1947, registers of members (5) 1906-37, accounts rendered books (7) 1853-1917, ledgers (6) 1932-57, Govan Ironworks statement book 1935-52 and monthly journal 1942-52, Govan Colliery day books (5) 1857-92, journals (8) 1849-58, 1863-1904, cash books (10) 1871-83, 1890-1929, other financial records (9 vols) 1930-55, sales book 1825-7, pig iron sales books (10) 1942-57, sales and stock books (8) 1898-1901, 1903-18, stores letter books (2) 1948-52, sales and output books (33) 1866-1923, analysis records (15 vols) 1882-1958, pig iron analysis records (19 vols) 1903-58 and production books (5) 1929-58, oncost records (28 vols) 1865-76, 1900-21, 1934-55, other production records (24 vols, etc) 1927-58, colliery pay sheet abstracts 1855-68, 1872-5, 1886-99,

Govan Colliery pay books (147) 1855-1927, wages records (24 vols) 1871-91, 1894-1903, 1907-61, time books (3) 1948-50, funeral fund roll books (4) 1841-66, accident report books, etc (8 vols) 1905-20, 1928-46, property records (2 vols) 1929-55, nd, misc corresp and papers (18 vols, etc) 1825-1952.
Glasgow University Archives and Business Record Centre (UGD/1). NRA 10828.

Agreements, papers rel to company reorganisation, plans of property, deeds and other legal papers (2 boxes, 27 bundles) 1776-1954.
Glasgow University Archives and Business Record Centre (UGD/191). NRA 13033.

Memorandum and articles of association 1873, 1906, certificate of incorporation 1906, minutes (1 vol) 1944-7, directors' reports and balance sheets 1908-52, share records 1939-52, record of capital reductions 1948-53, liquidation papers 1953-6, works accounts 1952-7, ironworks minutes 1955-62, pension and wages records c1950-60, insurance records 1898-1942, deeds and other legal and property records 1886-1955.
British Steel Records Centre, Shotton. NRA 36006.

Minutes 1954-62 and staff records 1946–c1960.
Scottish Record Office. NRA 35553.

Waste books (2) 1800-6, cash books (4) 1801-7 and pocket diary 1808 of William Dixon.
Scottish Record Office (CS 96/4379-85). *Court of Session Productions*, List & Index Society, special series vol 23, 1987, p146.

[177] **THOMAS DODWELL**, watch case turner, Coventry

Day book c1874-6, pattern books 19th-20th cent.
Coventry City RO: see *Accessions to repositories 1984*, p33.

[178] **J DONALD, FYFE & CO LTD**, iron and brass founders, Johnstone, Renfrewshire

Minute book from 1907, letter books (4) 1909-50, accounts rendered 1904-15, ledgers (2) 1919-52, cash books (3) 1919-54, sales and purchase records (10 vols) 1919-59, cost books (3) 1918-44, pay books (2) 1935-40; James Donald & Son printed catalogues (2) of patterns 1869.
In private possession. Enquiries to NRA Scotland (survey 636). NRA 15465.

[179] **DANIEL DONCASTER & SONS LTD**, steel mfrs, Sheffield

Directors' minutes and related corresp (2 vols, etc) 1932-59, directors' salary records 1931-6, letter book 1869-71, general corresp and papers 1874-7, 1904-74, profit and loss accounts, balance sheet values, etc 1936-60, private ledgers (8) 1844-89, 1891-1933, nominal ledgers (6) 1846-1932, journals (2) 1902-25, private journals (3) 1902-30, day books (4) 1829-36, 1897-8, 1919-25 and summary (1 vol) 1900-33, monthly account books (2) 1912-30, cash books (7) 1830-74, 1916-28, bank books (2) 1829-41, 1843-53, sales ledgers (13) 1829-99, order

and contract books (20) 1881-1939, purchase ledgers (2) 1850-9, 1902-13, trade receipts books and other stock records (23 vols, 1 bundle) 1864-1932, memoranda books (3) 1940-4, forge department private ledgers (3) 1902-30 and journals (2) 1906-30, analysis books, melt books and other technical records (19 vols and bundles) 1873-1941, wages records 1889-1912, 1930-6, other staff records 1909-45, plant and machinery valuations (3 vols) 1928-48, scrapbook 1898-9 and misc papers 1864-75; call books, notebooks, diaries and corresp of CM Mallinson 1911-46 and notebooks, call notes and misc corresp and papers of BW Doncaster 1920s-1949.
Sheffield Archives (LD 368-78 and Donc. 1-174). NRA 4808.

Notebooks (2) rel to the firm's business 1917-36, sales ledgers (6) 1881-92, 1899-1923, records of customers and sales (2 vols, 1 item) 1815-1928, price lists from 1806 and price book 1910-13, order books (3) 1915-20, nd, Swedish iron contracts (13 vols, etc) 1865-1940, purchase journal 1917-23, steel ledger 1909-10, Swedish iron stock book and conversions 1913, steel melting mixes (2 vols, etc) 1893, 1901-14, nd and analysis books (3) 1918-39, other misc technical records, plans of works and misc photographs, papers and printed items rel to the firm and the steel industry 19th-20th cent.
Kelham Island Industrial Museum, Sheffield (Daniel Doncaster Collection). NRA 34125.

[180] **DONCASTER WIRE CO LTD**, wire rope mfrs, Doncaster, Yorks

Memorandum and articles of association 1920, corresp, agreements and memoranda (4 vols and files) 1904-55, balance sheet 1906-7, schedule of standing expenses 1918, cash and wages book 1929-30, purchase and sales acounts (7 vols) 1909-11, 1922-57, inventories and valuations of mills 1925 and other misc property records 1910-c1937, printed technical tables 1920s.
Doncaster Archives Department (DY.BRI/12). NRA 21369.

[181] **DORMAN LONG & CO LTD**, ironmasters, steel and wire mfrs, bridge builders and constructional engineers, Middlesbrough

Records 1880s-1970s incl memorandum and articles of association 1889, 1933, directors' minutes (9 vols) 1889-1956, general meeting minutes (1 vol) 1890-1956, committee minutes (7 vols) 1922-68, debenture stockholders' meeting minutes (1 vol) 1915-36, register of directors (1 vol) from 1901, directors' reports 1890-1966, annual reports and accounts and proceedings of general meetings 1891-1939, share registers (c200 vols) 1920-38, 1954-69, dividend and interest books (42) 1950s-1960s, share bonus issue sheets (10 vols) 1960, printed papers rel to capitalisation 20th cent, bank ledgers (4) 1937-49, purchase books (10) 1944-65, contract sheets (3 vols) 1924-6, 1940s, constructional steelwork orders (12 vols) 1904-36, other order records (30 vols) from 1930s, make and work books (c350) 1925-1950s, materials ledgers

(*c*20) 1903-29, wire department letter books (2) 1899-1913, ledgers (2) 1900-31, private journals (3) 1900-41 and monthly account book 1902-31, other production records from 1920s, laboratory letter, report and analysis books (8) 1898-1963, papers (1 file) and press cuttings (11 vols) rel to Sydney Harbour Bridge 1924-32, drawings registers (11) 1902-70, copies of leases, conveyances, etc (3 vols) *c*1883-*c*1954, registers of property (2 vols) and rent book 1940s, copies of company publications, etc (7 vols) 1890-1967.
Cleveland Archives and *British Steel Northern Regional Records Centre, Middlesbrough.* Enquiries to Cleveland Archives. NRA 35680.

Memorandum and articles of association 1889, directors' minutes (1 vol) 1956-70, reports and accounts 1954-66, drawings for bridge contracts (28 boxes) *c*1915-69, photographs of bridges 1924-81.
British Steel East Midlands Regional Records Centre, Irthlingborough. NRA 35550.

Mainsforth Colliery accident report books (10) 1928-43, colliery wages book 1953-7.
Durham County RO (NCB 13/57-67). NRA 19490.

[182] **DOWLAIS IRON CO**, iron and steel mfrs and colliery proprietors, Merthyr Tydfil, Glam

Minutes (1 vol, 1 item) 1792-3, out-letter books (2) 1782-94, 1874-83, in-letter books (over 830) 1792-1917, Cardiff agency letter books (24) 1819-25, 1848-93, London letter books (*c*250) 1837-1919, other letter books (*c*90) 1824-5, 1888-1919, profit and loss accounts, financial analyses, statements of stock, etc (1 box, 1 vol) 1810-94, balance sheets and reports (1 box) 1834-84, private ledgers (2) 1843-8, 1863-75, accounts ledgers (2) 1834-59, bank book 1824, lists of firm's stocks, securities and credits (1 file, 2 items) 1848, 1850, papers rel to taxes and royalties (1 box) 1818-98, bills of costs (1 box) 1803-9, 1824-34, 1846-99, contract records (1 vol, 1 bundle, 1 file, 9 items) 1852-6, 1867, cost and output records (1 box) 1816-1900, assay book 1865-9, foundry book 1912, reports and notes rel to Dowlais and other ironworks, furnaces, processes, etc (2 boxes) *c*1800-1900, patents, specifications and related corresp and papers (1 box) 1853-1900, salaries ledgers and registers (5) 1882-1925, papers rel to wage rates, employee sick fund, etc (2 boxes) 1845-1907, beer issue records (2 vols) 1907-16, schedule and inventory of Dowlais Works 1848, papers rel to expenditure on building work (1 vol, 5 items) 1848-61, memoranda rel to repairs on managers' houses (1 vol) 1881-1914, deeds, legal papers, memoranda, corresp, etc rel to properties (8 boxes) 18th-20th cent, corresp and papers rel to quarries (1 box) 1875-94, collieries (1 box) 1815-1903 and railways, canals and waterworks (10 boxes) 1790-1914, plans, sketches and related papers 1761-1930, photographs 19th-20th cent; misc Guest family papers (1 box) 1807-1907, accounts and papers of the executors and trustees of Sir JJ Guest (1 box) 1816-90, papers rel to local institutions and events at Dowlais and Merthyr Tydfil (8 boxes) 19th cent.
Glamorgan Archive Service (D/DG). NRA 7863.

Records 19th-20th cent incl memorandum and articles of association, certificates of incorporation and change of name and minutes (2 vols, etc) 1899-1974, letter books (5 boxes) 1837-67, and plans and drawings rel to locomotives built at Dowlais (12 boxes) *c*1900-29.
British Steel Records Centre, Shotton. NRA 36010.

See also Guest, Keen & Nettlefolds Ltd.

[183] **N DOWNING & SONS LTD**, ironfounders, Stockton-on-Tees, co Durham
Agreement to dissolve partnership 1880, directors' minutes (1 vol) 1915-27, day books (3) 1879-1916, patents (4) 1889-1926, advertising leaflets, etc (11 items) 1896-1926, nd.
Cleveland Archives (U/ND). NRA 34084.

[184] **DRYAD METAL WORKS**, architectural metal workers, Leicester

Design sample books (9) early 20th cent, 1930s, work book *c*1920-68, drawings (1 vol) of plate in Leicestershire churches late 19th-early 20th cent, brochures, press cuttings and other printed material (3 files, *c*10 items).
Leicestershire RO (DE 2883, 2895). NRA 32558.

[185] **DUDLEY & SON**, shovel mfrs, Chesterfield, Derbys

Corresp, bills and receipts (368 items) 1837, 1843-67, nd, account book 1894-8.
Derbyshire RO (D1096 Z). NRA 8918.

[186] **DUMBARTON WELDLESS TUBE CO**, Dumbarton

Share ledger 1910-11, seal books (2) 1905-15, agreements 1910, nd, letter books (2) 1910-12 and general corresp 1912, corresp rel to trade mark 1917, accounts 1911-14, general ledger 1910-15, journal 1910-15, cash book 1910-15, receipts 1910-14, sales day book 1910-11, purchase ledger 1910-12, wages book 1910-12, property records 1906-12.
Glasgow University Archives and Business Record Centre (UGD/309/82). NRA 33916.

[187] **DUNFORD & ELLIOT (SHEFFIELD) LTD**, steel and motor cycle mfrs, Sheffield

Memorandum and articles of association 1952, board minutes (6 vols) 1902-47, 1968-76, general meeting minutes (1 vol) 1913-32, register of members, etc *c*1902-21, annual returns 1935-53, private ledgers (5) *c*1902-39, *c*1958-68, nd, pension fund deed rules 1976, valuations 1962, 1965.
Sheffield Archives (Hadfields records) . NBA 34874.

[188] **FREDERICK DYSON & SONS LTD**, ironfounders, Leeds

Bills (2) 1873, 1882, wages books (10) 1882-1905, 1912-49.
West Yorkshire Archive Service, Leads (Acc 1564). NRA 33802.

[189] **EADIE BROS & CO LTD**, ring and ring traveller mfrs, Paisley, Renfrewshire

Minutes (2 vols) 1958-78, statements of account 1891, 1904, balance sheets and profit and loss accounts 1908-76, letter books (12) 1868-1904, private ledgers (9) nd, general ledgers (6) 1909-48, private journals and cash books (9 vols) nd, journal 1926-33, day books (42) 1932-62, cash books (16) 1928-73, other financial records (7 vols) 1939-51, 1968, sales and purchase ledgers (15) 1913-72, order books (9) 1915-47, 1967-9, sales analysis book 1964-8, stock books (67) 1913-52, wages and salaries records (17 vols, 1 bundle) 1880-4, 1890-1905, 1925-50, insurance and balance book 1903-47, misc corresp and papers 1871-1981, Peter Eadie's notebooks (2) 1865-1913 rel to accounts, sales, plant and property.
Paisley Museum and Art Galleries (PMD 2). NRA 33885.

[190] **EARL OF DUDLEY'S ROUND OAK WORKS LTD** (afterwards **ROUND OAK STEEL WORKS LTD**), iron and steel mfrs, Brierley Hill, Staffs

Records 18th-20th cent incl directors' minutes (12 vols) 1891-4, 1897-1980, general meeting minutes (1 vol) 1897-1948, directors' attendance book 1891-4, share ledger 1891-4, cash book 1920-9, summary of makes 1932-4, 1942-6, list of sections 1936, section books (3) 1962-8, clerks' wages book nd, plant ledger 1916-23, inventories (2 vols) 1896, 1923, leases, conveyances, etc (c14 boxes) 1797-1985, scrapbooks (4) 1892-1910, 1978-82 and drawings and photographs.
British Steel Records Centre, Shotton. NRA 36008.

Memorandum and articles of association 1897, minutes, board papers, corresp and other corporate records 1945-86.
British Steel East Midlands Regional Records Centre, Irthlingborough. NRA 35551.

Notebook rel to cost of making steel ingots 1896, loop line machine day books, etc (42 vols) 1869-90, stores records (7 vols) 1864-1909, colliery records (c160 vols) 1842-91.
Dudley Archives and Local History Service (Acc 8945). NRA 35551.

Misc records 19th-20th cent incl loop line machine day book 1875, inventory and valuation nd, corresp, plans and leases 1865-1907; Level Furnaces mining accounts, leases and plans 1800-87.
Dudley Archives and Local History Service.

[191] **EATON & BOOTH**, steel tilters and forgers, Sheffield

Ledgers (4) 1890-1946.
Sheffield Archives (Acc 1990/83).

[192] **EBBW VALE STEEL, IRON & COAL CO LTD**, Ebbw Vale, Mon

Memoranda book 1796-1819, letter book 1824-7, journals (3) 1791-6, 1814-15, 1917-28, account of weekly costs 1926-8, papers rel to Sir Frederick Mills's visit to USA and Canada (1 vol) 1929, press cuttings book 1935-6.
Gwent RO (D 2472). NRA 34982.

Ledgers (8) 1805-33.
Public Record Office (C 114/124-7).

Agreements with railway companies (7 items) 1869-81, agreements, corresp and other papers rel to purchase of shares in other companies 1859-1936, deeds, legal papers and corresp rel to the purchase of the company's assets by Richard Thomas & Co Ltd and Partridge, Jones & John Paton Ltd (c100 items) 1936-8, particulars of sale of premises incl Golynos Ironworks 1867-8, deeds and schedules of deeds, etc 1674-1936.
Gwent RO (D 394). NRA 9872.

Abersychan Works waste book 1853-82, blast furnace production records (2 vols) 1859-79, account of iron made and materials used 1877-81, account of materials raised at Cwrt Llan Coed Rhych 1853-62.
Gwent RO (D 38.369-72, 374). NRA 28.

Colliery pay books (2) 1874-5, 1882.
Gwent RO (D 2145). NRA 14003.

Colliery pay books (3) 1875-81.
Gwent RO (Acc 2567).

Abersychan collieries' deed book 1900-12.
Glamorgan Archive Service (D/D X 423/4).

[193] **EGLINTON IRON CO**, pig iron mfrs, Lugar, Ayrshire

Cash book 1870s, receipt books (2) 1859, 1867-8, invoices 1868-86, nd, report book rel to Lugar Works 1875-6.
Cumnock and Doon Valley District Library. NRA (Scotland) (survey 2873). NRA 30698.

[194] **ELKINGTON & CO LTD**, silversmiths, electroplated ware and hot pressings mfrs, Birmingham

General corresp (11 bundles) 1837-48 incl accounts c1838-41, corresp and papers, etc mainly rel to patents and electroplating (10 vols) 1836-1950, seals (31 items), ledgers (3) 1852-77, plate trade ledger 1858-64, number books (2) 1868, 1882, pattern books (7) 1904-40, French specifications and orders (copies) 1837-42, printed patents, licences and specifications, etc nd, drawing books (25) 1840-1939, nd, deeds (6 items) 1841-4, trade catalogues nd, photographs (4 vols) c1905, nd and press cuttings.
Victoria & Albert Museum, Archive of Art and Design (AAD 3-1979). NRA 28682.

[195] **ELLIOTTS METAL CO LTD**, copper and brass tubes and plates mfrs, Birmingham

Memorandum and articles of association 1874, 1928, minutes (10 vols, 1 file) 1868-1942, seal book 1928-44, corresp and agreements rel to manufacturing and supplies of equipment, orders, etc (1 bundle, 2 items) 1864, 1909-25, tenders, specifications, reports and estimates, etc rel to

machinery and plant (1 bundle) 1876-1920,
inventory of plant (1 vol) 1929, corresp and other
legal papers, mainly rel to premises (23 bundles and
files, 14 items) 1832-1970; misc records of William
Cooper & Goode Ltd (2 vols, 1 bundle, 4 items)
1910-25, and of Hughes-Stubbs Metal Co Ltd
(2 vols, 1 bundle, 4 items) 1906-27.
Birmingham Central Library Archives Division
(MS 1422). NRA 32859.

[196] **ENGLISH COPPER CO**, Aberavon, Glam

Records (20 items) 1840-80 incl prospectus 1845,
contracts, specifications, etc 1854, stocktaking lists
1879-80, iron and tin yields 1858-9, lists of tinplate
costs 1853-9, inventory of chemical laboratories
1878, and parliamentary and legal papers 1840-8.
National Library of Wales (DT Eaton Papers).

[197] **JOHN ENGLISH & CO**, needle, pin and
fish hook mfrs, Feckenham, Worcs

Records 16th-20th cent incl business and family
corresp 18th-20th cent, letter books (11)
1838-1916, ledgers (2) 1891-1903, outwork ledgers
(7) 1804-50, bought ledger 1872-3, rent ledgers (3)
1820-90, payments book 1843-50, account and cash
books (8) 1785-6, 1806-49, 1868-1915, order books
(6) 1816, 1836-1908, letter books (orders) (2)
1838-46, 1886-92, despatch books (2) 1878-83,
1888-92, invoices (1 box) 1849-56, corresp, orders
and other papers rel to American business
(*c*22 boxes) 1839-84, Liverpool agent's shipping
records (3 boxes) 1848-59, memoranda book
1817-31, wages books (3) 1851-72, deeds 16th-19th
cent, price lists rel to needles and fishing tackle
1805-52 and other English family papers.
Redditch Central Library. NRA 1471.

Records of the firm and the Gutch family
(*c*4,000 items) 17th-20th cent incl corresp and
papers of the firms of John English and Gutch
(*c*500 items) 19th cent, letters to the Gutch family
about an amalgamation of their business (*c*55 items)
1900-2, articles dissolving partnership of John
English and JB Toulmin 1810, ledgers (3) *c*1781-98,
*c*1806-70, account books (2) 1788-1807, receipts
(*c*1,250 items) 1815-24, 1830-5, order book
1852-79, stock book 1890-1900, patents and
specifications 1841-2 and royal warrant 1837.
Hereford and Worcester RO, Worcester (705:89). NRA
1471.

[198] **ETNA IRON & STEEL CO LTD**, steel
mfrs, Craigneuk, Lanarkshire

Letter books (13) 1904-15, journal 1936-47, day
books (12) 1894-1929, account books (3 boxes)
1928-32, sales records (17 vols) 1901-49 incl copy
contract books (5) 1901-9 and invoice books (4)
1909-49, sales and purchase abstract book 1922-35,
purchase contract book 1926-31, copy order books
(4 boxes) 1901-32, produce books (27) 1936-49,
stock book 1921-43, stocktaker's despatch book
1913, way bill book 1907-8, goods received book
1914, time and day books (4) 1934-41, tonnage pay
books (7) 1935-44.
Scottish Record Office. NRA 35553.

Day books (5) 1942-75, order books (115) 1938-75.
Motherwell Public Library. NRA (Scotland) (survey
3046). NRA 31889.

Contract of copartnery 1889 and papers rel to
company registration 1914.
In private possession: see PL Payne, *Colvilles and the
Scottish Steel Industry*, 1979, p431.

[199] **ALLEN EVERITT & SONS LTD**, brass
and copper tube mfrs, Smethwick, Staffs

Memorandum and articles of association 1890,
1926, directors' minutes (1 vol, 1 file) 1910-42,
general meeting minutes (1 vol) 1890-1931, deeds
and legal papers (3 bundles, 7 items) 1800-1944,
printed catalogue 1920.
Birmingham Central Library Archives Division
(MS 1422). NRA 32859.

[200] **JOHN GEORGE FEARN**, jeweller and
goldsmith, London

Ledgers (2) 1819-41, day books (2) 1827-42, diaries
(3) 1832-58, stock book 1827-41.
Public Record Office (J 90/875-7, 879-90). NRA
35889.

[201] **FIRMIN & SONS LTD**, button and metal
badge mfrs, London and Birmingham

Deeds of copartnership 1749, 1812-37, papers rel to
formation of limited company (5 items) 1874-5,
memorandum and articles of association 1875-1969,
directors' minutes (2 vols) 1875-82, draft minutes
(11 vols) 1875-1948, general meeting minutes
1883-4, 1889-1961, share records (6 vols)
1875-1969, dividend account books (2) 1875-1942,
partnership accounts, etc 1826, 1870-4, annual lists
and summaries of accounts 1871-2, 1875-9,
1959-63, statements of debts and assets 1873-4,
private letter book 1875-82, misc corporate records,
circulars, etc 1849, 1875-1910, general ledgers (3)
1852-62, 1876-1902, private ledgers (7) 1831-73,
1928-33, nd, bought ledger 1839-40, Birmingham
ledger 1907-42, private journal 1935-54, cash books
(4) 1836-1971, bank books (4) 1845-51, 1853-61,
list of creditors 1874, legal corresp, accounts and
papers in case of Firmin *v* Firmin *c*1836-77, order
books (2) 1754-90, 1811-18, sales account book
1797-1837, commission account book 1846-1957,
traveller's dissection book and sale summaries
1952-62, die books (5) *c*1893-1927, pattern and
crest books (7) *c*1799-1937, receipts for stock, jobs
done and misc family corresp 1811-72, royal
warrants, advertisements, copies of bills, etc from
1796, trade mark certificate 1917, deeds, legal,
family and estate corresp and papers rel to the
Firmins and their business 1638-1971, nd.
Westminster City Archives, Victoria Library. NRA
28631; BAC *Company Archives* no 212.

[202] **JOHN PARSONS FIRMSTONE**,
ironmaster, Sedgley, Staffs

Papers rel to his partnerships in Highfields
Ironworks 1811-45 and in Glasgow Ironworks Co

1834-8, papers rel to his bankruptcy 1822, ledger 1803-21, day book 1803-21, business and personal accounts, bills and receipts 1810-39, order book 1827, memoranda books *c*1820, valuations of Highfields Ironworks 1818, 1858, executors' papers from 1858, deeds and related papers for Highfields and other Firmstone family properties 1698-1916.
Staffordshire RO (D 695/1/9). NRA 10593.

[203] **FIRTH, DUNLOP & RANKEN LTD** (afterwards **DUNLOP & RANKEN LTD**), constructional steel and steel roof mfrs, stockholders and merchants, Leeds

Directors' minutes (4 vols) 1911-80, register of directors' holdings (1 vol) 1967-77, register of members (2 vols) 1911-80, share certificate books (3) 1911-79.
British Steel East Midlands Regional Records Centre, Irthlingborough. NRA 35555.

[204] **THOS FIRTH & SONS LTD**, mfrs of steel edge tools, ordnance and railway tyres and axles, Sheffield

Records from 1841 incl articles of partnership 1858, 1875, board minutes (11 vols) 1881-1966, general meeting minutes (2 vols) 1881-1975, rough minutes (2 vols) 1886-1901, board and committee papers from 1889, preference share applications book 1907, secretary's private memoranda book 1881-8, balance sheets, accounts and related papers 1887-1964, private ledgers (5) 1859-*c*1867, 1882-7, 1893-1936, nominal ledgers (6) 1881-1952, private journals (4) 1881-1947, cash books (6) 1841-4, 1881-8, 1900-68, bank books (4) 1842-8, 1881-1911, stocktaking books (7) 1881-6, 1895-1940, Salamander Works ledger 1903-9, patents register and papers 1909-43, wages books (2) 1844-6 and from 1859, employee agreements 1859-1860s and register 1880s-1920s, and deeds, agreements, inventories, etc from 1850s.
Sheffield Archives. NRA 28631; BAC *Company Archives* no 372.

Misc sales analysis books and order books *c*1850-80, photographs nd.
Kelham Island Industrial Museum, Sheffield.

[205] **HARRY FISHER & CO LTD**, steel and file mfrs, Sheffield

Corresp (23 vols) between Harry Fisher and his chief clerk 1890-1901, copies (2 vols) of letters and memoranda to firm's agent in Odessa 1904-9, letter books (10) 1958-77, nd, misc corresp (3 bundles) 1915-19, 1967-72, ledgers (4) 1900-20, 1930-56, day books (5) 1949-76, cash books (8) 1912-64, order books (21) 1890-3, 1895-6, 1904-6, 1954-71, quotations book 1903-10, purchase journals (2) 1942-64, despatch record book 1910-16, misc administrative and accounting records (26 vols) 1912-78, catalogues and price lists (1 bundle) nd.
Sheffield Archives (MD 6651-6753). NRA 23246.

[206] **JOHN FOLKES (LYE FORGE) LTD**, mfrs of iron and steel forgings, Lye, Worcs

Records incl stock and expenses book 1791-1806, 'account of labour and work' *c*1877, wages book from 1901, diary of William Russell, master hammer-man, 1784-1817 and diary or memoranda book of Constantine Folkes from *c*1833.
Folkes Group plc: see JFA Mervyn, *Looking back 250 years at Lye Forge*, 1949. Enquiries to the Chairman.

[207] **WILLIAM & DAVID FORBES**, coppersmiths, London

Ledgers (2) 1771-84 and indexes (2), day books and journals (5) 1771-86, cash books (6) 1773-88, account book for bills, bonds and debentures 1780-5, order books and journals (15) 1773-89, receipt book 1775-9, record of goods received and supplied (21 vols) 1779-86, metal record books (12) 1778-84, incidents books (2) 1777-83, notebooks (34) 1774-85, wages books (9) 1778-90, orders from the Royal Navy and other customers, bills, receipts, wages accounts, inventories and misc papers mainly rel to the business (*c*17,500 items) 1768-94, business letter book 1778-82, business and personal corresp (*c*1,070 bundles) 1773-1815 and domestic accounts (10 vols) 1775-8 of William Forbes.
Scottish Record Office (GD 171/6-1079, 1408-1882). NRA 15476.

[208] **FORD FORGE & IRONWORKS**, Ford, Northumb

Ledgers (2) 1770-4, day books (2) 1770-4 incl inventories of stock 1770-1, receipts and disbursements (2 vols *passim*) 1768-74.
Northumberland RO (2/DE/2/64-5, 2/DE/16/12-5). NRA 10635.

[209] **SAMUEL FOX & CO LTD**, steel mfrs, Stocksbridge, Yorks

Board and committee minutes (13 vols, 1 box) 1884-1971, general meeting minutes (3 vols) 1872-1970, directors' attendance books (2) 1928-71, share registers (7) 1871-1914, dividend books (3) 1872-1915 and other share records (5 vols) 1915-51, register of mortgages 1921-48, balance sheets 1872-1915, 1948-66, corresp (2 vols) 1847-87, letter books (4) 1869-87, index to letters 19th cent, annual returns (3 vols) 1872-1916, register of seals 1941-59, private ledgers (5) 1871-1909, 1913-36, general ledgers (3) 1909-13, 1948-70, private journal 1905-13, journals (6) 1871-1913, cash books (6) 1874-80, bank books (34) 1904-15, bill book 1882-93, capital expenditure account (1 vol) 1909-13, other accounting records (8 vols) 1909-62, sales and invoice records (9 vols) 1871-1913, price lists and circulars 1892-1936, patent specifications (7 vols) and illustrations (2 vols) 1852-80, patents, agreements and other legal records 1853-1948, trade marks register (2 vols) 1852-1890s, photographs of industrial processes (4 vols) 20th cent, wages records (9 vols) 1884-1928, benefit fund records (10 vols) 1880-1938, works extensions capital accounts

(4 vols) 1906-36, works inventory 1915, property ledger c1870, deeds 1604-1942, register of deeds (2 vols) 1876-c1891, printed papers from 1895; financial papers of Samuel Fox and his executors (18 vols) 1875-1926.
Sheffield Archives and *British Steel Northern Regional Records Centre, Middlesbrough.* Enquiries to Sheffield Archives. NRA 35686.

Minutes (1 vol) 1970-80, registers (2) of directors and directors' interests 1948-77.
British Steel East Midlands Regional Records Centre, Irthlingborough. NRA 35548.

[210] **JOHN FREEMAN & COPPER CO**, copper mfrs, Llansamlet, Glam

Assignments of shares (1 file, 4 items) 1758-1824, articles of partnership (1 file) 1844, papers rel to lawsuit, dissolution of partnership, sale of company's assets, etc (9 vols, 58 files and envelopes, c450 items) 1846-84, memoranda book 1863-4, ledger 1860-84, account book 1851-4, loan accounts (1 vol) 1853-4, 1858, cash books (3) 1860-84, bank books (2) 1861-83, cheque book 1851-4, accounts for copper sold (1 vol) 1844-9, misc accounts and related papers (19 files and envelopes, 102 items) 1847-84, insurance papers (12 items) 1859-61, deeds and related papers (32 files, 72 items) 1702-1837.
Glamorgan Archive Service (D/DXhr). NRA 33987.

[211] **GARDINER, SONS & CO LTD**, constructional steelwork mfrs and art metal workers, Bristol

Minutes, share and other corporate records 1893-1971, ledgers, journals, day books, cash books and other accounting records 1860-1970, sales and stock records c1880-1970, agreements with employees and agents 1904-57 and other staff records 1892-1967, deeds 1822-74 and other property records 1874-1960s, photographs of premises and employees, catalogues and papers rel to company history 1860s-1960s.
The Company: see *Business in Avon and Somerset.*

[212] **GARNOCK, BIBBY & CO LTD**, wire and hemp rope mfrs, Liverpool

Minutes (2 vols) 1892-1959, Companies Act registers (2) 1892-1959, share certificate book 1923-51.
Doncaster Archives Department (DY.BRI/16). NRA 21369.

[213] **GARRARD & CO LTD**, goldsmiths and jewellers, London

Gentlemen's ledgers listing individual accounts (96 vols) 1735-61, 1765-1846, 1869-82, 1899-1948, workmen's ledgers (5) 1766-73, 1778-1816, day books (6) 1777-1806, 1815-16, 1874-9, daily

account books (2) 1797-1801, stock ledger 1747-62, stock book 1797-1808, corresp and papers (22 items) rel to John Wakelin's debtors 1790-1814.
Victoria & Albert Museum, Archive of Art and Design. Access restricted. Enquiries in writing to the Archivist in Charge, Archive of Art and Design.

[214] **GARTON & KING LTD**, ironfounders, Exeter, Devon

Partnership and other agreements (11) 1832-1925, minutes (1 vol) 1925-81, register of members and share ledger (2 vols) 1924-72, letter book 1900-18, corresp (2 bundles) 1843-1903, seal register 1944-80, accounts and reports 1919-79, liquidation papers 1979-81, ledger 1863-70, private ledger 1900-9, day books (2) 1865-8, 1898-1900, cash books (2) 1841-8, 1863-8, bank books 1847-50, c1939-45, sales of stoves account (1 vol) 1851-1903, sales day book 1900-15, register of stockists 1897, price books (5) 1848-1900, estimate books (4) 1849-c1880, 1902-12, order books (14) 1910-11, 1925-45, catalogues and price lists 1869-1931, stock records 1927, 1970-8, patents (2) 1911, nd, foundry cost time book 1900-21 and costing book 1917-23, wheel pattern book c1900-40, plans and drawings of products (c540 items) 1844-1929, nd, apprenticeship indentures 1868-1965, wages books (24) 1890-1978, tax records nd, inventories and valuations (6) 1840-1960, foundry plans (2 rolls) 1800-1979, rent account book 1849-63, tenancy agreements 1940s-1950s, deeds and related papers 1869-1939, photographs and papers rel to firm's history 1792-1977; Taylor & Bodley (Exeter) Ltd misc records 1867-1945 incl balance sheets 1893-1941, cost book 1897-1941 and machinery plans 1867-1923.
Devon RO (2783 B). NRA 22194.

[215] **GIBBONS family**, iron and coal masters, Kingswinford, Staffs

Partnership accounts of Thomas, William and Benjamin Gibbons (1 vol) 1779-1805, ledger (of Benjamin Gibbons?) 1776-1822, business corresp and papers mainly of John Gibbons (3 portfolios) 1816-58 incl cash account 1816-17, Level Ironworks sale catalogue 1816, Corbyns Hall furnaces and foundry balance sheets and other financial papers (1 bundle) 1826-41, Level Forge and Mill quarterly yields, balance sheets, details of stock, prices, etc (1 bundle) 1827-44, and printed papers rel to iron prices (1 bundle) 1825-31; other family corresp and papers 19th-20th cent.
In private possession. Enquiries to the Historical Manuscripts Commission. A photocopy of the partnership accounts is in Staffordshire RO (D1046).

Business, family and estate papers (126 vols and bundles) 1618-1943 incl Corbyns Hall furnace balance sheet 1830, ironworks and colliery inventories and valuations 1833, 1841, corresp, papers and deeds rel to works and machinery 1833-85 and catalogues and plan rel to dismantling of furnaces 1898; inventory of equipment at Level furnaces 1828, and other misc papers rel to ironworks and collieries 19th cent.
Staffordshire RO (D695/1/12). NRA 10593.

Cradley forges record of stock and yield (1 vol) 1805-12.
Dudley Archives and Local History Service (Acc 8440).

Business and family corresp and papers (1 box) 18th-19th cent, mainly of and rel to William Gibbons of Bristol *c*1750-*c*1807.
In private possession. Enquiries to the Historical Manuscripts Commission.

Family and estate corresp, accounts, wills, plans, deeds, etc (1 deed box) 1520-1860.
Untraced. NRA 149.

[216] **JAMES GIBBONS LTD**, mfrs of locks and architectural ironmongery, Wolverhampton, Staffs

Legal papers rel to incorporation (7 items) 1920, private ledgers (3) of FJJ Gibbons 1883-1912, summary of sales 1896-1927, costings and sale prices (1 vol) 1931-40, inventory and valuation of buildings, plant, tools, etc (2 vols) 1931, pattern and design books for locks, church furnishings, ironmongery, etc (8 vols) *c*1850-1941, nd, patents and related corresp and papers (7 vols and bundles) 1884-1953, wages book 1883-9, sick and benefit fund accounts (1 vol) 1898-1931 and sports and social committee minutes (1 vol) 1934-54, photographs (2 boxes, 16 vols, etc) 20th cent, press cuttings of advertisements (7 vols) 1928-65, history of the firm 1960, printed catalogues and other misc material 1856-1973.
Staffordshire RO (D 3146). NRA 21360.

[217] **GIBSON BROTHERS**, chain and nail mfrs and ironmongers, Bedlington, Northumb

Journals (2) 1853-60, 1868-75, journal of petty accounts 1916-17, ledgers (2) 1879-87, 1918-23, sales day book 1881-7.
Northumberland RO (2375). NRA 35876.

[218] **WILLIAM GILBERTSON & CO LTD**, tinplate mfrs, Pontardawe, Glam

Board and general meeting minutes (4 vols) 1909-34, board minutes (1 vol) 1934-6, general meeting minutes (1 vol) 1935-48, register of mortgages 1931-6, annual returns (1 file) 1933-45, liquidator's diary 1946-8.
British Steel Records Centre, Shotton. NRA 36012.

Ledger 1861-3, journals (4) 1916-25, cash books (12) 1914-27, stock ledgers (14) 1865-1920, departmental accounting and stock records (5 vols) 1918-27.
West Glamorgan Archive Service (D/D X 259). NRA 36132.

[219] **GILLETT & JOHNSTON LTD**, clock mfrs and bellfounders, Croydon, Surrey

Register of bells cast (1 vol) 1877-1919, notes rel to work on bells (1 vol) 1879-1907, tuning books (19) 1907-51, press cuttings, photographs, etc (7 vols) 1919-52, misc printed papers (10 items) 1920-85, corresp rel to the records (1 file) 1976-83.
Croydon Local Studies Library (AR1). NRA 35125.

[220] **GLAHOLM & ROBSON LTD**, wire and hemp rope mfrs, Sunderland, co Durham

Directors' minutes (4 vols) 1899-1947, general meeting minutes (3 vols) 1899-1963, registers (5) of members 1899-1958, directors and managers 1935-50 and directors' holdings 1910-61, annual and other accounts (74 items) 1899-1962, share records (2 vols, 1 file) 1918-63, works information books (2) 1922-55, superannuation records *c*1939-60, misc catalogues, photographs, etc *c*1914-1960s.
Doncaster Archives Department (DY.BRI/17). NRA 21369.

[221] **GLENBUCK IRON WORKS**, Glenbuck, Ayrshire

Letter book 1807-11.
Edinburgh University Library (Gen 700 F).

[222] **GLYNBEUDY TINPLATE CO LTD**, Brynamman, Carms

Board minutes (1 vol) 1910-34, general meeting minutes (1 vol) 1890-1930.
British Steel Records Centre, Shotton. NRA 36012.

[223] **GOLDENHILL COBALT CO**, Swansea, Glam

Balance sheets, corresp and papers (1 file) 1906-9, agreements rel to purchase of company (1 envelope) 1905, memoranda book of JH Williamson rel to metallurgical experiments mid 19th cent.
University College of Swansea Library (Yorkshire Imperial Metals Ltd). NRA 14358.

[224] **GEORGE GOODMAN LTD**, mfrs of pins, jewellery and hair curlers, Birmingham

Nominal ledger 1900-10, private ledgers (2) 1911-13, 1928, expenses account 1923.
Birmingham Central Library Archives Division (MS 1707). NRA 36183.

[225] **GRAHAMSTON IRON CO LTD**, ironfounders, Falkirk, Stirlingshire

Memorandum and articles of association 1951 and certificates of incorporation 1959-65, board minutes (1 vol, etc) 1914-91, general meeting minutes 1912-59, annual accounts 1901-29, other corporate papers 1930-91, private ledgers (2) 1870, 1881-93, private cash books (2) 1880-1, 1966-77, cash books (3) 1881-1914, 1957-82, account book 1914-56, monthly record of goods shipped 1893-1943, list of total sales and output 1868-1976, lists of snap plates and pipes 19th cent, foundry ledger accounts 1876, production notebook 1904, furnace books (2) 1912-22, 1937-44, other production records 1926-87, pattern books (5) 1893-1973, pensions and retirement benefits records 1950-85, insurance records 1871-1987, valuations and inventories 1955-68, product catalogues *c*1927-84, papers rel to company history 1940-83, misc corresp and papers 1931-92.
Falkirk Museum (A623). NRA 36538.

[226] **JAMES GRAY & SON LTD**, manufacturing ironmongers, Edinburgh

Copartnery contracts, agreements and related corresp (16 items) 1883-1900, balance sheets and profit and loss accounts, etc (30 items) 1883-1903, customer account book 1867-73, valuation of machinery and fittings 1876, wages book 1866-71, catalogue c1900, photograph of premises nd, misc corresp and papers (21 items) 1871-1903; J Sibbald & Sons ledger 1831-7.
Scottish Record Office (GD 262). NRA 10797.

[227] **GREEN'S PATENT TUBE CO LTD**, brass tube mfrs, Birmingham

Directors' and finance committee minutes (1 vol) 1866-79.
Birmingham Central Library Archives Division (MS 1422). NRA 32859.

[228] **PASCOE GRENFELL & SONS**, copper smelters, Swansea, Glam

Partnership records, articles of association and related legal papers (1 vol, 13 items) 1803-91, directors' minutes (1 vol) 1890-7, agendas (1 vol, 1 item) and attendance book 1890-2, reports (4) by and to the board 1891-2, general meeting proxies (8 items) 1892, share records (4 vols, 3 items) 1890-2, office letter book 1883-92, liquidation records (1 box, 3 items) 1882-97, papers rel to New Minera Mining Co (11 items) 1888-92, private ledger 1830-55, ledgers (30) 1856-79, journal 1856-79, waste books (30) 1830-90, cash books (2) 1891-3, bill books (5) 1879-93, bank books (10) 1887-97 and cheque books (4) 1891-7, misc financial papers (95 items) 1831-97, sales book 1885-92, invoice book 1891-3, export ledger, sales book and cash book (3 vols) 1890-3, accounts (3 vols) of copper ore deliveries 1783-93, stock book 1889-92, stock accounts (2 vols) 1890-2, records of managers' and clerks' salaries in Swansea and London 1892, deeds, plans and other Swansea and London premises records 1802-92, plan of company housing nd, rent account 1890-2.
University College of Swansea Library (Grenfell MSS). NRA 26521.

Annual accounts and balance sheets, sales and smelting records (1 vol) c1836-92.
Hertfordshire RO (D/ERv/B1). NRA 26768.

Memorandum and articles of association 1888, abstracts of title, etc to Llansamlet premises (1 bundle) 1835-92.
Birmingham Central Library Archives Division (MS 1422: Williams, Foster & Co). NRA 32859.

Deeds, corresp and plans rel to Middle Bank Works and London premises 1828-20th cent.
University College of Swansea Library (Williams, Foster papers). NRA 14358.

[229] **GRICE, GRICE & SON LTD**, brass and copper tube mfrs, Birmingham

Memorandum and articles of association and certificate of incorporation 1904, directors' and

general meeting minutes and agenda (2 vols) 1904-28, register of directors 1904-21, directors' attendance book 1904-20, report on accounts for 1929, legal agreements (1 bundle) 1918-23.
Birmingham Central Library Archives Division (MS 1422). NRA 32859.

[230] **GROVELAND IRON WORKS**, Tividale, Staffs

Records 1849-57 incl letter books, ledger, cash book, bill book, order book, etc, sales books (2), receipts, purchase journal, stock books, yield books and ticket books.
Public Record Office (J 90/899-914).

[231] **GROVESEND STEEL & TINPLATE CO LTD**, Gorseinon, Glam

Board and general meeting minutes (6 vols) 1904-48, share register (1 vol) 1904-21, other share and debenture records (10 vols) 1922-46, register of documents sealed 1938; Raven Tinplate Co Ltd minutes, etc (5 vols) 1895-1942; Wellfield Galvanising Co Ltd minutes, etc (5 vols) 1908-40; Whitford Steel Sheet & Galvanising Co Ltd minutes, etc (5 vols) 1909-39.
British Steel Records Centre, Shotton. NRA 36012.

[232] **GUEST & CHRIMES** (formerly **CHRIMES BROS**), brassfounders and mfrs of valves and water meters, Rotherham, Yorks

Corresp and accounts (c170 items) 1821-47, ledgers (3) 1816-35, 1852-5, day book 1821-3, desk diaries (5) 1868-82, notebooks (2) rel to prices, etc c1842-51, price lists, catalogues and advertisements c1840-70, stocktaking book 1847-53, patent specification 1861, apprenticeship agreements (27) 1844-7, printed staff regulations (10 items) 1854, tenancy agreement 1848, expenses of buildings and equipment (1 vol) 1851.
Rotherham Metropolitan Borough Archives (33/B). NRA 17718.

[233] **GUEST KEEN & NETTLEFOLDS LTD**, iron and steel mfrs, colliery owners and fastening mfrs, Birmingham, Cwmbran, Mon and Cardiff, Glam

Records 19th-20th cent incl minute books from 1900 and annual reports from 1902, Patent Nut & Bolt Co memorandum of association 1864 and minutes 1864-c1900, Nettlefolds Ltd board minutes 1880-94, general meeting minutes (1 vol) 1880-1902, plans of works and premises from c1854, catalogues of products from 1826, Joseph Chamberlain's notebook rel to Nettlefolds Ltd 1866-92 and bolt mill manager's commonplace book 1910-17.
GKN plc: see Edgar Jones, *History of GKN*, 2 vols, 1987-90.

Nettlefolds Ltd Birmingham sub-committee minutes 1920-2, annual general accounts (4 vols) 1880-1934 incl balance sheets 1893-1904, nominal ledgers (2) 1938-46, general journals (3) 1880-1936, investment

ledger 1894-1904, departmental accounts, balance sheets and ledgers (7 vols) 1893-1936, private journals and ledgers rel to screws and wire (8 vols) 1880-1936, London Works creditors' ledger 1919-46, trial balance books (2) 1903-34, cash books (4) 1904-25, 1945-8, screw wire profits and sales statistics (1 vol) 1895-1933, wages books (2) 1932-48 and register of employees late 19th-early 20th cent, Cwmbran Works rent books (5) 1915-18, King's Norton site plans and drawings (88 items) 1867-1980.
Birmingham Central Library Archives Division (MSS 298, 780, 1407). NRA 30297.

GKN (Fasteners) Ltd registers (2) of drawings and particulars of screws 19th cent and 1894-1921, plans and drawings of machinery (110 items) 1870-1949, nd, patent specifications, corresp and related papers (10 vols, 17 bundles and items) c1850-1963, trade catalogues and price lists (15 items) 1887-1952.
Walsall Archives Service (Accs 283, 287, 311). NRA 33234.

GKN (Bolt & Nut) Ltd memorandum and articles of association 1962-3, GKN bolt and nut section committee minute book 1927-33, reports, balance sheets and trade accounts 1912-48, ledgers (5) 1925-61, cash books (3) 1926-64, records rel to staff, income tax and social activities 1919-71, registers of plant (2 vols) c1927-72, photographs of works, machinery and staff (12 vols, etc) c1900-1980, misc printed material c1955-63; records of other subsidiaries 1865-1969.
Walsall Archives Service (Accs 265, 280, 313). NRA 23872.

Patent Nut & Bolt Co records rel to Monmouthshire works and collieries, etc 1867-1944 incl Cwmbran Works general manager's monthly reports and financial statements 1921-43, summaries of expenditure on plant and works 1920-6, bolt works, iron works and foundry quotations, corresp and specifications 1896-1905, output records 1896-1921, analyses of steel 1924-33, staff and wages records 1871-1944, and deeds, plans, corresp and papers rel to Cwmbran estate and works 1867-c1938.
Gwent RO (D409, D503). NRA 9557.

Cwmbran general manager's notebook 1921-30.
Gwent RO: see *Report 1980* and *1981*.

East Moors Works records 1878-1981 incl blast furnace and other production records 1908-78, notebooks (5) of statistics, etc 1902-28, plans, drawings and record cards c1900-1981, deeds and property records 1878-1978 and photographs of East Moors and other works 1888-1978.
British Steel Records Centre, Shotton. NRA 36010.

See also Dowlais Iron Co.

[234] GUEST, WHITEHOUSE & WILKINSON, ironmasters, Redfield, Glos

Articles of partnership 1778, legal agreements, corresp and papers (7 items) 1777-82, account of goods supplied by Thomas Whitehouse 1777-8, production and costs schedule nd, labour account 1777-8.
Public Record Office (C 108/84, 135).

[235] JJ HABERSHON & SONS LTD, steel rollers and mfrs, Rotherham, Yorks

Balance sheets, partnership, profit and loss and trading accounts, etc (c7 bundles) 1848-86, 1908-27, statement of assets and liabilities 1920, private ledger 1905-19, bank book 1916-19, weekly cost accounts (1 bundle) 1924-8, stock sheets (1 bundle) 1920, agreements (3) 1919-20, vouchers for building work and machinery and plant installation (1 bundle) 1911-13 and other misc premises records 1926-48, photographs of works (1 vol, etc) 1890-1955, misc printed brochures 1920-1960s, papers (1 bundle) rel to history of company and Habershon and Walker families 1860s-1940s; Sheffield and District Rolling Mills Proprietors' Association papers 1910.
Sheffield Archives (389/B). NRA 28062.

Plans of Holmes Works 1822-60.
Rotherham Metropolitan Borough Archives (382/F).

[236] HADFIELDS LTD, steel mfrs and mechanical engineers, Sheffield

Board and committee minutes (14 vols) 1888-1968, shareholders' minutes (3 vols) 1889-1979, agenda books (8) 1888-1960, register of seals (2 vols) 1940-73, share records (36 vols) 1906-39, nd, corresp (3 boxes) of Sir RA Hadfield 1885-90, nd, annual accounts (1 vol) nd, private ledgers (13) 1887-1966, nd, expenditure book 1920-1, private cash books nd, bank books (5) 1897-1931, private invoices outwards (11 vols) 1901-44, nd, projectiles orders (7 vols) 1901-45, nd, government contracts (1 vol) 1918-42, pension fund and suggestions box records 1938-79, inventory and valuation (5 vols) 1948.
Sheffield Archives (Hadfields records). NRA 34874.

Technical records nd.
Kelham Island Industrial Museum, Sheffield.

[237] R HOOD HAGGIE & SON LTD, wire and hemp rope mfrs, Newcastle upon Tyne, Northumb

Memorandum and articles of association 1951, directors' minute book 1958-61, general meeting minute book 1901-63, directors' and shareholders' attendance registers (2 vols) 1901-63, registers of directors, transfers, etc (8 vols) 1901-66, annual reports and accounts 1902-59, wire rope order book 1918-19, memoranda books (4) 1909-33, c1955, consultants' reports 1959-62, corresp and papers rel to employees, property, etc 1905-61, inventories 1901, 1941, visitors' book 1959-72, catalogues, press cuttings, etc 1923-66, nd, photographs 19th cent-1972; Cardiff office records incl agent's letter book 1909-12, customers' order book 1908-14, binder twine sales day book 1912-59, and wages book 1912-63.
Doncaster Archives Department (DY.BRI/20). NRA 21369.

[238] HALLAMSHIRE STEEL & FILE CO LTD, steel rollers, forgers and tilters, and shovel plates mfrs, Sheffield

Memorandum and articles of association 1873, 1918, directors' minutes (9 vols) 1873-1960, private

minutes (1 vol) 1953-9, general meeting minutes
(2 vols) 1873-1969, agenda book 1951-4, directors'
reports and accounts, etc (1 vol) 1875-1938, register
of members 1873-98, register of transfers
1874-1959, dividend lists (2 vols) 1874-1946,
debenture register 1879-80, annual returns (1 vol)
1938-41, letter books (6) 1873-8, 1885-96, 1937-9,
private ledgers (2) 1873-95, journals (3) 1884-1940,
day book 1865-82, cash books (6) 1887-94,
1913-34, 1942-8, bill book 1873-1914, town ledgers
(5) c1890-1904, 1934-41, country ledger c1903-41,
bought ledgers (3) c1924-41, departmental ledgers
(4) nd, customer accounts (3 vols) 1942-6, order
book 1872-6, stock book 1873, general production
analysis (1 vol) 1873-1940, salaries book 1873-1918,
wages book 20th cent, superannuation fund minutes
(1 vol) 1950s; Thomas Lawrence & Co Ltd minutes
(1 vol) 1900-3.
Sheffield Archives and *British Steel Northern Regional
Records Centre, Middlesbrough.* Enquiries to Sheffield
Archives. NRA 35682.

Certificate of incorporation 1873, certificate of
change of name 1958, minutes (1 vol) 1960-80,
register of directors 1948-60, register of members
(2 vols) 1954-81, register of seals 1955-76, accounts
1969-73.
*British Steel East Midlands Regional Records Centre,
Irthlingborough.* NRA 35555.

[239] **HALLS PATENT ANCHOR CO LTD**,
Sheffield

Memorandum and articles of association 1908,
board and general meeting minutes (3 vols)
1892-1948, register of members, etc 1892-1939,
register of directors early 20th cent, share certificate
books (2) 1892-1930, letter book 1892, ledger
1892-1900, day book 1892-9, cash book 1892-1910,
bank book 1911-54, reference order books (2)
1892-1921, invoice book 1897-1902, table of patent
stocked anchors nd.
Dudley Archives and Local History Service (Acc 8264).
NRA 25008.

Certificate of incorporation 1892, minutes (1 vol)
1949-76, register of members 1936-73, reports and
accounts, annual returns, etc 1960, 1969-75, ledger
1951-76, cash book 1955-67.
Sandwell Local Studies Centre (FH Lloyd Collection).
NRA 33404.

[240] **CT HALSTED**, ironfounder, Chichester,
Sussex

Memoranda and account books (2 vols) c1857-73.
West Sussex RO (Add MSS 2729-30). NRA 7796.

[241] **HAMILTON & PURVIS**, ironfounders,
Hexham, Northumb

Ledgers and other papers 1864-7.
Northumberland RO (ZLK Misc).

[242] **HAMPTON LOADE IRONWORKS**,
Chelmarsh, Salop

Corresp rel to Hampton Loade and Eardington
forges (1 bundle, 1 item) late 19th-early 20th cent,
account books (3) 1828-55, quarterly statements (4)
1860, receipt books (3) 1847-66, payments books
(2) 1859-69, price list of old iron and lead nd,
charcoal books (2) 1835-66, abstract of leases 1853
and terrier of Eardington Forge 1889.
Shropshire RO (SRO 5586/10/1/1-19). NRA 11576.

Stock account book 1803-36.
Shropshire RO (SRO 5686).

[243] **HANSON, DALE & CO LTD**, lead mfrs,
Huddersfield, Yorks

Articles of partnership, memorandum and articles of
association and related papers (14 items)
1845-1966, minutes (3 vols) 1899-1966, share
register 1899-1966, misc corporate and share
records (13 bundles and items) 1866-1965, private
ledgers (7) 1870-1973, day book 1834-6, cash book
1903-6, petty cash book 1922-35, contract books (3)
1892-1939, sales record book 1905-12, customer
address book 1914-20, stock books (2) 1897-1939,
warehouse diary 1944, making books (9) 1890-3,
1907-8, 1913-19, 1925-73, press books (3) 1927-45,
maintenance records (7 vols) 1921-34, 1946-73,
corresp, specifications, drawings, advertisements and
other papers (c160 bundles and items) rel to sales,
delivery and production 1847-1970, official returns
(3 vols) 1917-18, 1939-43, wages books (16)
1864-87, 1896-1973, time book 1926-34,
valuations, plans and other premises records
(14 bundles and items) 1847-1973, diary 1897,
photographs (2 vols) nd; Lead Manufacturers'
Association, etc, records (12 bundles and items)
1906-62.
West Yorkshire Archive Service, Kirklees (B/HD). NRA
34068.

[244] **JOHN HARDMAN & CO LTD**, mfrs of art
metalwork, church furnishings and stained glass,
Birmingham

Records from 1838 incl letters from clients and
manufacturers, memoranda, invoices, receipts, cost
and work sheets, etc (174 boxes) 1841-1907, letter
books 1865-1946, ledgers 1838-1920, metalwork
sales day books 1838-49, 1854-75, 1881-1904,
1908-10, nd, glass sales day books 1863-1914,
decoration day books 1845-50, 1892-1920, order
books 1845-1914, cost sheets 1845-1914, job
indexes 1843-1940 and inscription books 1875-99.
Birmingham Central Library Archives Division
(MS 175).

Warehouse books for metalwork c1865-1914 and
stained glass 1865-1949, working drawings for
metalwork from c1838, brass rubbings from 1843,
drawings and cartoons for stained glass (several
thousand items) from c1845.
*Birmingham Museum and Art Gallery, Fine Art
Department.*

Working drawings for stained glass and other ornamentation in the new Houses of Parliament, etc (120 items) 1835-55.
House of Lords RO (Hist Coll 130). *Guide to historical collections of the nineteenth and twentieth centuries, 1978*, p18.

[245] **HARDY & PADMORE LTD**, ironfounders, Worcester

Memorandum and articles of association 1893, 1956, directors' and general meeting minutes (2 vols) 1893-1942, register of members and shares 20th cent, register of seals 1964-7, ledger 1906-21, letters patent, assignments and specification 1877, deeds, abstracts of title, plans, land tax papers, etc (c320 items) c1808-1965.
Hereford and Worcester RO, Worcester (705:578). NRA 15931.

[246] **JOHN HARPER & CO LTD**, ironfounders, Willenhall, Staffs

Records (21 vols, 1 box) 19th-20th cent incl memorandum and articles of association 1888, minutes from 1912, directors' meeting reports, special resolutions and misc corporate records 1895-1917, letter book 1916-21, corresp and papers rel to accounts, patents and trade marks 1891-1921, balance sheets and annual accounts (1 vol) 1909-18, private ledger 1888-1901, summary of stock (1 file) 1911, and inventory of land, buildings and plant 1897.
Walsall Archives Service (Accs 315, 369, 461). NRA 27139 (partial list).

[247] **HARRINGTON IRON & COAL CO LTD**, Harrington, Cumberland

General meeting minutes (1 vol) 1908-9, branch railway private ledger 1921-8, plan 1910.
British Steel East Midlands Regional Records Centre, Irthlingborough. NRA 35548.

Directors' minutes (1 vol) 1908-9.
British Steel Northern Regional Records Centre, Middlesbrough. NRA 35686.

See also Workington Iron & Steel Co Ltd.

[248] **HARRISON, AINSLIE & CO LTD** (later **CHARCOAL IRON CO LTD**), pig iron mfrs, Barrow-in-Furness and Backbarrow, Lancs

Memorandum and articles of association 1917, directors' minutes (1 vol) 1917-71, share registers (2) 1879-93, 1917-61, share certificate book 1917-58, profit and loss accounts, etc 1910-50, letter books (9) 1892, 1908-19, nd, general corresp (11 files) 1907-1960s, papers rel to liquidation 1967-71, ledgers (2) 1873-1919, 1962-9, journal 1928-68, cash books (3) 1863-74, 1919, 1954-68, receipts and invoices 1917-60, contract details 1876-7, order books (5) 1922-63, records of ore deliveries (12 vols) 1858-79, 1902-60 and pig iron deliveries (32 vols, etc) 1920-70, stock books, etc (38 vols) 1868-77, 1899-1900, 1908-68, furnace records (1 box, 30 vols, etc) 1878-92, 1900-55,

other production records (7 vols) 1879-1958, analysis records 1897-1964, trade mark registration and related corresp 1918, plans and drawings (63 items) 1919-63, nd, staff records (16 vols, etc) 1919-65, nd, insurance policies 1917-20, rent receipts book 1919-38, surveys and valuations (3 items) 1921-60, misc corresp and papers c1889-1960s.
Cumbria RO, Barrow (BDB/2). NRA 35757.

Legal papers 1890-1906.
Lancashire RO: see *Annual Report 1974*, p18.

[249] **WILLIAM HARRISON & SONS (FALKIRK) LTD**, bolt and nut mfrs, Falkirk, Stirlingshire

Balance sheets, accounting records and tax returns (3 vols, etc) 1918, 1922-59, purchase ledger 1910-20, sales book 1880-1904, wages books (2) 1923-59, corresp and papers rel to Camelon Works, plans of premises, etc 1894, 1918-20, 1964, photograph of A Harrison, co-founder, c1910, typescript article on history of company c1965.
The Company. Enquiries to NRA (Scotland) (survey 1851). NRA 22137.

[250] **HARTS HILL IRON CO LTD**, iron mfrs, Brierley Hill, Staffs

Minutes (3 vols) 1906-44, register of members, etc (1 vol) 1906-54, statements of account, balance sheets, etc 1906-65, share transfer certificates 1910-32, internal order book 1948-52, corresp and papers (c30 files, envelopes, etc) rel to board meetings, customers, taxation, insurance, etc 1914-70, technical drawings nd, deeds and related papers (1 file, 1 bundle) 1846-1900, 1917-63.
Dudley Archives and Local History Service (D/HA, Accs 8264, 8740). NRA 14389.

[251] **MATTHEW HARVEY & CO LTD**, mfrs of coach and harness furniture and motor body fittings, Walsall, Staffs

Order book 1904-23, price books (3) nd, deeds and associated papers (108 items) rel to premises 1750-1930.
Walsall Archives Service (Accs 136/1-4, 454). NRA 21950.

[252] **RALPH HEATON & SONS**, coiners, Birmingham

Letter book 1855-7, ledgers (4) 1852-62, 1868-77, 1881-8, journal 1853-7, cash books (3) 1852-65, wages books (2) 1840-73.
Birmingham Central Library Archives Division (MS 1010). NRA 32202.

[253] **RICHARD HEMMING & SON**, needle and fish hook makers, Redditch, Worcs

Creditors' ledger and petty account book 1819-40, accounts (c200 items) late 18th-early 19th cent, notices (c30 items) rel to fraudulent use of firm's name 1833-41, misc letters and papers (15 items)

1797-1823, nd; William Gould, needle maker, account book 1794-1819.
Hereford and Worcester RO, Worcester (899:567). NRA 17902.

[254] **ROBERT HEWETSON**, nailer, Cockermouth, Cumberland

Account books (4) 1848-72, ledger 1850-72.
Cumbria RO, Carlisle (D/HM/12). NRA 21925.

[255] **HEXHAM FOUNDRY**, iron and brass founders, Hexham, Northumb

Ledgers (2) 1829-34, stock accounts (2) 1832-3, misc accounts, vouchers and corresp (*c*100 items) 1832-5.
Northumberland RO (ZLK BA). NRA 35878.

[256] **HEYWOOD & PORTEOUS LTD**, ironfounders, Gomersal, Yorks

Letter book 1913-18, cash book 1912-19, income tax returns 1915-17, quotations books (2) 1911-15, stock books 1913-20, carriage of goods book 1928-9, misc catalogues, list of overseas buyers, etc 1900-21.
West Yorkshire Archive Service, Kirklees (KC 123). NRA 28280.

[257] **ALFRED HICKMAN LTD**, iron and steel mfrs, Bilston, Staffs

Records incl board minutes (3 vols) 1882-1925, directors' agenda book 1882-3 and share ledger 1892-1919 incl records of the Staffordshire Steel & Ingot Iron Co Ltd, employees' share register 1919-20, register of mortgages 1917-19, records of capital expenditure 1919-38, register of mortgages 1917-19, liquidation accounts 1925, private ledgers (6) 1907-25, ledgers (3) 1882-91, 1899-1907, bank ledgers (2) 1910-20, Spring Vale furnace accounts (2 vols) 1919-26, private wages books (9) 1915-31, and wages books (2) 1882, 1919.
Wolverhampton Borough Archives and *British Steel East Midlands Regional Records Centre, Irthlingborough.* Enquiries to Wolverhampton Borough Archives. NRA 35554.

[258] **FRANCIS HIGGINS & SONS LTD**, silversmiths, London

Costing book 1893-1940.
Westminster City Archives, Marylebone Library (D/Misc 88). NRA 714.

[259] **HILL family**, ironmasters, Merthyr Tydfil, Glam

Letter book of Richard Hill 1786-92, Plymouth Ironworks furnace accounts (4 vols) 1787-1813.
National Library of Wales (MSS 15334-6, 15338).

Plymouth Forge Co partnership papers and deeds 1805-19.
Glamorgan Archive Service (BRA 2515).

Personal account book of Anthony Hill 1809-41.
Glamorgan Archive Service (D/D X 357/1). NRA 5196.

Business diary of Anthony Hill 1852.
Glamorgan Archive Service (D/D X 123/4).

[260] **N HINGLEY & SONS LTD**, chain and anchor mfrs and iron masters, Netherton, Worcs

Records 19th-20th cent incl memorandum and articles of association (8 vols) 1890-1963, board papers incl associate companies (7 boxes, 2 bundles) 1884-1935, agenda books (2) 1910-45, directors' reports (1 vol) 1957-8, registers (2) of directors 1901-57 and directors' holdings 1945-68, annual returns (1 vol) 1937-47, share records (8 vols, 1 file, 1 bundle) 1890-1968, letter books of directors (16) 1894-1934, secretaries (5) 1909-19 and Sir George Hingley (5) 1902-8, letter book 1933-6 incl record of credit notes 1937-45, corresp and papers mainly 20th cent, profit and loss accounts and balance sheets (5 boxes, 4 vols) 1875-1910, general ledgers (6) 1878-1961, journals (2) 1867-79, transfer journals (6) 1875-1957, day books (2) 1900-11, credit day books (4) 1910-59, cash books (33) 1878-80, 1899-1961, other accounting records (4 boxes, 16 vols, 4 files, etc) 1914-64, sales ledgers (22) 1863-1960, sales journals (29) 1879-1931 and day book 1943-63, chain works sale books (3) 1912-25, bought ledgers (7) 1902-36 and journals and day books (20) 1890-1945, purchase ledgers, journals and day books (8) 1949-64, order books (15) 1911-55, other records of orders 20th cent, commission accounts (4 vols) 1925-60, contract books (15) 1907-49, list of debtors 1914-61, receipt book 1954-6, delivery dockets (3 vols) 1955-8, patents, royalty accounts and related corresp and papers (4 boxes) *c*1892-*c*1933, cost book 1910, cost journal 1923-4, pig iron books (2) 1908-23, staff, wages and superannuation records (35 vols, 7 files and bundles, etc) 1906-73, nd, inventory and valuation 1890, deeds (2 bundles) 1896-1966, catalogues mainly 20th cent, photographs (2 boxes) of chains, anchors and machinery late 19th-early 20th cent, press cuttings (2 vols) rel to death of Sir George Hingley 1918; Chain & Anchor Co Ltd ledger and bought journal 1902-6, Old Hall Iron Works day book 1912, summary accounts (1 vol) 1926-57 and puddling book 1928-34.
Dudley Archives and Local History Service (Accs 8264, 8495, 8741, 8921, 8926, 8944). NRA 25008 (partial list).

[261] **THOMAS HOLCROFT & SONS LTD**, hollow-ware mfrs and ironfounders, Ettingshall, Staffs

Corresp (2 bundles) 1904, 1908-9, estimates books (16) 1890s, 1903-15, 1941-54, order books (3) 1878-81, 1940-1, 1960-7, cost books (2) 1905-8, stock books (2) 1897-1915 and cards 1935-54, castings books (3) 1890s-1910, index of castings produced 1900s, repairs books 1924-5, lorry record book 1934-9, technical drawings, blueprints, etc (5 boxes, 3 items) 1908, 1960s, sketch books, etc (10 vols, 1 file) nd, stress data from experiments on iron bars 1901, work done and wages records (11 vols) 1898-1907, 1956-62, misc legal agreements,

deeds, etc 1774-1911, nd, price lists and catalogues
(4 items) 1891-1920.
Wolverhampton Borough Archives (DB/3).
NRA 23035.

[262] JEREMIAH HOMFRAY & CO,
ironfounders, Merthyr Tydfil, Glam

Articles of copartnership 1786 and legal papers
mainly rel to partnership dispute (2 files or bundles)
1796-1823; Homfray family and estate papers
19th-20th cent.
Glamorgan Archive Service (D/D Pe). NRA 8735.

Bills of lading (5 items) 1788.
Glamorgan Archive Service (D/D Xhy 1/1-5).

Accounts and corresp 1786-8.
National Library of Wales (MS 15593).

[263] HENRY HOPE & SONS LTD (formerly
CLARKE & HOPE), metal window mfrs and
horticultural builders, Smethwick, Staffs

Copies of directors' minutes (7 files) 1928-68,
corresp and papers rel to mergers, takeovers and
subsidiary companies (33 files) 1909-68, letter book
1882-92, reports (4) on overseas visits by company
officials 1908-9, 1926, 1952, 1961-4, balance sheets
and accounts (101 items) 1899-1925, order books
(5) 1818-58, 1862-98, corresp and papers (5 files)
rel to contracts and price regulation 1843, 1940-64,
tables of tonnage output 1921-50, corresp and
papers rel to wages and salaries (3 files) 1909-30,
1937-41, 1958-60 and to a strike 1933 (4 files),
corresp, plans and press cuttings (1 file) rel to land
and premises 1919-36, 1964, corresp and papers
(1 file) rel to the second world war 1940-4,
catalogues, newsletters and other printed material
1874-1968, photographs (2 vols, etc) 19th
cent-1967; Henry Hope's diary 1866, drawings (48)
by him for a printed book on horticultural buildings
1874.
Birmingham Central Library Archives Division
(MS 1056). NRA 32204.

[264] JOHN I HOPPER LTD, wire rope mfrs,
Thornaby-on-Tees, Yorks

Minute book 1894-1953, register of directors nd,
share records (1 file) 1914-46, letter book 1909-20,
directors' reports, balance sheets, etc (1 box,
1 bundle, 5 items) 1895-1970, ledger 1895-1911,
private journals (2) 1930-80, cash books (4)
1894-1913, 1959-79, purchase ledger 1895-1915,
sales book 1904-10.
Strathclyde Regional Archives (TD 914/7).
NRA 30664.

[265] HORSEHAY CO LTD, ironfounders and
engineers, Horsehay, Salop

Order books (18) 1886-90, 1899-1922, price list
c1900, drawings (3 boxes) of machinery and
buildings from 1903, wages book nd, photographs
and misc papers late 19th-20th cent.
Ironbridge Gorge Museum. NRA 34679.

See also Coalbrookdale Co Ltd.

[266] HOSKINS & SEWELL LTD, bedstead
mfrs, Birmingham

Records c1868-1970 incl minutes, share records,
corresp, accounts, pattern books, catalogues and
photographs.
Birmingham Central Library Archives Division
(MS 1088).

[267] J HOYLAND (afterwards **GEORGE
TUCKER & CO**), mfrs of steel, files and saws,
Sheffield

Ledger 1786-94.
In private possession. Microfilm in Sheffield Archives
(N 535). *Catalogue of business and industrial records in
Sheffield City Libraries*, p41.

[268] WILLIAM HUME & CO, brassfounders,
Port Glasgow and Greenock, Renfrewshire

Balance sheets (1 vol) 1878-1924, estimate books
(2) 1928-34 incl sketches and specifications.
In private possession. Enquiries to NRA (Scotland)
(survey 1036). NRA 19008.

**[269] WILLIAM HUNT & SONS, BRADES,
LTD**, edge tool mfrs, Oldbury, Worcs

Articles of partnership, memorandum and articles of
association and related papers (c10 items) 1860-88,
letter book 1896-1922, business diaries (51)
1877-1927, interleaved copy of firm's tool catalogue
c1900-39.
Hereford and Worcester RO, Worcester (705:886).
NRA 20871.

[270] B HUNTSMAN LTD, steel mfrs, Sheffield

Register of members and share ledger 1918-28,
letter books (4) 1872-1913, register of seals
1921-50, private ledger 1870-98, nominal ledger
1874-95, ledgers (4) 1788-1806, 1817-80,
1888-1917, weekly accounts (2 vols) 1886-1900,
order books (3) 1797-1814, details of steel returned
and summaries of transactions (1 vol) 1884-1903,
stock books (2) 1843, 1899-1930, notebook rel to
scrap metal 1930-3, test record book 1910-44,
wages book 1901-52, printed account in French of
Huntsman steel 1792.
Sheffield Archives (LD 1612-24, MD 7171).
NRA 34837.

Board and general meeting minutes 1918-54, private
ledgers (2) c1918-47, plant register c1918-58.
Sheffield Archives (Hadfields records). NRA 34874.

[271] T & J HUTTON & CO LTD, scythe and
sickle mfrs, Ridgeway, Derbys

Cash, sales and other account books (22)
1891-1973.
Derbyshire RO (D3206).

[272] WILLIAM HUTTON & SONS LTD,
silverplaters, Sheffield

Misc papers rel to incorporation 1931, cash books
(4) 1933-60, bank statements 1960, price books (5)

*c*1894, 1914-27, nd, price list 1901, list of customers 1914, description book 1901, foreign letters and orders (1 vol) 1939-40, sales journal 1939-60, patent 1856, technical notebook *c*1888-9, calculation books (18) 1921-65, numbers index books (2) nd, stock sheets 1933-53, wages book 1904-9, wages summary 1949-53.
Sheffield Archives (James Dixon records). NRA 34873.

Leases, indentures, copies of letters and accounts, notes on firm's history, etc (20 vols, files and items) 1733-1921, notes by RS Hutton on technical matters (7 vols and files) 1904-21.
Sheffield Archives (MD 6107-26). NRA 23246.

[273] **IBBOTSON BROS & CO LTD**, steel, file and saw mfrs, Sheffield

Board meeting minutes (1 vol) 1872-87, register of members, etc (3 vols) 1874-1923, share ledger 1872-99, list of shareholders 1872-6, register of share transfers 1873-98, dividend and interest book 1883-93, balance sheets 1872-98, expenditure ledgers (3) 1893-1939, misc letters, catalogues, etc (8 items) 1825-*c*1950.
Sheffield Archives (LD 1145-55). NRA 12302.

Memorandum and articles of association with related papers 1872-1939, board and general meeting minutes (4 vols) 1888-1972, attendance lists 1904-58, list of documents sealed 1941-51, registers of members and transfers, certificates and other share records (9 vols and bundles) 1899-1954, lists of dividends and interest (1 vol) 1898-1937, balance sheets (1 vol) 1901-39, annual accounts (2 parcels) 1939-55, journals, cash books and other accounting records (14 vols) 1919-72, corresp with trade associations (4 folders) 1942-62, trade mark letter book 1921-45, machinery stock books (3) 1914-39, salaries and wages books (30) 1901-72.
Jonas Woodhead & Sons plc. Enquiries to Sheffield Archives. NRA 34878.

[274] **ILLIDGE & SONS**, brassfounders, Wolverhampton, Staffs

Royalties ledger 1887-91, cash book 1857-63, sales day books (3) 1827-54, 1866-1914, patents and specifications (19 items) 1886-1913, misc corresp and papers (11 items) 1866-1915.
Staffordshire RO (D 1297). NRA 25289.

[275] **INSHAW SEAMLESS IRON & STEEL TUBES LTD**, Craigneuk, Lanarkshire

Memorandum and articles of association 1905, balance sheet 1905, agreements mainly with Coltness Iron Co Ltd 1908-10, corresp and papers rel to liquidation (1 file) 1909-11, inventory of movable plant, machinery and utensils 1909.
Strathclyde Regional Archives (TD 1090). NRA 33980.

[276] **INVERNESS FOUNDRY CO**, Inverness

Minutes 1894-1900.
Scottish Record Office (GD 296/320). NRA 19358.

[277] **ISLIP IRON CO LTD**, iron ore proprietors and smelters, Islip, Northants

Memorandum and articles of association 1903, 1930, 1962, certificate of incorporation 1916, board and general meeting minutes (2 vols) 1903-39, registers of directors (2 vols) 1903-69 and members (2 vols) 1903-71, share certificate and transfer registers (2) 1903-52, share ledgers (2) 1903-52, balance sheets and directors' reports 1904-30, profit and loss accounts 1917, papers rel to investments and capitalization 1919-20, annual returns 1933-51, private ledger 1933-41, accounts 1928-32, purchases journal 1924-32, furnace accounts 1917, register of mining employees 1904-47, mineral leases book 1876-96.
British Steel East Midlands Regional Records Centre, Irthlingborough. NRA 35554.

Records incl notes of minerals raised (3 vols) 1906-52, wages sheets 1904-12 and wages book 1942-7.
Northamptonshire RO (Acc 1965/116). NRA 4039.

[278] **JACKSON, ELPHICK & CO LTD**, bath founders and enamellers, Birkenshaw, Lanarkshire

Minute books (2) 1905-36, agenda books (2) 1905-36, corresp, papers and photographs (1 box) 1899-1939, nd.
Glasgow University Archives and Business Record Centre (UGD 116). NRA 21284.

[279] **W & T JACKSON & CO LTD**, brass, bronze and aluminium founders and engineers, Leicester

Day books (33) 1899-1968, cash books (9) 1918-62, credit and debit books (3) 1932-51, 1969-70, price lists (3) 1899-1902, sales, purchase and order records (17 vols) 1918-66, specifications for mixing alloys (6 items) mid 20th cent, wages books (17) 1914-56, holiday credit books (2) 1957-78.
Leicestershire RO (DE 4166). NRA 36909.

[280] **JAHNCKE LTD**, tin box mfrs, London

Articles of association, patents, draft annual reports and accounts, etc (1 bundle) 1878-95, directors' and general meeting minutes (9 vols) 1893-1961, committee minutes (2 vols) 1894-9, directors' attendance book 1935-61, register of members (3 vols) 1894, 1896-1960, share and debenture records (3 vols, 1 file, 1 item) 1889-1924, 1951-60, annual returns 1925-53, corresp and papers rel to conversion to private company 1931 and liquidation *c*1950-60, accounting, order and sales records (18 vols and files) 1922-62, production line estimates 1950s, wages, salaries and staff benevolent fund records (17 vols and files) 1926-60, deeds and papers rel to premises 1822-1960.
Hackney Archives Department (D/B/BRY/4/8). NRA 24149.

[281] **GJ JAQUIN**, upholsterers' button and nail mfrs, London

Business corresp (1 bundle) 1829-60, partnership account 1855-9 and notice of dissolution of

partnership 1860, trading account 1876-8, business and family bills (1 bundle) 1864-98, patents and related corresp, drawings, etc (1 bundle) 1850-65, trade labels, cards, engraved plates, etc (2 bundles) *c*1850-*c*1900, papers rel to equipment and premises (3 bundles) 1860-1927, family corresp and papers (5 bundles, 7 items) 1852-1902.
Hackney Archives Department (D/B/JAQ). NRA 35033.

[282] **JENKS BROTHERS LTD**, small tool mfrs, Wolverhampton, Staffs

Minutes (3 vols) 1912-54, share registers (3) 1912-58, annual returns (1 vol) 1919-32, private ledger 1912-37, private journal 1912-34, purchase ledger 1922-38, patents 1901, 1920, catalogues 1940s.
Wolverhampton Borough Archives (DB/24). NRA 31835.

[283] **CHRISTOPHER JOHNSON (CUTLERS) LTD**, Sheffield

Letter books (10) 1849-60, 1875-90, 1897-1905, travellers' itineraries (2 vols) 1885, 1914, pattern and price list nd, printed pattern books nd, misc papers (3 items) 1881, 1883, nd.
Sheffield Archives (MD 2366-78, 2690-1; Printed Books 739.07 SQ). NRA 23246.

Misc accounting, sales and order records (7 vols and bundles) 1947-63, pattern books (3) *c*1854, *c*1910, nd, register of Australasian trade marks *c*1906-34, inventories (2) 1939, *c*1970.
Sheffield Archives (Wostenholm records, 1989 deposit). NRA 17831.

[284] **THOMAS JOHNSON & CO**, braziers and ironmongers, London

Journals (2) 1815-17, 1826-31, corresp (1 bundle) incl orders from customers *c*1820-1833, misc bills, receipts and notes (3 bundles, etc) 1782, 1807-33.
Public Record Office (C 107/51-3).

[285] **JOHNSONS OF HENDON LTD**, assayers and photographic chemists, London

Assay records of Johnson & Sons (Assayers) Ltd 1785-1892, with corporate, accounting, sales and other records for the assaying and photographic businesses from 1876.
The Company. NRA 28631; BAC *Company Archives* no 420.

[286] **JONES, BURTON, PARRY & KYRKE**, ironfounders, Ponkey, Denbighs

Records (1 vol) 1828-32 incl articles of copartnership 1828, assignment of share in profits 1828, proposals rel to reshaping the partnership 1830, resolutions adopted 1830, papers rel to the lease of the works and collieries and subsequent legal dispute 1828, 1830 and schedule of debts 1831.
Cardiff Central Library (MS 5.142).

[287] **JONES & LLOYD LTD**, anchor and chain mfrs, Cradley, Worcs

Letter books (4) 1904-5, 1909, ledgers (3) 1874-1909, 1912-47, account book 1950-6, cash books (3) 1928-46, order books (4) 1905-61, invoice and quotation books (9) 1901-14, other order and sales records (13 boxes, 29 files) 1891-1965, chain books (10) 1927-62, wages books (10) 1934-62, other staff records (3 vols) 1932-59, product catalogues 20th cent.
Dudley Archives and Local History Service (Accs 8191-8211, 8577). NRA 33560.

Letter books (30) 1905-6, 1909-20, 1931-52, cash books (2) 1905-17, 1949-52, order books (12) 1912-64, invoice ledger 1941-9, invoice and quotation books (16) 1900-12, 1920-2, price lists and publicity material (*c*40 items) 20th cent.
Hereford and Worcester RO, Worcester (705: 670). NRA 13987.

[288] **JONES & WILLIS LTD**, church furniture and metal work mfrs, Birmingham

Pattern books (6) and catalogues (22 vols) *c*1847-1931.
Birmingham Central Library Archives Division.

[289] **E JOPLING & SONS LTD**, steel castings mfrs, Sunderland, co Durham

Records incl minutes, balance sheets, reports and wages books *c*1897-1982; Jopling family papers and patents 1857-1943, photographs of plant, etc 1950s.
Tyne and Wear Archives Service (Accs 2028, 2481).

[290] **JOHN JOWETT** (formerly **MARSHALL & JOWETT**), mfrs of tools and sheep shears, Sheffield

Letter books (5) 1879-93, ledger 1843-65, cash book 1845-65, order books (2) 1845-71, invoice books (2) 1844-56, trade list of tools nd, papers rel to trade marks, building works, etc (1 parcel) 1920s, wages book 1844-60.
Sheffield Archives (Sis 46, 83-91). NRA 4869.

[291] **ROBERT KELLY & SONS LTD**, tool mfrs and cutlers, Liverpool

Share register 1916-34, private ledgers (4) 1908-53, ledgers (8) 1929-53, cash books (8) 1875-86, 1917-54, bank accounts, etc (2 vols) 1935-9, bill books (4) 1881-8, 1934-54, sales and purchase records (3 vols) 1942-56, workshop ledger 1939-41, wages records (1 vol, 1 bundle) 1954-62, misc corresp, photographs and papers (1 box, 3 vols, 1 bundle, 3 items) 1912-45, nd.
Liverpool RO (Acc 3289). NRA 35528.

[292] **H KENNEDY & SONS**, ironfounders and agricultural engineers, Coleraine, co Londonderry

Corresp (8 bundles) 1870-8, accounts for foundry fittings (1 vol) 1853-8, used cheques and cheque books (5 bundles) 1871-91, delivery notes (9 vols) 1873-97, misc letters, accounts, receipts and price lists (1 bundle) 1864-86.
Public Record Office of Northern Ireland (D 1036). NRA 34899.

Corresp and accounts (c50 items) 1820-86.
In private possession. Copies are in the Public Record
Office of Northern Ireland (T 1391). NRA 34899.

[293] ARCHIBALD KENRICK & SONS LTD,
hardware and hollow-ware mfrs, West Bromwich,
Staffs

Records incl dividend account book 1888-1912,
papers rel to shareholdings 1889-1934, balance
sheets 1827-31, 1953-65, accounts 1923-5, corresp
rel to trade associations, etc (3 boxes) c1903-52,
account books (6) 1812-51, 1868-1918, 1942-57,
ledgers from 1886, hollow-ware waste book
1891-1900, cash books (2) 1835-41, 1919-29, bank
books, etc (1 box, 7 vols) 1823-44 and 20th cent,
customer account books (4) 1828-43, 1912-35,
commission journal (1 vol) 1937-9 and ledger
(1 vol) 1937-54, sales and salaries records, etc
(1 bundle) 1818-19, 1863-81, vouchers and
accounts (1 bundle) 1886-93, sales summaries
1877-1966, other sales records (2 boxes, 16 vols,
12 files) 20th cent, stock books (16) 1814, 1829-30,
1893-1928, 1956-61, enamel notebook 1871-5,
production ledgers (2) 1873-94 and from 1902,
corresp and papers rel to production (25 box files)
1876-c1957, designs and specifications, etc
(4 bundles) 1870s-1900s, licences and misc legal
agreements 1881-1921, hiring books (2) 1827-65,
leases and other legal papers 1793-1915, inventory
and valuation 1832-65, insurance policies and
agreements (1 bundle) 1887-c1924, plans of works
and offices nd, catalogues and price lists
c1845-1964, misc corresp and papers from 1794.
Black Country Museum, Dudley. NRA 33584.

Directors' minutes from 1883.
The Company. NRA 33584.

Diary of Archibald Kenrick c1786-8.
In family possession. Enquiries to the Historical
Manuscripts Commission. NRA 33584.

[294] JOHN KENYON & CO, saw, file and edge
tool mfrs, Sheffield

Minute book 1909-30, agreement with Engineering
& Mercantile Co Ltd 1928, private ledger 1911-30,
bill book 1912-30, other accounting records (4 vols)
1926-30, receiver's corresp and statements
(3 bundles) 1929-30.
Sheffield Archives (244/B). NRA 22734.

**[295] KESWICK SCHOOL OF INDUSTRIAL
ARTS,** metal workers, Keswick, Cumberland

Trustees', management and committee minutes
(17 vols) 1884-1971, half-yearly accounts 1907-57,
balance sheets and profit and loss accounts 1925-58,
director's and manager's reports 1946-58, letters to
superintendent and director, etc 1899, 1915-58,
letter book 1925-7, ledgers (2) 1906-33, day book
1917-24, weekly expenditure book 1900-1, cash
books (3) 1919-46, bank books (2) 1919-41, bills
and vouchers 1893-9, 1905-14, letters to customers
(4 vols) 1906-1911, letters from customers and
suppliers 1894-1914, sales ledgers (2) 1906-7,
1925-43, sales analysis books (6) 1927-46, purchase

day book 1922-47, stock book 1925-34, cost book
1907-12, metal books (2) 1907-19, production day
books (8) 1903-6, 1911-51, work book c1912, time
book nd, design drawings (270 items) 1922-62, nd,
receipts for wages 1899, wages books (5) 1920-46,
nd, corresp and papers rel to property 1892-1957,
price lists and publicity material 1900-35, 1984,
photographs of founder, school and products (1 vol,
19 items) c1920-35, visitors' book c1891-1909, press
cuttings (2 vols) 1884-1984, misc papers incl
histories of the school 1884-1984.
Cumbria RO, Carlisle (DB/111). NRA 35360.

[296] KETTERING IRON & COAL CO LTD,
iron mfrs, Kettering, Northants

Memorandum and articles of association 1960,
minutes (5 vols) 1876-1940, 1954-69, register of
directors 1889-1964, register of members 1960-4,
share transfer register 1876-1967, share certificates
1950-68, annual returns 1944-69, register of seals
1956-68, private memoranda 1876-8, balance sheets
1879-98, half-yearly and quarterly accounts and
statements 1895-1950, private ledgers (2) 1872-83,
manager's reports 1876-86, cost analyses and
production data c1933-66, salaries ledger 1872-6,
wages books (2) 1878-87, leases (1 vol, 1 item)
1886, 1934-76.
*British Steel East Midlands Regional Records Centre,
Irthlingborough.* NRA 35554.

[297] KINGS NORTON METAL CO LTD, metal
and ammunition mfrs, Birmingham

Memorandum and articles of association 1890,
minutes (6 vols) 1890-1928, general meeting agenda
book 1890-1921, report and accounts 1890-1,
register of documents sealed 1890-1909, printed
tables of prices and production quality 20th cent,
photographs (10 items) 1918-20, 1926-7, typescript
history of the firm c1930, printed report of the
works reservists' fund 1899-1902.
Birmingham Central Library Archives Division
(MS 1422). NRA 32859.

[298] KIRKSTALL FORGE LTD, mfrs of iron,
steel and axles, Leeds

Proceedings of meeting to form limited company
1905, partners' minutes 1907-8 and committee
memoranda 1907-28, directors' minutes (3 vols)
1908-50, shareholders' meeting minutes (2 vols)
1908-50, works committee minutes (1 vol) 1942-5,
war relief fund minutes and register 1939-46,
registers of members (2 vols) 1908-49 and other
share records 1923-59, misc legal papers and
taxation records 1856, 1918-47, analysis of capital
and production expenses 1873-87, balance sheets
and profit and loss accounts (8 vols) 1878-1964,
auditors' report and accounts 1907, analysis of
balance sheets 1908-66, seal register 1919-50,
private ledgers (12) 1839-81, 1890-1950,
impersonal ledgers (2) 1906-16, 1945-50, ledgers
(41) 1800-9, 1845-1945, petty ledger 1809-12,
private journals (4) 1884-1907, 1919-59, impersonal
journal 1906-19, general journals (5) 1938-62, cash
books (30) 1808-1966, commission accounts (4 vols,

1 file) 1893-1924, waste books (11) 1779-80, 1784-94, 1799-1803, 1808-10, misc corresp and papers rel to financial matters (19 vols and bundles) 1908-63, sales records (17 vols) 1879-1965, purchase journals and other supplies records (18 vols and files) 1911-66, coal ledger 1809-16, order book 1809-10, railway tenders and orders (1 vol) 1862-71, costing and quotations records (22 vols) 1849-1904, 1911-58, departmental waste books (32) 1908-64, departmental special expenditure accounts (7 vols) 1891-1915, departmental sales day sheets, invoices and corresp rel to orders (40 boxes) 1935-43, Bradford iron warehouse waste books (2) 1824-32, accounts (1 vol) for goods sent to warehouses 1832-8, technical notes, engineering plans and drawings (34 boxes, *c*30 rolls, 1 vol, etc) 19th-20th cent, traffic records (4 vols) 1947-67, wages and salaries books (15) 1794-1809, 1924-46, accident report book 1910-37, office diaries (30) of GL Hamer 1927-56, firm's Home Guard records 1941-3, corresp and papers rel to property and plant 1838-1965, misc printed papers, photographs, etc *c*1900-60.
West Yorkshire Archive Service, Leeds (Kirkstall Forge records). NRA 6539.

Letter books (10) 1793-1823, 1880-93, 1897, 1910, letters (2 packets) 1871-8, 1920, private ledgers (2) 1812-39, ledgers (4) 1779-99, petty ledger 1800-8, waste books (2) 1796-7, 1803-5, sales accounts, etc (1 vol) 1797-1808, specifications, freight charges, etc (1 vol) 1822-5, costings books (4) 1835-48, 1861, 1872-1900, stock books (7) 1831, 1839-45, returns books (2) 1855-63, 1875-85, index of drawings 1906-22, inventories (2) 1783-92, valuation 1868, Home Guard record of service 1941-4, catalogues, price lists and other printed papers from 1822, scrapbooks (2) rel to firm's history from 1779; Thomas Butler's cash book 1813-30 and journals of tours of ironworks, etc (7 vols) 1815-29.
GKN Axles Ltd, Leeds. Enquiries to West Yorkshire Archive Service, Leeds. NRA 6539.

Spencer family papers rel to Kirkstall and other forges, comprising articles of partnership 1676-1753, corresp 1705-1832, legal papers 1623-1754, account books (3) of Kirkstall Forge 1700-57 and other accounts 1662-1752, and deeds 1632-1775.
West Yorkshire Archive Service, Bradford (Sp St/5/5). NRA 6959.

Butler family papers rel to ownership and management of Kirkstall Forge, comprising memorandum and articles of association 1908-45, letter book of AE Butler 1857-61, corresp, memoranda and other papers of HM Butler rel to management and finance 1906-43, financial summary 1879-1935, annual reports and statements of account 1934-64, axle shop log book 1876-7, axle account book 1919-27, misc business corresp and papers 1818-1948, and Butler family papers 1785-1965.
West Yorkshire Archive Service, Leeds (Butler papers). NRA 20242.

[299] **ALEXANDER KIRKWOOD & SON,** medallists and engravers, Edinburgh

Profit and trading accounts 1920-58, analyses of income and expenditure 1962-5, letter book, ledger and journal (1 vol) 1827-35, ledgers (12) 1831-1917, *c*1929-64, journals, day books and die cutting account books (70) 1840-1971, cash books (4) 1843-65, 1916-19, Post Office day book 1913-27, purchase tax books (3) 1941-54, order books (10) 1832-6, 1927-64, index of medals ordered 19th-20th cent, corresp and sketches, etc rel to medals and patterns *c*1855-96, wages books (3) 1922-64, maps and plans 1817-19, index of seal impressions 19th-20th cent, misc family and business papers 18th-20th cent.
The Company. Enquiries to NRA (Scotland) (survey 1189). NRA 19055.

Postmark books (21) 1828-1919.
Scottish Record Office (GD1/1134). *Keeper's Report 1991-2*, p37.

[300] **KNIGHT family,** ironmasters, Wolverley, Worcs

Deeds of copartnership and related partnership and legal papers (*c*80 items) 1851-80, general accounts (*c*140 items) for Stour Vale, Bringewood and other ironworks and forges 1726-1849, abstracts of accounts for Cookley Ironworks 1859-78, summary of output at Knight forges, etc 1796; Knight family corresp, papers and deeds 1568-1909.
Hereford and Worcester RO, Worcester (Knight Papers). NRA 1522.

[301] **JOHN KNOWLES (WEDNESBURY) LTD,** gas fittings mfrs, Wednesbury, Staffs

Private ledgers (2) 1869-1911.
William Salt Library, Stafford (122/70).

[302] **KYNOCH LTD,** ammunition, nail and wire mfrs, Birmingham

Copy deed of partnership 1883, memorandum and articles of association 1884, 1897-1929, certificate of incorporation 1899 and other papers (2 items) rel to formation and reconstruction of the company 1884, 1897, minutes (15 vols, 1 file) 1884-1929, general meeting agenda (1 vol) 1885-97, seal books (2) 1887-97, share transfer fees account book 1927-9, dividend warrants (2 bundles) 1891, private ledger 1887-90, bank books (2) 1884-91, financial corresp and papers (3 files) 1919-29, ammunition order book 1894-1926, agreements, leases, patents and other legal papers (2 vols, 2 bundles, 1 item) 1884, 1897-1921, valuation of Lion Works 1884, sale particulars and plans of premises 1900, 1906, catalogues, price lists, press cuttings and other printed material and photographs 19th-20th cent, Lion Works Mens Sick Club minutes (1 vol) 1910-25, Kynoch Estate Co Ltd directors' minutes (1 vol) 1899-1901; personal and family papers and photographs of George Kynoch (3 folders) late 19th cent.
Birmingham Central Library Archives Division (MS 1422). NRA 32859.

Medical care committee minutes (1 vol) 1893-1904.
Birmingham Central Library Archives Division (MS 1341). NRA 29847.

[303] **LAKE & ELLIOT LTD**, iron and steel founders, jack and cycle tool mfrs, Braintree, Essex

Survey book (products) 1913-24, 1935, drawings of machinery and components (124 items) 1907-34, nd, plan of Albion Works 1913, catalogues, price lists and brochures (76 items) 1919-61, press cuttings books (2) 1895-1911, 1921-2, photographs (2 folders) 1916-17.
Essex RO, Chelmsford (D/F 26). NRA 21791.

[304] **LANARKSHIRE STEEL CO LTD**, steel mfrs, Motherwell, Lanarkshire

Memorandum and articles of association 1897-1954, board and general meeting minutes 1889-1980, agenda book 1936-47, register of directors 1979, register of directors' holdings and interests 1934-56, directors' reports 1889-1953, list 1906 and registers c1918-1979 of members, share registers and ledgers 1899-1967, special resolutions, agreements, conveyances, etc 1899-1918, annual returns 1935-52, letter books (4) 1889-1916, analysis of capital expenditure 1898-1954, income tax calculations 1941-55, balance sheets 1968-9, monthly balances 1932-57, ledgers 1897-1957, journals (9) 1897-1957, cash books 1897-1968, accounts paid and received 1957-68, sales book 1938-52, cost records 1937-66, stock book 1907-17, universal beam mill books (2) 1960-1, output books and related records 1934-71, register of employees 1900-77, salaries books (9) 1903-59, plant inventory c1969, photographs, plans and corresp 1912-71.
Scottish Record Office and *British Steel East Midlands Regional Records Centre, Irthlingborough*. Enquiries to the Scottish Record Office. NRA 35553.

Records incl financial records (4 boxes) 1933-74, test house records (2 boxes) 1911-75, trade union, medical and related staff records (12 boxes) 1908-78, and deeds, agreements and cost records (10 boxes) 1899-1932.
British Steel Records Centre, Shotton. NRA 36006.

Loose-leaf book of statistical and other data nd.
In private possession: see PL Payne, *Colvilles and the Scottish Steel Industry*, 1979, p431.

[305] **CHARLES LANE & SONS LTD**, nail mfrs, Leeds
Bad debts register incl settlements and dividends 1868-98, nail sheet orders (1 vol) 1873-90, wire purchase contract and delivery book 1921-37, papers rel to new buildings (1 packet, 3 items) 1890-1906.
West Yorkshire Archive Service, Leeds (Acc 1477). NRA 34512.

[306] **LECLERE & BRAY**, engravers and chasers of silver, Sheffield

Day books (2), order books (3) and invoice books (2) 1868-87, glass negatives of engraved articles nd.
Sheffield Archives (LD 1437-44). NRA 15624.

[307] **H LEES & SONS LTD**, iron and steel mfrs, Ashton-under-Lyne, Lancs

Minutes (1 vol) 1885-1950, letter books (6) 1861-1907, other corporate corresp (1 file) 1923, nd, account book 1894-7, ledger 1857-1911, cash books (10) 1846-59, 1881-1918, bank book 1863, quotations 1856-63, stock balance 1862-78, accident book 1926-8, deeds and papers rel to property dispute, etc 18th-19th cent, valuation of premises 1872; corresp, papers and photographs of Lees family 18th-20th cent.
Tameside Archive Service (DDL, Acc 2198). NRA 32971.

[308] **SAMUEL LEWIS & CO LTD**, chain, nail and rivet mfrs, Netherton, Worcs

Directors' minutes (1 vol) 1899-1937, general meeting notices 1908-37, balance sheets, profit and loss accounts, etc 1899-1975, ledgers (4) 1894-1946, order book 1839-41, stock lists 1855-66, 1919-22 and books (2) 1930-9, patents and trade mark certificates, etc (6 bundles, 6 items) 1877-1938, wages book 1931-7, site plans (2) 1863-5, insurance policy records (11 items) 1904-32, misc corresp and papers from 1831, price lists and trade catalogues 1785-1988, photographs of employees, products, premises and exhibitions 1953-90, nd.
Black Country Museum, Dudley (1990/106). NRA 10098. A microfilm of the firm's records to 1965 is in Hereford and Worcester RO, Worcester (970:5:381).

[309] **LEYS IRON WORKS**, Kingswinford, Staffs

Account book 1829-37.
Staffordshire RO (D 695/1/9/83). NRA 10593.

Plan, particulars and contract of sale of Leys Iron Works 1899, deeds and agreements (30 items) 1828-1901.
Dudley Archives and Local History Service (Accs 6442-73).

[310] **LINCOLN FILE, STEEL & CUTLERY CO LTD**, Lincoln

Purchase ledger c1883-7.
Lincolnshire Archives (LPC 3/4/3). NRA 6578.

[311] **LION FOUNDRY CO LTD**, ironfounders, Kirkintilloch, Dunbarton

Copartnery contract (1 bundle) 1880-1, shareholders' minutes 1950-2 and directors' reports, etc 1947-8, share register 1893-1936, share applications (1 bundle) 1893-6, dividend statements (1 bundle) 1893-1912, trading accounts, balance sheets and profit and loss accounts, etc (4 bundles, etc) 1881-1916, 1945-52, private memoranda book 1880-2 and private letter book 1881-99, papers rel to company registration (1 bundle) 1893-4, merger papers 1935, ledger balances 1894-1915, ledgers (3) 1880-1, 1933-5, 1948-63, cash books (2) 1880-4, 1912-26, bank account books (7) 1921-43, order books (18) 1910-75, customer credit book 1910-42,

contract corresp (1 bundle) 1897-1914, cost books
(3) 1908, patent specifications and related corresp
(1 bundle) nd, sketch book of products 1896,
drawings incl band stands 1895-1939, building
fronts 1911-58, power stations 1942-69, drinking
fountains 1910-38, bus stations 1928-40, entrance
canopies 1911-58, gates and railings 1938-67, lamp
pillars 1924-38, monuments 1934, shelters 1904-77,
stairs 1915-81, local and misc orders 1913-68 and
bridges 1929-55, plans and photographs mainly of
premises, products and clients' properties 1904-79,
catalogues, brochures and publicity sheets, etc
1923-85, nd, misc records 1917-87, press cuttings
1919-73 and misc papers 1881-1984.
William Patrick Library, Kirkintilloch (A 10). NRA
36230.

Designs of band stands (*c*150 items) *c*1900-30,
catalogues (19 items) *c*1900-60.
Strathclyde Regional Archives (TD 898). NRA 15357.

Wagons inward and outward records (2 vols)
1931-64, photographs, drawings and pamphlets
*c*1890-1930s, nd.
Glasgow University Archives and Business Record Centre
(UGD/107). NRA 15357.

[312] LISTER & WRIGHT LTD, goldsmiths, Birmingham

Private ledger 1905-22, apprenticeship indentures
(2) 1885, 1892, legal agreement 1913.
Birmingham Central Library Archives Division (MS
752). NRA 30308.

[313] LLANELLY COPPER SMELTING CO, Llanelly, Carms

Minute and account book 1861-72, plans (2) *c*1865.
West Glamorgan Archive Service (D/D Xav).

[314] LLANGENNECH TIN PLATE CO, Llangennech, Carms

Corresp, patent licences, agreements, deeds and
leases (2 boxes) 1858-1907.
*Baker Library, Harvard University, Cambridge,
Massachusetts*: see *Manuscripts in the Baker Library*,
4th edn 1978, p286.

[315] FH LLOYD & CO LTD, mfrs of steel castings, Wednesbury, Staffs

Records from 1881 incl directors' minutes (17 vols)
1895-1921, 1935-53, 1964-78, register of directors
(1 vol) 1888-1915, directors' attendance and agenda
books (3) 1923-55, 1972-4, letter books (3)
1888-1921, directors' reports and accounts 1921-78,
share and mortgage records (*c*45 vols, bundles,
folders, etc) 1888-1981, misc corporate corresp and
papers (*c*60 vols, bundles, folders, etc) 1910-71,
accounts (1 box) 1881-1930, private ledger 1888-96,
nominal ledgers (6) 1904-47, deposit account book
1898-1910, cash books (20) 1918-70, other
accounting records (12 vols) 1925-76, notes of
business trips (4 vols) 1901-55 and record of
companies dealt with 1954-9, stock book
1897-1951, foundry memoranda book from 1895,

papers rel to steel castings (8 folders) nd, misc
production records (8 bundles and folders) 1914-18,
1940-8, papers rel to patents and agreements
(3 boxes) from 1920s, wages and staff records
(8 vols and bundles) 1919-44, plant and property
records (8 vols and files) *c*1895, *c*1902-12,
*c*1927-1973, publicity material, house journal and
other printed papers *c*1907-82.
Sandwell Local Studies Centre (Accs 8707, 8810,
9337). NRA 33404 (partial list).

Cardiff Works records 1963-82.
Glamorgan Archive Service: see *Accessions to
repositories 1989*, p42.

Corresp, agreements, etc rel to foundry at
Chittaranjan, India (13 files) 1953-75.
British Library, Oriental and India Office Collections
(MSS Eur D 1198). NRA 34758.

[316] LLOYD & LLOYD LTD, iron tube mfrs, Birmingham

Memorandum and articles of association 1898,
certificate of incorporation 1898, prospectus 1899,
minutes (1 vol) 1924-40, reports to management
committee 1899-1902, register and returns of
directors and secretaries 1919-68, annual summaries
1914-68, mortgage debenture deed 1898,
agreements (2 items) 1859, 1898, partners' corresp
1870-80, other corresp 1880-1921, letter book
1870-80, papers rel to amalgamation 1902, private
ledger 1824-62, private journal 1824-75, record of
cash received 1872-9, account book 1889-1927,
papers rel to iron tube and coal prices 1872-7, works
reports (1 folder) 1884-1903, result of experiment
on iron and steel bars 1876, papers rel to tube
weights nd, specifications 1877, 1888, patent 1864,
agreements, licences and other papers rel to electric
welding 1885-97, workmen's letters and addresses
1859, agreement with foreman 1864, agreement,
rules and regulations of Albion Works Sick Club
1887-8, registers (2) of deeds *c*1799-1930, lists of
deeds (2 items) *c*1897, 1903, licence to assign
Cardiff premises 1903, warehouse and office
notebooks 1897-1925, catalogues (4 items) 1891-2,
cuttings and pamphlets rel to competitors
1888-1905, scrapbook 1863-93, diaries (3) 1874-6,
personal notebook of SS Lloyd nd; Henry Howard &
Co partnership agreement 1869, deed of dissolution
1870, other agreements (2 items) 1870, trade
account 1870.
*British Steel East Midlands Regional Records Centre,
Irthlingborough*. NRA 35554.

See also Stewarts & Lloyds Ltd.

[317] LOCKE, BLACKETT & CO LTD, lead mfrs, Newcastle upon Tyne

Memorandum and articles of association and related
papers 1891-1966, directors' minutes (4 vols)
1891-1974 and papers (55 items) 1931-8, general
meeting minutes (1 vol) 1891-1965 and papers
(36 items) 1892-1927, letter books (2) 1898-1903,
corresp (30 files) 1891-1938, 1950-66, registers of
directors, shareholders and debenture holders

(7 vols, 1 file) 1891-1967, share registration and transfer records (4 vols, 33 items) 1891, 1909-1960s, mortgage deed and related papers (1 file) 1906-22, seal register 1891-1952, draft accounts, income tax papers and misc financial records (6 files) 1913-66, balance sheets 1891-1974, private ledgers (3) 1891-1938, costs ledgers (3) 1904-6, 1943, journal 1929-31, papers rel to foreign agencies (1 file) 1918-36, legal case papers (1 bundle) 1908, insurance register, etc (1 vol, 1 file) 1930-8, wages ledger 1851-2, salaries ledger 1891-1937, papers rel to staff gratuities (1 vol, 89 items) 1926-44, inventory, plans and other papers rel to Gallowgate Works (84 items) 1900-33, deeds, agreements and related corresp and papers 1694-1937.
Tyne and Wear Archives Service (Acc 1512/7147-9645). NRA 32095.

[318] **LOCKE, LANCASTER & WW & R JOHNSON & SONS LTD**, lead mfrs and merchants, London

Memorandum and articles of association 1929, resolutions 1905, 1908, board minutes (2 vols) 1917-49, committee minutes (1 vol) 1910-33, general meeting minutes (1 vol) 1914-61, register of shareholders (1 vol) 1930-47, corresp (12 items) 1868-72, letter books (2) 1898-1900, balance sheets and accounts 1926-40, private ledgers (5) 1891-1930, cash ledger 1872-80, expenditure ledger 1886-93, bank ledger 1942-4, private journals (2) 1878-9, 1881-6, account books (2) 1881-90, cash books (6) 1893-1936, Millwall Works ledger 1913-62 and costs records (1 vol, 12 rolls) 1900-38, other production records (5 vols, 10 files, 80 items) 1843-6, 1866, 1905-27, 1960, wages and salaries records (56 vols, 1 file, 1 roll, 5 items) 1893-1902, 1906-7, 1911-50, register of deductions and payments under the Truck Act 1896, insurance register 1924-9, agreements, licences, etc 1872-1909, misc premises records 1911, 1937-51, misc photographs, printed papers and papers rel to company history *c*1873-1972; Hill family corresp and papers 1793-1945.
Tyne and Wear Archives Service (Acc 1512/9646-10252). NRA 32095.

WW & R Johnson & Sons articles of partnership 1867, partner's account 1823-9, vouchers (1 file, 35 items) 1794-1818, measuring books (2) 1795-6, 1802, release from agreement 1836, legal papers (2 files, 1 item) 1831, taxation papers (1 file) rel to estate of Robert Johnson 1863-89.
Tyne and Wear Archives Service (DX 25). NRA 34471.

[319] **LONGFORD WIRE CO LTD**, wire drawers, Warrington, Lancs

Minutes 1874-86, 1921-78, agenda book 1938-50, share register 1899-1950, directors' annual statements 1886-1959, cash, order and stock books 1940-9, plans and drawings nd, salaries, wages and related records 1938-86, misc corresp and papers *c*1874-1960, catalogues, advertising material, photographs, etc nd.
Warrington Library (MSS 2637-51). NRA 36703.

[320] **LORN FURNACE CO**, iron smelters, Bonawe, Argyll

Contracts and corresp (1 vol) 1752-1813, letter books (2) 1786-1812 incl accounts 1781.
National Library of Scotland (MSS 993-5).

Records 1753-1813 incl assignment of share in ironworks 1771, assignment of lease 1813 and misc papers (6 items) 1753-76.
Cumbria RO, Barrow (Z 28-Z 71 *passim*). NRA 35515.

[321] **LOW MOOR CO LTD**, ironmasters and coal owners, Bradford, Yorks

Private ledger 1888-1928, ledgers (9) 1876-1929, private journals (2) 1888-1928, cash book 1931-5, sales and purchase ledgers (4) 1929-53, stock books (3) 1795-1887, puddlers' journal 1914-18, forge wages book 1915-17, visitors' book 1851-1939, cottage rents (1 vol) 1925-7.
West Yorkshire Archive Service, Bradford (LMI; Miscellaneous MSS C/33). NRA 34868.

Corresp, accounts, papers rel to iron and coal taxes, etc *c*1778-*c*1805.
York Minster Library (Hailstone MSS 5.16, 5.31, 6.12, PP5, 70, 73).

Letter book rel to financial matters 1825-9.
Sheffield Archives: see *Catalogue of business and industrial records in Sheffield City Libraries*, 1971, p41.

Corresp and papers rel to coal on Low Moor estate 1781-7, legal case papers 1821, report and plans rel to coal and iron mines at Low Moor and elsewhere 1886.
Wakefield Libraries Department of Local Studies (Goodchild Loan MSS: Iron MSS). NRA 23032.

[322] **CHARLES LOWCOCK**, sickle and reaping hook mfrs, Dronfield, Derbys

Statement of profits 1897, balance sheet 1934, income tax papers 1898, 1903, 1906, bank books (6) 1876-1908, order book late 19th cent, misc trade mark and other papers (16 items) 1891-1905, insurance receipts and certificates (39 items) 1891-1906, deeds and other property records (27 items) 1843-1907, misc Lowcock family papers 1880-1921.
Derbyshire RO (D2810). NRA 35793.

[323] **LOWICK GREEN SPADE FORGE**, Lowick, Lancs

Sales book 1875-98, wages book 1864-83.
Cumbria RO, Barrow (BDB/19). NRA 35515.

[324] **EDWARD & WILLIAM LUCAS LTD**, spade and tool mfrs, Sheffield

Articles of association, debenture certificates and misc papers (1 bundle) 1908-50, nd, summaries of accounts (1 vol) 1890-1907, company accounts ledger 1908-21, general ledger 1907-22, ledger nd.
Sheffield Archives (SJC 97-101). NRA 11376.

[325] **WALTER ADAMS LYNDON**, edge tool mfr, Birmingham

Ledger 1837-44, journal 1837-43.
Birmingham Central Library Archives Division (MS 224). NRA 29847.

[326] **JOHN LYSAGHT LTD**, ironmasters, steel mfrs and constructional engineers, Bristol and Scunthorpe, Lincs

Minutes (8 vols) 1881-1917, 1921-40.
GKN plc: see Edgar Jones, *History of GKN*, vol 2, 1990.

Corresp and papers rel to proposed establishment of steelworks in Lincolnshire (2 boxes) 1904-8, steelworks committee minutes and papers (4 boxes) 1917-24, general manager's corresp files (10 boxes) 1919-45, capital expenditure records and invoices (14 boxes) 1912-67, private ledgers (10) 1912-66, cash books (7) 1908-12, 1947-70, other ledgers, journals and accounts (2 boxes, 13 vols, 3 files) 1913-22, 1932-70, receipts for payments (6 files) 1908-12, purchase records (23 vols) 1908-12, 1934-55, sales records (36 vols) 1912-24, 1932-61, delivery books (23) 1959-68, cost records (4 boxes, 23 vols) 1912-39, 1951-6, mill work book 1915-19, salaries and wages records (1 box, 8 vols) 1908-44, misc records (1 box) 1914-40; Nettleton Mine accounting and misc records (6 vols) 1944-69.
British Steel East Midlands Regional Records Centre, Irthlingborough. NRA 35549.

Nettleton Mine accounts and other papers 1923-69.
Lincolnshire Archives (MISC DEP 316). *Archivists' Report 26, 1975-7*, p28.

[327] **MACCLESFIELD COPPER CO**, Macclesfield, Cheshire

Committee book 1774-1833.
John Rylands University Library of Manchester (EHfM4). NRA 35446.

[328] **McHUTCHEON & CO**, galvanizers, tinners and enamellers, Glasgow

Private journal and ledger 1908-14.
Strathclyde Regional Archives (T-MS 320). NRA 19243.

Minutes (1 vol) 1930-64, register of members 1930-62 and misc corporate records c1930, 1933, 1961-7.
British Steel East Midlands Regional Records Centre, Irthlingborough. NRA 35553.

[329] **FREDERICK MACKAY**, coppersmith, Gateshead, co Durham

Order books (3) 1871-1906, memoranda rel to manufacture of copper boilers, stock, etc from 1885.
Tyne and Wear Archives Service (Acc 668). NRA 8919.

[330] **J & J McKEOWN LTD**, ironfounders, engineers and saw mill owners, Belfast

Ledgers (6) 1902-52, day books (5) 1922-41, cash books (8) 1899-1913, 1917-46, building society account book 1875-8, wood sales book 1917-31, wages book 1910-12.
Public Record Office of Northern Ireland (D 2619). NRA 34896.

Letter books (3) 1876-1905.
In private possession. Copies are in the Public Record Office of Northern Ireland (T 2385). NRA 34896.

[331] **THOMAS McLAREN & SONS LTD**, brass and iron founders, Galashiels, Selkirkshire

Order books (2) 1880-6, cost books (2) 1927-42, notebook of stock and experiments 1911-40, notebook rel to cylinders 1892-1918, record of quantities 1925-6, pattern books (6) 1916-53, notebook of employee 1862, notebook of charitable donations 1928-42, misc corresp and notebooks nd.
Glasgow University Archives and Business Record Centre (UGD/276). NRA 15227.

[332] **MADELEY WOOD CO**, iron mfrs, Madeley, Salop

Partnership agreements (2 items) 1776, account of stock holders c1770, inventories (2) of plant and land c1770.
Shropshire RO (SRO 1987/60). NRA 35748.

Account book 1790-7.
Shropshire RO (SRO 271). NRA 11563.

[333] **MANGANESE STEEL CO LTD**, steel mfrs, Sheffield

Journal and private ledger 1902-67.
Sheffield Archives (Hadfields records). NRA 34874.

[334] **GEORGE MARSDEN & SONS**, sheet metal workers, Manchester

Day book 1887-1923.
Rolls-Royce Enthusiasts Club. Enquiries to the Warden, The Hunt House, Paulerspury, Northants. NRA 35052.

[335] **MARSH BROTHERS & CO LTD**, steel, cutlery and tool mfrs and merchants, Sheffield

Partnership deeds, articles of agreement and legal papers (4 bundles, 43 items) 1828-1907, memorandum and articles of association 1907-65, papers rel to formation of limited company (10 vols, bundles and items) 1895-1908, misc papers (5 bundles) mainly rel to Effingham Steel Works & Rolling Mills Co Ltd 1892-1911 and Sheffield Steelmakers Ltd 1904-5, partnership accounts, cash books and stock balances (11 vols) 1810-70, accounts and balance sheets, trading statements, etc 1917-66, income tax papers (2 bundles) 1873-4, 1889-96, bill book 1864-99, general expenses receipt book 1871-93, bank books 1866-96, bills and corresp (1 folder) 1879-1908, additional corporate

and accounting records (3 vols, 14 files, etc)
1959-79, corresp and papers rel to British sales and
orders (9 vols, 8 bundles and files) 1836-48,
1874-81, 1948-61, corresp and papers rel to foreign
trade (26 vols, bundles and items) 1819-94, agency
agreements and related papers (14 bundles and
items) 1864-1960, cost and prices records,
calculations, test notes, etc (11 vols and bundles)
c1854-1927, works cash book and expenses ledger
1828-35, works notebooks (3) 1893-6, 1910-11, nd,
papers rel to high speed steel technology (2 bundles,
8 items) 1909-41, wages books (2) 1887-1906,
insurance policies (1 bundle, 8 items) 1847,
1877-99, deeds 1853-1957, valuations of works and
misc premises records (39 items) 1853-61, plans and
photographs of premises 1864-89, 1939-63, nd,
misc papers rel to firm's and Marsh family history
(48 bundles and items) 1852-1963, catalogues,
advertisements and price lists c1845-1954, nd.
Sheffield Archives (Marsh records). NRA 4806.

Letters to American firms and agents (1 bundle)
1863-7, prices book 1849-64, price lists,
memoranda, etc (1 bundle) 1857-9, stock list 1848,
time books (2) 1942.
Sheffield Archives (MD 1485-6, 6773-6). NRA
23246.

[336] **MARSHALL & BOYD**, ironfounders, Hull,
Yorks

Hope Ironworks cash book 1867-71.
Brynmor Jones Library, Hull University (DX/60).
NRA 10731.

[337] **MARSHALL & EDGAR**, ironfounders,
Dundee

Order book 1836-47, time book 1845-7.
Dundee University Library. NRA 15466.

[338] **JOHN MARSTON LTD**, sheet metal
workers, bicycle and radiator mfrs, Wolverhampton,
Staffs

Memorandum and articles of association 1895,
1927, corresp and other legal papers rel to
establishment of company (1 bundle, 4 items) 1895,
directors' and general meeting minutes (3 vols)
1895-1936, copy minutes (3 folders) 1927-42, seal
book 1899-1944, catalogues, advertisements, etc
(4 vols, 17 items) 1920s-1930s, deeds (2) 1895.
Birmingham Central Library Archives Division (MS
1422). NRA 32859.

[339] **MARTIN, HALL & CO**, cutlery mfrs and
silversmiths, Sheffield

Financial memoranda (1 vol) 1921-4, order book
1891-1902, description books (3) 1886-91, 1920s,
pattern books (12) 1869-76, 1892-1932, costings
book 1922-4, catalogues (3) c1900, c1910.
Sheffield Archives (COBB 3). NRA 34872.

[340] **GEORGE JOHN MASON & SON**, metal
workers, Leicester

Ledgers (2) 1895-1901, 1906-11, day book
1906-10, week books (3) 1877-98, job and sales
book 1878-93.
Leicestershire RO (24 D 60). NRA 6263.

[341] **HENRY MAXWELL**, spur maker, London

Sales ledger 1824-8, royal warrants, etc (3 items)
1824, nd.
H Maxwell & Co Ltd. NRA 11120.

[342] **C MEADOWS & CO LTD**, steel forgers
and rollers, Sheffield

Articles of association (3 packets) 1891, minutes
(2 vols) 1891-1953, annual accounts and balance
sheets (4 vols) 1891-1926, financial corresp
1922-46, private cash book 1913-37, bank
statements 1928-51, stock accounts 1924-39,
managers' and clerks' wages book 1915-46,
specifications for new plant 1925 and deeds from
c1835, employers' association circular letters 1933-6.
Sheffield Archives (BDR). NRA 15735.

Board and general meeting minutes 1953-68,
register of members, etc 1891-1950, share transfers
(1 folder) nd.
Sheffield Archives (Aurora II). NRA 26201.

[343] **MEARS & STAINBANK
(WHITECHAPEL BELL FOUNDRY)**, bell
founders, London

Letter books 1894-c1939, agreement with St Paul's
Cathedral 1709, ledgers from 1837, purchases and
sales day books 1837-1939, estimate books
1880-c1939, setting books from c1761, plans and
drawings mid 19th-20th cent, church bell inscriptions
(4 vols) c1840-90, photographs from c1890,
catalogues and other printed material from c1860.
The Foundry. Enquiries to Tower Hamlets Local
History Library and Archives. NRA 10815.

[344] **MELINGRIFFITH CO LTD**, tinplate mfrs,
Whitchurch, Glam

Corresp (6 bundles) 1771-5, 1783-6, 1790-5,
balance and sustenance book 1781-91, receiver's
account 1880, receipt books (2) 1776-7, 1783-4,
cash book 1782-3, orders cash books (2) 1782-4,
1792-4, 1805, accounts of iron received (2 vols)
1822-4, 1828-31, bolt iron accounts (1 vol) 1782-3,
stock accounts (1 vol) 1795-6, stock list 1864, works
accounts (1 vol) 1770, accounts (2 vols) for tin
house 1850-9 and forge mills 1852-3, New Steam
Mills costings 1854, accounts (2 items) of work done
in Old Forge 1833-4 and New Steam Mills 1853-6,
wages and works shop books (5) 1782-9, medical
notes (1 vol) c1900, construction and maintenance
accounts (1 vol) 1769, inventories (2) of stock and
equipment 1776-7, 1783-4, canal memoranda book
1826-7, farm book 1800-1 and farm sale account
1824.
Dyfed Archives Service, Carmarthen (Trostre
Collection).

Day book 1790-1, carpenters' and masons' day book
1790, cash book rel to Melingriffith and the
Pentyrch Ironworks 1822-31, forge and mill
accounts 1790-1, 1792-3, 1806-7, freight, coal,
charcoal and delivery accounts 1790-1, 1806-7, misc
ledger sheets (5) 1806-7, order book 1786-91,
invoice book 1835-8, cordwood and timber delivery

book (Melingriffith and Pentyrch) 1850-79, works
diary 1779, half-yearly cost book 1924-34, daily
production (1 vol) 1786-7 and mill production
records 1806-7, forge stock (1 vol) 1790-1 and mill
stock records (2 vols) 1790-1, 1806-7.
Welsh Industrial and Maritime Museum, Cardiff (Acc
1991/25/1-11). NRA 34788.

Corresp with Bristol partners (4 bundles) 1773-83,
1796-1806, accounts, letters and advice notes
(15 items) from Bristol partners 1770, 1773-4,
1810-11, letters from Machen Forge (1 bundle)
1782-4.
Glamorgan Archive Service (D/D Mg). NRA 33989.

Account book c1779-80.
Glamorgan Archive Service (D/DX 809).

Board and general meeting minutes (6 vols)
1888-1939, share ledgers (2) 1889-1939, statement
of accounts and balance sheet ledger 1889-1934,
liquidator's book 1939-40.
British Steel Records Centre, Shotton. NRA 36012.

[345] **MELYN TINPLATE CO LTD**, Neath,
Glam

Memorandum and articles of association 1920,
directors' and shareholders' minutes (3 vols)
1903-20; Leach, Flower & Co directors' and general
meeting minutes (3 vols) 1865-1905; Villiers Tin
Plate Co Ltd shareholders' minutes (1 vol)
1887-1909.
Glamorgan Archive Service (D/D Xgu). NRA 33986.

[346] **MEPHAN-FERGUSON LOCK BAR
PIPE CO LTD**, Tipton, Staffs

Certificate of incorporation 1904, minutes (2 vols)
1907-19, agenda books (2) 1904-17, board and
general meeting papers 1910-19, list of members
and other share records 1904, register of members
1905-12, balance sheets and profit and loss accounts
1905-16, annual summaries 1914-17, agreements,
conveyances and corresp 1903-17, account rel to
formation of company 1904, ledger and journal
(2 vols) 1904-19, cash book 1913-18, statement of
iron and steel contracts 1905-6, corresp rel to
foreign markets 1905-11, patents, licences and
corresp 1896-1910, valuation and inventory of works
1904-16, catalogue of plant and machinery 1917.
*British Steel East Midlands Regional Records Centre,
Irthlingborough.* NRA 35554.

See also Stewarts & Lloyds Ltd.

[347] **MERSEY WHITE LEAD CO LTD**, lead
and paint mfrs, Warrington, Lancs

Memorandum and articles of association (2 vols,
3 items) 1870, 1889-1908, directors' minutes
(4 vols) 1889-1972, register of directors 1901-48,
share and mortgage registers (6 vols) 1889-1959,
other share records (177 items) 1889-96, annual
accounts, etc (2 vols, 22 items) 1889-1916, annual
returns (1 vol) 1949-69, general corresp (73 items)
1886-1931, seal book 1947-63, taxation papers
(122 items) 1901-26, capital account ledger 1889-90,
bad debt ledger 1890-1955, receipts (1 vol, 33 items)

1889-91, 1899, bill book 1899-1942, sales corresp
(2 files) 1926-9, lead deliveries (2 vols) 1889-90,
1920-8 and purchase records (1 file) 1889-90, stock
book 1890-2, production costs (1 item) 1889, assay
reports (1 vol) 1898-1909, memoranda book
1922-46, notes rel to stack process (2 items) c1890,
stack books (6) 1908-57, technical reports, etc
(1 vol, 80 items) 1927-35, valuation of works 1948,
photographs mainly rel to lead manufacture
(17 items) 1950s, misc corresp and papers (2 vols,
1 file, 62 items) 1889-1956.
Tyne and Wear Archives Service (Acc 1512/10253-
800). NRA 32095.

[348] **MESSENGER & CO LTD**, horticultural
builders, heating engineers and ironfounders,
Loughborough, Leics

Balance sheets 1880-3, 1931-58, private ledgers (3)
1886-97, 1902-16, 1951-61, general ledgers (4)
1875-90, day book 1885-1958, cash books (7)
1945-71, bank book 1954-5 and statements 1974-5,
bought ledgers (3) 1886-95, 1901-38, purchase
books (8) 1943-70, sales day books (3) 1966-70,
invoice day books (6) 1923, 1951-60, contract books
(5) 1866-77, 1920-3, 1945-57 and files (c200)
1886-1958, plan and contract record books (10)
1903-13, 1920-63, contract letter book 1920-35,
boiler order books (8) 1903-58, estimate books (6)
1907-51, cost books (5) 1885-9, 1904-5, 1909-10,
quotations book 1903-7, customers' accounts (1 vol)
1967-9, price lists (2) 1925, heating lists (9)
1895-1901, 1907-61, claims book 1907-53, glass
empties book 1929-41, stock analysis book 1945-56,
address book c1920-35, wages books (4) 1956-63,
deeds, articles of apprenticeship, legal and property
corresp, etc (c150 items) 1875-1973, plans (c163) of
conservatories, greenhouses, etc c1920-1946,
drawings and photographs (120 items) 1939-63.
Leicestershire RO (DE 2121). NRA 26186.

[349] **MILLER & CO LTD**, ironfounders and
chilled iron roll mfrs, Edinburgh

Directors' minutes (1 vol) 1897-1947, share transfer
book 1899-1920, letter book 1901-14, ledger
1892-1921, private journal 1898-1913, journals (2)
1867-84, 1900-56, cash book 1867-77, sales records
rel to scrolls and wheel presses 1883-96, foreign
sales book 1903-6, purchase book 1889-90, furnace
contract book 1892, scrapbook 1879-86 incl
sketches of plant and machinery, record of wage
increases (1 vol) 1876-96.
The Company. Enquiries to NRA (Scotland) (survey
260). NRA 10788.

[350] **MILLOM AND ASKAM HEMATITE
IRON CO LTD**, pig iron mfrs, Millom,
Cumberland

Records from 1890 incl board and general meeting
minutes (14 vols) 1890-1958, agenda books (13)
1890-1958, registers (15) of members 1919-51,
registers (4) of mortgages and debentures
1890-1947 and other share records 1916-64, letter
books (4) 1908-52, registers (6) of probates
1897-1951, ledgers (16) 1899-1950, journals (41)

1890-1949, cash books (17) 1896-1962, accounts owing books (2) 1912-26, invoice books (11) 1928-42, advice books (10) 1928-63, contract books (7) 1910-59, delivery books (6) 1926-60, stock books (5) 1900-51, cost books (5) 1915-35, furnace sales journal 1891-7, furnace daily report books (27) 1938-68, wages records (8 vols) 1898-1964, misc corresp and papers 1890-1968; Cumberland Iron Mining & Smelting Co Ltd minute book 1879-90. *Cumbria RO, Barrow* (BDB/47). NRA 17337; *Report of the County Archivist* June 1974, p3.

Records 19th-20th cent incl memorandum and articles of association (3 items) 1890-1919, misc corporate records, deeds and other legal papers rel to property, and papers rel to foreign subsidiaries. *Cumbria RO, Barrow* (BD/HJ 164-173). NRA 32581.

[351] **MILNWOOD IRON & STEEL CO LTD**, Mossend, Lanarkshire

Directors' and shareholders' minute book 1886-91. *Strathclyde Regional Archives* (T-MS 322). NRA 19243.

[352] **MINERA LEAD SMELTING WORKS**, Minera, Denbighs

Ledgers (2) 1787-1800, journals (2) 1782-1800, sales accounts 1797-9, smelting account 1796-7, valuation of lead and ore 1797, assignment of premises 1799; Bagillt Lead Smelting Works journal (1 vol) 1782-4 incl stock inventory 1781 and manager's accounts 1785-1800; misc legal, estate and lead mining papers 1785-1806. *Public Record Office* (C 104/29). NRA 36224.

[353] **WILLIAM MITCHELL (PENS) LTD**, steel pen mfrs, London

Annual accounts nd, ledger [of the firm?] 1836-59, work books (9) 1900-3, 1908-10, nd, work returned book 1907-17, make book 1921, samples of labels (5 drawers) c1938-53, workmen's fund annual accounts 1938-44, 1950, photographs (1 parcel) c1900, personal papers of William Mitchell (1 bundle) 1830s-1840s. *British Pens Ltd.* Enquiries to the Business Archives Council. NRA 26587.

[354] **MONKLAND IRON & STEEL CO LTD**, Calderbank, Lanarkshire

Trustees' minutes (1 vol) 1861-6. *Strathclyde Regional Archives* (T-BK 142). NRA 15348.

[355] **MONKS, HALL & CO LTD**, iron and steel mfrs, Warrington, Lancs

Records 1874-1969 incl articles of association 1878, 1955, minutes (8 vols) 1892, 1897-1965, agenda book 1931-4, directors' attendance book 1919-36, register of directors (2 vols) 1924-45, annual list of members 1887-1915, debenture book 1900, share ledger 1889-1932, share call book 1903, share

transfer records (c5 vols) 1879-1936, register of returns of allotments (2 vols) 1901-6, directors' reports 1919-45, secretary's letter books (3) 1910-13, nd, auditors' reports 1897-1910, balance sheets, statements of accounts, etc 1875-1935, interest on loans (1 vol) 1887-1915, income tax returns 1882-1910, private ledgers (2) 1909-15, 1921-4, cash books (2) 1874-5, 1883-9, stock book 1882-1910 and RT Thomas' business diaries (1 box) 1895-1902; Church Ironworks Co Ltd board minutes (2 vols) 1909-36, register of members, etc (1 vol) 1909-36. *British Steel Records Centre, Shotton.* NRA 36012.

Memorandum and articles of association 1897-1962, board minutes (1 vol) 1965-80, general meeting minutes (1 vol) 1911-80, register of directors 1948-81, register of seals 1968-73. *British Steel East Midlands Regional Records Centre, Irthlingborough.* NRA 35552.

[356] **F MOODY & CO LTD**, straw-plait mill and hat iron mfrs, Luton, Beds

Ledgers (4) 1854-1903, journal 1893-1903, bills and accounts (1 bundle) 1844-64, cash book 1905-13. *Luton Museum and Art Gallery.* NRA 203.

[357] **WILLIAM HENRY MOORE & SONS**, non-ferrous metal mfrs and wire drawers, Birmingham

Accounts (2 items) of money due to Edward Moore on dissolution of partnership 1832, receipts (3 items) for purchases of metal 1873, 1887, notebooks (2) rel to orders, costings and ingredients 1833-88, stock book 1829-42, price lists, handbooks, tables and other printed papers (1 vol, 15 items) 1851-1951. *Birmingham Central Library Archives Division* (MS 1731). NRA 36648.

Bordesley deeds and schedules of deeds and documents 1825-1953. *Birmingham Central Library Archives Division* (MS 193). NRA 29847.

[358] **JOHN MORGAN & CO**, iron and tinplate mfrs, Carmarthen

Letter book 1759-62, accounts (2 vols) 1807-8, 1839, tinplate accounts (1 vol) 1800-6, Whitland forge and other accounts (2 vols) 1802-10, charcoal accounts 1807-8, day books (4) 1839-40, accounts and corresp with London agent (1 vol, 7 items) 1801-9, 1812-15, nd, London sales accounts (3 items) 1813-16 and price list 1816, accounts of debts due to the foundry (1 vol, etc) 1832-5, production records (1 vol) 1839-40, records of tinplate production (3 items) 1812-20 and rolling mill production (1 vol) 1841, stock inventory of Blackpool, Carmarthen, Kidwelly and Llandyfân works (1 vol) 1799-1800, stock accounts (1 vol, 1 item) 1808, 1814, Kidwelly Works stock book 1839 and daily output figures 1840-1, Gwendraeth Works forge book 1839-40, Gwendraeth Works and other weekly pay bills (5 vols) 1838-9, inventory of

work done at Kidwelly Works (1 vol) 1840 and corresp rel to plant, inventories and leases (9 items) 1745-1839; Morgan family and business accounts (3 vols) 1800-15, estate and household cash book 1812-21 and executors' papers (1 vol, etc) 1805, 1808-18.
National Library of Wales (Griffith E Owen Collection).

[359] **MORLAIS TIN PLATE CO LTD**, Llangennech, Carms

Directors' and general meeting minutes (4 vols) 1893-1916, 1928-40, registers of directors and shareholders and other share records (11 vols, 1 file) 1894-1950, balance sheets 1894-1951, private letter book 1910-51, letter books (13) 1936-50, ledgers (5) 1880, 1894-1951, journal 1894-1951, cash books, etc (12 vols) 1894-1951, bills receivable 1880-97, invoice books (6) 1930-51, other sales records (6 vols, etc) 1929-51, stock and weighbridge records (3 vols) 1930-51, acid yield account book 1894-1941, other production records (2 vols, etc) 1939-41, wages and staff records (8 vols, etc) 1901-51, works inventory 1894, site plans and tracings c1915-48, insurance book 1941, misc corresp and papers (10 files) c1910-51; corresp and papers rel to Llanelli Steel Co Ltd 1907-49.
University College of Swansea Library. NRA 14358.

[360] **ABEL MORRALL LTD**, needle mfrs, Redditch, Worcs

Private ledgers (9) 1876-82, 1894-1970, nominal ledgers (6) 1934-68, London and RFS ledger 1939-44, ledgers (4) 1912-20, 1930-63, private journals (2) 1898-1919, other journals (6) 1915-68, day books (2) 1910-44, cash books (19) 1892-8, 1910-74, sales, order and costings records (6 vols) 1912-59, expenditure and travellers' costs (2 vols) 1909-44, salaries and time books (10) 1906-52, valuation book 1921.
Hereford and Worcester RO, Worcester (b705:1151). NRA 34885.

[361] **JOHN MORRISON & SONS**, brassfounders, Paisley, Renfrewshire

Letter book 1859-77, private ledgers (4) 1894-1922, ledgers (11) 1859-69, 1872-1903, 1907-23, day book 1878-82, plumber's cash book 1860-77, time book 1890-7, photographs of products, etc c1880-1900.
Morrison & Macdonald (Paisley) Ltd. Enquiries to NRA (Scotland) (survey 670). NRA 16016.

[362] **MORRISTON & MIDLAND TINPLATE WORKS LTD**, Swansea, Glam

Account books (2) 1878-85, bank and cheque books (4) 1876-80, 1889-1900, receipt books, etc (2 vols, etc) 1886, 1896, stoppages timetable 1934-5, misc corresp 1875-83.
University College of Swansea Library. NRA 14358.

[363] **MOSS BAY HEMATITE IRON & STEEL CO LTD**, Workington, Cumberland

Directors', shareholders' and works committee minutes (4 vols) 1881-1915, index to minutes (1 vol) 1881-90, directors' agenda book 1891-1912, letters received (2 files) 1891-5.
Cumbria RO, Carlisle (DB/118). NRA 35358.

Rough minutes (1 vol) 1891-1911, blast furnaces sales book 1879-80, cost comparisons (6 items) 1910-29.
British Steel East Midlands Regional Records Centre, Irthlingborough. NRA 35548.

Pig iron cost book 1879-80.
British Steel Northern Regional Records Centre, Middlesbrough. NRA 35686.

See also Workington Iron & Steel Co Ltd.

[364] **MUNTZ'S METAL CO LTD**, copper and brass tube and aluminium castings mfrs, Smethwick, Staffs

Memorandum and articles of association and related papers (1 vol, 7 items) 1863-1921, minutes of general meetings (1 vol) 1864-1923 and board committee (1 vol) 1921-6, directors' reports (1 vol) 1864-1904, share records (1 folder) early 20th cent, corresp and papers rel to reconstruction of the company (1 bundle) 1890, balance sheets and accounts (5 items) 1893, 1906, 1911, dividend warrants (1 bundle) 1903-8, report on samples of Nicro copper 1907, salaries and wages books (7) 1915-28, deeds, legal corresp and papers, etc (7 bundles and folders, 8 items) 1888-1919, printed history of the company c1930; bankruptcy papers of WG Owen, late company secretary (1 bundle) 1870-5, reports and papers rel to Sir GA Muntz's inspection of American metal working practices (1 bundle) 1902.
Birmingham Central Library Archives Division (MS 1422). NRA 32859.

[365] **MUSSELBURGH WIRE MILLS CO LTD**, Musselburgh, Midlothian

Minute book 1878-81.
Scottish Record Office (CS 96/487). *Annual Report 1979*, p25.

[366] **FT MYERSON LTD**, iron plate and sheet metal workers, London

Sales accounts ledgers (5) 1909-71, order ledgers (2) 1889-1929, orders supplied books (8) 1939-62.
Greater London RO (Acc 2169/115-129). NRA 34765.

[367] **NANTYGLO & BLAINA IRONWORKS CO LTD**, iron mfrs and colliery proprietors, Nantyglo and Blaina, Mon

Balance sheets and financial statements (14 items) 1872-82, accounts and cost synopses (4 items) 1872-3, account of rails bought and sold c1873 and papers rel to sale of iron stocks (13 items) 1879-83, misc sales and purchase records (35 items) 1862-79,

statements of iron production and coke consumption (7 items) 1873-4, lists of staff and agents and related papers (12 items) 1872-1904, summaries of pay books, wage-cost calculations, etc (29 items) 1871-4, corresp rel to Blaina Workmen's Sick Fund 1874, inventories (3) of stock and plant 1874, nd, papers rel to premises in Monmouthshire and London incl mineral workings (66 items) 1848-1900, nd, leases and agreements with railway companies (c40 items) 1863-1902.
Gwent RO (D 397). NRA 9471.

Directors' report 1873, general meeting reports and papers and misc corresp rel to shares (27 items) 1873-81, financial reports and balance sheets (9 items) 1873-80.
Gwent RO (D 390/1-4). NRA 14003.

Committee minutes 1875, particulars of properties 1872, report on surface estate 1880, mining reports 1918.
Welsh Industrial and Maritime Museum, Cardiff (Acc 72.84 I). NRA 28631; BAC *Company Archives* no 131.

[368] **ISAAC NASH (BELBROUGHTON) LTD**, scythe mfrs, Belbroughton, Worcs

Letter books (3) 1918-19, 1936-9, ledgers 1874-1945, day books (8 vols, 1 file) 1877-9, 1919-52, account book 1935-45, investors' account book 1918-24, accounts analysis books (2) 1946-54, cash books 1873-6, 1912-54, copies of credit notes 1937-9, sales ledger 1915-51, bought ledger 1909-21, purchase analysis books (4) 1928-42, stock book 1928-42, repairs analysis book 1928-46, wages books 1875-7, 1913-18, 1928-48, trade mark papers 1896-1929, deeds and accounts (c25 items) 1793-1872, price list and misc papers 20th cent.
Hereford and Worcester RO, Worcester (705:616). NRA 12323.

[369] **NEATH ABBEY IRON CO**, iron mfrs, marine and locomotive engineers, Neath, Glam

Engine plans (1 file, 891 items) 1792-1882, shipbuilding and marine engineering plans (3 files, 743 items) 1817-83, locomotive and railway engineering plans (1 file, 446 items) 1826-92, gas installations plans (4 files, 387 items) 1820-62, plans of the works and plant (2 files, 143 items) 1813-81.
West Glamorgan Archive Service (D/D NAI). NRA 26202.

Further plans 1802-90.
West Glamorgan Archive Service: see *Accessions to repositories 1990*, p45.

[370] **NEATH STEEL SHEET & GALVANISING CO LTD**, Neath, Glam

Records (28 boxes) from 1896 incl articles of association 1896, board minute books 1898-1962, general meeting minute book 1896-1965, register of members and share ledger 1896-1956, share transfer certificates 1897-1941 and private ledgers (6) 1896-1952.
British Steel Records Centre, Shotton. NRA 36013.

Board minute book 1970-80, register of members 1959-81.
British Steel East Midlands Regional Records Centre, Irthlingborough. NRA 35555.

[371] **NEEDHAM, VEALL & TYZACK LTD**, cutlery mfrs, Sheffield

Minute book 1889-1906, papers rel to purchase of Joseph Hayward & Co 1902, ledger 1879-93, cost, price and pattern books (11) 1890s-1982, patent and agency papers 1865-1926, agreements with employees 1915-18 and wages book 1915, catalogues and other printed papers 20th cent; EM Dickinson customer reference book 1875-88; Nixon & Winterbottom Ltd pattern book 1862-1918; Saynor, Cooke & Ridal agency agreements, trade mark certificates, etc 1882-1948; WT Wheatley Bros trade mark papers 1878-1934.
Sheffield Archives (NVT; Acc 1986/36). NRA 34855.

[372] **NEVILL, DRUCE & CO**, copper and lead smelters, Llanelly, Carms

Resolutions of Messrs Daniell, Savill, Guest & Nevill (2 vols) 1804-34, annual meeting minutes of Sims, Willyams, Nevill, Druce & Co (1 vol) 1837-50 incl colliery, silver house and lead works accounts, letter books (8) of the Nevill family and other business associates 1797-1813, 1823-53, trade and domestic accounts of Richard Nevill (1 vol) 1808-16, Llanelly Copper Works ledger 1823-57, abstracts of accounts for copper works and collieries (2 vols) 1811-13, 1816-18, copper works accounts (3 vols) 1807-34, 1854-74, sales book 1862-3, order book 1848-70 and produce book 1865-70, copper works and collieries stock books (2) 1835-52, copper and other ore records (9 vols, 121 items) 1850-76, other shipping records (1 vol) 1838-40; Llanelly Lead Works purchase books (2) 1859-75, receipt books (2) 1862-72 and produce books (2) 1864-72; specifications of plant and equipment at the copper and lead works and collieries (2 vols) 1830-69, deeds, legal papers and related corresp (c2,800 items) 1701-1910; colliery accounts and other records (10 vols) 1803-20, 1836, 1850-80; shipbuilding specifications 1865-73.
National Library of Wales (Nevill, Druce & Co). NRA 34638.

[373] **RICHARD NEVILL & CO LTD**, ironfounders, Llanelly, Carms

Board minutes (2 vols) 1903-46, general meeting minutes (1 vol) 1888-1947, agenda books (2) 1909-24, register of members (3 vols) 1888-1906, share ledger 1888-1931, register of share transfers (1 vol) 1888-96, register of mortgages (1 vol) 1892-1921, annual returns 1925-46, ledgers (22) 1924-71, cash books (3) 1931-45, order book 1907-13, order register 1915-27, schedule of plant at Gowerton nd.
British Steel Records Centre, Shotton. NRA 36012.

[374] **NEW BRITISH IRON CO**, iron and steel mfrs, Corngreaves, Staffs

Bank account books (3) 1881-7, Corngreaves Works departmental cost sheets (8 items) and stock return sheets (5 items) 1842-3, printed legal papers rel to the British Iron Co c1830.
Sandwell Local Studies Centre (BS/NB). NRA 32391.

[375] **NEWEY BROTHERS LTD**, mfrs of metal fasteners, Birmingham

Cash books (2) 1868, 1899-1901, sales accounts, day books and customer records (15 vols) 1867, 1878-80, 1892-1909, 1928, purchase records (5 vols) 1864-70, 1896-8, 1920-2, 1934, record of war shares 1918, product transfers 1923, wages and production statistics (2 vols) 1921-6.
Birmingham Central Library Archives Division (MS 1707). NRA 36183.

[376] **NEWLAND CO**, iron mfrs, Newland and Nibthwaite, Lancs

Balance sheets, accounts and corresp (29 items) 1785-1832, inventories of goods (3 items) 1745-9, legal papers, etc (51 items) 1743-1838.
Cumbria RO, Barrow (BDX 38/19, 21, 24). NRA 32580.

[377] **NEWMILL IRONWORKS**, ironfounders and mechanical engineers, Elgin, Moray

Journal 1879-82, cash books (2) 1855-78 incl apprentices' wages 1867, order book 1856-8, sales book 1865-7, material book 1878-9, plans 1884, 1922.
In private possession. Enquiries to NRA (Scotland) (survey 592). NRA 14947. See also *Textiles and Leather,* entry 167 (James Johnston & Co) for other records relating to the early history of this firm.

[378] **NEWPORT TINPLATE CO LTD** (formerly **ABERCARN TINPLATE CO LTD**), Abercarn, Mon

Board minutes (1 vol) 1895-1901, board and general meeting minutes (1 vol) 1902-15, register of documents (1 vol) 1874-1926, register of deeds (1 vol) 1874-1922.
British Steel Records Centre, Shotton. NRA 36012.

[379] **NEWTON, CHAMBERS & CO LTD**, ironfounders, gas and water engineers, colliery owners and chemical mfrs, Sheffield

Drafts and copies of partnership agreements, etc (20 items) from 1881, memoranda of partners' weekly meetings (2 vols) 1863-87, directors' minutes (8 vols) 1881-1953, works advisory committee minutes (10 vols) 1940-53, letter and memoranda books (27 vols, etc) 1825-31, 1866-91, 1894-1915, register of mortgages 1882-95, secretary's reports 1917-24, auditors' reports 1900-22, misc administrative papers 1940-57, balance sheets 1860-1927 (incl abstract 1797-1821), 1940s-1960s, nominal and other accounts (7 vols, 1 binder)

1868-80, 1896-1948, private ledgers (7) 1805-1929, nominal ledgers (2) 1924-48, private journals (6) 1861-81, 1901-56, nd, day books (40) 1793-1852, cash books (2) 1802-11, 1876-1903, bank book 1856-60, other accounting records (12 binders) 1960s-1980s, corresp with agents, gas companies, waterworks, foundries, etc (141 files) 1793-1850, sales ledgers (3) 1793-1806, 1871-82, purchase books (2) 1822-6, 1891, order books (3) 1820-5, 1876-8, vouchers (9 files) 1795-1849, despatch and transport records (6 vols, 1 file) 1795-7, 1837-40, 1864-6, 1875-1909, stock books (9) 1799-1829, 1874, 1880-1, furnace books and other production records (6 vols) 1817-20, 1826-37, 1880-91, costings (1 binder) 1930-49, corresp and papers rel to the Delta process (6 files) 1937-55, production reports 1900-13, works diaries (2) 1909, 1912, plant records (3 binders) 1930s-1940s, record of terms of employment (1 vol) 1863-77, salaries and wages ledger 1867-78, 'tommy' shop records 1801-48, misc social and publicity records (3 vols, 4 files) 1923-61, deeds, agreements, etc 1792-1964, misc corresp and papers (21 files) 1795-1861, maps and plans 1836-1972, catalogues, price lists, etc 1845-1938, nd, press cuttings 1883-1955, photographs and glass negatives 1867-1968, nd; colliery records 1795-1964, chemical department records 1893-1942, Newton and Chambers family corresp and papers 1774-1874, papers rel to firm's history and archives 18th-20th cent.
Sheffield Archives (TR). NRA 8131.

Colliery records 1872-1957.
Sheffield Archives (NCB 609-875). NRA 14792.

Misc colliery records 19th-20th cent.
Sheffield Archives (MD 3586). NRA 23246.

[380] **NORTH EASTERN STEEL CO LTD**, steel mfrs, Middlesbrough

Memorandum and articles of association 1881, directors' minutes (1 vol) 1881-7, board and general meeting minutes (1 vol) 1914-35, directors' reports and balance sheets 1903-16, seal register 1899-1925, proposal for merger with Dorman Long 1923, journal 1917-28, departmental ledgers (4) 1905-23, estimates and quotations book c1914-36, materials ledger 1921-4, Acklam Works journal 1889-1923, purchase order books (17) 1912-39 and cost ledgers (4) 1913-23, metallurgical notebooks c1900.
British Steel Northern Regional Records Centre, Middlesbrough. NRA 35680.

[381] **NORTH LONSDALE IRON & STEEL CO LTD**, Ulverston, Lancs

Board minutes 1933-46 and general meeting minutes 1873-1946.
Cumbria RO, Barrow (B/BD 47): see *Accessions to repositories 1976*, p24.

Memorandum and articles of agreement 1894, directors' meeting papers 1936-47, reports and balance sheets 1912-50, list of shareholders and financial statement (2 items) 1950, letter rel to amalgamation 1931, cost sheets, etc (1 file) 1922-3,

deeds and papers mainly rel to property (2 boxes, 1 bundle) 1911-45.
Cumbria RO, Barrow (BD/HJ boxes 154-6, 169, 173). NRA 32581.

[382] **THOMAS NOWILL & CO**, cutlery mfrs, Sheffield

Account book 1788-1801, ledgers (5) and day books (5) 1786-1825, retail sales, disbursements, etc (2 vols) 1806-13, order book 1819-21, corresp 1819-21, 1849-51, wages books (8) 1786-1850, accounts (1 vol) of apprentices' keep 1814-43.
Sheffield Archives (LD 192-215). *Catalogue of business and industrial records in Sheffield City Libraries*, p21 and *Guide to the manuscript collections in the Sheffield City Libraries*, p63.

[383] **OAK FARM CO**, ironworks and colliery owners, Kingswinford, Staffs

Corresp (350 items) mainly of Sir John Gladstone and WE Gladstone with the company's manager James Boydell, agents for the company, solicitors and others 1838-61, out-letter books (3) of Sir John Gladstone concerning the company 1843-8, deed of partnership 1845, memoranda (19 items) 1836-56, accounts (1 bundle) 1836-56, bank book 1847-9, description and valuation of Oak Farm estate 1856, report on the company's works and mines 1858, misc papers 1829-65.
Clwyd RO, Hawarden (Glynne-Gladstone MSS 2892-2926). NRA 14174.

Corresp, financial and legal papers and deeds (100 bundles and items) of Sir Stephen Glynne and his trustees rel to the company and its estate 1835-75.
Clwyd RO, Hawarden (D/HA). NRA 9839.

Corresp and papers (2 bundles, 9 items) of CB Trevor Roper as a partner in the company 1844-9, incl valuation of works 1846, statement of company's affairs 1847 and report by committee of creditors 1848.
Clwyd RO, Hawarden (D/PT/1058-68). NRA 1127.

[384] **JAMES OAKES & CO**, ironworkers, Alfreton, Derbys

Private ledger and account book 1886-1908.
Derbyshire RO (D2468Z). NRA 8918.

[385] **OATEY & MARTYN LTD**, ironfounders and stove mfrs, Wadebridge, Cornwall

Pattern shop order books (11) c1850-1926, specification book c1880.
Cornwall RO (AD 661/1-12). *List of Accessions April 1982-March 1983.*

[386] **OLD CASTLE IRON & TINPLATE CO LTD**, Llanelly, Carms

Memorandum and articles of association 1896-1935, papers rel to the foundation of the company (2 bundles) 1866-7, directors' minutes (24 vols) 1867-1939, general meeting minutes (3 vols)

1867-1938, agenda books (3) and other meeting papers 1925-39, register of directors 1901-31, directors' attendances and fees (2 bundles) 1872-1905, 1912-14, directors' reports (2 bundles, 2 files, etc) 1868-1932, register of members incl share ledger (2 vols) 1866-1938, numerical register nd, summary of capital and lists of members, etc (5 bundles) 1867-1936, other share and dividend records (5 vols, 1 box, 1 bundle, etc) 1866-1937, reports and accounts (18 files, etc) 1929-38, profit and loss accounts 1922, balance sheets (2 bundles) 1866-1914, 1918-28, registers of confidential reports (3) 1894-1921, letter books (5) 1870-1913, 1920-30, general corresp and agreements (c34 files, 27 bundles, etc) 1869-1944, other corporate papers (1 box) 1862-1919, personal and nominal ledgers (3) 1934-50, cash ledgers (4) 1898-1935, ledger balances 1866-76, journals (6) 1915-40, cash books (2) 1934-40 and related records (1 bundle) 1928, trade accounts (2 bundles) 1867-1928, cost accounts (9 bundles) 1867-1928, order books and other sales and purchase records (6 vols, 2 bundles, 1 file) 1935-9, bill book 1867-1938, lists of creditors (2 bundles) 1866-1929 and debtors (2 bundles) 1867-1929, records of tin and terne plate shipped (2 bundles) 1871-92, cost book 1907-10, stock records (1 vol, 23 files, 1 bundle, etc) 1867-88, 1922-47, misc production and mill output records (8 items) 1876, 1882, 1898-1908, distribution sheets (1 bundle) 1871-6, patents, etc (1 envelope, 1 item) 1877, 1903-37, trade mark certificates (1 bundle) 1884-6, 1891, wages records (2 vols, 3 files) 1931-47, agreements with the workforce (5 items) 1895-1901, inventories of tools (1 bundle, etc) 1867, tenders and specifications for new plant (9 files, etc) 1936-9, insurance policies (2 bundles, etc) 1898-1936, deeds 1866-1910.
University College of Swansea Library. NRA 8486.

[387] **OLD PARK SILVER MILLS LTD**, metal and silver rollers and nickel silver mfrs, Sheffield

Private ledger 1883-1925, wages books 1883-91.
Sheffield Archives. NRA 28631; BAC *Company Archives* no 447.

Directors' minutes (2 vols) 1908-46, general meeting minutes (1 vol) 1884-1983, register of members 1891-1961, register of transfers 1884-1961.
Untraced. NRA 28631.

[388] **OMOA IRON WORKS**, Cleland, Lanarkshire

Ledger rel to customers in England and Ireland 1796-1805.
Scottish Record Office (CS 96/1925). *Court of Session Productions*, List & Index Society, special series vol 23, 1987, p128.

[389] **ORMESBY ROLLING MILLS LTD**, steel rollers, Middlesbrough

Directors' and shareholders' minutes 1909-53, register of members and share ledger 1909-47, register of seals 1932-53, private ledger 1910-53, impersonal ledger 1910-34, private journal 1910-53,

capital expenditure on Talbot continuous process
(1 vol) 1909-17, manufacturing ledger 1909-27.
*British Steel Northern Regional Records Centre,
Middlesbrough.* NRA 35685.

[390] **SAMUEL OSBORN & CO LTD**, mfrs of
steel, files, tools and springs, Sheffield

Board minutes (1 vol) 1916-34, decisions book
1942-8 and report book 1906-8, letter books (13)
1852-65, 1902-11, private letter books (4) of Samuel
Osborn 1873-91, register of agreements 1909-54,
balance books and sheets 1887, 1891-1920, private
and partnership ledgers (7) 1860-76, 1891-1906,
1916-19, departmental and impersonal ledgers (4)
1874-1919, other ledgers (12) 1928-69, partnership
journals (8) 1869-72, 1874-1919, departmental and
general journals (2) 1899-1920, cash books (7)
1852-66, 1963-9, bought journal 1901-5, letters and
orders from China (2 bundles) 1868-9, overseas
trade and agency ledger and journals (5) 1897-1956,
cost books (4) 1877-85, 1891-2, stock journals (2)
1887-1951, technical notebooks, analysis books,
mixture books, etc (10 vols) 1896-1929, wages and
other staff records (11 vols and files) 1875-1972,
inventories of works 1889, 1896, rent books (2)
1903-19, press cuttings, scrapbooks and other
printed papers 1873-1967.
Sheffield Archives (Osborn 1-137). NRA 21582.

Records 1859-1970s incl articles of partnership
1897, 1903, memorandum and articles of
association 1905 and special resolutions 1920-50,
letter book 1882-1902, seal book 1906-37, trading
and profit and loss accounts and balance sheets 1856
and from 1866, dividend account book 1906-16,
private ledgers (4) 1875-90, 1906-27, private journal
1875-90, abstract book 1876-7, agency and tenancy
agreements 1901-1960s, corresp and papers mainly
rel to overseas trade (1 box) late 19th-early 20th
cent, misc corresp, agreements, insurance policies,
etc (1 envelope) 1877-1905, patents, specifications
and related papers 1859-1960s, spring cost book
1877-81, plant accounts (4 vols) 1869, 1872,
stocktaking books (2) 1874-1903, salaries lists
1904-15, deeds, etc c1875-c1912, and catalogues
late 19th-early 20th cent.
Sheffield Archives (Aurora III). NRA 26201.

Misc circulars, price lists, advertisements, etc
(3 bundles) 1875-88.
Sheffield Archives (MD 1195-7). NRA 23246.

[391] **OUSEBURN LEAD CO**, lead mfrs,
Newcastle upon Tyne

Directors' minutes (1 vol) 1884-1967, register of
directors and shareholders (1 vol) 1885-9, share
transfer register (Acc 1 vol) 1887-1940.
Tyne and Wear Archives Service (Acc 1512/10801-3).
NRA 32095.

[392] **OVERTON & HIGGINS**, saddlers'
ironmongers, Walsall, Staffs

Corresp (28 bundles) 1904-15, cash book 1906,
orders sent and received, invoices, bills and related
corresp (30 bundles) 1909-17, corresp and journey

lists of sales representatives (5 bundles) 1912-15,
despatch and parcel books (7) 1912-14, firm's price
lists, designs and illustrations (13 bundles and items)
1902, 1907, nd, trade catalogues of suppliers and
competitors (c100 items) 1882-1911.
Walsall Archives Service (Acc 185/2-4). NRA 23873.

[393] **OWEN & FENDELOW**, tool mfrs,
Wolverhampton, Staffs

Orders day book 1811-58.
Wolverhampton Borough Archives (DB/24/393). NRA
31835.

[394] **TW PALMER & CO (MERTON ABBEY)
LTD**, mfrs of iron gates, fences and railings, and
constructional engineers, Merton, Surrey

Deeds of partnership, etc (11 items) 1894, 1909-41,
profit and loss accounts, balance sheets and related
corresp (2 vols, 155 items) 1894-1943, ledger,
journal, day books and cash book (5 vols)
1894-1913, order book from 1894, papers rel to
publicity, staff and premises 1923-69, photographs
1908, 1920s-1968.
Surrey RO, Kingston upon Thames (2044). NRA
23776.

[395] **PARK GATE IRON & STEEL CO LTD**,
Rotherham, Yorks

Articles of partnership, dissolution of partnership,
etc (3 vols, 2 items) 1833-47, directors' minutes
from 1864, statistics of costs, sales, stock, wages, etc
(3 vols) 1847, 1850, 1853, order book 1864-5,
Admiralty contract 1872, plans (2) 1861, 1871,
wages books (2) 1863, 1869.
Untraced. NRA 4872.

Register of members (21 vols) 1919-51, share
certificate counterfoils (1 vol) 1948-51, records of
stockholders and transfers, etc (1 vol, c6 bundles)
20th cent.
Rotherham Metropolitan Borough Archives and *British
Steel Northern Regional Records Centre, Middlesbrough.*
Enquiries to Rotherham Metropolitan Borough
Archives. NRA 35683.

[396] **WILLIAM PARK & CO**, iron and steel
forgings and edge tool mfrs, Wigan, Lancs

Report and accounts (1 vol) 1955, account book
1824-56, cost books (2) 1929-30, employee returns
(3 vols) 1916-18, recreation club records (1 vol,
3 files) 1937-56, plant registers (3) 1933-48,
photographs mainly of products and premises
(35 items) c1900-68, publicity material (3 vols)
1967-80, company histories (2 items) 20th cent,
Park family papers (1 vol) 19th cent.
Wigan Archives Service (D/DY PW). NRA 35098.

[397] **A & F PARKES & CO LTD**, spade, shovel
and edge tool mfrs, Birmingham

Minutes (2 vols) 1901-25, cash book 1910-22, press
cuttings (1 vol) 19th-20th cent.
Wigan Archives Service (D/DY PW/F2). NRA 35098.

[398] **HP PARKES & CO LTD**, chain mfrs, Cradley Heath, Staffs

Minutes (1 vol) 1956-65, register of members and share ledger 1905-54, nominal ledger 1894-1929, other accounting records (6 vols) 1920-66, invoice book 1918-61, wages book 1925-40.
Dudley Archives and Local History Service (Acc 8264). NRA 25008.

[399] **F PARKIN & SONS LTD**, iron and brass founders, Exeter, Devon

Ledgers (13 vols, 1 bundle) 1847-1952, day books (44) 1847-1954, cash books (25) 1862-70, 1887-93, 1898-1959, bill books (2) 19th cent, 1892-1919, misc accounting records (7 vols) 1911-60, bought ledgers (5) 1877-88, 1893-9, 1922-41, order books (3) 1934-7, 1950, traveller's notebook 1868, journey books (11) 1891-1908, 1919-58, catalogues and lists of items manufactured and stocked 19th cent, wages books (5) 1877-1903, 1919-40, property records (4 vols, 1 bundle) 1892-1955.
Devon RO (68/18). NRA 34802.

Corresp, technical plans, catalogues and property records 1860s-1956.
Ironbridge Gorge Museum (Acc L448).

[400] **F PARRAMORE & SONS LTD**, ironfounders, Chapeltown, Yorks

Papers rel to directors' and general meetings (143 items) 1925-41, balance sheets, trading and profit and loss accounts and related papers (99 items) 1924-68, nominal ledgers (4) 1908-67, private ledger 1924-62, cash books (3) 1908-43, sales day book 1912, sales invoices (1 vol) 1915-17, munitions of war day book 1915-19, misc papers rel to patents, production and taxation 1909-59, nd, wages books (7) 1917-65 and related papers (1 bundle) 1961-70, agreements, etc (31 items) 1905-53, nd, insurance policies (18) 1907-44, inventories and valuations (2) 1968-9, plans (7) 1922-38.
Sheffield Archives (LD 2118-44). NRA 24514.

[401] **PARTINGTON STEEL & IRON CO LTD**, steel mfrs, Irlam, Lancs

Minute books (2) 1916-29, committee minutes 1910-12, 1920-7, scheme of arrangement 1928, loan records (2 vols) nd, capital account ledger 1911, nominal ledger 1930, departmental ledger 1920, pension records nd, improvements and extensions accounts 1929.
British Steel Records Centre, Shotton. NRA 36007.

Comparative profit and loss accounts (1 vol) 1914-27, account and day books (42 vols) 1903-29, 1933-4.
Warrington Library (MSS 2405-6). NRA 36069.

[402] **PARTRIDGE, JONES & CO LTD**, iron mfrs and colliery proprietors, Varteg and Golynos, Mon

Partnership agreements (2 items) 1872-4, memorandum and articles of association 1874, certificate of incorporation 1902, board and general meeting minutes (2 vols) 1898-1921, directors' reports and balance sheets (6 items) 1876-1917, misc share records (17 items) 1883, 1892-1920, agreements rel to plant at Varteg and Golynos works, leases and other premises records 1864-1962; Varteg and Plas-y-coed colliery balance sheets (2 items) 1872-5, mineral leases and wayleaves (66 items) 1871-1918.
Gwent RO (D 394). NRA 9872.

Further records 1914-63.
Gwent RO: see *Accessions to repositories 1989*, p43.

[403] **MARY PARTRIDGE**, awl mfr, Bloxwich, Staffs

Account books (2) c1830, c1850.
Walsall Archives Service (Acc 59). NRA 23874.

[404] **PATENT TYPE FOUNDING CO LTD**, London

Minute book 1857-74.
Guildhall Library, London (MS 18790).

[405] **WILLIAM PATTERSON LTD**, wire and sheet metal workers, Newcastle upon Tyne

Letter books 1947-51, financial records 1881-1976, order books 1922-74.
Tyne and Wear Archives Service (Acc 2305).

[406] **PAYTON PEPPER & SONS LTD**, manufacturing jewellers, Birmingham

Records 19th-20th cent incl minute books from 1898, pattern books late 19th-20th cent, shipping export book 1896, printed catalogues 20th cent and deed of apprenticeship of Charles Payton 1826.
The Company. Enquiries to the Managing Director.

[407] **PEARSON & KNOWLES COAL & IRON CO LTD**, iron mfrs and colliery proprietors, Warrington, Lancs

Articles of association 1874, board minutes (4 vols) 1874-97, 1916-28, 1958-70, general meeting minutes (1 vol) 1874-1921, board and general meeting minutes (2 vols) 1930-58, debenture and bond holders' minutes nd, committee minutes 1874-1927, board papers 1958-66, scheme of arrangement 1928, private ledgers (2) 1883-1909, 1930, private journal 1925-30, orders journal 1925-30, sales analysis 1888, salaries books (5) 1879-1908, 1919-31, valuation of stock 1937, Dallam Works plant book 1903-19, coal department private ledger 1910.
British Steel Records Centre, Shotton. NRA 36007.

Colliery quantity books (5) 1883-1937.
Lancashire RO (NCPk). NRA 12638.

[408] **PEGLERS LTD**, brassfounders, Doncaster, Yorks

Minutes (5 vols) 1914-63 and related papers (3 vols, 11 items) 1921-4, 1935-60, 1971, share records

(10 vols, 1 bundle) 1914-67, register of seals
1935-57, balance sheets and profit and loss accounts
(1 vol) 1934-50, private ledgers (3) 1901-49 and
related papers (2 bundles) 1904-16, 1932-3, cash
books (3) 1919-50, 1957-9, bill book 1901-54,
plating department statement book 1927-40, wages
and salaries books, absentee registers, works notices,
etc (26 vols, 3 files, 1 bundle) 1918-74, valuation
(1 vol) of materials, stock, wages, etc 1886-7,
inventory and valuation (1 vol) of plant and
machinery 1904-5, catalogues, house magazines,
pension scheme papers and other printed material
1898-1982.
Doncaster Archives Department (DY/PEG). NRA
30361.

[409] PENSNETT COLLIERY & IRON WORKS, Pensnett, Staffs

Personal ledgers (2) 1888-1905, 1910-24, journals
(2) 1901-10, 1920-5, purchase day book 1919-25,
wages books for forge (3 vols) 1859-81, furnace
(3 vols) 1845-52, 1859-83 and colliery (21 vols)
1848-51, 1874-1945, other workmen's accounts
(1 vol) 1876-1912.
Dudley Archives and Local History Service (D/LU).
NRA 21951.

[410] PENTYRCH IRONWORKS, Pentyrch, Glam

Cash book 1790-3, memoranda book 1807-28 rel to
Pentyrch and Melingriffith tinplate works.
Glamorgan Archive Service (D/D Xn 3, CL
MS 1.710).

Cash book 1822-31 and cordwood and timber
delivery book 1850-79 rel to Pentyrch and
Melingriffith tinplate works.
Welsh Industrial and Maritime Museum, Cardiff (Accs
1991.25/7,9).

Foundry account book 1850-1.
Dyfed Archives Service, Carmarthen (Trostre 40).

Manager's commonplace book 1781-1834.
Cardiff Central Library (MS 4.1000).

[411] JOHN PERKS & SONS LTD, edge tool mfrs, Wolverhampton, Staffs

Day book 1793-1833, ledgers, cash books and
purchase and sales records (49 vols) 1933-59, order
books (4) 1853, 1872, 1879-92, 1908-15, 1927-35,
quotations book 1951-60, pattern books (3)
1901-27, trade mark books (2) 1877-1926, misc
notes, press cuttings, etc (1 file) 1930s, catalogues
(19) 20th cent.
Staffordshire RO (D 1007). NRA 22207.

[412] PERRAN FOUNDRY, ironfounders and steam engine builders, Perranarworthal, Cornwall

Ledgers (2) 1842-59, 1872-81, journal 1877-81,
cash journal 1878-83, cash book 1877-9, delivery
book 1879-81, wages book 1878-81.
Cornwall RO (CF 4004-10). NRA 34797.

Corresp 1872-3, price list 1874, plan *c*1880, lease
1882.
Cornwall RO (M 252/49, M 253/5, SHM 660,
X 197).

[413] PERRY & CO LTD, steel pen and cycle chain mfrs, Birmingham and London

Records 19th-20th cent incl prospectus 1876,
memorandum and articles of association 1876,
board and general meeting minutes 1875-1965,
management committee minutes 1926, board
transfer books (5) 1876-1905 and papers 1906-37,
directors' attendance books nd, reports to
shareholders 1877-9, reports of general meetings
1902-45, agenda books 1926-58, statement of
profits 1859-75, profits and home trading accounts
1906-27, balance sheets and profit and loss accounts
1890-1945, share transactions records 1901-40,
records of stock prices 1876-1958, papers rel to
directors' and families' stockholdings 1904-59,
papers rel to office procedures 1891, 1897-1903,
agency agreements from 1879, other agreements
1839-43, 1866-1964, papers rel to amalgamations
and acquisitions 1876, 1904, 1928-64, accounts of
Frankfurt business 1873, payment guarantee 1929,
record of orders 1864-71, specifications
abridgements for writing instruments, chains and
velocipedes to 1936, registered designs for pens and
pencils, etc 1862-91, corresp and papers rel to trade
marks and patents 1836, 1865-8, 1959-64,
appointment of works manager 1901, papers rel to
London premises 1866, illustrated price list 1868,
press cuttings (2 vols) 1890-1945, photograph of
factory 1956; Alfred Sommerville & Co trading
figures 1888-1906, trade marks *c*1880, price lists of
Josiah Mason and others *c*1862.
Manchester Central Library Local Studies Unit
(M501/PE). NRA 35782.

[414] PICKERSGILL & FROST LTD, stove and grate mfrs, Langley Mill, Derbys

Articles of association 1897, private ledger
1897-1913, ledgers (9) 1888-91, 1937-56, cash
books, day books and other accounting records
(34 vols) 1916-67, memoranda rel to prices,
measurements, specifications, etc (several vols, 1 file)
19th-20th cent, catalogues and price lists (3 files,
1 bundle) *c*1910-1960s, other sales, order, invoice
and production records (*c*77 vols, etc) *c*1938-1960s,
wages and time books (39) 1907-64, rents book
1947-57, photographs (1 file) 19th-20th cent.
Derbyshire RO (D626). NRA 34310.

[415] JOHN PLAYER & SONS LTD, ironfounders and tinplate mfrs, Clydach, Glam

Private letter books (3) *c*1884-1939, other letter
books (42) 1862-96, 1938-50, account books (2)
1859-68, 1899-1919, private ledgers (2) 1861-91,
1909-41, ledgers (11) 1861-1946, works ledgers (9)
1876-1951, journals (6) 1861-76, 1886-99,
1904-36, works journals (6) 1876-1940, day books
(6) 1861-87, 1913-33, cash books (7) 1861-82,
1900-10, 1924-46, works cash books (8) 1876-92,
1900-15, 1937-52, contract books (2) 1898-1913,
1922-30, estimate book *c*1867, specifications books
(15) 1884-1934, order books (14) 1861-95,
1904-12, 1925-59, invoice books (22) 1862-88,
1914-51, corresp rel to foundry orders and supplies
1874-1925, stock books (6) 1881-1940 and

inventories (2 items) c1870, 1881, castings books (2)
1864-8, plate books (4) 1891-2, 1908-11, 1915-21,
yield books (20) 1908-12, 1922-54, make books
(27) 1914-55, moulders' output books (2) 1873-8,
1895-1904, wages and salaries books (63) for
foundry, works, etc 1855-1940, time books (8)
1864-5, 1870-5, 1936-46, Factory Act register
1868-78, other staff records 1905-41.
University College of Swansea Library. NRA 14358.

[416] **POLLIT & WIGZELL LTD**, ironfounders
and engineers, Sowerby Bridge, Yorks

Specifications (4 vols) 1849-1927.
In private possession. Photocopies in West Yorkshire
Archive Service, Calderdale (MISC:261). NRA
21161.

Engine specifications 1905-13.
West Yorkshire Archive Service, Bradford (59D90).

[417] **PONTYPOOL IRON & TINPLATE
WORKS**, Pontypool, Mon

Partnership deeds (25) 1851-67, directors' minute
books (2) 1886-96, directors' reports and balance
sheets (23 items) 1891-1919, debentures 1855,
1887, misc deeds, agreements, etc rel to premises,
mineral property and railway companies (c50 items)
1772-1911.
Gwent RO (D394). NRA 9872.

Account book 1855.
National Library of Wales: see *Annual Report 1954-55*,
p32.

Papers rel to dispute with the Newport,
Abergavenny & Hereford Railway Co (3 boxes)
1846-53, mortgages and leases (3 boxes) 1850s.
Birmingham University Library (Nineteenth-Century
Industry Collection, boxes 1-6). NRA 31928.

[418] **JOHN PRICE**, nailmaker, Llangollen,
Denbighs

Accounts (2 vols) c1858-1902.
Clwyd RO, Ruthin (DD/DM/1014). NRA 34287.

[419] **PRIESTFIELD IRONWORKS**,
Wolverhampton, Staffs

Memoranda and account book of William Ward rel
to ironworks and collieries mainly 1843-8, misc
memoranda and papers (21 items) 1825-48, press
cuttings, etc c1840s.
Staffordshire RO (D4617). NRA 3515.

[420] **ROBERT PRINGLE**, pewterer, London

Ledgers (3) 1866-72, 1911-13.
Hackney Archives Department (D/B/PRI). NRA
30851.

[421] **PROTECTOR LAMP & LIGHTING CO
LTD**, miners' lamp mfrs, Eccles, Lancs

Minutes, etc 1882-1940 and from c1960, share
records 1899-1926, annual accounts, etc 1884-1913,

letter books 1895-1926 and other corporate records
1893-1926, ledgers, journals and other accounting
records 1876-1954, patents list 1911, staff records
1900-50.
The Company. NRA 28631. BAC *Company Archives*
no 169.

[422] **JOHN RABONE & SONS LTD**, steel and
wooden rule mfrs, Birmingham

Minutes (2 vols, 1 bundle) 1910-63, directors'
agreements, annual accounts, etc (3 bundles,
25 items) 1922-63, papers (2 bundles) rel to
purchase of Edward Preston & Sons Ltd 1932, office
circulars (2 vols) 1940-51, summary accounts and
balance sheets (1 vol) of tapes and steel rules
department 1877-1911, ledgers (5) 1817-60,
1865-9, town and country ledgers (2) 1869-72,
private ledgers (5 vols, 1 bundle) 1872-1931,
1948-51, nominal ledgers (8) 1910-60, account
ledgers (2) 1948-64, cash books (7) 1846-70,
1910-41, 1950-64, trade statistics (1 vol) 1817-72,
information about customers (5 vols) 1877-93, order
book 1895-6, consecutive numbers order books (2)
1868-1964, quotations books (3) 1902-33, wood
cost book 1877-1958, bought ledgers (2) 1872-6,
1879-81, commissions ledger 1915-55, misc letters,
memoranda, shipping documents, catalogues, etc
(2 vols, 2 bundles, 1 item) 19th-20th cent, stock
books (19) 1846-1974, patent and trade mark
records (1 vol, 14 bundles, 14 items) 1756,
1894-1949, wages books (2) 1870-81, staff records
(6 vols) 1911-38, plant valuation (1 vol) 1936,
inventory and valuations (3 vols, 1 bundle) of
Hockley Abbey Works 1914-19, 1947, history of
firm (1 vol) 1984; Rabone Chesterman Ltd misc
corporate records 1963-83; James Chesterman & Co
price list 1872-4 and order book 1895-1953;
Edward Preston & Sons Ltd shareholders' minutes
1898-1940.
Birmingham Central Library Archives Division
(MS 1522). NRA 33241.

[423] **RAINE & CO LTD**, iron and steel mfrs,
Swalwell, co Durham

Records incl directors' minutes 1957-68, list of
members 1891-1957, financial records 1882-1972
and photographs c1882-1972.
Tyne and Wear Archives Service (Acc 2529).

[424] **RALPH & JORDAN** (afterwards
JA JORDAN & SONS LTD), enamellers, hollow-
ware mfrs, tinners and galvanisers, Bilston, Staffs

Order book 1907-9, orders completed day book
1910-12, order and despatch record 1911-15, sales
day books (2) 1896-1901, sales record 1916-23,
refunds book 1895-1911, enamelling day book
1907-13, materials and maintenance record
1911-17, piece work accounts (3 vols) 1912-16,
1937, wages sheets (2 vols) 1917-20.
Staffordshire RO (D 1521). NRA 20732.

[425] **NC READING & CO LTD**, gold and silver jewellery, chain and bracelet mfrs, Birmingham

Corresp (1 bundle) 1903-19, partnership ledger 1903-20, private ledgers (2) 1888-1921, day books (9) 1912-53, journals (10) 1919-67, cash books (8) 1914-65, sales ledgers (6) 1911-47, bought ledgers (6) 1911-57, customer accounts totals (3 vols) 1924-9, 1933-42, order books (3) 1912-26, price lists (3) *c*1899, *c*1921, *c*1940, gilding department register 1887-1921, cost book *c*1952-62, pattern book *c*1920, time book 1910-13, wages books (7) 1895-8, 1916-22, 1926-56; personal share ledger of partner in the firm 1916-24.
Birmingham Central Library Archives Division (MS 1574). NRA 36657.

[426] **REDBOURN HILL IRON & COAL CO LTD**, ironmasters and coal merchants, Scunthorpe, Lincs

Board and general meeting minutes (5 vols) 1872-1925, index to minutes nd, directors' attendance book 1918-24, register of members and share ledger (1 vol) 1905-24, annual list and summary of shares 1909-24, register of deeds and documents (1 vol) 1879-1934, photographs of works (12 vols) 1914-20.
British Steel Records Centre, Shotton. NRA 36012.

[427] **REDBROOK TINPLATE CO LTD**, Redbrook, Glos

Memorandum of association (2 items) 1883, legal papers (6 items) rel to sale of works 1861, corresp and papers incl inventories of stock (4 bundles, 44 papers) rel to bankruptcy of the firm occupying the works 1847-69, misc deeds, abstracts of title, mortgages, plans and inventories (90 items, 2 envelopes) 1712-1948.
Gloucestershire RO (D637-8, D2441). NRA 1374.

Redbrook Ironworks accounts (1 vol) 1778-99.
Gloucestershire RO (D326/Z4). NRA 5482.

Memorandum and articles of association 1957, output records (2 vols) 1924-61, technical papers and drawings (13) rel to engines and motors, fuel and water use 18th cent, 20th cent, deeds (*c*90) 1739-19th cent.
Gloucestershire RO (D2166). NRA 23788.

[428] **JOHN REDGATE**, ironfounders and stove mfrs, Nottingham

Account and stocktaking book 1808-1913, trading accounts 1903-4, day book 1833-6, apprenticeship indenture 1854, photographs (8) of works, etc *c*1891–*c*1933.
Nottinghamshire Archives (RGA). NRA 6885.

[429] **AR REDHOUSE & CO**, ironworkers, Hildersham, Cambs

Day books (2) 1882-5, 1889-95, account book 1884-1901.
Hertfordshire RO (D/ESn B5-7). NRA 22786.

[430] **REDPATH, BROWN & CO LTD**, structural steel mfrs and constructional engineers, Edinburgh

Board, general meeting and committee minutes (20 vols) 1896-1967, register of mortgages 1886-1907, share registers (2) 1903-68, balance sheets 1820-58, prospectus, annual reports and balance sheets 1896-1970, other corporate and share records 1938-77, ledgers (9) 1940-70, bill books (3) 1897-1939, sundry cost statements 1914-67, return of sales 1946-70, job books (2) 1954-69, bridge contract records (12 boxes) 1937-71, annual certificates, etc 1938-67, staff records (8 boxes, 2 files) 1946-76, plant register cards (1 box) *c*1913-1970, papers and photographs rel to firm's history (1 box) 1909-63, photographs of bridges, etc 1924-81, press cuttings 1962-81.
British Steel East Midlands Regional Records Centre, Irthlingborough. NRA 35550.

[431] **HANS RENOLD LTD**, driving chain mfrs, Manchester

Records 19th-20th cent incl memorandum and articles of association 1903-22, board and general meeting minutes 1903-32, head office meeting minutes (10 vols) 1910-28, managing director's council minutes from 1928, other departmental and committee minutes 1910-18, balance sheets and trading accounts 1903-22, notes on the organisation of commercial and technical offices 1906 and other organisational records (20 vols, etc) 1909-30, papers rel to liquidation and merger with Coventry Chain Co Ltd 1927-35, accounts (1 binder, etc) 1903-29, 'carry forward' statements 1903-22, papers rel to accounting system 1913, expense rates 1913-21, draft private ledgers (2) 1913-14, chart of annual chain sales 1880-97, daily record of orders and sales 1905-8, monthly sales statistics 1882-1910, sales bulletins 1911-24, testimonial 1911, diagram of cost system 1908, paper by Hans Renold rel to engineering workshop organisation 1913, instruction cards for chain assembly 1913-49, applications books and drawings 1909-22, patents 1865, 1885-1910, technical papers 1912-40, payroll *c*1906, terms of employment 1896, 1914-22, factory plans 1913-14, photographs of employees and premises (1 vol, 3 items, etc) from *c*1900, scrapbook 1896-1907, catalogues and related notes 1885-1937, misc papers and publicity material 1900-37.
Manchester Central Library Local Studies Unit (M501/HR). NRA 35782.

[432] **GEORGE RESTALL**, tinsmith, Stratford-upon-Avon, Warwicks

Account book 1829-37.
Shakespeare Birthplace Trust RO, Stratford-upon-Avon (ER 124). NRA 4523.

[433] **T REYNOLDS & SON**, ironfounders and shell moulders, Little Harrowden, Northants

Account book 1911-18, ledgers (2) 1867-71, 1912-13, cash books (2) 1898-1922, foundry and

farm orders, accounts, invoices, corresp, etc
(11 bundles) 1908-35, foundry wages books (8)
1901-3, 1906-8, 1912-27, farm wages books (10)
1911-25, farm inventory 1880-9, price lists, etc of
other firms (120 items) 1927-31, nd, misc corresp
and papers (c60 items) 1882-1932, trade magazines
1928-30.
Northamptonshire RO (1978/32). NRA 22313.

[434] **RHYMNEY IRON CO LTD**, iron and steel
mfrs and colliery proprietors, Rhymney, Mon

General meeting minutes (1 vol) 1903-37, minute
books (3) 1914-26, letter books (46) of the
Rhymney Works 1857-9, 1903, 1910-20 and
London office 1911-12, ledger 1848-61, works
ledgers (9) 1836-64, iron ledgers (7) 1863-70,
1877-96, coal and coke ledgers (14) 1860-1910,
company journals (2) 1850-64, works journals (8)
1836-52, London office journals (8) 1836-82,
1886-1909, cash book 1860-5, bank books (2)
1877-1912, 1916-19, account books (2) 1886-1913,
accounts of bricks received (1 vol) 1879-80,
accounts of iron, steel, clay, limestone, coal and coke
produced and consumed (1 vol) 1886-9, invoice
books (9) 1836-66, iron and steel invoice books (12)
1866-82, 1884-91, coal and coke invoice books (9)
1860-84, 1887-1901, bills payable (1 vol) 1841 and
receivable (1 vol) 1840-63, inventory of stock (1 vol)
1848, insurance policies (7 items) 1870-87, indicator
diagram book for furnaces 1876-8, 1889-90, plans
and elevations (3) of the works c1880 and index
book to plans and drawings 1875-9, plans of mineral
estate (53 items) 1837-53, misc deeds, leases and
related corresp and papers 1825-1922; colliery
corresp, accounts, sales, production, staff and other
records 1885-1939.
Glamorgan Archive Service (D/D Rh). NRA 6686.

Balance sheets 1898-1914, register of leases
1837-1934.
Glamorgan Archive Service (D/D PD 52-3). NRA
35920.

Colliery cost books (12) 1920-31.
Glamorgan Archive Service (D/D NCB). NRA 12820.

[435] **RICE & CO**, ironfounders, Northampton
Travellers' ledgers (3) 1868-72, catalogues,
photographs, etc c1900-1970s.
Northamptonshire RO (Acc 1978/157). NRA 22277.

[436] **ROBERTS & BELK LTD**, silversmiths and
cutlery mfrs, Sheffield

Cost books (3) for tableware and cutlery
c1895-c1936, cutlery pattern books (3) 1881-1954,
pattern cards and drawings, etc of silverware
(37 boxes, 9 folders) 19th-20th cent, photographs of
products (2 drawers) early 20th cent.
Sheffield Archives (LD 1959-64 and 1988 deposit).
NRA 34827.

[437] **WILLIAM ROBERTSON LTD**, steel mfrs,
Warrington, Lancs

Minute books (5) 1899-1910, 1936-70.
British Steel Records Centre, Shotton. NRA 36007.

[438] **GEORGE W ROBSON**, sheet metal
workers, Sunderland, co Durham

Ledger 1898-1927, time book 1913-20.
Tyne and Wear Archives Service (DX91). NRA 22717.

[439] **JOHN ROBY LTD**, brassfounders, Rainhill,
Lancs

Minutes (2 vols, etc) 1914-66, share ledgers (2)
1956 and register of members nd, balance sheets, etc
(1 box) 1910-65, private ledger 1914-41, enquiries,
quotations and bills (39 boxes) 1929-65, legal papers
incl some rel to patents (1 box) 1829-1962, plans
(1 box) nd, catalogues (1 box) c1940-60, misc
corresp and papers (1 vol, 2 folders) 1884-1965.
*National Museums and Galleries on Merseyside,
Merseyside Maritime Museum* (D/B boxes 1-45). NRA
35598.

Cash books 1913-41, work books 1888-1903, wages
books 1873-1916.
St Helens Local History and Archives Library. NRA
24416.

[440] **JOSEPH RODGERS & SONS LTD**,
cutlery mfrs and silver platers, Sheffield

Records (30 boxes, 15 vols, 1 bundle) 1871-1977
incl minutes (3 vols) 1871-87, 1905-43, dividend
book 1890-8, register of mortgages (1 vol)
1891-1934, share and other corporate records
(18 vols) 1925-68, ledgers and other account books
(8) 1918-70 and inventory and valuation (1 vol)
1909-57.
Sheffield Archives (Rodgers records, 1988 deposit).
NRA 16915.

Corresp and orders (9 bundles) 1817-53.
Sheffield Archives (MD 6205-13). NRA 16915.

Returns of shareholders 1914-33, balance sheets,
trading and profit and loss accounts, lists of debtors
and creditors, etc 1926-67.
Sheffield Archives (Wos.R.176-7). NRA 17831.

Silver estimates book 1926-46, calculation books (2)
c1926-33.
Sheffield Archives (James Dixon records A115, B194,
B524). NRA 34873.

[441] **ROSE STREET FOUNDRY &
ENGINEERING CO LTD** (formerly
**NORTHERN AGRICULTURAL IMPLEMENT
& FOUNDRY CO LTD**), iron and brass founders,
shipbuilders, agricultural and motor engineers,
Inverness

Memorandum and articles of association, reports,
balance sheets and profit and loss accounts (1 file)
1895-1959, scroll minutes 1880-1910 and minute
books (8) 1872-1909, 1917-51, accounts 1922-48,
customers' books (2) 1924-57, works orders
1928-45, drawing registers and drawings of welding
machines (microfilm) from 1923, patent
specifications and apprenticeship indentures
(1 bundle) 1939-60, plans of premises 1892-4,
photographs (3 vols) of premises and welding

equipment *c*1890-1960, sale and works notices *c*1920, 1947-8.
A1 Welders Ltd. Enquiries to NRA (Scotland) (survey 2566). NRA 27016.

[442] ROUGH HILLS IRONWORKS,
Wolverhampton, Staffs

Schedule of payments by John and William Firmstone for the purchase of the works 1816-20 and account of payments 1819-21, profit account of furnace and colliery 1804-10, colliery ledgers (2) 1803-15, inventory of works *c*1812 and account of money owing for furnace repairs (1 item) 1812, misc corresp and bills (13 items) 1801-35 incl notes on the history of the works.
Public Record Office (C 108/111).

Inventory of works 1821, measurements at works 1820.
Staffordshire RO (D 695/1/9/21). NRA 10593.

[443] RUGELEY SHEET IRON & TIN PLATE CO LTD, Rugeley, Staffs

Prospectuses, corresp and misc papers *c*1870-2.
Staffordshire RO (D531/M/B/9). NRA 3515.

Customers' and suppliers' ledgers 1872-3.
Staffordshire RO (4975). NRA 3515.

[444] AM RUSSELL LTD, wire workers and agricultural implement mfrs, Edinburgh

Directors' minutes (2 vols) 1947-68, balance sheets (2 vols) 1911-38, cash books (3) 1882, commission book 1882, leases and other legal papers (1 bundle) 1894-6, 1948.
The Company. Enquiries to NRA (Scotland) (survey 2212). NRA 24140.

[445] JAMES RUSSELL & SONS LTD, wrought iron and steel mfrs, Wednesbury, Staffs

Certificate of incorporation 1868, minutes (3 vols) 1868-1939, registers of directors (2) 1868-1929, 1945-67, register of members 1959-67, register of debentures nd, investment book 1923-31, annual returns 1950-65, private ledger (jointly with John Russell & Co Ltd) 1931-46, patent papers 1836-86.
British Steel East Midlands Regional Records Centre, Irthlingborough. NRA 35554.

[446] JOHN RUSSELL & CO LTD, iron and steel tube mfrs, Walsall, Staffs

Memorandum and articles of association 1876, 1915, board and general meeting minutes (4 vols) 1876-1939, registers of directors (2) 1939-68, register of members 1868-1963, share transfer register and misc share records 1875-1952, share ledgers (5) 1877-1948, seal books (2) 1931-45, balance sheets and annual accounts 1929-31, company regulations 1895, corresp 1933-8, private ledger (jointly with James Russell & Sons Ltd) 1931-46, ledger 1867-72, commercial and premises agreements 1876-8, piece work rate and product price lists (1 vol) 1865-86, salaries book 1900-32,

inventory of Alma Works 1864; auditors' report and accounts for John Russell Western Australia 1904-16.
British Steel East Midlands Regional Records Centre, Irthlingborough. NRA 35554.

[447] RUTLAND FOUNDRY CO LTD,
ironfounders, Ilkeston, Derbys

Sales ledgers, invoice books, drawings, wages records, etc 1907-74.
Derbyshire RO (D2950). *Guide to the Record Office*, 1992, p123.

[448] SIR B SAMUELSON & CO LTD,
ironmasters, Middlesbrough

Board and general meeting minutes (1 vol) 1887-1935, ledgers (2) 1907-23, letter book of Francis Samuelson 1886-1905.
Cleveland Archives and *British Steel Northern Regional Records Centre, Middlesbrough*. Enquiries to Cleveland Archives. NRA 35680.

[449] JOSEPH SANKEY & SONS LTD, pressed steel and hollow-ware mfrs, Bilston, Staffs and Hadley, Salop

Records *c*1870-*c*1975 incl share records (7 vols) 1902, 1913-30, ledgers, journals and other accounts (24 vols, etc) 1880-1950s, sales and purchase records (16 vols) 1870-1958, size book of drawings and specifications 1927, wages and salaries books (5) 1889-1942, inventories of machinery and plant, etc (*c*10 vols) 1901-1940s, printed catalogues, instruction manuals and photographs; ledger rel to Joseph Sankey's estate 1886-1906; Hadley Engineering Co Ltd share records (1 vol) 1911.
Wolverhampton Borough Archives. NRA 33376.

Minutes 1902-40.
GKN Sankey Ltd: see Edgar Jones, *History of GKN*, Vol 2, 1990.

Copies of minutes and other corporate records, sales, production, technical, staff and publicity records, mainly rel to Castle Works, Hadley, 1914-1970s.
Shropshire RO (SRO 4898).

[450] SAUNDERS, SHEPHERD & CO LTD,
manufacturing jewellers and goldsmiths, London

Minute books (3) 1916-71, share registers (2) 1906-11, *c*1950-66, balance sheets and profit and loss accounts (2 vols) 1914-42, trust deeds (2 items) 1916, 1926, corresp rel to acquisition of WH Wilmot Ltd (1 file) 1959, accounting records (3 vols) 1935-60, cost and sales book 1945-59, other sales records (3 vols, 3 files, etc) 1954-70, pattern books (2) 1913-60, nd, registers (2) of designs 1875-1921, plate licences (1 bundle) 1905-47, sketch book nd, insurance papers (1 file) 1908-11, photographs of premises, etc 20th cent, catalogues, misc corresp and papers from 1897.
The Company. Enquiries to the Chairman. NRA 33985.

[451] **SCHNEIDER, HANNAY & CO**, iron mfrs,
Barrow-in-Furness, Lancs

Ledgers (2) 1858-65.
Cumbria RO, Barrow (Z1998). NRA 35515.

[452] **SCOTTISH TUBE CO LTD**, iron and steel
tube mfrs, Glasgow

Memorandum and articles of association 1912,
directors' minutes (5 vols) 1912-40, general meeting
minutes 1919-40, registers of directors (2) 1912-68,
returns of directors 1950-68, share and transfer
registers (11) 1896-1959, debenture register
1898-1908, seal book 1912-47, private ledger
1912-35, papers rel to company history (1 file)
*c*1930.
British Steel East Midlands Regional Records Centre,
Irthlingborough. NRA 35554.

See also Stewarts & Lloyds Ltd.

[453] **SEAHAM HARBOUR IRON CO LTD**,
iron mfrs, Seaham, co Durham

Prospectus 1859, agreements (2 bundles, 3 files)
1854-60, 1866, 1869, accounts and estimates
(3 bundles, 6 items) 1860-1, reports, etc on blast
furnaces (3 files, 8 items) 1859-62 and iron
production costs (1 item) 1864.
Durham County RO (D/Lo/B 348-63). NRA 11528.

[454] **SEARLE & CO LTD**, jewellers and
silversmiths, London

Ledgers (19) 1896-1948.
Guildhall Library, London.

[455] **SEATON CAREW IRON CO LTD**, iron
mfrs, West Hartlepool, co Durham

Memorandum and articles of association 1882,
1924, directors' minutes (2 vols) 1882-1919,
workmen's compensation book 1915-28.
British Steel Northern Regional Records Centre,
Middlesbrough. NRA 35685.

[456] **SEEBOHM & DIECKSTAHL LTD**, steel
mfrs and converters, Sheffield

Shareholders' minutes (1 vol) 1899-1920.
Sheffield Archives (Aurora II). NRA 26201.

[457] **SHANKS & CO LTD**, brassfounders,
sanitary engineers and sanitary ware mfrs, Barrhead,
Renfrewshire

Minutes (2 vols) 1934-71, letter books (6)
1887-1938, private ledgers (5) 1866-1965, private
journals (2) 1898-1937, 1953-60, journal 1907-43,
sales and purchase ledgers (2) 1920-46, record of
suppliers (1 vol) 1884, notebook incl drawings of
John Shanks 1897-8, patents (5 vols) 1862-1913 and
patent applications 1877-1925, plans mainly of coal
and ironstone pits 1849-1939, nd, pottery works
inventories and valuations (2 items) 1949, catalogues

incl some of other firms 1852-1963, photographs rel
to history of company (1 album) 1856-1960.
Armitage Shanks Ltd. Enquiries to NRA (Scotland)
(surveys 767, 943). NRA 17519.

[458] **SHAW & FISHER**, Britannia metal mfrs,
Sheffield

Letters from other firms 1841-56, invoices and bills
1832-57, designs, advertisements and related papers
1843-50, apprenticeship indentures nd.
Sheffield Archives (TC 1056-8, 1072-3, 1092).
Catalogue of business and industrial records in Sheffield
City Libraries, p33.

[459] **H SHAW (MAGNETS)**, magnet and ships'
compass mfrs, Sheffield

Day books (14) 1870-2, 1896-1909, 1914-53, cash
books (3) 1930-57, sales ledgers (7) 1856-1966,
purchase ledger and journal (2 vols) 1930-65,
weekly sales and receipts (3 vols) 1913-54, order
books (3) 1956-69, account book rel to loans made
and rent paid 1896-1936.
Sheffield Archives (HSM 1-33). NRA 34854.

[460] **JOHN SHAW & SONS,**
WOLVERHAMPTON, LTD, tool mfrs,
Wolverhampton, Staffs

Articles of partnership and association, agreements,
etc (1 bundle, 20 items) 1815, 1876, 1886-1937,
directors', shareholders' and committee minutes
(5 vols) 1887-1949, agenda book 1905-19, general
meeting papers (6 bundles) 1928-32, register of
bonds 1888, register of members (9 vols)
1888-1954, share transfer ledger 1888-1918, annual
returns 1926-38, seal book 1888-1919, draft
accounts, trial balances, memoranda and other share
and accounting papers (*c*177 bundles and items)
1906-26, corresp and misc papers (105 items)
1810-1953, memoranda books (4) *c*1850-4,
1876-85, 1911-12, private ledgers (14) 1808-42,
1848-52, 1887-98, 1933-44, nd, cash books (6)
1809-14, 1835-90, bill books (3) 1805-8, *c*1815-19,
1844-9, misc account books (5) 1813-15, *c*1868-82,
nd, misc sales agreements, trade mark papers, etc
(23 items) 1801-1939, address book 1880, order
books (20) 1809-20, stock books (6) *c*1805, 1823-5,
1838, personnel books (7) *c*1887-1936, corresp rel
to life insurance policy (58 items) 1855-73, misc
catalogues, deeds, photographs and papers rel to
firm's history 1732-1973.
Wolverhampton Borough Archives (DB/24). NRA
31835.

[461] **W SHAW & CO LTD**, steel castings mfrs,
Middlesbrough

Accounts 1889-1951.
Cleveland Archives

[462] **SHEEPBRIDGE ROLLING MILLS LTD,**
ironmasters, Chesterfield, Derbys

Records 19th-20th cent incl memorandum and
articles of association 1939, 1957, directors' minutes

(11 vols) 1864-1970, general meeting minutes
(1 vol) 1930-70, register of directors or managers
(3 vols) 1901-67, register of members and share
ledgers 1864-1964, other share records from 1914,
debenture records 1866-1949, annual reports,
balance sheets and accounts 1864-1967, chairman's
list (1 vol) 1878-85, secretary's and directors' papers
and reports 1950-61, evidences of title (3 vols)
1867-1937, register of seals 1949-67, nominal
ledgers (15) 1864-1960, dead ledger sheets 1933-52,
day books (3) and journals (3) 1929-52, cash books
(7) and sheets 1924-56, rates book 1900-5, wagon
books (5) 1925-37, sales analysis 1944-7, purchase
ledger 1946-54, list of accounts to be paid 1951-3
and appropriation of wages book 1945-50.
Derbyshire RO (D3808) and *Stanton plc*. Enquiries to
Derbyshire RO.

Memorandum and articles of association 1965,
register of members, share certificates, etc (2 vols)
1966, creditors' account book 1971-4, cash book
1967-75.
Sheffield Archives (MD 7081 *passim*). NRA 34857.

Electrician's memoranda book 1932-53, work books
1958-66, engineering drawings (38 rolls) 1890-1970,
photographs and other misc records 20th cent.
Derbyshire RO (D985, D1016, D1413, D1438,
D2563).

[463] **SHEFFIELD SMELTING CO LTD**
(formerly **READ & CO**), precious metal smelters
and refiners, Sheffield

Records 1781-1960 (*c*900 vols, bundles and items)
incl partnership deeds and related papers (16 items)
1831, 1846, 1860-89, memorandum and articles of
association 1889-90, 1909-54, directors' log books
(4) 1896-1902 and index (1 vol), attendance book
1905-10 and other directors' records (3 items)
1896-8, 1904, share transfers (2 vols) 1890-1929,
general corresp and memoranda 1791-2, 1814,
*c*1824-1924, summary of partners' accounts, etc
1837-47, profit and loss accounts 1849-69,
accounting and stock records 1781-1923, corresp
and papers rel to overseas sales, clients and business
trips abroad 1867-1960, home sales and purchase
records 1846-1929, assay and other technical
records 1848-1928, staff records 1846-1924, nd,
premises records 1781-1913, papers rel to fraud and
theft (9 bundles) 1863, 1890-1952, misc papers and
photographs 1795-1951, nd; records of
Birmingham, London and Sheffield branches
1815-1948; records mainly rel to the takeovers of
Charles Cooper & Son, Birmingham (23 bundles
and items) 1871-3, nd and of EW Oakes & Co
(*c*60 vols, bundles and items) 1869-1902; papers of
the Read and Wilson families 1772-1959.
Sheffield Archives (SSC). NRA 489.

John Read's ledger 1771-84, day book 1779-82 and
stock book 1779-83.
The Company. Microfilm in Sheffield Archives. NRA
489.

[464] **SHELDON, BUSH & PATENT SHOT
CO**, lead smelters, sheet and shot mfrs, Bristol

Share capital summary 1911, letter books (2)
1836-46, 1912-29, agreements, settlements and
contracts 1881-1920, accounting records
1808-*c*1971 incl private ledgers (4) 1864-*c*1971,
cash books (2) 1889-1921 and bills of lading (1 vol)
1808-23, sales and purchase ledger 1962-77, annual
price lists 1832-44, stock book 1959-84, licences
(3 items) 1877-1944, wages, pension and insurance
records 1941-65, nd, plans, valuations and other
property records 1876-1941, auction catalogue of
machinery 1851, photographs of premises, etc
(2 vols) 1960s-1982, misc papers rel to company
history (1 file) *c*1782-1960s.
The Company: see *Business in Avon and Somerset*.

Letter books (3) 1927-9, ledger 1891-*c*1929, town
ledger 1878-90, country ledgers (2) 1886-*c*1896,
glass ledger *c*1849-89, day books (2) 1909-21,
1928-36, town and country day books (20) 1931-42,
cash books (5) 1922-43, bought books (2) 1931-6,
costs ledger 1888-*c*1921.
Bristol RO (38701).

[465] **SHELTON IRON, STEEL & COAL CO
LTD**, iron and steel mfrs and colliery proprietors,
Stoke-on-Trent, Staffs

Memorandum and articles of association 1889-1950,
minutes (7 vols) 1852-85, 1889-1970, local
directors' minutes (2 vols) 1900-7, private minute
book 1944-68, directors' fees (2 vols) 1908-9, 1942,
share registers (4) 1913-19, nd, registers of transfers
(4) 1890-1969, share certificates 1920-67, dividend
reports 1917-39, annual reports, balance sheets and
accounts 1889-1970, summaries of results 1961-4,
secretary's letter books (16) 1908-24, general
manager's letter books (7) 1912-23, letter book
1911-34, agreements with subsidiaries 1904-14,
private ledgers (3) 1899-1911, 1917-70, class ledger
1890-6, ledger 1868-73, general ledgers (2) 1891,
1917-24, journals (9) 1890-1904, 1919-72, account
book 1891-1912, cash book 1890-1, petty cash book
1924-39, cash received and paid (8 vols) 1945-65,
compensation cash books (8) 1905-47, bill book
1889-1913, royalty accounts 1898-1920, tax papers
1890-1971, insurance records 1925-57, misc
accounting and financial records 1905-*c*1970, sales
ledgers (9) 1945-61, ledgers of pig iron sales
1917-65, bought ledgers (11) 1943-62, production
ledger 1955-71, output and stock control records
(2 vols) 1934-54, cost books and related records
1923-70, output books 1943-7, blast furnace
consumption records 1935-63, and other technical
records 20th cent, wage books (2) and other staff
records 1938-61, deeds and legal papers 18th-20th
cent.
British Steel Records Centre, Shotton. NRA 36011.

Certificates of incorporation 1889, 1956, directors'
minutes (1 vol) 1970-80, general meeting minutes
(1 vol) 1930-80, register of seals 1932-70.
*British Steel East Midlands Regional Records Centre,
Irthlingborough*. NRA 3555.

Engineering drawings and site plans (43 items)
1911-71.
Staffordshire RO (D4677). NRA 30941.

[466] SHOTTON BROS LTD, ironfounders, Oldbury and Halesowen, Worcs

Directors' and general meeting minutes (3 vols) 1900-52, ledger 1899-1917.
Dudley Archives and Local History Service (Acc 8512).

[467] SHOTTS IRON CO LTD, ironfounders and coal masters, Shotts, Lanarkshire

Copartnery contract 1825-6 and deeds of accession 1825-39, sederunt books and minutes (19 vols) 1824-1958, registers (5) of shareholders and transfers 1871-1923, annual reports (1 vol) 1871-1951, monthly reports mainly rel to blast furnaces and mines (1 vol) 1851-5; colliery records 1906-46.
Scottish Record Office (GD1/3, CB21). NRA 34387.

[468] SHUTT & MARSHALL, harness furniture mfrs, Walsall, Staffs

Corresp and orders (13 bundles) 1885, 1912-14, orders received (7 bundles) 1885, 1913-15, sales ledger *c*1895-1904, bills payable (2 bundles) 1893, 1911, stock sheets 1900, draft returns and price list nd.
Walsall Archives Service (Acc 185/1). NRA 23873.

Profit and loss account book 1872-97.
WA Goold (Holdings) Ltd. Enquiries to the Chairman and Managing Director. NRA 32064.

[469] STEPHEN SIMPSON LTD, gold and silver wire and thread mfrs, Preston, Lancs, and London

Account with Simpson & Rook (1 vol) 1880-97, nominal, creditors' and debtors' ledgers (10) 1849-1915, other financial records (13 vols) 1936-64, invoice books (2) 1911-14 and analysis books (5) 1935-69, stock books (3) 1913-67, returns book 1932-44, embroidery ledgers (4) 1904-15, designs, instructions and samples (1 vol) *c*1914-42, wages books (16) 1863-7, 1913-61, valuation of works 1903, photographs of gold thread work (1 album) early 20th cent, published history of Simpson family 1922.
Lancashire RO (DDX 1876). NRA 35008.

[470] W & G SISSONS LTD (formerly **ROBERTS, SMITH & CO**), silverplaters, Sheffield

Partnership deeds 1786, 1826, 1834, papers (1 envelope) rel to amalgamation with International Silver Co 1933, share ledger *c*1884-1935, letter books (7) 1869-75, 1890-1900, 1907-16, 1932-5, misc letters and agreements 1764-early 20th cent, case for counsel 1843, income tax papers (1 bundle) 1849-83, ledgers (9) 1786-1884, 1893-1903, private ledgers (2) 1901-39, bank books (5) 1843-1939, bill books (2) 1831-9, 1887-1935, cash books, accounts, etc (22 vols, 4 envelopes) 1802-1956, sales day book 1820-5, sales accounts (1 vol) 1893-1935 and ledgers (3) 1899-1947, bought ledgers and purchase records (12 vols) 1931-50, prices records (8 vols) 1890s-1932, estimates books (7) 1867, 1888-1939, orders day book 1928-36, foreign orders book

*c*1928, invoice records (9 vols, 1 envelope) 1825-1942, lists of products (2 vols, 1 packet) 1839, 1860s, nd, patent 1798, specifications 1836, 1840, 1945-6, trade mark registration certificates, etc (2 bundles) 1909-46, pattern books and designs (*c*33 vols and folders) 1798-1933, nd, stock books (20) 1787, 1833-86, 1932-5, technical notes 1917, nd, work books (2) 1896-9, wages books and other staff records (11 vols, bundles and envelopes) 1907-59, accounts and vouchers for building work 1813-14, *c*1881, valuation 1887-8, leases and papers rel to London premises 1879-94, press cuttings 1889, photographs of products, etc, nd, executorship, trusteeship and charity records 1821-47, 1867, 1899-1940.
Sheffield Archives (Sis 1-45, 47-82, 95-188; Acc 1986/109). NRA 4869.

[471] SKINNINGROVE IRON CO LTD, iron and steel mfrs, Skinningrove, Yorks

Directors' minutes (8 vols) 1880-1947, register of transfers 1916-63, shareholders' ledger 1913-*c*1945, private ledgers (6) 1880-1947, ledger 1923-35, personal ledger cash book 1936-70, annual accounts 1937-67.
British Steel Northern Regional Records Centre, Middlesbrough. Enquiries to Cleveland Archives. NRA 35684.

Memorandum and articles of association 1880, certificate of incorporation 1880, directors' minutes (1 vol) 1947-79, general meeting minutes 1880-1978, register of directors 1932-79, register of seals 1936-79, board papers, annual returns, accounts and pension fund papers *c*1963-72.
British Steel East Midlands Regional Records Centre, Irthlingborough. NRA 35555.

[472] JOHN & DANIEL SMALLWOOD, mfrs of metal and wooden rules, squares and levels, Birmingham

Wages books (3) 1884-1900.
Birmingham University Library. NRA 32504.

[473] SMITH, FLETCHER & CO, wire workers, Edinburgh

Letter book 1853-7, private ledgers (2) 1899-1924, purchase ledgers (2) 1854-9, 1876-85, wages book 1894-1910.
In private possession. Enquiries to NRA (Scotland) (survey 2397). NRA 25416.

[474] SMITH & McLEAN LTD, galvanisers, Glasgow

Contract of copartnery and related papers (5 items) 1861-6, memorandum and articles of association 1900-60, minute books 1895-1973, notices of meetings 1895-1947, board and general meeting papers and other corporate records 1957-74, share register 1901, letter books 1895-1914, annual reports and accounts 1894-1967, annual returns 1959-69, balance sheets 1925-67, papers rel to profits (1 file) 1920-57, private ledgers 1895-1916,

private journal 1872-7, misc accounting and production records 1880-1935, agreements with other firms 1920s-1930s, wages book 1881-8, records rel to purchase by David Colville & Sons Ltd *c*1919, papers rel to company history 20th cent.
Scottish Record Office and *British Steel East Midlands Regional Records Centre, Irthlingborough.* Enquiries to the Scottish Record Office. NRA 35553.

[475] **SMITH & PEPPER**, manufacturing jewellers, Birmingham

Letter books (9) 1902-39, notebooks (5) 1921-38, diaries (2) 1913, 1930, ledgers (3) 1903, 1925-36, day books (11) 1921-37, cash books (11) 1899-1911, 1914-36, petty cash book 1902, analysis book 1939, estimate books (5) 1919-35, sales ledgers (7) 1899-1902, 1904-6, 1925-32 and day books (3) 1900-8, purchase ledgers (3) 1926-37 and day books (18) 1900-33, order books (12) 1906-13, 1918-39, approval books (54) 1913-39, large invoice books (69) 1908-39, receipts (5 vols, 1 file) 1911-34, memorandum of goods books (22) 1921-39, parcel receipt books (12) 1919-36 and despatch book 1904, jobbing books (50) 1918-39, stock books (4) 1903-37, design books (2) 1899, 1902, patents (1 envelope) 1907-13, salaries book 1917, attendance books (3) 1922-35, misc papers *c*1914-20, printed books, etc 1906-39.
Jewellery Quarter Discovery Centre, Birmingham (1990 F). NRA 35797.

[476] **SAMUEL & WILLIAM SMITH**, ironmasters, Sheffield

Technical notebook of Samuel Smith 1794, observations (2 items) on iron production *c*1800, copy letter 1808.
Birmingham Central Library Archives Division (MS 1513). NRA 29847.

[477] **SMITH & WELLSTOOD LTD**, ironfounders, stove and range mfrs, Bonnybridge, Stirlingshire

Memorandum and articles of association, etc (3 bundles) *c*1881-1938, nd, minute books (8) 1888-1954, register of directors and managers 1880-91, share records (12 vols) 1888-1950, corresp and papers (*c*2 boxes, 9 bundles) 1855-1979, private ledgers (6) 1887-1958, export order books (4) 1882-3, 1893-1901, address book of agents and customers nd, cost book 1906-7, minute books (3) rel to staff pension scheme and Wellstood Club 1945-63, book of feus, leases and telephone agreements *c*1900-60, catalogues of products 1851-*c*1940, nd, company magazines (1 bundle) *c*1920-50; business diaries (2) of GA Ure 1917-47, personal cash book of George Ure *c*1930.
The Company. Enquiries to NRA (Scotland) (survey 2198). NRA 15350.

[478] **WH SMITH & CO (WHITCHURCH) LTD**, agricultural engineers and ironfounders, Whitchurch, Salop

Ledgers (5) 1879-84, 1895-1910, day book 1861-3, journal 1859-64, WH Smith's private journal with

analysis of balance sheets 1897-1904, bank book 1886-8, invoice books (347) 1876-1909, proposals (1 vol) for gas light in Whitchurch with notes by William Smith rel to bad debts, etc nd, specifications for iron ordered (1 vol) 1852-72, stock book 1873, foundry day book 1842-4, patents and related papers (22 items) 1860-1, 1896, specifications for erection of new premises (3 items) 1878-9, catalogues, photographs and other printed papers (22 items) *c*1870-1937; Smith family papers 1901-42.
Shropshire RO (SRO 2500, 2510). NRA 34474.

[479] **THOMAS SMITH'S STAMPING WORKS LTD**, drop forgers, Coventry

Minute books (8) 1896-1964, attendance books (3) 1943-64, seal books (3) 1896-1923, private ledgers (4) 1896-1937, nominal ledgers (2) *c*1928-35, 1950-8, journal 1896-1918, private accounts (2 vols) 1905-35, cash books (12) 1937-66, sales and purchase ledgers (5) *c*1920-41, time books and salaries and wages records (*c*19 vols) 1927-66, property and plant register 1920.
Coventry City RO (Acc 425, 634). NRA 30530.

Memorandum and articles of association 1919, minute book 1953-64, register of seals and mortgages 1923-69, accounts and returns 1951-73, misc records 1950s-1980s.
Clwyd RO, Hawarden (AN 2830/20-21). NRA 35998.

[480] **SMITHS' IRONWORKS**, Chesterfield, Derbys

Letter book of Ebenezer Smith 1805-15, partnership ledger 1815-33, journey book 1824-33.
Sheffield Archives (SSC 75-7). NRA 489.

[481] **SNEDSHILL IRON CO LTD**, wrought iron mfrs, Snedshill, Salop

Partnership deed 1856, minute book 1883-91, register of members 1880-1916, register of transfers 1882-1916, shareholders' address book 1902, 1911-42, share certificates, etc 1881-1916, balance sheets (1 vol) nd, statement of accounts 1888, misc corporate records 1884-8, register of deeds 1836-87, title deeds and related papers 1883-7, rental 1880-8.
Ironbridge Gorge Museum (1986.11842); and see BAC *Company Archives* no 359.

[482] **WALTER SOMERS LTD**, engine and marine forgings mfrs, Halesowen, Worcs

Order books (54) 1887-1957.
Dudley Archives and Local History Service. NRA 23244.

[483] **SOUTH DURHAM STEEL & IRON CO LTD**, iron and steel mfrs, Stockton-on-Tees, co Durham

Memorandum and articles of association 1898, 1928, 1956, trust deeds 1900-58, directors' minutes (8 vols) 1898-1970, shareholders' minutes (2 vols)

1899-1967, register of directors (2 vols) 1901-47, shareholders' attendance book 1929-57, annual reports, accounts and general meeting proceedings 1900-39, register of shareholders 1898-9, register of share transfers (4 vols) 1906-16, mortgage register nd, probate list 1950s, letter books (4) 1898-1905, 1919-29, annual lists and summaries (8 vols) 1939-51, register of documents sealed (2 vols) 1899-1950, balance sheets and profit and loss accounts 1899-1919, 1928-34, analyses of accounts (1 vol) 1899-1909, auditors' reports (6 vols) 1899-1954, private ledgers (8) 1898-*c*1956, private journals (6) 1898-1950, misc stock and production records (4 vols) 1917-*c*1940, plant ledgers (4) 1904-29, salaries books (8) 1906-37.
British Steel Northern Regional Records Centre, Middlesbrough. Enquiries to Cleveland Archives. NRA 35685.

[484] **SOUTH YORKSHIRE IRONMASTERS' SYNDICATE**, Sheffield

Yorkshire ledgers (14) 1690-1765 and journals (11) 1690-1763, Derbyshire and Nottinghamshire ledgers (2) 1750-66 and journals (2) 1750-73.
Sheffield Archives (SIR 1-29). NRA 34877.

See also Staveley Coal & Iron Co Ltd and Kirkstall Forge Ltd.

[485] **SOUTHERN & RICHARDSON LTD** (formerly **WILSON & SOUTHERN**), cutlery mfrs, Sheffield

Quotations and prices book 1845-54, trade mark records 1886-1956.
Sheffield Archives (NVT 16-17). NRA 34855.

Ledger 1832-56, account books (2) 1830-44, invoice book 1837-42, customer reference book 1839-45, stock book 1856-67, pattern books (5) 1856-1914, nd incl price lists, invoices, lists of customers, etc. *Untraced.* NRA 4868.

[486] **SPARK BRIDGE AND DUDDON IRONWORKS**, Sparkbridge, Lancs

Account books (4) 1750, 1755-65, 1772-9.
Lancashire RO (DDX 192). NRA 16881.

[487] **SPEAR & JACKSON LTD**, saw and edge tool mfrs, Sheffield

Articles of partnership and related papers (3 bundles, 3 items) 1824-96, memorandum and articles of association 1937, papers (1 bundle) rel to formation of limited company 1904-5, directors' minute book 1905-36, directors' reports and accounts 1937-55, share and debenture records (7 vols, 4 bundles) 1847-1937, letter books (3) 1812-16, 1852-8, 1905-24, papers (4 files) rel to proposed amalgamations, etc 1913-25, partnership ledger 1833-93, private ledgers (4) 1892-1941, departmental accounts ledger 1909-46, private journals (2) 1873-1915, bank books (3) 1886-7, 1922-41, bill book 1857-84, sales and purchase ledger 1828-31, papers (1 bundle) rel to prices of steel and tools 1888-1900, catalogues and price lists

(7) 1880-1932, consignment records (2 vols, 1 file) 1903-23, papers rel to Russian agency (8 files) 1913-49 and to trips abroad by LJ Combe (8 vols, 3 files) 1905-34, misc papers rel to trade marks (5 vols, etc) *c*1860-1922, notes of specifications, costings, work done, etc (6 vols) *c*1839-1913, machinery stock book 1925, wages and salaries books (2) 1883-1906, agreements with agents and staff (2 bundles) 1920-32, nd, misc property records (2 bundles, 1 item) 1868-1915, press cuttings (4 vols) 1879-1925, misc papers rel to firm's history (1 bundle, 6 items) 1812-1930; Drabble & Sanderson letter book 1904-20, ledger 1918-22 and misc papers (2 files) 1913-26.
Sheffield Archives (SJC). NRA 11376.

Wednesbury Works memoranda book containing information about rival firms 1921-8.
Staffordshire RO (D 4583). NRA 3515.

[488] **JOHN SPENCER LTD**, engineers and iron and steel tube mfrs, Wednesbury, Staffs

Memorandum and articles of association 1898-1957, board and general meeting minutes 1898-1939, 1958-80, special resolutions 1908-1930, registers of directors (2) 1901-35, 1948-80, registers of members (2) 1935-71, share certificates 1963-9, annual summaries 1912-33 and returns 1963-70, seal books (2) 1961-71, nd, wages books (2) 1930-43, accident records 1960-6, works regulations *c*1890, plan and particulars of Globe Tube Works 1880, 1931-45.
British Steel East Midlands Regional Records Centre, Irthlingborough. NRA 35554.

See also Stewarts & Lloyds Ltd.

[489] **MATTHIAS SPENCER & SONS LTD**, mfrs of files, steel and mining equipment, Sheffield

Board and general meeting minutes (3 vols) 1929-77, register of members 20th cent, journal and ledger 1757-95, memoranda book 1830-49, cost book for factoring business in France 1880s-1920s, post book 1944-68, salaries ledger 1961-71, general corresp and papers 1950s-1970s.
Sheffield Archives (LD 1925-8 and 1984 deposit). NRA 34866.

[490] **STAFFORDSHIRE BOLT, NUT & FENCING CO LTD**, Darlaston, Staffs

Articles of association 1867, 1902, 1919-20 and certificate of incorporation 1867, directors' minutes (3 vols) 1897-1943, share registers (2) 1867-1943 and ledger 1867-1929, corresp rel to shares in Midland Bolt, Nut & Rivet Co (5 items) 1919-29, private ledger 1929-40, registers of bills (2) 1868-1911, bank books (2) 1889-97, plan of premises with copy agreement for water extraction 1904, schedules of deeds (2 items) *c*1928 and corresp rel to rents (7 items) *c*1923-8.
Walsall Archives Service (Acc 265, 280, 313). NRA 23872.

[491] STAVELEY COAL & IRON CO LTD, ironfounders and colliery proprietors, Staveley, Derbys

Ironworks balance sheets (1 vol) 1841-63, capital account (1 vol) 1841-65, private ledgers (4) 1841-64, general ledgers (4) 1838-40, 1842-64, journals (13) 1841-64, cash books (2) 1856-64, salaries book 1856-62, farm balance sheets 1856-68; company records incl memorandum and articles of association 1863-1931, minute books from 1863, general meeting minute books from 1864, directors' meeting reports 1927-51, share records 1889-1957, annual reports, accounts and balance sheets 1863-1950, profit and loss accounts, estimates and summaries 1865-1950, seal books (4) 1888-1949, chairman's lists (4 vols) 1920-42, tax papers 1912-53, solicitors' accounts 1965-91 and diaries (13 vols) 1921-45, capital, general and private ledgers from 1864, farm ledger 1864-1906, journals and cash books from 1864, list of small debtors 1868-89, summary accounts from 1922, other accounting records 20th cent, sales, purchase and bought ledgers from 1872, other purchase records 1937-60, furnace book 1856-66, castings and pig iron day books 1943-50, castings and sundry accounts 1877-94, cost books and related papers *c*1858-99, 1913-20, 1940-53, production records 1942-61, returns book, etc 1856-79, stock sheets, valuations and inventories 1901-48, trade mark, patent and other legal papers from 1867, salaries records from 1896 and other staff records from 1872, Devonshire Works and other premises records 1906-20, estate records from 1863 and scrapbook 1878-1908; records of colliery and other subsidiaries from 1856.
Derbyshire RO (D3808) and *Stanton plc*. Enquiries to Derbyshire RO.

Furnace journal 1772-97 incl orders 1806-8, furnace account 1784-1806; cost book *c*1880-1901 incl capital accounts 1864-1900.
Sheffield Archives (SIR 30-32). NRA 34877.

Corresp, agreements, accounts, trade catalogues and brochures (1 box) 1908-54.
Derbyshire RO (D1721).

Records 20th cent (8 boxes, 20 rolls) incl development plan 1954, laboratory records 1922-73, graphs and plans 1928-69, photographs 20th cent and printed material 1938-57.
Derbyshire RO (D1185).

Markham Colliery records 1897-1950.
Derbyshire RO: see *Accessions to repositories 1973*, p38.

Warsop Main Colliery deputation meeting minute book 1940.
Nottinghamshire Archives (NCB 12/1). NRA 6885.

See also South Yorkshire Ironmasters' Syndicate and Kirkstall Forge Ltd.

[492] STEEL COMPANY OF SCOTLAND LTD, steel mfrs, Glasgow

Certificate of incorporation 1872, memorandum and articles of association 1936, 1954, minute books (20) 1872-1947, board papers (13 vols) 1920-56,

directors' attendance books (2) 1935-60, share register 1907-20, list of shareholders 1905-34, transfer register 1920-34, dividend book 1916-40, debenture stock records (3 vols) 1895-1934, directors' reports (3 vols) 1872-1911, reports and accounts 1912-48, letter books 1871-2, 1879-1916, private ledgers (11) 1871-1929, nd, journal ledgers (19) 1872-1962, balance books (4) 1907-50, private cash book 1872, nd, cash books (23) 1927-61, order book 1932-5, acceptance books (5) and indexes (2) 1899-1916, Hallside and Blochairn works production, delivery and prices records 1897-1939, abstracts of production, costs and sales 1915-35, melting shop cost books (3) 1917-27, rolling shop records (7 vols) 1896-1900, 1924-34, job books (3) 1893-1954, specifications (1 vol) *c*1876-88, agreements rel to Siemens process (1 vol) 1872-80, records rel to processes and experiments (1 vol) 1874-1916, engineer's sketch book *c*1868-73, salaries books (4) 1880-1949, Blochairn Works valuation 1935, deeds *c*1872-*c*1947, early historical records (1 file), press cuttings books, photographs and other printed material 1872-1960.
Scottish Record Office and *British Steel East Midlands Regional Records Centre, Irthlingborough*. Enquiries to the Scottish Record Office. NRA 35553.

Memorandum and articles of association 1936, 1954, minute books (2) from 1947, general meeting minute book *c*1942-69, register of directors *c*1950-69, register of members *c*1935-55, valuation of site and plant at Blochairn 1935, summary of deeds 1879; Hallside Works records incl chief draughtsman's corresp and job number quotations, etc (1 box) 1909-70, drawing office corresp and job number files (23 boxes) 1875-1980, sketch files nd, works engineer's corresp (15 boxes) 1946-71 and job numbers files (4 boxes) 1956-70, boiler certificates nd, contractors' records (2 boxes) 1973-8, patents, photographs and printed material.
British Steel Records Centre, Shotton. NRA 36006.

Corresp and misc papers of Sir Andrew McCance as director (3 files, 3 items) 1941-63.
Glasgow University Archives and Business Record Centre (UGD/104). NRA 27344.

[493] STEEL, PEECH & TOZER LTD, steel mfrs, Sheffield

Records 20th cent incl register of members 1916-17, journals (4) 1929-37, tenders for orders (3 vols) 1951-5, engineering department order books (3) 1909-18, cold rolling mill time book 1950-61 and photographs of processes (4 vols) 20th cent.
Rotherham Metropolitan Borough Archives and *British Steel Northern Regional Records Centre, Middlesbrough*. Enquiries to Rotherham Metropolitan Borough Archives. NRA 35686.

Board minutes (1 vol) 1932-80, register of directors 1948-64, register of members 1932-68.
British Steel East Midlands Regional Records Centre, Irthlingborough. NRA 35548.

Memorandum and articles of association 1875, resolution of change of name 1883, register of mortgages 1876-92.
Rotherham Metropolitan Borough Archives (348/Z). NRA 12413.

[494] **STEVEN & STRUTHERS LTD**,
brassfounders and engineers, Glasgow

Letters rel to bells (1 file) nd, order book
1902-1930s, bell books (7) 1838-20th cent, cocks
and valves book 1937-40, large foundry books (2)
1916-43, memoranda and despatch books (4)
1874-1956, letters patent, specifications, orders,
photographs, etc (2 boxes) nd, plans and technical
drawings (3 boxes, 36 items) 1901-60, pay book
1911-19, catalogues (2 boxes) 1930.
Glasgow University Archives and Business Record Centre
(UGD/17). NRA 13692.

[495] **A&J STEWART & MENZIES LTD**,
ironfounders and iron and steel tube mfrs, Glasgow
and Coatbridge, Lanarkshire

Memorandum and articles of association 1890,
directors' minutes (5 vols) 1890-1902, agenda books
(2) 1890-1903 and attendance book 1895-1902,
agenda papers for annual general meetings 1880-90,
register of directors 1901-5, registers of members (8)
1886-96, 1901-3, misc share records 1883-91,
balance sheets and profit and loss accounts 1883-97,
reports and accounts 1891-1925, letter books (3)
1886-90, 1895-1902, minutes of agreement
1882-92, private ledger 1882-95, general ledger
1889-92, private journal 1882-93, journal 1889-92,
day book 1889, private cash book 1882-9, cash
books (5) 1887-9, other accounting records
1882-91, sales and purchase ledgers (4) 1889-92,
licences 1880-5, income tax payments 1886-90,
valuation 1890.
Scottish Record Office and *British Steel East Midlands*
Regional Records Centre, Irthlingborough. Enquiries to
the Scottish Record Office. NRA 35554.

Memorandum and articles of association, notices of
general meetings and related corresp (*c*20 items)
1882-91, photographs of senior management
(3 items) nd.
Mitchell Library, Glasgow (MS 121). NRA 34175.

Sederunt book of trust for debenture holders
1901-3.
Strathclyde Regional Archives (T-MS 327). NRA
19243.

See also Stewarts & Lloyds Ltd.

[496] **STEWARTS & LLOYDS LTD**, iron and
steel tube mfrs and colliery proprietors, Glasgow,
Birmingham and Corby, Northants

Memorandum and articles of association 1964,
registers of minutes (2) 1903-52, board minutes
(14 vols) 1903-62, agenda books (5) 1903-67,
attendance books (3) 1932-67, general meeting
minutes 1890-1948, reports and papers (2 files)
1890-1939, committee, local board, trust and
subsidiary company minutes, etc 1903-70, register of
directors or managers 1926-45, share records
1896-1967, balance sheets and profit and loss
accounts (2 bundles) 1904-29, directors' reports and
accounts (2 files) 1914-25, chairman's papers
1927-69, annual reports 1930-66 and accounts
1935-47, seal books (4) 1890-1904, 1932-67,
register of agreements 1906-32 and agreements rel

to overseas interests 1902-41, corresp rel to assets
1902-8, other corresp (3 files) 1921-31, confidential
booklets 1927-73, accounts rel to Birmingham and
Coombs Wood works 1903-29, private ledgers (12)
1903-29, 1951-66, final account ledger *c*1909-27,
transfer ledger 1851-1927, private journals (11)
1890-1959, private cash book 1903-10, cash books
(20) 1920-64, order books for limestone and
ironstone (2) 1931-5, costs and selling prices (1 vol)
1904-14, papers rel to home and foreign agencies
(2 files) 1902, home and foreign currency
agreements (5 bundles, 2 files) 1903-32, record of
strip received (1 vol) 1908, slag delivery book
1918-35, material prices (1 vol) 1914-20, welding
pluck list 1909, salaries book rel to Imperial Tube
Works 1900, salaries books (25) rel to managers and
office staff at Clyde Tube Works 1890-1930, salaries
books (9) rel to other works 1901-43, salaries
committee minutes (18 vols) 1933-70, records rel to
employee trust, benefit and pension funds, etc
*c*1914-70, patents (1 file) 1906-16, agreements
mainly rel to licences and railway companies (1 box)
1894-1939, feu payments for Clyde Tube Works
*c*1908-35, register of leases *c*1906-36, register of title
deeds for England 1900-32, deeds and other legal
papers rel to property 1810-1967, plans and papers
rel to Coombs Wood 1867-1932, drawings and
specifications rel to Corby Works *c*1922-80, report
on office accommodation in Birmingham 1912,
papers rel to Cardiff warehouse (1 envelope)
1897-1913, warehouse profit and loss accounts
1907, 1912-25, press cuttings (3 vols, 1 file)
1903-50, photographs of Clyde Tube Works (1 vol)
1900-30, photographs of plant, manufacturing
processes and staff *c*1930-1977, papers rel to
company history (1 file) 1825-*c*1953, misc papers
1906-*c*1960, records of overseas subsidiaries
1908-73; papers rel to Tube Makers Association
1879-1931 and Scottish Steel Makers Association
(4 files) *c*1908-57; papers of Sir Frederick Scopes rel
to his history of the Corby Works *c*1890-1970.
British Steel East Midlands Regional Records Centre,
Irthlingborough. NRA 35554.

Share records (82 boxes) 1916-71; Calder Works
financial and cost records 1936-65, tube stock books
(4) 1903-23 and other stock records 1952-62, plant
books (10) 1881-93, 1913-55 and plant register
1935-70; Clyde Tube Works management committee
meetings records 1900-57, production records
1952-66, engine drawing 1896, plant books (12 vols,
etc) 1877-1945, abstract of buildings taken down
1890-6, plan book 1901-13; Sun Foundry plant
books (2) 1869-1905.
British Steel Records Centre, Shotton. NRA 36009.

[497] **J STOKES & SONS**, cart hame and chain
mfrs, Walsall, Staffs

Account of work completed (2 vols) 1871-84, misc
photographs late 19th cent.
Walsall Archives Service (Acc 496). NRA 21950.

[498] **ANDREW STRANG & CO LTD**,
ironfounders, Hurlford, Ayrshire

Minute books (3) 1898-1957, share registers (2),
certificate books (3) and transfers nd, account book

1866-8, ledgers (4) 1886-1912, purchase ledgers (3) 1896-1934 and books (6) 1891-1942, order books (2) 1890-7, engineering sales book 1914, price books (2) 1921-60, cost book 1923-9, time and wages books (5) 1882-1903, canteen bills (1 envelope) nd, abstracts of sales, wages and production 1885-1932, inventory of foundry, plant and equipment 1896-1934, deeds nd, plans and photographs, etc 1904, nd, pamphlets rel to history of company.
Dick Institute, Kilmarnock. NRA (Scotland) (survey 2326). NRA 15351.

Secretary's letter book 1913-44, account books (6) 1920-61, private ledgers (3) 1885-90, 1914-24, 1938-44, ledger 1936-46, journals (3) 1881-92, 1895-1944, cash books (4) 1884-97, 1904-11, purchase ledger 1891-6, purchase books (2) 1898-1910, 1942-52, purchase classification books (3) 1943-61, sales books (14) 1890-1954, stock books (2) 1898-1937, cost books (2) 1921-35, castings book 1898-1900, propeller book 1924-65, time and wages books (11) 1903-49, payroll sheets (3 files) 1959-68.
Untraced. Enquiries to NRA (Scotland) (survey 618). NRA 15351.

[499] **PETER STUBS LTD**, steel, file and watchmakers' tool mfrs, Warrington, Lancs

Articles of partnership, etc 1845-65, general corresp incl orders 1777-1900, 1933, account book 1776-8, day books (17) 1788-91, 1802-39, cash books (4) 1805-9, bank books (10) 1791-1813, 1820-47, sales ledger 1806-8, sales books (3) 1778-82, 1828-30, file orders 1780-1882, order and payment books (12) 1801-16, bill books (2) 1815-57, despatch book 1811-15, account with carrier 1824-9, steel deliveries book 1834-40, stock book 1830-3, production statistics (6 vols, 1 item) 1815, 1820-37, workmen's ledgers (3) 1824-40, forgers' weekly record (4 vols) 1828-36, cutters' work lists (1 box) 1805-7, debt and stoppage book 1808-20, papers rel to trade mark disputes 1831, 1842-3, castings wages book 1826-52, piece work rates list 1884, apprenticeship indenture 1839, ground rent for premises 1802-61, rent book rel to firm's property 1812-41, fire engine inspection reports 1825-7, catalogues and price lists incl some of other firms (2 boxes) 1775-1909, nd, papers rel to company history 1841-1905; diary of W Stubs 1841 and private accounts of Stubs family 1798-1849.
Manchester Central Library Local Studies Unit (L24/1).

Records 1797-1813 incl invoices and receipts.
Prescot Museum of Clock and Watch Making: see *Friends of the National Libraries Annual Report 1984*, p13.

[500] **STUBS, WOOD & CO**, wire drawers and pin mfrs, Warrington, Lancs

Letter book 1814-24, general corresp incl orders (19 boxes) 1814-27, cash book 1815-31, petty cash disbursements (3 vols) 1814-22, bank book 1827-31, account of pins straightened (1 vol) 1816-17, record of debts (1 vol) 1817, sales and purchase ledger 1814-24, sales day book 1814-21,

pin warehouse order books (2) 1814-29, travellers' order books (3) *c*1822-8, carriage books (2) 1814-27, coal and slack book 1829, headers' books (5) 1814-15, 1824-9 and hiring books (3) 1821-9, pointers' books (3) 1814-29, head cutters' books 1814-29, whiteners' books (3) 1814-26, stickers' books (3) 1814-17, 1826-8, drawers' book 1822-9, rent book 1828-9.
Manchester Central Library Local Studies Unit (L24/2).

[501] **WILLIAM SUGG & CO LTD**, gas light and heating appliance mfrs, London

Directors' minutes 1881-1907 and from 1964, share transfer papers 1910-60, other corporate records from 1955, pension fund records 1960s-1970s.
Thorn EMI Heating. NRA 28631; BAC *Company Archives* no 374.

[502] **JOHN SUMMERS & SONS LTD**, steel mfrs, Shotton, Flints

Records 19th-20th cent incl memorandum and articles of association 1898-1954, agenda book 1897-1908, directors' attendance books (2) 1925-58, directors' emoluments 1948-70, registers of members and stock, share and debenture ledgers from 1898, debenture stock registers (2) 1899-1923, ordinary and preference share transfer registers 1946-67, nd, dividend lists (4) 1898-1931 and other share records (*c*250 boxes and bundles) 1898-1978, seal registers (5) nd, annual reports and accounts 1909-70, balance sheets and profit and loss accounts 1904-15, 1937-44, secretary's administrative files, general corresp and papers, Shotton Works secretary's papers and papers rel to subsidiaries 1944-74, legal agreements 1895-1979, tax records 1933-41, office expenditure summaries 1910-13, ledger balances 1874-5, private ledgers (3) 1896-1925, extracts from private ledger 1888-1912, nominal ledger 1942-57, private journals (3) 1859-1914, cash ledger 1939-40, cash books (6) 1906-69, accounts 1937-9, overdue accounts 1875-7, misc accounting records 1935-58, corresp, contracts and specifications rel to orders 1907-40 and other sales and purchase records 1960-9, nd, private stock and production ledger 1859-1914 and other stock and production records 1928-69, trade mark and patent records 1876-1978, wages registers (12) 1904-44, income tax papers 1904-7, workmen's bonus book 1913-19, Stalybridge Works wages ledgers nd and other staff records 1912-69, nd, property records incl those of Sealand Tenants Ltd 1871-1978; misc Summers family papers 1896, 20th cent incl corresp of Henry Hall Summers 1933-5.
British Steel Records Centre, Shotton. NRA 36011.

Minutes.
British Steel plc. Enquiries to the Records Centre, Shotton. NRA 36011.

[503] **WJ SUTTON LTD**, manufacturing jewellers, Birmingham

Directors' and general meeting minute book 1935-78, papers (8 items) rel to registration of the company 1935, general account book 1904-90, bank

books, etc (7 vols, 1 bundle) 1917-79, stocktaking
book 1939-85, trade mark registration papers
(6 items) 1910, 1936-8, misc staff and tax records
1937-85, printed papers and photographs 1900-89
incl illustrations of watch chains and bracelets early
20th cent.
The Company. Enquiries to the Chairman. NRA
33778.

[504] **R SYKES & SON LTD**, chain mfrs, Cradley
Heath, Staffs

Directors' and general meeting minutes (2 vols)
1901-66, private ledger 1941-63, cash books (3)
1958-65, sales journal 1954-61, other sales records
(2 vols, 13 bundles) 1954-64, product catalogue nd.
Dudley Archives and Local History Service (Acc 8264).
NRA 25008.

[505] **JOHN TAYLOR & CO (BELL
FOUNDERS) LTD**, Loughborough, Leics

Records 18th-20th cent.
The Company. Closed to research.

[506] **TAYLOR & SONS LTD**, ferrous and non-
ferrous castings mfrs, Briton Ferry, Glam

Letter book of HF Taylor 1898-1904, general
corresp and papers (*c*40 items, 8 files, 5 plans)
1884-1939, corresp and papers rel to George
Leyshon's patent tinning process (16 items) 1882-4
and foreign patents (24 files, 10 items) 1883-96,
sketch books (26) 1889-1941, photographs nd.
West Glamorgan Archive Service (D/D Ta). NRA
36130.

[507] **RB TENNENT LTD**, ironfounders and steel
roll mfrs, Coatbridge, Lanarkshire

Minute books (3) 1901-45, minutes, agendas and
accounts (1 box) 1960-72, registers of members (2)
1900-41, letter books (2) 1888-90, 1901-16,
company corresp and other papers 1911-76, balance
sheets 1901-14, 1920-40, reports, financial
statements and legal papers *c*1945-60, private
ledgers (3) 1901-16, 1929-48 and journals (4)
1901-49, investment book 1925-34, bank books (27)
1946-70, sales ledgers (2) 1844-1949, day books (2)
1940-3 and analysis books (57) 1904-62, order
books (8) 1933-45, 1963-5, cost books (11)
1914-47, charge books (10) 1914-44 and other
production records 1958-79, private wage analysis
books (4) 1910-60, register of plant 1942, glass
negatives of plant, machinery, foundry samples and
the Tennent family; Roll Makers Association of
Great Britain minutes, corresp, reports, etc 1934-5,
1952-62.
The Company. Enquiries to NRA (Scotland) (survey
2582). NRA 27041.

[508] **WILLIAM TERRELL & SONS LTD**, wire
and hemp rope mfrs, Bristol

Registers of directors and members (2 vols)
1886-1915, nd, register of transfers 1880-1932,
share ledger 1888-1959, register of mortgages

1874-1950, balance sheets 1889-1958, private
ledgers (2) 1879-1958, journal 1880-1961, cash
books (3) 1920-63, bill books (2) 1843-1930, prices
files 1940-64, estimate book 1908, cordage book
*c*1814, stocktaking notebook 1925-53, policy register
1884-1915, valuations (2) of plant and machinery
1875, 1878, site plans 1928, 1951, photographs
(2 vols) 1920, 1950, misc papers 1822-1961.
Bristol RO (Acc 21790). NRA 15592.

Directors' minutes (4 vols) 1880-1962, misc share
records, corresp and papers 1940-64.
Doncaster Archives Department (DY.BRI/29). NRA
21369.

[509] **THAMES BANK IRON CO LTD**,
ironfounders, London

Directors' minutes from 1911, annual reports and
balance sheets 1918-21, price lists and catalogues
(23 items) 1899-1955, particulars of agency
agreement and legal corresp rel to infringement of
patents 1923, staff records 1918-47, corresp and
deeds rel to London premises 1871-1919, plan of
Old Barge Iron Wharf *c*1900.
In private possession. Enquiries to the Business
Archives Council. NRA 20500.

[510] **THARSIS SULPHUR & COPPER CO
LTD**, mine owners and copper smelters, Glasgow

Board minutes from 1866, directors' annual reports
from 1867.
*Tharsis plc: see Archives of the British Chemical
Industry 1750-1914*, ed PJT Morris and CA Russell,
1988, pp184-5.

Report of general meetings 1872-4, directors'
attendance registers (2) 1882-95, letter books (44)
1857-1930, reports to auditors 1893-1906, credit
receipts book 1930-9, weekly list of absentees (1 vol)
1907-16.
Glasgow University Archives and Business Record Centre
(UGD/57). NRA 21850.

Works plans and leases at Jarrow, Hebburn and
Newcastle upon Tyne, and related papers,
1869-1947, nd.
Durham County RO (D/X 244). Morris and Russell,
ibid.

[511] **EC THEEDAM LTD**, sheet metal workers
and ironmongers, Dudley, Worcs

Cash books (2) 1947-50, lists of suppliers with
related corresp and papers (6 vols) 1869-1952, lists
of goods supplied (3 vols) 1915-40, nd, pattern and
costing books (13 vols, 1 item) 1889-1948, stock
books, etc (6 vols) 1927-54, catalogues and price
lists (1 box, *c*10 items) 19th-20th cent, notes on
firm's history.
Dudley Archives and Local History Service (Accs 8217,
8220). NRA 33551.

[512] **THOMAS & CLEMENT LTD**, iron and
brass founders, Llanelly, Carms

Articles of partnership 1874, draft proposals for a
foundry and list of stock 1874, memorandum and

articles of association and agreement for the transfer of the business 1907, shareholders' dividend ledger 1874-1907, schedule of partners' dividends with summary accounts *c*1907, balance sheet and misc financial papers (3 items) 1908, papers rel to the misappropriation of company funds (1 vol, etc) 1907-8.
Dyfed Archives Service, Carmarthen (DB/48). NRA 29913.

Minutes, corresp, ledgers, accounts and photographs *c*1890-1956.
Dyfed Archives Service, Carmarthen (DB/48 addnl).

[513] GEORGE & RICHARD THOMAS LTD, ironmasters, Bloxwich, Staffs

Corresp 1874-1903, invoices 1872-9, 1889-1900, abstract of expenditure on raw materials and vouchers, etc from suppliers 1898-9, specifications of tank engines *c*1875, catalogues, price lists, etc of suppliers late 19th cent, colliery plan 1928 and misc papers 1861-7.
Staffordshire RO (D 1281). NRA 17398.

Bills and receipts for mineral carriage, etc (80 bundles) 1873-1900.
Walsall Archives Service (Accs 37, 252). NRA 33233.

[514] RICHARD THOMAS & CO LTD, iron, steel and tinplate mfrs, Lydney, Glos and Swansea, Glam

Records 18th-20th cent incl board minutes (12 vols) 1884-1965, finance committee minutes (2 vols) 1926-34, 1940-5, abstract of minutes (1 file) 1930-57, register of directors (3 vols) 1902-47, directors' attendance book 1918-23, directors' reports and accounts (2 files) 1936-9, reports of general meetings 1920-30, proceedings of tinplate conferences (1 vol) 1934, register of mortgages and charges 1884-1939, private ledgers (16) 1898-1906, 1912-66, cash ledgers (2) 1892-5, 1936-45, ledger 1901-26, copy ledger 1913-27, private journal 1884-8, other ledgers and accounting records 1921-1970s, Abercarn Works sales, production, technical and staff records 1920s-1970s and inventory 1912-39, indenture and agreement ledger 1853-99, employment, earnings and accidents registers (6) 1942-64, copy documents books for various works (14 vols) 1868-1928 and deeds and legal papers 1754-1980s; Alyn Steel Tinplate Co Ltd minutes, etc (3 vols) 1896-1939; Edlogan Tinplate Co Ltd copy documents book 1870-1924 and inventory 1908-46; Ely Tinplate Co Ltd copy documents book 1872-1927 and inventory 1908-43; South Wales Steel & Tinplate Co Ltd copy documents books (3) 1828-1914.
British Steel Records Centre, Shotton. NRA 36012.

Lydney leases and related papers (2 files) 1876, 1889, 1896 and plans of works (2 items) 1939; scrapbooks (2) compiled by RB Thomas rel to his business and other interests *c*1894-*c*1916.
Gloucestershire RO (D 4880). NRA 3514.

See also Baldwins Ltd.

[515] THOMAS THOMAS, nailmaster, Dudley, Worcs

Cash books (2) 1838-47, 1850-4.
Staffordshire RO (3166/4/2-3). NRA 21622.

[516] ARCHIBALD THOMSON, BLACK & CO LTD, wire rope mfrs, Glasgow

Corresp (1 file) 1938-61, balance sheets and accounts, etc 1909-33, 1952-3, general ledger 1938-40, sales ledger 1916-34, manual 1948-9, notes on wire ropes nd.
Glasgow University Archives and Business Record Centre (UGD/42). NRA 10832.

Minute book 1903-39, register of members nd.
In private possession. A microfilm is in Glasgow University Archives and Business Record Centre (UGD/42/32).

[517] TINSLEY ROLLING MILLS CO LTD, steel mfrs, Sheffield

Minutes (6 vols) 1874-1955, register of members and share ledger (2 vols) 1897-1920, dividend register 1902-19, letter book incl misc corporate papers 1901-18, private ledgers (2) 1874-1928, day book 1838-74, cash book 1896-1913, technical notebook 1902-25, factory plans (13) 1899-1956, nd, photographs (131 items) *c*1906-62, centenary brochure 1946.
Sheffield Archives (LD 2259-78). NRA 34975.

Register of directors 1948, seal book 1972-7, pension scheme minutes 1962-78, nd, valuations of plant 1936-65.
Sheffield Archives (Hadfields records). NRA 34874.

[518] TITANIC STEEL & IRON CO LTD, Coleford, Glos

Letters (5) 1868-74, list of shareholders 1871, list of customers 1869-71, quotation book and index (2 vols) 1867-70, record of weights of steel melted and fuel costs 1867-70, lists of contracts and purchases 1870 and stock 1874, advertisements, price lists and testimonials (13 items) 1867-70.
Sheffield Archives (MD 1193-4). NRA 23246.

[519] JOSHUA TODD & SON, ironfounders, Summerbridge, Yorks

Ledgers (12) 1904-14, 1920-5, 1932-54, draft ledger 1925-43, day books (2) 1931-41, 1956-7, order books (2) 1955-6.
West Yorkshire Archive Service, Leeds (Acc 1335, 1934). NRA 31016.

[520] TOMLINSON family, braziers and tinplate workers, Stafford

Account book 1768-9, ledgers (5) 1793-1823, day books (5) 1809-39; family corresp (2 items) 1797, 1817.
Staffordshire RO (D 256, D 616). NRA 23051.

[521] **JOHN S TREGONING & CO LTD**,
tinplate mfrs, Llanelly, Carms

Account books (5) 1907-36, ledgers (9) 1869-78,
1890-3, 1907-55, journals (11) 1869-81, 1891-7,
1907-55, cash books (7) 1894-1911, 1930-55, order
books, etc (6 vols, 8 files) 1857-1935, other sales
records (5 vols, 5 files) 1926-52, forge account book
1857-1911, weekly report books (3) 1893-6, 1901-6,
1926-31, consignment books (2) 1889-95, extract
book 1927-36.
University College of Swansea Library. NRA 8486.

[522] **TRENT IRON WORKS**, ironfounders,
Scunthorpe, Lincs

Furnace driving book 1864-70.
South Humberside Area AO (511). *Summary guide*,
1989.

Accounts rel to furnace building, etc and legal case
papers 1866-9.
Wakefield Libraries Department of Local Studies
(Goodchild Loan MSS: Iron MSS). NRA 23032.

[523] **TRURO SMELTING CO**, Truro, Cornwall

Black tin account book 1840-1.
Cornwall RO (X363/5). NRA 5235 (Summary of
accessions Oct-Dec 1970).

[524] **THOMAS TUCKLEY**, nailmaker, Coleshill,
Warwicks

Ledger 1857-92.
Warwickshire RO (CR 2314/1).

[525] **THOMAS TURTON & SONS LTD**, file,
tool and spring mfrs, Sheffield

Memorandum and articles of association 1886-1921,
board minutes (3 vols) 1885-1957, 1966-8, board
and general meeting agenda books (4) 1890-1958,
share ledger 1886-1964, registers of shareholders
and transfers (2 vols) 1886-1969, annual return of
shareholders 1886-1926, letter book 1912-33,
general corresp and papers (3 boxes, 8 parcels, 7 box
files) 1921-1960s, balance sheets, trading accounts,
profit and loss accounts and related papers (8 vols,
1 bundle, 1 envelope) 1886-1966, private ledgers (2)
1905-63, ledger 1886-1920, departmental accounts
(1 vol) 1894-1947, record of expenses (1 vol)
1902-29, South American sales journal 1909-19,
record of contracts (1 vol) c1888-96, file department
stock book 1874, patents, assignments, agreements,
trade mark papers, etc (2 boxes, 1 parcel, 1 item)
1831-1938, daily production totals (1 vol) 1924-55,
weights of various types of steel (3 vols) 1877-1944,
plans and papers rel to new premises 1960s.
Sheffield Archives (Stephenson, Blake records). NRA
35036.

[526] **SAMUEL TYZACK & CO LTD**, iron and
steel founders and concrete products mfrs,
Sunderland, co Durham

Letter book 1869-1914, annual returns (2 vols)
1900-29, accounting and wages records (4 vols)
1928-52, catalogues and brochures (14 items)
1940s-1970.
Tyne and Wear Archives Service (DX64). NRA 22561.

[527] **UNION IRON CO**, Rhymney, Mon

Account book 1800, account of iron made (1 vol)
1801-5, furnace log book 1801-4, finers' metal stock
book 1819-24.
Cardiff Central Library (MSS 1.465, 4.560-2).

Legal papers rel to dissolution of partnership
1805-7.
National Library of Wales (John Lloyd MSS). NRA
34436.

Balance sheet 1824-5, inventory of stock 1825, sale
particulars of works (2 items) 1824-5.
Public Record Office (C 107/84).

[528] **UNITED WIRE LTD**, wire drawers and
mfrs, Edinburgh

Memorandum and articles of association 1897,
directors' and shareholders' minutes (12 vols) from
1897, share registers (3) 1898-1916 and list of
shareholders 1930-42, annual reports and accounts
from 1899, specifications of metals and alloys 1916,
salaries books (2) 1912-51, printed history of
company 1947; Patent Process Wire Weaving Co
salaries book 1899-1918; minutes, etc of wire
manufacturers' trade associations 1899-1920.
The Company. Enquiries to NRA (Scotland) (survey
763). NRA 17522.

[529] **GEORGE URE & CO LTD**, ironfounders,
Bonnybridge, Stirlingshire

Memorandum and articles of association, etc
(1 bundle) 1884, letter books (3) 1873-84, 1913-19,
papers rel to liquidation 1890, profit distribution
book 1873-84, day books (3) 1869-72, cash books
(2) 1861-9, 1873-81, order book 1867, invoice book
1870-2, stock books (2) 1860-71, 1873-84, cost
book nd, piece work books (2) 1863, 1867, salaries
book 1869-73.
Smith & Wellstood Ltd. Enquiries to NRA (Scotland)
(survey 2198). NRA 15350.

[530] **VALE family**, curl blade and awl makers,
Bloxwich, Staffs

Business and rent accounts (4 vols) 1854-65,
1876-1900, 1909-19.
Walsall Archives Service (Acc 59/27-30). NRA 23874.

[531] **JOHN VESSEY & SONS LTD**, steel mfrs,
Sheffield

Board and general meeting minutes (5 vols)
1903-78, register of members (2 vols) 1921-73,
share ledger 1904-49, share certificate book
1904-62, private ledgers (3) 1908-57, sales and
purchase records (5 vols, 1 bundle) 1927-58, salaries
ledger 1961-71, general corresp and papers
1950s-1970s.
Sheffield Archives (LD 1929-35a and 1984 deposit).
NRA 34866.

[532] **VICTORIA TUBE CO LTD**, Tipton, Staffs

Minutes (1 vol) 1898-1921, attendance book
1927-38, register of directors and managers 1901-4,
register of members 1898-1925, private ledgers (2)
1910-19, 1927-41, ledgers (5) 1932-48, cash books
(4) 1898-1904, 1919-40.
*British Steel East Midlands Regional Records Centre,
Irthlingborough.* NRA 35554.

See also Stewarts & Lloyds Ltd.

[533] **VIVIAN & SONS**, copper smelters, Swansea,
Glam

Draft minutes of directors' meetings early 20th cent,
list of stock holders of Hafod Works 1820-1, corresp
and papers rel to restructuring of capital (1 file)
1897-1906, other corresp and papers (2 files)
1909-34, annual accounts (10 items) 1856, 1867,
c1870-9, lists (2) of company liabilities 1877-8 and
assets 1878, audit of accounts (1 file) 1925, notes rel
to Cornish ore sampling 1809-12, sales 1814-26 and
purchases 1848-79, accounts (2) of ore sold 1821
and copper sold 1852, records of annual trade
transactions (1 vol) 1846-79, notes on Cornish ore
production (3 items) 1720-1800, calculations rel to
smelting in Anglesey (3 items) 1805-11, list and
valuation of stock at Forest Mills (2 items) 1820,
account of copper stocks at Hafod 1822, misc
papers (c24 items) rel to Hafod Works and Forest
Mills 1811-99; copper trade and mining papers
1792-1827, colliery accounts and records 1864-89;
minutes (1 item) of the [Cornish] Miners'
Committee 1810; Vivian family, business and estate
papers 19th-20th cent incl business notebook of
HH Vivian 1841-87.
National Library of Wales (Vivian Papers). NRA
25196.

Accounts (2) of copper and copper ore bought
1727-84; Hafod Works memoranda book 1834-9,
record of ore sampled 1838-9, notes on smelting
1873-1902 and observations on the Works 1844;
notes on Cwmavon Mill 1846 and description of the
Penclawdd, Llanelly and Risca works 1811.
National Library of Wales (MSS 15103-10,
15112-17).

Draft deed of partnership of Vivian & Sons (1 file)
1868, corresp rel to Margam and Hafod copper
works (4 bundles) 1889, 1905-6, 1910, corresp and
papers rel to operations at Port Talbot, Aberavon
and Morfa (9 bundles, 1 item) 1867-1913, cost
statements rel to Margam Works and Morfa Colliery
(3 files) 1905, 1910-11, reports (2) on the White
Rock Works 1910 and on ore mining in the USA,
Peru and Chile 1861; business notebooks (9) of
AP Vivian 1851-1923.
Glamorgan Archive Service (D/DGV).

Partnership papers 1843-59, patent specifications
and licences rel to new processes 1844, 1870-1,
leases of land, minerals and premises, mainly in
Wales and London, 1736-1947, misc plans and
estate papers c1860-1914.
University College of Swansea Library (Whiterock
Collection). NRA 14358.

Taibach Works cash book 1838-1942, Morfa Works
construction costs 1834; Copper Trade Association
minutes 1824-9.

University College of Swansea Library (Hugh Vivian
Collection). NRA 14358.

Corresp rel to the company 1903-5.
University College of Swansea Library (Graham Vivian
Collection). NRA 14358.

Licences (c1 bundle) rel to premises in Cornwall
1899-1913, deeds, plans and papers (1 bundle) rel
to premises at Llansamlet 1858-1925.
Birmingham Central Library Archives Division (MS
1422: British Copper Manufacturers Ltd). NRA
32859.

[534] **JOHN WAINE & SONS**, ironfounders and
lock mfrs, Willenhall, Staffs

Foundry day books (6) 1893-1916, 1926-50.
Staffordshire RO (D 3085). NRA 25290.

[535] **JOHN NEWMAN WAITE**, coppersmith and
ironmonger, Norwich, Norfolk

Accounts and stock book 1840-7.
Norfolk RO: see *Accessions to repositories 1989*, p33.

[536] **TN WALDRON LTD**, metal stampers and
piercers, Birmingham and Stratford-upon-Avon,
Warwicks

Records (c56 vols) 1910-56 incl expenditure ledgers
(3) 1910-53, expenditure day book 1910-21, sales
day books (11) 1910-19, 1930-56, and job books (2)
1913-27.
Shakespeare Birthplace Trust RO, Stratford-upon-Avon
(DR 614). NRA 33328.

[537] **WALKER BROTHERS LTD**, iron and steel
mfrs and galvanisers, Walsall, Staffs

Articles of association 1896, 1908, 1938, directors'
reports and accounts and other misc corporate
records 1940-64, corresp (3 files) 1948-56, private
ledgers (3) 1939-64, cost analyses (1 vol) 1892,
1899, staff records (2 vols, 4 items) 1938-c1960,
agreement with Walsall Sanitary Authority 1881,
valuations of works and related reports (15 vols and
items) 1891, 1938-61, plans (9) of works mid 20th
cent, catalogues and other printed material
1895-1962.
Walsall Archives Service (Acc 486). NRA 29859.

[538] **WALKER & HALL** (formerly **BINGHAM &
HALL**), cutlery mfrs and silver platers, Sheffield

Capital account ledger 1842-53, employment
contracts book 1875-83.
Sheffield Archives (MD 6189-90). NRA 23246.

[539] **SAMUEL WALKER & CO**, ironfounders
and steel refiners, Rotherham, Yorks

Business journal (1 vol) 1741-92.
Institution of Mechanical Engineers Library. A
photocopy is in Rotherham Metropolitan Borough
Archives (394/Z). A slightly different version
extending to 1833 is printed in *The Walker family,
iron founders and lead manufacturers, 1741-1893*, ed
AH John, 1951.

MS 'Sketch of the proceedings of the Foundry, etc'
1741-60 by Samuel Walker, bound in extra-
illustrated copy of John Guest, *Relics and records of
men and manufactures . . . of Rotherham . . .*, 1866.
Rotherham Metropolitan Borough Archives.

Proposals for conduct of the business and division of
responsibilities among partners *c*1785.
Rotherham Metropolitan Borough Archives (328/Z).
NRA 12413.

Articles of partnership and deeds 1757-1828.
Sheffield Archives (WC 2701-26 *passim*). *Catalogue of
business and industrial records in Sheffield City
Libraries*, 1971, p19.

[540] **WALKERS, PARKER & CO LTD**, lead
mfrs, Elswick, Northumb

Partnership agreements 1799, 1814, 1824-5, 1860,
board minutes (8 vols) 1889-1939 and index
1926-39, general meeting minutes (2 vols, 2 files)
1889-92, register of directors (1 vol) 1903-39,
register of shareholders (4 vols) 1889-1938 and
index *c*1920, agreements, etc rel to shares and
debentures (278 items) 1886-1934, share values
ledger 1918-19, trust deeds (36 items) 1889-1974,
letter books (4) 1778-89, 1840, misc corresp and
related papers (170 items) 1845, 1899-1979,
agreements (50 items) 1897-1935, legal papers rel to
corporate, patent and trade mark disputes (8 files,
3 items) 1885-1938, profit and loss accounts (2 vols,
2 items) 1780-1800, 1815-31, balance sheets
(3 vols, 2 items) 1902, 1913-38 and related
accounting records (16 items) 1875-88, 1901-3,
1931, private ledgers (2) 1888-1949, nominal
ledgers (2) 1889-1948, ledgers (9) 1778-1814,
1822-32 and indexes (3 vols) *c*1790-*c*1814, journals
(7) 1779-82, 1798-1802, 1839-42, 1947-8, petty
cash books (2) 1934-45, bank cash book 1945-6,
record of lead sheet and pipe sales (1 file) 1901-11,
record of lead and antimony purchases (3 vols)
1907-22, shipment register 1956-73, cost
calculations (3 vols, 1 file) 1907-9, 1924-40, papers
rel to shot production, smelting and refining
processes (3 vols, 6 files, 2 items) 1893-1948, assay
register 1912-28, stock books and ledgers (12)
1784-91, 1840, 1854-1914, 1927-48, wages books
and related papers (16 vols, 23 items) 1778-82,
1925-68, welfare accounts, accident books and other
staff records (7 vols, 144 items) 1799-1820,
1914-74, deeds, corresp, photographs, etc rel to
Elswick Works 1778-1966; Chester Works private
ledger 1884-1914, stock records (2 vols) 1885-1928,
wages ledger 1839-40 and misc corresp, plans,
deeds, etc 1837, 1884-*c*1960; Hull Works misc
corresp, memoranda, taxation papers, etc 1905-46;
Lambeth Works record of lead delivered (1 vol)
1874-83, production memoranda (4 vols)
1895-1937, technical notes (1 vol, 1 file) 1915-22,
works register 1946, inventory and valuation 1889,
papers rel to sales and repair of premises and
equipment (1 vol, 2 files) 1884, 1933-4, 1938-40
and misc corresp, agreements, deeds, photographs,
etc 1879-1947; Dee Bank Works production
memoranda (2 files, 3 items) 1892-1930s, corresp
mainly rel to property (7 files) 1889-1976, valuation
reports, etc (4 files) 1926-62, plans (14) 1888-1953,

deeds, agreements, etc 1859-1952 and misc records
1895-1952; misc papers rel to Walker family and
history of firm 18th-20th cent.
Tyne and Wear Archives Service (Acc 1512/10868-
12703). NRA 32095.

Misc papers rel to Walker family lead interests
1778-1960s incl articles of partnership and related
papers (6 files, 1 item) 1841, 1869, 1888-92, legal
charges rel to formation of new partnership (8 files,
1 bundle) 1824-5, deeds, assignments and other
legal and property papers 1778-1907 and papers rel
to history of family and firm 20th cent.
Tyne and Wear Archives Service (Acc 1555). NRA
8919.

'Minutes relating to the Lead Manufactory'
1778-1893.
Untraced: see *The Walker family, iron founders and lead
manufacturers, 1741-1893*, ed AH John, 1951.

[541] **THOMAS WALMSLEY & SONS LTD**,
iron mfrs, Bolton, Lancs

Account book 1872-87, nominal ledger *c*1900-40,
order sheet *c*1870, price list 1877-91, address book
nd, summary of work done 1872-7, cost
memorandum 1867, puddling department costs
*c*1880, pig iron test book 1874, wages list 1869-81,
attendance book 1887-8, sick and accident society
minute book 1903-14, bank book 1891-1910 and
rules *c*1880, inventories and valuations (3 items)
1877-1906, corresp, plans and other papers rel to
property 1870-1917, publicity leaflets (3 items) nd,
misc corresp and papers 1858-1917.
Bolton Archive Service (ZZ/395). NRA 34858.

[542] **JOHN WALTON & CO**, lead smelters and
merchants, Castleside, co Durham

Out-letter books (5) 1874-85, 1888-91.
Durham County RO (D/X 884). NRA 32512.

[543] **WARDROBE & SMITH LTD**, steel mfrs,
Sheffield

Day books (3) 1871-80, 1887-93, 1902-5, sales
ledgers (2) 1871-86, 1944-57, price book
1887-1955, price lists and circulars (1 bundle)
1930s-1940s, invoice journal 1956-9, converting
ledger 1854-61, furnace production book
1866-1954.
Sheffield Archives (LD 1936-44). NRA 34866.

[544] **WARNER & CO LTD**, refined pig iron mfrs,
Middlesbrough

Memorandum and articles of association 1874,
1900, 1953, directors' minutes (2 vols) 1900-51,
general meeting and committee minutes (3 vols)
1901-68, share ledgers, registers and related papers
(15 vols, 8 files and bundles) 1900-68, letter books
(2) 1883-1913, seal register 1900-60, annual
reports, accounts and balance sheets 1901-55,
foreign ledgers (2) 1900-46, impersonal ledgers nd,
journals (6) 1900-82, cash books (12) 1915-67, bill
books (2) 1902-31, debts analysis book 1953-64,
misc accounts (1 vol) 1883-1900, purchase ledgers

and journals (11) 1900-55, sales ledgers and journals (11) 1912-67, order books (6) 1908-14, 1936-57, despatch books (3) 1879-90, 1893-1905, 1952-6, stock book 1879-1926, materials received (1 vol) 1952-5, patents (1 folder, 2 items) 1859-74, 'make of iron' books (9) 1883-1926, misc production records (6 vols) 1881-1945, wages books (8) 1936-50, misc records rel to premises, etc 1896-1977, advertisements, articles rel to processes and other printed papers 1874-1938, nd.
Cleveland Archives (U/WA). NRA 34097.

[545] WAVERLEY IRON & STEEL CO LTD, iron and steel mfrs, Glasgow

Memorandum and articles of association 1894, 1900, minutes (1 vol) nd, directors' report, manager's report and profit and loss account 1904, misc corresp, specifications and plans (1 bundle) *c*1901-4, misc commercial agreements (1 bundle) 1899-1900.
Glasgow University Archives and Business Record Centre (UGD 259/16).

[546] WEBSTER & CO LTD, wire and hemp rope mfrs, Sunderland, co Durham

Private ledger 1882-1902, ledgers (9) 1848-1914, day books (23) 1820-1926, private journal 1882-1902, journals (2) 1864-93, cash book 1780-91, order books (3) 1890-1903, 1918-21, shipping and export ledger 1914-27, stock books (2) 1898-1904, 1915-20, stock account and valuation 1885, time books (8) 1865-1916, register of young employees, accidents, etc 1914-57, scrapbook 1906-23, misc business and legal corresp and papers, plans, photographs.
Tyne and Wear Archives Service (Acc 569). NRA 22975.

Memorandum and articles of association 1899, 1959, directors' minute book 1899-1959, other corporate and share records (*c*15 vols and files, etc) 1907-68, administrative corresp and papers 1943-68, factory register 1958-65, inventory and valuation 1935.
Doncaster Archives Department (DY.BRI/30). NRA 21369.

[547] WEBSTER & HORSFALL LTD, wire and wire rope mfrs, Birmingham

Records from 1801 incl memorandum and articles of association (1 box) 1892-1954, minute books (two series) from 1892, letter books (7) 1840-9, 1858-60, 1863-4, 1890-9, Atlantic cable corresp and papers and related research papers (1 box) 1864-1903, nd, other corporate records from 1945, ledgers (3) 1892-1914, private ledger of Joseph Webster III 1801-50 incorporating production statistics for 1777-1814, accounts, costs and data (*c*33 bundles) 1920-48, day book 1904-8, cash book 1898-1903, steel production records (1 vol) 1848-51, wire production records (1 vol) 1859-61, output analysis book 1948-55, price calculations (1 vol) 1806-32, sales and purchase contracts (2 vols) 1899-1923, other sales records 1920,

1948-76, technical records 1870-1930s, patents, specifications and related corresp (1 vol, 4 items) 1853-1913, wages and salaries records (10 vols) 1898-1953, nd, other staff records from 1940, Amalgamated Society of Wire Drawers subscription records for Hay Mills (1 vol) 1893-8 and Birmingham district (1 bundle) 1929-31, deeds, corresp and papers rel to premises, plant and estates at Penns, Plants Brook and Hay Mills, Warwicks 19th-20th cent; business and personal corresp and papers of the Webster and Horsfall families 19th-20th cent; letter book of TC Batchelor 1884-93, Latch & Batchelor Ltd corresp and papers (1 box) from 1889 and other corporate records from 1954.
The Company. Enquiries to the Chairman. NRA 33688.

[548] WELLINGTON TUBE WORKS LTD, Tipton, Staffs

Directors' minutes (1 vol) 1959-80, attendance book 1906-39, registers of members (1 vol) 1927-79, of documents (1 vol) *c*1940-56 and of probates (1 vol) 1943-59, private ledgers (4) 1906-40, nominal ledgers (2) 1923-33, ledger summaries 1930-3, journal 1948-56, cash books (13) 1914-71, stock book 1933-40, salaries books 1928-32.
British Steel East Midlands Regional Records Centre, Irthlingborough. NRA 35554.

See also Stewarts & Lloyds Ltd.

[549] HENRY WHITE & CO LTD, steel mfrs and founders, Pontymister, Mon

Memorandum and articles of association 1903, directors' reports, statements of accounts and balance sheets (21 items) 1904-25, auditors' report 1905, corresp rel to supply of castings to Admiralty (10 items) 1902-8, apprenticeship indentures 1879-1901, particulars 1897 and agreement 1903 rel to sale of the works, inventories (2) 1897-1903, insurance policies, misc agreements and licences rel to new processes, etc (*c*1 bundle, 12 items) 1898-1918.
Gwent RO (D 394). NRA 9872.

[550] WHITECROSS CO LTD, wire and iron mfrs and colliery proprietors, Warrington, Lancs

Board and general meeting minutes (7 vols) 1887-1970, register of directors nd, register of members and ordinary shares nd, monthly summary of earnings 1959-61.
British Steel Records Centre, Shotton. NRA 36007.

[551] WHITEHAVEN HEMATITE IRON & STEEL CO LTD, Cleator Moor, Cumberland

Balance sheets and profit and loss accounts 1861-2, misc accounts 1849-61, receipts 1854-62, agreement and other legal papers (3 items) 1858-61, valuation of plant and sundries 1862.
Cumbria RO, Carlisle (DB/61/2). NRA 35352.

[552] **WHITEHEAD & HAYNES**, sheet iron
mfrs, Tipton, Staffs

Bought day book 1854-72.
Dudley Archives and Local History Service (Acc 7317).

[553] **WHITEHOUSE family**, ironmasters,
Sedgley, Staffs

Letter books (2) 1904-8, 1918-20, invoice book
1917-18, business and personal diaries of Benjamin
Whitehouse (16 vols) 1877-1913, photographs of
Priorsfield Ironworks and employees c1890-1910,
cards of other firms (1 bundle) late 19th-20th cent;
corresp and papers of Whitehouse family 19th-20th
cent.
Staffordshire RO (D 683). NRA 9415.

[554] **WICK IRON CO**, iron smelters, Wick, Glos

Accounts (66 items) 1785-1816, particulars of rents
1818, plans of alterations to the rolling mill c1800.
Bristol RO (HA/B/10-12). NRA 7286.

[555] **WIGAN COAL & IRON CO LTD**, iron and
steel mfrs and coal proprietors, Wigan, Lancs

Records 1865-1952 incl board minutes (18 vols)
1865-1952, indexes (5 vols) 1865-1920 and agendas
1870-1926, general meeting minutes (5 vols)
1865-1952, register of directors or managers
1902-48, share ledgers (4) from 1869, indexes to
share ledgers and registers of members (4 vols) nd,
annual lists and summaries of members (26 vols)
1881-1941, registers (6) of transfers 1866-1931, lists
of stocks and debentures 1866-93, directors' and
auditors' reports and resolutions, balance sheets and
accounts 1869-1929, analysis of profit and loss
accounts 1865-1930, half-yearly statements
1870-1924, secretary's corresp (1 box) 1877-1927,
seal books (2) 1893-1936, private ledgers and
indexes 1865-70, 1876-95, ledger and index
1871-83, private journal 1865-1951, journal
1870-81, salaries and commission ledger 1897-1919.
British Steel Records Centre, Shotton. NRA 36007.

Records (185 items) 1860-82 incl memorandum and
articles of association 1865 and special resolutions
(3 items) 1866-8, directors' minutes (2 items) 1877
and draft minutes (12 items) 1878-9, 1882, reports
and resolutions 1868-82 and corresp and papers
mainly rel to meetings, shares and accounts.
Wigan Archives Service (D/DX EL, boxes 156-7).
NRA 19719.

Articles of association 1893-4, special resolution
1870, directors' and auditors' reports and balance
sheets 1868-94, monthly financial statements
1874-80, misc corresp and papers c1867-1930.
Wigan Archives Service (D/D HAI, boxes 3, 14).
NRA 13277.

Certificate of incorporation 1865, index to board
minutes c1890, balance sheets, directors' and
auditors' reports (35 items) 1867-1938, core plan
1924.
Wigan Archives Service (D/DY WC). NRA 13277.

Colliery records 1866-1951 incl letter book 1923-5,
sales cash book 1903-39, brick sales books (5)

1904-51, pit get records 1866-1930, colliery reports
and statistics 1924-43, wages records (2 vols)
1897-8, 1917-31, trespass book 1870-1921, rents
payable 1911-39 and legal papers rel to property
disputes 1879-89.
Lancashire RO (NCWi). NRA 12638.

Records 1870-96.
Lancashire RO (DDX/127). *Guide to the Lancashire
Record Office*, 1985, p165.

Stock book 1872-1940, wages books (2) 1874-85,
1888-1906, misc papers and photographs
(c20 items) mainly 1890-1930.
Cumbria RO, Barrow (BDB/43). NRA 35756.

[556] **ERNEST WILKES LTD**, ironfounders and
colliery plant mfrs, Pelsall, Staffs

Letter books (7) 1889-1938, ledgers (14)
1895-1943, day books (4) 1909-34, cash books (2)
1893-1925, notebook rel to settled accounts 1906-8,
order, despatch and invoice counterfoil books (15)
1891-1914, pattern shop book 1881-2, pulley books
(2) 1899-1958, fitting shop books (2) 1909-10,
1916-18, smiths' book 1929-38, foundry books (3)
1967-8, 1971-3, nd, design books (7) 1887-1914,
1939-48, 1965-6, technical notebooks (7) 1905-7,
1915-20, 1929-38, drawings (17 vols, 12 bundles,
1 item) 1896-1973 incl Hamstead Colliery
machinery 1896-1942 and compound bull engine
for East Warwickshire Waterworks c1897, printed
publicity material (1 bundle).
Walsall Archives Service (Acc 180, 217). NRA 26575.

[557] **JOSHUA WILKINSON**, vice and anvil
maker, Dudley, Worcs

Letters, bills, orders and other papers (c40 items)
1841-5.
Dudley Archives and Local History Service (Acc 8397).

[558] **WILKINSON SWORD CO LTD**, gun and
sword makers, London

Gun barrel books (5) 1807-93, 1900-6, sword proof
registers (136) from 1854, registers of firearms (3)
from 1920, royal warrants (18) 1863-1985.
Wilkinson Sword Ltd, Acton. Enquiries to the Sales
Administration Manager. NRA 33607.

[559] **WILLENHALL FURNACES LTD**,
ironmasters and colliery proprietors, Willenhall,
Staffs

Partnership agreements and dissolution (3 items)
1855-9, 1868, memorandum and articles of
association 1876, partners' corresp (168 items)
1854-70, balance sheets and accounts 1854-69,
directors' report and accounts 1879, inventories and
valuations (10 items) 1857-81, deeds (17 items)
1857-79, misc printed papers 1855-78.
Staffordshire RO (D 595). NRA 7280.

[560] **EDWARD WILLIAMS**, bicycle chain wheel
and crank mfrs, Smethwick, Staffs

Corresp and printed papers rel to the Williams
family partnership (3 bundles, 1 item) 1911-20,

general corresp and papers (20 bundles and files) 1883-1952, balance sheets (2 files) 1896-1905, 1909-13, private ledgers (5) 1896-1921, nd, ledgers (7) 1898-1924, nd, day books (19) 1904-12, 1923-6, day and analysis books (39) 1912-32, journals (3) 1908-22, 1924-42, credit books (9) 1908-12, 1922-32, cash books (28) 1863-1964, bank and memoranda book 1893-5, bills, receipts and vouchers (173 bundles) 1862-1918, sales ledgers (11) 1908-15, 1923-39 and day books (7) 1902-6, 1933-9, nd, purchase ledgers (3) 1907-31 and day books (15) 1896-1930, bought, export and misc ledgers (9) 1923-39, orders (1 bundle) and order books (24) 1874-1956, customer records (2 vols) 1894, nd, petrol and carbide stock book 1912-29, technical notebooks (7) 1863-72, *c*1887-95, 1905 and drawings, etc (39 bundles) 1888-*c*1975, corresp and papers rel to patents and trade marks (32 bundles and items) 1884-1973, nd, wages books and other staff records (18 vols, 1 bundle, 4 items) 1884-1932, nd, deeds, premises records, insurance papers and legal agreements (1 vol, 3 bundles, 2 items) 1847-1925, price lists and trade catalogues, etc (39 items) 1869-1953, scrapbooks and misc records (5 vols, 15 bundles and items) 1888-1976, nd, photographs of staff and premises (3 vols, etc) *c*1910-18, nd, manuscript history of the firm and Williams family 1800-1925 and related papers (1 vol, 6 folders, 1 envelope); Williams family papers (33 bundles and items) 1828-1970.
Staffordshire RO (D 4466). NRA 29552.

[561] **WILLIAMS, HARVEY & CO LTD**, tin smelters, Liverpool

Register of directors or managers nd, dividend notices (1 vol) 1927-9, private letter book 1903-12, private ledger 1888-1901, merchants' ledger 1907-11, salaries book 1911-29.
Liverpool RO (Acc 3872). NRA 35529.

Letters received (1,122 items) 1914-21.
Cornwall RO (H 211). NRA 655.

[562] **JOHN WILLIAMS (WISHAW) LTD**, steel, wire and nail mfrs and ironfounders, Wishaw, Lanarkshire

Annual reports and accounts and misc corporate records 1921-82, private ledgers (6) 1898-1978, nominal ledger 1900-7, sales and purchase journals (3) 1894-1911; James Shortland & Co Ltd misc corporate records 1920, 1969-81, private ledger 1906-15.
Sheffield Archives (TW 479-83, 591-606). NRA 34879.

[563] **WH WILMOT LTD**, gold chain and watch bracelet mfrs, Birmingham

Directors' minutes (1 vol) 1903-70, share register 1903-59 and certificates 1916-1960s, annual returns 1963-8, papers rel to company reorganisation (1 file) 1969, private ledger 1944-58, other accounting records (3 files) 1968-73, sales records (1 vol, 10 files, 1 bundle) *c*1960-70, production records

(2 files) 1968-9, employment and wages records (2 files) 1969-71, printed catalogues 1920s-1960s, photographs mainly of staff and products 19th-20th cent.
Saunders, Shepherd & Co Ltd. Enquiries to the Chairman. NRA 33985.

[564] **WILSON family**, steel drawers, silverplaters and snuff mfrs, Sheffield

Business records from 1746, mainly rel to manufacture and sale of snuff after 1775, but incl steel drawing ledger 1746-61, bill book 1763-89, travellers' ledgers (12) *c*1762-75, sales day books from 1770 and inventories of saws, files, plated goods and casting furnace stock 1772, 1774.
Wilsons & Co (Sharrow) Ltd. Enquiries to the Chairman. NRA 7795.

[565] **WINFIELDS ROLLING MILLS LTD**, metal rollers, Birmingham

Directors' and general meeting minutes (8 vols) 1898-1977, register of directors 1901-76, share register (1 vol) 1898-1976, certificates (1 folder) 1929-71 and transfer committee minutes (1 vol) 1961-71, legal agreements rel to staff assurance scheme (5 items) 1960-4.
Birmingham Central Library Archives Division (MS 1422). NRA 32859.

Memorandum and articles of association 1898, printed report 1897 and prospectus 1898, statement of dividends 1898-1927, misc accounts 1929-35, cost analysis book 1899-1915, deeds and legal agreements (26 items) 1824-1935, sale catalogues, price lists, plans, etc 1833-1956.
Birmingham Central Library Archives Division (MS 322). NRA 30292.

[566] **T WINKLES & CO**, gilt chain and jewellery mfrs, Birmingham

Letter books (2) 1927-8, 1933-5, statements of accounts (2 bundles) 1897-1917, 1946-57, private ledger 1900-36, ledgers, day books and cash books (13) 1919-58, invoice book 1939-58, accounts owing and list of stock (1 vol) 1903-6, list of debtors and creditors (1 vol) 1907-33, stock book late 19th cent-1958, patent and trade mark papers (7 items) 1872-1917, corresp rel to licences to manufacture jewellery in wartime (1 file) 1942-4, wages book 1918-57, products leaflet *c*1901, photographs (3) of workshop 1920s.
Birmingham Central Library Archives Division (MS 1610). NRA 36184.

[567] **WINTER & CO**, founders, coppersmiths and worm makers, London

Time and pay books (2) 1800-3.
Public Record Office (C 103/68).

[568] **STEPHEN WITHAM**, ironmaster, Leeds

Ledger 1854-73.
West Yorkshire Archive Service, Leeds (Brooke, North & Goodwin Collection). *Sources of business and industrial history in Leeds Archives Department*, p19.

[569] WOLVERHAMPTON CORRUGATED IRON CO LTD, galvanised iron mfrs, Wolverhampton, Staffs and Ellesmere Port, Cheshire

Memorandum and articles of association 1893, 1950, minute books (3) 1893-1970, register of directors 1893-1906, register of directors and managers nd, share records (2 vols) nd, accounts, balance sheets, etc 1908-69, annual returns 1957-70, wages book 1914-19.
British Steel Records Centre, Shotton. NRA 36011.

[570] ISAIAH WOODALL & SONS LTD, hearth furniture mfrs, Dudley, Worcs

Cash books (8) 1907-47, sales ledgers (6) 1903-24, sales accounts (4 vols) 1905-29, crate accounts (2 vols) 1907-28, recipients of firm's catalogues (1 vol) 1910-30, other sales, purchase and production records (12 vols, 1 bundle) 1912-58, wages books (17) 1913-51, catalogues and photographs of products (33 vols, 7 files, 2 bundles) 20th cent.
Dudley Archives and Local History Service (Accs 8239, 8244). NRA 33552.

[571] WOODHOUSE & CO, brassfounders, Doncaster, Yorks

Balance sheets (1 vol) 1884-91, 1906-8, cash book 1878-85, bank books (3) 1886-92 and counterfoil books (3) 1891-3, receipted accounts (1 bundle) 1890-4, memorandum rel to employees and wages 1890-1, firm's catalogue 1893, trade cards (10) 20th cent, press cuttings rel to labour dispute, etc (1 vol) 1898-1904, photographs *c*1890-1950s.
Doncaster Archives Department (DY.Wo). NRA 30359.

[572] WORKINGTON FOUNDRY, Workington, Cumberland

Account books (4) 1820-1, 1823-34, ledgers (2) 1820-36, castings day books (2) 1822-7 and payment books (2) *c*1820, nd, cash books (2) 1821-34, order book 1838-43, stock book 1821 and account 1830, castings registers (2) 1821-9, castings cost records (3 vols, etc) 19th cent; plans (6 items) of Seaton Ironworks 1792-4, 1816; family and estate papers of the Curwen family 14th-20th cent.
Cumbria RO, Carlisle (D/Cu). NRA 11185.

[573] WORKINGTON IRON & STEEL CO LTD, Workington, Cumberland

Memorandum and articles of association 1933, directors' and shareholders' minutes (3 vols) 1912-81, agenda book 1912-19, directors' attendance book 1912-81, register of directors 1941-81, register of members 1933-71, profit and loss accounts, etc (1 box) 1919-60, ledgers (13) 1917-67, journals (13) 1935-64, analysis book 1870-1, contract records (1 vol, etc) 1918-62, production records (12 vols, etc) 1920-74, drawings mainly of rails and fishplates (7 boxes) 1893-1960, compendium of engineering information (2 vols) nd, staff records 1914-73, plans, maps and photographs of works, pits and quarries (11 boxes, 4 vols, etc)

1850s-1980, works bulletin (18 vols, 6 items) 1946-68; records of subsidiary companies 1901-60.
British Steel East Midlands Regional Records Centre, Irthlingborough. NRA 35548.

Directors', shareholders' and works committee minutes (3 vols) 1909-21.
Cumbria RO, Carlisle (DB/117). NRA 35357.

Records 1896-1923 incl some of predecessor and associated companies.
Cumbria RO, Carlisle: see *Report of the County Archivist* June 1982, p5.

[574] WORRALL, HALLAM & CO, steel wire mfrs, Sheffield

Annual accounts 1897-1939 incl winding-up of firm, private ledger 1897-1934, stocktaking returns 1901-37.
Sheffield Archives (MD 3642). NRA 23246.

[575] WORSLEY MESNES IRONWORKS LTD, ironfounders and engineers, Wigan, Lancs

Letter book 1909-18, order books (9) 1887-1956, specifications (3 folders, etc) 1887-1902, 1914-58, patents (2 items) 1891, 1906 and related corresp 1912-14, list of drawings (1 vol) from 1887, drawings and diagrams of engines, etc 1874-1963, nd, sketch books (20) 1892-1959, publicity material (15 items) 1889-1905, nd, and misc corresp (2 items) 1911-16; Winding Engine Manufacturers Association corresp 1895-1920.
Museum of Science and Industry in Manchester. NRA 29504.

Sales letter book 1929-37 and order books (74) 1904-64, reverser book 1890-1953, progress book 1956-9, standards book 1940, specifications 1907-27, test reports (1 vol) 1948, drawing books (7) 1902-63, drawings (1 bundle) 1963, lists of drawings 1904-1921 and record of drawings sent to shops 1952-9, general index nd.
Wigan Archives Service. NRA 36424.

[576] GEORGE WOSTENHOLM & SON LTD, cutlery mfrs, Sheffield

Records (*c*870 vols, files and bundles) 1766-1985 incl memorandum and articles of association, agreements and misc papers rel to shares (39 items) 1875-90, 1907, 1985, draft board minutes (1 vol) 1866-90, share ledgers (2) 1907-18, managing director's corresp 1888, nd, secretary's and other letter books (8) 1870s-1908, 1913-17, 1920s, 1950s, secretary's register, agenda and minutes (4 vols) 1880s-1920s, balance sheets, profit and loss accounts, trading accounts, etc (5 files) 1876-1972, ledgers (4) 1829-31, 1895-1920, bank books (5) 1907-32, lists of customers (1 vol) 1870s-1890s, register of display cards and boards 1870s-1930s, testimonials (2 vols) *c*1900-68, country sales cash books (2) 1911-16, order books (6) 1913-28, receipts from suppliers (4 vols) 1911-15, shipping books (2) 1913-19, American agency records 1850-63, 1895-1929, Australian agency records 1885-1927, pattern books (16) 1817-*c*1950, index of

pattern numbers 1896, razor production book 1897-1902, annual stock books (47) 1913-64, apprenticeship indentures (8) 1766-1872, indebted workmen's undertakings (1 vol) 1860-84, works benevolent fund accounts 1888-1934, misc corresp and papers rel to employees (1 bundle) 1872-7, nd, price lists and related papers from 1843, and George Wostenholm's private journal 1860 and accounts 1865.
Sheffield Archives (Wos.R). NRA 17831.

[577] **GEORGE WRIGHT (ROTHERHAM) LTD**, ironfounders and stove mfrs, Rotherham, Yorks

Records c1850-1960 incl ledgers, account books and catalogues.
Rotherham Metropolitan Borough Archives.

[578] **JOSEPH WRIGHT & CO LTD**, chain mfrs, Tipton, Staffs

Corresp and related papers (61 bundles and items) 1882-1915, misc drawings, specifications, etc (20 items) 1855-93, nd.
Sandwell Local Studies Centre (BS/W). NRA 34048.

Invoices (1 box, 2 vols) 1960-1.
Dudley Archives and Local History Service (Acc 8264). NRA 25008.

[579] **WRIGHTS' ROPES LTD**, wire and hemp rope mfrs, Birmingham

Directors' minutes (6 vols) 1899-1954, register of directors, share records, etc (13 vols, 1 file, 3 items) 1923-64, annual reports and accounts (2 vols, 5 bundles) 1898-1963, returns rel to orders and deliveries (1 file) 1963-5, patent specifications (32 items) 1796-1906, production record book 1915-25, staff and charitable records (2 vols, 6 files) 1945-64, price lists, catalogues and papers rel to firm's history (c25 files and items) 1880-1954.
Doncaster Archives Department (DY.BRI/31). NRA 21369.

[580] **YNISCEDWYN IRON, STEEL & COAL CO LTD**, Yniscedwyn, Brecon

Memorandum and articles of association and related papers and accounts 1870-1, directors' report and accounts 1875, misc notices rel to meetings and shares (7 items) 1873-6, corresp with Thomas Cook Davies & Co 1871-2 and George Blizard & Co 1875, legal papers (7 items) 1871-6, leases and abstracts of title, etc (c30 items) 1837-76, nd.
National Library of Wales (SL Beaumont 50-102). NRA 26130.

Special resolutions 1867, agreement with railway company 1869, mineral lease 1839.
National Library of Wales (Hereford City Library [1961 donation]).

Special resolutions 1869-73, deeds and agreements (6 bundles) 1837-83.
West Glamorgan Archive Service (D/D YS).

[581] **J YOULE & CO LTD**, brassfounders and miners' lamp mfrs, Rotherham, Yorks

Memorandum and articles of association 1912, register of members and share ledger 1912-86, misc share records (19 items) 1924-82, trading accounts and balance sheets (31 items) 1905, 1935-65, order books (2) 1896-8, 1906-13, wages books (6) 1915-52, premises records, etc (18 items) 1892-1939.
Rotherham Metropolitan Borough Archives (298/B). NRA 32671.

[582] **YSTALYFERA IRON CO**, Swansea, Glam

Deeds of settlement (2 items) 1838, 1842, directors' minutes (1 vol) 1838-59 and general meeting minutes (1 vol) 1839-54, corresp and papers 1839-95 of Rawson family as principal shareholders incl managing director's reports, accounts and balance sheets.
In private possession. Enquiries to West Yorkshire Archive Service, Leeds. NRA 9568.

MECHANICAL ENGINEERING

[583] **ABERDEEN TRAWL OWNERS & TRADERS ENGINEERING CO LTD**, ship repairers and marine engineers, Aberdeen

Directors' and general meeting minutes (2 vols) 1900-52, directors' minutes (1 vol) 1952-71, printed accounts 1905-52, general ledger 1901-48, cash book 1928-68.
Aberdeen University Library (MS 3248). NRA 30007.

[584] **DANIEL ADAMSON & CO LTD**, boilermakers, mechanical engineers and ironfounders, Newton and Dukinfield, Cheshire

Memorandum and articles of association 1937, 1964, directors' minutes 1916-21, share records 1914-70, company assets 1913, 1954, accounts and ledgers 1890-1963, corresp rel to turbine orders 1939-58 and papers rel to Indian business nd, production records 1958-62, patents 1853, 1878, drawings of boilers and steam turbines 1920-60, wages and other staff records 1920-63, conveyances and indentures 1865-1914, insurance valuations nd, catalogues nd.
Museum of Science and Industry in Manchester (EN 14/1-14). NRA 29507, 22050.

Letter books (5) 1853-89, 1897-1908, order book 1870-1, patent specifications (3 vols, etc) 1852-87, index to drawings (2 vols) 1851-1945, plans of furnace and ironworks (3 items) 1885, nd, catalogues (2 items) 1869, nd, press cuttings (3 vols, etc) 1866-93.
Greater Manchester RO. NRA 29656.

[585] **AILSA SHIPBUILDING CO LTD**, Troon, Ayrshire

Minute books (9) 1901-76, board papers 1957-65, registers (4) of members, directors, etc 1901-78, annual list and summary (2 vols) 1911-30, annual returns 1911-64, directors' reports, accounts and balance sheets 1923-61, private letter book 1902-11, corresp and memoranda c1939-71, private ledgers (7) 1887-1965, private journals (5) 1887-1959, cost book 1910-19, estimate books 1954-80, company diaries and data books 1887-1947, particulars book 1883-1910, engineers' record book 1910-82, agreements, specifications and guidance drawings nd, wood and spar book 1901-10, builders' certificates 1919-57, licence agreements 1951-61, ship plans 1887-1980, other technical records 1921-68, salaries books (10) 1909-65, Ayr and Troon plant valuation books (11) 1906-66, corresp and papers rel to premises and workmen's houses c1918-62, photographs nd; Barclay & Co (Kilmarnock) Ltd corporate records 1933-67, ledgers 1934-71, corresp and agreements 1896-1934.
Glasgow University Archives and Business Record Centre (GD 400). NRA 18721.

Ship plans 1887-1964.
Scottish Maritime Museum, Irvine.

[586] **AIMERS, McLEAN & CO LTD**, mechanical engineers and machinery mfrs, Galashiels, Selkirkshire

Memorandum and articles of association 1921, directors' minutes 1921-67, balance sheets and profit and loss accounts 1896-1972, letter book 1916-27, misc accounts 1929-67 and audit papers 1978-82, private ledgers (2) 1896-1938, nominal ledgers (2) 1919-61, cash books (11) 1932-82, sales ledgers (4) 1922-79, sales day books (2) 1901-64, sales books (36) 1879-1969, contract corresp 1920-79, sales analyses 1947-68, purchase day books (11) 1921-68, purchase books (20) 1895-1968, stock book 1933-48, prime cost books (2) 1878-1907, materials books (9) 1918-58, castings book 1950-70, registers of gear wheel contracts (2) 1885-1956, notebook rel to steam engine orders 1907-50, calculations book for mill shafting and gearing 1864-71, drawings of mills and dyeworks (765 items) 1845-1979, mills and dyeworks machinery (95 items) 1867-1964, water turbines (30 items) 1864-1916, nd, horizontal steam engines (161 items) 1877-1948, nd, vertical steam engines (38 items) 1872-1920, boiler installations (51 items) c1865-1970, machinery drives and shafting (35 items) 1867-1947, winches and cranes, etc (43 items) 1865-1947, public wash-houses and laundries (42 items) 1914-61, iron works and other property (34 items) 1875-1969, and other industrial premises, plant and machinery (c400 items) c1850-1980, specifications (2 vols, 10 items) 1868-1972, pattern catalogues (3 items) 1879, shop sketch books (4) 1904-23, patents incl some for other firms (15 items) 1884-1928, other technical corresp and papers 1891-1968, registers (12) of young persons and accidents 1868-1957, apprenticeship indentures 1932-52, weekly payrolls

1934-80, plant inventories and valuations (3 items) 1900-66, valuations of customers' woollen mills, etc (3 vols, 48 items) 1900-67, misc maps and plans (15 items) 1851-c1940, catalogues and publicity material, etc (1 vol, 40 items) 1890-c1930, nd, photographs mainly of products and works 1884-1970s, misc papers 1927-65.
Borders Region Archive (D/30). NRA 15224.

[587] **AITCHISON, BLAIR LTD**, marine engineers, Clydebank, Dunbarton

Copartnery contract 1904 and minute of dissolution 1909, minutes (2 vols) 1909-49, balance sheet 1908, papers rel to post-war recapitalisation (1 file) 1945, final accounts 1934-64 and monthly accounts 1946-69, private ledgers (6) 1905-57, journals (2) 1909-67, sales ledgers (2) 1919-50, sales and purchase records (25 vols) 1919-66, cost books (10) 1904-69, job books (3) nd and sheets 1913-61, engine costs breakdown (1 vol) 1950-1, notebook of proposed engines and ships 1906-13, notebook of air pumps manufactured nd, abstracts of weights of machinery 1926-65, engineering drawings 20th cent, specification nd, notebooks (2) with details of engines built nd, data books (2) of engineers and draughtsmen nd, notebooks (2) of A Blair junior mainly rel to boilers nd, wages records 1949-68, record of apprentices 1936-56, valuation books (3) 1904-54, legal papers rel to factory 1904.
Strathclyde Regional Archives (TD 550). NRA 18287.

[588] **ALBION MOTORS LTD**, commercial vehicle mfrs, Glasgow

Records incl partnership agreement 1900, minute books from 1902, register of seals from 1902, balance and stock sheets (1 file) 1900-1, sales record cards (1 bundle) 1900-5, job book 1903-5, cost books (4) 1902-22 and sheets (1 file) 1914-20, 1936-57, labour cost book 1902-17, salaries book 1915-17, plan and papers rel to premises 1899-c1900, annual historical notes, statistics and photographs (3 vols) from 1899.
Moat Park Heritage Centre, Biggar. NRA 10509.

[589] **J GORDON ALISON & CO LTD**, engineers, ironfounders and ship repairers, Birkenhead, Cheshire

Directors' minutes (1 vol) 1894-1927, cost books (3) 1883-4, 1906-7, 1909-10, dry-docking notebooks (4) 1915-55, engineering drawings c1870-1969.
National Museums and Galleries on Merseyside, Merseyside Maritime Museum (D/AL). NRA 23096.

[590] **WILLIAM ALLAN & CO LTD**, marine engine builders, Sunderland, co Durham

Directors' minutes 1894-1900, general meeting minutes 1888-94, register of shareholders nd, letter books 1888-1915, profit and loss accounts and balance sheets 1888-1900, liquidation papers 1900, accounts receipt book 1889-1909, contract books and agreements 1889-1929, employment record books 1888-1924, valuations 1888-1915, plans of

works nd, misc papers 1888-1924, photographs 1888-1912.
In private possession: see Ritchie.

[591] ALLEN-LIVERSIDGE LTD, acetylene gas apparatus mfrs, London

Corresp and papers rel to formation of the company 1910, minutes (2 vols) 1910-24, procedures book 1929, price lists, catalogues and photographs 1920s-1930s.
BOC Group plc. Enquiries to the Business Archives Council. NRA 26123.

[592] ALLEY & MACLELLAN LTD, engineers and shipbuilders, Glasgow and Worcester

Directors' minute books (5) 1903-72, general meeting minute books (2) 1903-60, salaries book 1916-24.
Glasgow University Archives and Business Record Centre (UGD/23). NRA 21581.

Directors' minute book 1955-66, executive committee minute book 1959-61, share ledger and register of members 1945-60, seal book 1903-66, sales ledger 1943-52, purchase ledger 1939-52, press cuttings book 1903-38.
Strathclyde Regional Archives (TD 500). NRA 16124.

[593] EDWIN AMIES & SON LTD, mfrs of paper making machinery, Maidstone, Kent

Memorandum and articles of association 1950, corresp 1915-83, sales ledgers and day books (13) 1881-8, 1897-1972 and misc accounting records (7 vols) 1928-74, order books (5) 1895-1902, 1932-55, nd, customer address book nd, machine parts book 1919-51, watermark plates books (9) nd, watermark rubbings (7 boxes, 1 vol, 14 bundles) 1878, nd, wages books (8) 1866-72, 1902-9, 1928-76.
Centre for Kentish Studies, Maidstone (U 2852).

[594] ANGULAR HOLE DRILLING & MANUFACTURING CO LTD, tool mfrs, Beeston, Notts

Memorandum and articles of association 1901, 1962, board and general meeting minutes (3 vols) 1894-1949, share registers (2) *c*1916-56, seal book 1962-85, annual reports 1932-6, 1946, day books, invoices, insurance policies and inspection certificates 1981-6.
Nottinghamshire Archives (DD 1596). NRA 34950.

[595] S APPLEYARD & CO, machine tool mfrs, Halifax

Sales day book 1898-1916, technical drawings (103) of machinery 1903-53, nd, production notebooks (2) nd, address book nd.
West Yorkshire Archive Service, Calderdale (AP). NRA 30592.

[596] ARMSTRONG SIDDELEY MOTORS LTD, motor car mfrs, Coventry

Memorandum and articles of association 1906-49, minute books (4) 1906-56, register of directors 1919-46, attendance books (2) 1919-35, notices of general meetings, etc (4 items) 1912, 1917-18, *c*1950, registers of members and other share records (9 vols, 18 bundles and items) 1906-50, general corresp (19 vols and files) 1945-58, seal registers (3) 1906-38, 1946-54, private ledgers (3) 1910-17, 1922-7, impersonal or nominal ledgers, etc (27 vols) 1912-59, 1965-72, transfer journals (3) 1945-59, analysis ledger of overheads and expenses 1955-7, balance sheets, accounts and other financial corresp and papers 1906-66, cash books (3) 1919-49, sales ledger 1953-5, stores ledger 1953-9, corresp rel to supply of engines, chassis and parts (4 files) 1910-11, staff and wages records (2 vols, 159 items) 1890, 1917-70, corresp and plans rel to premises (10 files, 9 items) 1948-56, legal agreements, deeds and related papers 1772-1962.
Coventry City RO (Accs 1060, 1128, 1150 and 1207). NRA 28350.

Car delivery record book 1928, car and chassis record book 1933-46.
Museum of British Road Transport, Coventry.

[597] SIR WG ARMSTRONG, WHITWORTH & CO LTD, shipbuilders, steel mfrs, engineers and armament mfrs, Newcastle upon Tyne

Records incl board and general meeting minutes 1882-1949, executive and other committee minutes 1912-64, board agendas 1882-1924, directors' and shareholders' attendance books 1883-1940, register of directors nd, share register nd, register of seals 1882-1947, annual reports 1883-1943, agreements 1880-1927, ledgers 1847-1947, journals 1882-1929, cash books 1847-1952, launching books 1920-4, salaries books 1897-1940, apprenticeship registers 1856-61, 1896-1928, accident registers 1907-32 and compensation reports 1912-33.
Tyne and Wear Archives Service: see Ritchie.

Records incl articles of association nd, board papers 1899-1912, annual reports and accounts 1900-12, 1915-27, London office notebook 1886-1934, papers rel to ships built at Elswick and Walker yards 1883-1920 and other misc production records; Elswick Works account book 1848-81, register of activities 1860-1911, order book 1847-54, ships' cost book 1897-1909, shipyard report books (2) 1883-1913.
Cambridge University Library (Vickers Archives). NRA 27797.

Lord Rendel's business corresp and papers (*c*8,943 items) 1863-1913.
Tyne and Wear Archives Service (Acc 31). NRA 31574.

Private ledgers (3) 1898-1928, journals (2) 1899-1929.
Sheffield Archives (MD 200). NRA 36163.

Ships' particulars books nd, naval architect's notebook 1911-30, launch data nd, steam trial data

1894-6, 1907-25, notes and plans rel to guns
1880-1960.
National Maritime Museum Manuscripts Section: see
Ritchie.

Ship plans 1853-1912 and photographs 1882-1902.
Tyne and Wear Museums Service: see Ritchie.

Records 1930-8, nd, incl order books, cost sheets,
components lists and specifications, drawing
registers and sketch books and photographs.
Glasgow University Archives and Business Record Centre
(GD 329): see Scottish Record Office *Annual Report*
1980, p25.

Scotswood Works plans (10) 1911-27, nd, Walker
yard berth and wharf charts (26) 19th-20th cent.
Tyne and Wear Archives Service (Accs 1990, 2171).
NRA 8919.

Machinery shop work book 1847-52, Elswick Works
plans (14) 1837-1969, photographs and printed
papers 1838-1979.
Tyne and Wear Archives Service (Acc 1975). NRA
31850.

[598] **SIR WILLIAM ARROL & CO LTD**,
engineers, bridge builders and crane mfrs, Glasgow

Register of directors 1921-4, share and dividend
records (13 vols) 1893-1951, annual accounts
(1 vol) 1900-12, ledgers (2) 1887-93, journal
1889-92, private journals (2) 1919-35, cash books
(14) 1879-1915, bill books (3) 1878-86, tenders and
estimates (53 bundles) 1891-1911, nd, other sales
and purchase records (4 vols) 1925-41, contract and
material cost books (15) 1892-1928, payments to
soldiers (1 vol) 1916-18, staff salaries books (7)
1921-44, accident book 1946-9, plan of Dalmarnock
Iron Works c1920, misc corresp and papers (15 files,
1 bundle) 1892-3, 1921-7, photographs and glass
plate negatives (3 albums, etc) 1884-1918, nd,
scrapbooks (2) 1881-1922; financial records, order
book, cost books, pay books, etc rel to Tower Bridge
(1 box, 14 vols, 6 bundles, etc) 1889-94; ledger
abstracts, contracts, cost books, specifications, etc
rel to Tay Bridge (1 box, 3 bundles) 1882-7;
accounts, contracts, engineer's files, corresp, etc rel
to Benue Bridge (22 files, 1 bundle, etc) 1926-33.
Strathclyde Regional Archives (TD 208, 1128). NRA
28632.

Calculations and drawings rel to Inchinnan airship
shed 1915-17.
National Monuments Record of Scotland. NRA
(Scotland) (survey 3029). NRA 20373.

Photographs of construction work and products 20th
cent.
In private possession. Enquiries to NRA (Scotland)
(survey 740). NRA 19459.

[599] **ATHERTON BROS LTD**, textile machinery
mfrs, Preston, Lancs

Articles of association 1896, 1898, letter books (51)
1900-30, ledgers (3) 1904-32, day books (2)
1893-1927, cash books (7) 1912-60, order and
counterfoil books (30) 1869-1930, contract books
(6) 1880-1939, invoice books (13) 1899-1931,

delivery books (3) 1872-9, 1896-7, 1910-14, job
books (5) 1879-98, railway day books (3)
1890-1904, loom order day book 1896-1900,
production day book 1913-28, plans and drawings
1897-1900, wages books (3) 1882-96, 1911-12,
1939-40, inventory and valuations 1894, 1900.
Lancashire RO (DDAt). NRA 21461.

[600] **AUDLEY ENGINEERING CO LTD**,
mechanical engineers, Newport, Salop

Letter book 1906-8.
Shropshire RO (SRO 3354). NRA 11563.

[601] **DAVID AULD & SONS LTD**, valve mfrs,
Glasgow

Minutes (1 vol) 1911-76, register of members, etc
1911-76, sketches and calculations for orders
(6 vols) 1879-88, pattern makers' order book
c1881-2, patent specifications (14) 1856-86,
sketches of patents (2 vols) c1864-72, notebook of
formulas with tables of production and materials
bought c1917, misc corresp, papers and photographs
(c20 files, envelopes, etc) rel to patents, contracts,
etc 1901-68.
David Auld Valves Ltd. Enquiries to NRA (Scotland)
(survey 3033). NRA 31882.

[602] **AUSTIN & PICKERSGILL LTD**,
shipbuilders and ship repairers, Sunderland, co
Durham

SP Austin & Son Ltd annual reports 1900-54,
register of directors 1901-48, ship plans 20th cent;
William Pickersgill & Sons Ltd partnership articles
1885, 1895, directors' meeting minutes 1925-54,
register of members and share ledger 1908-58,
summary of share capital 1926-38, seal book
1951-7, balance sheets 1885-1907, private ledger
1880-1901, private journal 1901-8, directors'
personal cash books 1880-1910, ship plans 20th
cent, wages book 1898-1916; Austin & Pickersgill
Ltd debenture interest register 1954-75, journal
1974-85.
Tyne and Wear Archives Service: see Ritchie.

Ship plans (Pickersgill) (23 items) c1880-96.
Durham County RO (D/AP/1-15). NRA 31633.

Ship plans 1919-50.
Tyne and Wear Museums Service.

Ship plans nd.
National Maritime Museum Manuscripts Section.

Drawings of ships' fittings (several hundred items)
nd.
Dundee District Archive and Record Centre. NRA
20370.

[603] **AVELING & PORTER LTD**, road roller
and agricultural machinery mfrs, Rochester, Kent

Records from 1857 incl articles of association 1919,
1928, 1950, trust deeds 1963, 1966, register of
directors (1 vol) 1900-32, directors' attendance book
1895-1946, cancelled mortgage debentures
(3 boxes) 1895, share transfer and other registers

(10) 1933-60, misc legal and share papers (74 items) 1857-c1910, suppliers' ledger 1860-2, customers' ledger 1894-7, other accounting, sales and purchase records from 1921, royalty books from c1870, order books (24) 1929-63, despatch books 1859-1920s, engine parts books 1899-1935, production and stock records from c1919, drawings registers c1860-c1940, drawings from c1890, register of employees (1 vol) 1890-1933, salaries, wages and other staff records from 1912, leases and agreements (21 items) 1863-1911 and schedule of deeds, etc to 1932.
Lincolnshire Archives (AB). NRA 18981.

Specifications, tenders, etc 1948-57.
Lincolnshire Archives (Misc Don 550). *Archivists' Report 28, 1982-3*, p14.

[604] **W & T AVERY LTD**, scale, weight, and weighing machine mfrs, Smethwick, Staffs

Secretary's department corresp and papers (2 vols, 11 parcels, 3 folders) c1900-61, annual reports and accounts (1 box file) 1907-58, other corporate records 1921-1950s, balance sheets, accounts and related papers, incl subsidiaries' (4 vols, 9 parcels, 6 folders) 1891-1947, private ledgers (30) 1890-1947, nominal ledgers (4) 1908-14, 1930-52, other ledgers (11) 1865-76, 1905-16, 1919-46, day book 1873-6, cash books (8) 1896-1946, other accounting records 1916-59, bought ledger 1905-20, sales ledgers (3) 1911-15, 1919-26, 1933-6, customer order and enquiries book 1896-1907, weighbridge order books (2) 1888-1901, 1912-14, automatic orders summary books (4) 1903-9, 1916-44, commission books (2) 1910-13, contracts (1 vol, 1 folder) 1853-1920, 1939-46, price book 1904-19, costings of fine balances (1 vol) 1910-12, private costs book 1914-17, machine numbers books (6) 1901-34, record of autolever scales made 1915-21, pig iron stocks and coke received (3 vols) 1937-44, patent records 1920s-1930s, staff records c1919-53, rent accounts (1 folder) 1901-9, premises and plant records (2 vols, 1 parcel) 1912-34, nd, deeds, agreements and legal papers (5 parcels, 4 bundles, 2 folders and loose items) c1787-c1947 and misc records (2 vols, 1 box, 4 folders) c1891-1955, nd.
Birmingham Central Library Archives Division (MS 1588). NRA 36399.

Records incl purchase and expense account book 1898, automatic orders summary book 1900, prices records (3 vols) 1875, c1880, 1897, record of machines passed (1 vol) 1889-92, railway department letter book 1892, inventory and valuation 1890, Avery family account books from c1851, press cuttings, publicity material and photographs.
Avery Historical Museum, Smethwick. Enquiries to the Curator. NRA 30129.

[605] **AVONSIDE ENGINE CO LTD**, locomotive builders, Bristol

Specifications 1895-1934, locomotive registers nd, weight diagram books c1915-1934, locomotive enquiry proposals c1900-1935, drawings 1885-1935, photographs 1893-1933.
Leeds Industrial Museum.

[606] **BABCOCK & WILCOX LTD**, boilermakers and electrical and mechanical engineers, London, Glasgow and Renfrew

Memorandum and articles of association 1891-1982, certificate of incorporation 1979, board minutes (42 vols) 1891-1985 and copies (18 vols) 1969-78, general meeting minutes from 1900 and attendance register 1891-1982, resolutions 1913-78, registers of directors (2) 1926-83 and attendance books (6) 1955-87, register of holdings in subsidiary and associated companies 1890s-1950s, register of directors' holdings 1950s-1960s, records of share prices (2 vols) 1911-55, other share records 1953-83, audited annual accounts (microfiches) 1933-88, annual returns, etc 1950-80, agreement with Singer Manufacturing Co 1881, agreements rel to licences 1891-1982, seal books (6) 1941-83, general corresp c1880-91, management meeting minutes (24 vols) 1930-83, other management and secretarial papers 1940-82, intimation notes and circulars 1900-84, other corporate records 1924-c1989, financial statements 1887-91, ledgers 1920s-1950s, other financial papers 1951-c1979, royalties ledger 1903-64, customer account ledgers (2) c1910-1920s, contract record books and notes (16 vols, etc) 1899-1966, order books for economisers (21) 1887-1938, stokers (5) 1897-1918, superheaters (5) 1899-1919, heaters (2) 1904-18, air heaters (1) 1925-58, cranes (4) 1905-36, marine boilers (1) 1892-5, ash handling plant (6) c1910-69 and purifiers (1) 1901-14, conveyor department order books (14) 1903-58, other order books (34) 1905-77, agency agreements 1886-1983, home and export diaries (92) 1904-41, Glasgow office sales records 1910-58, other sales records 1899-c1979, purchase ledger 1917-66, boiler stock book 1900-c1920, London contract job books from c1881, Glasgow and Renfrew job books (46) from 1881, jobs record books (7) 1900-6, indexes to job books (4) 1883-1903, stoker job books (25) 1899-1975, marine and boiler job book 1889-1925, misc job book c1915-18, job inspection records 19th cent-1977, monthly reports of jobs completed 1889-90, list of marine boilers 1889-1904 and list of Royal Navy vessels with Babcock boilers 1896-1966, boiler cost book 1909-18, statistical summaries of production and sales, etc 1908-71, patents 1873-1912, 1937-60, pattern book c1870, standard boiler drawings c1899-1904, drawing numbers books (12) c1890-1951, other technical records c1860-c1979, summary of wages books (2) 1897-1908 and wages book 1944-9, drum department piecework rate book 1905, pension and insurance records 1912-85, other staff records 1907-87, property records 1891-1983, photographs mainly of products, works and staff 1890s-1970s, product catalogues and price lists, etc c1890-c1979, press cuttings and releases (3 vols, 1 box file, etc) 1891-1987, visitors' books, etc 1941-83, papers rel to company history 1940-80; personal and business papers 1875-c1899 of Charles Knight incl his corresp with G Babcock and S Wilcox; technical papers (41 vols and index) 1867-c1969 rel to company history collected by Harold Morris; records 1933-85 of the Water Tube Boilermakers Association; records of US parent company and

home and foreign subsidiary and associate companies 1880s-*c*1989.
Glasgow University Archives and Business Record Centre (UGD/309). NRA 33916.

Diaries and letter books of pattern shop employee 1916-68.
Strathclyde Regional Archives (TD 646). *Accessions to repositories 1980*, p50.

[607] **WG BAGNALL LTD**, locomotive engineers, Stafford

Private ledger and annual balance sheets 1889-1924.
Staffordshire RO (D 4338/A/7). NRA 29538.

Workmen's day book 1915-25, photographs (12) of railway engines early 20th cent.
Staffordshire RO (D 709). NRA 3515.

[608] **BAGSHAWE & CO LTD**, ironfounders and mfrs of mechanical handling equipment and conveyors, Dunstable, Beds

Memorandum and articles of association, etc 1906-70, minutes (2 vols, 1 box) 1906-53, registers (3) of members, debenture holders and preference shareholders 1906-66, share certificates, transfers and related papers 1906-70, annual returns 1907-47, papers (16 files) rel to takeover by Thomas Tilling Ltd 1952-4, balance books (3) 1898-1932, balance sheets and accounts 1895-1968, private ledgers (5) 1906-67, other accounting records (20 vols, 1 box) 1939-68, order and invoice records (1 box, 1 cabinet) 1905-68, catalogues and other advertising literature of the firm and competitors 1891-1970, drawings, memoranda, calculations books and other production records (9 boxes) 1923-70, nd, wages and personnel records (10 boxes) 1907-70, plans and misc premises records 1901-72, photographs of premises, products, staff, etc *c*1906-1972, papers rel to history of firm (2 box files, etc).
Bedfordshire RO (BG). NRA 34778.

[609] **BAILEY, PEGG & CO LTD**, engineers and ironfounders, Brierley Hill, Staffs

Order forms, corresp and telegrams (11 bundles) 1857-8, 1863-4, 1872, 1893-4, 1900, order books (21) 1877-91, invoice books, invoices and delivery notes from suppliers (2 vols, 165 bundles, etc) 1887-1904, receipts for goods delivered (23 bundles) 1892, 1895, misc accounts, vouchers and counterfoils (5 vols, 2 bundles) 1872-95, stock books (8) 1864-7, 1877-87 and lists (1 bundle) 1886, yield books (3) 1861-7, 1880-1, production books (56) 1872-92, furnace books (2) 1864-73, records of iron supply and use (2 vols) 1866-77, time books (65) 1875-99 and sheets (1 bundle) 1884, sick club receipt books (8) 1867-78, registers of employees 1868-78, misc printed material 1867-1903.
Staffordshire RO (642). NRA 8749.

[610] **BAILLIE & SONS**, mechanical engineers, millwrights and iron and brass founders, Bessbrook, co Armagh

Certificate of registration 1917, misc corresp (1 bundle) 1913-60, nominal ledgers (6) 1903-24 and index 1916-21, personal ledgers (4) 1919-45, cash books (3) 1901-19, 1942-6, bank lodgement book and cashed cheques (1 vol, 1 bundle) 1953-6, order books (11) 1901-6, 1916-52, sales, despatch and invoice records (13 vols, 2 bundles, 11 items) 1910-53, stock book 1906-52, wages books (9) 1904-45, work and time books (17) 1921-53, misc records (2 vols, 2 bundles, 22 items) 1913-46, catalogues and other printed papers 1864-*c*1900, nd.
Public Record Office of Northern Ireland (D 3638). NRA 34976.

[611] **WILLIAM BAIRD & SON LTD**, steel roof and bridge builders, Glasgow

Memorandum and articles of association 1925, directors' and shareholders' minutes (1 vol) 1925-51, letter book 1907-14, general corresp (1 file) 1913-65, legal corresp and papers (1 bundle, 4 envelopes) 1909-24, ledger 1910-24, private journal 1910-24, order books (2) 1884-1980, enquiries, tenders and contracts (4 vols or bundles) 1910-13, cost and estimate book 1928-50, work schedules, etc (1 bundle) 1928-65, specifications 1927, nd, patents, etc (3 bundles, 1 item) 1881, 1910-12, plans rel to contracts 1910-72, employment and wages records 1910-75, plans of works and machinery 1917-73, photographs (3 albums, 3 bundles, etc) *c*1894-1971, reports and publicity material *c*1900-64.
Glasgow University Archives and Business Record Centre (UGD/138). NRA 25598.

[612] **JOHN BAKER & BESSEMER LTD**, railway wheel, tyre and axle mfrs, Rotherham, Yorks

Directors' minute book (Henry Bessemer & Co Ltd?) 1892-1912, register of members and other share records (8 vols) 1920-64, guard book 1922-9, balance sheets, ledgers, cash books and other accounting records (12 vols) 1929-69.
Rotherham Metropolitan Borough Archives and *British Steel Northern Regional Records Centre, Middlesbrough*. Enquiries to Rotherham Metropolitan Borough Archives. NRA 35678.

John Baker & Co Ltd draft balance sheets 1911-27, corresp with Ministry of Munitions and Inland Revenue nd and papers rel to takeover of Henry Bessemer & Co Ltd 1927-9; papers rel to taxation, nationalisation, etc 1938-53.
Rotherham Metropolitan Borough Archives (Hart, Moss & Copley Papers). NRA 19377.

[613] **BAMBOO CYCLE CO LTD**, cycle mfrs, Wolverhampton, Staffs

Memorandum and articles of association 1894, draft agreements, prospectuses, etc rel to formation of the company 1895, minutes (2 vols), directors' attendance book and papers rel to board and general meetings and liquidation of the company 1895-8,

letter books (4) 1895-7, corresp 1895-9, share records 1895-8 incl journal, allotment book and register of members, register of mortgages and charges 1897, ledger 1895-7, cash books (3) 1895-8, bank book 1896-8, balance sheets (2) 1896-7, estimates 1896-7, receipts 1896-8, trading profit and loss accounts 1895-7, Wolverhampton and London works weekly reports 1897-8, reports on machines and parts 1897-8, patents and specifications 1895-8, schedule of deeds 1898, press cuttings book and misc printed material.
Northamptonshire RO (1958/21). NRA 20202.

[614] ANDREW BARCLAY, SONS & CO LTD, locomotive builders and mechanical engineers, Kilmarnock, Ayrshire

Nominal ledgers (4) 1912-58, day books (19) 1875-1929, sales ledgers (8) 1886-1959, enquiries book 1937-61, contract lists 1858-1961, contract books (3) 1908-19, locomotive contract and repair records (61 files) 1939-66, misc order books (17) 1884-1926, despatch books (2) 1900-13, purchase ledgers (7) 1887-1959, stock books (2) 1892-1918, analysis of foundry charges and costs (1 envelope) 1898-1907, foundry cost books, etc (8 vols) 1920-5, misc cost records (21 vols, 1 envelope) 1911-59, quantities lists 1902-5, nd, smiths' forging books (16) 1876-86, 1893-1934, specification books for locomotives (56) 1878-1970, locomotive repairs (4) 1898-1948, engines, etc (25) 1885-1951 and pumps (5) 1901-47, drawing office requisition books (29) 1906-49 and misc records 1868-1923, memoranda and calculation books 1903-43 and log books (2) 1918-50 of drawing office employee, tracing list books (14) 1903-54, locomotive tracing index books (27) nd, locomotive and machinery requisition books (4) 1884-1900, sketch books for quotations (6) 1896-1937, outward sketch books (20) 1890-1936, misc sketch book 1908-9, locomotive sketch books (7) 1934-63 and sketches for shops (37 vols) 1910-44, locomotive drawings nd, records mainly rel to premises (8 bundles) 1900-21, advertisement books (5) 1912-61, photographs mainly of locomotives, engines and machinery *c*1877-1962, press cuttings, product catalogues and periodicals *c*1900-70.
Glasgow University Archives and Business Record Centre (GD 329, RHP 53894-55548). NRA 36388; and see Scottish Record Office *Annual Report 1980*, p25.

[615] BARCLAY, CURLE & CO LTD, shipbuilders and ship repairers, engineers and boilermakers, Glasgow

Partners', directors' and general meeting minutes (11 vols) 1860-79, 1884-1939, corresp rel to general meetings 1902-4, share records (3 files) 1901-6, 1909-12, balance sheets and accounts (18 vols, 1 bundle) 1886-1932, directors' financial corresp (1 file) 1933-7, summary capital accounts (Elderslie Dockyard) (2 vols) 1959-60, allocation journal 1962-3, cash books (4) 1947-62, accounts rendered book 1953-5, sales day book (Elderslie) 1958-61, ship data book 1845-1904, engine data books 1927-70, docking books (11) 1909-74, contract cost books (5) 1941-64, material transfer books

(Elderslie) (2) 1954-7, corresp and papers rel to agreements, contracts, estimates, staff, plant and machines, etc (*c*20 bundles) 1868-1967, ship and engine plans 1860-1975, labour transfer books (Elderslie and Clydeside repair works) (4) 1945-63, private wages books (3) 1871-1912, 1921-4, plant registers (Elderslie) (3) 1912-31.
Strathclyde Regional Archives (TD 232, 265, 269). NRA 19955; and see Ritchie.

Ship plans 1850-1939.
National Maritime Museum Manuscripts Section.

[616] BARFORD & PERKINS LTD, road roller and agricultural machinery mfrs, Peterborough, Northants

Records from 1911 incl articles of association 1911, minutes (2 vols) 1912-30, register of members, share ledger, etc (2 vols) 1912-29, nominal ledgers (2) 1911-23, private ledgers (2) 1911-34, record of engines supplied (1 vol) *c*1919-37 and stock lists (11) *c*1931.
Lincolnshire Archives (AB). NRA 18981.

See also Aveling & Porter Ltd.

[617] BARKER & CO (COACHBUILDERS) LTD, London

Balance books (2) 1797-1835, sales ledgers (22) 1799-1907, photographs (*c*50) of motor vehicles *c*1930-40.
Science Museum, Department 5. Enquiries to the Science Museum Library. NRA 28472.

[618] BARON & HOGARTH LTD, reed and heald mfrs, Kendal, Westmorland

Ledger 1938-62, day books (9) 1856-64, 1918-31, cash books (8) 1928-55, sales and purchase ledgers (3) 1920-8, order books (6) 1848-55, 1915-56, purchase analysis books (4) 1929-61, vouchers (4 bundles) 1953-70, remittance advice notes 1971, wages books (5) 1951-61, postage book 1961, address book nd.
Cumbria RO, Kendal (WDB/44). NRA 35280.

[619] BARR, THOMSON & CO LTD, mechanical engineers, Kilmarnock, Ayrshire

Minutes (1 vol) 1897-1905, ledger 1951-69, account book 1978-80, wages book 1897-1900, plant registers (2) 1899-1979, nd.
The Company. Enquiries to NRA (Scotland) (survey 2731). NRA 28975.

[620] BARRY, HENRY & COOK LTD, mechanical engineers, Aberdeen

Records 20th cent.
Aberdeen University Library (MS 3348). *Accessions to repositories 1990*, p1.

Records 19th-20th cent incl notes on investments *c*1890-1917, contracts (2 items) 1890-6, drawings 1898-1902, 1914-15, management efficiency report 1890, wages list 1896-7, apprenticeship indenture

1914, lists of products, prices and mill machinery
(3 items) 1901-10, photographs (4 albums)
1911-18.
Aberdeen Art Gallery and Museums. NRA 34749.

Plans of machinery (3 drawers) 1895-1900,
1929-45, catalogues of patterns 1899-1913, c1970.
Grampian Regional Archives. NRA 19078.

[621] **BARTRAM & SONS LTD,** shipbuilders and
ship repairers, Sunderland, co Durham

Letter books 1911-46, private letter book 1956-69,
ships' accounts 1943-66, journals 1865-75, 1936-68,
ship plans 19th-20th cent, salaries ledgers 1938-51.
Tyne and Wear Archives Service: see Ritchie.

[622] **JOHN C BEADLE LTD,** motor car body
builders and engineers, Dartford, Kent

Private ledgers (4) 1895-1914, purchase tax slips
1962-3, sales ledger and summaries 1945-7, bought
ledgers (2) 1942-6, expenditure ledger and sheets
1964-5, order book 1899-1905, corresp rel to weight
and price of vehicles 1920, delivery books 1964,
production estimates 1964-5 and job numbers nd,
plans, technical drawings and photographs (11) early
20th cent, 1960s-1970s, wages, tax and national
insurance records (5 vols) 1927, 1930, 1942-6,
1958-63, photographs and promotional material
early 20th cent-1954.
In private possession. Enquiries to Centre for Kentish
Studies, Maidstone. NRA 29612.

[623] **JOHN BEATSON,** ship repairers, London

Ledger 1831-54, journal 1835-58.
Southwark Local Studies Library: see *Guide to London
local history resources: Southwark,* p6.

[624] **BELLISS & MORCOM LTD,** engineers,
boilermakers and turbine mfrs, Birmingham

Records 19th-20th cent incl board minutes (2 vols,
1 folder) 1900, 1907-32, committee minutes
(22 vols) 1902-59, general meeting minutes (1 vol)
1899-1949, register of directors and managers
(1 vol) 1901-15, letters from JS White to GE Belliss
(1 folder) 1888, papers rel to Belliss *v* White
(1 folder) 1890, share certificates (1 vol) 1893,
prospectus 1899, corresp rel to dividends, etc
(1 folder) 1898-1916, registers of documents (1 vol)
from 1892 and documents sealed (2 vols) 1909-49,
balance sheets 1863-5, 1893, 1900, notes rel to
profits, costs, etc (1 folder) 1887, private ledger
1893-1900, list of orders awaiting completion 1892,
estimate of costs (1 folder) 1886-8, patents (1 box)
19th-20th cent, patents book from 1893,
assignments of patent rights and goodwill (6 folders)
1893-9, technical notes and calculations, etc (c8 vols
and folders) 1877-1908, nd, costs and valuations of
stock and buildings (1 folder) 1885-91, lists of
agreements, patents and apprenticeship indentures
1896, 1899, staff agreements (1 box and
c28 bundles) 1856-20th cent, assignment of
indentures of apprenticeship (1 folder) 1895, wages
and salaries records (3 vols, 2 folders) 1874-93,

1899-1913, 1927-41, benevolent and
superannuation fund minutes (2 vols) 1902-71,
notebook of FO Everard rel to personnel and pay
1909 and letters to him from GE Belliss and
A Morcom (1 folder) 1899-1905, papers rel to a
strike at the firm (3 folders) 1887, visitors' book
1901-32, deeds and other property records
1836-1946, photographs of products, works and
staff (33 vols) 1890-1953, reports, catalogues, press
cuttings and other printed papers 19th-20th cent,
histories of the firm and biographies of J Belliss and
A Morcom, GE Belliss's indenture of apprenticeship
1855, private letter book 1873-91, private cash book
1880 and personal account book 1884-94, personal
accounts of R Bach (1 vol) 1853-6 and A Morcom
(1 vol) 1884-94, and personal notebooks (3) of
A Jude 1901-39.
Birmingham Central Library Archives Division
(MS 1708). NRA 36181.

[625] **EH BENTALL & CO LTD,** ironfounders
and agricultural machinery and implement mfrs,
Heybridge, Essex

Articles of association 1909, 1946, minutes (1 vol)
1875-1901, ledgers (2) 1808-10, 1815-23, cash
book 1886-8, sales ledger 1895-1935, bought ledger
1925-30, export orders book 1923-34, costing books
(4) c1846-1907, prices book for other
manufacturers' products c1877-89, patent
specifications 1843-6, motor department journal
1906-16, motor tool book 1916-20, production
census 1947-54, salaries books (3) 1905-8, 1944-9,
memoranda books (2) of William Bentall 1807 and
EH Bentall c1836-63, catalogues, prospectuses and
other printed material c1800-c1939.
Essex RO, Chelmsford (D/F 1). NRA 9819.

Ledger 1810-14.
In private possession. A microfilm is in Essex RO (T/B
229/2).

[626] **FH BENTHAM LTD,** hackle, gill and wool
comb mfrs, Bradford, Yorks

Ledger incl profit and loss account 1887-94, journal
1879-85, bill book 1890-8, balance sheets and misc
accounting records (6 vols and bundles) 1891-1921,
order books (5) 1871-1910, 1920-33, sales ledger
1879-84, invoice books (3) 1891-7, stock and plant
inventories (5 vols) 1890-1902 and misc stock sheets
1903-44, advertising material 1875-1933; Bramham
& Henderson ledger 1880-2.
West Yorkshire Archive Service, Bradford (A2). NRA
29411.

[627] **BERGIUS CO LTD,** marine motor
engineers and engine mfrs, Glasgow

Minute book 1915-19, private ledgers (4) 1905-51,
journal 1915-24, drawings of engines, launches, etc
and catalogues from c1910, photographs of works,
offices, launches, etc (1 box, 2 albums) c1910-20,
nd.
Kelvin Diesels Ltd. Enquiries to NRA (Scotland)
(survey 1044). NRA 19047.

[628] **JAMES BERTRAM & SON LTD**, engineers and paper machinery mfrs, Leith, Midlothian

Articles of association 1908, minutes (1 vol) 1891-1958, share registers (5) 1891-1948, annual reports and balance sheets 1868-1963, accounting records (28 vols) 1935-66, order books (30) 1869-1963, price journals (90) 1920-62 and pricing books (5) 1950-63, other sales records (11 vols) 1945-68, specifications, operations manuals, etc 1932-71, list of paper machinery constructed 1847-1972, patents, etc 1894-1939, plans of machines and mills (c310 items) 1858-1971, nd, drawings and technical notes 1933-76, wages ledger 1945-61, time journals (19) 1947-62, sketch of foundry c1891, plant book 1933-44, catalogues and publicity material (3 files, 12 items) 1881-c1930, nd, photographs mainly of machinery (6 albums, etc) 1894, nd, misc corresp and papers 1897-1950.
Scottish Record Office (GD1/779, GD 284, RHP 50001-284, 69795-834). NRA 18883, 21901.

[629] **BERTRAMS LTD**, engineers, machine tool and paper machinery mfrs, Edinburgh

Share registers (8) c1888-1941, dividend books (2) 1910-29, annual reports 1957-79, balance sheets and profit and loss accounts 1939-66, secretary's letter books (4) 1888-92, ledgers (3) 1910-35, journal 1888-1900, order books (38) 1920-69, sales commission book 1920-81, production evaluation 1974, technical notebooks (4) c1880-97, 1946-65, drawings of papermaking and other machinery (377 items, microfilms) 1863-1970, drawings registers (24) 1891-1983, corresp and papers rel to patent agreements 1949-50, salaries books (3) 1889-1928, wages book 1938-40, valuations of machinery and works (3 items) 1886-c1918, plans of works and paper mills 1885-1964, photographs, product catalogues and publicity material, etc c1888-1971, nd, corresp and papers rel to company history c1860-1950, nd; James Milne & Son Ltd and Davis & Primrose Ltd drawings (149 items, microfilms) 1878-1932.
Scottish Record Office (GD 419, RHP 48902-8, 72624-73149). NRA 10971.

Minute books from 1888, account and balance sheet 1854-6, balance book 1894-1913, private letter book 1896-1902, day books from 1919, cash books (19) 1882-1952, bill books (2) 1868-1920, sales ledger 1919-35, purchase ledgers (3) 1898-1904, 1911-18, stock book 1915-18, cost ledger 1907-29 and paper machine cost books (8) 1920-9, job and contract books (c65) c1927-50, brass castings books (2) 1920-31, technical letter book of works manager 1905-6, wages books (46) 1890-4, 1899-1903, 1907-47, record of skilled work 1924-9 (1 item), improvements to works (1 vol) 1924-30.
In private possession. Enquiries to NRA (Scotland) (survey 322). NRA 10971.

[630] **JOHN BETTRIDGE & SON**, agricultural engineers and implement mfrs, Wellesbourne Hastings, Warwicks

Ledgers and account books (5) 1892-1954, journal 1928-38, wages book 1871-1908, printed volume of machinery designs c1870.
Warwickshire RO (CR 1358). NRA 26335.

[631] **BEYER, PEACOCK & CO LTD**, locomotive engineers, machine tool mfrs and steel founders, Manchester

Articles of association 1883, 1902, directors' minutes (23 vols) 1854-63, 1902-58, general meeting minutes (3 vols) 1927-59, chairman's agenda books (15) 1932-62, reports, accounts and financial statements 1935-64, tax returns 1867-1916, register of assets 1854-1908, agreement with J Gerrard & Sons Ltd 1919, general corresp and corresp diaries (7 vols, etc) 1901-57, account books (5) 1854-1901, cash books (6) 1854-61, 1870-1921, 1939-50, locomotive order books (123) 1854-1966, machine tool order books (12) nd, corresp rel to orders received 1854-61, tender book 1955, cost books (16 vols, etc) 1854-94, 1935-59, materials books (9) 1887-1914, 1920-62, machine tool specifications nd, general arrangement drawings for locomotives nd, valve diagrams (5 vols) 1886-1926, index to drawings (2 vols) nd, drawing office books (29) 1854-1965, draughtsmen's notebooks (16) 1893-1912, other technical records rel to boilers, engines and wheels nd, wages books (22) 1854-1928, inventory and valuation (2 vols) 1953, locomotive and engine price lists 1870s-1890s, misc trade catalogues nd, company's quarterly review, other printed material and unpublished company histories; day books (2) 1850-75 and corresp 1855-63 of C Beyer, notebook 1864-85 of R Peacock.
Museum of Science and Industry in Manchester (BP). NRA 32285.

[632] **SAMUEL BIRKETT & SONS (CLECKHEATON) LTD**, brass founders and valve mfrs, Cleckheaton, Yorks

Articles of partnership 1903, memorandum and articles of association 1912, share register 1906-7, register of members, etc 1912-18, balance sheets 1897-1914, ledgers, day books and cash books (31 vols) 1932-78, sales brochures 1930, 1952, valuation of Marsdens' engineering works 1926.
West Yorkshire Archive Service, Kirklees (B/SB). NRA 34065.

[633] **BIRMINGHAM RAILWAY CARRIAGE & WAGON CO LTD**, railway rolling stock builders, Smethwick, Staffs

Memorandum and articles of association 1907, directors' minute, agenda and attendance books (4) 1855-65, secretary's corresp (17 files) 1927-55, managing director's corresp (12 files) 1943-60, account of joint stock capital 1900-2, share records (62 vols and bundles) 1854-1960, seal books (4) 1910-34, ledgers (4) 1855-73, 1881-92 and indexes (4) nd, day books (6) 1932-58, journals (4) 1855-95, wagon rents and sales ledgers (11) 1937-52, cash books (4) 1935-55, misc financial records (16 boxes and vols) 1880-1961, invoice books (5) 1928-50 and memoranda (2 files) 1925-52, tender books (22) 1897-1946, order books (22) 1909-54, enquiry books (3) 1935-9, estimate books (6) 1883-1914, contract books (5) 1935-8, nd, agreements 1904-9, plant and material purchase

books (4) 1911-18, 1941-61, wagon hire records (6 vols) 1865-1908, nd, wagon description books (2) 1912-37 and weight book 1910-16, machine books (2) 1928-31, cost books (5) 1946, nd, despatch book 1953-6, repair book 1918-21, stock account books (4) 1920, 1941-4, 1950, stores record book 1934-40 and sales book 1944-5, other corresp and papers rel to orders and deliveries (17 files and bundles) 1928-58, customs papers (1 box) 1930s, house rents (6 files) 1924-51, misc staff records 1944-58, glass plate negatives and prints of rolling stock, etc (91 boxes).
Staffordshire RO (D 831, D 4663). NRA 21615.

[634] **BIRMINGHAM SMALL ARMS CO LTD**, rifle, cycle, tool and aircraft component mfrs, Birmingham

Memorandum and articles of association 1906, 1948, directors' and shareholders' meeting minutes (19 vols) 1879-1972, Small Heath works committee agenda book 1902-6, papers rel to directors' fees, salaries and terms of employment, etc 1951-75, secretary's printed circulars (2 vols) nd, general corresp and papers incl board papers, annual reports and accounts, chairmens' speeches and general meeting papers 1890-1978, nd, cycle steering lock royalty accounts 1896-9, legal agreements, licences, etc 1885-1972, corresp and papers rel to trade marks, inventions and patents 1882-1965, valuations of premises and other fixed assets, deeds, etc 1919-76, printed books, magazines, catalogues and pamphlets 1855-1982, photograph albums, scrap books, press cuttings and misc papers 1877-1977.
Solihull Central Library. NRA 29220.

Directors' meeting minutes (3 vols) 1876-87, 1901-6, 1917-20, Small Heath works committee minutes (2 vols) 1882-7, 1893-6, annual reports 1948-72, corresp and invoices 1897, railway and shipping ledgers 1926-9, cycles journal 1919-35 and cash book 1931-7, specifications, service charts, instruction manuals, spares lists, etc 1940s-1960s, wages books 1883-94 and salary records 1894-8, gun department wages book 1906-10 and salary records 1919-22, cycle department wages book 1906-10 and salary records 1907-11, plans, valuations and deeds or premises 1895-1972, public relations department corresp and press cuttings, scrapbooks, photographs of products and personnel, etc 1940s-1960s.
Birmingham Central Library Archives Division (MS 137). NRA 36662 (partial list).

Committee minutes and misc board and committee papers 1907-45, reports to board 1907-60, corresp (12 files) 1897-1943, nd, annual reports and chairmens' speeches (50 items) 1912-72, financial papers 1877-1938, misc legal agreements and administrative papers (30 bundles and items) 1873-1956, nd, departmental reports (22) c1906-20, technical papers (18 items) 1933-59, nd, salaries ledgers (2) 1889-1937 and misc staff records (1 file) 1903-61, papers rel to plant and premises (81 items) 1897, 1910-51, inventory of machine tools at Small Heath 1892-1905, printed books and papers 1913-73, nd.
Warwick University Modern Records Centre (MSS 19). NRA 17830.

Small Heath deeds 1895-1972.
Birmingham Central Library Archives Division (MS 1477). *Annual report 1989-90.*

[635] **BISHOP BROS**, engineers and ironfounders, Wellington, Somerset

Letter books (3) 1907-12, 1920-7, ledgers (5) 1878-87, 1900-26, day books (10) 1903-6, 1909-29, receipts and vouchers (3 vols) 1911-15, 1920, estimates and specifications (1 vol) 1919-20, time books (9) 1917-29.
Somerset Archive and Record Service (DD/SIAS). NRA 28391.

[636] **BLAIR, CAMPBELL & McLEAN LTD**, brewers' and distillers' engineers, Glasgow

Minutes (3 vols) 1905-34, private ledgers (2) 1858-1904, reports to Mirrlees Watson Co Ltd 1899-1900.
Glasgow University Archives and Business Record Centre (UGD 116). NRA 21020.

Cost books (5) 1931-46 and schedules, etc (8 boxes, 1 file) 1946-65.
Glasgow University Archives and Business Record Centre (UGD 118/6). NRA 14656.

[637] **R BLEZARD & SONS**, millwrights, Preston, Lancs

Account books (6) 1838-41, 1851-61, 1877-1911, day book 1851-4, notes of work done and estimates of repairs (1 vol) 1868-89.
Lancashire RO (DDX 142). NRA 16737.

[638] **BLIGH BROS**, coachbuilders, Canterbury, Kent

Bill book 1891-1902, order book 1894-1907.
Centre for Kentish Studies, Maidstone (U 2103). NRA 20944.

[639] **BLUEMEL BROS LTD**, cycle, motor and motor cycle accessories mfrs, Wolston, Warwicks

Articles of partnership 1891, memorandum and articles of association 1913, share prospectus 1913, directors' minutes (3 vols) 1913-48, annual reports 1913-59, agreements, deeds, etc (15 bundles and items) 1896-1941, trade catalogues 1902-c1950, press cuttings (2 vols) 1924-68; Dover Ltd memorandum and articles of association 1897, directors' minutes (1 vol) 1897-1914, press cuttings (6 vols) 1897-1960.
Untraced. Formerly with the Company: see Lane.

Overseas sales ledger 1914-67.
Coventry City RO: see *Accessions to repositories 1989*, p31.

[640] **ROBERT BOBY LTD**, agricultural implement, handling equipment, and malting and distillery machinery mfrs, Bury St Edmunds, Suffolk

Board minutes (6 vols) 1898-1962, general meeting minutes (1 vol) 1898-1956, annual accounts

1948-64, quarterly reports 1946-62, papers
(3 envelopes) rel to production 1939-45 and to
firm's history nd.
Cambridge University Library (Vickers Archives
220-83, 605, 717, 771, 1212-18, 1769-85). NRA
27797.

Order books (35) 1866-7, 1872-91, 1896-1909,
technical drawings 1927-45, plant and implement
valuations (1 vol) 1871-80, photographs early 20th
cent.
Suffolk RO, Bury St Edmunds (E5/2/6.1, HC537,
K770). NRA 5499.

[641] **BOMFORD & EVERSHED LTD**,
agricultural machinery mfrs, Salford Priors,
Warwicks

Memorandum and articles of association 1904-64,
board minutes (4 vols) 1904-69, general meeting
minutes (1 vol) 1904-71, directors' reports and
papers (6 files, 2 items) 1949-72, annual returns
(1 vol) 1929-48, share certificate book 1904-42,
dividend books (3) 1943-54, misc papers rel to
general meetings 1907-15, 1938-70, letter books (2)
1900-3, 1907-19, misc administrative corresp and
papers (2 files, 6 items) 1908-60, financial
statements 1910, 1936-74, private ledger 1940-56,
nominal ledgers (3) 1908-34, 1946-56, cash books
(3) 1935-49, auditors' and other financial records
1908-12, 1940-61, agreements and related papers
(c18 files) 1909-77, estimates books (3) 1903-40,
sales, purchase, order and contract records (c13 vols,
c60 files) 1935-77, requisition books (74) 1948-68,
patents, specifications and related papers
(c285 items) 1872, 1895-1967, plant and store
registers (4) 1919-39 and related papers
c1910-1972, production memoranda (4 vols)
1963-73, drawings (41 files, etc) c1890-1960, sketch
books (2) 1911-38, testing and design records
1944-69, staff records 1919-76, premises and estate
records c1905-1977, catalogues, advertisements, etc
1902-71, photographs (several hundred)
c1860-c1970, notes and papers rel to firm's history
c1860-1978; Bomford and Evershed family papers
1849-1977.
Rural History Centre, Reading University (TR BOM).
NRA 21009.

[642] **BOROUGH STEAM WHEEL WORKS**,
engineers, London

Minutes (2 vols) 1856-7, letter books (5) 1855-62,
corresp (c4 boxes) 1856-60, ledgers (15) c1854-63,
journals (5) 1854-62, day books (3) 1854-7, 1863,
cash books (11) 1854-63, bill books (2) 1855-8,
bank book nd, waste book 1856-8, order books (6)
1856-63, order slip books (16) 1857-63, invoice
books (2) nd, order and delivery notes (several files)
1859-60, nd, returns book 1858-63, goods receipts
and diaries (1 box) nd, stock book 1859-61, piece
work book 1857-63, wages books 1855-63, misc
books and papers 1846-59, nd, incl papers of
Saliomia Sterne, partner in the firm.
Public Record Office (J 90/1152-98). NRA 35175.

[643] **BOULTON, WATT & CO** (afterwards
JAMES WATT & CO), steam engine builders and
ironfounders, Smethwick, Staffs

Records of the firm (c550 vols, c70,000 items)
1757-1900 incl letter books (c160) 1775-1895,
original out-letters (18 vols) 1758-1898, letters from
partners, employees, regional agents, customers,
suppliers and others (many thousand items)
1770s-1870s incl the Murdock family 1779-1837,
John Rennie, George Rennie and Sir John Rennie
1784-1842, John Southern 1778-1815, John and
William Wilkinson 1770-1811, Thomas Wilson
1777-1810 and corresp between Matthew Boulton,
MR Boulton, James Watt and James Watt junior
c1775-c1830, balance books (2) 1779-89, ledgers
(17) 1777-8, 1795-1863, account books (c23)
1795-1850, 1868-72, journals (11) 1766-74,
1810-48, cash books (35) 1795-1863, bank book
1832-40, bill books (2) 1827-53, waste book 1757,
corresp and papers rel to business in Cornwall
(2 boxes) 1775-1805, abstract of sales 1821-6,
enquiries book 1879-88, order books (c50)
1790-1890, estimates (5 vols, c50 bundles)
1788-1877, agreements for engines (c240 items)
mainly 1777-99, delivery and carriage records
(c8 vols) 1819-28, 1835-46, 1876-9, 1886-93,
patents and related papers (1 box) 1769-84, corresp
and papers rel to Hornblower v Boulton (1 box)
1779-99, pattern books (8) 1762-1844 and indexes
(16 vols) 1803-83, drawings (c37,000 items)
18th-19th cent, drawing ledger 1882-94, calculation
and blotting books and other technical notebooks
1779-1867, misc papers rel to Cornish engines
(3 vols) 1779-94, engine books (23) 1797-1873,
boat engine books (17) 1821-53, 1868, engine day
books (10) 1792-1809, 1814-34, 1837-48, 1875-83,
boilers made at Soho (3 vols) 1806-52, castings
records (12 vols) 1802-56, 1874-94, foundry day
books (10) 1795-1839 and day book drawings
(2 vols) 1786-1841, 1864-75, foundry accounts
1795-7 and analysis of foundry accounts 1811-12,
fitting records (28 vols) 1796-1863, c1887, 1891-5,
corresp and papers rel to gas lighting (1 box) mainly
1785-1837, to British and foreign mints and mint
machinery (1 box) 1787-1843, and to French Walls
Steel Works (1 box) 1815-65, staff agreements, work
contracts, etc (1 box, 20 bundles, 46 items)
1778-1848, wages and piece work records (c23 vols)
1795-7, 1802, 1815-52, 1866-88, inventories
(15 vols) 1783-93, 1797-1800, 1805-40, 1879,
1897, building and machinery accounts (3 vols)
1802-52, rentals and rent ledgers (10) 1811-66,
photographs of works, machinery, etc (1 box) c1895,
c1900, and scrapbooks (2) 1777-1884.
Birmingham Central Library Archives Division
(Boulton & Watt Collection). NRA 14609.

Boulton family, business and estate corresp and
papers c1751-c1863 incl Boulton & Fothergill letter
books (9) 1757-81, ledgers (2) 1776-82, journals (3)
1776-83, day book 1779-81 and cash books (5)
1762-82; Soho Mint letter books (9) 1805-8,
1820-45, ledgers (9) 1791-1846, journals (5)
1791-1803, 1808-19, 1830-41, day books (10)
1791-1813, 1820-49, cash books (3) 1820-34,
1845-9, weight, delivery and consignment books (6)

1797-1809, time and wages books (8) 1798-1801, 1806-9, 1825-47, misc business records (c16 vols) 1792-1848, coinage patents (6) 1790-1807, and papers rel to British and foreign mints and coinage (20 boxes) nd; letter books of Matthew Boulton (12) 1766-73, 1780-99, 1808-9, MR Boulton (3) 1815-19, 1825-43, the Soho Works (3) 1827-30, 1833-40, the London agency (1) 1832-6 and rel to buttons (1) 1822-5; ledgers of Matthew and MR Boulton (10) 1775-1816, 1825-41, journals (3) 1774-1817, bill book 1804-5, cash books and cash accounts (c25 vols) 1768-1844 and Boulton, Watt & Co trade accounts (1 box) 1794-1840; papers rel to James Watt (1 box) 1778, directions for building steam engines (1 vol) nd, performance record of Cornish engines (2 vols) 1783-90, papers rel to steam engines and agents (2 boxes) 1819-39, nd, works technical records rel to boilers and valves (1 box) nd, rolling mill records (2 vols) 1805-18, building and machinery records (1 vol) 1798-1822, inventories (4) 1782-1841, nd, other records rel to Soho Works (1 box) nd, and papers rel to the Assay Office (2 boxes) nd, Cornish mines and copper smelting (2 boxes) nd, and the parliamentary enquiry into gas lighting (1 box) 1809; general corresp of Matthew and MR Boulton arranged alphabetically (48 boxes) c1753-c1842, and corresp with individuals incl John Fothergill (1 box) nd, Samuel Garbett (3 boxes) 1765-1806, Pascoe Grenfell (1 box) nd, James Keir (1 box) 1772-1810, John Rennie (1 box) nd, John Roebuck (1 box) nd, James Watt and James Watt junior (9 boxes) 1768-1848, John, Thomas and William Wilkinson (1 box) nd, Thomas Wilson (1 box) 1778-1812 and John Woodward (5 boxes) 1793-1810; notebooks of Matthew Boulton (96 vols) 1751-1804 and diaries mainly of Matthew and MR Boulton (2 boxes) 1766-1849.
Birmingham Central Library Archives Division (Matthew Boulton papers). NRA 9497.

Papers of James Watt comprising personal corresp (1 vol, c4,300 items) 1761-1819 incl letters from Joseph Black, Matthew Boulton, James Lind, John Roebuck, James Watt junior and Josiah Wedgwood, press copy letters (6 vols, 1 bundle, 2 folders) 1779-1819, journal notebooks (9) 1776-85, accounts (2 vols, 1 bundle, 20 items) 1757-64, 1773-5, 1786-7, 1806-17, notebook of experiments 1765-1814, commonplace book 1782-1812, business papers rel to scientific instrument making and civil engineering surveys (5 vols, 2 bundles, 220 items) c1755-1774, technical, business and legal papers rel to steam engines (19 vols, 14 bundles, 25 items) 1766-1809 incl papers and drawings concerning a fire engine for the Carron Co 1766, patents, patent specifications and drawings 1767-87 and papers in the cases of Boulton *v* Bull and Boulton and Watt *v* Hornblower and Maberly 1769-99, and misc papers (5 vols, 10 bundles and rolls, 75 items) c1765-1818 incl papers rel to patents and business matters c1800, steam engines 1802-3 and drawings 1812-18; papers of James Watt junior comprising personal corresp (1 bundle, 150 items) 1788-1839, press copy letters (2 vols, 5 bundles) 1794-1817, and misc papers (7 vols, 1 parcel, 16 bundles, rolls and files, c105 items) 1796-1848

incl a short history of the steam engine c1825, papers rel to steam navigation 1829, 1837 and a list of employees of the firm 1808-30; other Watt family papers 1729-1870.
Birmingham Central Library Archives Division (James Watt papers). NRA 22549.

Watt family, business and estate corresp and papers c1638-c1852 incl Boulton, Watt & Co articles of copartnership, agreements, etc 1779-1849 and balance sheets, accounts, and papers rel to sales and manufacture (c7 bundles) 1778-1820; James Watt's journal notebooks (10) 1768-74, 1786-7, 1795-1803, ledgers, cash books and other accounts (c23 vols) 1757-1808, notebooks of experiments (3) 1770-81, c1786-9, 1795-7, engine performance book 1774-81 and details of Cornish engines (18 items) 1775-1800; James Watt junior's business ledger 1794-1801 and notebooks (c24) rel to Soho Foundry engine orders, experiments, etc 1796-1835.
Birmingham Central Library Archives Division (Boulton & Watt Collection: Muirhead). NRA 14609.

Misc corresp, papers and press cuttings 1761-1923 incl letters and papers rel to a steam engine for a Spanish customer (50 items) 1790-4, Cornish engine book c1780-90, notes and calculations rel to engine parts (1 vol) 1780-3 and prices of engine parts, ironmongery, etc (1 vol) c1830.
Birmingham Central Library Archives Division (MSS 49, 59, 80, 82, 127, 131, 1381). NRA 14609.

Drawings, blueprints and tracings.
Birmingham Museum of Science and Industry.

Misc letters and papers (15 items) 1779-98, drawings (38 items) 1825-82, nd.
Sandwell Local Studies Centre (Accs 2460-2511, 3887). NRA 9198.

Particulars of costs of engines (2 items) 1800, 1802, drawings (21 items) 1795, nd.
Institution of Mechanical Engineers Library. NRA 9515.

Pattern book of silver and Sheffield plate for Matthew Boulton c1785.
Victoria & Albert Museum, Department of Designs, Prints and Drawings (E. 2060-1952).

Copies of letters from Boulton & Watt mainly to their Cornish agent Thomas Wilson (11 vols) 1780-1803, original letters to Wilson (80 items) 1800-3.
Cornwall RO (X208, X318). NRA 34747.

[644] ORIGINAL BOWER, millwright and textile machinery mfr, Lockwood, Yorks

Account books (7) 1854-90, jobbing book 1873-86, letters, invoices and receipts 1864-86, wages books (10) 1856-7, 1863-5, 1869-89.
West Yorkshire Archive Service, Kirklees (KC 127). NRA 28281.

[645] J & T BOYD LTD, textile machinery mfrs, Glasgow

Letter books (63) 1895-1956, corresp (over 70 files) 1914-45, ledgers (18) 1868-1961, journals (3)

1895-1900, 1930-45, charges account book 1870-92, order books (30) 1933-66, purchase books (22) 1918-59, specifications books (26) 1876-1959, packing books (5) 1894-1916, stock books (4) 1874-88, nd, cost books (18) 1905-6, 1917-18, 1933-54, nd, job numbers books (18) 1903-49, machine work day books (19) 1873-1949, foundry day books (7) 1889-1935, misc production records (13 vols) 1924-53, nd, pattern sketch books (3) nd, lists and registers of drawings and blueprints 1874-1945, memoranda books (6) *c*1872, 1888-1949, wages and salaries books (73) 1885-1969, misc price lists and other printed material.
Strathclyde Regional Archives (TD 226). NRA 20912.

Additional records 20th cent.
Strathclyde Regional Archives: see *Annual Report 1987*, p7.

[646] JOSEPH BRADDELL & SON LTD, gun makers, Belfast

Gun stock books (7) 1888-1957, guns and cartridges in storage (1 vol) 1920-7, work book 1907, time book 1903-6, brief MS history of firm 1811-1982.
The Company. Enquiries to the Public Record Office of Northern Ireland. NRA 34901.

[647] ISAAC BRAITHWAITE & SON ENGINEERS LTD (afterwards **IBIS ENGINEERS LTD**), laundry engineers and mill furnishers, London and Kendal, Westmorland

Directors' minutes 1909-63, report and accounts 1955-60, account book 1887, ledgers 1892, 1912-1970s, other financial records from 1927, sales registers and stock books (6 vols) 1904-*c*1964, other sales records 1921-62, purchase record and list of presses 1912-39, cost book 1888-94, engineer's balance sheets and accounts 1911-63, data from experiments 1887, patents, specifications and related papers 1884-1905, 1929-41, wages books (11) 1854-7, 1916-56, bonus scheme papers (3 files, etc) 1910-60, other staff records 1915-62, rent roll 1859-1930, inventory and valuation 1964, price lists from 1921, photographs of laundry machinery nd, misc corresp and papers from 1913.
Cumbria RO, Kendal (WDB/57). NRA 35282 (partial list); *Report of the County Archivist* May 1980 p5, Sept 1980 p10.

Articles of association 1888, 1909, directors' minutes 1964-5, annual reports and balance sheets 1889-1962, report rel to liquidation 1965, private ledgers (2) 1893-1938, letters to I Braithwaite 1908-9 and misc corresp 1930-56.
Cumbria RO, Kendal: see *Report of the County Archivist* May 1979 p8, March 1991 p12.

[648] BRAMLEY ENGINEERING CO LTD, stone-working machinery mfrs, Leeds

Purchase ledgers (2) 1899-1906, wages book 1945-61, plans and photographs (25) 1862-1963.
West Yorkshire Archive Service, Leeds (Acc 2509). NRA 26087.

[649] BRIGHAM & COWAN LTD, ship repairers, South Shields, co Durham

Directors' minute book 1901-36, general meeting minute book 1901-53, agenda book 1901-53, preference share register 1912-55, dividend book 1931-57, register of seals 1901-37, private ledger 1924-44, impersonal ledger nd, private cash book 1929-41, inventory 1912, mortgages, agreements and debentures 1901-41.
In private possession. Enquiries to Tyne and Wear Archives Service; and see Ritchie.

Foreman shipwright's work journal 1919-39.
Tyne and Wear Archives Service (Acc 1810/9). NRA 8919.

[650] BRISTOL AEROPLANE CO LTD, aircraft mfrs, Bristol

Minutes 1910-63, share records 1921-64 and other corporate records 1910-72, ledgers, journals, cash books and other accounting records 1910-70, sales analysis 1939, production and technical records nd, staff records 1919-20, 1957, photographs of engines, staff and premises nd.
Rolls-Royce plc, Bristol: see *Business in Avon and Somerset*.

[651] BRITISH PISTON RING CO LTD (afterwards **BRICO ENGINEERING LTD**), engine components mfrs, Coventry

Directors' minutes, ledgers, balance sheets, photographs and misc printed papers 20th cent.
The Company: see Lane.

[652] BROWN BROTHERS & CO LTD, hydraulic engineers and ironfounders, Edinburgh

Report and accounts (1 bundle) 1905, corresp rel to steering gear incl AB Brown's patent (2 bundles) 1896-7, 1900-5, notes and calculations on steam steering (1 bundle) nd, Brown family and misc papers *c*1890-1901.
Edinburgh City Archives (Acc 84). NRA 30720.

Product catalogues incl drawings (6 items) 1928-39, nd.
Scottish Record Office (GD 1/779/47-52). NRA 21901.

[653] DAVID BROWN, gear and pattern maker, Huddersfield, Yorks

Day book 1869-76.
West Yorkshire Archive Service, Kirklees (KC 313/2/6). NRA 13680.

[654] GEORGE BROWN & CO (MARINE) LTD, shipbuilders, Greenock, Renfrewshire

Partnership contract 1918, memorandum and articles of association 1936, corporate corresp and papers 1916-83, balance sheets 1903-4, 1957-78, ledgers (13) 1902-4, 1958-75, journals (1 box, 11 vols) 1900-15, 1958-70, cash books (11) 1958-70, balance books (4) 1916-40, estimate books (3)

1930-63, notebook of shipowners approached
1906-7, stock records (3 vols) 1904, 1939-68, cost
books (2) 1919-51, particulars books (2) 1901-14,
list of vessels built 1899-1983, plans and technical
papers rel to ships 1901-83, standard plans of
fittings on small ships (5 boxes) 1900-63, wages
books (6) 1904-63 and wages analysis 1969-73,
leases and plans 1900-67, valuations of plant,
machinery and premises 1900-58, glass negatives of
ships (2 boxes) 1904-12, misc corresp and papers
c1909-81.
Strathclyde Regional Archives (TD 865). NRA 36383.

[655] **JOHN BROWN & CO LTD** (formerly
JAMES & GEORGE THOMSON LTD),
shipbuilders and engineers, Clydebank, Dunbarton

Board and general meeting minutes, directors'
reports, balance sheets and valuations, etc 1896-9,
1906-68, board committee minutes (3 vols) 1910-52
and papers 1883-1968, agenda book 1924-59 and
reports 1930-1, 1961-2, directors' attendance books
(7) 1890-1955, debenture stock prospectus 1890,
directors' letter books (17) 1857-86, 1905-56,
secretary's letter books (36) 1929-64, official letter
books (3) 1909-17, 1951-2, other letter books (67)
1930-66, shipyard diaries (3 vols) 1871-1968,
registers of corresp (2) c1945-65, purchase
agreement with parent company 1899, papers rel to
company registration 1906-8, other administrative
records (185 files) 1903-69, financial statements
(5 vols) 1868-1914, misc account books (14)
1872-81, 1890-1965, accounts abstract books (14)
1946-62, working papers rel to annual accounts
1935-56, private ledgers (2) 1848-85, ledgers (17)
1847-1961, journals (12) 1847-54, 1879-1953,
private cash sheets 1888-1941, cash books (23)
1847-80, 1889-1959, records of fixed charges and
overheads 1897-1959 and general charges 1920-62,
other financial records (8 vols, 79 files) c1901-69,
debtors' books, ledgers and journals (22 vols)
1899-1963, debtors' claim books (10) 1904-64 and
payment books (13) 1906-63, estimate books (15)
1883-1967, papers rel to tenders and contracts, etc
(237 files) 1886, 1892-1968, tender books (13)
1888-1963, profit and loss contract registers (2)
c1899-1931, contract instalments c1919-57 and
rebates c1913-56, steel contract books (2) 1929-57,
iron and steel order books (46) nd, sundry order
books (10) 1923-63, quotations books (4) 1939-66,
enquiries rel to vessel construction 1907-13,
acceptance letter books (40) 1920-62, Admiralty
payments (6 vols) 1900-46, stock sheets 1930-62,
contract cost registers (5) 1899-1946, abstract cost
books (11) 1871-1945, progressive cost books (399)
1887-1966, wages cost books (20) 1896-1965, cost
books for engines and water turbines (17) 1928-61,
boilers (17) 1881-3, 1892-5, 1904-59 and hulls (12)
1912-61, finished cost books (34) c1898-1959, nd,
estimate and cost comparisons (246 vols) c1913-62,
misc cost records c1883, 1929-62, abstracts of
sectional weights nd, record of weights worked into
hulls 1889-1938, engines and boilers 1935-67 and
plant and machinery 1952-67, general calculation
books (12) c1877-1951, specification books (103)
1895, 1901-66, engine particulars books (99)
c1881-1945, particulars of ships (52) c1872-1970,

drawings of engines and ships 1852-1965, small boat
plans and standard tracings c1900-50, papers rel to
ships (435 files) 1890-1970, records rel to turbines
and generators 1903-61, misc technical papers
1887-1959, agreements with personnel 1877-1928,
income tax records 1907-21, 1940-53, pay books
(13) 1853-71, 1900-56, wages books, etc (44 vols)
1880-1900, 1945-61 and abstracts 1930-58, wages
analysis records 1910-57, records of wage rates
1889-1970, salaries books (9) 1880-1955, charges
book 1872-80, time books (12) and piece work
books (10) 1948, pay bill books (14) 1905-67,
record of workers employed on individual contracts
1914-71, other staff records 1903-61, corresp,
papers and plans rel to shipyard and plant (39 files)
1884-1967, plant and property registers (2)
1899-1946, corresp and papers rel to Clydebank
property (11 files) 1882-5, 1913-52, valuation books
for shipyards and engine and boiler works (24)
1884-1938, other papers rel to rating and valuation
(5 files) 1901-62, insurance records 1872-c1965,
photographs mainly of ships (218 vols) c1881-1972,
illustrated brochures 1907-c1970, launch invitations
1906-66, press cuttings (19 vols) 1880-1964,
periodicals and publications rel to ships 1893-1969,
papers rel to company history c1852-1970.
Glasgow University Archives and Business Record Centre
(UCS 1). NRA 14659; and see Ritchie.

Clydebank summary ledgers (2) and journal
1899-1937, photographs of ships 1890s-1940s.
Sheffield Archives. NRA 28631; BAC *Company
Archives* no 372.

Riveters' books (2) 1906-7.
Scottish Record Office (CS 96/4820-1). *Annual Report
1979*, p25.

Hydrodynamics records nd.
National Maritime Museum Manuscripts Section.

Plans of HMS *Australia* 1911-13.
Strathclyde Regional Archives (TD 232/140).

See also John Brown & Co Ltd, steel mfrs, Sheffield.

[656] **BROWNLIE & MURRAY LTD**, structural
engineers, steel roof and bridge builders, Glasgow

Certificate of incorporation 1918, consultative
committee minutes 1955, balance sheets and profit
and loss accounts (1 bundle) 1906-33, Henry
Murray's account book 1900-4, ledgers (3) 1936-64,
cash books (4) 1939-63, bank books (4) 1898-1901,
order books (24) 1901-71, estimates (10 vols, 3 files)
1899, 1910-59, sales day books (2) 1923-53,
corresp, quotations, specifications, drawings and
photographs rel to plant and machinery (26 bundles
and files) 1922-44, other sales records (15 vols)
c1931-66, order progress records 1921-53, other
production records (2 vols) 1953-7, design
calculations (15 vols) 1939-61, James Murray's
drawings notebooks (2) c1870-80, 1925, papers and
drawings rel to patent application by Henry Murray
1905-6, drawings of machinery and buildings
1899-1972, nd, other technical records (4 vols)
1931-63, wages books (4) 1912-18, 1951-64,
inventory and valuation of works (2 items) 1898,
1941, catalogues incl some of other firms (24 items)

1895-1951, photographs of buildings and staff
c1910-73, scrapbooks (2) 1880-1973, misc papers
1910-73.
Strathclyde Regional Archives (TD 575). NRA 22611.

[657] **BUCK & HICKMAN LTD**, machine and
hand tool mfrs, importers and distributors, London

Ledgers (6) 1889-1915, stocktaking files (13)
1938-56, lease and plan 1927, catalogues (6)
1889-1934.
The Company. Enquiries to the Chairman. NRA
19270.

[658] **SAMUEL BUCKLEY & CO LTD**, machine
tool mfrs, Ashton-under-Lyne, Lancs

Minutes (4 vols) 1892-7, 1908-73, register of
members and share ledger 1892-1973, share
certificates 1892-1948, annual returns 1913-44, cash
book 1879-85, trade account 1958-73, stocktaking
book 1876-89, catalogues of tools late 19th cent,
c1950.
Greater Manchester RO (B3). NRA 29688.

[659] **BURMAN & SONS LTD**, mfrs of sheep and
barbers' clippers, motor cycle gearboxes and steering
gear, Birmingham

Memorandum and articles of association 1897-1957,
papers rel to acquisition by Vono Industrial Products
(3 files, 1 bundle) 1951-7, private ledger 1875-1937,
client ledger 1896-1956, technical and patent papers
(4 files, 4 bundles, 2 items) 1931-52, salaries books
(2) 1945-54, deeds and sale particulars (4 bundles,
2 items) 1800-1965, history of firm (1 file) 1944.
Birmingham Central Library Archives Division
(MS 1728). NRA 36182.

[660] **BUTTERLEY CO LTD**, engineers,
ironfounders and colliery owners, Butterley, Derbys

Minutes 1878-1957, registers of shares, etc
1888-1936, letter books 1894-1927 and other
corporate records from 1887, ledgers, journals and
other accounting records 1796-1952, coal sales and
mineral rents 1793-1802, 1849-68, 1889-1928,
production records 1765, 1810-1959, plans
1835-1940, staff records c1804, 1830-1947,
premises and property records, patents and other
legal papers 1597-1944, catalogues, price lists and
other printed papers 1886-1967, nd.
Derbyshire RO (D356, D503): see BAC *Company
Archives* no 608.

Returns of land damaged by the company 1857-96
and measurements of coal worked 1880-91.
Derbyshire RO (N33/1). NRA 32965.

[661] **BUTTERS BROTHERS & CO LTD**, crane
builders, Glasgow

Board meeting papers (6 files) 1968-74, corresp and
reports (9 files) 1942, 1963-77, ledgers (5) 1912-61,
cash books (14) 1936-69, accounts (8 files)
1963-72, order books (30) 1898-1955, purchase and
sales ledgers (16) 1937-56, hire books (5) 1929-56,

cost books (17) 1915-45, job books (67) 1919-80,
job descriptions book 1909-46, print books (18)
1890-1979, specifications (28 files) 1921-53, repair
books (5) 1947-52, wages records (7 vols, etc)
1937-64, catalogues, photographs, etc 1922-69, nd.
Glasgow University Archives and Business Record Centre
(UGD 151). NRA 21018.

Memorandum and articles of association 1939,
1963, board minutes, reports and papers 1964-75,
annual reports and accounts 1964-70.
Sheffield Archives (TW 193-5). NRA 34879.

[662] **CALEDON SHIPBUILDING &
ENGINEERING CO LTD**, Dundee

Directors' minutes and balance sheets (5 vols)
1896-1948, hull and machinery specifications
1900-66, offset books (7) 1909-48, data books (10)
1907-44, engines trial data books nd, hull and
engine drawings 1876-1976, visitors' books 1941-80,
photographs c1900-75, publicity material and press
cuttings c1870-1974.
Dundee District Archive and Record Centre. NRA
21655; and see Ritchie.

[663] **CAMMELL LAIRD & CO LTD**, steel mfrs,
shipbuilders and railway carriage mfrs, Sheffield and
Birkenhead, Cheshire

Records c1810-1989 incl board minutes of Charles
Cammell & Co Ltd from c1864 and Cammell Laird
& Co Ltd from 1903, ledgers, accounts and related
papers from c1810, contracts and estimates from
1833, design, estimating and planning department
records from c1880, specifications books, trial trip
reports and vessel particulars and dimensions from
c1850, patents and tenders, etc c1911-35, boiler
report books, records of propeller and hull design
and testing, etc 19th-20th cent, ship plans, engine
drawings, etc from c1840, plant and machinery
records from c1860, photographs 19th-20th cent
and press cuttings books from 1902.
Wirral Archives Service (ZCL). NRA 26265 (partial
list); *Accessions to repositories 1991*, p39.

Letters, agreements, contract pads, patent files,
engine plans, machinery specifications and deeds
1822-1984.
*National Museums and Galleries on Merseyside,
Merseyside Maritime Museum*.

Ledger of construction costs 1860-4, repairs order
book 1856-1911, ledgers (2) of ships' fittings
c1899-1915, vessel particulars and dimensions
1855-1910, offset book 1914-36, dimensions book
1878-92, data books (4) 1856-1964, book of
elements 1837-96, misc engine plans and drawings
1884-1949, details of launching ceremonies
1927-67, trial trip reports (1 vol) 1910-15, press
cuttings books (21) 1902-81.
Williamson Art Gallery and Museum, Birkenhead.
NRA 30901.

Records incl misc legal, share and financial papers
nd, salaries journals (2) 1880-1906, staff and
executive lists (3 vols) late 19th-early 20th cent,
registers (2) of deeds and agreements to 1915 and
Dronfield deeds (2 boxes).
Sheffield Archives (MD 200). NRA 36163.

[664] **CAMPBELTOWN SHIPBUILDING CO LTD**, Campbeltown, Argyll

Register of ships launched 1878-80, letter books (9) 1878-1920, tender books (2) 1907-13.
In private possession. Enquiries to NRA (Scotland) (survey 1370). NRA 19995.

Lists and details of vessels built 1878-1921, plans and drawings of the yacht *Glenesta* 1901, plans of buildings nd, photographs *c*1896-1913.
Argyll and Bute District Archives (DR 4/10). NRA 27756.

Data book of vessels built 1900-11, list of vessels built nd.
Argyll and Bute District Archives (DR 1/106/27-8). NRA 25012.

[665] **DAVID CARLAW & SONS LTD**, envelope machinery mfrs, motor and mechanical engineers, Glasgow

Ledgers, day books and cash books (22 vols) 1930-70, envelope machine order book 1961, customers' accounts 1944-7, cost books (5) 1934-56, specifications 1926, drawing office registers (6) 1917-76, pattern books (2) 1920-9, plans and drawings 1889-1946, sketches (26) of slitting machines 1931-2, wages books (9) 1925-53, personnel record cards 1947-8, works estimates and measurements 1897, photographs of engines, machinery, premises and the Carlaw family 1888-1951, catalogues (1 file) nd, desk diaries (11) of JS Carlaw 1955-65, printed history of company 1960, misc papers (1 vol, etc) 1888-1948.
David Carlaw Engineering (Glasgow) Ltd. Enquiries to NRA (Scotland) (survey 1924). NRA 18742.

Order books (65) 1936-61 and index (1 vol) 1948-53, other sales records (2 vols) 1936-67, cost books (2) 1934-8.
Strathclyde Regional Archives (TD 935). NRA 33978.

[666] **JAMES CARR & SONS**, gunsmiths, Birmingham

Ledger 1891-1910, sales day book 1894-7.
Birmingham Central Library Archives Division (MS 88). NRA 29847.

[667] **JH CARRUTHERS & CO LTD**, pump and crane mfrs, Glasgow

General memoranda book 1897-1922, policy records incl employers' association papers (1 bundle) 1911-12, commercial agreements (2 bundles) 1897-1947, private letter books (3) 1916-43, corresp (1 bundle) 1929-35, profit and loss account 1915, ledgers (2) and journal 1886-1919, misc accounts 1906-18, bill book 1898-1922, invoices (2 files) 1972-6, contracts (2 bundles) 1904-50, order books (160) 1886-1975, order notebooks (5) 1889-1957, centrifugal pump orders (2 files) 1957-64, commission book 1910-28, agency price list *c*1919-24, production census returns (1 bundle) 1908-37, stock records 1933-56, materials lists and books (48 vols and items) *c*1898-1945, materials cost books (7) 1913-25, filter books (6) 1897-1961,

pump registers (2) 1891-1912, 1949-59 and test records (46 vols, 28 files, etc) 1890-1970, patents, etc (3 bundles, 1 item) 1897-1950, technical notebooks (10) 1907-78, technical subject files (47) and papers (6 items) 1898-1980, shop on-cost wages books 1912-41, other wages and pay books (26) 1926-54, staff list 1886-1953, machinery valuation book 1889-1953, inventory and valuation of Polmadie Works 1921, photographs, brochures and other printed papers 1901-87, nd.
Glasgow University Archives and Business Record Centre (UGD 333). NRA 35796.

[668] **ALEX CHAPLIN & CO LTD**, engineers and crane mfrs, Glasgow

Letter books (2) 1878-93, 1913, register of engines made and sold 1857-1917, cranes order book 1906-7, capstan and sundry order books (2) 1903-16, gear book 1922, job files (5 boxes) *c*1920-7, lists of jobs carried out (2 files) 1895-1931, rough calculations and estimates (1 vol) 1919-30, crane test log books (2) 1924-32, drawing office letter books (13) 1910-29, sketches and drawings of cranes (12 vols) 1893-1930 and parts (2 bundles) 1912-28.
Leicestershire RO (28D69/92-105). NRA 23956.

[669] **J CHIDGEY & SON**, millwrights, Watchet, Somerset

Day book 1865-75, estimates book 1887-1913.
Somerset Archive and Record Service: see *Proceedings of the Somerset Archaeological and Natural History Society*, vol 121, 1977, p140.

[670] **GEORGE CLARK LTD**, marine engine builders, Sunderland, co Durham

Private cash books (2) 1895-1910, index to contracts (1 vol) 1883-1907, corresp rel to boiler patent 1934-6, engine plans *c*1880-20th cent, misc plans *c*1894-1927, photographs 1887-1960.
Tyne and Wear Archives Service (Acc 1993). NRA 30899; and see Ritchie.

[671] **CLARKE, CHAPMAN & CO LTD**, mechanical engineers, Gateshead, co Durham

Records 19th-20th cent incl memorandum and articles of association 1893, 1946, board and general meeting minutes 1893-1948, share records 1893, balance sheets 1893-1967, seal book 1918-21, letter books and corresp 1889-1913, ledgers and cash books 1892-1947 and other financial records *c*1890-1969, order book nd, cost accounts 1953-69, patent register 1901-55, sketch books nd, time and motion analyses 1928-31, indexes of employees 1894-1951, accident books 1907-29, compensation register 1907-48, trust deeds 1971-7, and photographs 19th-20th cent.
Tyne and Wear Archives Service (Accs 2505, 2786, 2803).

[672] **CLARKE, CLULEY & CO LTD**, cycle mfrs and engineers, Coventry

Draft articles of partnership, etc 1900, memorandum and articles of association 1925, 1955, private ledgers (6) 1903-65, cash books (14) 1913-71, petty cash books (9) 1938-85 and vouchers 1947-8, accounts, draft accounts and balance sheets 1931-73, bank books (7) 1899, 1907-10, 1917-37, 1952-65, cheques out register 1950-3, bank statements 1928-9, 1937-8, 1942-3, nominal ledger sheets 1965-82, invoice books (3) 1931-41, order book 1927-40, orders, quotations and specifications (145 items) 1974-84, parts order books (13) 1920-41, sales ledgers and day book and sold ledgers (33 vols, 1 bundle and loose sheets) 1904-73, sales summaries 1917-65, purchase journals, ledgers, day book and sheets (41 vols, 6 items) 1922-74, bought ledgers 1904-33, goods received books (5) 1933-43, material control charts (3 items) 1966-8, stock lists 1934-7, censuses of production, etc (23 items) 1924-5, 1944-63, deeds of apprenticeship and personnel records 1965-79, wages ledgers, salaries account books and sheets, payroll analyses, tax receipts and other financial papers 1908-20, 1927-83, premises records 1913-63, farm account book 1948-53, legal corresp and papers 1903-79 incl some rel to patents, cycle sale catalogues (3) 1902-5 and misc papers 1934-53; financial and legal papers of the Cluley family 1929-65.
Coventry City RO (Acc 1233). NRA 31555.

[673] **TAW CLARKE LTD**, engineers and founders, Leicester

Letter books (2) 1901-5, letters received (2 files) 1905-6, 1947-9, ledgers and other accounts (7 vols) 1865-9, 1875-96, 1900-30, invoice books (2) 1901-5, job books (2) 1862-80, 1903-8, papers and plans (4 files) rel to patents and designs 1880-1927, engineering notebook 1895-9, wages books (3) 1885-1910, foundry time sheets 1901-2, papers (2 vols, 2 files) rel to income tax, premises, etc 1873-1907.
Leicestershire RO (17 D 61). NRA 21694.

[674] **CLAYTON & SHUTTLEWORTH LTD**, agricultural engineers, Lincoln

Registers (15 vols) of steam engines, threshing machines, etc *c*1840-1938, building books (28) 1881-1931, sales register 1877-1928, parts register *c*1900-30, report on reorganisation of Stamp End Works 1919.
Rural History Centre, Reading University. NRA 21007.

Agency agreements (2 vols) 1894-1931.
Lincolnshire Archives (Marshall 13-14). NRA 35742.

Large collection of industrial drawings.
In private possession: see Lincolnshire Archives Committee *Archivists' Report 16, 1964-5*, p44. Enquiries to Mr R Hooley, Technical Librarian, CGT, Waterside South, Lincoln.

[675] **CLAYTON, SON & CO LTD**, boiler and gasometer mfrs, Leeds

Records late 19th-20th cent (290 vols, 16 boxes, 20 parcels) incl general ledgers from 1873, impersonal ledgers 1913-62, cash books 1884-92 and from 1939, general sales books from 1910, gasholder sales books from 1908, purchase analysis books from 1924, purchase journals from 1949, order books from 1922, contracts books from 1903, goods inwards books from 1948 and wages books from 1880.
West Yorkshire Archive Service, Leeds. NRA 21365.

Further records incl order books 1876-1917 and sketch books 1876-1945, plans of boilers and gasholders nd and staff records, photographs, etc.
The Company. Enquiries to West Yorkshire Archive Service, Leeds. NRA 21365.

[676] **CLEVELAND BRIDGE & ENGINEERING CO LTD**, bridge builders and general engineers, Darlington, co Durham

Directors' minutes (8 vols) 1893-1920, 1948-77, shareholders' minutes (4 vols) 1899-1969, statutory register 1893-1910.
British Steel East Midlands Regional Records Centre, Irthlingborough. NRA 35550.

Orders and unsuccessful tenders (354 items) 1900-51.
Durham County RO (D/CB). NRA 35676.

[677] **CLIFTON & BAIRD LTD**, machine tool mfrs, Johnstone, Renfrewshire

Letter book 1945, contract books for machines built (21 vols) 1908-71 and for repairs (22 vols) 1931-71, job books (18) for subcontracted work 1918-71, quotation and specification books (63) 1921-66, technical drawings and photographs from 1908.
The Company. Enquiries to NRA (Scotland) (survey 760). NRA 17525.

[678] **CLIMAX ROCK DRILL & ENGINEERING WORKS LTD**, Redruth, Cornwall

Minutes (2 vols) 1913-36, order books (4) 1874-1903, 1907-9, wages book 1875-8, inventory and valuation of works 1949.
Cornwall RO (X 542). NRA 5235.

[679] **VICTOR COATES & CO LTD**, engineers and boilermakers, Belfast

Order books 1893-9.
In private possession. Microfilm in the Public Record Office of Northern Ireland (Mic 163): see *Deputy Keeper's Report 1960-5*, p131.

[680] **COCHRAN & CO (ANNAN) LTD**, engineers, shipbuilders and boilermakers, Annan, Dumfriesshire, and Birkenhead, Cheshire

Articles of association 1937, 1968, board and general meeting minutes (11 vols) 1898-1966,

accounts and balance sheets 1897-1968, cost and
profit book 1901-4, auditors' notebooks (2) 1901,
1919-20, agreements (2 bundles, 1 envelope)
1931-65, letter books (7) 1900-23, papers rel to
merger (1 file) 1969-70, private ledgers (3)
1899-1911, 1948-59, ledgers (4) 1883-94,
1899-1908, private journal 1898-1908, sales and
purchase ledgers (2) 1898-1908, materials ordered
records (4 vols) 1899-1918, registers of machinery
owners (3) c1920, nd, costs for orders 1878-9,
registers of boilers (3 vols, 1 envelope) 1880-3,
1907-78, boiler test certificates (1 vol) 1899-1912,
trial reports 1937 and drawings (microfilm)
1899-1980, works industrial council minutes
1918-69, staff records (13 vols) 1955-71, corresp
and papers rel to property (2 bundles, 9 envelopes,
etc) 1895-1971, leaflets and catalogues (2 drawers)
1906-64, photographs and slides of products, works
and staff c1885-1969, nd, visitors' book 1938-61,
misc corresp and papers (1 envelope, etc)
1899-1930, press cuttings (1 vol) 1968-9.
NEI International Combustion Ltd. Enquiries to NRA
(Scotland) (survey 2336). NRA 24816.

Drawings and specifications of steamships
(microfilm) 1898-1901.
National Library of Scotland (Acc 7366). *Annual
Report 1978-9*, p65.

[681] **JOHN COCHRANE & CO LTD**,
ironfounders, boilermakers and pump mfrs,
Barrhead, Renfrewshire

Letter books (3) 1905-12 and corresp (10 files)
1921-7, quotation book 1897-1900, order book
1918-27, foundry costs summary 1920-1,
photographs mainly of engines and other products
manufactured (1 box, 1 album, 9 envelopes)
c1910-50, publicity material 1884-1925, nd.
Glasgow University Archives and Business Record Centre
(GD 329/10). NRA 36388.

[682] **COCHRANE SHIPBUILDERS LTD**,
Selby, Yorks

Articles of association 1951, board and general
meeting minutes 1912-62, register of directors'
holdings and interests 1948-60, share records
1915-51, annual returns 1917-67, company tax
corresp 1937-60, financial statements and balance
sheets 1898-1961, bill book 1905-59, other
accounting records 1914-69, purchase and sales
records 1932-75, contracts books 1901-52,
comparative statement book 1924-56, prime cost
books c1904-70, calculations books c1915-60,
weights and quantities estimate book 1912-68,
specifications and tracings c1955-70, particulars
books 1891-c1965, naval architects' data books
1898-1955, tonnage and dimensions books
c1915-42, loft offset books 1914-60, sketch books
nd, wage rate books 1914-59, demarcation
agreements and corresp 1932, establishment charges
books 1909-61, inventory and valuations 1921-52,
photograph albums nd, press cuttings c1927-65.
The Company: see Ritchie.

Lines plans 1884-1937, 1950-5.
National Maritime Museum Manuscripts Section.

[683] **JOSEPH COCKSHOOT & CO LTD**,
coach and motor body builders and automobile
engineers, Manchester

Articles of partnership 1873, 1878, memorandum
and articles of association 1959, share registers (3)
1895-1959 and share certificate counterfoils
1895-1959, balance sheets 1883, 1904, 1907-14,
1968 and statements of account 1915-67, directors'
reports 1898-1968, record of carriages sold 1877-86,
records of sales 1934-59, agency agreements
1919-49, index to customers nd, production
notebooks (4) 1884-93, 1904-39, corresp and
papers rel to production 1914-18, 1939-65, list of
work done for Rolls Royce nd, patents (3 items)
1867, sketch books (2) c1900-8, carriage and car
body specifications and drawings late 19th-early 20th
cent, nd, apprenticeship indentures (2 items) 1850,
1875, wages and salaries books (10) 1911-61, papers
rel to employee welfare and social club, etc
1882-1961, illustration of carriage works c1865 and
papers mainly rel to premises 1905-70, nd, product
catalogues, etc (4 items) 1905-c1953, photographs
of products, premises and employees (7 vols, etc)
c1880-1968, nd, corresp and papers mainly rel to
company history and relations with Rolls Royce
1894-1979; papers rel to trades unions and trade
associations (5 items) 1914-28, nd.
Museum of Science and Industry in Manchester (TR1).
NRA 32235.

[684] **J COLLINS & CO**, coachbuilders, Oxford

Day book 1858-64; day book of JJ Coles,
coachbuilder, 1819-32.
Bodleian Library, Oxford (MSS Eng.misc.c. 258-9).

[685] **JOSEPH COLLIS LTD**, mechanical
engineers, ironfounders and ironmongers, Strood,
Kent

Records mainly post-1914 but incl accounts from
mid 19th cent and deeds from 1752.
Rochester upon Medway Studies Centre (DE 113,
DE 122).

[686] **CHARLES CONACHER & SON**,
coachbuilders, Blairgowrie, Perthshire

Register of hours worked 1860-1914 incl accounts
1864-6, job descriptions and specifications.
Dundee District Archive and Record Centre
(GD/Mus 58). NRA 20370.

[687] **CHARLES CONNELL & CO LTD**,
shipbuilders, Glasgow

Memorandum and articles of association 1958,
directors' minutes 1958-71, production meeting
minutes 1966-7, private letter books 1867-1953,
J Baird Smith letter books (6) 1889-1915, Charles
Connell's private letter book 1898-1908, other letter
books (256) 1880-1968, general corresp 1942-68,
ledgers (9) 1865-1925, day books (8) 1886-1957,
journals (9) 1877-1950, cash books (2) 1867-85,
balance books (11) 1881-1937, account books (3)
1869-1920, accepted offer letter books (62)

1877-1968, tenders accepted 1960-8, abstract of
ships' cost accounts 1880-9, ship account books (79)
1885-1959, stock books (3) 1938-54, engineers'
letter books (35) 1899-1958, drawing office letter
books (62) 1915-66, materials orders, specifications
(3 vols) and corresp rel to ships nd, hull drawings
1924-60, pay books (155) 1885-1966, registers of
apprentices (5) 1895-1937, property account books
1895-1958, photographs 1943-53.
Strathclyde Regional Archives (T-CO and UCS
2/140/1-2). NRA 16063.

[688] **COOCH & SONS LTD**, agricultural
engineers and wagon builders, Northampton and
Harlestone, Northants

Articles of partnership 1906, financial statements
1917-26, nominal, bought and general ledgers (7)
1891-1912, 1937-50, 1961-9, account books (3)
1847-73, 1929-38, 1959-63, cash books (22) 1846,
1865-92, 1915-66, letter books (4) 1902-8,
1913-16, 1919-24, sales registers, etc (13 vols)
1800-1949, ledgers (13) 1874-1956, day books (54)
1869-77, 1890-1955 and journals (2) 1945-58,
purchase day books (2) 1891-1910, 1945-7,
testimonials (119 items) 1850-1929, notebooks (7)
of Henry Cooch 1875-6, 1881-2, 1884-90, materials
book 1927-50, particulars book 1891-1923, patents
(4) 1800, 1911-14, wages books (5) 1871-5,
1900-26, 1942-52, factory registers and related
papers (4 vols, 3 items) 1902-45, misc property
papers (1 bundle, 1 item) 1891, 1902, advertising
leaflets, price lists and other printed papers
1841-1971.
Rural History Centre, Reading University (TR COO).
NRA 21206.

[689] **CORNWALL BOILER CO LTD**,
boilermakers, Camborne, Cornwall

Private ledger and journal 1895-9.
Cornwall RO (X 542/11). NRA 5235.

[690] **COSENS & CO LTD**, marine and general
engineers, Weymouth, Dorset

Records 1868-1970 incl directors' and general
meeting minutes, share records, annual reports and
accounts, ledgers, journals, day books, staff records,
press cuttings, and photographs.
The Company. NRA 28631; BAC *Company Archives*
no 253.

[691] **WILLIAM COTTON LTD**, hosiery
machinery mfrs, Loughborough, Leics

Order books (5) 1914-54, frame books (3)
1896-1956, corresp and papers (22 items) rel to
patents 1890-1905, design drawings (56 items)
1901-40, nd, photographs (83 vols) of machinery
1903-54.
Leicestershire RO (DE 711 and 3305). NRA 31374.

[692] **COWANS, SHELDON & CO LTD**,
engineers and crane mfrs, Carlisle, Cumberland

Records 19th-20th cent incl partners' minutes
(2 vols) 1866-93, partnership ledger 1858-72 and

accounts 1858-62, order books 1908-37, nd,
contract files nd, estimate weight books (32)
1929-46 and finished weight book nd, enquiry
registers (6) 1908-63, memoranda book 1891-1913,
materials sheets, cost and progress sheets nd,
engineers' calculation books (324) 1928-66, nd, test
record book 1928-32, drawings registers (3)
1868-1936 and drawings nd, cloth tracings record
books (2) 1898-1903, wages books nd, deeds and
related papers 1623-1845, publicity material and
photographs of cranes 20th cent.
Cumbria RO, Carlisle (DB/40). NRA 35350. *Report of
the County Archivist*, Dec 1987, p10.

Directors' minutes from 1955, general meeting
minutes from 1964, deeds and other property
records 19th-20th cent.
NEI plc, Newcastle upon Tyne: see BAC *Company
Archives* no 164.

[693] **E & W COWARD**, bobbin mfrs, Finsthwaite,
Lancs

Stott Park Mill ledgers (11) 1908-66.
Cumbria RO, Kendal: see *Report of the County
Archivist*, Jan 1987, p15.

[694] **COWARD, PHILIPSON & CO LTD**,
bobbin mfrs, Keswick, Cumberland

General ledgers (2) 1872-1906, day books (2)
1872-91, account books (4) 1867-1900, annual
inventories and lists of debts owing to company
(2 vols) 1877-1907, wages book 1888-95, misc
catalogues, photographs, papers rel to sale of
premises, etc 1872-1959.
Cumbria RO, Carlisle (DB/2). NRA 17337.

[695] **COX & CO (ENGINEERS) LTD**,
shipbuilders and ship repairers, Falmouth, Cornwall

Directors' minutes 1909-39, private ledgers
1909-43, journal from 1918, cash book 1923-37,
order books c1890-1960, photographs nd.
A&P Appledore (Falmouth) Ltd: see Ritchie.

[696] **AF CRAIG & CO LTD**, oil refinery, sugar
and textile machinery mfrs and ironfounders,
Paisley, Renfrewshire

Minutes (5 vols) 1895-1974, share receipts (2 boxes)
1902-12, balance sheets (1 box) 1904-12, directors'
letter books (2) 1921-44, corresp (12 boxes) 1923-45,
private ledgers (2 vols, etc) 1896-1978, ledgers (11)
1901-3, 1920-79, day books (18) 1930-82, cash books
(20) 1913, 1922-79, other financial records (7 boxes)
1897-1966, order books (47) 1878-81, 1914-71,
quotations books (80) 1933-4, 1946-82, invoice books
(54) 1941-77, stock books (7) 1884, 1919-60, cost
books (33) 1940-80, job cost books (49) 1908-78, job
books, etc (11 vols) 1868-92, 1951-79, calculations
books (150) 1925-81, machine registers (2) c1910-57,
drawings 1930-40, nd, microfilm of drawings and
indexes 1962-75, staff records (43 vols) 1885-1973,
stock books and inventories of plant and machinery
(10 vols) c1902-69, sugar estate books (5)

*c*1899-1948, photographs of premises and machinery 1896-1965, company notices, catalogues and misc papers 1868-1982.
Glasgow University Archives and Business Record Centre (UGD/173, UGD/185). NRA 26838.

Financial, sales, production, technical, staff and misc records 1936-82.
Paisley Museum and Art Galleries. NRA 33887.

[697] **CRAIG & DONALD LTD**, engineers and machine tool mfrs, Johnstone, Renfrewshire

Records 1709-1975 incl register of directors' holdings 1948-63, balance sheets and profit and loss accounts 1966-73, job order books (8) 1895-1919, lists of machinery users and catalogues nd.
Glasgow University Archives and Business Record Centre (UGD/175, UGD/275). NRA 26837 (partial list).

Engineering drawings 1900-30.
Museum of Science and Industry in Manchester. NRA 22050.

[698] **CRAVEN BROS (MANCHESTER) LTD**, machine tool makers and crane builders, Reddish, Lancs

Directors', local board and general meeting minutes (9 vols) 1886-1959, local board letter book 1916-18, registers of members, etc (2 vols) nd, corresp received (7 files) 1930-43, corresp, agreements, etc rel to acquisition of other firms 1928-31, balance sheets, balance books, annual accounts and profit and loss accounts 1860-1967, ledger 1864-81, trading account (1 vol) 1892-7, misc accounting records 1928-53, cost book 1868-73, commissions record 1902-30, papers rel to enquiries, orders, tenders and contracts (*c*50 files, etc) 1911-43, papers rel to overseas agencies 1920s-1930s, nd, salaries books (2) 1911-45, photographs of machinery (over 70 vols) 1885-1957, nd, catalogues nd, press cuttings (8 vols, 1 packet) nd.
Museum of Science and Industry in Manchester (CB). NRA 29508.

Sales book 1942-3, crane order books (14) 1898-1931, cost books (12) 1897-1928, job file 1930, sketch books (43 boxes) 1866, 1878-*c*1931, drawings of electrical parts (1 box) *c*1902-3, 1920, lists and indexes of drawings (10 vols)) *c*1930-44.
Leicestershire RO (28D69/106-124). NRA 32956.

Order book 1853-62.
Manchester Central Library Local Studies Unit: see *Accessions to repositories 1974*, p43.

Directors' and general meeting minutes, directors' attendance book and share certificate books 1942-70.
Staveley Industries plc. NRA 28631; BAC *Company Archives* no 44.

[699] **JOHN CROWN & SONS LTD**, shipbuilders and ship repairers, Sunderland, co Durham

Register of members and share ledger 1903-46, private ledgers 1903-46, private journals 1903-60, statements of account 1903-43, ship contracts

1908-22, dimensions book 1880-1925, drawing office offset books 1927-46, ships' tonnages 1947-61, plans 1908-22, photographs 1947-60.
Tyne and Wear Archives Service: see Ritchie.

Ship plans 1905-49.
Tyne and Wear Museums Service.

[700] **CUNLIFFE & CROOM LTD**, machine tool mfrs, Manchester

Directors' and general meeting minutes (3 vols) 1897-1964, register of members, etc (1 vol) 1897-1952, register of seals (1 vol) 1954-64.
Staveley Industries plc. NRA 28631; BAC *Company Archives* no 44.

[701] **DAIMLER CO LTD**, motor car mfrs, Coventry

Daimler Motor Syndicate Ltd memorandum and articles of association 1893, minute book 1893-5, directors' attendance book 1893-5, agenda books (2) 1894-5, share records (3 vols) 1893-5, nd, letter book and papers rel to winding up of the syndicate 1895-6, trustees' agenda book 1895-6, balance sheet nd, accounts (2 items) 1894-5, bank books (4) 1893-6, misc specifications, plans and other corresp and papers 1893-6; Daimler Motor Co Ltd memorandum and articles of association 1896, agenda and general manager's report 1896, annual reports 1897-1904, drawings, descriptions of cars and misc papers (*c*1 file) 1896-1902; corresp of FR Simms rel to the firm (*c*2 files) 1895-1902.
London University Library (Simms Papers). Access restricted. NRA 9402.

Memorandum and articles of association 1959, minutes (7 vols) 1903-14, agenda books (3) 1913-24, share records (21 vols, 20 files) 1896-1915, corresp (1 box, 6 vols, *c*220 files) 1911-42, liquidator's record book and related papers 1910-11, profit and loss accounts (2 vols) 1906-18, private ledger 1913-29, parts sales ledger 1933-4, bus despatch notes and car assembly lists (26 bundles) 1928-49, agreement books (4) 1896-1927, legal papers, agreements and deeds (113 items) 1861-1940.
Coventry City RO (Acc 594, 699, 1358). NRA 30533.

Minutes (11 vols) 1896-1932, sales ledgers (15) 1951-66, vehicle despatch notebooks (19) 1934-68, technical drawings nd, handbooks and brochures (31 bundles and items) 1897-1973.
Jaguar plc, Coventry. NRA 29220; and see Lane.

[702] **WILLIAM DALE & SONS**, agricultural implement mfrs, Alderley Edge, Cheshire

Ledgers (34) 1794-1921, Dale family papers 18th-20th cent.
John Rylands University Library of Manchester. NRA 354.

[703] **EDWIN DANKS & CO (OLDBURY) LTD**, boilermakers, Oldbury, Worcs

Memorandum and articles of association (3 items) 1896-1960, board and general meeting minutes

(13 vols) 1896-1972, directors' agenda books (4) 1896-1960, attendance books (4) nd and papers 1897-1914, registers of directors (3) 1901-60, directors' shareholdings (1) 1938-61 and shareholders (1) 1896-1956, other share records 1898-1971, annual reports and accounts 1901-10, 1967-71, annual returns and summaries 1903-72, company registration papers 1917-71, register of seals 1896-1904, agreements 1901-12, 1955-62, contracts (10 items) 1906-56, works committee minutes (2 vols) 1896-1901 and papers 1902-12, works manager's reports 1911-16, corresp rel to quality control 1912, patent papers 1909-67, drawings 1873-1933, nd, misc technical papers 1895-1970, directors' salaries ledger 1903-44, service agreements 1896-1910, plans and papers rel to premises 1905-68, product catalogues 1911-1970s, press cuttings 1905, misc corresp and papers 1896-1969.
Glasgow University Archives and Business Record Centre (UGD/309/78). NRA 33916.

[704] **DARLINGTON RAILWAY PLANT & FOUNDRY CO LTD**, Darlington, co Durham

Memorandum and articles of association with related papers 1899-1977, directors' minutes (4 vols) 1913-67, shareholders' minutes (1 vol) 1899-1966, management committee minutes (1 vol) 1975-7, directors' attendance book 1967-78, seal book 1953-81, register of members and share ledger (3 vols) 1899-1979, annual lists of shareholders and summaries of share capital (3 vols) 1905-35, papers mainly rel to share capital 1899-1938, dividend book 1903-48, annual returns 1936-68, annual accounts and directors' reports 1900-79, private ledger 1902-25, general ledgers (2) 1899-1909, cash book 1899-1901, bought ledger 1899-1901, stock book 1960-3, inventory 1919, valuation 1937, estimate for sand plant 1956.
Sheffield Archives (TW 216-48). NRA 34879.

[705] **DAVEY, PAXMAN & CO LTD**, boilermakers and steam engine mfrs, Colchester, Essex

Debenture stock transfer records (3 vols, 14 items) 1898-1944, private ledgers (3) 1894-8, 1906-13, 1921-30, trading accounts (2 vols) 1918-43, patent for improved grain drying apparatus 1867, specification book c1925, estimating department price list c1925, misc administrative records (5 vols, 10 files, 50 items) 1880-1962, photographs (12 vols, c550 items) 1897-1958, brochures, press cuttings, etc 1875-1965.
Essex RO, Colchester (D/F 23). NRA 21788.

[706] **DAVIDSON & CO LTD**, ironfounders and mfrs of fans and tea-drying equipment, Belfast

Corresp (1 vol, 2 bundles) 1870, 1899-1900, 1936-40, diary of SC Davidson's business trip to the United States 1899, telegraphic code book nd, patent specifications (11 vols) 1870-1928, minutes (1 vol) of building extension committee 1899, record (1 vol) of progress on new foundry 1909-10, photographs (36 vols) of works, staff and products

1886-1939, glass plate negatives (39 boxes) nd, catalogues and other printed papers 1896-c1972, scrapbooks (13) containing corresp, catalogues, brochures and press cuttings 1880s-1971, papers (4 vols) rel to tea trade 1864-c1940.
Public Record Office of Northern Ireland (D 3639). NRA 34897.

Davidson family papers 1865-1954 incl SC Davidson's Indian diaries 1865-71 and technical notebooks and drawings 1886-1921, and printed papers rel to firm 1890-1954.
Public Record Office of Northern Ireland (D 3642).
Deputy Keeper's Report 1983, pp14-15.

[707] **SAMUEL DENISON & SON LTD**, weighing and testing machine mfrs, Leeds

Cash book 1886-91, machine order books (20) 1863-73, 1883-91, 1898-1960, journal 1943-5 and indexes (2) nd.
West Yorkshire Archive Service, Leeds (Acc 1463). NRA 34490.

[708] **WILLIAM DENNY & BROTHERS LTD**, shipbuilders and engineers, Dumbarton

Bills, receipts and letters 1818-34, cash book 1827-32, petty expenses book 1828, bank book 1827-8, scantling books 1819-50, nd, specifications, tenders and certificates of construction c1804-34, misc details rel to construction and repairs 1822-34.
Scottish Record Office (GD 260/7): see Ritchie.

Awards committee minutes (3 vols) 1884-1931, private Admiralty letter book 1906-8, letter books (6) 1845-6, 1962-3, private ledgers (36) 1845-1921, ledgers (15) 1844-1910, journals (25) 1844-1949, bills receivable (1 vol) 1903-12, accounts rendered (2 vols) 1905-28, bank books (5) 1917-52, estimate books (11) 1872-89, tendering records (2 vols) 1862-1922, contract books (9) 1880-1921 and envelopes c1850-1941, cost books (22) 1885-1937, nd, instalments and extras books (3) 1914-44, estimates, trials and production books (4) 1913-33, finished weights book nd, forgings books (2) 1925-32, particulars books (2) 1862-80, nd, wages and materials books (16) 1844-1940, nd, salaries books (2) c1877-1907, certificates of character 1890-1913, inventories 1871-9, allocation and rent book for workmen's houses 1868, press cuttings (4 vols) 1884-1939, photographs 1870-1957; William Denny's jottings books 1863-75, John Denny's private notebook 1883-1921.
Glasgow University Archives and Business Record Centre (UGD 3). NRA 10829; and see Ritchie.

Sir Maurice Denny's private letter books (35) 1911-55.
Glasgow University Archives and Business Record Centre (DC 114). NRA 30891.

Trial, launch and data books, specifications, ship and engine plans 1854-1963, press cuttings and photograph albums 1881-1957.
National Maritime Museum Manuscripts Section: see Guide to the Manuscripts in the National Maritime Museum, vol 2, 1980.

Ship model tank data 1883-1983.
Denny Tank, Dumbarton: see Ritchie.

[709] **S DEWDNEY & SONS**, ship and boat builders, Brixham, Devon

General ledgers (2) 1877-1901, coal account book 1886-93.
Devon RO (2448B). NRA 4613.

[710] **DOBSON & BARLOW LTD**, cotton machinery mfrs, Bolton, Lancs

Memorandum and articles of association and debenture trust deeds 1907, ledger 1945-9, contract registers (82) 1857-1969, summary books (25) 1881-1953 and index books (9) c1885-1900, 1906-17, foreign contract books (25) 1879-1937, machine order books (181) 1851-1954, customers' letter code book c1880, machinery calculations books (18) 1896-c1930, patents and specifications, etc (1 vol, 11 bundles) 1869-1931, valuation of works (1 vol) 1907, machinery inventory books (2) c1945-9, price lists (3 items) c1895-9, catalogues and publicity material (93 items) c1900-69, photographs of machinery and factories, etc (2 albums, etc) 1897-1927, copies of deeds and agreements (1 vol) 1797-1863, misc papers 1873-1967.
Lancashire RO (DDPSL/2). NRA 20296.

Agreements and contracts (1 vol) 1856-8, quotation (1 item) 1813, sales memoranda book 1866-94, corresp and papers mainly rel to employees (31 items) 1797, 1819-68, nd, deeds and legal papers (11 items) 1706-1820, other property records (3 items) 1830-49, nd; cash account books (15) of Benjamin Dobson 1835-46.
Bolton Archive Service (ZDB). NRA 27108.

Diaries of Sir BA Dobson 1869-74.
In family possession: see *Dictionary of Business Biography*, ed DJ Jeremy, vol 2, 1984, p116.

[711] **A DODMAN & CO LTD**, mechanical engineers and boilermakers, Kings Lynn, Norfolk

Ledgers 1879-1930, drawings (c7,000) of boilers, food processing machinery and drainage equipment 1867-1940, pay books 1893-1923, misc letters, specifications, plans, catalogues, etc (c50 items) nd.
Lynn Museum. NRA 33429.

[712] **BRYAN DONKIN CO LTD**, mechanical and gas engineers and valve mfrs, London and Chesterfield, Derbys

Records incl minutes (1 vol) from late 19th cent, record of work undertaken at Bermondsey factory (2 vols) 1835-41, finished work book 1927-36, impressions of dies (1 vol) 1845-1950, drawings register incl record of plant and equipment (1 vol) 1811-59, and misc photographs, printed papers, etc 19th-20th cent.
The Company. Enquiries to the Sales and Marketing Coordinator.

Engineering drawings, etc (c145 items) 1795-1887, nd.
Derbyshire RO (D1851). NRA 34311.

Corresp and letter books of Bryan Donkin 1810-23.
Derbyshire RO.

[713] **WH DORMAN & CO LTD**, engine, machine tool and printing machine mfrs, Stafford

Balance sheets, etc 1934-57, private ledgers and ledger sheets (6 vols, etc) 1886-1962, nominal ledgers (14) 1912-65, personal ledger 1944-55, private journals (2) 1911-21, 1954-8, cash books (4) 1897-1904, 1958-66, misc financial papers 1937-63, customer enquiries (11 vols) 1962-7 and sample corresp with customers (4 files) 1943, 1962-8, lists of foreign sales 1953-4, engine records (216 vols) 1913-56, corresp, minutes, reports, etc of small engine development and experimental departments 1948-68, technical records, drawings and blueprints (24 bundles, etc) 1930-46, legal corresp and papers rel to Constantinesco's gun-firing apparatus (6 files) 1917-36, financial records rel to sports and welfare activities (6 vols) 1945-65, inventories, schedules and valuations of plant, machinery and stock (7 vols) 1922-55, instruction manuals, publicity material, etc 20th cent, photographs (13 vols, etc) 1919-68.
Staffordshire RO (Acc 1256, D 3886). NRA 17397.

[714] **DOUGLAS & GRANT LTD** (afterwards **LEWIS C GRANT LTD**), engineers and mill machinery mfrs, Kirkcaldy, Fife

Copartnery contracts and agreements, etc 1851-1915 incl draft memorandum and articles of association 1890s, accounts and balance sheets 1918-26, papers of LC Grant rel to company policy and reorganisation (1 file) c1897-1926, ledgers (70) 1926-52, cash statement 1846, order book 1854-6, sales book 1879-1907, estimate books (4) 1892-1900, 1921-42, sales and purchase day books (8) 1936-61, corresp and papers mainly rel to mill machinery (29 files) 1887-1956, engine diagram book 1867-1918, specification book c1923-40 and index 1913, engineering sketch books (20) 1903-26, technical and personal memoranda books of LC Grant (20 vols) 1923-52, apprentice book 1920-51, fire insurance specification 1921, valuations and inventory of plant and machinery 1927-50, catalogues and price lists (2 bundles) 1909-64, catalogues of other firms (3 bundles) c1900-56, photographs (6 albums, 2 folders, etc) of engines, mills, employees and works, etc 1873-1920s, misc corresp and papers 1863-1969; letters to Lewis Grant (1 bundle, 20 items) 1883-4, 1892-1908 and letter book of CE Douglas 1914-15.
Dundee University Library (MS 45). NRA 20217.

Minutes from 1950, private ledger 1926-62, general ledger from 1962, order books from 1926, estimate books from c1942, technical notebook of Robert Douglas 1856.
The Company. Enquiries to NRA (Scotland) (survey 1336). NRA 20217.

Drawings (c60) c1870-1925 of engines and engine components.
Royal Museum of Scotland.

[715] **DOUGLAS, LAWSON & CO LTD**,
engineers and pulley makers, Birstall, Yorks

Memorandum and articles of association 1923, letter
books (2) 1903-44, corresp, bills and misc papers
(2 files) 1900-8, corresp rel to winding up of firm
1970, papers rel to investments, stocks and income
tax (6 files, 12 bundles) 1893-1944, balance sheets
and accounts (2 files) 1892-1926, accounts (2 files)
1900-44, private ledger 1900-8, ledgers (2 vols,
2 files) 1895-1945, day book 1889-90, cheque
counterfoils 1890-8, dispatch book 1905-13, index
of firms supplied (2 vols) 1904-50, list of goods sold
(1 vol) 1949-69, papers rel to patents, trade marks,
agreements, etc (1 file, 1 item) 1923-70, monthly
costs book 1907-13, costs of labour and material
(1 vol) 1889-95, job records (4 vols, c9 boxes)
1890-1, 1902-70, stocktaking file 1901-5, notes rel
to pulleys (2 vols, 1 file) 1906-11, 1940s, reports,
etc on costs, procedures and productivity c1949-62,
time books (3) 1914-20, wages and salaries books
(12) 1890-1915, plant registers (2) 1944-70, misc
price lists, etc 1880s-1930s.
West Yorkshire Archive Service, Kirklees (KC 488).
NRA 36687.

[716] **WILLIAM DOXFORD & SONS LTD**,
shipbuilders and marine engineers, Sunderland, co
Durham

Directors' meeting minutes 1891-1966,
WT Doxford private letters 1889-1908, other private
letters 1903-61, registers of members and share
ledgers 1900-36, balance sheets 1864-1956, private
ledgers 1891-1969, ledgers 1834-82, ships'
particulars books 1871-1969, register of turret-deck
vessels 1892-1904, ships' contracts 1894-1970,
wages summary books 1863-1958, photographs
1840-1969.
Tyne and Wear Archives Service: see Ritchie.

Ship plans 1858-1951, photographs 20th cent.
Tyne and Wear Museums Service.

[717] **DRONSFIELD BROTHERS LTD**, textile
machinery mfrs, Oldham, Lancs

Directors' minutes (1 vol) 1919-34, registers (3) of
directors and shareholders 1917-1950s, balance
sheets (2 vols) 1891-1960, ledger 1889-1900, bank
book 1903-44, other accounting records (13 vols)
1919-82, stock books (2) 1891-1981, work
completed books (3) 1921-3, 1961-82, details of
machines produced (6 vols) nd, plant repairs book
1917-66, visitors' books (6) 1955-83, wages books
and other staff records (13 vols) 1888-1900,
1912-44, 1968-72, catalogues, advertisements and
photographs 1957-79, nd.
Oldham Archives Service (MISC/38). NRA 29985.

[718] **DRUMMOND BROTHERS LTD**, lathe
and machine tool mfrs, Guildford, Surrey

Memorandum and articles of association 1916,
certificate of registration and special resolutions
1905-8, directors' minutes (2 vols) 1907-23, general
meeting minutes (1 vol) 1902-19, share certificate
book 1902-8, stock list 1933, engineering drawings,

plans and related papers (5 boxes, 7 files, 6 items)
c1937-1970s, plans of premises 1928-75,
photographs and slides c1900-79, handbooks,
publicity material and other printed papers 1909-81.
Surrey RO, Guildford (1550). NRA 31430.

Share transfer journal nd.
Staveley Industries plc. NRA 28631; BAC *Company
Archives* no 44.

[719] **DUBS & CO**, locomotive builders, Glasgow

Order books (5) 1870-3, 1882-4, 1890-1, contract
lists to 1903, cost books (47) 1870-c1900,
specifications to 1903, salaries books (4) 1864-79,
inventories (33 vols) 1865-1902.
Glasgow University Archives and Business Record Centre
(UGD/9). NRA 10858.

Drawings 19th-20th cent.
Glasgow University Archives and Business Record Centre
(RHP 56501-12). NRA 36388.

Records incl glass plate negatives 1865-1903.
Mitchell Library, Glasgow.

Order books (2) 1864-1903.
National Railway Museum, York. NRA 28465.

Specification books (5) nd.
*DeGolyer Library, Southern Methodist University,
Dallas, Texas.*

See also North British Locomotive Co Ltd.

[720] **ROBERT DUNCAN & CO LTD**,
shipbuilders, Port Glasgow, Renfrewshire

Memorandum and articles of association 1890, with
special resolution 1908, misc corresp incl liquidator's
valuations 1915-52, share records (2 vols) 1908-39,
cost books (77) 1863-1931, ships' papers incl
agreements, specifications, corresp, etc 1916-31,
corresp, plans, etc rel to plant and property
1907-26, deeds 1845-1917.
Glasgow University Archives and Business Record Centre
(GD 320). NRA 19046.

Ship plans 1920-31.
National Maritime Museum Manuscripts Section: see
Ritchie.

[721] **DUNFORD BROTHERS LTD**,
ironmongers and colliery equipment mfrs, Newcastle
upon Tyne

Articles of partnership (1 file), directors' minutes
1926-60, register of directors' holdings and interests
1948-65, balance sheet 1905, private letter book
1900-18, misc corresp and notes (38 items)
1900-41, nd, petty ledger 1872-4, private ledgers (5)
1875-88, 1890-9, 1905-15, 1940-9, details of
greasers installed in collieries (1 vol, 2 items)
1887-1907, 1935, deeds of premises (3 files,
27 items) 1911, 1921-39.
Tyne and Wear Archives Service (1705). NRA 28367.

[722] **DUNLOP, BREMNER & CO LTD**,
shipbuilders, Port Glasgow, Renfrewshire

Memorandum and articles of association 1911 and
special resolution 1918, directors' minutes 1911-25,

agenda book and papers, etc 1912-25, register
(2 vols) 1912-24 and lists of shareholders nd, share
certificate book 1911-19, reports and annual
accounts 1912-17, finance account copying book
1914-25, private copying book 1911-25, cash book
1911-23, instalment book 1911-25, copy contract
sales book 1912-25, progressive cost book and
contract costs register (2 vols) 1911-26, particulars
rel to purchase and valuation of works 1911.
Glasgow University Archives and Business Record Centre
(GD 320, UGD/223). NRA 19046.

[723] **DURSLEY PEDERSEN CYCLE CO**,
Dursley, Glos

Private ledgers (2) 1899-1917, patents, agreements
and licences (2 bundles) 1893-1906, corresp and
papers rel to manufacture of and legal dispute about
three-speed gear hub (4 bundles) 1903-7, misc
papers (2 items) 1903-4.
Gloucestershire RO (D3310/2). NRA 23970.

[724] **WILLIAM DUTCH**, shipbuilder, Tayport,
Fife

Account book 1828-30, ledgers (6) 1816-22,
1827-30, waste books (3) 1819-20, 1829-30, work
books (5) 1817-25, 1828-30, wages account books
(8) 1816-31.
Scottish Record Office (CS 96/2087-96, 3037-49).
Court of Session Productions, List & Index Society,
special series vol 23, 1987, p280.

[725] **EAGLE ENGINEERING CO LTD**,
mechanical engineers, Warwick

Memorandum and articles of association and related
papers (1 file, 1 item) 1911-66, minutes (1 vol,
1 file) 1929-43, 1966, reports, accounts, agenda, etc
1917-66, fees and dividends book 1949-67, private
ledger 1911-18, expenses ledger 1960-6, journals (3)
1910-66, cash books (7) 1957-67, order and record
books (44) 1905-65, sales corresp (4 boxes) 1963-6,
sales ledger 1922-33 and ledger sheets 1966-8,
purchase journal sheets 1942-8, price books (8)
1934-61, production records (31 files) 1941-9,
specifications, agreements, etc (133 items) 1948-68,
visitors' books, photographs, etc (26 vols, 2 files)
1918-69, advertising leaflets, press cuttings, etc
1946-70.
Warwickshire RO (CR 1372). NRA 26336.

[726] **EARLE'S SHIPBUILDING &
ENGINEERING CO LTD**, shipbuilders, marine
engineers and boilermakers, Hull, Yorks

Annual reports and balance sheets, etc (9 items)
1892-8, lists of shareholders (2 items) c1899, nd,
proposed scheme for reconstruction c1898, draft
balance sheets (9 items) 1863-71, cost estimates
(1 bundle) c1893, plan of PS *Lady Tyler*, annual
records of workmen's compensation 1905-9, terms
and forms of apprenticeship (10 items) c1890,
statement of firm's claim rel to HMS *Endymion* and
HMS *St George* c1893, abstract of sale agreement
with valuation summary and financial details 1871,
deeds and legal papers rel to the company and its

property 1858-1900, description of the firm's works
1887, notes on firm's history 1858-80.
Brynmor Jones Library, Hull University (DEA). NRA
12336.

Annual reports 1872-92.
Town Docks Museum, Hull: see Ritchie.

[727] **WILLIAM ELDER & SONS LTD**,
ironfounders, engineers and agricultural implement
mfrs, Berwick-upon-Tweed, Northumb, and
Glasgow

Memorandum and articles of association 1910,
minutes (1 vol) 1910-16, register of shareholders
1910, annual summaries of shares and share capital
1911-30, receipts and expenditure book 1910-15,
ledgers (3) 1910-14, journal 1904-72, day book
1889-1919, cash book 1910-14, sales book 1910-14,
purchase book 1910-14, stock book 1911-16,
product catalogues (3 items) early 20th cent,
photographs of premises and products early 20th
cent, misc corresp 1875-1938.
Berwick-upon-Tweed RO (BRO.126). NRA 35362.

[728] **ELLIOTT & GARROOD LTD**, marine and
general engineers, brass and iron founders, Beccles,
Suffolk

Memorandum and articles of association 1897,
directors' agenda book 1898-1901, directors' reports
and misc papers 1908-57, summary of accounts
1890-7, private ledgers (2) 1923-46, ledgers (6)
1897-1917, customers' ledgers (3) 1878-95,
1900-55 and accounts 1917-c1958, bought ledgers
(6) 1909-60, bank book 1899-1900, other
accounting records (7 vols) 1915-64, goods inward
book 1953-9, order books (9) 1910-11, 1932-57,
price book c1922-56, works ledgers (47)
1901-c1959, capstan and boiler stock registers
(7 vols) 1896-1910, capstan registers and indexes
(27 vols) 1884-1952, rough specification book 19th
cent, capstan specification book 1892-1902, capstan
rough plans book 1888-90, plans and drawings
(microfilm) 1925-67, staff salary account book
1949-55, inventories and valuations 1920, 1941.
Suffolk RO, Lowestoft. NRA 20609.

[729] **ELSWICK-HOPPER CYCLE & MOTOR
CO LTD** (formerly **F HOPPER & CO LTD**),
Barton upon Humber, Lincs

Records 1907-71 incl articles of association 1908,
directors' minutes from 1907, reports to directors
from 1924, corresp from 1909, private ledgers from
1914, other ledgers from 1907, journals 1928-59,
cash books 1909-32 and daily sales summaries from
1918.
South Humberside Area AO (351).

[730] **ENGLISH DE LAVAL STEAM TURBINE
CO LTD** (afterwards **ALBION TURBINE CO
LTD**), Leeds

Corporate and financial papers (1 folder)
1898-1924, register of members, etc (1 vol)
1900-67, share certificate book 1899-1965, corresp

and agreements with other firms (1 bundle) 1898-1912, order notebooks (2 boxes) 1901-23, cost of sundries books (3) 1899-1910, time ledgers (10) 1899-1912.
West Yorkshire Archive Service, Leeds (Greenwood & Batley). NRA 21361.

[731] **DAVID ETCHELLS & SON**, machine tool mfrs and ironfounders, Darlaston, Staffs

Account book for foundry supplies 1906-12, wages book 1885-9, publicity material c1890-c1930.
Walsall Archives Service (Acc 487). NRA 29635.

[732] **R & J EVANS & CO LTD**, shipbuilders, ship repairers, engineers and boilermakers, Liverpool

Articles of association 1899-1900, directors' minutes 1911-21, combined share ledger 1914, balance sheets 1901-8, 1916, contract 1893, legal papers 1902-4, liquidation papers 1911.
National Museums and Galleries on Merseyside, Merseyside Maritime Museum. NRA 24291 (partial list); and see Ritchie.

[733] **JAMES EVERETT**, agricultural engineers, Little Baddow, Essex

Ledgers (6) 1904-55, cash books (4) 1907-17, 1922-9, day books, etc (14) 1917-50, stock journals (3) 1903-6, 1910.
Essex RO, Chelmsford (D/F 7). NRA 21784.

[734] **FAIRBAIRN, LAWSON, COMBE, BARBOUR LTD**, textile machinery mfrs, Leeds and Belfast

Articles of association 1890-1959, board minutes (8 vols) 1900-69, committee minutes (1 vol) 1926-41, general meeting and shareholders' minutes (2 vols) 1900-51, directors' attendance book 1900-52, share records (11 boxes and vols) 1924-70, company secretary's papers (12 boxes, files, etc) 1900, 1924-74, agreements (2 boxes, etc) 1906-47, annual reports, accounts and balance sheets 1901-67, profit and loss accounts (2 vols) 1910-30, balance book 1848-62, amalgamated working account book 1910-30, private ledgers (4) 1852-62, 1910-31, ledgers (6) 1920-33, 1952-5, journals (4) 1848-62, 1930-3, head office ledgers and journals (3 boxes) 1900-39, Belfast branch nominal ledger 1953-5, cash books (11) 1919-46, register of interest 1922-31, bill book 1926-38, purchase ledger 1931-8, sales journals (2) 1931-5, order and specifications records (c100 vols) 1846-1970, cost books (2) 1862-88, machinery designs and drawings (4 vols, 4 files, etc) 1863-1952, Belfast drawing office books (24) 1904-55, contract material book 1934, wages and salaries books (12) 1870-4, 1929-49, 1965-6, Belfast salaries books and tax and personnel files (1 parcel) 1918-55, other staff records (4 vols) 1881-1965, visitors' book 1868-1930, deeds, schedules and misc property records 1701-1964, photographs, press cuttings, catalogues and other printed material c1880-1970s, papers rel to company history 1843-1967.
West Yorkshire Archive Service, Leeds (Fairbairn Lawson records). NRA 14292.

Memorandum and articles of association 1890, 1900, minutes of Combe, Barbour & Combe Ltd and Belfast branch of Fairbairn, Lawson, Combe, Barbour Ltd (7 vols) 1890-1924, 1935-51, corresp and papers rel to amalgamation (40 items) 1900-1, register of members 1890-9, share ledger 1890-9, list of shareholders 1911, general corresp (14 vols, etc) 1904-50, profit and loss returns (1 vol) 1891-9, private ledgers (6) and indexes 1886-1931, private journals (4) 1890-6, 1904-33, journals (2) 1941-51, debit and credit accounts (1 vol) 1897-1928, cash books (7) 1916-53, bill books (3) 1891-1947, bank books (5) 1933-46, weekly summary accounts (3 vols) 1929-53, order book and index 1860-8, other order, sales and purchase records (14 vols) 1919-53, lists of patents 1884-1900, corresp rel to patents (2 vols) 1904-22, machinery drawings (1 vol) 19th cent, stock ledger 1865-90, materials in stock (3 vols) 1905-51, misc stock and production records 1929-52, wages books (14) 1888-1928, 1941-5, misc staff records 1938-50, misc property records 1848-1900; additional records (c1,000 items) c1896-1963 incl corresp and personnel files 1918-57 and accounts 1960-3.
Public Record Office of Northern Ireland (D 769, D 2288). NRA 34903.

[735] **FAIRFIELD SHIPBUILDING & ENGINEERING CO LTD** (formerly **JOHN ELDER & CO**), Glasgow and Chepstow, Mon

Partnership agreements and other directors' papers 1868-1906, board minutes 1889-94, 1899-1966, general meeting minutes (1 vol) 1930-55, directors' registers (2) 1901-48 and attendance books (2) 1922-48, registers of members (3) 1889-1935 and share ledger 1889-1904, preference share registers and ledgers (4) c1889-1935, other share records (4 vols, etc) c1930-1966, reports and balance sheets 1878, 1890-1962, registers of seals (2) 1898-1937, registers of probates and administration (4) 1928-66, black list (1 vol) 1871-88, specimen document book c1889-1940, secretary's private letter book 1888-1918 and memoranda book c1920, yard diary 1915-54, private ledgers (13) 1889-1960, public ledgers (7) 1927-35, other ledgers (2) 1931-63, journals (44) 1905-65, cash books (9) 1905-47, sundry account books (39) 1921-44, record of accounting procedures (1 vol) late 19th cent, contract accounts (11 vols) 1903-48, other records rel to contracts and agreements 1925-59, nd, estimates book 1896-1903 and drawings 1962-8, enquiries for ships, machinery and related records (213 files, etc) 1956-64, sales and purchase records (3 vols) 1924-50, stock ledger c1920-30, charges book 1921-30 and charge comparisons 1929-33, contract, material, vessels' wages, progressive and finished cost books (115) c1861-1946, material transfer books (11) 1931-48, specifications 1887-1969, nd, model records (1 vol, 1 file) c1900-56, engine department output books (5) 1909-31, credits (6 vols) 1907-31 and cost books (10) 1873-1931, pay book 1930-1, wages cost books (4) 1907-21 and labour transfer books (2) 1936-41, register of licensed turbines 1904-45, boiler department credits (3 vols) 1907-22 and cost books (5) 1873-85, 1898-1926, other departmental job

and cost books (3) 1916-36, shipyard managers' papers (40 files) nd, papers rel to output and vessels built 1870-1953, patent royalty returns 1917-34, offset books (5) nd, launch books (6) 1881-1928, trials books (3) nd, crew manuals (5 vols) nd, maiden voyage report books (3) 1925-9, technical reports and corresp 1924-9, misc papers rel to gas tankers (25 files) 1959-63, plans of ships 1869-1966 and registers of plans (35) nd, engine and boiler arrangements 1863-1906 and registers of engine drawings (3) 1871-1917, engine and boiler details 1870-1966, machinery instruction books (9) 1958-61 and particulars notebooks (4) 1922, wages sheets 1926-30 and weekly cost analysis 1933-54, weekly returns of employees 1895-1914, apprenticeship certificates (8 vols) 1913-49, labour transfer books (6) 1931-48, staff notices 1912-46, insurance books (2) 1896-1911, inventory 1926, photographic prints and negatives of ships, shipyard, machinery and staff, etc 1861-1970, photograph albums of launches (10) 1948-65, press cuttings and publicity material 1880-1962, misc papers rel to shipping c1851-1954.
Strathclyde Regional Archives (UCS 2). NRA 14659; and see Ritchie.

Board papers 1941, memoranda book 1869-1916, reports and annual accounts 1930-63, general corresp 1937-62.
Glasgow University Archives and Business Record Centre.

Financial records, order books and wages and salaries books rel to Chepstow Works (30 vols) 1919-73.
Gwent RO (D 2025). NRA 26306.

Plans and designs (27 items) mainly of ships 1827-1944.
Strathclyde Regional Archives (TD 232/71-97). NRA 12501.

Plans of ships 1870-1910.
National Maritime Museum Manuscripts Section.

[736] **FALMOUTH DOCKS & ENGINEERING CO LTD**, ship repairers, Falmouth, Cornwall

Directors' minutes 1859-1951, management committee minutes 1847-1915, share transfer register from 1859, journal 1918-27, revenue cash book 1926, docking books 1930-59, details of ships repaired 1940-51, photographs nd.
A & P Appledore (Falmouth) Ltd: see Ritchie.

[737] **J FARRAR ENGINEERING CO LTD**, dyeing machinery mfrs, Halifax, Yorks

Memorandum and articles of association 1921, 1927, ledgers and other accounting records (7 vols) 1927-62, purchase and sales ledger incl trading accounts 1899-1934, other purchase, sales and order records (30 vols, 2 files) 1917-65, diaries of JF Pell, sales representative, 1922-33, patent specifications and related papers (8 bundles and items) 1868-1933, notebooks rel to, and technical drawings of, machinery 1912-68, nd, publicity material, press

cuttings and photographs (9 vols and bundles, c130 items) 1922-30, nd.
West Yorkshire Archive Service, Calderdale (FA). NRA 28000.

[738] **FAWCETT, PRESTON & CO LTD**, marine and hydraulic engineers, Liverpool and Bromborough, Cheshire

Board and general meeting minutes and related papers (8 vols, etc) 1888-1965, register of managers and directors 1905-47, share registers (2) 1905-49 and certificate book 1949-57, shareholders' attendance register 1906-56, annual reports, etc (44 items) 1913-47, balance sheets, annual and profit and loss accounts, etc 1925-60, private ledgers (3) 1905-60, journals (5) 1932-60, cash books (4) 1953-67, order books (10) 1872-1914, estimate book 1947, engine books (3) 1813-63, 1870-1962, engineers' notes (1 vol) 1873-99, drawings 1845-1903 and index 1894, deeds and legal papers, etc 1778-1958, inventories (4 items) 1888-1938, photographs mainly of products and machinery 1910-58, nd, press cuttings (4 vols, etc) 1923-67, visitors' books (3 vols, etc) 1942-66, publicity material, misc corresp and papers 1862-1964.
National Museums and Galleries on Merseyside, Merseyside Maritime Museum (B/FP) NRA 35368.

[739] **FELLOWS & CO LTD**, shipbuilders and ship repairers, Great Yarmouth, Norfolk

Partnership deeds (3 items) 1829, 1842, misc board papers 1899-1951 incl draft minutes 1899, directors' attendance book 1949-57, letter books (7) 1859-1926, annual accounts incl corresp (1 bundle) 1904-45, ledgers (7) 1828-1964, investment and property ledgers (2) 1879-98, 1948-65, cash books (3) 1879-94, 1900-67, day books (8) 1828-91, bank books 1827-1945, labour accounts (1 vol) 1867-73, caulker's accounts (1 bundle) 1911, vouchers (3 bundles) 1884-90, 1950-2, lists of vessels built 1837-1904, registers of vessels docked (3 vols) 1881-1946, stock books and lists (28 vols and bundles) 1819-1940, agreements, estimates, surveys and related papers (13 vols and bundles) 1825-1921, smacks' day books (2) 1880-6, shipbuilding and repair job papers (c150 bundles) 1853-1964, corresp with other firms and misc business papers, etc (c27 bundles) 1825-1955, lists of employees (3 bundles, 1 item) c1939-50, leases (2 bundles) 1884-1904, papers rel to acquisition of interest in RW Crabtree & Sons, marine engineers (1 bundle) 1930-3.
Norfolk RO (PR/DM). NRA 27693; and see Ritchie.

Directors' minutes 1960-70.
Richards (Shipbuilders) Ltd.

Ship plans nd.
Maritime Museum for East Anglia, Great Yarmouth.

[740] **FERGUSON BROTHERS (PORT GLASGOW) LTD**, shipbuilders and ship repairers, Port Glasgow, Renfrewshire

Directors' minutes 1912-55, balance sheets 1905-38 and other financial records 1903-63, estimate books

(5) 1920-37, cost books (291) 1903-60, particulars books, specifications and technical data nd, design, proposal and guidance drawings nd, hull and engine drawings 1903-58, publicity material nd, photographs 1910-63.
Glasgow University Archives and Business Record Centre (GD 321). NRA 21654; and see Ritchie.

[741] ALEXANDER FINDLAY & CO LTD, structural engineers and bridge builders, Motherwell, Lanarkshire

Letter book 1909-12, ledgers (3) 1897-1912, journals (2) 1934-42, 1970-7, day book 1942-51, cash books (9) 1933-76, directory of customers' estimates 1881-1941, estimate books (6) 1937-70, contract index notebooks 1946-74, sales books (2) 1947-59, purchase books (2) 1964-71, job number books (5) 1894-1949.
Motherwell Public Library. NRA (Scotland) (survey 3046). NRA 31889.

Order book index of jobs completed 1888-1923, order book from 1953, enquiries book 1933-8.
The Company. Enquiries to NRA (Scotland) (survey 988). NRA 18738.

Illustrated catalogues (6) *c*1920-60, nd.
Strathclyde Regional Archives (TD 492). NRA 12501.

[742] FLEMING & FERGUSON LTD, shipbuilders and engineers, Paisley, Renfrewshire

Articles of association 1946, directors' minute book 1895-8, register of shareholders, etc 1895-9, corresp and company reports 1927-49, dredger cost book 1901-7, job specification and measurement book nd, steel and timber weights job book nd, trial book nd, misc specifications, plans, maps, etc 20th cent, photographs nd.
Paisley Museum and Art Galleries. NRA (Scotland) (survey 575). NRA 14816.

Material cost books (16) 1913-61, outside order books (3) 1931-55, vessel particulars nd, hull and engine plans 1886-1944.
Glasgow University Archives and Business Record Centre (UGD/130, UGD/207). NRA 14816.

[743] GEORGE FLETCHER & CO LTD, sugar machinery mfrs, Derby

Register of members and share ledger (2 vols) 1909-36, letter book *c*1947-57, private ledgers (2) 1907, nd, nominal ledgers (2) 1909-19, private journal 1955-68, financial statements *c*1935-40, order books (61) 1914-67, order index book 1910-60, shop lists (9 vols) 1947-52, work in progress ledger *c*1930-40, records of projects and tenders 1959-80, engineering drawings (*c*225 folders) 1925-65, photographs (8 boxes, 4 vols, 7 files) late 19th-20th cent, brochures, advertisements, etc 20th cent.
Derbyshire RO (D2653B). NRA 871.

[744] FLETCHER, JENNINGS & CO, locomotive builders, Whitehaven, Cumberland

Order book 1861-1921.
National Railway Museum, York.

[745] FLITT MOTOR CO (formerly AE GRIMMER & CO), cycle mfrs and motor engineers, Ampthill, Beds

Corresp and papers (1 vol, *c*12 bundles, *c*130 items) rel to administration and closure of firm mainly 1939-50, balance sheets and trading accounts 1924-48, account books (5) 1906-19, 1939-44, day books (2) 1903-5, 1946-8, petty cash book 1925-38, receipts and payments books (5) 1917-32, 1939-51, parcels book 1910-14, motor repair book 1912-14, wages books (2) 1932-48, corresp, leases, etc (1 bundle, 27 items) rel to premises 1909-55.
Bedfordshire RO (X 291/253). NRA 23303.

[746] FODENS LTD, commercial vehicle mfrs, Sandbach, Cheshire

Prospectus 1902, memorandum and articles of association (3 items) 1887-1952, directors' minutes (3 vols) 1970-80, register of directors 1919-80, registers (3) of shareholders 1935-64, share transfer certificates (20 items) 1889-1901, other share records (1 vol, 2 items) 1902-25, reports of annual general meetings 1919-32, directors' reports 1904-36, balance sheets and profit and loss accounts 1892-1936, agreements 1887, 1901, royal warrant 1928, investment accounts (2 vols, 2 items) 1902-57, general ledger 1902-24, private cash book 1978-80, bank books (2) 1902-3, 1912, cost book *c*1874-1910, vehicle sales records 1921-4, vehicle and chassis building records (79 vols, etc) 1902-66, product manuals 1945-72, nd, drawings incl index books (29) 1870s-1950s, letter rel to patent 1890, wages and salaries books (3) 1911-33, other staff records (6 items) 1939-41, papers rel to property (10 items) 1887-1936, photographs mainly of vehicles and engines 1901-54, cartoons rel to sales and production (1 vol) 1930s, company histories, publicity material and misc papers 20th cent.
Cheshire RO (DFO). NRA 35031.

[747] FOLLOWS & BATE LTD, horticultural and domestic machinery and implement mfrs, Manchester

Records 1882-1968 incl minutes, share ledger, register of mortgages, annual reports and accounts, private ledgers, cash book, catalogues, and price lists.
Qualcast (Lawn Mowers) Ltd. NRA 28631; BAC *Company Archives* no 388.

[748] FORWARD ENGINEERING CO (formerly TB BARKER & CO), mechanical engineers, Birmingham

Directors' and general meeting minutes (1 vol) 1898-1905, share records (3 vols) 1898-1902, corresp (1 box) *c*1890-1905, bank books (2 vols) 1892-8, record of invoices (1 vol) 1889-99, salaries

book 1897-1900, patents, hire agreements, contracts, etc (5 bundles) 1881-1903, insurance policies (1 bundle) c1898-1901; personal bank book of HB Graham, director, 1901-2.
Birmingham Central Library Archives Division (MS 1422). NRA 32859.

[749] **WILLIAM FOSTER & CO LTD**, agricultural engineers, Lincoln

Letter books (5) 1961-2, sales and order records (11 vols and files) 1931-61, specifications book 1897-1951, registers (8) of threshers, chaff cutters and straw elevators 1860-1960, stock books (6) c1900-40, pattern books, drawings, etc (10 boxes, 8 vols, 15 rolls, 7 bundles, etc) 1903-60, printed papers, photographs, etc (4 bundles) 1901-38.
Lincolnshire Archives (Rundle). NRA 14280.

Photographs (1 vol, 1 folder) showing development of Foster tank mainly 1915-18, and other misc papers 1910-63 of William Rigby, chief draughtsman to the firm.
Lincolnshire Archives (Rigby). NRA 14280.

Balance sheets and reports 1878-1960.
Lincolnshire Archives: see Archivists' Report 24, 1972-73, p50.

Register of male employees in protected occupations 1918.
Lincolnshire Archives (Misc Dep 213). *Archivists' Report 20, 1968-69*, p41.

Drawings (c70) of Foster tanks c1915-18, records (several box files) rel to tank production c1939-45.
Tank Museum, Bovington. NRA 14263.

Records rel to production of portable steam engines and traction engines.
Newcomen Society, London: see Lincolnshire Archives Committee *Archivists' Report 21, 1969-70*, p10.

[750] **W & J FOSTER LTD**, knitting machine mfrs, Preston, Lancs

Stock account book 1896-1946, stock book 1941, wages books (2) 1889-1912, 1918-24, diaries (2) and misc papers of James Foster 1862-97, papers (1 bundle) rel to firm's centenary 1961.
Lancashire RO (DDX/438). NRA 17070.

[751] **JOHN FOWLER & CO (LEEDS) LTD**, agricultural machinery mfrs and locomotive builders, Leeds

Partnership book 1863-83, company book 1862-1931, articles of partnership, memorandum and articles of association and related papers (33 files and items) 1862-1965, registers of directors (2) 1929-72, share ledger 1886-1901, share allotment book 1886-7, 1965 and other share and dividend records (9 vols, 27 files, bundles and items) 1886-1974, draft report on company's position 1935, annual financial statements and related papers (1 vol, 100 files and items) 1860-74, 1887-1935, investment records (33 files, bundles and items) 1887-1947, monthly expenditure summaries 1974, private ledgers (2) 1886-1912, 1947-73, ledgers,

journals and cash books (22) 1937-73, misc sales records (2 vols, 2 files) 1938-73, graph showing numbers of ploughing tackles despatched 1868-1917, corresp, papers and agreements mainly rel to overseas business (116 files and items) 1868-1935, 1968-71, analysis (1 vol) of costs and prices 1913-18, Steam Plough Works administration book 1914, patents, specifications and related papers (3 vols, 1 bundle, 133 items) 1847-1929, engine, locomotive and general product registers (6) 1895-1968, engine details books (15) 1893-1923, shop and locomotive building books (20) 1922-43, nd, locomotive department files (c500) 1945-68, particulars and dimensions books (5) 1885-1930, registers (2) of designs 1883-1914 and modifications 1953-63, misc technical records (1 file, 8 items) 1852-1963, drawing registers (11) 1860s-1960s, drawing office sketch books (11) 1921-66, drawings, tracings and prints (over 10,000 items) from 1860s, misc staff records (10 vols, 14 files and items) 1874-1930, 1951-72, inventory of Steam Plough Works 1895, corresp, deeds and papers rel to British and overseas property (52 files and items) 1868-1938, 1972-5, photographs of products (79 vols, c300 items) c1862-c1970, catalogues, instruction manuals, house journals, etc (c220 vols, files and items) 1874-1971, printing proofs and artwork (7 vols, c1,850 items) c1860-1950, misc papers mainly rel to company's history (31 files and items) 1850-1948.
Rural History Centre, Reading University (TR FOW). NRA 21065.

Memorandum and articles of association 1886, 1951, board minutes (1 vol) 1964-81, register of members, etc (1 vol) 1977-9, annual accounts, directors' reports, annual returns, etc (8 files) 1943-82.
Sheffield Archives (TW 300-11). NRA 34879.

[752] **DOUGLAS FRASER & SONS LTD**, ironfounders, engineers and textile machinery mfrs, Arbroath, Angus

Memorandum and articles of association 1905-60, minute books (3) 1905-68, register of directors 1903-61, letter books (3) 1880-1916, memoranda books (4) 1955-64 and index, private ledgers (7) 1878-1965, journals (6) 1878-1942, 1954-68, misc financial and legal corresp and papers 1857-1959, maps and plans 1837-1948, photographs c1920-1963.
Dundee University Library (MS 42). NRA 17171.

Notebooks (42) rel to engineering sub-contract work 1932-56, technical drawings 20th cent.
Giddings & Lewis-Fraser Ltd. NRA (Scotland) (survey 873). Enquiries to Dundee University Library. NRA 17171.

[753] **JOHN FULLER & CO**, coachbuilders, Bristol

Letter books (3) 1815-28, 1919, ledgers (4) 1915-20, account books (2) 1815-38, cash day book 1815-33, sales ledger 1897-1919, stock book 1816, memoranda book 1897, drawings, engravings and photographs of coaches (2 parcels) 18th-20th cent, photographs of firm's premises (1 vol) c1892.
Bristol RO (Acc 28049). NRA 4891.

[754] **S & A FULLER LTD** (afterwards **KINGSMEAD MOTOR CO LTD**), coachbuilders, Bath, Somerset

Directors' minutes (1 vol) 1943-63 and other corporate records 1913, 1939-76, order book 1815-19, carriage designs nd, employee obituary 1832, apprenticeship indenture 1871 and other staff and pension fund records 1930-76, corresp and plans rel to premises 1864-5, 1954-68, price lists 1937-58, photographs of vehicles, premises and staff *c*1896-1970, press cuttings 1853-1953, booklet and papers rel to company history 1955, nd.
The Company: see Business in Avon and Somerset.

[755] **FULLERTON, HODGART & BARCLAY LTD**, engineers and mining machinery mfrs, Paisley, Renfrewshire

Minutes 1892-1969, corresp 1888-1977, accounting records 1850-1977, order books 1865-1975, specifications and patents 1871-1977, drawings of plant and machinery 1866-*c*1967, wages and salaries records 1919-77, photographs of machinery *c*1910-61, catalogues and misc papers 1884-1964, nd.
Glasgow University Archives and Business Record Centre (UGD/120). NRA 17534.

Letter offer books (15) 1934-9, nd, order books (27) 1917-40, abstract order book 1865-1941, enquiry books (2) 1940-50, engine sales books, etc (11 vols, etc) 1921-63, job books (54) 1888-1961, cost books (24) 1900-67, record of labour and weights for metal castings (1 item) 1908, parts list 1911-16, engine number book nd, printed engine drawings (1 vol) 1887, patent drawings nd, drawing number book 1906-18, pay books 1938-64, catalogues *c*1910-20.
In private possession. Enquiries to NRA (Scotland) (survey 750). NRA 17534.

[756] **GALLOWAYS LTD**, engineers and boilermakers, Manchester

Out-letter and estimate book 1840-63, notebook 1831-3, diary 1856 and reminiscences *c*1890 of John Galloway.
In private possession. Enquiries to Chetham's Library, Manchester. NRA 470. Loose copies of the out-letters and estimates are in the John Rylands University Library of Manchester.

Plans and drawings (*c*650 items) 1866-1921.
Museum of Science and Industry in Manchester. NRA 32284.

[757] **GALLYON & SON**, gunsmiths, Cambridge

Sales ledgers 1878-1937, 1954-8, register of pistols sold or hired out 1903-18, sales register 1916-20.
Cambridgeshire RO, Cambridge (R83/15). *Annual Report 1983*, p17.

[758] **SAMUEL GALTON**, gunsmith, Birmingham

Letter books (2) 1741-51, business and legal papers rel to his gunmaking business in partnership with

James Farmer (3 bundles, 9 items) 1754-76, misc personal papers 1735-90 and other deeds and family papers 13th-19th cent.
Birmingham Central Library Archives Division (Galton MSS). NRA 6576.

[759] **L GARDNER & SONS LTD**, mechanical engineers, Patricroft, Lancs

Order books (3) 1905-18.
Museum of Science and Industry in Manchester (EN 11). NRA 29510.

[760] **RICHARD GARRETT ENGINEERING LTD**, agricultural and general engineers, Leiston, Suffolk

Memorandum and articles of association 1897, directors' attendance books 1857-1980, ledgers 1845-1924, day books 1887-1933, bill books 1881-1929, register of charitable donations 1860-1914, order books 1895-1928, costing and pricing books 1860-*c*1903 and calculations 1898-1931, stock books 1913-31, registers of engines and machines built 1860-*c*1903, monthly output summaries 1903-28, memoranda books rel to products and overseas customers nd, specifications, technical drawings, registers of costings, forgings, etc nd, sketch book 1909-49, testing records, logsheets, product files, etc incl some rel to munitions 1914-18, patents 1842-74, journeymen's ledgers 1869-1915, wages and salaries books 1888-1936, valuation of buildings and fixtures 1866, inventories of plant and machinery 1877-1924, canteen book 1921-5, accounts of housing repairs 1919-21, catalogues from 1859, photographs and publicity material.
Suffolk RO, Ipswich (HC 30). NRA 30268.

[761] **GATESIDE MILLS CO LTD**, shuttle and bobbin mfrs, Gateside, Fife

Sales day books (36) 1893-1971, purchase day books (21) 1901-69, bobbin block book 1948-9.
St Andrews University Library (MS 38110-68).

[762] **ALFRED J GENTLE**, founders and general engineers, St Albans, Herts

Sales ledgers (8) 1888-1904, 1937-40, 1958-72, other accounting and sales records (30 vols) *c*1950-1972, estimates, orders, invoices and machinery plans (1 vol, 1 bundle, 1 file) 1942-69, wages books (11) 1962-72.
Hertfordshire RO (D/EGt). NRA 22053.

[763] **RC GIBBINS & CO**, crane mfrs, tool mfrs and engineers, Birmingham

Private ledgers (2) 1869-1911.
Birmingham Central Library Archives Division (MSS 665, 787). NRA 30305.

[764] **GEORGE GIBBS LTD**, gun and rifle makers, Bristol

Registers of weapons bought and made (2 vols) from 1904, tools and designs pattern book *c*1894-1927.
IM Crudgington Ltd: see Business in Avon and Somerset.

[765] **GILBERT GILKES & GORDON LTD,**
water turbine and pump mfrs, Kendal, Westmorland

Estimate books (14) 1931-64, wages books (17)
1873-81, 1890-1949, printed company history 1975.
Cumbria RO, Kendal (WDB/29). NRA 35281.

[766] **GIMSON & CO (LEICESTER) LTD,**
ironfounders and mfrs of engines, boilers and
electric lifts, Leicester

Memorandum and articles of association and misc
legal papers 1896, 1932, register of members, share
ledgers and related papers (8 vols, files, etc)
1896-1948, statements of account (132 items)
1884-1962, private ledgers (2) 1895-1945, bank
books (2) 1865-70, 1923-4 and ledger 1914-30, lift
books (231) 1885-1971, out-orders books (72)
1908-78, drawing office order books (32) 1924-78
and drawing numbers books (5) 1878-1946, site
notebook c1880, engine register 1887-1914, lift
plans (32 files) 1921-78, misc order and production
records 1890-1914, SA Gimson's notebooks (2)
1907-45, wages books (10) 1921-44 and misc staff
records 1872-1965, publicity material, photographs,
etc 1865-1984.
Leicestershire RO (DE 3034). NRA 30450.

Minute book 1896-1950.
The Company. Microfilm in Leicestershire RO
(MF 472).

[767] **GLASGOW RAILWAY ENGINEERING
CO LTD,** railway wheel, spring and axle mfrs,
Glasgow

Memorandum and articles of association 1900,
minute books (2) 1901-55, share register 1909-46,
memorandum of special resolutions from 1919,
statements of account (12) 1945-59.
Glasgow University Archives and Business Record Centre
(UGD/100/3). NRA 14667.

[768] **GH GLEDHILL & SONS LTD,** cash
register and time clock mfrs, Halifax, Yorks

Company returns (1 file) 1891-1949, letter book
1916-28, share records (2 vols, 2 files) 1896-1948,
account books (15) 1891-1963, day books (2)
1901-11, 1916-22, bank books (9) 1899-1914 and
statements (1 bundle) 1915-16, private ledger
1938-57, ledger balance 1932-7, profit estimate
book 1915-21, trade ledgers (2) 1907-57, sales
ledgers (27) 1896-1905, 1927-57, sales registers (2)
1888-1904, purchase ledger 1958-77, purchases
dissection sheets 1938-45, order books (16)
1948-79, costings books (7) 1892-1930, stock books
(5) 1891-3, 1896-1906, 1941, nd, output book
1907-8, index to patents book 1883, corresp, plans,
drawings and other papers rel to designs and
products (55 vols, files, etc) 1903-69, serial numbers
of machines manufactured (8 vols, 4 drawers)
1896-1970s, geographical index of completed
machines nd, machinery repair book 1891-7,
maintenance service handbooks (2) 1966-78 and
contracts register 1977-83, time books (7)
1890-1910, wages records (4 vols, 1 file, etc)
1912-72, accident books (4) 1924-68, valuations of

works 1921, 1939-49, press cuttings book 1901-8,
catalogues, pamphlets and other printed papers
c1920-70; British Machine Co Ltd register of
members and transfers 1897-1935 and accounts
1897-1913, Stockall-Brook Time Recorders Ltd
minute book and misc papers 1907-12.
West Yorkshire Archive Service, Calderdale (GLE,
MISC 467). NRA 24971.

[769] **GLENFIELD & KENNEDY LTD,**
hydraulic engineers and ironfounders, Kilmarnock,
Ayrshire

Kennedy's Patent Water Meter Co Ltd minute book
1865-82, The Glenfield Co minute books (3)
1865-1903 and share registers (3) c1865-99,
amalgamation meetings (1 vol) 1899-1901, minute
books (16) 1903-44, directors' agenda books (2)
1898-1904, 1908-9, memoranda books (2)
1870-1905, share registers and ledgers (11)
1887-1950, investment register c1920-60, letter
book 1943-4, reports (1 vol) on various companies
1927-46, register of seals 1909-50, private ledgers
(4) 1900-43, ledger account summaries (2 vols)
1882-99, 1937-48, journals, cash books, etc (4 vols)
1915-44, sales and purchase ledgers (4) 1925-37,
estimate books (2) 1912-19, general order books
(359) 1872-6, 1882-95, 1944-70, order books
classified geographically (257) 1883-1944, order
books classified by product or customer (148)
1877-1944, misc order books (6) 1904-44, jobs
completed book 1878-9 and index books (2)
1906-45, job cost books (73) 1906-49, log books of
work done, etc (26 vols) 1881-1906, nd, tracings
sent out (18 vols) 1880-1911, lists of patterns and
indexes of drawings (8 vols) 1884-1922, nd, wages
record (9 vols) 1887-1942, plant records (4 vols)
1868-1901, glass negatives (20 boxes) from c1930,
printed catalogues (c50) from c1889, history of
company 1852-1952; Compagnie Francaise
d'Appareils Glenfield & Kennedy SA minute book
1906-12 and misc financial records.
*Glasgow University Archives and Business Record
Centre.* NRA 16124.

[770] **GLOUCESTER RAILWAY CARRIAGE &
WAGON CO LTD,** rolling stock mfrs, Gloucester

Records 18th-20th cent incl memorandum and
articles of association 1860-1962, directors' minutes
(25 vols) 1860-1962, executive committee minutes
(1 file) 1945-8, board meeting agendas (20 vols,
3 files) 1867-1962, board meeting papers,
chairman's corresp, etc 1917-49, directors' reports
and statements of accounts (2 bundles) 1860-1960,
reports of general meetings (58 items) 1862-1955,
annual reports, accounts and related papers (12 vols,
2 files, 11 items) 1860-1961, registers of
stockholders, shareholders and transfers and related
papers (23 vols, 1 file, 78 items) 1860-1968,
debenture records (5 vols, 8 bundles, 2 items)
1864-1950, income tax returns (2 bundles)
1860-1919, income tax and corporation tax appeal
papers 1920-5, financial guarantees, agreements, etc
(3 bundles, 19 items) 1880-1962, ledger 1881-4, bill
books (2) 1869-1955, corresp and papers rel to
holdings in other companies, agency agreements,

wagon leases and sales, etc (9 files, 15 bundles, 162 items) 1877-1968, contracts, specifications and related papers (9 vols, 13 files, 6 bundles, 65 items) 1887-1966, order books (100) 1905-69, patents, licences and assignments (53 items) 1890-1947, drawing office requisition books (258) 1914-81, registers of drawings (10 vols) 1871-1980, engineering drawings (12 vols, 72 rolls) c1895-1982, superannuation fund, sports and social clubs and misc staff records 1875-1969, deeds, leases, building contracts, agreements rel to services, etc 1784-1970, inventories and valuations 1884-1943, plans of premises 1902-71, insurance policies 1902-68, photographs of rolling stock, premises, etc 1862-c1970, and catalogues, brochures, technical literature and press cuttings 1854-1978.
Gloucestershire RO (D 4791). NRA 32937 (partial list).

Photographs and negatives of products.
National Railway Museum, York.

[771] **B GOODFELLOW**, engineers, boilermakers and ironfounders, Hyde, Cheshire

Drawings (c760) of machinery for textile factories, collieries, waterworks, electricity stations, etc 1875-1905, nd.
Museum of Science and Industry in Manchester. NRA 32350.

[772] **GOODWIN BARSBY & CO LTD**, asphalt and quarry plant mfrs, Leicester

Records 1877-1975 incl memorandum and articles of association 1908-55, board and committee minutes (5 vols, 1 packet) 1953-75, other corporate and share records 1920-75, dividend account book 1919-29, balance sheets, statements of account, etc 1914-71, ledgers (8) 1896-1968, other accounting records 1950s-1970s, tender and estimate books (5) 1963-9, patent records (2 files) 1877-1915, machinery work record books (26) 1888-1960s, stone breakers (1 vol) 1882-1902, wages books (4) 1929-60, personnel files nd and deeds (2 boxes).
Leicestershire RO (DE 3731, 3816, 3850, 3928). NRA 33634 (partial list).

Coke breakers (1 vol) 1902-7, machine record files from 1947.
The Company. NRA 33634.

[773] **DAVID GORRIE & SON**, engineers, coppersmiths and cleaning and dyeing machinery mfrs, Perth

Corresp, orders, estimates and specifications (4 bundles) 1893-1954, vouchers (5 bundles) 1914-52, drawings of machinery and plans of company and customers' premises 1891-1937, nd, photographs incl glass plate negatives and illustrations mainly of machinery 1899-1944, nd, catalogues, price lists and publicity material incl some rel to other firms (63 items) 1903-54, nd.
Perth and Kinross District Archive (MS 6). NRA 34707.

[774] **GOSLING & GATENSBURY LTD**, ceramic machinery mfrs, Hanley, Staffs

Letter books (2) 1939-48 and corresp with overseas customers and agents c1948-54, sales ledgers (10) 1895-1952, invoice books (36) 1895-1948, bought cash books (3) 1946-62, wages books (16) 1944-52.
Staffordshire RO (D 3236). NRA 22213.

[775] **GOURLAY BROTHERS & CO (DUNDEE) LTD**, shipbuilders and engineers, Dundee

Memorandum and articles of association (1 bundle) 1904 and other papers rel to the partnership and incorporation (2 bundles) 1903-7, minutes (1 vol) 1904-8, legal corresp and papers, etc (1 bundle) 1893-8, business corresp (1 bundle) 1901-8, balance sheets and trade accounts (1 bundle) 1903-4, liquidation papers (2 bundles) 1907-10, inventories and valuations 1900-8, catalogue of plant and machinery 1909, yard plan 1908, shipyard leases (1 bundle) 1870-1904, Gershom Gourlay's trust corresp and papers 1901-8.
Dundee University Library (MS 57/2). NRA 20766.

Ship plans 1859-1908.
Dundee District Archive and Record Centre. NRA 28255.

Ship plans 1890s.
National Maritime Museum Manuscripts Section: see Ritchie.

[776] **GRAFTON CRANES LTD**, crane mfrs, Bedford

Plans and technical drawings (145 items) of cranes, premises and plant 1893, 1901-60, nd; Bedford Engineering Co technical drawings (202) of cranes, etc 1895-1931, nd.
Bedfordshire RO (Z 331). NRA 6970.

Order book 1932-c1960, crane lists 1947-c1960, tracing register 1930-61.
Leicestershire RO (DE 1930). NRA 33075.

[777] **GRANGEMOUTH DOCKYARD CO LTD**, shipbuilders, ship repairers and marine engineers, Grangemouth, Stirlingshire

Records 19th cent-1972 incl accounts, instructions, regulations, ships' log books, records of ship repair, sea trials, dock improvement and hours worked, ships' log books and plans, and staff ledgers.
Falkirk Museum (A53, A56, A94). NRA 18888.

Drawings of ships (c150 items) c1870-1941.
Central Regional Council Archives Department. NRA 24511.

[778] **WILLIAM GRAY & CO LTD**, shipbuilders, ship repairers and marine engine builders, West Hartlepool, co Durham

Ships' particulars books 1885-1961, new ships' book 1916-28, yard book 19th cent, offset book c1930-56, launch notebook 1888-1932, trials notebook 1885-1960, marine engine works corresp 1885-95,

specifications and plans 1940-61, nd, press cuttings books 1885-1937, other printed material and photographs 1955-63.
Hartlepool Maritime Museum: see Ritchie.

Labour cost book 1898-1924.
Northumberland RO.

Yard books nd.
Hartlepool Central Library.

[779] **M & W GRAZEBROOK LTD**, heavy engineers and boilermakers, Netherton, Worcs

Share certificate counterfoils (2 vols) 1914-46, corresp and papers (1 bundle) rel to trade marks and brands 1887-1943, legal agreements (1 bundle) 1891-1950, income tax papers (1 bundle) 1940-4, plans and papers (2 files, 1 envelope, 7 items) rel to firm's landed property 1809-20, 1902-52.
Dudley Archives and Local History Service (Acc 8710). NRA 33583.

[780] **R & H GREEN & SILLEY WEIR LTD**, ship repairers, London

Directors' minutes 1899-1970, agenda book 1910-38 and attendance books 1915-77, registers of directors and transfers, etc 1911-74, directors' reports and accounts, etc 1912-35, letter book 1910-18 and corresp 1914-63, ship repair agreements 1921-64, accounting records 1910-79, staff records 1898-1973, press cuttings 1916-22.
National Maritime Museum Manuscripts Section: see Ritchie.

[781] **THOMAS GREEN & SON LTD**, mechanical engineers and ironfounders, Leeds

Articles of association 1904, directors' attendance book 1944-62, general meeting attendance register and visitors' book 1923-63, papers rel to board meetings, agency agreements and reorganisation of capital 1951-9, share register 1879-1937, annual lists of shareholders 1919-34, accounts and balance sheets (2 boxes) 1932-70, cash analysis books (10) 1948-59, order book 1875-92, costings and parts book c1938-41, misc patent records 1856, 1872, 1908-9, indexes of drawings c1882-1941, machinery record sheets 1940-5, insurance policy register 1881-1901, testimonials 1881-99, catalogues and photographs 20th cent.
West Yorkshire Archive Service, Leeds (Acc 1927). NRA 20241.

[782] **WW GREENER LTD**, gunsmiths, Birmingham

Day book 1886-8.
Birmingham Central Library Archives Division (MS 1168). NRA 29847.

[783] **TW GREENWELL & CO LTD**, ship repairers, Sunderland, co Durham

Records 1901-73 incl ledgers 1902-57, cash and account books 1928-68, purchase and sales ledgers and journals 1901-73, particulars of dry-docked

vessels 1925-64 and papers rel to dry dock construction 1922-54.
Tyne and Wear Archives Service: see Ritchie.

[784] **GREENWOOD & BATLEY LTD**, mechanical engineers and machine tool mfrs, Leeds

Prospectus 1888, directors' minutes (5 vols) 1888-93, 1902-53, partnership and directors' salary agreements (13 items) 1860-1918, register of directors' holdings and interests 1948-67, share transfers and certificates (7 boxes, 2 files) 1888-c1963, debenture transfer register 1895-1945, registers (4) of probates, etc 1889-1969, other share and debenture records (1 vol, 1 bundle, 3 folders, 3 items) c1906-1963, register of mortgages and charges 1893, annual returns (1 parcel) 1889-1971, letter books (2 boxes, 4 vols) 1873-1925, nd, seal books (2) 1948-62, Chancery bill of complaint 1846, corresp and papers (55 files) rel to administrative, legal and financial matters 1863-1942, c1952-1972, annual report and balance sheets 1889-1971, auditors' report and accounts (1 box, 28 vols) 1888-1935, 1960-4, papers rel to capital reorganisation (1 parcel) 1961-3, profit and loss account ledger 1884-1914, investments ledger 1889-1930, private ledgers (2) 1906-20, nd, ledger 1856-88, ledger balances (8 items) 1908-9, balance book and private journal (1 vol) 1856-88, journals (2) 1919-63, cash books (7) 1866-73, 1900-4, 1907-10, 1919-21, accounts rendered book from 1902, order books (62) 1856-1927, 1952, printed order slips (59 vols, 1 bundle) 1881-1921, 1944-5, carriers' delivery books (45) 1877-1934, misc sales and invoice records (7 vols, 2 bundles) 1902-4, 1909-10, 1916-47, corresp, tenders, contracts, specifications, etc (71 files) 1871-1939, index books of orders, drawings and photographs (10 boxes) 1859-1923, nd, drawing office registers and roll books (1 box) nd, drawings nd, patents, trade mark papers, manufacturing agreements, etc (3 bundles, c47 items) 1863-77, 1886-1971, departmental cost ledgers (21) 1911-17, summary departmental cost accounts (1 vol) 1910-11, cost of sundries books (137) 1890-1917, parts order and cost sheets (16 bundles) 1938-56, cartridge and rifle department records (6 vols) c1899-1945, explosives licences (1 packet) 1923, register of tools 1859-82, time ledgers (199) 1856-1913, time book 1946-7, papers rel to property (4 bundles, 1 packet) 1863-1919, c1940-1963, photographs (51 vols, 20 boxes, 2 files) 1859-1972, nd, catalogues, circulars and other printed papers 1860-1927, nd, memorial volume rel to Thomas Greenwood 1873.
West Yorkshire Archive Service, Leeds (Greenwood & Batley records). NRA 21361.

[785] **JT GREENWOOD & SONS**, coachbuilders, Carmarthen and Llandilo, Carms

Account book 1897-1916, misc notebooks, plans and papers (35 items) c1900, plans (4) of firm's workshop 1969.
Welsh Folk Museum, Cardiff (MSS 2523, 2566, 2622). NRA 31986.

Accounts, day book and catalogues 1897-1937.
Dyfed Archives Service, Carmarthen: see *Quarterly newsletter March 1981*, p7.

[786] **ALFRED GRINDROD & CO LTD**, heating and ventilation engineers, Sheffield

Cash books (6) 1893-1965, sales ledger 1889-1921, prime cost ledger 1903-40 and day books (5) 1896-1916, 1952-67, purchase day books (32) 1909-51, other sales and purchase records (9 vols) 1919-67, order books (7) 1924-69, wages books (5) 1915-66.
Sheffield Archives (LD 1842-77, MD 6969-98). NRA 34836.

[787] **GROSE LTD**, coachbuilders, motor engineers and automobile distributors, Northampton

Cash books (5) 1957-73, purchase ledger journal 1963-72, wages book 1904-8, typescript history of firm c1976.
Northamptonshire RO (1978/143). NRA 22316.

Albums (5) containing photographs of vehicles and premises, misc letters, price lists, advertisements, etc 1878-1978.
The Company. Enquiries to Northamptonshire RO. NRA 22316.

[788] **GROVER & CO LTD**, general engineers and machinists, London

Records from 1862 incl minutes, corporate agreements, share records, annual reports and accounts, private ledgers, sales statistics, price lists and catalogues, specifications, patents and production corresp, and plans and drawings of machinery and premises.
The Company. NRA 28631; BAC *Company Archives* no 224.

[789] **GN HADEN & SONS LTD**, heating engineers, textile machinery mfrs and millwrights, Trowbridge, Wilts

Partnership agreements, share certificates, papers rel to capital, etc (14 bundles and items) 1855-c1961, partnership ledgers of WN Haden (2 vols) 1892-1921, order books (9) 1821-90, estimates (1 vol) 1824-42, customers' accounts (1 vol) 1824-43, pattern book c1830, prices book c1860-95, patents and related papers 1829-53, nd, machinery drawings (c40 items) 1780-1932, corresp and papers rel to individual installations and repairs (8 bundles and items) 1838-1922, misc staff records (21 bundles and items) 1821-1964, inventory of Trowbridge factory 1892 and other premises records (15 items) c1870-1965, corresp and papers rel to the firm's history and the Haden family c1780-1980, photographs of products and work done 1879-1965, printed technical and publicity material c1840-1964.
Wiltshire RO (WRO 1325). NRA 12587. A few of the above records are photocopies of originals in the possession of Haden Young Ltd or elsewhere.

Lincoln branch corresp, drawings and plans 1950s-1960s.
Lincolnshire Archives (HADEN; Misc Dep 258).
Archivists' Report 22, 1970-1, p63, 24, 1972-3, p50, 27, 1977-82, pp28, 43, 29, 1983-4, p21.

[790] **JOHN HAIGH & SONS LTD**, ironfounders and textile machinery mfrs, Huddersfield, Yorks

Letter books (14) 1890-1, 1893, 1900-8, balance books (2) 1892-1905, ledger 1876-1900, nominal ledger 1892-6, journals (5) 1871-9, 1893-6, day books (20) 1876-84, 1887-1915, cash books (3) 1882-9, 1893-1908, purchase ledger 1883-8, purchase day books (2) 1893-6, 1902-7, sales journal 1896-1903, receipts (28 files) 1895-6, 1899-1914, stock book 1872-83, stocktaking book 1882-94, castings ledger 1884-1900, description of machinery 1930s, misc publicity material and other printed papers (2 bundles, 7 items) 1895-1950s, wages books (3) 1886-98, premises records (3 items) 1913-1950s; Chadwick Machine Co Ltd corresp c1912-67, misc sales and production records 1900-83, publicity material 1925-61, misc staff records 1919-60, inventories and other papers rel to premises 1892-1960, misc records 1899-1972; Haigh-Chadwick Ltd annual reports, misc corresp, statistics and printed papers 1971-86.
West Yorkshire Archive Service, Kirklees (B/HC, KC 411). NRA 34067.

[791] **ALEXANDER HALL & CO LTD**, shipbuilders, Aberdeen

Directors' meeting minutes 1904-14, letter book 1868-71, private ledger 1872-9, register of ships built 1811-1958, cost books 1817-90, offset book c1868-93.
Aberdeen City Archives: see Ritchie.

[792] **ROBERT HALL & SONS (BURY) LTD**, loom and weaving machinery mfrs, Bury, Lancs

Articles of association 1894, balance sheets 1860-3, letter book 1854-79, home accounts (44 vols) 1865-1968, foreign accounts (24 vols) 1869-1946, private ledger 1877-94, general ledgers (4) 1880-96, 1909-15, home ledgers (6) c1888-92, 1903-61, foreign ledgers (3) c1887-92, 1896-1926, nominal ledgers (7) 1862-1952, bank books 1844-80, order books (26) 1856-1958, bill book 1877-93, stock book c1854 and sheets 1963, castings account book 1844-5, cost book 1931-5, moulders' weights book 1958-70, particulars of machines and looms 1865-85, lists of wheel patterns, working exhibits and drawings c1800-late 19th cent, indexes to blueprints (2 folders) nd, wages books (32) 1837-1969, staff analysis books (2) 1889-1960, valuations of tools, stock, plant and premises (3 vols) 1861-77, 1886-1941, plan of foundry 1879, papers rel to extension of premises late 19th cent, deeds and other property records 1686, 19th-20th cent, catalogues and wallcharts, etc (2 vols, 5 binders, 10 items) late 19th cent-c1910, photographs of mill (4 items) nd, glass plate negatives (192 boxes) and index nd; papers rel to Hall family.
Lancashire RO (DDH1). NRA 34993.

General ledger 1895-1902, estimate books (23) 1930-56, loom order books (2) 1895-1904, job order books (2) 1927-32 and details books (3) 1903-35, indexes to order books (2) 20th cent, check books (2) 1914-50, cost books (4) 1903-4, 1912-30, sketch books (34) c1893-1955 and plans of

machinery (3 items) 20th cent, index to drawings
late 19th cent, misc papers and index books (6 vols)
20th cent.
Bury Archive Service (BRH). NRA 34905.

[793] **HALL, RUSSELL & CO LTD**,
shipbuilders, Aberdeen

Partnership minutes (1 vol) 1865-97, register of
directors 1901-46, summaries of share capital
1909-48, private ledgers 1880-97, private journals
1879-97, account book of insurance premiums and
feu duties paid *c*1897-1904, cost books *c*1875-1938,
particulars book 1938-53, calculation book 1942-55,
machinery particulars 1923-58, notebooks *c*1924-60,
details of wage rates 1880-1912, register of engine
works wages 1880-1941, apprentice book
1869-1922, photographs nd.
Aberdeen City Archives: see Ritchie.

Records of shipyard wages incl rates of pay
1880-1952.
Grampian Regional Archives.

Contracts and agreements 1954-64, ship plans nd,
photographs of ships and yard 20th cent.
Scottish Record Office (GD 313). NRA 20367.

Drawings 1945-82.
Aberdeen Art Gallery and Museums. NRA 34453.

[794] **WILLIAM HAMILTON & CO LTD**,
shipbuilders, Port Glasgow, Renfrewshire

Directors' minutes (1 vol) 1904-75, reports and
annual accounts 1951-65, corresp 1949-64, cash
books (4) 1929-46, estimate books (5) 1912-22, cost
books (128) 1913-63, particulars books (3)
1877-1950, list of ships built 1914-63, ships' papers
and plans 1944-63.
Glasgow University Archives and Business Record Centre
(GD 320, UGD/223). NRA 19046.

Ship plans 1920-40.
National Maritime Museum Manuscripts Section: see
Ritchie.

[795] **JAMES HAMMOND**, coachbuilder,
Gainsborough, Lincs

Ledger 1861-8.
Lincolnshire Archives (Brace 24). *Archivists' Report 13,
1961-2,* p48.

[796] **HA HAMSHAW LTD**, coachbuilders and
motor engineers, Leicester

Ledgers (4) 1910-36, cash books (18) 1911-56,
bank accounts 1960-1, enquiries books 1909-15,
order books (31) 1927-58, sales books (28)
1925-50, lists of debtors and creditors 1950-2,
corresp and papers (2 vols, *c*65 items) rel to
agreements, specifications, patents, etc 1880-1957,
wages books (10) 1908-59, insurance records
(146 items) 1905, 1927-56, plans and photographs
(2 vols, 28 items) of factory and vehicles late 19th
cent-1936, typescript history of firm 1946.
Leicestershire RO (4 D 61, DE 1518). NRA 21685.

[797] **HARDING (LEEDS) LTD**, textile pin and
machinery accessory mfrs, Leeds

Memorandum and articles of association 1892-1919
and related corresp 1892-1908, agreements with
subsidiaries 1892-1910, directors' and shareholders'
minutes (4 vols) 1892-1966, draft minutes (1 vol)
1892-1901, special resolutions 1894-5, 1899-1908,
share records (12 vols, 3 bundles) 1892-1949, seal
register 1892-4, annual returns and summaries
(2 vols) 1911-48, corresp and papers (6 bundles) rel
to tax, insurance, etc 1903-4, 1915-62, annual
reports and balance sheets, etc (1 vol and loose
items) 1896-1939, ledgers (3) 1863-95, private
ledgers (7) 1892-1968, private journals (2)
1892-1902, cash books (2) 1893-5, 1933-57,
transfer journal 1948, bank book 1916-17, trading
accounts (2 vols) 1896-1941, sales ledger 1892-7,
invoice books (4) 1910-12, letter book rel to orders
1913, patents (1 vol) 1850-75, scrapbook of printed
machinery drawings *c*1857-80, deeds, papers rel to
works extensions and other property records
(6 bundles) 1845-1935, notes on history of firm
*c*1956; Robert Cook & Co (Hathersage) Ltd articles
of association 1899 and private ledger 1900-19,
James Rhodes & Co minutes, share records, seal
register, ledger and journal (6 vols) 1892-5,
Richardson, Child, Christy & Co minutes, share
records, seal register, ledger, journal and bank book
(10 vols) 1892-5 and stock account books (3)
1889-92.
West Yorkshire Archive Service, Leeds (Accs 2392,
2959, 3039). NRA 33803.

[798] **HARLAND & WOLFF LTD**, shipbuilders
and engineers, Belfast and Glasgow

Records 19th-20th cent incl directors' meeting
minutes 1907-28, accounts 1863-1970, agreements,
specifications and corresp rel to licences, etc
1921-79, rigging plans 1860-99, wages books
1861-1952, reports on works and buildings 1921-57
and trade union corresp 1911-38.
Public Record Office of Northern Ireland (D 2805).
NRA 32782; and see Ritchie.

Estimating books (Govan yard) 1923-50, misc
notebooks rel to contracts *c*1905-53.
*Glasgow University Archives and Business Record
Centre.*

Ship folders *c*1913-51, plans of slipways nd.
Ulster Folk and Transport Museum, Holywood.

[799] **HARRISON, McGREGOR & GUEST
LTD**, agricultural implement mfrs, Leigh, Lancs

Records 1875-20th cent incl board and general
meeting minutes (11 vols) 1891-1955, drawings of
machinery, wages book 1889-98, catalogues and
publicity material and photographs.
Wigan Archives Service (D/DY HMG). NRA 35097;
Accessions to repositories 1988, p29.

[800] **HARVEY & CO LTD**, engineers,
ironfounders and general merchants, Hayle,
Cornwall

Minutes (3 vols) 1845-52, 1863-99, directors'
agenda book 1899-1922, registers of members and

share ledgers (5) 1883-1904, 1922-66, notebook rel to shareholders and capital 1893, letters received, with related reports, etc (186 bundles) 1829-1904, letter books (234) 1791-6, 1809-1904, 1923-35, papers rel to legal cases (18 bundles and items) 1812-16, 1828-9, 1865-c1900, misc corporate papers (103 items) 1852-1904, corresp, share certificates and debentures for mining and misc companies (325 items) 1867-1929, ledgers (60) 1809-1907, cash books (30) 1809-1905, Truro branch ledgers and cash books (6) 1935-52, journals (17) 1809-1904, receipt and disbursement books (4) 1811-25, debit and credit books (7) 1823-8, 1838-63, 1879-82, 1890-1916, debt books (3) 1859-78, bankers' interest books (2) 1827-63, bill books (2) 1827-84, stem books (21) 1825-8, 1836-42, 1857-72, 1882-3, 1891-2, 1901-7, misc accounts (4 vols) 1848-56, 1876-87, 1891-3, statements of account (7) 1895-1904, mining account books, reports, prospectuses, etc (23 vols, files, etc) 1819-1928, corresp, accounts, coal books, freight books, etc rel to the company's shipping and shipbuilding interests (c18 vols, c36 items) 1835-1944, cost books (6) 1828-39, 1848-54, order book 1853-62, price book 1862-85, contract letter book 1844-51, contract book 1865-77 and ledgers (2) 1860-85, waste book 1874-5, stock inventories (46 vols) 1815-1904, misc corresp, specifications, catalogues, etc (c65 vols, bundles and items) 1845-1934, apprenticeship indentures (84 items) 1823-93, factory abstract pay book 1890-1904, valuations of premises (12) 1841, 1864-97, estate rent books (5) 1862-1907 and accounts and rentals (c88 items) 1868-1920, deeds, etc 1688-1934, maps and plans 1810-1946, misc papers mainly rel to local and company history 19th-20th cent.
Cornwall RO (H). NRA 655.

Additional corresp (56 items) 1829-49, 1887-8, 1895, 1900.
Cornwall RO (X 681/1-56). *List of accessions 1983-84*, p2.

Inventories of stock 1812-19, 1835-9, 1843-8.
Cornwall RO (X 475). NRA 5235 (Summary of accessions Oct-Dec 1975).

Engineering drawings c1860-1908.
Cornwall RO (X 725). *List of accessions 1985-86*, p1.

[801] **HARVEY ENGINEERING CO LTD**, sugar machinery mfrs, Glasgow

Letter book 1889-1911, order books (8) 1861-71, 1886-98, 1901-6 and related memoranda 1869-71, drawing office order books (69) 1872-1930, drawing office notebook 1905-20, dimension and repair books (25) 1851, 1872-3, 1880-7, drawing catalogue books (2) 1851-70, sketch book 1896-1910.
Glasgow University Archives and Business Record Centre. (UGD/118). NRA 14656.

[802] **JOHN HASTIE & CO LTD**, ships' steering gear mfrs and engineers, Greenock, Renfrewshire

Minutes (1 vol) 1915-52 and agenda book 1899-1953, agreements (8 items) 1904-23, other corporate corresp and papers 1918-41, misc

financial records 1910-50, general order books (12) 1892-1947, order books for screw gears (8) 1873-1924, steam gears (14) 1907-57 and hydraulic gears (4) 1919-69, pump book 1920-9, rudder calculations books (35) 1929-64, drawing registers for steam gears (18) 1900-59, hydraulic gears (6) 1923-42 and pumps (13) 1927-42, misc drawing registers (7) c1890-1976, product drawings (c13,000 items) 1870s-1928, nd, patents and related legal papers 1883-1926, lists of staff nd, plans of works (11 items) 1906-11, 1945, nd, microfilms of drawings and order books (7 boxes, 6 spools, 2 envelopes) nd, photographs of ships nd, publicity material and instruction books (27 items) 19th cent-1970s.
Glasgow University Archives and Business Record Centre (GD 444). NRA 36364.

Shareholders' and directors' minutes and papers 1972-6, registers of members (2) 1918-75, dividend registers (2) 1953-72, register of seals 1972-5, receipts (microfilm) 1964-6, patent specification 1884, pay book 1845-53, misc papers (8 files) 1952-76.
In private possession. Enquiries to NRA (Scotland) (survey 3031). NRA 14825.

[803] **HATHORN, DAVEY & CO LTD**, pumping engine mfrs, Leeds

Order books (34) 1852-1937, prime cost books (45) 1910-37, shop tracing books (17) 1875-1939, test books (7) 1904-39, sketch books (2) c1876-98, 1937-8, drawings (several hundred) nd, photograph albums (2) nd, press cuttings book 1904-15, printed catalogues, etc 1899-c1948.
West Yorkshire Archive Service, Leeds (HD). NRA 25021.

[804] **GEORGE HATTERSLEY & SONS LTD**, textile machinery mfrs, Keighley, Yorks

Memorandum and articles of association 1888, 1954, partnership, agency and other agreements (17 bundles, envelopes, etc) c1865-1974, directors' minutes (2 vols) 1888-1984, managers' minutes (1 vol) 1976, register of directors 1901-10, share records (8 vols and files) 1889-1985, office memoranda, notes on business visits, etc (10 vols) 1868-1979, letter and memoranda books (10) 1824-68, 1882-1908, general corresp (75 files and envelopes) 1829-1980, corresp and purchase files (989) 1950-85, balance sheets and trading accounts (115 items) 1889-1980, ledgers (10) 1797-1851, 1866-88, private ledgers (5) 1881-7, 1890-1971, nominal ledgers (3) 1909-70, day books (9) 1793-8, 1806-26, 1958-60, 1976-82, cash books (14) 1795-1837, 1872-5, 1878-81, 1951-85, journals (5) 1914-32, 1955-78, bank books (10) 1869-73, 1928-34, bill books (4) 1814-57, 1922-82, misc accounting records (9 vols) 1815-39, late 19th cent-1963, order books (c240 vols, etc) 1817-1981, prices records (15 vols) c1899-1979, information rel to customers, competitors and the textile industry (48 vols, files, etc) 1876-1975, catalogues and advertising material (112 vols, bundles and items) 1898-1981, purchase and production analysis

records (9 vols) c1900-1973, stocktaking records
(52 vols) 1863-7, 1889, 1901-81, drawings,
instruction manuals and other technical records
(34 vols, files, etc) 1867-1980, patents (83 items)
1853-1928, litigation and other legal records
(c32 bundles and envelopes, etc) 1823-1981,
salaries, wages and directors' expenses books (21)
1808-37, 1873-4, 1900-81, apprentice books and
employee registers (9) 1818-1981, pension scheme
and social club records (19 vols, files, etc) 1951-78,
plans, valuations and other property records
19th-20th cent, papers rel to firm's history
1847-1980, photographs c1882-1970s; Hattersley
family personal and executors' corresp and papers
1841-1974.
West Yorkshire Archive Service, Bradford (32D83).
NRA 29694.

American patent specifications (34 bundles), indexes
(2 vols), photographs (1 packet).
Bradford Industrial Museum. NRA 29694.

[805] R & W HAWTHORN, LESLIE & CO
LTD, shipbuilders, Newcastle upon Tyne

Articles of association, agreements and other
corporate papers (19 files, etc) 1886-1920,
partners', directors' and general meeting minutes
(1 vol) 1885-91, directors' minutes (8 vols)
1885-1938, committee minutes (5 vols, 1 file)
1899-1926, board agendas (1 vol) 1905-18
and papers (1 vol, 2 files) 1920-40, seal book
1901-36, directors' reports (10 vols) 1897-1926,
directors' letter books (4) 1888-1915 and corresp
(8 files) 1886-1916, misc papers rel to shares
(11 files, 14 items) 1886-1951, secretary's letter
books (18) 1886-1914, bank letter books (4)
1888-1912 and other company corresp (23 files,
1 bundle, etc) 1886-1946, balance sheets and profit
and loss accounts 1871-1948, private ledgers (5)
1883-1940, departmental ledgers (4) 1919-31,
St Peter's Works ledger balances (17 files) 1886,
1891-4, private journals (3) 1885-1942, other
journals (3) 1915-47, cash books (16) 1885-8,
1890-2, 1901-50, St Peter's bills receivable (2 vols)
1885-1925 and payable (1 vol) 1901-4, misc
financial records 1885-1945, marine engine order
books (2) 1882-1916, order books (2) 1921-54,
sales and Admiralty ledgers (5) 1913-32, purchase
and sales journals (5) 1921-36, engine contracts
(1 bundle) 1873-92, Hebburn yard tenders (9 vols)
1904-27 and cost book 1884-1900, ships' particulars
books (5) 1886-1942, ships' specifications, launch
particulars and engine work records (75 vols)
1914-62, trial trip data (1 vol) 1886-1900, delivery
books (2) 1915-60 and other production records,
patents and licences (14 files, 21 items) 1843-1947,
apprenticeship records (1 vol, 4 bundles and files,
etc) 1819-1960, wages, salaries and other staff
records (4 vols, 18 files and bundles, etc)
1871-1945, plant inventories and valuations
(13 vols, 6 files, 3 items) 1885-1939, capital costs
and rentals for electrical power (1 vol) 1902-23,
deeds and property agreements 1829-1962, papers
rel to company history, publications and
photographs 1865-1976, nd, employers' association
papers (20 files, etc) 1898-1959; private corresp and

papers of Sir Benjamin Browne and Benjamin
Browne junior 1900-24.
Tyne and Wear Archives Service (Acc 962 and 1248).
NRA 678.

Data sheets (3 vols) 1926-64, launch data notebook
nd, builders' certificate book nd.
Tyne and Wear Archives Service (Acc 1836). NRA
23331.

Locomotive order books c1835-1959, drawing office
registers 1872-1959, drawings and photographs nd.
National Railway Museum, York.

Ship plans (c240 items) 1854, 1885-1921.
National Maritime Museum Manuscripts Section: see
Ritchie.

Photographs 1877-1929.
South Tyneside Central Library.

Misc drawings.
Monkwearmouth Station Museum.

[806] HAYWARD-TYLER & CO LTD, pump
mfrs and mechanical engineers, Luton, Beds

Articles of partnership (6 items) 1864-99, minute
books (6) 1905-49, out-letter books (10) 1871-1930,
memoranda book, corresp and papers 1874-c1940,
balance sheets 1923-34, private account books (3)
1915-52, private journal 1899-1934, private ledger
1951-4, bill book 1883-1913, royalty books (3)
1878-1900, bank books (4) and related papers
1858-1916, purchase day books (2) 1931-5, order
book 1937 and misc sales corresp and papers
1869-1910, production totals books (4) 1902-6,
price books (2) 1882-1900, stock inventories (5)
1855-1908, pattern book 1907-8, work contracts
1878-1918, misc soda water production records
1837, 1878-1931, patents 1840-1929, drawing office
sketch copy books (10) 1896-1922, out-letter books
(2) rel to staff 1896-1908, wages and salaries books
(7) 1886-1947, registers of employees (4) and misc
staff records 19th-20th cent, agency agreements
1876-1936, licences, etc 19th-20th cent, deeds, legal
papers and bills, London and Luton premises
records c1854-1933, catalogues and photographs
19th-20th cent; records of subsidiary and associate
companies 1864-1945, nd.
Bedfordshire RO (SP). NRA 24356.

[807] HEAD, WRIGHTSON & CO LTD,
engineers, ironfounders and bridge builders,
Thornaby-on-Tees, Yorks

Directors' minutes (6 vols, 1 envelope) 1890-1903,
1907-36, general meeting minutes (1 vol)
1890-1933, committee minutes (1 vol) 1939-61,
directors' attendance registers (2) 1890-1920,
corresp (1 bundle) rel to dissolution of partnership
1889-1900, misc corresp (2 bundles) 1853-98,
1929, share records (14 vols, bundles and items)
1865-1961, balance sheets, private journal, misc
accounts and related papers (c25 vols, bundles and
items) 1860-1961, contracts letter book 1889-1943,

rough order book for chains 1870-1, order book 1877-1902, order books (94) 1922-79, patent records (*c*24 items) 1869-1904, wages books (32) 1916-82, new starters register 1921-61, corresp rel to property (2 bundles) 1897-9, 1910-23, maps, plans and diagrams (31 items) 1853-1939, nd, deeds (*c*70) mainly rel to property 1808-1945 and schedules (8) of deeds 1840-1935, photographs of staff, works and products mainly 20th cent, printed papers 1894-1979; Stockton Steel Foundry Co Ltd directors' minutes 1906-33 and balance sheets and reports 1935-46.
Cleveland Archives (U/HW). NRA 34098.

[808] **JOSHUA HEAP & CO LTD**, screwing machine and tool mfrs, Ashton-under-Lyne, Lancs

Share certificates (2 items) 1878, 1885, annual returns 1878-93, exhibition certificates (5 items) 1876-82, 1920s, assignment of patent 1883, price lists and catalogues incl some of competing firms 1895-1912, nd, misc papers (2 items) 1902, 1959; Hall family papers 1923-39.
Tameside Archive Service (DD/238). NRA 34898.

Directors' and general meeting minutes from 1875, share records 1876-1952, other corporate records 1874-1904, financial records from 1899, works plans 1917, 1958.
In private possession. NRA 28631; BAC *Company Archives* no 208.

[809] **HEDGES & SON**, ironfounders, engineers and agricultural implement mfrs, Bucklebury, Berks

Sales ledger 1736-46.
Berkshire RO (D/EX 223). NRA 3501.

Sales ledgers (2) 1746-73.
In private possession. Microfilm in the Rural History Centre, Reading University. NRA 21006.

Sales ledgers (2) 1882-7.
Rural History Centre, Reading University. NRA 21006.

[810] **DAVID & WILLIAM HENDERSON & CO LTD**, shipbuilders, Glasgow

Liquidation accounts 1935-6, particulars of vessels built 1834-1931, particulars books 1863-91, contract notebook nd, plans of lands feued 1880, historical notes nd.
Glasgow University Archives and Business Record Centre (UGD 239). NRA 21083; and see Ritchie.

Memorandum and articles of association 1900, directors' report and balance sheet 1912, legal corresp and papers 1851-1935, corresp and papers rel to sale of yard to National Shipbuilders Security 1936, Meadowside yard and other deeds 1880-1925.
Strathclyde Regional Archives (T-BK 160). NRA 15348.

Plans of dock installations *c*1880-1962, corresp with Drysdale & Co Ltd rel to dock pumps 1930.
Strathclyde Regional Archives (TD 44). NRA 15409.

Plans of yachts and sailing vessels 1887-99.
National Maritime Museum Manuscripts Section.

[811] **ALFRED HERBERT LTD**, machine tool mfrs, Coventry

Memorandum and articles of association, etc 1894-1980, minutes (25 vols and files) 1894-1980, papers rel to reconstruction and liquidation 1974-82, register of directors (1 vol) 1911-65, registers of members (60 vols and files) 1894-1975, share certificate books (6) 1905-44, registers of transfers (3 vols) 1944-80 and of debentures (2 vols) 1960-81, mortgages (1 vol) 1967-70 and probates (1 vol) 1968-80, misc debenture papers 1960-80, corresp with shareholders, stockholders, banks, etc 1948-81, seal books (7) 1918-48, 1957-80, annual returns (1 vol, 1 file) 1930-9, 1976-81, balance sheets, accounts, monthly group accounts, etc (1 vol, *c*210 files and bundles) 1887-1980, private ledgers (4) 1894-1974, investment ledgers (2) 1939-43, 1963-80 and related papers 1954-76, ledgers (12) 1902-76, ledger sheets *c*1912-73, cash books (2) 1939-51, purchase, sales and agency agreements (2 files) 1939-79, cost ledgers (5 vols) 1942-8 and print-outs (3 vols) 1950-2, stock books (2) 1887-1901, plant books (25) 1887-91, 1906-48, machine testing book 1897, plans and elevations of machine tools (13 sets) 1912-33, personnel records 1941-82, records of joint shop stewards' committee (43 vols, 3 bundles) 1942-80, furniture and fittings valuation books (7) 1918-47, misc corresp, agreements, etc 1908-78, machine tool catalogues and other printed papers 1897-1984; records of subsidiaries 1899-1980.
Coventry City RO (Acc 586, 926, 1330, 1512, 1558, 1618). NRA 30534.

Corresp, memoranda and other papers of Sir AE Herbert (11 boxes, 6 items) 1917-59, some rel to machine tool production.
Shakespeare Birthplace Trust RO, Stratford-upon-Avon (DR 526). Access to material under fifty years old restricted. NRA 27931.

Misc corresp, notes and printed articles by Sir AE Herbert, etc (2 boxes) mainly 1911-57, incl balance sheet of Herbert & Hubbard 1887-8 and agreement for establishing Alfred Herbert Ltd 1894.
In private possession. Enquiries to Shakespeare Birthplace Trust RO. NRA 27931.

[812] **JOHN HETHERINGTON & SONS LTD**, textile machinery mfrs, Manchester

Comber order books (16) 1905-63, catalogues and sales literature (6 items) 1930s.
Lancashire RO (DDPSL/19). NRA 20296.

Machinery inspection reports 1927.
Museum of Science and Industry in Manchester (TX 2/3). NRA 29510.

[813] **JOSEPH HIBBERT & CO LTD**, textile machinery mfrs, Darwen, Lancs

Directors' minutes (1 vol) 1903-40, impersonal ledger 1898-1913, catalogues, manuals and sales leaflets (26 items) *c*1920-69.
Lancashire RO (DDPSL/9). NRA 20296.

[814] **HICK HARGREAVES & CO LTD**, engineers, boilermakers and locomotive builders, Bolton, Lancs

Corresp (c1,800 items) 1854, 1860-1, balance book 1936-42, cash books (4) 1919-41, credit ledgers (2) 1911-29, debit ledgers (sales) (9) 1906-32, sales day book 1928-34, enquiry books, order books and related records (15 vols) 1915-65, lists of engines built 1835-1916, nd, engine smiths' books (8) 1864-88, engine renewal books (7) 1871-1971, engineers' copy books (109) 1891-1927, engine size books (2) 1896-1937, engine work ordered out (3 vols) 1896-1928, engine files (30 vols) 1927-67, Hick-Breguet condenser order and production records (26 vols) 1914-33, millwrights' copy, estimates and fitting books, etc (56 vols) 1887-1959, power station files (51 vols) 1930-80, bolt books (7) 1902-27, misc lists and indexes (6 vols) 1871-1933, engineering drawings 1819-1966, drawings lists and catalogues (20 vols) 1832-1940, wages books (25) 1925-42, piece work registers (2) 1902-17, analysis of work accounts 1906-9, repair work books (2) 1915-16, glass negatives (c800 items) 1873-1936, engineering publications 1942-63.
Bolton Archive Service (ZHH). NRA 27111.

Locomotive drawings (45 items) 1831-54.
Museum of Science and Industry in Manchester. NRA 22050.

[815] **CHARLES HILL & SONS LTD**, shipbuilders and ship repairers, Bristol

Articles of partnership 1825, 1839, minutes (1 vol) 1920-49, letter book 1856-78, private ledgers 1872-1900, journals 1819-22, 1826-7, materials and labour books 1799-1817, building accounts 1793-1836, ship plans 18th-20th cent, wages books 1775-1817, mould loft and dock plans and papers c1819-23, photographs nd.
National Maritime Museum Manuscripts Section: see Ritchie.

[816] **HILL & ROBINSON**, engine and boiler mfrs, Coseley, Staffs

Records continuing those of John Wassell's Union Engine Factory incl ledger 1838-58, cash books (2) 1835-59, pocket account books (2) 1857, order books (2) 1851-7, workmen's time book 1841-58, tenancy agreement, legal papers and related corresp (1 bundle) 1853, misc bills and receipts (3 bundles) c1853-9.
Public Record Office (J 90/166). NRA 35890.

[817] **JOHN HIND & SONS LTD**, engineers and machine makers, Belfast

Order books (5) 1900-16, agreement 1884, deeds and share certificates (17 items) 1883-95, notes on firm's history.
Public Record Office of Northern Ireland (D 2037). NRA 34894.

Corresp, patents, specifications, draft deeds, etc (1 bundle) 1868-1919.
Public Record Office of Northern Ireland (D 1326/3/8). NRA 34894.

[818] **HOAD & SONS**, coachbuilders and wheelwrights, Portsmouth, Hants

Ledgers (7) 1851-1980, day books (12) 1910-11, 1914-80, account book for horsedrawn vehicles supplied on credit 1886-1913, other accounting records (11 vols) 1911-79, estimate and specifications records (12 vols, c610 items) 1895-1984, order books (15) 1909-11, 1921-81, invoice books (3) 1893-1909, 1932-4, 1947-77, copies of letters to suppliers (1 vol) 1894-1919, suppliers' catalogues and corresp (c430 items) 1897-1980, stocktaking books (2) 1935-79, time books and sheets (3 vols, 10 bundles) 1909-44, wages books (12) 1935-79, misc staff records (1 vol, 35 items) 1903-51, rent books and other premises and insurance records (c15 vols, c12 bundles, c150 items) 1879-1981, photographs (c140 items) of vehicles and premises c1900-86; Hoad family papers 1777-1984.
Portsmouth City RO (1433A). NRA 32364.

[819] **GEORGE HODGSON LTD**, loom mfrs, Bradford, Yorks

Directors' reports and statements of account 1899-1930, corresp and reports on state of firm (c3 files) 1905-17, business, estate and personal letter books of George Hodgson (2) 1914-21, private ledgers (4) 1895-1930, expired agreements (1 bundle) nd, stock-in-trade account and working plant 1898, catalogues c1913-18.
West Yorkshire Archive Service, Bradford (32D83/53). NRA 29694.

[820] **HOFFMANN MANUFACTURING CO LTD**, ball bearing mfrs, Chelmsford, Essex

Letters mainly from customers and suppliers (568 files) 1897-1904, corresp, patent and sales agreements, income tax papers, etc (312 files) 1896-1970.
Essex RO, Chelmsford (D/F 18). NRA 27214.

[821] **HOLDEN & BROOKE LTD**, pump mfrs, Manchester

Records from 1882 incl articles of partnership and association, directors' minutes, agreements, balance sheets, accounts, sales corresp, specifications and patents, salaries books, property agreements and papers, and RG Brooke's pump diagram book and letter books.
The Company. NRA 28631; BAC *Company Archives* no 561.

[822] **HOLLAND & HOLLAND LTD**, gun and rifle makers, London

Records from c1854 incl directors' minutes (2 vols) 1909-33, 1959-64, letter book of Henry Holland 1895-1922, register of investments 1899-1957,

register of probates 1899-1959, ledgers (3) 1880-91, 1904-8, 1910-17, audit ledger 1919-26, sundries ledger 1931-7, day books (c23) 1901-73, dividend account cash book 1914-60, account expenses (4 vols, etc) 1904-60, information rel to customers (2 vols) c1890-1910, nd, sales and export accounts (1 vol) 1914-39, yearly sales ledger from 1931, register of firearms transactions (5 vols) 1937-56, order books (c70) from c1854, case books (2) 1908-39, rifle regulators' notebooks (2) c1905-8, 1912-14, sketch book c1900-11, test book 1933-60, repair books (5 vols, etc) 1893-5 and from 1918, trade mark papers (1 bundle) 1886-1924, indenture 1880, salary and wages book 1920-31, papers rel to property (2 bundles) 1910-c1922, visitors' books (3) 1928-82 and photographs, press cuttings, catalogues, etc c1898-1990.
The Company. Enquiries to the Business Archives Council. NRA 35073.

[823] **HOLMAN BROS LTD**, engineers and ironfounders, Camborne, Cornwall

Cash book 1894-1901, foundry day books (2) 1863-74, 1892-6, job book 1903-11.
Cornwall RO (X 475, X 542). NRA 5235.

[824] **THOMAS HOLMES & JOHN PYKE**, coachbuilders, London

Day book 1792-7.
Guildhall Library, London (MS 5643A). *Guide to archives and manuscripts in Guildhall Library*, 1989, p87.

[825] **WC HOLMES & CO LTD**, gas plant mfrs and engineers, Huddersfield, Yorks

Memorandum and articles of association 1910-63, letter books (4) 1895-1905, balance sheets, accounts and misc financial papers 1890-6, day book 1871-8, standing charges 1909-10, costings books (2) c1880-90, 1900-3, list and valuation of valves in stock 1894, technical and misc letters and papers (11 items) 1834-1912, catalogues and other printed papers 1851-1981, photographs of staff, works and installations c1880-c1960.
West Yorkshire Archive Service, Kirklees (KC537). NRA 35363.

[826] **JOHN HOLROYD & CO LTD**, engineers and tool mfrs, Milnrow, Lancs

Records 19th-20th cent incl directors' minutes (5 vols, etc) 1899-1964, trading figures 1909-19, agreement 1947, letter rel to overtime 1879, works inventory and valuation 1907, catalogues (3 items) 1888-1906 and photographs of exhibition stands 1906-58.
Manchester Central Library Local Studies Unit (M501/HR). NRA 35782.

[827] **HOLTZAPFFEL & CO**, mechanical engineers and lathe and tool mfrs, London

Articles of partnership 1794, 1804, cash book 1812-20, register of lathes made 1798-1928, account

for tools and appliances 1893, inventory and valuation of stock, materials and equipment 1800, leases (6) 1825-95, personal vouchers and receipts (6 bundles) 1830-5 and other misc business and family letters and papers 1786-1847, notes rel to firm's history 20th cent.
Guildhall Library, London (MSS 9475, 21515-33). NRA 31286.

Ledgers (3) 1811-12, 1815-16, 1819-22, customers' journal 1892-7.
Edinburgh University Library (Gen 879-82). *Index to manuscripts: first supplement*, 1981, p273.

[828] **HOOPER & CO (COACHBUILDERS) LTD** (formerly **ADAMS & HOOPER**), London

Order books (10) 1879-1920, invoice books (2) 1864-1907, sales records (over 35 vols and files) 1922-56, delivery registers (3 vols) 1877-93, 1903-44, record of work done (1 vol) 1840-4, prime cost book 1828-45, smith's journeyman's prices (1 vol) from c1855, specifications (1 vol) 1895-8, designs for monograms, etc (1 vol) 1890-1937, production records, drawings and photographs (16 vols, c4,200 items) 1925-59.
Science Museum, Department 5. Enquiries to the Science Museum Library. NRA 13485.

Letter and estimate book 1818-20, list of customers 1878-9, list of bad debts 1854-94, stocktaking list 1873-4, misc estimates, advertisements and staff records (45 items) c1855-93.
Westminster City Archives, Victoria Library (Accs 324, 738). NRA 13485.

Order books (2) 1930s-1959, corresp rel to Rolls-Royce and Bentley cars 1940s-1960s.
Rolls-Royce Enthusiasts Club. Enquiries to the Warden, The Hunt House, Paulerspury, Northants. NRA 35052.

[829] **RICHARD HORNSBY & SONS LTD**, mfrs of steam, oil and gas engines, Grantham, Lincs

Records from 1854 incl ordinary share ledger and register of members (1 vol) c1880-1920, letter books (2) 1880-1918, annual reports from 1891, ledgers (6) c1897-1931, summary account 1898-1900, agency agreements (3 vols) 1898-1916, invoice book 1910, statistics of sales, stock, wages, etc 1905-21, shipping specifications (1 envelope) 1890-5, misc commercial papers (1 folder) c1918-19, thresher register 1854-1906, engine registers (9) 1873-1913, oil and gas engine registers (over 160) from 1892, experiment and test records (c14 vols) from 1893, engine construction costing book 1909, engineer's corresp 1897-1905 and instructions 1909, weekly output statistics (4 vols) 1897-1903, plant requisitions 1910-19, motor car data book 1905-21, pattern mark books (4) 1892-c1905, drawings, tracings and blueprints from c1870, wages records (21 vols) 1883-1941, employees' letters 1898-1907, valuation records 1882, 1888-92, visitors' book 1881-1918, photographs from c1885, press cuttings 1902-18, printed summary of legal case 1906 and catalogue and price lists 1919.
Lincolnshire Archives. NRA 11143 and *Archivists' Report 21, 1969-70*, pp11-14.

Memorandum and articles of association 1879,
annual reports (1 vol) 1880-1917.
*National Museums and Galleries on Merseyside,
Merseyside Maritime Museum* (B/VF/2/2/2). NRA
29901.

See also Ruston, Proctor & Co Ltd.

[830] **HORSELEY BRIDGE & ENGINEERING
CO LTD** (afterwards **HORSELEY BRIDGE &
THOMAS PIGGOTT LTD**), Tipton, Staffs

Managing directors' monthly reports, annual
reports, etc (7 files) 1920-54, balance sheets and
related papers (19 files) 1846-7, 1858, 1875-1944,
corresp and papers rel to accounts, financial
statements and annual general meetings 1916-51,
share records (5 vols, 4 files) 1874-1944, papers rel
to shares, sales and other financial affairs (10 files)
1927-58, secretary's and works manager's reports,
management and works committee minutes, etc rel
to office reorganisation (8 files) 1919-29, private
ledgers (5) 1893-1925, private cash book 1912-27,
creditors' ledgers (7) 1951-68, sales ledger 1935-43,
contract books and order books and registers
(5 vols) 1929-56, nd, other papers rel to orders
(27 boxes, 3 files) 1929-52, misc production and
stock records (16 vols and files) 1843-1947, contract
drawings (1 bundle) 1968, deeds, agreements and
patents (35 items) 1865-1923, inventory and
valuations of plant, etc 1896, 1906, plans of
premises (12 items) 19th cent, nd, Horseley Works
visitors' book 1949-57, photographs (12 vols, etc)
*c*1920-63, company secretary's unofficial diaries
(4 vols) 1892-1928, press cuttings, publicity
material, notes on company history, etc 1881-1986.
Staffordshire RO (D 1288, 3142, 4469, 4819). NRA
17387.

See also Thomas Piggott & Co Ltd.

[831] **HOWARD & BULLOUGH LTD**, textile
machinery mfrs, Accrington, Lancs

Partnership deeds (2) 1857, 1863, letter books (4)
1881-95, 1908-9, profit calculations (1 vol) 1864,
balance books (2) 1893-1907, 1934-8, private ledger
1863-6, impersonal ledgers (3) 1871-1909, 1931-50,
impersonal accounts (5 vols) 1896-1912, 1940-6,
other accounting records (57 vols) 1908-59, order
and specification books (2) 1857-60, 1869-71, order
books (51) 1871-1945, jobbing order books (100)
1927-57, specification books (2) 1907-11, 1927-40,
estimate and quotations registers (33) 1920-4,
1930-57, summary of prices (1 vol) 1905-31, types,
totals and values of machines ordered (32 vols)
1891-8, 1903-62, agents' export registers (5)
1902-15, 1927-45, catalogues and sales literature
1888-1967, agreements, patent records, etc (2 vols,
5 files) 1863-1934, production meetings minutes
(1 vol) 1894-1921, production notebook 1882-1921,
munitions production records (3 vols) 1936-45, staff
and wages records (17 vols) 1891-1956, inventory
books (21) 1882-1952, buildings and machinery
insurance register 1899-1926, fixed stock and
buildings summary book 1892-7, notebooks, price
lists, photographs and other misc records (67 vols,
files and items) 1851-*c*1965.
Lancashire RO (DDPSL/3). NRA 20296.

[832] **THOMAS HUDSON LTD**, boilermakers,
Coatbridge, Lanarkshire

Minutes (2 vols) 1903-33, private ledgers (4)
1899-1965, ledgers (13) 1896-1976, day books (21)
1888-1986, journal 1896-1945, cash books (15)
1893-1985, estimate books (28) 1905-16, invoice
books (15) 1876-1977, goods received books (4)
1897-1913, steel purchase book 1904-29, works cost
books (22) 1888-1922, specification and materials
books (5) 1891-5, materials books (27) 1897-1923,
1963-80, pay books (12) 1894-1980, time books
(38) 1877-86, 1889-1980, catalogues, etc (4 items)
1897-1930.
Glasgow University Archives and Business Record Centre
(UGD/99). NRA 21184.

Plans (343) of products 1896-1946, nd.
In private possession. Enquiries to Glasgow University
Archives and Business Record Centre.

[833] **HUDSWELL CLARKE & CO LTD**,
locomotive builders, Leeds

Order books 1861-1961 (copies).
National Railway Museum, York.

Specifications, locomotive registers, drawings and
photographs nd.
Leeds Industrial Museum.

[834] **HUMBER GRAVING DOCK &
ENGINEERING CO LTD**, ship and engine
repairers, Immingham, Lincs

Minutes 1909-37, agenda books 1909-35, corresp
nd, ledgers 1910-40, journals 1909-73, salary and
wages records 1926-47, vouchers books 1913-18.
South Humberside Area AO: see Ritchie.

Directors' minutes 1909-20.
Public Record Office (RAIL 1057/3270-2).

Photograph albums *c*1960.
Immingham Museum.

[835] **HUMBER LTD**, cycle and motor car mfrs,
Coventry

Records incl minutes from *c*1900.
Peugeot Talbot Motor Co Ltd. Enquiries to the
Company Secretary.

[836] **EDWARD HUMPHRIES LTD**, steam
engine and threshing machine mfrs, Pershore, Worcs

Steam engine register 1885-1906.
Rural History Centre, Reading University. NRA 21013.

Threshing machine registers (2) 1871-1933.
Untraced. Microfilms are in the Rural History
Centre, Reading University. NRA 21013.

[837] **HUNSLET ENGINE CO LTD**, locomotive
builders, Leeds

Order books from 1897, specifications 1875-1940,
locomotive registers from 1865, weight diagram
books from 1877, drawings 1865-1959, paint shop

records 1899-1935, locomotive enquiry proposals *c*1900-1955, photographs from 1865.
Leeds Industrial Museum. Copies of order books 1865-1971 are in the National Railway Museum, York.

[838] **R HUNT & CO LTD**, engineers, ironfounders and agricultural implement mfrs, Earls Colne, Essex

Memorandum and articles of association 1899, 1950, minutes (1 vol) 1899-1941, financial statements, profit and loss accounts, expenditure analysis, etc (7 vols) 1872-1928, general account book 1823, 1845-55, private ledgers (5) 1886-1953, capital ledgers (2) 1887-1931, journal 1936-48, cash books (6) 1886-1909, 1925-34, 1943-8, sales ledgers (38) 1849-56, 1863-1952, sales day books (205) 1908-67, sales analysis books (19) 1872-6, 1884-1950, sales and wages summary (9 vols) 1899-1940, other sales records (11 vols, 1 bundle) 1885-1919, purchase day books (6) 1937-47, bought ledgers (10) 1863-1942, other purchase records (23 vols, 1 bundle) 1895-1939, customer orders (41 vols, 1 file) 1889-1918, internal orders (81 vols) 1902-14, index books of terms (8) *c*1885-1897, 1906-8, specifications (8 vols) 1870s-1904, costing records (23 vols, 5 files) 1885, 1891-1909, other order, price and despatch records (17 vols, etc) 1880s, 1904-64, stock books (36 vols, 1 bundle) 1911-19, 1939-49, drawings (1 bundle, 1 item) 1891, 1903-9, machinery construction books (11) 1870s-1932, foundry, turnery and misc production records (12 vols, 14 files, 3 bundles) 1870-4, *c*1890-1908, 1913-55, labour books (45) 1906-16, misc staff records (9 vols and bundles) 1870, 1897-1918, 1930s, valuations and schedules of works, plant and equipment (6 vols) *c*1880-1946, property account and rent books (11) 1899-1944, photographs (*c*1,000 items) 1860s-1950s, firm's and competitors' publications nd; Hunt family papers (2 vols, 17 bundles) 1896-1941, nd.
Rural History Centre, Reading University. NRA 21003.

Records 1892-1989 incl directors' attendance books 1920-60, 1979-83, accounts 1963-79, delivery registers 1892-7, shipping register *c*1901, disintegrator registers 1894-1947 and catalogues 1928-86.
Essex RO, Chelmsford (A7886, A7932, A7950, A8102).

[839] **HUNTS**, millwrights, machinists and implement agents, Soham, Cambs

Ledgers (4) 1832-52, 1879-1903, day books (8) 1830-51, 1864-91, 1897-1922, misc papers (8) *c*1880-1901, 1933.
Cambridgeshire RO, Cambridge (773). NRA 24574.

[840] **HUTCHINSON, HOLLINGWORTH & CO LTD**, loom mfrs, Dobcross, Yorks

Share application books (2) 1874, 1880, balance sheet 1879, account book 1860-1, misc accounts (2 bundles) 1873-85, bank books (4) 1909-28, cash book 1929-35, diary 1873 incl orders for machinery,

patent records (8 items) 1876-88, moulding department notebook 1913-15, wages books (45) 1861-1961, misc corresp, papers and catalogues (*c*25 vols and items) 1862-1960, other business, legal and property papers mainly of James Hollingworth (*c*116 items) 1845-1939.
Saddleworth Museum and Art Gallery (M/HUT). NRA 11134.

Foreign ledgers (2) *c*1920-36, prices for sundries (1 vol) *c*1917-31, goods book 1928-35, loom books (15) 1881-1917, catalogues 1898, nd.
Leeds University, Department of Textile Industries. NRA 32465.

Papers rel to takeover by George Hattersley & Sons Ltd (1 bundle) 1963-9, loom orders and specifications (12 vols, files and bundles) 1897-*c*1970, catalogues, photographs, etc 1889, 1904, 1960s-1970s.
West Yorkshire Archive Service, Bradford (32D83/54). NRA 29694.

[841] **HYDRAULIC ENGINEERING CO LTD**, hydraulic machinery mfrs and ironfounders, Chester, Cheshire

Memorandum and articles of association 1874, 1950-8, board, committee and general meeting minutes 1886-1938, reports, accounts and balance sheets 1886-1977, register of directors 1901-77, preference share register 1892-1966, register of seals 1887-1984, machinery registers 1877-1984, drawing office order books 1911-26 and order cards *c*1922-56, drawings from *c*1920, plans of premises 1906-40, misc printed papers 1920-40.
In private possession. NRA 28631; BAC *Company Archives* no 193.

Records 1874-1971 (127 vols, 33 items) incl ledgers, order books and plans.
Chester City RO (CR 256): see *Archives and records of the city of Chester*, pp106-7.

[842] **IMPERIAL TYPEWRITER CO LTD**, typewriter mfrs, Leicester

Memorandum and articles of association and agreement 1908, annual reports and accounts 1952-65, nominal ledgers (7) 1906-37, cash books, bill books, bank journals and other financial records (24 vols, 1 file) 1920-67, corresp files 1929-*c*1957, sales returns (2 vols) 1913-28, export contracts and corresp (1 file) 1912-53, home and export reports (1 vol) 1929-31, patent ledgers (2) 1908-18, wages and staff insurance records (4 vols) 1922-38, photographs, company magazines, etc 1911-1960s.
Leicestershire RO (DE 1535 and 3413). NRA 32955.

[843] **A & J INGLIS LTD**, shipbuilders and engineers, Glasgow

Financial statistics (1 file) 1925-30, private estimate letter book 1881-93, private cost ledger *c*1860-83, cost ledger 1863-92, finished engine weights books (4) 1865-*c*1925, trials books (2) 1881-1917, specifications (2 vols) 1865-78, nd, trial diagrams and statistics (4 vols) 1878-1908, drawings of fittings

(3 vols) 1898-1921, misc plans (2 boxes) nd, inventory of titles (1 vol) *c*1885.
Strathclyde Regional Archives. NRA 15402.

Partnership agreements 1868-83.
Glasgow University Archives and Business Record Centre (UGD/69). NRA 21083; and see Ritchie.

[844] INTERNATIONAL HARVESTER CO OF GREAT BRITAIN LTD, agricultural equipment mfrs, London

Memorandum and articles of association 1906, 1946, board and general meeting minute book 1907-25, annual profit and loss accounts and financial statements 1906-49, financial report 1918, general ledgers (14) 1912-60, general and agents' journals (9) 1907-*c*1922 and cash books (17) 1919-37, goods registers (2) 1924-32, publicity material, technical literature and photographs from *c*1918, further records from 1960.
Rural History Centre, Reading University. NRA 29100.

[845] JACKSON & BROTHER LTD, engineers and ironfounders, Little Bolton, Lancs

Directors' minutes (1 vol) 1911-42, wages records (8 vols) 1864-1913, inventories and valuations 1893, 1909, 1960, notebook of TC Jackson *c*1830.
Museum of Science and Industry in Manchester (MP/JB). NRA 29505.

Stock book 1842, inventory of machinery and tools 1872, misc photographs of foundry *c*1910, printed list of wage movements in engineering industry 1897-1925.
Bolton Archive Service (ZJE). NRA 19836.

[846] WJ JEFFERY & CO LTD, gun and rifle makers, London

Records from *c*1889 incl minutes and agenda (2 vols) 1924-9, 1949-54, register of members, etc (1 vol) 1918-31, private ledger 1946-57, cash books 1889-99, 1956-60, sundries book 1897-9, sales, purchase and order ledgers, day books and journals *c*1891-*c*1912 and from 1919, repairs book 1911-17, stock books (12) 1894-1963, export stock book and related papers 1929-61, stock book journal 1938-48, stock index 1947, storage book 1919-50, testimonials and photographs (1 vol) *c*1913-41, catalogue 1924-5 and advertisements (1 vol) *c*1930-9.
Holland & Holland Ltd. Enquiries to the Business Archives Council. NRA 35073.

[847] J JOICE & SON, coachbuilders, Basingstoke, Hants

Balance sheets 1914-15, 1917, 1931, cash book 1896-9, ledgers and other accounts (10 vols) 1913-59, sales journal 1927-42, stock inventories 1888, 1913-31, nd, pocket books (4) of John Joice 1884, 1887-9.
Hampshire RO (32M65). NRA 25332.

Day book 1884-7.
Hertfordshire RO (D/ESn B12). NRA 22786.

[848] JOINTLESS RIM LTD, cycle wheel mfrs, Birmingham

Private ledger 1906-61, journal 1906-61, cash book 1906-60.
Greater London RO (BTR Industries Ltd). NRA 24145.

[849] EVAN JONES & SON, mechanical, cycle and motor engineers and ironmongers, Caernarvon

Journals (12) 1870-1904, 1911-12, 1922-43, day books (17) 1909-49, customers' account ledgers (17) 1869-1957, shop ledgers (6) 1870-1913, cycle sales ledgers (3) 1899-1916, purchase journals (4) 1917-35, receipts and payments books (7) *c*1895-1936, misc accounts, etc (*c*22 vols) 1886-*c*1951, order and letter books (3) 1908, 1939, 1950-1, duplicate postcard book 1898-9, stocktaking books (12) 1906-11, 1935-52, diaries (3) 1899, 1901-2, misc advertisements, photographs, etc 1891-1912, nd; Welsh Cycle Co Ltd receipts and payments book 1900-3.
Gwynedd Archives and Museums Service, Caernarfon (XD/31, XS/2208). NRA 30921.

[850] KAY & BACKHOUSE LTD, agricultural and dairy engineers, York

Ledgers (20) 1891-1969, bill book 1894-7.
Brynmor Jones Library, Hull University (DX/122/2-22). NRA 10731.

[851] HW KEARNS & CO LTD, machine tool mfrs, Darlaston, Staffs

Minutes (6 vols) 1907-73 and other corporate records 1907, 1939-73.
Staveley Industries plc. NRA 28631; BAC *Company Archives* no 44.

[852] KEATS & BEXON LTD, shoe machinery mfrs, Stafford

Balance sheet and profit and loss account 1894, debenture 1909, general ledger 1896-1903, cost and selling prices of firm's machines and parts (2 vols) 1901, inventory and valuation 1895, misc leases, agreements, etc (1 bundle) 1904-26, catalogues (5) 1897-9, nd.
Staffordshire RO (D 955). NRA 17379.

[853] KERR, STUART & CO LTD, locomotive builders and mfrs of railway equipment, London and Stoke-on-Trent, Staffs

Order books, cost books, weight diagram books, shipping specification books, locomotive enquiry proposals, drawings and photographs 1891-1930.
Leeds Industrial Museum. Copies of order, costing and specification books are in the National Railway Museum, York.

[854] JOSEPH KILNER & SON, heald and slay mfrs, Honley, Yorks

Account books (5) 1874-1924, day books (4) 1868-94, cash book 1898-1914, bank and cheque

books 1905-26, delivery record books (4) 1902-24, receipts, bills, delivery notes, invoices and corresp (14 bundles) 1876-89, 1900-25, notebooks (4) containing names, addresses, etc 1870, 1876-8, nd, telephone book 1899-1902, production notebook 1864-5, diaries (2) 1904, 1909, misc printed papers 1912-19.
West Yorkshire Archive Service, Kirklees (B/JHK, B/K). NRA 34070.

[855] **JOHN G KINCAID & CO LTD**, marine engineers and boilermakers, Greenock, Renfrewshire

Board minutes 1887-98, 1906-66, general meeting minutes 1920-52, private letter books 1894-1917, 1954-75, ledgers and cash books 20th cent, sales ledger 1948-56, material cost books 1901-67, abstracts of costs books 1920-42, contracts letter book 1928-37 and files 1950-68, engine enquiries 1940-55, specification books c1915-70, engine register nd and drawings 19th-20th cent, wages and salary records 1919-60, stock list and valuation of tools and machinery 1860-70, inventories and valuations 1917-30, misc corresp 1917-30, publicity material and photographs nd.
Strathclyde Regional Archives. NRA 18890 (partial list); and see Ritchie.

Papers rel to formation of the company 1887-8, reports and balance sheets 1894, 1934-58, misc corresp 1922-53.
Glasgow University Archives and Business Record Centre.

[856] **HJH KING & CO LTD**, mechanical engineers, Nailsworth, Glos

Engineering memoranda book of Henry JH King 1866-93.
Gloucestershire RO (D2794/28). NRA 17634.

Product drawings of engines, clutches, winding gear, governors, etc 1892-1915.
Gloucestershire RO (D2625). *Handlist*, 1990, p102.

[857] **CHARLES LACK & SONS LTD**, agricultural engineers and brassfounders, Cottenham, Cambs

Corresp, minutes and papers rel to winding up of the firm 1946-68, register of directors and members 1916-46, balance sheets and accounts 1946-64, day books (14) 1913-27, petty cash books (4) 1917-41, bought, sold and stores ledgers and journals (16 vols) 1915-37, estimates books (3) 1892-1912, invoice books (4) 1917-42, job ledger 1872-85, job books (8) 1934-47, material allocation books (14) 1928-42, wages records (23 vols) 1912-48, misc photographs, brochures, etc c1921-63.
Cambridgeshire RO, Cambridge (768). NRA 29253.

[858] **SIR JAMES LAING & SONS LTD**, shipbuilders and ship repairers, Sunderland, co Durham

Directors' meeting minutes 1898-1913, 1943-54, registers of members 1898-1938, private letter book 1916-31, balance sheets 1882-1947, annual

statements books 1916-39, ledgers 1818-1967, cash books 1944-67, cost books 1864-1966, ships' particulars books 1794-1962, general arrangement plans 1926-63 and contracts 1848-1967, wages records 1800-1933, plant book 1899-1933, photographs 1889-1971; Philip Laing's account books 1846-91.
Tyne and Wear Archives Service: see Ritchie.

[859] **LAMBERTON & CO LTD**, mechanical engineers, Coatbridge, Lanarkshire

Statement of affairs 1888-1905, profit and loss accounts 1890-1908, balance sheets, etc (3 files) 1955-8, letter books (9) 1874-82, 1888-9, corresp, some with foreign clients (4 files) 1911, 1915, abstracts of distributive accounts (4 items) 1904-40, ledgers (7) 1876-1969, other accounting records (6 vols) 1954-62, invoice books (5) 1874-7, 1905-15, order books (3) 1876-1900, foundry order book 1904-13, sales book 1924-40, cost books (44) 1898-1964, works account books (3) 1883-1939, work schedule 1877-85, job books and ledgers (10) 1879-1961, specifications books (4) 1879-1936, abstract of goods book 1906-15, wages books and sheets (25 vols, 3 bundles) 1874-1924, 1939-62, inventories 1880-90, 1936, measurements of premises 1904-11, legal papers 1903-5, photographs and glass negatives c1890-1960, misc corresp, papers and photographs (3 filing cabinets) 1928-60.
The Company. Enquiries to NRA (Scotland) (survey 2065). NRA 23491.

[860] **LANCELEYS LTD**, engineers and ironfounders, Chester, Cheshire

Account books (3) 1881-1909, drawings of seed machines, mill and pumping machinery, etc (7 bundles) 1874-1948.
Chester City RO (CR 77 and 90). *Archives and records of the city of Chester*, p107 and *Accessions to repositories 1970*, p20.

[861] **JJ LANE LTD**, general engineers and boilermakers, London

Letter books (2) 1873-4, firm's catalogues and brochures c1878-c1902, particulars of sale on closure of firm 1957.
Greater London RO (B/LAN). NRA 7562.

[862] **JOHN LANG & SONS LTD**, machine tool and lathe mfrs, Johnstone, Renfrewshire

Minute book of joint production advisory committee 1942-9, private ledgers (8) 1892-1957, ledger, journal and cash book (1 vol) 1916-19, order books (47) 1883-1945, monthly sales and purchase records, etc (3 vols) 1894-1951, diagrams (9 boxes) nd, salaries book 1936-42, benevolent fund ledger 1944-52, photographs of founder, workforce, works and products c1890-1970, product catalogues and other printed material c1890-1969, nd.
Glasgow University Archives and Business Record Centre (UGD/48). NRA 16053.

Partnership agreements (4 items) 1888-1916, annual report books (2) 1883-1901, private journal 1937-9,

order books (14) 1904-5, 1945-62, testimonials books (2) 1891-1904, 1907-22, cast book 1874-80, specifications book 1883-5, stock book (machine parts) 1934-51, machine index books (6) nd, time book 1874, notes rel to Halsey-Weir bonus system 1898, salaries book 1926-35, inventory and valuation 1885.
In private possession. Enquiries to NRA (Scotland) (survey 665). NRA 16053.

Minute book 1962-85, register of members 1959-81, other corporate records (1 file) *c*1967-80, trade mark registrations and patents 1939-67; Wickman Lang Ltd memorandum and articles of association 1916-66, minute books (2) 1964-85, registers of members and directors (2 vols, etc) *c*1952-82, other corporate records (3 files) *c*1965-85, letters patent, trade marks and related corresp 1939-77.
Coventry City RO (Acc 1140). NRA 28002.

Records *c*1940-79 incl certificates of incorporation (2 items) 1959, 1965, operator's manuals and parts lists, plans of works and photographs of products.
Strathclyde Regional Archives (TD 995). NRA 12501.

[863] **LANSTON MONOTYPE CORPORATION LTD**, composing machine mfrs, London

Records incl board minutes (incomplete series) from *c*1897, misc corresp early 20th cent, and patent records from *c*1900.
In private possession. Enquiries to the Historical Manuscripts Commission.

Records incl ledgers.
Merrion Monotype Trust. Enquiries to the Historical Manuscripts Commission.

[864] **ASA LEES & CO LTD**, textile machinery mfrs, Oldham, Lancs

Memorandum and articles of association 1931, machine order books for cotton gins (5) 1903-38, openers and lap machines (18) 1878-1941, carding engines (12) 1884-1942, slubbing, intermediate and roving frames (15) 1875-1944 and components (27) 1895-1944, mules (8) 1883-5, 1894-1913 and components (158) 1865-1952, ring spinning and doubling frames (6) 1903-39, reeling machines (2) 1910-52 and drawing frames (2) 1906-26, order sheets 1914-40 and summaries for carding engines (4 vols) 1891-1928, job order books (14) 1919-52, stock order notebooks (11) 1904-46, calculation books for mules (5) 1908-45, job work notebook 1900-29, production notebooks for carding engines (23) 1890-1940, mule shafts (3) 1902-7, 1912-16, frames gearing (3) 1905-7, 1911-26 and speed frames 1895-6, production details book for twiners 1907-26, details book for ring spinning and doubling spindles 1909-26, details (5 vols, etc) 1897-1932 and setting out books (5) 1906-32 for ring spinning and doubling frames, plates and patterns books (11) 1903-37, plans, drawings and specifications *c*1900-52, parts schedules and product catalogues (47 items) *c*1890-1948 and misc records *c*1900-52.
Lancashire RO (DDPSL/4). NRA 20296.

[865] **ALFRED LENG**, coachbuilders, Pontefract, Yorks

Cash book 1909-11, memoranda rel to coachbuilding work (3 vols) 1889-1927, notes, sketches, bills, etc *c*1905-30, catalogues (*c*35) and other printed papers *c*1880-1933.
West Yorkshire Archive Service, Wakefield Headquarters (C776). NRA 20126.

[866] **LILLESHALL CO LTD** (formerly **EARL GOWER & CO**), engineers, iron and steel mfrs and colliery proprietors, Priors Lee, Salop

Records (*c*65 vols, 39 boxes, etc) 1660-1981 incl partnership agreements and papers 1764-1878, minutes 1840, 1878, memorandum and articles of association 1878-80, corresp and other corporate records from 1880, agreements and contracts 1883-1932, papers rel to debentures 1888-1928, journals from 1935, misc accounts from 1794, pig iron cost book 1886-90, steel monthly cost book 1886-9, costs ledger 1890-4, hot metal analysis books (2) 1909-25, diary of steel rolling department 1910, summary of work manufactured, weight of steel work on order, etc (1 vol) 1886-1917, engine plans 1907-12, patent records 1892-1909, staff records from 1900, deeds, legal and other papers rel to estates, premises and mines (*c*30 boxes, 133 items) and other mining and brickmaking records 18th-20th cent.
Ironbridge Gorge Museum. Partial description: BAC *Company Archives* no 359.

Articles of association 1880, 1947, 1972, directors' minutes (7 vols) 1891-1951, general meeting minutes, etc (9 vols) 1899-1914, 1947-64, board agenda books (7) 1881-1957, directors' register 1903-45 and attendance books (3) 1903-63, share and debenture records 1916-77, annual accounts 1905-81, agreements 1920-33, register of seals and deeds 1907-63, report on Lilleshall rolling mills 1963, invoice books 1972-6, sales ledger 1896-1912, purchase ledger 1955-7, railway costs 1932-47, bar annealing cost book 1942-5 and account book 1942-4, process costs 1940, raw materials book 1899-1942, water record book 1955-80, staff records 1942-58, nd, capital costs book for plant 1939-40, inventories and valuations 1907-82, estate accounts and rentals 1926-79, misc papers 1929-76.
Ironbridge Gorge Museum (1986.11842).

Further estate records (25 boxes).
Ironbridge Gorge Museum.

[867] **LINKLETERS PATENT SHIP FITTINGS CO LTD**, North Shields, Northumb

Deed of partnership 1913, registers of directors and annual returns (2 items) 1934-48 and other company registration and share records 1926-55, profit and loss accounts, etc 1907-34, 1957, war damage claims (1 bundle) 1919-22, ledgers (3) 1913-22, 1926-47, journals (3) 1915-42, cash books (8) 1917-55, lists (2) of creditors and debtors 1912, bank account books (6) 1912-32, order book 1910-21, contract sheets (2) 1929, stock list 1912, stock and work in progress sheets (16 items)

1924-40, patents and Board of Trade certificates (c50 items) 1884, 1906, 1913-30, wages book 1934-9, income tax papers and other tax records (30 bundles) 1909-37, legal papers and corresp rel to works (26 items) 1913-15, trade circulars 1910-75, photographs 1900-40, papers rel to James Linkleter and the history of the firm (1 bundle, 28 items) 1907-64.
Tyne and Wear Archives Service (Acc 694). NRA 21124.

[868] **RA LISTER & CO LTD**, agricultural engineers, dairy utensil and diesel engine mfrs, Dursley, Glos

Register of members (2 vols) 1893-1931 and of directors (1 vol) 1922-36, directors' reports, corresp, accounts and balance sheets (14 bundles, 3 files) 1929-49, ledgers (5) 1892-1931, insurance policies (1 vol) 1934, wages, salaries and pensions records (4 vols, 2 files, 1 bundle) 1894-9, 1909-59.
Gloucestershire RO (D3310). NRA 23970.

[869] **LITHGOWS LTD**, shipbuilders and ship repairers, Port Glasgow, Renfrewshire

Directors' minutes and board papers 1919-68, register of shareholdings incl values and depreciation of ships c1878-1908, shareholdings and investments in subsidiaries, etc 1911-69, investment registers 1947, administrative papers 1875-1970, balance sheets and profit and loss accounts 1876-1968, private ledgers (2) 1890-1910, general ledgers (8) 1906-51, journals (10) 1917-58, private day books (2) 1896-1920, private cash books (3) 1910-47, account book 1874-1908, other financial records 1876-1969, private letter books rel to quotations (3) 1911-26, estimates and enquiries c1939-69, cost books and records 1875-1961, yard diaries (3) 1906-40, outfit, extra and timber index books (14 vols) 1917-47, particulars books 1907-46, ships' papers 1875-1970 and plans 20th cent, wages records 1893-1968, other staff records 1902-68 incl apprenticeship registers (19) 1902-50, valuations and related papers rel to property and plant 1875-1970, press cuttings and publicity material 1952-72, photographs nd.
Glasgow University Archives and Business Record Centre (GD 320, UGD 223). NRA 19046.

Sir James Lithgow's personal corresp and papers and biographical papers 1891-1969.
Glasgow University Archives and Business Record Centre (DC/35). NRA 30494.

Ship plans 1920-45.
National Maritime Museum Manuscripts Section: see Ritchie.

[870] **LLANDOVERY WEIGHING MACHINE CO**, weighing machine mfrs, Llandovery, Carms

Minutes (1 vol) 1908-18, accounts (1 vol) 1888-1907, misc accounts, share transfers, etc (24 items) 1903-42.
National Library of Wales (DTM Jones Collection 6876-6901). NRA 37182.

[871] **LLOYDS ENGINEERING & FOUNDRY CO LTD**, Abercarn, Mon

Memorandum and articles of association 1896, bank book 1895-6 and cancelled cheques 1895-8, corresp (68 items) with solicitors 1895-8, corresp (38 items) rel to contracts and work carried out 1890-6, valuations and lists of work and stock 1896-7, misc papers (7 items) 1892-7, nd.
Gwent RO (D 1718). NRA 14003.

[872] **LOBNITZ & CO LTD**, shipbuilders and engineers, Renfrew

Partnership minutes (1 vol) 1890-5, directors' minutes (4 vols) 1895-1957, board and administrative papers 1912-68, register of transfers and annual returns 1900-60, balance sheets and working papers 1873-1964, ledgers (5) 1895-1960, register of imported materials 1934-63, estimates and enquiries working papers 1957-64, cost books (2) 1885-9, list of ships built 1848-1960s, contract books (17) 1899-1965, salary book 1930-59, apprentices' time books (6) 1907-33, insurance register c1945, photographs 1859-1963.
Glasgow University Archives and Business Record Centre (UCS 4) NRA 14659.

Ship plans 1928-59, nd.
Glasgow University Archives and Business Record Centre (UGD 130/3). NRA 14316.

[873] **LOCKWOOD & CARLISLE LTD**, piston ring, spring and valve mfrs, Sheffield

Agreements, etc (1 bundle, 1 envelope, 2 items) 1886-1918, ledgers (15) 1882-1956, day books (18) 1883-1956, cash books (6) 1958-68, purchase ledger 1943-53, box account ledger 1948-55, order books (46) 1878-80, 1888-1941, letter book 1894 and other misc records rel to orders 1935-45, shipping books (10) 1913-63, reports (4 vols) on ships' and colliery engines 1924-66, registers (29) of ships' names, order numbers, etc 1901-70, patent specifications (2 boxes) 1832-1945, wages books (7) 1892-9, 1946-67, misc corresp and papers rel to premises 1898-1941, catalogues, photographs, etc 1870s-1950s.
Sheffield Archives (S10). NRA 34876.

[874] **LONDON & GLASGOW ENGINEERING & IRON SHIPBUILDING CO LTD**, Glasgow

Boiler works and engine department ledger 1910-14, inventories and valuations 1910-12.
Harland & Wolff plc: see Ritchie.

Ship plans c1865-95.
Strathclyde Regional Archives (TD 232). NRA 12501.

[875] **LONDON GRAVING DOCK CO LTD**, ship repairers, London

Minutes 1890-1980, agenda books 1928-77, share records 1890-1979, annual returns 1890-1928, annual reports 1931-66, balance sheets 1914-72, chairman's statements 1897-1973, accounts 1890-1982, ledgers 1947-71, journal 1940-79, job

books 1966-78, wages records 1939-74, plant and machinery registers 1940-74.
National Maritime Museum Manuscripts Section: see Ritchie.

[876] LONGWOOD ENGINEERING CO LTD, mechanical engineers, Huddersfield, Yorks

Minutes (1 vol) 1902-37, registers (2) of directors and annual returns 1920-65, secretary's corresp files (2) 1903-25 incl reports and balance sheets, private ledger 1902-36, monthly summaries book 1903-63, stock book 1905-20, stock and wages expenditure book 1921-63, valuations (4 vols) of buildings, plant and machinery 1916-68.
West Yorkshire Archive Service, Kirklees (KC 17). NRA 31065.

[877] JAMES F LOW & CO LTD, engineers and textile machinery mfrs, iron and brass founders, Monifieth, Angus

Directors' and general meeting minutes (4 vols) 1920-70, production meeting minutes 1961-2, registers (4) of shareholders 1902-71, transfers 1903-61 and directors' holdings 1948-71, note of capital expenditure 1905-25, private ledgers (2) 1902-39, other financial records (7 vols) 1929-71, order records (11 vols, etc) 1913-36, purchase day books (2) 1918-40, bills of material 1946-55, machinery books (5) 1870-1959, specifications and descriptions rel to carding machines (11 vols, etc) 1862-1976, preparing machines (16 vols) 1911-56, spinning frames (20 vols, etc) 1850-1966, winders (5 vols) 1912-69 and crimpers, etc (1 vol) 1925-66, operating instructions for machinery 1946-59, drawing office index 1867-1955, drawings of tools and machinery (294 items) 1857-1959, patent book 1924-60, plans (3) of foundry buildings 1908-68, photographs of machinery (109 items) 1928-*c*1950, papers rel to company history and Low family, etc *c*1902-84.
Dundee University Library (MS 89). NRA 17647.

Sales and purchase ledgers (3) 1953-62, bills receivable (1 vol) 1924-69, wages books (7) 1944-63.
In private possession. Enquiries to NRA (Scotland) (survey 865). NRA 17647.

[878] LUCAS INDUSTRIES LTD, bicycle, automotive and aerospace components mfrs, Birmingham

Records incl directors' and shareholders' minutes from 1897, board papers (microfilms) from 1939, share register 1897-1905, share registers (microfilms) from 1905, reports and accounts from 1898, inventory of plant and equipment 1897; Joseph Lucas Ltd directors' minutes 1952-66.
The Company. Access restricted. Enquiries to the Assistant Company Secretary.

Trade catalogues and photographs.
British Motor Industry Heritage Trust, Gaydon, Warwicks.

Arrangement for division of partnership profits 1883, balance sheet and statement of affairs

(2 items) 1884-5, letter book (Harry Lucas) 1880-5, sales account book (Joseph Lucas) 1860-72, cost book (Harry Lucas) 1872-*c*1882.
Untraced: see H Nockolds, *Lucas: The First 100 Years*, vol 1, 1976.

[879] LUKE & SPENCER LTD, abrasive and grinding wheel mfrs, Altrincham, Cheshire

Minutes, annual reports, etc (6 vols, 1 file) 1877-1961, secretary's letter book 1884-1913, share certificate book 1961-72, balance ledger 1901-63, balance sheets, accounts, etc 1954-61, staff records 1937-81.
Unicorn Industries plc. NRA 28631; BAC *Company Archives* no 263.

[880] LUMSDEN MACHINE CO LTD, grinding machinery mfrs, Gateshead, co Durham

Financial, sales, technical and staff records 1906-92.
Tyne and Wear Archives Service (Acc 2769). *Annual review 1992-93*, p12.

[881] DJ MACDONALD LTD, textile machinery mfrs, Dundee

Job order books (4) 1894-1952, machine order book 1982-6, stock books (3) 1956-89, costings records, parts lists and instructions *c*1900-84, plans and drawings *c*1893-1956, drawing office indexes (2 vols) 1920s, nd, wages book 1907-12, employee register 1892-1984, list of apprentices 1926-84, photographs (139 items) mainly of machinery, the MacDonald family and employees *c*1891-1956, nd, catalogues and misc papers 1884-5, 1920s-1930s, nd; account of DJ MacDonald's life *c*1933.
Dundee University Library (MS 93). NRA 34355.

Private ledger 1908-20, ledgers (2) 1910-33; political corresp and papers of DJ MacDonald incl papers rel to industrial affairs (1 bundle) 1883-1934.
In private possession. Enquiries to NRA (Scotland) (survey 2032). NRA 23016.

[882] JOHN McDOWALL & SONS, engineers and woodworking machinery mfrs, Johnstone, Renfrewshire

Memoranda book mainly rel to works and machinery 1875-1929, corresp and price list 1857, product catalogues (4) 1865-6, 1871, 1927, photographs (*c*1,000) of works and products from *c*1880.
Thomas White & Sons Ltd. Enquiries to NRA (Scotland) (survey 721). NRA 16014.

[883] McGREGOR & BALFOUR LTD, shuttle makers and mill furnishers, Dundee

Letter books (3) 1902-13, 1920-3, journals (2) 1925-32, corresp and orders (4 files) 1902, 1907-8, 1916, Calcutta order books (3) 1909-13, 1916-25, pattern order books (5) 1936-74, works plan *c*1900.
Dundee District Archive and Record Centre (GD/MB, GD/Mus 114). NRA 25491.

[884] McKIE & BAXTER LTD, marine engine builders, Paisley, Renfrewshire

Memorandum and articles of association 1927, list of shareholders 1931-67, letter books (11) 1905-10, 1914-16, balance sheets 1955-66, tenders (1 vol) 1914-19, lists (2) of engines built 1896-1968, machinery register 1896-1968, engine particulars (1 vol) 1910-27, misc engine cost records 1916-31, corresp rel to Admiralty vessels (2 bundles) 1914-17, ship and engine plans c1896-1967, indicator cards and trial results 1915-52, publicity material and photographs c1914-54; plans of engines built by Muir & Houston, Campbell & Calderwood Ltd, etc from c1899.
Strathclyde Regional Archives (TD 820, TD 827). NRA 28628.

Particulars books 1922-4, corresp and data c1920-39, ship plans 1921-33.
National Maritime Museum Manuscripts Section: see Ritchie.

[885] JAMES MACKIE & SONS LTD, flax, jute and hemp machinery mfrs, Belfast

Records (142 vols, 13 files, 17 items) 1892-1983 incl articles of association 1897, letter book 1910-16, ledgers 1892-1965, journals 1909-38, bill books 1903-56, flax account book 1914-16 and notebook rel to Russian flax industry 1903-13.
Public Record Office of Northern Ireland (D 3964). *Annual accessions 1992-93: private records.*

[886] McKITTERICK, ARMOUR & CO, engineers, millwrights and boilermakers, Newry, co Down

Letter book with accounts 1905-7.
Public Record Office of Northern Ireland (D 3628). *Deputy Keeper's Report 1983*, p47.

[887] P & W MACLELLAN LTD, engineers, railway rolling stock builders, nut and bolt mfrs, Glasgow

Copartnery contracts and agreements (4 items) 1870-93, memorandum and articles of association 1890, annual reports and balance sheets (82 items) 1890-1953, investment registers (2) 1898-1956, letter books (3) 1867-87, 1906-11, agency and other legal agreements, etc (1 vol, etc) 1905-36, private ledgers (7) 1842-1907, ledgers (13) 1858-1953, private journals (8) 1873-1902, 1910-55, journals (9) 1873-1909, 1931-60, cash books (5) 1839-47, 1873-96, bill books (2) 1834-46, 1885-90, teak contract books 1866-1910, bridge contract books (3) 1851, 1875-1962, contracts, tenders and specifications (4 files) 1861, 1871-1910, drawings (4) of Singapore suspension bridge 1968, patents (6 bundles) 1909-45, wages book 1864-70, yard plans (4) 1868-1933, nd and other property records 1909, 1919-48, photographs (1 album, etc) mainly of wagons and premises 1880-1945, nd, misc corresp and papers (1 vol, 8 files) 1876-1967; sales ledger 1822-31 and stock inventory 1830-2 of Donald MacLellan, hardware merchant.
Glasgow University Archives and Business Record Centre (UGD/153). NRA 17521.

Balance sheets (9 files) 1958-75, profit abstracts 1890-1947, accounting records (21 vols, etc) 1920-78, bill book 1890-1972, order books (3) 1834-46, 1904-5, c1972, stock books (14) 1909-62, cost book 1851-2, drawing office tracing book 1883-93, pension scheme cash book 1952-64, diagram of Clutha Works 1887, catalogue 1897.
In private possession. Enquiries to NRA (Scotland) (survey 764). NRA 17521.

[888] JOHN McNEIL & CO LTD, engineers and sugar machinery mfrs, Glasgow

Order books (48) 1887-1935, progressive costing books (50) 1905-52, registers of drawings (3) 1881-1958 and sketch tracings (8) 1941-59, estate order books (9) 1882-1958.
Glasgow University Archives and Business Record Centre (UGD/118/5). NRA 14656.

[889] MACTAGGART, SCOTT & CO LTD, mechanical engineers, Loanhead, Midlothian

Minutes of agreement of copartnery 1899, letter books (3) 1898-1917, pay books (2) 1899-1914.
The Company. Enquiries to NRA (Scotland) (survey 2560). NRA 27010.

[890] A & J MAIN & CO LTD, structural engineers, steel building and bridge mfrs, Glasgow

Directors' and general meeting minutes (3 vols) 1896-1920, share records (6 vols, etc) 1896-1949, directors' roll 1896-1966 and register 1901-46, balance sheets (44 vols) 1873-1920, annual returns 1906-15, dividend account books (2) 1896-1919, register of seals 1920-5, private ledgers (3) 1878-94, 1896-1922, ledger and annual balances (2 vols) 1896-1922, private journals (3) 1887-1914, statement of tonnage, sales and distribution of profits (1 item) 1904-12, patent rel to iron fences 1863, inventories and valuations 1877-9, 1906-8, machinery and plant record books (2) 1908-18, historical account of Germiston Works 1883-1923, catalogues and photographs of products 1864-c1903, nd, misc corresp and papers c1858-1966.
Strathclyde Regional Archives (TD 143). NRA 16544.

[891] MALDON IRON WORKS CO LTD, ironfounders, agricultural engineers and wagon builders, Maldon, Essex

Cash books (22) 1873-7, 1883-7, 1891-1947, retail, wholesale and warehouse ledgers (18) 1873-1942 and day books (48) 1911-42, statistics books (3) 1876-1940, misc records (9 vols) 1926-54.
Essex RO, Chelmsford (D/F 11). NRA 28631; BAC *Company Archives* no 156.

Cash books (4) 1873-1900, retail and wholesale ledgers (4) 1874-92, 1912-23, carriage book 1874-c1936, misc records (6 vols) 1914-15, 1932-51.
Maldon Museum. NRA 28631 *ibid.*

[892] **MANLOVE, ALLIOTT & CO LTD**, laundry machinery and hospital equipment mfrs, Nottingham

Registers of members (1 vol) 1896-1940 and debentures (2 vols) 1916-26 and related papers (5 bundles, 3 items) 1896-1951, ledgers (4) 1890-1948, private journal 1906-39, bill book 1889-1952, accounts with War Office and Ministry of Supply 1919-44, Willingdon laundry purchase accounts 1940-51, drawing office list books (6) 1894-1905, legal agreements and related corresp (57 items) 1909-42, patents (2 items) 1874, 1932, catalogues and printed material 1860-1957.
Nottingham University Library (A1). NRA 9182.

[893] **MANNING, WARDLE & CO LTD**, locomotive builders, Leeds

Order books 1861-1926 (copies), schedules of painting details nd.
National Railway Museum, York.

Working drawings (c350 items) 1863-1920, nd.
National Museums and Galleries on Merseyside, Merseyside Maritime Museum. NRA 29901.

Drawings 1860-1925, photographs nd.
Leeds Industrial Museum.

[894] **MARKHAM & CO LTD**, steam engine and colliery equipment mfrs, constructional and mechanical engineers, Chesterfield, Derbys

Corporate records incl memorandum and articles of association 1889, 1925, directors' minutes (3 vols) 1889-1958, general meeting minutes (1 vol) 1891-1925, company returns (2 vols) 1895-1928 and agency agreements from 1900; photographs of colliery equipment and construction projects c1900-1960s.
The Company. Enquiries to the Business Archives Council. NRA 21986.

Records (52 boxes, 37 vols, 15 rolls) 19th-20th cent incl accounting records 1872-1965, sales and purchase records 1900-46, production records 1863-1954, plans 20th cent, wages and other staff records 1890-1943, and plant and premises records 1876-1921.
Derbyshire RO (D2102, D2881). NRA 21986 (partial list).

[895] **MARSHALL, FLEMING & CO LTD**, engineers and crane mfrs, Motherwell, Lanarkshire

Articles of association 1938-48, minute book 1915-57, notices of annual meetings (1 vol) 1919-64, share records (4 vols) 1915-78, corresp and agreements 1915-62, annual returns, balance sheets, profit and loss accounts, etc (6 files, 2 bundles) 1916-78, capitalisation files (2) 1937-8, 1960, revenue and trade account books (2) 1912-34, private ledgers (2 vols, 2 files) 1915-78, ledgers (4) 1910-34, 1973-9, journal 1915-78, cash books (19) 1912-78, purchase and sales ledgers (6) c1934-81, order books (3) 1890-1932, sales books (6) 1900-64, purchase and estimate books (19) 1936-82, jobs cost books, etc (31) 1924-82, report

on crane design 1965, wages records (18 vols, etc) 1913-82, insurance policies 1916-60, crane catalogues nd, photographs of cranes and machine shop nd.
Glasgow University Archives and Business Record Centre (UGD/242). NRA 30967.

[896] **MARSHALL, SONS & CO LTD**, mfrs of steam and traction engines, threshing machinery and boilers, Gainsborough, Lincs

Memorandum and articles of association 1862-81, board minutes (2 vols) 1862-1900, share records 1930s-1970s, directors' and auditors' reports 1901-31, private ledger 1900-29, balance ledger 1900-22, dividend ledger 1913-28, petty cash books (2) 1889-91, 1903-9, other accounting records 1951-74, sales schedule 1910, patent 1876, other patent and trade mark records 1963-71, pensions records 1948-1970s, plant books 1900-2, misc records 1960s-1970s.
Lincolnshire Archives (Marshall, 2 Marshall). NRA 35742.

Agency agreements (3 vols) 1880-1930, sales ledger 1921-30, engine building books (70) 1864-99, 1912-68, threshing machine and other building books (9) 1865-70, 1876-1911, 1942-9, summary engine registers (4) 1863-94, 1897-1903, 1910-59, technical notebook c1880-1901, employee registers and apprenticeship records (14 vols) 1872-1950, inventories and valuations (21 vols) 1899-1937.
Rural History Centre, Reading University. NRA 21237.

Memorandum and articles of association 1936-70, board minutes (1 vol) 1966-81, general meeting minutes (1 vol) 1936-81, registers (2) of directors and members 1936-79, annual returns, papers rel to liquidation, etc 1948-82.
Sheffield Archives (TW 376-389). NRA 34879.

Foundry order book 1889-91.
Lincolnshire Archives (Misc Dep 543).

Engineer's notebook c1900.
Lincolnshire Archives (Misc Don 499). *Archivists' Report 27, 1977-82*, p37.

[897] **MARTIN'S CULTIVATOR CO LTD**, agricultural engineers, Stamford, Lincs

Letter books (5) 1907-8, cash books (17) 1909-30, 1939-62, other accounting records (16 vols) 1918-60, purchase ledgers (10) and day books (6) 1899-1901, 1910-54, sales ledgers (44) 1902-5, 1930-54 and journals (2) 1899-1905, order books (16) 1903-14, invoices (44 vols, 2 files) 1916-17, 1948-66, consignment books (10) 1911-19, 1951, misc records mainly rel to customers and sales (c15 vols, 2 boxes, 1 file) 1910-56, stock books (22) 1903, 1920-71, wages books (7) 1905-15.
Lincolnshire Archives (MAM). NRA 23818.

[898] **JOHN MASON** and **JAMES DAVENPORT**, machine mfrs, Rochdale, Lancs

Mason's letter books (3) 1838-57, corresp with Davenport (1 bundle) 1846 and other corresp (2 parcels) 1849-55, Davenport's letter book 1873-88

and letters sent (2 items) 1835, royalty return 1855, machinery diagrams and patents (6 items) 1842-61, nd, agreement with foreman 1841, lease of premises 1820, misc printed papers (1 pamphlet, 1 item) 1814, 1852; papers of Mason, Davenport and Whitehead families 1633-1916.
Manchester Central Library Local Studies Unit (L29).

[899] **ALEXANDER MATHER & SON LTD**, ironfounders, oatmeal mill mfrs and general engineers, Edinburgh

Account books (14) 1905-44, ledgers (6) 1934-70, cash books (11) 1936-66, order books (8) 1941-66, estimate books (16) 1928-71, cost books (19) 1903-72, job sheets (10 vols) 1890-1962 and account books (4) 1926-68, work records (3 vols) 1922-48, drawings mainly of machinery (c2,100 items) 1859-1961, nd, wages and salaries records (10 vols) 1928-70, apprentice registers (2) 1896-1938, reports and valuations, etc (4 vols) 1937-65, nd, product catalogues (2) c1897-1900, glass plate negatives of mills and machinery (59 items) c1900-40.
Scottish Record Office (GD 295, RHP 50285-52397, 52725-30). NRA 18882.

[900] **MAUDSLAY SONS & FIELD LTD**, mechanical and marine engineers and boilermakers, London

Collected records 1807-1902, incl memorandum and articles of association 1889, corresp, notes, etc rel to estimates, orders, technical matters, etc (c130 items) 1807-90, lists of vessels fitted with Maudslay engines, paddle wheels and propellers 1841-94, patents (4) 1816, 1839, 1883, technical notebooks (4) 1830s, notebook of Joshua Field c1851-2, notebook of Charles Sells, chief draughtsman, 1851-3, and photographs of premises and products.
Science Museum Library (MAUD).

Corresp and papers of Joshua Field mainly rel to marine, railway and other engines, boilers, etc (2 vols) c1806-72, estimates for machinery and misc notes (1 vol) 1812-c1828, Field's diary of tour in Midland manufacturing districts (2 vols) 1821, misc printed works.
Science Museum Library (FIELD). NRA 25397.

Notebooks (12) of Charles Sells c1842-1851, 1853-83.
Science Museum Library (SELLS). NRA 36698.

Corresp, notes, specifications, etc (c72 items) and drawings 1805-75.
Science Museum Library (MSS 419, 1258-96).

Drawings, etc (c66 items) rel to ship engines and boilers 1818-55, 1885-91, nd.
Science Museum Library (1993-404, 1993-576, 1993-1594).

[901] **MAVOR & COULSON LTD**, electrical and mining machinery mfrs, Glasgow

Board minutes (4 vols) 1897-1927, agenda book 1942-9, register of directors 1901-32, registers of members (2 vols) 1897-1907, 1924-8, transfers

(2 vols, etc) 1916-36, 1948-64, dividends (1 vol, etc) 1897-1952 and seals (2 vols) 1897-1953, annual summaries (5 vols) 1908-47, directors' reports and accounts 1948-61, monthly balances 1907-66 and accounts 1931-42, letter books (2) 1888-1929, private ledgers (3) 1887-1946, capital ledger 1901-35, private journals (3) 1896-1910, 1924-64, journals (3) 1931-53, registers of coal cutters and conveyors (2 vols) 1934-8, patent registers (16 vols) 1891-1950, wages and pension fund records 1927-64, inventories and valuations 1950-8, misc papers (4 files, etc) c1897-1980, statistical graphs 1913-52, product catalogues and misc leaflets (7 files) 1894-1936, nd, negatives and lantern slides (c10,000 items) late 19th-20th cent.
Strathclyde Regional Archives (TD 279). NRA 17523.

Minutes (7 vols) 1927-64, registers of seals (2 vols) 1920-78 and mortgages (1 vol) 1896-1933, private ledgers (5) 1892-1906, 1947-71, general ledgers and transfers 1920-31, 1949-76, journals (3) 1949-72, cash books (17) 1948-65, negatives of drawings c1919-70, salaries records 1896-8, employment training cards 1897-c1950, pension fund records (4 vols) 1948-76, letter book of HA Mavor rel to American visit 1890, apprentices' magazine (48 vols) 1917-64.
Anderson Mavor Ltd. Enquiries to NRA (Scotland) (surveys 2601, 3237). NRA 27341.

[902] **MAXIM NORDENFELT GUNS & AMMUNITION CO LTD**, London

Minutes (2 vols) 1888-98, secretary's private letter books (microfilm) 1888-1913, contracts received (1 vol) 1888-9, patents (2 vols) 1883-93, stock held by agents and for trials (1 vol) 1887-91, recollections of firm by GR Shields 1892-7, misc papers (2 envelopes) nd; Maxim Gun Co Ltd minutes (2 vols) 1884-9; Nordenfelt Guns & Ammunition Co Ltd minutes (2 vols) 1886-9, contracts (1 envelope) 1885-8 and plans of submarines (1 envelope) 1886-7.
Cambridge University Library (Vickers Archives). NRA 27797.

[903] **MAY & JACOBS LTD**, coachbuilders, Guildford, Surrey

Deed of partnership 1909, articles of association 1911, bank book 1928-9, sales ledgers (2) 1847-50, 1897-1908, bought ledger 1921-6, corresp (40 items) mainly rel to appointment as carriage makers to Duke Ernest of Saxe-Coburg-Gotha 1887-1902 and to unauthorised use of royal arms 1915, misc business and family papers 1881-1954.
Surrey RO, Guildford (176, 1235, 1236). NRA 17913.

Specifications book 1883-91, designs for carriages (3 vols) 1899, nd, drawings (1 vol) of crests and monograms for use on carriages c1860-1910, misc typescript and printed papers (16 items) 1882-1927.
Guildford Museum (LG 1629). NRA 17913.

[904] **MECCANO LTD**, machine tool and
mechanical toy mfrs, Liverpool

Memorandum and articles of association 1908-12,
directors' minutes, attendance books and register
1944-65, committee minutes 1962-4, balance sheets
and profit and loss accounts, etc 1903-76, directors'
reports 1949-70, annual returns 1960-9, legal
corresp and papers 1915-79, administration
information cards 1919-65, other corporate records
1920-66, monthly accounts 1904-5, 1912, 1975-7,
other financial records 1929-77, sales agreements,
etc 1928-72, sales and stock records 1955-80, patent
records 1925-74, specifications and drawings, etc
1968-77, pensions and other staff records 1945-79,
deeds and other papers rel to property 1882-1974,
factory plans 1971, press cuttings 1933-79, publicity
material, photographs and misc papers 1925-81.
National Museums and Galleries on Merseyside,
Merseyside Maritime Museum (DME). NRA 36257.

[905] **MECHANS LTD**, general engineers,
Glasgow

Articles of association 1904, minutes 1904-57,
corresp *c*1960-3, private ledger 1893-9, account
book *c*1900-19, accounts and balance sheets
*c*1945-57, machinery and plant accounts 1938,
register of new employees 1957-63, catalogue *c*1900.
Staffordshire RO (D1288). NRA 17387.

Misc agreements 1886, production census 1907,
particulars of output 1939-45, press cuttings,
historical notes and printed material 1909-46, nd.
Strathclyde Regional Archives (TD 985). NRA 12501.

[906] **JAMES MELROSE & SONS**, engineers
and ironfounders, Hawick, Roxburghshire

Balance sheets and trading accounts, etc (6 bundles)
20th cent, letter book 1938-42, misc corresp and
papers (4 bundles) 1897-1908, papers mainly rel to
taxation (1 bundle) 1904-20, estimate book 1874,
cost book 1916-37, foundry accounts (1 bundle)
20th cent, estimates, specifications and plans
(4 bundles) *c*1870-97, plans (366) of machinery,
mills, etc 1867-1940, nd, advertising material and
photographs (1 bundle) 19th-20th cent.
Scottish Record Office (GD 276, RHP 20176-541).
NRA 16191.

Plans (101) of machinery and buildings *c*1863-1910,
nd.
In private possession. Enquiries to NRA (Scotland)
(survey 680). NRA 16117.

[907] **METROPOLITAN RAILWAY**
CARRIAGE & WAGON CO LTD, railway
carriage and rolling stock mfrs, Birmingham

Records from 1867.
Metro-Cammell Ltd. Microfiche of specifications,
drawings and photographs 1867-1940 is in
Birmingham Central Library Archives Division
(MS 99). NRA 29847.

[908] **MIDDLEMORE'S (COVENTRY) LTD**,
motor and cycle accessories mfrs, Coventry

Records from *c*1890 incl directors' minute books
and agendas and catalogues.
In private possession: see J Lowe, *Guide to sources in*
the history of the cycle and motor industries in Coventry
1880-1939, 1982. Enquiries to Coventry City RO.

[909] **MILLBROOK ENGINEERING CO LTD**,
iron and brass founders and engineers, Landore,
Glam

Abstract of partnership agreement 1863,
memorandum and articles of association 1901,
promissory notes to shareholders 1902 and share
transfer certificates 1903-50, general meeting papers
and directors' reports 1908, 1942-9, private letter
book 1899-1908, letter books (2) 1902-44, corresp
mainly with customers and suppliers (65 files)
1879-1951, profit and loss accounts and balance
sheets (53 items) 1898-1950, ledgers (2) 1863-93,
1915-27, other accounting records (5 vols) 1927-54,
order, sales and purchase records (9 vols) 1922-56,
costing records (2 vols, 1 item) 1925-8, 1944-52,
stock book 1932-5, records of pot shop production
(1 vol) 1952-4, drawings of machine parts (40 vols,
etc) *c*1920-55, draft patent specifications for tinning
machinery and related corresp 1896, 1910, 1932,
wages records (4 vols) 1925-54, valuations, plans,
leases and other premises records 19th-20th cent,
trade brochures, etc (1 box) *c*1930; papers rel to
trade associations 1923, 1935-6.
University College of Swansea Library (Millbrook
Collection). NRA 14358.

[910] **GEORGE F MILNES & CO LTD**, tramcar
and railway rolling stock mfrs, Hadley, Salop

Directors' minutes (1 vol) 1905-17, registers (3) of
directors or managers 1905, members 1905 and
shareholders 1905-8, balance sheets 1902, 1906-16,
annual summaries, etc 1910-16, misc papers rel to
takeover by United Electric Car Co Ltd 1903, 1905,
corresp, plans, leases, etc rel to building of Hadley
Works 1899-1900, inventory of stock and plant early
20th cent.
Lancashire RO. NRA 26268.

Photograph albums (2) rel to opening of the Hadley
Works 1900 and products 1902.
Untraced. Copies are in Wirral Archives (ZME) with
other photographic and printed material rel to the
firm. NRA 26268.

[911] **MIRRLEES WATSON CO LTD**, engineers,
sugar machinery and pump mfrs, Glasgow

Letter books (16) 1903-36, 1949, letters from
Indian offices and other businesses (23 files)
1926-36, order books (40) 1840-1966, invoice books
(3) 1900-2, quotation books (2) 1919-21, estimate
books (2) 1933, 1958, price lists and specifications
1938-41, job books (88) 1897-1957, order/job books
for work by other companies (126) 1922-40, job
schedule books, etc (512) 1906-67, production
order books (7) 1966-74, machinery testing
notebook 1894-1910, foundry test book 1937-66,

quantities book 1933-4, record of experimental goods 1938-59, copy books and files (15) 1935-66, sketch and drawings index books (18) 1841-1966, roller books (5) and list of mills and rollers 1904-64, sugar bulletins 1925-36.
Glasgow University Archives and Business Record Centre (UGD/62, UGD/118/2,8). NRA 10851, 14656.

[912] **C MOODY & SON**, cutlers and gunsmiths, Romsey, Hants

Ledger 1905-32, day books (5) 1872-7, 1883-9, 1896-1900, 1935-61, shop books (15) 1934-60, corresp and vouchers (1 bundle) 1927-53, nd, accounts and orders rel to cartridges and explosives (2 bundles, 5 items) 1937-52, permit register 1941-50, rent book 1922-31.
Hampshire RO (194M85). NRA 28675.

[913] **HERBERT MORRIS LTD**, mfrs of cranes, conveyors and boilers, Loughborough, Leics

Board agenda book 1927-33, private ledgers (4) 1907-15, 1918-44, cash books (6) 1902-5, 1918-20, 1939-51, other accounting records (4 vols) 1919-58, copies of corresp with potential customers (1 bundle) 1905-19, sales and purchase records (5 vols) 1917-55, order books (36) 1903-40 and index 1924-5, stock order books (9) 1903-49, suppliers' code book c1960, factory empties and returns book 1944-6, pattern book c1911, template and jig record books (2) 1900-9, specifications records (18 vols, 3 files) c1906-1960, drawings books and lists (77 vols) 1908-52, drawings and blueprints incl some for subsidiaries (526 rolls, 6 boxes, 1 file, 66 items) c1896-1967, visitors' book 1925-8, photographs and negatives c1900-50, advertising material and other printed papers 1902-60.
Leicestershire RO (28D69, DE3409). NRA 32956.

[914] **JOHN MORRIS & SONS LTD**, fire engineers and fire appliance mfrs, Salford, Lancs

Return sales book 1911-13, patent specifications (9) 1895-1905, papers rel to insurance policies (1 vol) 1920-39, visitors' book 1936-58.
Salford Archives Centre (U 35). NRA 19178.

[915] **FRANK MORTLOCK & SONS**, agricultural engineers, Lavenham, Suffolk

Day book 1899-1906, ledgers (2) 1906-12, 1915-27, corresp, invoices, misc papers and photographs 1924-c1975.
Suffolk RO, Bury St Edmunds (HC 502/1-6). NRA 3517.

[916] **MURRAY & PATERSON LTD**, engineers, Coatbridge, Lanarkshire

Minute book 1900-17, agenda book 1900-1, register of directors 1902, private ledgers (4) 1897-9, 1901-28, private journals (2) 1898-1923, cash books (10) 1888-1950, contract book 1900-1, estimate book 1892-1901, sales books (2) 1897-1916, bill book 1868-1924, cost book 1951-65, materials book

1900-1, weight books (57) 1901-72, specification books (8) 1890-1922, drawing books (2) 1900-11, list of machinery 1891-2 and index of drawings (1 vol) 19th cent, wages books (3) 1900-24, inventories (2 vols) 1896, 1900-6, photographs of machinery c1890-1950, notice book 1925-35, product catalogues (4 items) c1870-92.
In private possession. Enquiries to NRA (Scotland) (survey 1030). NRA 18910.

Specification books (10) 1902, 1922-56, drawings (5 shelves) nd, photographs of workshops, machinery and products (5 boxes, 645 items) 1936-83.
Strathclyde Regional Archives (TD 264). NRA 18910.

[917] **MUSGRAVE & CO LTD**, mfrs of gates, structural ironwork and air-conditioning equipment, Belfast

Certificates of incorporation 1872, 1905, 1924, minutes (5 vols) 1872-1943, registers of members, etc (2 vols) 1926, 1948-50, share certificate books (2) 1872-1947, letter book 1881-93, balance sheets, trading and profit and loss accounts, etc c1920-60, private ledger 1923-46, order books (c70) c1899-c1964, corresp and papers rel to sales and orders (4 boxes, 28 files) 1940-61, designs, drawings, index books, etc (2 boxes, 5 vols, 1 bundle) c1896-1958, visitors' book 1949-52, misc staff records 1922-65, deeds, leases, plans and other papers rel to property (1 vol, 2 bundles, 24 items) c1858-1953, catalogues, advertisements and photographs c1914-65.
Public Record Office of Northern Ireland (D 1991). NRA 34900.

[918] **JOHN MUSGRAVE & SONS LTD**, mechanical engineers, Bolton, Lancs

Records 19th-20th cent incl mill books (26) 1899-1914, pipe books (65) 1879-1914, engine book c1880-1926, drawings (c10,000 items), registers (2) 1920-7 and lists of drawings from 1850.
Bolton Archive Service (ZMU). NRA 34860.

Drawings (c110 items) 1890-1912, nd.
Museum of Science and Industry in Manchester. NRA 32351.

Order book nd, drawings of engine parts (24 items) 1891, 1905.
Royal Commission on the Historical Monuments of England, Salisbury (George Watkins Collection).

[919] **NALDER & NALDER LTD**, mechanical engineers, Challow, Berks

Memorandum and articles of association 1958, share records (1 file, 1 bundle, 1 item) 1866-1955, letter books (32) and files (10) 1865-6, 1878-1949, registers (4) of incoming corresp 1889-1900, 1938-55, statements and balance sheets 1876, 1896, 1906-59, general ledger 1857-66, day book 1906-21, cash books (3) 1904-45, bill books (3) 1876-1967, bank books (4) 1899-1928, analysis books (2) 1908-55, stock books and registers (25) 1866-1952, order registers (33) and files (145) 1871-1961, nd,

general sales and purchase records (8 vols) *c*1860,
1870-1967, estimates (24 vols) 1889-1949, cost
books (15) 1864-1944, piecework prices 1907,
1914, incoming invoices and analysis books (5 vols,
131 files) 1889-1932, outgoing invoices (58 vols)
1874-1949, requisition books (5) 1910-35,
consignment and haulage records (7 vols)
1892-1932, 1959-64, reminder book 1911,
manufacturing and order books (71) 1862-*c*1940,
costing register 1899-1906, foundry costing books
1957-9, brewing room diaries 1928, 1948, 1950,
1952, assembly work books 1957-9, wages and
production analysis books 1911-55, pattern registers
(6) nd, drawings register 1888-1916, wages book
1857-60, misc staff records 1870-1950,
photographs, misc records, etc 20th cent.
Rural History Centre, Reading University (T 74/9,
TR NAL). NRA 21004.

[920] **NAPIER & MILLER LTD**, shipbuilders,
Old Kilpatrick, Dunbarton

Details of ships built and related drawings
1896-1910, details of vessels launched and annual
shipbuilding reports 1899-1930, ship plans 1908-26,
offset book *c*1877-98, ships' particulars book
1899-1915, misc papers rel to Napier, Shanks & Bell
1878-97, legal corresp rel to sale of Napier & Miller
assets and sale catalogue 1931; Henry Napier's
business and personal corresp and papers
1870-1958.
*Glasgow University Archives and Business Record
Centre.* NRA 21743.

Lists of ships built incl tonnages, costing and profits
1879-1930, ship details book nd, specifications,
technical particulars, data sheets, etc *c*1880-1930,
ships' particulars book 1915-30, launching books
nd, trials book 1877-96, specifications for buildings,
yard plan, etc 1877-*c*1923, photographs 1886-1928.
Glasgow Museum of Transport. NRA 21743; and see
Ritchie.

[921] **R NAPIER & SONS LTD**, shipbuilders and
engineers, Glasgow

Records incl business corresp and papers
1849-1909, diary 1866, technical specifications of
costs of ships 1865-79, misc cost records 1844-71,
trial book incl technical specifications 1843-6, press
cuttings books 1865-1900; Robert Napier's
personal, family and legal corresp and papers
1812-76, James R Napier's corresp and papers
1836-80 incl letter books 1857-9, 1866-71, business
diary 1865 and technical memoranda books and
papers 1836-72.
*Glasgow University Archives and Business Record
Centre.* NRA 21743.

Misc administrative papers 1814-77, vessel
memoranda books, ship plans, trials book and sketch
books nd, note and sketch book 1866-9, piecework
rates books *c*1880, details of yard machinery 1872,
photographs 1866-1900; James R Napier's letter
book 1863-4.
Glasgow Museum of Transport. NRA 21743.

[922] **NASMYTH, WILSON & CO LTD**,
locomotive, hydraulic and general engineers, Eccles,
Lancs

Letter books (6) 1838-40, day book 1837-54, bill
book 1840-1, order books (3) 1836-59, sales books
(4) 1837-61, 1870-7, record of locomotives sold
(1 vol) *c*1867-1922, specifications letter book
1875-8, manager's production notes, drawings and
photographs (2 vols) *c*1886-94, plans rel to
installation of machinery (38 items) 1850-2, nd,
catalogues (3 items) *c*1849-81, nd.
Salford Archives Centre (U 268). NRA 33743.

Misc corresp of James Nasmyth (*c*80 items) 1848-89
and his partner in the firm (*c*20 items) 1834-84.
Salford Archives Centre (U 312, U 313). NRA 19178,
NRA 33747.

Notebooks, etc of Nathan Walker partly rel to boilers
and locomotives (14 vols, 39 items) 1875-1939.
Salford Archives Centre (U 49). NRA 19178.

Locomotive specifications books (copies)
1839-1938.
National Railway Museum, York.

Locomotive drawings (180 items) 1917-38.
Science Museum, Department 5. Enquiries to the
Science Museum Library.

Drawings (702 items) 1796-1885, nd, mainly by
James Nasmyth.
National Library of Scotland (MSS 3241-3).

Partnership deeds (3 items) 1842-50.
Lancashire RO (DDX 260): see *Guide to the
Lancashire Record Office*, 1985, p166.

See also HMC *Papers of British Scientists*, 1982,
under James Nasmyth.

[923] **NEILSON, REID & CO**, locomotive
builders, Glasgow

Private journals (2) 1850-6, nd, order books (2)
1880-1, contract lists to 1903, cost and weight books
(5) 1889-90, specifications to 1903, inventories and
valuations (8 vols) 1874-1902, autobiographical
notes nd.
Glasgow University Archives and Business Record Centre
(UGD/10). NRA 10858.

Drawings 19th-20th cent.
Glasgow University Archives and Business Record Centre
(RHP 56531-57010). NRA 36388.

Records incl duplicate order book 1871-6, works list
to 1864, weight diagram books, unexecuted designs
and glass plate negatives 1864-1903.
Mitchell Library, Glasgow.

Order books (2) 1863-1903 and drawings nd.
National Railway Museum, York. NRA 28465.

See also North British Locomotive Co Ltd.

[924] **NICHOLLS & SONS LTD**, coachbuilders
and motor engineers, Bedford

Ledgers (2) 1895-1911, 1922-8, book of designs for
horse-drawn vehicles nd.
Bedfordshire RO (DDX 128). NRA 15785.

[925] **NOBLE & LUND LTD**, machine tool mfrs, Felling, co Durham

Order books, plans and photographs 1889-1968.
Tyne and Wear Archives Service (Acc 2742, 2748).
Annual review 1992-93, p12.

[926] **NORTH BRITISH LOCOMOTIVE CO LTD**, locomotive builders, Glasgow

Prospectus 1903, general meeting minutes, etc
(1 file) 1957-66, board papers (40 files) 1953-66,
annual reports 1903-66, notices to shareholders, etc
1903-64, share registers (9 vols, etc) 1920-62,
directors' reports and balance sheets 1903-48,
liquidators' papers (60 files) 1959-66, ledgers and
other financial records 1952-62, contract books (10)
1914-45, order books (3) 1927-40, other sales
records (2 vols) 1946-8, cost books (27) 1909-46
and day books (9) 1909-21, cost and weight books
(39) c1903-25, licence agreements (8 files) 1949-62,
pension fund records (11 files) 1945-68, inventories
(4 vols) 1903-7, 1915-22, illustrated company
history nd.
Glasgow University Archives and Business Record Centre
(UGD/11). NRA 10858.

Corresp register 1910-13, contract tracing registers
(7) 1904-58 and tracing list 1919-50, drawing office
registers (18) 1910-62, drawings of locomotives 20th
cent, mechanical standards books (2) nd and misc
printed specifications 1895-1957.
Glasgow University Archives and Business Record Centre
(GD 329, RHP 58121-59263). NRA 36388.

Memorandum and articles of association 1903,
prospectus 1903, applications for shares 1903,
directors' reports and balance sheets 1903-48, profit
and loss accounts of predecessor companies
1898-1903, corresp and papers rel to contracts and
orders (2 files) 1911-42, review of locomotive
industry 1909-11.
Glasgow University Archives and Business Record Centre
(UGD/109/2). NRA 21082.

Records 1903-62 incl Atlas Works order book
1903-7, engine order records 1903-61, steaming and
delivery record (1 vol) 1928-51, output statistics
1904-48, weight diagram books and glass plate
negatives.
Mitchell Library, Glasgow.

Order books 1903-47.
National Railway Museum, York. NRA 28465.

Plans of Atlas and Hyde Park works (12 items)
1893-1954.
Strathclyde Regional Archives (TD 50). NRA 10858.

[927] **NORTH BRITISH MACHINE CO LTD**,
cycle and sewing machine mfrs, Glasgow

Articles of association 1909, balance sheets (2 files)
1917-40, private ledgers (4) 1906-38.
Strathclyde Regional Archives (TD 268). NRA 18734.

[928] **NORTH EASTERN MARINE ENGINEERING CO LTD**, marine engineers,
boilermakers and forgemasters, Wallsend, Northumb
and Sunderland, co Durham

Records 1865-1957 incl memorandum and articles
of association 1865, minutes 1865-1924, share
registers 1912-24, corresp and publicity material
1865-1957 and engine plans c1880.
Tyne and Wear Archives Service. NRA 30899 (partial
list); and see Ritchie.

[929] **NORTH SOMERSET ENGINEERING CO**, Keynsham, Somerset

Ledgers (3) 1901-11, 1920-60, day book 1921-3,
misc accounts, etc (1 vol) c1868-1918.
Bristol RO (Acc 38097): see *Business in Avon and
Somerset.*

[930] **ALBERT OAKLEY LTD**, agricultural and
motor engineers, iron and brass founders, Hurst
Green, Sussex

Account books 1890-1924.
East Sussex RO (Acc 2596). *Annual Report 1980*, p9.

[931] **OSGERBY family**, coachbuilders, Beverley,
Yorks

Financial records and estimate and pattern books
c1863-1940.
Humberside County AO: see *Accessions to repositories
1983*, p28.

[932] **DAVID OWEN & SON**, threshing machine
mfrs, Newtown, Montgom

Letter books (2) 1921-43, account books (3)
1860-95, 1910-17, 1933-58, time sheets 1945-58,
misc corresp and papers (1 folder) 1916-57,
notebook of J Lewis rel to threshing, etc 1914-21.
National Library of Wales (A 1982/55). NRA 26130.

[933] **OXFORDSHIRE STEAM PLOUGH CO
LTD** (afterwards **JOHN ALLEN & SONS
(OXFORD) LTD**), mechanical engineers,
agricultural machinery mfrs and contractors, Oxford

Minutes (1 vol) 1915-49, private ledgers (6)
1897-1954, nominal ledgers (2) 1905-51,
investments ledger 1915-26, journal 1898-1915,
financial statements (4 vols) 1897-1942 and misc
related papers 1888-1911, patent specification 1910,
drawings register nd, drawings nd, manufacturing
working papers 1920s-1930s, nd, wages book
1901-3, valuation of firm's assets 1905, deeds
(2 bundles) 1706-1926, advertising and technical
literature, photographs and glass negatives.
Rural History Centre, Reading University (TR ALS).
NRA 35053.

[934] **PALMERS SHIPBUILDING & IRON CO
LTD**, shipbuilders, engineers and iron and steel
mfrs, Jarrow and Hebburn, co Durham

Letter book of Sir CM Palmer 1877-89, wages book
1889-1916, foremen's salaries book 1921-8, yard

plan *c*1885, scrapbook 1850-1907, photographs
(1 vol) *c*1910.
Bede Gallery, Jarrow: see Ritchie.

Construction costs (2 vols) 1906-8, 1911-28,
corresp, estimates, specifications, designs, etc
*c*1920-9, working charges and running expenses
(1 file) 1931-2, shipyard rates of pay (1 item)
1901-32.
Tyne and Wear Archives Service (Acc 1479). NRA
27193.

Foreman shipwright's work journal 1905-9,
blacksmith's piecework book 1914-20.
Tyne and Wear Archives Service (Acc 1810/5-6). NRA
8919.

Annual reports and accounts 1865-93, list of ships
built 1851-1933, the *Palmer Record* (3 vols) 1902-6,
photographs nd, history of firm 1909.
Cambridge University Library (Vickers Archives).
NRA 27797.

Records incl annual reports and accounts
1899-1929, ledgers nd and ships' plans early 20th
cent.
National Maritime Museum Manuscripts Section: see
Ritchie.

Corresp and business papers of Sir CM Palmer
(1 vol) 1845-98.
Tyne and Wear Archives Service (Acc 1357). NRA
26002.

[935] **J PARKINSON & SON (SHIPLEY) LTD**,
machine tool mfrs, Shipley, Yorks

Records incl day book 1874-8, advertising material
and brochures 20th cent and photographs 20th cent.
West Yorkshire Archive Service, Bradford (51D84).

[936] **PARNALL & SONS LTD**, iron and brass
founders, scale mfrs and shopfitters, Bristol

Corporate corresp and papers 1939-44, expense
account ledger 1922-37, order sheets 1934-7,
apprenticeship indenture 1869, register of works
employees 1887-1906, photographs of products and
employees from *c*1920, price lists and catalogues
from 1905, misc printed material rel to company
history 1952-1980s.
The Company: see Business in Avon and Somerset.

Private ledgers (2) 1889-1920, account books (2)
1920-46, mortgages, deeds, papers rel to sale of
business and property to W & T Avery Ltd, etc
(3 parcels) 1889-*c*1914.
Birmingham Central Library Archives Division
(MS 1588). NRA 36399.

[937] **JAMES PARRY**, coachbuilder, Chester,
Cheshire

Account book 1825-40.
Chester City RO (CR 230). NRA 25024.

[938] **PATENT SHAFT & AXLETREE CO
LTD**, railway rolling stock mfrs and bridge builders,
Wednesbury, Staffs

Memorandum and articles of association 1864,
1889, agreement rel to liquidation and sale of
company 1889, directors' minutes (12 vols)
1864-1969 and indexes nd, general meeting minutes
(1 vol) 1909-28, works committee minutes (1 vol)
1884-1911, register of directors or managers
1901-10, private ledgers (5) 1878-1929, excursion
account ledger 1868-9, private journals (2)
1879-1930, day book 1826-30, costing books (6)
1887-96, register of agencies 1911, patent
agreement 1901, trade mark registration certificate
1903, apprenticeship indenture 1857, wages books
(2) 1875-91, nd, plans (1 vol, 2 items) *c*1800, 1867,
*c*1917, inventories and valuations 1888-1900, copy
conveyance 1903, photographs (2 boxes, 1 vol,
*c*250 items) 1870-1953, catalogues and other printed
papers 1862-1931.
Sandwell Local Studies Centre. NRA 33405.

Deeds, leases, abstracts of title, etc (485 items)
1720-1922.
Staffordshire RO (D1376). NRA 28028.

[939] **PEACOCK & BINNINGTON**, agricultural
engineers, Brigg, Lincs

Sold ledgers (5) 1894-1923, day books (6) 1905-24,
1929-35, 1942-3, order books (43) 1900-36, repairs
order books (13) 1922-43, order book duplicates
(66 vols) 1900-48, invoices 1915-50, advice notes
1943-6, stock books (4) 1910-35, misc corresp,
indexes and other papers 1908-51.
Lincolnshire Archives (PB). NRA 35741.

[940] **FRANK PEARN & CO LTD**, pump mfrs,
Manchester

Memorandum and articles of association and
agreements 1894-1955, private ledger and journal
1878-84, impersonal ledger 1887-93, misc sales
corresp, advertisements, etc 1899-1943, salaries and
wages books (7) 1884-1920, 1951-3.
Holden & Brooke Ltd. NRA 28631; BAC *Company
Archives* no 561.

Drawings.
Greater Manchester RO.

[941] **PEAT & DREWERY**, millwrights and textile
machinery mfrs, Gildersome, Yorks

Accounts for work done (2 vols) 1895-1929, time
and wages day book 1911-20, misc letters and
photographs nd, deeds (21) 1716-1920.
Untraced. NRA 11904.

[942] **PECKETT & SONS LTD** (formerly **FOX,
WALKER & CO**), locomotive builders, Bristol

Order books, specification books, drawings and glass
negatives *c*1870-1960.
National Railway Museum, York.

[943] **PEMBERTON & SONS LTD**, loom mfrs, Burnley, Lancs

Order books (5) 1896-7, 1911-68.
Towneley Hall Art Gallery and Museums, Burnley.

Order books 1897-1901, 1909-60.
Weavers' Triangle Visitor Centre, Burnley.

[944] **PENMAN & CO LTD**, boilermakers and engineers, Glasgow

Memorandum and articles of association 1907, 1947, minutes (3 vols) 1942-76, management committee minutes 1969, directors' attendance book 1947-72 and registers (2) of shareholdings *c*1947-76, list of board members 1947-69, share ledger 1907-75, other share records (2 vols, etc) 1931-75, annual returns and accounts 1947-75, licence agreements 1945, 1969, general corresp and papers 1926-74, accounting records (3 vols) 1948-50, 1962-9, sales and purchase ledgers (5) 1948-63, invoice books (4) 1939-62, order books, etc (23 vols, 5 box files) 1886-1906, 1909-65, boiler contracts (257 files) 1931-71, agency agreements 1944-5, stores books (7) 1941-57, drawings mainly of boilers (1,062 items) 1908-66, nd, wages records (22 vols, etc) 1906-58, pension deeds 1956-7 and other staff records 1971-2, plan *c*1970 of works and papers rel to its closure 1973, photographs mainly of products and employees 1884-*c*1960, publicity material *c*1920-70.
Strathclyde Regional Archives (TD 244). NRA 18727 (partial list).

[945] **JOHN PERRY & CO**, shipbuilders, London

Contract book 1775-1807, memoranda book 1777-1801.
National Maritime Museum Manuscripts Section (SPB/27, 47). *Guide to the manuscripts*, vol 2, p144.

[946] **PETRIE & CO LTD**, engineers, Rochdale, Lancs

Records 19th-20th cent incl directors' minutes (2 vols) 1891-1941, register of directors 1907-41 and photographs of staff nd.
Manchester Central Library Local Studies Unit (M501/PC). NRA 35782.

[947] **JW PICKERING & SONS LTD**, ship repairers, engineers and ironfounders, Liverpool

Articles of association 1911, special resolution 1925, balance sheets and related papers 1912-19, payment ledger 1902, ledger 1911-23, cash books (2) 1887-9, *c*1943-62, estimates book 1884-1900, 1932-9, pay rates index book *c*1890-1940, apprenticeship applications 1903-16; JW Pickering's diary 1874.
National Museums and Galleries on Merseyside, Merseyside Maritime Museum (DX/210). NRA 30814.

[948] **RY PICKERING & CO LTD**, railway wagon, wheel and axle mfrs, Wishaw, Lanarkshire

Board minutes (3 vols) 1888-1934, agenda books (7) 1931-51, board papers 1951-61, registers of members and directors (6 vols) 1888-1934, share certificates (2 vols, 3 files) 1911-60, register of mortgages and debentures 1888-1937, letter books (2) 1913, 1921, corresp (48 bundles, etc) 1894-1950, private ledger 1888, private journal 1888, other financial records (18 vols, etc) 1923-69, estimate books (19) 1896-1960, card order books (21) 1889-1952, nd, order books (23) 1897, 1909-21, material order books (2) 1911-13, 1921-44, contract books (6) 1896-1938, enquiries records (23 vols) 1896-1969, stores day books (54) 1893-1950, deliveries day books (2) 1891-3, goods despatched and received (5 vols) 1918-28, 1952-4, railway rate book 1908-23, record of new wagons loaded 1927, other sales and purchase records (3 vols, etc) 1931-53, wagon register 1907-24, specification books (11) *c*1888-94, 1897-1941, repair schedules 1940-55, nd, drawing office weight books (2) 1892-3, drawings 20th cent, wages and salaries records (17 vols) 1910-52, accidents register 1898-1967, friendly society records (3 vols, etc) 1893, 1903-13, plans of premises 1932-52, nd, wagon plant book 1893-1924 and rent book 1897-1903, valuation of plant and machinery 1937, advertisements (2 folders) nd, photographs of rolling stock 1907-69, nd, misc papers 1951-73.
Glasgow University Archives and Business Record Centre (UGD/12). NRA 13688.

[949] **THOMAS PIGGOTT & CO LTD**, engineers, Birmingham

Directors' minutes (1 vol) 1905-13, directors' monthly reports and related papers (4 files) 1929-33, misc papers (4 files) rel to capitalisation and winding up of the company, etc 1892-1933, financial statements, etc (4 files) 1921-33, nd, nominal ledgers (2) 1906-28, private journal nd, records of gasholders and accessories produced 1845-1928, wages and salaries books (3) 1874-7, 1918-28, nd, valuation of plant, etc 1869, misc deeds, agreements, etc (17 items) 1854-1930, photographs of products, works and staff (6 vols, etc) 1902-36, publicity material and miscellanea 1874-1934; Guest, Keen & Piggotts Ltd misc papers 1925-35.
Staffordshire RO (D1288, 4469). NRA 17387.

See also Horseley Bridge & Engineering Co Ltd.

[950] **PILLATT & CO LTD**, ironfounders and mfrs of boilers, furnaces and incinerators, Stapleford, Notts

Corresp (*c*600 files) *c*1919-56, agreements, insurance policies, etc *c*1921-40, ledgers (9) 1903-34, cash books (15) 1903-7, 1910-49, day books (13 vols, 3 bundles) 1903-50, journals (2) 1910-18, order index cards (6 boxes) 1933-46, invoice books (5) 1910-36, delivery advice books (12) 1917-22, product drawings (*c*2,000) *c*1896-*c*1942, test sheets (4 files and parcels) *c*1908-39, work sheets listing components (17 boxes) 1910-45, photographs and other illustrations of products nd, testimonial letters received 1920-35, wages books (8) 1914-44.
Nottingham University Library (Pi). NRA 7062.

[951] **PLATT BROTHERS & CO LTD**, textile machinery mfrs and colliery proprietors, Oldham, Lancs

Memorandum and articles of association 1875-1939, directors' minutes, indexes and signature book (22 vols) 1897-8, 1923-57, shareholders' minutes (1 vol, etc) 1868-1902, 1931-50, committee minutes (13 vols) 1928-53 and papers 1941-52, share records 1926-65, balance sheets, directors' reports and annual returns 1844-1951, register of seals 1898-1939, agreements 1910-67, general corresp 1929-59, managing directors' papers 1952-67, ledgers (8) 1838-1948, journals (2) 1924-47, other financial records 1834-1968; general order books (9) 1884-1901, 1910-31, order books (550) and papers rel to mules and components 1859-1946, order books (incl components) for hopper feeders and openers (11) 1894-1947, bale breakers (5) 1901-47, openers (11) 1883-1948, exhaust openers (9) 1889-1937, scutchers (9) 1866-1912, scutchers, openers and lap machines (3) 1911-47, carding engines (31) 1859-61, 1865-1948, combing machines (4) 1890-1908, 1925-37 and rollers (4) 1894-1932, drawing frames (10) 1844-1903, 1913-39 and roller spindles (11) 1884-1929, slubbing, intermediate and roving frames (202) 1853-1941, ring spinning frames (67) 1862-1947, throstles and ring spinning frames (166) 1861-1935, ring spinning and doubling frames (127) 1870-1957, flyer and ring doubling frames (7) 1888-1929, chapon cop spinning frames (3) 1895-1955, worsted preparing machinery (2) 1894-1950, worsted spinning frames (3) 1864-1934, cop or bobbin reels (8) 1888-1949, yarn bundling presses (1) 1912-36, box details (2) 1897-1936, warping and beaming machines (5) 1878-1938, warping joiners (2) 1865-78, sizing machines (6) 1865-1938, shirley cages (2) 1929-47, pneumatic delivery boxes (3) 1928-47, looms (28) 1858-1943, cloth folding machines (2) 1892-1934, duplex cones (3) c1885, 1911-c1920, ribbon lap machines (8) 1895-1959, fancy woollen doublers (2) 1904-56 and sliver lap machines (3) 1935-59; headstock and stores books (16) for throstles, ring frames, etc 1893-1940, job books for willows and doublers (3) 1907-40, machine order and delivery books (57) 1881-1954, other order records (24 vols, etc) 1934-68, sales corresp (c50 files) 1932-49, corresp and papers of technical representatives 1945-59, overseas job books (8) 1873-1913, 1945-50, wheel job books (11) 1929-55, production books for drawing frames (47) 1854-1940, slubbing, intermediate and roving frames (84) 1855-1941, mules (44) 1877-1941, ring spinning and doubling frames (3) 1889-94, ring department works notebooks (7 vols, etc) 1886-1978, throstle and ring frame department letter books (5) 1908-33, misc production records 1847-1963, specifications for combing and worsted machines (46) 1865-1931, mules and twiners (167) 1843-1929, speed frames (41) 1873-1932, ring spinning and doubling frames (105) 1865-1933, looms (4) 1877-1931, other specifications records 1933-59, drawings rel to installation of cotton mules and twiners 1895-1933, drawings of machinery 1850-1959 and drawings registers (3) 1949-66, carding engine drawing schedule 1951-4, operating

instructions and service manuals 1897-1946, maintenance and servicing records c1920-65, misc technical corresp 1931-46, patents and related papers 1837-1949, wages and salaries records (78 vols or files) 1838-41, 1897-1958, overtime and special payment records (35 vols or files) 1884-1904, 1932-56, pensions and insurance records 1927-58 and records of Hartford Trust 1873-1948, inventories and valuations 1845-77, 1931-53, maps and plans of premises and property (39 items) c1850-1970, car insurance corresp 1945-59, catalogues and publicity material (188 items) 1897-1948, house journals 1935-73, visitors' books (3) 1934-52, photographic negatives record books (30) 1888-1946, misc papers and photographs 1847-1972; personal account book of John and James Platt 1854-66.
Lancashire RO (DDPSL/1). NRA 20296.

Operating instructions and service manuals (3 boxes) 1925-67, records of new employees (4 vols) 1915-80, apprentices' advance book 1929-68, discharge book 1927-47, Hartford Trust minute book 1895-1974, deeds and related papers (6 boxes) 1779-1945, nd, catalogues and publicity material (6 boxes) 1899-1969, misc papers and photographs (1 box) 1890-1957, nd.
Oldham Archives Service (MISC/14). NRA 35273.

Day book of John Platt 1813-23 and product catalogues nd.
Saddleworth Museum and Art Gallery (M/GX/T/BB 7-8). NRA 11134.

Mule order book 1855-6.
Museum of Science and Industry in Manchester (TX2/1). NRA 29510.

Building plans (2 vols) 1881-c1907.
Oldham Archives Service (Acc 1993.012).

[952] **PLENTY & SON LTD**, marine engine builders and pump mfrs, Newbury, Berks

Memorandum and articles of association 1890, 1911, minutes (2 vols) 1899-1902, 1938-49, letter books (2) 1916-21, share and debenture records (4 vols, 1 envelope) 1890-1950, balance sheets, reports and accounts 1892-1967, private ledgers (4) 1882-1919, cash books (2) 1943-64, income tax records, royalties, etc (1 bundle) 1935-40, enquiry, estimate and order books (20 vols) 1882-c1970, production records (16 vols) 1889-1967, engineering drawings, etc (1 vol, 9 bundles and files) 1900-65, patents (2) 1816, 1867, deeds (1 box) 1746-1891, drawings and plans of premises 1908-35 and inventory of property and plant (1 vol) 1916, manager's site notebook nd, catalogues, newsletters and publicity material 1806, c1900-80, photographs 1890s-1980; papers rel to the Plenty family 1790-1920, the Plenty lifeboat 1800-50 and misc organisations 1950s-1970s.
Plenty Mirrlees Pumps. Enquiries to the Business Archives Council. NRA 28135.

Engine plans (c10,000 items) 1900-40.
National Maritime Museum Manuscripts Section: see Ritchie.

Nordenfelt submarine drawings (12 items) 1880-9.
Science Museum Library.

[953] **H PLOWRIGHT & SONS**, ironfounders, agricultural and general engineers and ironmongers, Swaffham, Norfolk

Ironmongery sales ledgers (7) 1775-83, 1805-41, sales day book 1837-8, bought ledger 1802-40, receipts (3) 1840-1, catalogues and publicity material (*c*90 items) of Plowrights and other firms 1879-1940s.
Rural History Centre, Reading University (TR PLO). NRA 21069.

[954] **JAMES POLLOCK, SONS & CO LTD**, shipbuilders, London and Faversham, Kent

Walter Pollock's letter books 1938-46, accounting records 1916-54, sales and purchase records 1931-51, enquiries and estimates 1925-70, cost of vessels book 1885-1912, finished costs and weight book 1909-47, other cost records nd, stock and job records 1935-70, ship plans 1875-1970 and files nd, salaries records 1916-50, scrapbooks and publicity material nd.
National Maritime Museum Manuscripts Section: see Ritchie.

[955] **POND & SONS LTD**, ironmongers and mfrs of agricultural implements and dairy utensils, Blandford, Dorset

Corresp, accounts and ledgers 1808-1929.
Dorset RO: see *Report of the County Archivist*, Nov 1969, p4.

Account books (2) 1827-72, catalogues (7) *c*1835-1915, nd.
Rural History Centre, Reading University. NRA 21012.

[956] **HENRY POOLEY & SON LTD**, mfrs of scales and weighing machines, Birmingham

Finance committee agenda book 1934-45, mortgage debentures (1 bundle) 1897-9, debenture holders' meeting papers (1 envelope) 1905-10, papers rel to sale of business to W & T Avery Ltd (1 bundle) 1914, general agency papers (1 folder) 1921-49, quotation books (2) 1910-14, papers rel to experimental weighbridge (1 parcel) *c*1932, war relief accounts (1 parcel) 1914, apprenticeship agreements (2 parcels, 3 bundles) *c*1928-50, property records (1 bundle) early 20th cent.
Birmingham Central Library Archives Division (MS 1588). NRA 36399.

[957] **PORT TALBOT DRY DOCK CO LTD**, ship repairers, Port Talbot, Glam

Memorandum and articles of association 1903, board, general meeting and committee minutes (11 vols) 1901-40, 1955-69, general manager's reports and directors' meetings agenda books (3 vols) 1934-44, agenda register 1939-47, registers (2) of directors and managers 1901-11, 1956-7, register of directors' holdings 1951-9, registers of shares, debentures and dividends (5 vols) 1898-1925, annual lists and summaries (2 vols) 1901-19, private ledgers (2) 1898-1969, ledgers (4) 1900-5, 1931-59, journals (2) 1901-46, cash book

1946-57, misc financial records (2 vols) 1947-69, order and price books (2) and other purchase records (3 vols) *c*1940-71, salary register 1901-12 and paysheets (1 file) 1945, inventory and valuation 1941, stock and tool valuations (4 vols) 1965-9.
West Glamorgan Archive Service (D/D X 105). NRA 30557.

[958] **POWELL BROTHERS LTD**, mechanical and agricultural engineers and ironmongers, Wrexham, Denbighs

Memorandum and articles of association 1914, corresp (7 bundles) 1893, 1906-28, letter book 1909-20, summaries of shareholdings in firm (2 items) 1917, 1924, balance sheets, trading accounts and financial reports (2 files, 1 bundle, 1 item) 1894-1924, receipt and expenditure book 1850-7, accounts 1916-26, receipts and accounts (3 bundles, 5 items) 1889, 1891, 1904-27, misc accounting records (4 vols, 2 bundles, 2 items) 1918-*c*1930, counterfoil book 1917, income tax papers (1 bundle, 1 item) 1916-27, agreements (2 bundles, 2 items) for sale or hire of products 1912-25, record of standard parts and daily sales analyses (2 bundles) 1919-22, machinery drawings (6 bundles) 1923-7, price lists, brochures, photographs, etc (26 items) *c*1920-9, legal and property records (2 files, 33 items) 1892-1927; Powell family papers 19th-20th cent.
Clwyd RO, Ruthin (DD/DM/543, DD/DM/968). NRA 34293; *Annual report 1991*.

Monthly summaries (3 vols) 1874-5, 1892-4, nd, cash books (*c*21) 1875-95, 1910-27, private accounts paid (12 bundles) 1882-95, bank books (12) 1875-1900, cheque counterfoils (*c*33 bundles) 1871-1915, customers' ledgers (3) 1910-20, sales accounts (2 vols) 1912-20, other accounting, sales and order records (*c*13 vols) 1914-29, nd, stock books (4) 1893-1916, 1920-6, wages book 1901-7 and analyses 1915.
National Library of Wales. NRA 34184.

[959] **PRATCHITT BROS LTD** (later **APV MITCHELL DRYERS LTD**), mechanical engineers, drying and chemical plant mfrs, Carlisle, Cumberland

Balance sheets and profit and loss accounts, etc (3 vols) 1866-1954, letter books (35) 1859-62, 1866-7, 1871-1913, circular rel to merger 1970, account book 1846 incl foundry wages 1847-50, ledgers (3) 1859-70, 1906-49 and index *c*1900, day book 1897-1902, estimate book 1856-7, corresp, contract and specifications 1862, order pocket book 1902-3, traveller's notebook *c*1900-4, cost book 1852-5, works journals (3) 1887-1901, job books (6) 1859-65, 1874-9, 1923-33, engineering drawings (1 folder, 3 items) 1851-6, nd, wages books (5) 1865-82, inventory and valuation (1 vol) 1859, catalogues (23 items) 1860-1963, photographs of John Pratchitt and steam lorries (4 items) *c*1836-1907, exhibition medals (2 items) 1862, nd, and printed centenary history 1959.
Cumbria RO, Carlisle (DB/56). NRA 35353.

[960] **PRIESTLEY BROTHERS**, card mfrs and engineers, Halifax and Leeds

Letter books (2) 1890-6, ledgers (5 vols, 1 bundle) 1835-44, 1862-99, day books (4) 1859-74, 1888-92, invoice books (2) 1877-80, 1889-90, list of, and corresp with, European silk dressers 1889, particulars of stocks and shares held by LE Priestley (1 vol) 1882-3.
West Yorkshire Archive Service, Leeds. NRA 6540.

[961] **PRIESTMAN BROTHERS LTD**, contractors' plant and equipment mfrs, Hull, Yorks

Misc corporate records (c3 files, c26 items) 1900, 1945-86, bank statements nd, patent books (2) 1916-35, wages books (56) 1878-1942, workmen's registers (2) 1889-1929, 1941-61, apprenticeship indentures (1 bundle) 1903-42, superannuation and other staff records c1920-84, sales literature, manufacturing standards and misc papers nd.
Kingston upon Hull City RO (DBPm). NRA 28753.

[962] **PRINCE-SMITH & STELLS LTD**, textile machinery mfrs, Keighley, Yorks

Corresp 1900-1, 1965, ledger balances (1 vol) 1937-40, sales accounts (1 vol) 1928-44, order books (2) 1870-1, 1899-1907, memoranda (6 vols) rel to machinery 1876-81, 1892-1902, 1955-6, nd, specifications 1961-2, patents (25) 1945-60, visitors' book 1908-20, price lists and other printed papers 1925-66.
West Yorkshire Archive Service, Bradford (4D83). NRA 31930.

Annual stock summary book 1898-1931, order, sales, invoice and delivery records (35 vols, bundles and items) 1912, 1924-71, catalogues, sales and technical literature and other printed papers (76 items) 1918-67, photographs (c6 vols) c1900-55, glass negatives and register c1954-1968.
Lancashire RO (DDPSL/8). NRA 20296.

[963] **MA PRITLOVE**, coachbuilder, tyresmith and wheelwright, Chadwell Heath, Essex

Account book 1866-80.
Essex RO, Chelmsford (D/DU 1318/2). NRA 3505.

[964] **PULSOMETER ENGINEERING CO LTD**, mfrs of pumps, filters and refrigerating machinery, London and Reading, Berks

Records from 1872 incl memorandum and articles of association, special resolutions, etc 1877-1950, board minutes (14 vols) 1878-1968, general meeting minutes (1 vol) 1876-1964, directors' attendance books (2) 1878-1962, corresp rel to corporate business, etc 1875-1926, share summary (2 vols) 1902-33, dividend receipts 1905-11, seal books (2) 1878-1953, balance sheets, profit and loss accounts and related papers c1875-1919, 1962-8, orders received 1909, 1934-58, customer account ledger 1881-6, misc sales records from 1879, price lists and catalogues from 1875, patents, specifications and related papers 1872-1903, working instructions (3 vols) 1900-5, 1914-27, corresp rel to work not

paid for 1881-90, character register 1900-19 and other staff records from 1876, misc premises records from 1875, photographs from 1883 and press cuttings, advertisements, etc from 1879.
Berkshire RO and *SPP Ltd.* Enquiries to Berkshire RO. NRA 28631; BAC *Company Archives* no 279.

[965] **JAMES PURDEY & SONS LTD**, gun makers, London

Records 19th-20th cent incl legal papers rel to ownership of the business from 1857, corresp from late 19th cent, private accounts and balance sheets from 1880, ledgers from 1818, dimensions books from 1820 and staff and wages records from 1863.
The Company: see R Beaumont, *Purdey's: the guns and the family*, 1984. Closed to research.

[966] **QUALTER, HALL & CO LTD**, bulk mechanical handling engineers, Barnsley, Yorks

Minutes (1 vol) 1910-55, balance sheets and accounts 1875-88, 1902-17, 1940-72, private ledger 1910-55, cash book 1949-70, technical drawings (24 drawers) 1904-63, legal agreements, notes on the history of the firm, etc (1 file) 1870-1972, nd, photograph album c1890-1900.
The Company. Enquiries to Barnsley Archive Service. NRA 20542.

[967] **RAILWAY & GENERAL ENGINEERING CO LTD**, railway switch and crossing mfrs, Nottingham

Memorandum and articles of association with related papers 1900-71, directors' and shareholders' minutes (9 vols) 1900-75, directors' attendance book 1900-16, debenture trust deed 1916 and related papers 1972-5, share records (10 vols) 1900-78, register of mortgages and charges 1900-16, annual returns 1932-67, annual accounts and directors' reports with related papers 1928-79, private ledger 1958-79, misc agreements, etc rel to staff and premises 1909-71.
Sheffield Archives (TW 428-61). NRA 34879.

[968] **RALEIGH INDUSTRIES LTD**, bicycle mfrs, Nottingham

Certificates of incorporation (13) 1915-80, minutes (14 vols) 1891-1908, 1915-61, annual reports, balance sheets and accounts (6 items) 1889-90, 1926-30, 1976-80, financial statements (4) 1949-75 and auditors' reports 1926-30, receivers' accounts 1898-9, registers (2) of sealed documents 1934-74, ledgers (9 vols and loose items) 1888-1952, 1958-61, technical drawings 1960s-1970s, deeds, photographic plates and negatives (several thousand items), publicity material, press cuttings and other printed items 1890s-1980s.
Nottinghamshire Archives (DDRN). NRA 34479; A Millward, *The Raleigh archive: a detailed list of the contents*, 1987.

[969] **RAMAGE & FERGUSON LTD**, shipbuilders, Leith, Midlothian

Records incl agenda book 1892-1904, register of members, etc 1918-29, directors' private ledgers 1877-1903, quotations books 1888-1929, final cost books 1878-1916, particulars of vessels built 1878-1931 and trial trip particulars of engines and boilers 1896-1926.
Scottish Record Office (GD 339): see Ritchie.

[970] **F RANDELL LTD**, ironmongers and engineers, North Walsham, Norfolk

Proxy forms for ordinary general meeting (1 bundle) 1897, share records (3 bundles, 2 files, etc) 1897-1901, 1938-63, general corresp (2 files) 1897-1901, ledger 1897-1915, ledger summaries for Reepham branch (3 packets) 1940-1, summaries of accounts, etc (1 file) 1897-8, cash book 1932-40, account of cash drawn (1 vol) 1899-1919, bank books (4) 1897-1904, passed cheques (2) 1877, 1908, order and enquiry book 1956-63, list of stock prices (1 vol) 1906-67, stocktaking corresp (1 file, etc) 1897-1902, wages and other staff records (5 vols, 1 packet, etc) 1902, 1934-65, deeds and other premises records 1762-1965, misc papers from 1878.
Norfolk RO (BR 87). NRA 27692.

Articles of association 1897, 1954-5, directors' minutes (1 vol) 1897-1916, financial statements for directors' meetings (3 bundles) 1898-1914, balance sheets, reports, accounts, etc (2 bundles, 1 packet, etc) 1894-1914, 1921-39, customers' ledger 1837-44, private cash book 1897-1901, list of cheques passed 1859-70, stock lists from Reepham Works (3 vols) 1934-6, patents and related papers (1 packet, 2 items) 1873, 1881, 1890-5, corresp and papers rel to premises, etc (5 files, 2 bundles, 1 item) 1882-1900, wages and salaries accounts (2 vols) 1961-5; personal, legal and business papers of James Randell, his widow and executors (1 packet, 1 bundle) 1853-70.
In private possession. Enquiries to Norfolk RO. NRA 27692.

[971] **A RANSOME & CO LTD**, saw mill engineers and ironfounders, Newark, Notts

General and misc corresp and papers (6 boxes) 1898, 1911-29 incl share records 1915-18, specifications (6 items) 1911-26 and corresp rel to personnel 1915-24, customer order day books (15) 1855-66, 1870-97, corresp and papers rel to individual customers (*c*150 files) 1912-32, invoices (19 files) 1914-16, goods delivery ledgers (8) 1919-21, 1925-8, index of suppliers 1916-17, corresp rel to advertising (4 files) 1920s, journals (1 vol, 1 file) 1886-92, foundry day books (6) 1880-96.
Nottingham University Library (MS 428). NRA 33227.

[972] **RANSOMES & RAPIER LTD**, mfrs of railway plant, bridges and sluices, cranes and excavators, Ipswich, Suffolk

Records 1869-1986 incl certificate of incorporation 1896, board minutes 1896-1972, general meeting minutes 1897-1931, 1961-72, share registers and ledgers 1896-1958, seal registers 1896-1952, annual reports and balance sheets 1896-1933, directors' corresp and papers from 1878, ledgers, journals and cash books 19th-20th cent, order books and costing records from 1870, order abstract books *c*1875-*c*1961, commission claim books 1904-17, patents and agreements 1889-*c*1899, engineering drawings *c*1880-*c*1900, engineers' notebooks *c*1903-20, papers rel to the Shanghai-Woosung railway 1873-5, salaries records 1869-1956, plant and machinery records 1869-1943, plans of Waterside Ironworks from *c*1890 and photograph albums *c*1876-*c*1960.
Suffolk RO, Ipswich (HC 427). NRA 35179.

Records 1870-1926 incl mortgage of Waterside Ironworks, patents and Rapier family papers.
Suffolk RO, Ipswich (HB 439). NRA 7822.

[973] **RANSOMES, SIMS & JEFFERIES LTD**, agricultural engineers, Ipswich, Suffolk

Records 1785-1980 incl deeds of partnership and articles of agreement 1809-75, partnership book 1863-5, company books (2) 1884-1937, directors' minutes (1 vol) 1884-1937, reports of proceedings of directors' meetings (9 files) 1919-39, stock transfer register 1911-48, balance sheets and financial statements 1837-83, 1941-71, Ipswich and Bury St Edmunds financial statements 1915-45 and summaries 1909-46, Odessa branch financial statements 1892-1919, capital ledger 1865-83, private ledgers (9) 1884-1944, 1952-67, nominal ledger 1920-39, 'QQ' ledgers (2) 1920-54, memoranda account book 1895-1925, general account books (2) 1804-39, summaries of accounts and capital (1 vol) 1884-1901, cost accounts analysis books (5) 1885, 1936-9 and related papers (1 folder) 1856-78, Ipswich warehouse ledgers (2) 1916-47, journals (2) 1902-28 and regulations 1892, sales analyses 1871-1976, summary sales books (2) 1877-88, 1914-19, detailed sales books (50) 1906-55, price fluctuation statistics (1 folder) 1866-1927, order books, indexes, etc (*c*67 vols) 1917-68, goods despatch analysis books (2) 1866-82 and related notes (2 vols) 1861-91, export books (3) 1861-89, implement agencies books (11) 1914-50, notebook rel to business travels of James Ransome 1804, misc corresp and papers rel to sales and orders 1834-1969, show and exhibition records 1841-1965, trade mark and design registration and litigation papers (8 vols, 53 files and items) 1872-1932, engineering and other departments' production registers, customer indexes and related papers (54 vols) *c*1846-1948, engineering department turnery books (27) 1860-1949, report books (156) 1874-1910, despatch books (9) 1883-1932 and other records (10 vols) 1895-1946, parts registers, etc (17 vols and files) 1840-1956, trial and experiment records (10 vols, files, etc) 1838-89, 1902-15, 1944, 1963, engineer's notebook

1888-1908, drawings from *c*1840, drawings ledgers, registers and indexes (17 vols) 1834-1951, patents, specifications and related papers (*c*110 vols, files and items) 1785-1934, wages analysis sheets 1871-1939, salaries books (2) 1887-1907, 1926-40, lists of workmen (4) 1835, 1843, 1851, *c*1870, registers of workmen (6) 1859-1922, of apprenticeship indentures (1) 1838-72 and of boys entering firm (4) 1898-1966, employees' character references (2 files) 1900, 1917, notebook rel to labour relations 1887-1924, staff relief fund book 1817-36, invalids' book 1838-49, misc papers rel to personnel matters 1822-1969, notebooks (4) rel to sales, production, staff, etc 1833-1950, plans and particulars of works, etc (7 vols) 1846-1963, conveyance 1852, valuation records (7 files) 1895-1964, histories of the firm, research notes, etc 20th cent, catalogues, price lists, instruction manuals and other printed publicity and technical records from *c*1800, press cuttings from 1861 and photographs (*c*140 vols and many loose items) from *c*1856.
Rural History Centre, Reading University. NRA 20992; DR Grace and DC Phillips, *Ransomes of Ipswich: a history of the firm and guide to its records*, 1975.

Records from 1793 incl directors' minutes from 1884, directors' private memoranda 1892-1965, financial statements 1851-80, directors' reports and financial statements from 1883, memoranda books (3) 1890s-1920s, bad debts notebook 1878-1927, order book 1852-84, James Ransome's sketch book of plough designs early 19th cent, pattern books (2) 1849-1918, wages books (2) 1859-71, 1900-10, salaries books (2) 1863-86, 1908-26, fines account book 1883-1917, list of workmen 1793-1841, abstracts of apprenticeship indentures *c*1840-78 and works notices 1877-1953.
The Company. NRA 28631; BAC *Company Archives* no 467.

Grantham branch cash book 1930-7 and salaries book 1930-7.
Lincolnshire Archives (Ruston & Hornsby). NRA 11143.

[974] **RATCLIFFE & SON**, mechanical engineers and ironfounders, Malmesbury, Wilts

Day book 1870-81, diaries incl accounts (2 vols) 1885-99, bills and receipts (1 bundle) 1897-1901, specifications and estimates 1886-97.
Wiltshire RO (WRO 1269). NRA 24652.

[975] **JOHN READHEAD & SONS LTD**, shipbuilders, ship repairers and marine engineers, South Shields, co Durham

Memorandum and articles of association 1957, register of members 1909-58, letter books (33) 1896-1945, corresp (13 files, etc) 1914-64, private ledgers (4) 1865-1915, general, creditors' and debtors' ledgers (12) *c*1872-1963, private journal 1865-70, sundry journal 1912-57, cash books (9) 1882-1914, petty cash books (21) 1888-1915, bill books (2) 1875-95, bank books (14) 1904-58, accounts, vouchers and corresp rel to taxes, Admiralty, etc 1915-52, purchase and sales journals (8) 1938-63, contracts and related papers 1918-41,

cost books (210) and papers 1909-68, specifications (130 vols, 4 files) 1918-68, engine parts sketch books (29) 1883-1940, engine trials books (2) 1888-1908, boiler and engine details nd, ship plans 1879, 1902-68, yard plans 1813, *c*1870-1950, salaries books (18) 1886-1909, 1940-8, wages summary books (39) 1909-66, other staff records 1933-64, establishment charges 1914-18, 1955-63, ship and yard photographs 1863-1968, misc corresp, plans and legal papers 1891-1941, press cuttings 1939-66; Readhead family, estate and trust papers 1858-1936.
Tyne and Wear Archives Service (Acc 1061, Acc 2742). NRA 27128 and *Tyne and Wear Archives Service Annual Review 1992-93*, p18.

[976] **RECORD VANNER & SLIMER CO**, ore separation and dressing machinery mfrs, Minera, Denbighs

Certificate of registration 1917, general accounts (1 vol) 1916-50, orders and general accounts (2 vols) 1904-50, annual statements of trade accounts (1 bundle) 1915-29, bank book 1917-30, sales brochure *c*1930, patents (1 bundle) 1897-1913, plans (37 bundles) 1897-1950.
Clwyd RO, Ruthin (DD/WN). NRA 21864.

[977] **R & J REEVES & SON LTD**, ironfounders and agricultural implement mfrs, Bratton, Wilts

Articles of partnership 1881, 1896, memorandum and articles of association 1902, minutes 1903-70, register of members and directors 1903-60, seal book 1903-65, balance sheets, profit and loss accounts, etc 1881-1970, private ledgers (3) 1906-70, account book 1881-1901, royalty account book 1896-1907, cash books (19) 1897-1970, misc financial corresp and papers, etc 1883-1970, accounts (1 vol) for building, repair work and machinery 1843-6, building work and repair estimates (3 bundles) 1876-1914, sales ledgers (39) 1846-1957, sales day books (21) 1871-7, 1900-21, 1934-70, bought ledgers (26) 1871-1970, further sales and purchase records (*c*32 vols) 1926-70, bad debts accounts (1 vol) 1905-37, inventories and stock books (36) 1864-1959 and related papers (*c*6 bundles) 1891-1900, 1925-69, parts issued book 1952-3, registers of machines factored, etc 1939-70, machinery plans and drawings (1 bundle) 1883-1911, plant expenditure accounts (3 vols) 1902-10, wages and staff records 1863-1970, deeds, valuations of premises, etc 1874-1959, catalogues, price lists, etc 1890-*c*1920.
Wiltshire RO (WRO 951). NRA 21638.

Balance sheets and accounts 1894-1957, estimates, costings and sales records 1871-1965 incl sales day books 1871, sales and purchase corresp (28 files) 1922-51, stock and product records, material books and specifications *c*1900-50, manufacturing and production records 1848-1960, drawings (214 items) 1875-1943 and other technical records *c*1865-1960, wages and staff records *c*1871-1955, patents and legal papers 1854-1950s, premises records 1906-45, address book 1899-1920s, publicity material, catalogues and instruction books 1853-1960,

photographs (114 items) 1890s-1960s, historical notes on the firm by TH Gotch to c1952.
Rural History Centre, Reading University (HR 1318). NRA 21205.

[978] A REYROLLE & CO LTD, engineers, Hebburn, co Durham

Records incl letter books, financial records and photographs 1901-c1980.
Tyne and Wear Archives Service (Acc 1611).

[979] RICE & CO (LEEDS) LTD, hydraulic engineers, Leeds

Memorandum and articles of association 1900 and special resolutions 1908, 1930, capital account book 1893-1900, motor car account 1903, plant accounts (1 vol, etc) 1893-1963, machinery valuation 1907, drainage plan for Neville Works estate 1903, hydraulic tools catalogue mid 20th cent.
West Yorkshire Archive Service, Leeds (Acc 1643). NRA 34513.

[980] GEORGE RICHARDS & CO LTD, engineers and machine tool mfrs, Manchester

Corporate and share records (7 vols) 1885-1971.
Staveley Industries plc. NRA 28631; BAC *Company Archives* no 44.

[981] WESTLEY RICHARDS & CO LTD, gunmakers, Birmingham

Minutes (1 vol) 1872-99 incl liquidator's accounts 1899, journals (12) 1946-60, misc accounts (2 cupboards) to 1980s, gun order books (7) 1897-1960 and shotgun sales book 1979-87, customer ledgers (5) 1905-10, 1914-48 and indexes (5 vols), cost book 1839, stock books (2) 1835-9, 1898-1933, records of rifles, shotguns and pistols made and repaired (51 vols) c1830-1989, technical notebook, etc (1 vol) late 19th cent, royal warrants 19th-20th cent.
The Company. Access restricted. Enquiries to the Chairman. NRA 33397.

Ledger index from 1910, sales and purchase records 1922-59, job books (2) 1947-56, sundries book 1957-8, indexes (2 vols) 1950-7.
Holland & Holland Ltd. Enquiries to the Business Archives Council. NRA 35073.

[982] RICHARDSON & SON, coachbuilders and cycle mfrs, Uttoxeter, Staffs

Ledgers (29) 1883-1948, petty cash book 1885, estimate books (6) 1896-7, 1900-1, 1915-20, nd, carriage repair book 1880-7, job notebooks (4) 1909-20, 1927-33, drawings and photographs of carriages and other misc papers (1 bundle) c1900, trade catalogues, etc (7 bundles) c1890-1935, wages book 1912-48, papers mainly rel to the firm's business as undertakers (1 vol, 1 bundle) 1893-1933.
Staffordshire RO (D 617). NRA 7949.

[983] RIPPON BROS LTD, coach builders, Huddersfield, Yorks

Ledgers (2) 1894-1911, account book 1894-1903, day books (2) 1884-94, 1898-1902, cash books (7) 1898-1917, analysis book 1936-9, motor department sales and specifications (3 vols) 1905-13, sales book 1938-9, purchase day books (2) 1916-26, order books (2) 1907-10, 1914, tyres and tubes (1 vol) 1909-12, misc records (1 bundle) incl notebook of sketches and measurements 1870 and patent records 1895, 1920, Leeds shop diary 1914, memoranda book 1937-41, time book nd, deeds (3 boxes).
West Yorkshire Archive Service, Kirklees (B/RB). NRA 34071.

Records (9 boxes) 1892-1970s incl share register 1890s, sales records (2 vols, etc) 1907-71, nd, drawings and publicity material (2 vols, etc) 20th cent and glass negatives, etc (6 boxes) early 20th cent.
Rolls-Royce Enthusiasts Club. Enquiries to the Warden, The Hunt House, Paulerspury, Northants. NRA 34913.

[984] RITCHIE, HART & CO LTD, mfrs of heavy machinery, Belfast

Directors' minutes (2 vols) 1875-95, 1954-84, capital and share records (6 vols) 1881-1984, agreement 1953, letter books (3) 1898-1984, private ledger 1902-38, salaries and wages books (2) 1932-46, valuation and inventory 1902, advertising brochure c1950, speech on history of firm 1966.
Public Record Office of Northern Ireland (D 3872). Not available for research until listed. NRA 34902.

[985] CHARLES ROBERTS & CO LTD, railway wagon builders, Horbury, Yorks

Wagon order books 1893-1924, drawings and negatives c1893-1960.
National Railway Museum, York.

Private letter book of Charles Roberts 1888-92.
Wakefield Libraries Department of Local Studies (Goodchild Loan MSS).

[986] ROBERTSON & ORCHAR LTD, textile machinery mfrs, Dundee

Minutes (2 vols) 1898-1921, profit and loss accounts and balance sheets 1898-1907, private ledgers (2) 1889-96, 1921-37, wood prints and tracings of machinery (1 vol) 1907.
West Yorkshire Archive Service, Leeds (Acc 1323, 1325, 1341, 2371). NRA 14292.

See also Urquhart, Lindsay & Co Ltd.

[987] ROBEY & CO LTD, mechanical engineers, Lincoln

Records 19th-20th cent incl general meeting minutes (1 vol) c1910-30, draft minute books 1893-1963, other minutes nd, share records 1894-1935, accounts 1918-66, branch ledger 1896-1909, private cash registers 1894-1926, private account 1927-48, machinery order books c1880-c1970, shop order books nd, machinery and engine purchasers' books 1896-1961, register of foreign agencies and customers 1908-36, consignment books nd, registers of engines 1865-1931, boilers 1879-1924, boiler plates from 1917 and diesels 1930-74, weight books 1879-1954, patent specifications 1897-1967, pattern books 1896-1931, drawing registers nd, drawing office duplicates 1908-52, plans 19th-20th cent, register of employees 1895-1931, salary books 1896-1944, works department costs and expenses 1895-1908, building plan and cost books 1898-1923, inventories and valuations 1893, 1954 and printed papers 19th-20th cent.

Lincolnshire Archives (Robey). *Archivists' Report 27, 1977-82*, pp98-9, *28, 1982-3*, p13 and *29, 1983-4*, p17.

[988] **JOHN ROBSON (SHIPLEY) LTD**, diesel engine mfrs, Shipley, Yorks

Memorandum and articles of association 1906, 1916, annual reports and accounts (1 file) 1909-81, share and dividend records (13 vols, 3 bundles) 1906-74, registers of directors, annual returns and misc corporate records (1 vol, 2 bundles, 31 items) 1919-46, corresp files 1918-22, subject files (20) 1906-63 incl employee agreements (1 file) 1906-10 and corresp with architects and related papers (1 file) 1910-11, sole agency agreements (15) with other firms 1911-33, balance sheets and profit and loss accounts (1 bundle) 1903-69, ledgers (2) 1909-14, nominal ledgers (6) 1915-67, bank books (4) 1908-12, 1930-8, cash books, day books and misc accounting records (c30 vols, c4 files) 1915-88, sales and purchase ledgers, day books, etc (55 vols) 1897-1980, foundry day books, agents' registers, test reports and other production records (15 vols, etc) 1909-1980s, drawing office registers (3) 1908-59, sketch books (4) 1945-54, drawings (several thousand) of engines from 1908 and other drawing office records, salaries and wages books (50) 1908-79, factory act registers, card index of employees and other staff records 1930s-1981, publicity and advertising records, misc photographs and printed papers from early 20th cent; Yorkshire Engineering Co (Egypt) Ltd annual returns, register of directors, share counterfoils, etc 1911-46, legal and misc corresp and papers (28 files and bundles) 1907-39, balance sheets and trading and profit and loss accounts 1912-36, cash accounts, etc (4 files) 1911-15, bank book 1914-21, sales notes and contracts 1922-30.

West Yorkshire Archive Service, Bradford (19D91). NRA 34183.

[989] **ROLLS-ROYCE LTD**, motor car and aero-engine mfrs, Derby

Board minutes from 1906, corresp mainly post-1945, technical records and drawings mainly rel to aircraft engines 20th cent, staff records from 1906, photographs and publicity material.

Rolls-Royce plc, Derby. NRA 11562.

Records 19th-20th cent incl agreement between Royce Ltd and CS Rolls 1904, certificate of incorporation 1906, directors' files c1971, misc share

records nd, annual reports from 1906, early cheques drawn on FH Royce & Co Ltd and Rolls-Royce Ltd, test log book for Royce's petrol engine 1903, technical records and drawings rel to aircraft engines 20th cent, apprenticeship indentures 1906-39, papers rel to Derby site and premises 1906-7; corresp 1898-1926 and notebooks 1903-7 of Claude Johnson, and papers of Sir Arthur Sidgreaves and EW Hives, 1st Baron Hives.

Rolls-Royce Heritage Trust, PO Box 31, Derby. Enquiries to the Chairman. Other technical records are held by local branches of the Trust.

Guarantee books for Rolls-Royce and Bentley cars (20 vols) 1905-67, records of cars made (c500 boxes, 1 file) 1904-1960s, depot sheets (3 vols, 8 files) 1920s-1930s, technical corresp (c180 boxes) 1907-c1945 and drawings (c30,000 items) 20th cent, test records of experimental cars (392 vols) 1923-72, sales catalogues of Rolls-Royce and Bentley cars (3 drawers) from 1905, photographs and glass plate negatives of cars (c30,000 items), Shrewsbury factory records, Rolls-Royce instruction school reports (12 vols) 1929-39; corresp and papers of CS Rolls (18 vols, 1 folder, 1 item) 1896-1910, nd, Sir Henry Royce (23 boxes, 3 vols, 1 item) 1903-36 and EW Hives, 1st Baron Hives (7 vols and loose items) 1908-63.

Rolls-Royce Enthusiasts Club. Enquiries to the Warden, The Hunt House, Paulerspury, Northants. NRA 35052.

Further technical records after 1914 are in Brooklands Museum and time books are in Coventry City RO. These records relate only to the aero-engine side of the business.

[990] **ROSE, DOWNS & THOMPSON LTD**, engineers, ironfounders and mfrs of oil mill and hydraulic machinery, Hull, Yorks

Partnership papers 1871, 1894, corresp (c500 items) 1859-1912, nd, annual balance sheets 1860-2, 1864, 1872, half-yearly summaries 1874-83, ledger accounts (3 vols) 1790-1, 1838-45, 1866-78, bought journals (5) 1911-29, price books (3) 1859-78, nd, sales and publicity material, catalogues, etc (155 items), stock books (2) 1925-35, cost and charge books (17) in customers' series 1890-1905 and internal series 1889-1901, shop order books (81) 1875-1943, reference detail books by names of clients (36) 1876-1935, invoice book 1898-1902, estimates (80) 1882-90, nd, cost books (15) 1902-13, cost accounts of goods made by moulders 1853-65, accounts of iron made and sold 1872-4, papers rel to munitions production 1914-19, sketch books (7) 1939-45, patents, etc 1861-86, wages accounts 1859, piece work rates book nd, accounts rel to moulders' strike 1901, Old Foundry report 1865-7, valuations 1859-84, nd, plans and specifications 19th cent, deeds 1808-20th cent, reports, etc on machinery and tests 1884-1932, nd, James Downs' private cash books (2) 1861-75, papers rel to his appointment as manager 1859 and his dispute with JC Thompson 1872-8, history of the firm, historical files (8) and printed material, cricket club score book 1900-6.

Kingston upon Hull City RO (DBR). NRA 14470.

[991] **RG ROSS & SON LTD**, steam hammer mfrs, Glasgow

Order book 1902-39, costing books (9) 1856-1935, list of hammers built 1858-1906, corresp and drawings (4 files) 1937-65, nd.
Glasgow University Archives and Business Record Centre (UGD/118/7). NRA 14656.

[992] **ROVER CO LTD** (formerly **JK STARLEY & CO LTD**), mfrs of motor vehicles and bicycles, Coventry

Board minutes (12 vols) 1890-1972 and indexes 1958-71, executive directors' minutes (1 vol) 1961-6, general meeting minutes (2 vols) 1896-1972, register of directors (3 vols) 1901-48, directors' attendance books (2) 1948-72, nd, seal book 1896-1949, annual accounts 1932-57, estimated assets and liabilities (2 vols) 1906-31, private ledgers (3) 1890-1903, 1906-16, misc corporate and other records 1931-77, register of deeds, etc (1 vol) 1888-1941 and misc property records (4 vols) 1929-78.
Warwick University Modern Records Centre (MSS 226/RO). NRA 28571.

Catalogues, press cuttings, photographs, etc from c1904.
British Motor Industry Heritage Trust, Gaydon, Warwicks.

[993] **ROWHEDGE IRONWORKS CO LTD**, shipbuilders and marine engineers, Rowhedge, Essex

Records c1907-56 incl cash books nd, sales and purchase records nd, materials order books (c340) 1911, 1915-55, requisition books nd, specifications (3 binders) from 1911, sketch books (c20) 1907-56, corresp files rel to individual ships nd, wages and timekeepers' records nd and photographs (4 vols) nd.
Essex University Library. NRA 35364; and see Ritchie.

Specifications, plans and technical records nd.
National Maritime Museum Manuscripts Section.

[994] **JOSEPH ROWLINSON**, coach step mfr, Birmingham

Sales journal 1839-47.
Birmingham Central Library Archives Division (MS 804). NRA 29847.

[995] **ROYLES LTD**, iron and brass founders, engineers and calorifier mfrs, Irlam, Lancs

Prospectus 1900, articles of association 1900, board and general meeting minutes (3 vols) 1900-57, share records (4 vols, etc) 1900-53, balance sheets and profit and loss accounts 1950-65, fixed capital record 1900-1940s, letter book 1893-1909, register of seals 1902-33, account book 1901-5, private ledger 1895-8, impersonal ledgers 1900-57, private journal 1900-1960s, order books, etc (15 vols, etc) from 1898, sketch books (2) of John Royle 1875, 1883, brass foundry pattern register 1899-1943,

drawings of machinery (microfilms) from 1900, tracings records (12 vols) c1950-60, salaries books (7) 1900-46, wages books (2) 1957-61, photographs of machinery (7 albums) 1890s-1920s and of works (1 album) c1900, price lists, catalogues, printed material and misc papers 1874-1963.
The Company. Enquiries to the Business Archives Council. NRA 21363.

Memorandum and articles of association, certificate of incorporation and related papers (10 items) 1900-71, directors' reports and accounts 1941-75, ledgers (7) c1899-1909, cash books (6) 1911-34, sales books 1910-27, list of invoices (1 vol) 1879-81, stock book 1876-1908, nd, notes rel to reducing valve 1903-4, wages and salaries books, etc (2 vols) 1910-32, time book 1879-84, valuations of premises and machinery (1 vol) 1901-44, catalogues, patent applications and misc papers c1909-78.
Salford Archives Centre (U 117). NRA 21363.

[996] **RUBERY OWEN & CO LTD**, mfrs of motor vehicle components, steel roofing and fencing and machine tools, Darlaston, Staffs

Records from 1883 incl articles of partnership between JT Rubery and TW Rubery 1884, deeds of partnership between JT Rubery and AE Owen 1893 and dissolution of partnership 1911, management committee minutes (2 vols) 1912-22, directors' and general meeting minutes (1 vol) 1937-59, letter books (2) 1897-1912, copies of memoranda to and from AE Owen and AGB Owen (1 parcel) 1913-44, letters from accountants (1 bundle) 1895-1901, 1909, balance sheet 1909, trading accounts 1908-10, private ledgers (10) 1893-1929, cash books (c10) 1893, 1909-44, sales ledger 1883-93, sales journal 1899-1901, cost book and order book 1901, motor department cost book 1901, papers rel to patent for tubular steel billets (1 envelope) 1911, diary of works events 1903, deeds and plans of premises and property (c80 bundles) 19th-20th cent, valuation of property and plant 1901, quotations for new works premises (1 file) 1912, and catalogues and other printed papers from c1904.
Rubery Owen Holdings Ltd. Enquiries to the Chairman. NRA 33231.

[997] **RUDGE-WHITWORTH LTD**, bicycle and motorcycle mfrs, Coventry and Birmingham

Certificates of incorporation (4) 1894, 1934, annual reports and accounts (38 items) 1894-1932, balance sheets, etc (3 items) 1934-6, annual returns of members (14 items) 1898-1911, ledger 1933-7, printed catalogues, press cuttings and publicity material 1888-1958.
Nottinghamshire Archives (DDRN). NRA 34479; A Millward, *The Raleigh archive: a detailed list of the contents*, 1987.

Memorandum and articles of association and other misc corporate and financial records (14 items) 1887-8, 1894-5, plans of premises (4 items) 1911-16, nd, deeds 18th-20th cent.
Coventry City RO (Acc 849). NRA 32961.

[998] **HARRY N RUMSBY & SONS**, iron and brass founders, mfrs of stoves and agricultural implements, Bungay, Suffolk

Ledgers (8) 1819-33, 1887-1901, 1903-4, day books (2) 1923-45.
Suffolk RO, Ipswich (HC 406/2). NRA 7822.

[999] **GEORGE RUSSELL & CO LTD**, engineers and crane mfrs, Motherwell, Lanarkshire

Memorandum and articles of association 1902, special resolutions (2 items) 1908, 1919, order book 1875-80, plans of cranes 20th cent, abstract time book 1880, glass negatives mainly of overhead cranes (1 box) nd, catalogues and photographs of cranes (2 boxes, etc) 1920s-1960s, nd.
Strathclyde Regional Archives (TD 450). NRA 33977.

[1000] **RUSTON, PROCTOR & CO LTD**, agricultural and general engineers and boilermakers, Lincoln

Records from 1860 incl directors' attendance book 1899-1918, register of debentures 1895 with summary of transfers to *c*1918, capital expenditure records *c*1900-40, account book 1888-91, cash book 1870-95, agreements (5 vols) 1883-1937, engine registers (*c*15) 1860-1942, thresher registers (2) 1905-31, castings registers 1914, aeroplane records (3 vols) 1915-19, thresher spare parts list 1868-93, spare parts lists and sketch books *c*1905-50, stock orders (1 file) 1907-20, gas plant experiments 1912-37, plans and drawings from *c*1880, lists of tracings sent away (3 vols) 1912-31, time account 1864-8, doctor's account 1908-17, building and machinery cost records (*c*7 vols) 1883-1914, rent and agreement book 1913-31, photographs from *c*1880 and catalogues, price lists and other printed material from *c*1890; cash books (10) of JS Ruston 1897-1910, Ruston family trust ledgers (2) 1907-21; Andrews Ltd gas engine registers (2) 1894-1906 and experiments record 1899-1916.
Lincolnshire Archives. NRA 11143 and *Archivists' Report 21, 1969-70*, pp11-14.

Annual reports (1 vol) 1890-1966, agreements with Aveling Barford Ltd 1934-42 and Bucyrus-Erie Co 1929-65.
National Museums and Galleries on Merseyside, Merseyside Maritime Museum (B/VF/1/2/3, B/VF/2/3). NRA 29901.

Memoranda and articles of association *c*1919-74, war work order book 1938-44, drawings *c*1919-74, printed material 1926-34.
Rural History Centre, Reading University: see Ritchie.

See also Richard Hornsby & Sons Ltd.

[1001] **GEORGE SALTER & CO LTD**, bayonet, scale and spring balance mfrs, West Bromwich, Staffs

Partnership deeds and related papers (*c*12 items) 1863-1915, memorandum and articles of association 1915, nd, directors' minutes (2 vols) 1915-16, 1935-45, registers of members, loan stock and debenture records (3 vols, 1 bundle, 2 items)

1915-40, 1969, annual returns, balance sheets and accounts, etc 1872-7, 1885-1938, agreements and trading arrangements with other firms (33 bundles and items) 1881-1958, other legal records (5 bundles, *c*20 items) 1898-1928, 1970-1, private ledgers (9) 1905-68, nominal ledgers (2) 1909-22, 1964, bank ledgers (3) 1909-13, 1919-26, general and other ledgers (4) 1882-99, 1966-7, nd, cash books (22) 1858-69, 1881-1949, bank books (3) 1914-21, account books (2) 1894-1909, nd, other financial records (2 vols, etc) *c*1892-1956, bayonet trade records incl minutes, corresp, accounts, order book and cost book (10 vols, 21 bundles, 32 items) 1825-53, 1857-63, analysis books (17) 1855-1944, royalty book 1884-1900 and other records rel to sales (5 vols) 1875-9, 1894-1909, 1935-67 and production (3 vols, 2 bundles, 3 items) 1860s-1982, patents, Board of Trade certificates and related papers (42 bundles and items) 1846-1962, wages and salaries books (9) 1873-1900, 1929-45, other staff records *c*1876-1985, plant and premises records 1901-69, nd, visitors' book 1983-8, photographs of products, premises and staff late 19th-20th cent, catalogues, price lists, house magazines and other publicity material 1815-1987, press cuttings and scrapbooks 1915-1960s, papers rel to Salter family and company history 1782-1970; Salter Typewriter Co private ledger 1903-15, corresp and accounts (1 bundle) 1911-12, bank book 1912-17 and sales ledger 1904-12.
Staffordshire RO (D 4721). NRA 33839.

[1002] **SAMUELSON & CO LTD**, agricultural and general engineers, Banbury, Oxon

Memorandum and articles of association, corresp, partnership, share and patent records, legal papers, agreements, leases, etc (64 bundles) 1859-1907.
Oxfordshire Archives (Acc 344). NRA 35026.

Patents and specifications (43 items) 1863-86 with related papers (11 bundles and items) 1867-87, misc technical, personnel and other records (5 bundles, 28 items) 1860-1914.
In private possession. Photocopies of some items are in the Rural History Centre, Reading University. NRA 24718.

[1003] **SANDERSON & HOLMES LTD**, coachbuilders, Derby

Account books (26) 1889-1963, desk book 1887-1917, stock inventory nd, schedule of plant, machinery, etc 1897.
Derbyshire RO (D2696).

[1004] **SANDYCROFT FOUNDRY**, mfrs of mining machinery and electric motors, Sandycroft, Flints

Letters received 1875-90, order book 1886-7, sketches of crushing machinery 1878, foundry institute minutes 1875-83, catalogues, photographs, press cuttings, etc 1885-1923.
Clwyd RO, Hawarden: see *Guide to the Flintshire Record Office, 1974*, p113.

[1005] **SAVAGES' LTD**, agricultural engineers, boilermakers and fairground machinery mfrs, Kings Lynn, Norfolk

Records mainly 1880-1920 incl letter book, specifications book, engine register, engineering drawings (*c*400 items), drawings and designs for fairground carving, photographs (*c*100 items) of fairground rides, agricultural machinery, etc, wages book, register of employees, insurance policies, catalogues, and misc letters, agreements and leases.
Lynn Museum. NRA 33430.

[1006] **ARCHIBALD SCOTT LTD**, coach and motor vehicle body builders, Bellshill, Lanarkshire

Ledgers (2) 1877-1900, job ledgers (3) 1900-12, time books (83) *c*1880-1905, wages book 1932-40, architectural plans *c*1886-90, photographs of products, workshop, family and employees (1 album, *c*400 items) *c*1880-1977.
In private possession. Enquiries to NRA (Scotland) (survey 1900). NRA 22373.

[1007] **GEORGE SCOTT & SON (LONDON) LTD**, engineers and chemical plant mfrs, London and Leven, Fife

Memorandum and articles of association, etc (4 items) 1900, 1962-70, register of members 1900-76, balance sheets, etc 1914-57, agreements, etc (21 items) 1910-11, 1915-59, valuation, plan and leases of premises (5 items) 1923-43, nd, centenary history 1934; Ernest Scott & Co Ltd memoranda and articles of association 1908, 1962, certificate of incorporation 1908, special resolutions (3 items) 1941-70, register of members 1900-76, balance sheets 1914-57, agreements and corresp 1908-56. Combined records of both firms: papers rel to formation of holding company 1933, corresp rel to share transfers 1924, balance sheets, etc 1911-43, agreements (4 items) 1933-53, sales records (3 vols, etc) *c*1927-59, staff and salaries list 1930, catalogues, etc incl some of other firms (*c*40 items) 1921-68, notes rel to history of Balfour Group (18 items) *c*1960-8.
Scottish Record Office (GD 410). NRA 34481.

[1008] **SCOTT & SONS (BOWLING) LTD**, shipbuilders and ship repairers, Bowling, Dunbarton

Letter books (42) 1945-68, ledgers (7) 1857-78, 1937-72, day books (10) 1857-1962, journal, cash books and other accounting records (21 vols) 1917-70, purchase ledgers and invoice books (16) 1929-64, estimate books (2) 1885-1930, quotations books (3) 1936-56, contract files (78) from 1939, cost files (88) 1933-58, stock book 1926-42, block books (2) *c*1869-1959, specification letter book 1937-62, launch books (4) 1902-73, particulars books (69) nd, list of ships built 1851-1979, ship drawings 1915-61, time books (23) 1949-71, photographs, publicity material, press cuttings, etc *c*1850-1977.
Glasgow University Archives and Business Record Centre (GD 322, RHP 52660-724, 62053-7, 66690-702); and see Ritchie.

[1009] **SCOTTS' SHIPBUILDING & ENGINEERING CO LTD**, Greenock, Renfrewshire

Share records 1899-1964, letter books 1798-1945, corresp 1908-68, annual balances and profit and loss accounts 1859-1967, ledgers 1780-1967, journals 1802-1969, cash books 1851-1969, account books 1870-1959, cost books 1892-1969, enquiries, tenders, contracts, specifications and related corresp 1853-1969, ship and engine plans nd, salary books 1919-55, wages books 1903-69, pay bill books 1901-65, inventories and valuations 1906-68, photographs nd, press cuttings and publicity material 1918-61.
Glasgow University Archives and Business Record Centre: see Ritchie.

[1010] **SCRIVEN CROSTHWAITE LTD** (formerly **CROSTHWAITE FURNACES & SCRIVEN MACHINE TOOLS LTD**), machine tool mfrs, Leeds

Cash book 1944-6, customer accounts ledger 1936-44, machinery weights and components for despatch (1 vol) *c*1865 and reference book 1896-1900, classified offer books (2) 1913-60, sales ledger 1938-46, cost books (3) *c*1904-1917, nd, order books (7) 1870-1947, counterfoil order books (12) 1933-4, 1946-64, drawing office order books (3) 1906-23 and other order records (7 files, 1 bundle) 1920s-1940s, drawing ledger 1914-46, tracing books (7) 1910-50, drawing office item lists, etc (1 box, 2 vols, 11 files, 2 items) 20th cent, wheel books (4) 1901-15, nd, stockroom list nd, Scriven & Co catalogues (2) 20th cent, blueprints, photographs and glass negatives of machinery 20th cent, nd.
West Yorkshire Archive Service, Leeds. NRA 34672.

[1011] **ALEXANDER SHANKS & SON LTD**, engineers and ironfounders, Arbroath, Angus

Memorandum and articles of association nd, directors' minutes (2 vols) 1894-1904, 1939-51, share records (4 vols) 1894-1953, private ledger 1894-1907, apprenticeship records (1 vol) 1892-1910, inventories and valuations (2 vols, etc) 1883-1925, 1961-5.
Dundee University Library (MS 43). NRA 17169.

Order book 1882, price-fixing agreement with other firms manufacturing lawn mowers 1899, price lists (3) 1876-8, 1889, costings and specifications book 1859-77, technical details of grass cutting machine 1842, patents and royal warrant corresp and papers 1835, 1888-1955, parts lists, service manual, etc (4 items) *c*1900, plans of works *c*1880-1900, inventory of plant and machinery 1893, catalogues and advertising material 1859-1951, photographs of products and employees (2 vols) 20th cent, misc papers rel to history of the lawn mower (1 file) 1912-36.
Arbroath Signal Tower Museum. NRA (Scotland) (survey 2184). NRA 24032.

[1012] **SHARP, STEWART & CO LTD** (formerly **SHARP, ROBERTS & CO**), locomotive builders, Manchester and Glasgow

Order books (5) 1836-66 and drawings nd.
National Railway Museum, York. NRA 28465.

Records incl order book 1887-1903 and glass plate negatives 1888-1903.
Mitchell Library, Glasgow, Department of Science and Technology.

Drawings 19th-20th cent.
Glasgow University Archives and Business Record Centre (RHP 57021-58104). NRA 36388.

Visitors' books (3) for Manchester engineering works 1842-55.
Science Museum Library (MS 368). NRA 9524.

See also North British Locomotive Co Ltd.

[1013] **CC SHARPE & SONS**, millwrights and agricultural engineers, Donington, Lincs

Account books (2) 1909-10, 1913-15, day book 1909-11.
Lincolnshire Archives (LLHS 20). *Accessions to repositories 1963*, p31.

[1014] **JOHN SHEARD**, hackle, gill and wool comb mfr, Bradford, Yorks

Customers' account book 1859-71, order book 1863-92.
West Yorkshire Archive Service, Bradford (A2/32-3). NRA 29411.

[1015] **SHORT BROTHERS LTD**, shipbuilders, Sunderland, co Durham

Articles of partnership 1884, certificates of incorporation 1900, 1922, directors' minutes, etc (10 items) 1901, private letter books (2) 1906-14, diaries (2) 1881-2, legal corresp and papers (128 files, 907 items) 1877, 1896-1927, statements of capital and profits (2 items) 1891-1906, ledgers (8) 1870-85, 1891-1918, bill book 1871-4, day book 1918-63, quotations (3 vols, 1 file, 2 items) 1878, 1900-28, contracts and related papers (1 vol, 27 files, 243 items) 1870-1957, cost books (9) 1890-1911, 1916-24, corresp, agreements, etc rel to individual ships (35 files, 165 items) 1870-1957, ships' particulars books (2) 1890-1962, tonnage book 1909-38, specifications (1 vol, 5 files, 6 items) 1871-1916, patent papers (4 files, 27 items) 1886-7, 1909-10, wages books and summaries (11 vols, 3 files) 1883-5, 1906-62, production bonus record (1 vol) 1957-63, letter of appointment of shipyard manager 1900, joint agreement rel to dispute at shipyard (1 file) 1911, valuation of machinery, plant and stock (1 file) 1885, corresp and papers rel to premises and property (7 files, 36 items) 1896-1943; private notebooks of JY Short (11) 1880-98 and Thomas Short (7) 1894-1910.
Tyne and Wear Archives Service (Accs 714, 1391). NRA 22559.

Drawings 1924-46, photographs nd.
Tyne and Wear Museums Service: see Ritchie.

Ship plans (5 items) *c*1876-89.
Durham County RO (D/AP 23-27). NRA 31633.

[1016] **A & H SIMONETT (ENGINEERS) LTD**, textile machinery mfrs, Bradford, Yorks

Records 1900-72 incl textile machinery accounts 1910-45, other accounting records 1931-70, order books 1900-52, quotation books 1953-69, job books 1947-60, agreements 1931-47 and wages books 1943-7.
West Yorkshire Archive Service, Bradford (64D81, 57D83).

[1017] **WILLIAM SIMONS & CO LTD**, ship and dredger builders, Renfrew

Records incl annual summary 1949-58, ledger 1901-56, private contract books (15) 1899-1936, vessel costings 1915-55, specifications 1925-33, ship plans 1814-1961 and photographs 1889-1960.
Glasgow University Archives and Business Record Centre (UCS 4, UGD/114, UGD/130). NRA 14659, 14816, 21022; and see Ritchie.

Ship plans (7 items) 1814-64.
Strathclyde Regional Archives (TD 232). NRA 12501.

Plans and trial records of dredger *c*1927.
National Maritime Museum Manuscripts Section.

Ship photographs (267 items) 1890-1913.
Paisley Museum and Art Galleries.

[1018] **TH & M SIMPSON**, valve mfrs and sanitary and heating engineers, Loughborough, Leics

Ledger 1890-1903, day books (2) 1883-7.
Leicestershire RO (5 D 68). NRA 6263.

[1019] **SIMPSON-LAWRENCE LTD**, yacht fittings and marine hardware mfrs, Glasgow

Memorandum and articles of association nd, certificate of incorporation nd, minutes from 1967, register of members, directors, mortgages and annual returns from 1937, share certificates from 1938, annual accounts 1911-36 and from 1957, letter book 1908-9, private ledger 1901-12, day books (2) 1913-15, customer index cards *c*1938, wages book 1894-1901, record of salaries 1924, trade catalogues nd.
The Company. Enquiries to NRA (Scotland) (survey 3030). NRA 31768.

[1020] **SINGER & CO LTD**, cycle and motor car mfrs, Coventry

Records incl minutes from *c*1900.
Peugeot Talbot Motor Co Ltd. Enquiries to the Company Secretary.

[1021] **SINGER MANUFACTURING CO LTD**, sewing machine mfrs, Clydebank, Dunbarton

Records late 19th-20th cent incl board, executive committee and general meeting minutes (4 vols) 1917-73, share records, registers of members, letter

books, contracts, leases, etc 1883-1968, ledgers (6) 1955-73, cash books (7) 1871-81, 1952-63, bank credit and debit books (13) 1963-72, purchase and sales ledgers (10) 1957-62, claims and sales book 1961-2, factory and foundry department costs, etc 1886-91, 1901-3, estimates rel to factory and tenements 1882-6, list of foremen's wages 1903, inventory of tools and fixtures 1881, plans of tenements and foundry *c*1890-1900 and corresp and papers rel to history of company (2 files) 1867-*c*1970.
Singer Sewing Machines, Guildford. Enquiries to NRA (Scotland) (survey 2427). NRA 10852.

Invoice books (2) and orders 1941-62, price lists, parts lists incl original drawings for illustrations, service manuals, instruction booklets, catalogues and photographs, etc from 1879.
Clydebank District Library. NRA 10852.

Cash books (7) 1943-52, unclaimed wages ledgers, etc (38 vols) 1885-1967, retiring gratuities account books (6) 1925-50.
Glasgow University Archives and Business Record Centre (UGD/121). NRA 10852.

[1022] **W SISSON & CO LTD**, marine engine builders, Gloucester

Memorandum and articles of association 1904-43, directors' minutes (4 vols) 1938-65, registers of directors and managers (2 vols) 1904-35, share records (2 vols, 4 files) 1904-58, directors' and auditors' reports 1904, balance sheets and accounts (5 files) 1890-1963, private ledgers (3) 1904-67, journal 1937-68, private cash book 1946-69, register of engines constructed 1919-34, misc legal, financial and technical records 1904-68; notes, drawings, photographs, brochures, press cuttings, etc rel to firm's history collected by the Fowler family *c*1878-1982 incl design book of William Sisson from *c*1878.
Gloucestershire RO (D5748, D6093). NRA 32952.

[1023] **SKINNER, BOARD & CO LTD**, heating engineers and greenhouse mfrs, Bristol

Minutes from 1948 and other misc corporate records from 1902, private ledgers, cash books and other accounting records 1907-80, order books, etc 1893-1979, wages books, etc from 1893, catalogues (2) 1908, 1920s.
The Company: see Business in Avon and Somerset.

[1024] **SMEDLEY BROS LTD**, ironfounders and mfrs of grinding machinery, Belper, Derbys

Articles of association, misc accounts, order and stock books, plans, drawings and catalogues (*c*10 boxes) *c*1890-*c*1970.
Derbyshire RO (D982, D2790).

[1025] **A & W SMITH & CO LTD**, engineers and sugar machinery mfrs, Glasgow

Minute books (3) 1909-47, order books (39) 1845-1965, work register 1880-1934, job books (48) 1900-62, cost price books (27) 1906-34, production order books (18) 1954-74, record of blocks 1933-55, drawing registers (4) 1859-1959, valuation of plant and machinery 1897, photograph albums (5) 1907-24, nd.
Glasgow University Archives and Business Record Centre (UGD/118/1, 8). NRA 14656.

[1026] **SMITH BROS & CO (GLASGOW) LTD**, engineers and machine tool mfrs, Glasgow

Drawing office order books (3) *c*1890-1929, standard time books (2) 1925-31, index of work supplied *c*1890-1931.
Museum of Science and Industry in Manchester (EN 4). NRA 29503.

[1027] **HUGH SMITH & CO LTD**, hydraulic engineers and machine tool mfrs, Glasgow

Registers of members (2) 1903, 1955, private ledgers (2) 1904-47, ledgers (3) 1875-99, 1920-32, journals (5) 1896-1901, 1904-66, nd, cash books (14) 1878-1966, other financial records (16 vols) 1946-75, order books (38) 1891-1950, nd, sales ledger 1914-24, sales books (6) 1935-64, other sales records (12 vols) 1911-70, stock books (3) 1892-1912, 1927-55, materials books (20) 1875-1938, drawing office sketch books (3) 1894-1937, time books (9) 1875-92, 1903-19, 1937-8, wages and salaries records (8 vols) 1906-40, apprenticeship book 1886-1967.
Glasgow University Archives and Business Record Centre (UGD/182). NRA 10853.

Technical records.
Hugh Smith (Engineering) Ltd. NRA 10853.

[1028] **WILLIAM SMITH & SONS**, road sweeping machine mfrs, Barnard Castle, co Durham

Letter books (4) 1866-1904, general ledgers (2) 1925-45, sales ledgers (4) 1890-1930, order book 1889-1900, misc patents, drawings, photographs of machines, etc (2 vols, 2 bundles, 10 items) 1864-1911.
Durham County RO (D/WS). NRA 19308.

[1029] **SMITH'S DOCK CO LTD**, shipbuilders, ship repairers and marine engineers, North Shields, Northumb, South Shields, co Durham and Middlesbrough

Impersonal ledgers 1910-38, ship and engine ledgers 1912-40, cost books with particulars 1909-44, dock order books 1946-54, specifications 1911-64, calculations books 1910-70, capacity books 1930-69, general particulars booklets 1947-70, ship plans nd, builder's certificate books 1916-81.
Cleveland Archives: see Ritchie.

Ship plans 1908, 1920-79.
National Maritime Museum Manuscripts Section.

[1030] **THOMAS SMITHDALE & SONS**, mechanical engineers and ironfounders, Norwich

Letter books (4) 1850-76, 1886, income and expenditure account (1 vol) 1872-8, debtor and

creditor account (1 vol) 1876-81, general ledgers (8) 1859-61, 1863-6, 1869-84, Panxworth ledgers (2) 1873-5, 1881-3, bought ledgers (2) 1865-73, 1876-83, ledgers (2) showing time spent and materials used 1868-72, day books (4) 1871-2, 1875-6, 1878-86, order books (5) 1853-6, 1873-88, time and wages books (2) 1877-8, 1884-5, 1888-90, misc engineering drawings nd.
Norfolk RO (BR 136). NRA 34906.

[1031] JAMES SMYTH & SONS LTD, agricultural engineers, Peasenhall, Suffolk

Share corresp, etc 1908-9, 1927-31, profit and loss accounts and balance sheets 1924-31, account book incl valuation 1844-8, order books (66) 1847-1962, number books (20) for customers' orders 1836-71, boxes and frames 1873-1967, horse hoes 1897-1912, steerages 1916-59 and sketch work drills from 1878, work sheets 1959-62, engineering drawings (39) nd, patents, trade marks and related papers 1843-1939, price lists c1920-65, catalogues and manuals late 19th-20th cent, photographs 19th-20th cent, deeds c1700-1859, plan 1924, sale particulars 1968, press cuttings, corresp and notes rel to history of firm and misc papers.
Suffolk RO, Ipswich (HC 23). NRA 14308.

[1032] SPENCER (MELKSHAM) LTD, mfrs of conveyors and mechanical handling equipment, Melksham, Wilts

Records (c400 boxes, etc) c1890-1985, incl minutes, letter books, order and process books, specifications, plans and drawings, catalogues, photographs and personnel records.
Wiltshire RO (WRO 2516).

[1033] MH SPENCER LTD, reed and heald mfrs, Coventry

Stock books (2) 1882-9, 1922-39, notebooks (3) of customers' addresses, journeys, orders, etc 1887-95, 1906-24, nd, agreement rel to prices c1870, wages books (3) 1897-1906, valuation 1889, agreements (2) rel to property 1861, 1877, specification for building Priory Mill 1861, misc letters and circulars c1860-1920.
The Company: see Lane.

[1034] SPRINGALL family, agricultural engineers, wheelwrights and blacksmiths, Horsham St Faith, Norfolk

Ledgers (7) 1886-9, 1892-6, 1911-49, wheelwrighting day book 1882-91, customer payments accounts (5 vols) 1912-46 and misc sales and order records 1914-62.
Norfolk RO (BR 219). NRA 34907.

[1035] STANDARD ENGINEERING CO LTD, shoe machinery mfrs, Leicester

Nominal ledgers (13) 1903-51, private ledgers (4) 1920-62, cash books (20) 1918-65, depot cash books (14) 1905-62, bank books (2) 1923-7, book-keeping department corresp (2 files) 1940, foreign corresp (5 files) 1958-68, sold ledgers (4 boxes, 5 vols) c1900-66 and other sales, purchase, order and invoice records 1918-67, stock, costing, parts and prices records (c26 vols, bundles, etc) c1906-62, corresp and papers rel to patents, leasing of machinery, etc (15 files) c1907-52, plant books (2) 1910-25, plant inspection reports (c3 bundles) c1928-62, insurance policies, corresp, etc (3 boxes) c1930, wages books (39) 1902-68 and other staff records (8 files and bundles) 1930-73, catalogues, price lists, leaflets and negatives (11 boxes) c1930-50.
Leicestershire RO (DE 1620). NRA 21101.

[1036] STANDARD MOTOR CO LTD, motor car mfrs, Coventry

Directors' and general meeting minutes (20 vols) 1903-76, attendance books (2) 1912-28, register of directors and secretary 1948-9, records of board meetings rel to production, etc (1 vol) 1908-12, general managers' reports presented to board (23 files) 1964-6, reports and balance sheets (49) 1913-60, financial forecasts, analyses and budgets (6 files, 3 items) 1960-7, secretary's department records mainly arranged by subject (c1,000 files) 1934-70.
Warwick University Modern Records Centre (MSS 226/ST). NRA 28571.

Journals (15) 1929-53, general cash paid books (25) 1958-70, notices to staff 1944-61.
British Motor Industry Heritage Trust, Gaydon, Warwicks.

[1037] ALEXANDER STEPHEN & SONS LTD, shipbuilders, ship repairers and marine engineers, Glasgow

Minutes (3 vols) 1892-4, 1900-32, registers of members (2) 1900-23, annual reports and accounts 1901-53, letter books (78) 1856-1929, Burghead day books (3) 1824-51, private cash book 1873-9, general agreements for contracts (3 vols) 1899-1938, tender books (4) 1918-66, bills of sale (3 items) 1867-70, estimate book 1928-37, steel and iron books (2) 1898-1908, 1914-19, stock book 1963-4, works diary 1856-9, engine department wages book 1886-7 and time book 1907, wages summation book 1940-52, photograph albums of engine drawing office (12) 1952-60, nd and of ships' trials and interiors (36 vols) 1908-60, press cuttings (4 vols) 1883, 1957-9 and misc papers 1883-1964, papers rel to transport and electricity industry 1929-48; letter books (50) 1859-1932 and diaries (54) 1859-99 of various members of the Stephen family.
Glasgow University Archives and Business Record Centre (UGD/4, UGD/7, UGD/149/1). NRA 10830.

Board papers and reports, etc 1917-69, balance sheets 1901-53, reports and accounts 1962-7, general corresp (24 files) 1914-66, ledger 1848-50, accounts (2 vols) 1920-51, estimate books (6) 1906-42 and rough calculations books (10) 1901-37, enquiries, estimates and tenders (326 files) 1916-68, material and wages cost books (251) 1913-66, nd, engine cost books (100) c1929-63, misc cost records (66 vols) 1905-68, nd, engine job books (18)

1897-1930, patent 1862, specifications (166 vols, 221 items) 1862-1966, boat books (6) 1923-64, offset books (18) 1929-50, requisition books (9) 1934-67, spar books (3) 1906-47, timber books (5) 1908-66, launch particulars books (7) 1890-1963, engine trials books (3) 1885-1936, trial data and reports, etc 1904-66, voyage reports and log abstracts 1889-1954, lists of engine spares and tools (11 items) nd, boiler particulars nd, engine drawing office copying books (16) 1902-65, engine particulars (101 items) nd, technical corresp and papers (55 files) c1914-63, ships' papers (752 files) 1911-68, plans c1920-68, photographs of ships, etc nd and particulars, etc c1852-1968, engine drawings nd, valuation books (2) 1932-48, ships' insurances c1920-51, time and wages book 1865, labour statistics (10 vols) 1927-68, photographs of management and staff to 1968, other printed material 1896-1967, papers rel to company history c1850-1960, catalogues (2 items) nd; corresp, diaries, notebooks and misc papers of the Stephen family rel to domestic, social and business matters 1813-1946.
Glasgow University Archives and Business Record Centre (UCS 3). NRA 14659.

Records 19th-20th cent incl ledgers 1858-1932, journals 1892-1928, estimate books 1939-54, specifications, engineers' notes, corresp rel to ships, launch, trials, stability and particulars books, plans and photographs.
National Maritime Museum Manuscripts Section: see Guide to the manuscripts in the National Maritime Museum, vol 2, 1980, p76.

[1038] ROBERT STEPHENSON & CO LTD, locomotive builders and shipbuilders, Darlington and Hebburn, co Durham

Minutes nd, works ledger 1823-31, sales accounts 1886-1901, order books (14) 1832-49, 1853-68, description books (14) 1829-75, lists of engines finished 1824-1901 incl Stockton & Darlington railway locomotives, and of engine deliveries, etc 1837-1901, engine record book nd, Robert Stephenson's diary 1834, historical documents files (22) nd.
Science Museum, Department 5. Enquiries to the Science Museum Library. NRA 28464.

Copy accounts for Newcastle upon Tyne Works 1826-56, corresp rel to management of the firm, etc 1824-61 and other Pease family papers.
Durham County RO (D/PS). NRA 24239.

Engineering drawings (334) 1825-1956.
National Museums and Galleries on Merseyside, Merseyside Maritime Museum (Vulcan Foundry Collection). NRA 29901.

Locomotive weight book 1902-37, drawings registers 1902-63, drawings nd.
National Railway Museum, York.

Specification for steel screw steamer (1 vol) 1907.
Tyne and Wear Archives Service (Acc 1810/7). NRA 8919.

[1039] DUNCAN STEWART & CO LTD, engineers and sugar machinery mfrs, Glasgow

Minute book 1891-5, balance sheets and profit and loss accounts (1 bundle) 1902-17, private ledgers (2) 1912-20, 1938-40 and journal 1913-40, job books (6) 1931-43, salaries ledgers (2) 1892-1945, apprenticeship register 1919-39, photographs of steel works plant, sugar factory machinery, etc (3 albums) c1919-29, nd, press cuttings book 1886-1931.
Strathclyde Regional Archives (TD 158). NRA 10849.

Cost book 1881-1902.
Glasgow University Archives and Business Record Centre (UGD/52/1/1). NRA 10849.

[1040] WILLIAM R STEWART & SONS (HACKLEMAKERS) LTD, Dundee

Minutes from 1946, ledgers (2) 1926-52, sales ledgers (2) 1875-1903, sales day book c1939-60, order books (12) 1915-51, notebook and papers rel to weights of coverings 1911, time and wages book 1911-12.
Dundee University Library. NRA 19895.

[1041] JOHN STIRK & SONS LTD (afterwards COVENTRY MACHINE TOOL WORKS LTD), machine tool mfrs, Halifax

Memorandum and articles of association 1937, certificates of incorporation 1907, 1937, 1964, minutes (7 vols, 1 bundle) 1937-84, share registers and related records (6 vols, 2 bundles) 1907-80, register of mortgages 1965-70, company corresp (4 bundles) nd, annual returns and misc balance sheets 1934-84, private ledger 1899-1917, cash books (2) 1899-1910, sales ledger 1916-26, endowment insurance schedules (1 bundle) 1950-68, plans, inventories and valuations 1905, 1920, 1938-80; Northern Engineering Co ledger and day book 1906-27.
Coventry City RO (Acc 1052, 1142). Access restricted. NRA 28005.

[1042] STIRLING BOILER CO LTD, boilermakers, London and Glasgow

Memorandum and articles of association (2 items) 1898-1946 and certificates of incorporation (2 items) 1898-1937, board and general meeting minutes (5 vols) 1899-1977, directors' attendance book 1908-59 and agenda books (2) 1942-57, register of shareholders 1899-1905 and share transfer certificates nd, corresp rel to shareholders 1906-37, register of investments 1909-41, annual returns 1901-48 and accounts 1899-1975, registers of seals (2) 1901-63, agreements (2 items) 1906, 1952, financial records (4 vols, etc) 1934-59, nd, list of contracts 1898-1920 and other contracts records 1910-56, drawings for contracts nd, summaries of salaries 1907-40, corresp rel to freelance agents c1910-39, holiday fund accounts 1939-50, corresp rel to pensions 1930s, product catalogues, etc 1890s-1950s and advertisements (1 vol) 1950s, notes rel to company history 1969.
Glasgow University Archives and Business Record Centre (UGD/309/133). NRA 33916.

[1043] **STOCK GHYLL MILLS** (afterwards **HORRAX (AMBLESIDE) LTD**), bobbin mfrs, Ambleside, Westmorland

Mill letter books (4) 1911-18, laundry letter books (2) 1910-19, account books (3) 1892-1914, ledgers (5) 1866-96, 1906-12, 1920-43, day books (6) 1839-45, 1877-92, 1902-11, cash books (3) 1887-1906, bill book 1873-82, sales account 1928, order books (6) 1870-1903, 1926-68, mill sundries sales books (4) 1907-21, analysis books (3) 1902-37, cost book 1926-40, wages books (2) 1909-17, inventories and valuations of mill and stock 1920, 1947.
Cumbria RO, Kendal (WDB/3). NRA 35279; *Report of the County Archivist*, Nov 1988, p10.

[1044] **SS STOTT LTD**, ironfounders, millwrights and elevator and conveyor mfrs, Haslingden, Lancs

Minutes, share certificate book and related corresp and papers (2 vols, 2 bundles) 1938-69, goods received ledger 1900-2, engineering department order and contract books (8) 1933-48, elevator department drawings books (8) 1885-1970 and papers (2 files) c1945-8, quantities book 1910-17, pattern book 1922-44, patent records (3 items) 1910, 1916, machinery plans (8) 1893, time standards books (4) 20th cent, wages books (3) 1914-32, inventory of machines and related papers (1 file, 2 bundles) 1965-74, misc printed catalogues, etc 1905-16, nd.
Lancashire RO (DDX 1701). NRA 31459.

[1045] **STURMEY-ARCHER GEARS LTD**, cycle gear mfrs, Nottingham

Certificates of incorporation (5) 1903-77, minutes (1 vol) 1903-38, ledgers (2) 1909-27, publicity material, press cuttings, catalogues, etc 20th cent.
Nottinghamshire Archives (DDRN). NRA 34479; A Millward, *The Raleigh archive: a detailed list of the contents*, 1987.

[1046] **W & S SUMMERSCALES' SONS**, domestic machinery mfrs, Keighley, Yorks

Records 1888-1960s incl account book 1888-1924, specifications and costs 1894-1915 and wages books 1900-16.
West Yorkshire Archive Service, Bradford (46D78).

[1047] **SUN CYCLE & FITTINGS CO LTD**, Birmingham

Certificate of incorporation 1935, minutes (1 vol) 1935-55, ledgers (2) 1897-1919.
Nottinghamshire Archives (DDRN). NRA 34479; A Millward, *The Raleigh archive: a detailed list of the contents*, 1987.

[1048] **SWAN, HUNTER & WIGHAM RICHARDSON LTD**, shipbuilders, ship repairers and engineers, Newcastle upon Tyne and Wallsend, Northumb

Records 1860-1977 incl memorandum and articles of association, liquidation and flotation papers, etc

1899-1903, directors' minutes 1903-77, shareholders' minutes (1 vol) 1903-50, annual reports and accounts 1899-1953, private ledgers (5) 1903-56, private journals (4) 1903-52, journal (1 vol) 1957-60, bill book 1931-53, contract ledgers (10) 1882-1961, contract payments notebooks (2) 1860-80, corresp, draft contracts, agreements with purchasers of vessels, etc (7 files, 10 items) 1934-62, corresp rel to invoices and accounts (2 vols) 1951-7, particulars of licences and royalties (1 vol) 1931-60, ships' particulars books (12) 1873-1964 and notebooks (13) nd, launching and trials records (14 vols, 11 items) 1927-30, nd, particulars of floating docks (1 vol) c1901-61, misc production records 1909-56, nd, salaries records (9 vols, 13 files) 1882-1956 and other papers rel to wage rates, working conditions, etc (6 vols) 1903-6, 1915-55, valuations of building, plant and machinery and related papers (9 vols) 1899-1903, deeds, corresp, etc rel to Neptune yard (2 bundles) 1883-1913, and legal agreements, leases and misc corresp and papers rel to staff and premises 1864, 1901-61.
Tyne and Wear Archives Service (Accs 964, 1826, 1836, 2029, 2742, 2782). NRA 23331 and *Tyne and Wear Archives Service Annual Review 1992-93*, p18.

Salaries book 1875-98.
Tyne and Wear Archives Service (Acc 2263/1). NRA 8919.

[1049] **HENRY SYKES LTD**, pump mfrs, London

Memorandum and articles of association 1897, balance sheets, etc (3 vols) 1869-79, 1903-42, general ledger 1880-1902, private ledger 1895-1907, cash book 1923-38, hire and purchase record books (6) 1913-39, estimate books (11) 1924-58, wages book 1895-1909, salaries book 1928-55, works register 1916-17, 1944 with corresp rel to wage rates 1941-8, misc papers (1 folder, 2 items) rel to staff and property 1868-1943, catalogues, photographs and press cuttings (15 vols, 80 items) 1880-1950.
Greenwich Local History Library. NRA 26583.

[1050] **TANGYE LTD**, hydraulic and general engineers, Birmingham

Minute books, letter books and day books from late 19th cent, register of drawings from 1882, pulley block tracings (1 roll) c1946-7, printed catalogues 1891, 1914.
The Company. Mainly noted in RE Waterhouse, *A hundred years of engineering craftsmanship . . . Tangye's Ltd, Smethwick 1857-1957*, 1957.

Technical drawings and plans (150 rolls) 1874-1934.
Birmingham Central Library Archives Division: see Accessions to repositories 1972, p28.

[1051] **TAYLOR & CHALLEN LTD**, mechanical engineers and machinery mfrs, Birmingham

Memorandum and articles of association 1967, directors' minutes (2 vols, etc) 1947-85, shareholders' minutes (2 vols) 1890-1965, register of directors and secretaries 1931-80, directors' report book 1953-64, notices of company meetings (6)

1915 and notes of minutes, reports, and ledgers
(1 bundle) 1947, 1956, share records (4 vols, 2 files,
1 item) 1889-1980, misc annual accounts and
balance sheets (9) 1889-1976, general corresp
1966-85, corresp and legal papers rel to sale of the
business (1 file) 1979-80, plans of Hong Kong mint
(4 items) 1863-4, private salaries book 1962-6 and
insurance contributions book 1965-6, illuminated
address to JC Bayliss, works manager 1921, legal
agreements and corresp 1863-1980.
Birmingham Central Library Archives Division (MSS
1350, 1350A). NRA 32244.

Further records incl letter books of Joseph Taylor
1856-8, auction ledgers 1903-40, credit journals
1913-42, debit journals 1911-39, authorised
payments books 1915-46, invoice books 1907-38,
bought ledgers 1911-42, prime cost ledgers
1894-1929, foundry castings books 1937-47 and
wages books 1950-6, time book 1856-61;
autobiography and diaries of SW Challen
1891-1929.
Birmingham Central Library Archives Division.

[1052] TAYLOR & HUBBARD LTD, crane mfrs
and engineers, Leicester

Accounting records 1927-81, order books and cards
(2 boxes, 63 vols) 1894-c1965, foundry orders
received (1 box) 1962, works order files 20th cent,
purchase and sales books (10) 1974-9, sales
estimates 1930s-1940s, other sales records (1 box,
3 vols) 1934-45, 1978, diaries rel to special cranes
(3) 1907-16, crane and boiler registers (5)
c1880-c1960, standards books (2) c1899-c1959, tests
book, steam crane patterns, service manuals and
instruction books (2 boxes, 2 vols) 20th cent, other
production records (2 boxes, 7 vols) 1932-78,
drawings register 1888-1961, blueprint record books
(5) 1932-70, plans and technical drawings 19th-20th
cent, salaries and wages records (7 vols) 1973-9,
injuries book 1964-78, insurance records (1 box)
1970s, papers rel to closure, etc (5 boxes) 1976-80,
catalogues and other printed material (3 boxes) 20th
cent, photographs and glass negatives (5 boxes,
2 vols).
Leicestershire RO (DE 1405, 1930 and 3360). NRA
33075.

[1053] TAYLOR, LANG & CO LTD, textile
machinery mfrs and ironfounders, Stalybridge,
Lancs

Machinery order books (26) 1873-1936, mule job
book 1911-35, drawings (8 items) 1901-34, mule
catalogues (3 items) c1920-5.
Lancashire RO (DDPSL/7). NRA 20296.

**[1054] TEACHERS' BICYCLE & TRICYCLE
CO**, cycle mfrs and dealers, Woking, Surrey

Records (6 boxes) incl purchase instalment books
from c1885 and business corresp and financial
papers 1895-1903.
Surrey RO, Kingston upon Thames (2638).

**[1055] TEES SIDE BRIDGE &
ENGINEERING WORKS LTD**, steel bridge and
roof builders, engineers and contractors,
Middlesbrough

Private ledgers (2) 1898-1940, ledger 1932-4,
private journal 1896-1936, general journal 1950-7,
cash book 1963-7, purchases and sales summary
1950-69, sales journal 1965-70, order books (2)
1893-1914, 1945-53, plant order book 1947-74,
completed orders 1960s-1970s, stores issued (1 vol)
1967-70, prime cost ledgers (15) 1919-53, foundry
output (2 vols) 1926-49, bridge yard output 1932-5,
misc production records 1960s-1970s, wages and
salaries books (6) 1931-40.
*British Steel Northern Regional Records Centre,
Middlesbrough.* NRA 35680.

**[1056] THAMES IRON WORKS,
SHIPBUILDING & ENGINEERING CO LTD**,
London

Minute book incl annual reports and accounts
1899-1911.
Greater London RO (O/45/1). NRA 7562.

Memorandum and articles of association 1899,
directors' report 1898, corresp and papers rel to
share issue 1899, list of vessels and engines built by
firm nd.
Guildhall Library, London: see Ritchie.

[1057] THOM, LAMONT & CO LTD, engineers
and pump mfrs, Paisley, Renfrewshire

Minute books 1909-71, job books 1898-1971, pump
number books 1895-1971, technical drawings
1895-1971.
In private possession. Enquiries to NRA (Scotland)
(survey 663). NRA 16054.

**[1058] JOHN THOMPSON
(WOLVERHAMPTON) LTD**, boilermakers and
engineers, Ettingshall, Staffs

Articles of association 1918, corresp rel to the
formation of a public company 1935, minute books
(3) 1936-66, share prospectus and cash book 1936,
summary of securities held 1927-41, list of directors
1942-4, ledgers (2) 1900-3, 1906-10, bank
reconciliations 1945-7, order books (2) 1906-18,
purchase invoice book 1929-31, cost books (2)
1891-4, 1903-11, stock books of boiler works (35)
1909-44 and of other works and departments (18)
1917-44, boiler specifications 1890s and works
ledger 1908-12, test certificates 1909-13, record of
baths supplied (1 vol) 1894-1914, contracts and loan
agreements 1920s-1940s, nd, drawings of furnaces
(1 roll) 1935, staff, wages and pension records
1890-1952, property schedules, valuations and
premises records 1924-45, catalogues, brochures,
publicity material, etc c1910-45; papers of Sir
EW Thompson (8 files) 1942-54; records of
subsidiary companies 1901-66.
Wolverhampton Borough Archives (DB/5). NRA
23989.

[1059] **JOSEPH L THOMPSON & SONS LTD**, shipbuilders and ship repairers, Sunderland, co Durham

Minutes 1952-70, private letter book 1918-24, private ledgers 1875-94, 1926-33, other ledgers and journals 1944-69, annual statements 1894-1929, private accounts rel to new ships and repairs 1874-1901, ships' cost book 1871-1944, ships' particulars book 1846-83, records of ships built and annual tonnages (2 vols) 1846-1947, general measurement books 1889-1954, general arrangement plans 1941-5, ships' contracts 1935-70 and photographs 1930-69.
Tyne and Wear Archives Service.

Ship plans and specifications 1880-1956.
Tyne and Wear Museums Service: see Ritchie.

[1060] **JOHN I THORNYCROFT & CO LTD**, engineers, shipbuilders and motor vehicle mfrs, London and Southampton, Hants

Records from c1884 incl directors' reports and balance sheets 1901-65, share records 1904-66, administrative papers 20th cent, accounts 1901-65, private ledger 1904-10, order books 1884-1903 and indexes 1904-15, 1925-30, staff attendance registers 1911-20, inventory of Woolston Works 1904, plans of premises 1912-68 and advertisements, press cuttings and photographs 19th-20th cent.
Southampton City RO (D/VT): see Ritchie.

Records incl corresp, tenders, specifications, ship and design files, trial reports and technical notes, etc for the Chiswick, Woolston and Hampton yards c1880-1964, and corresp, memoranda and notebooks 1880-1960 of SW and KC Barnaby, the firm's chief naval architects.
National Maritime Museum Manuscripts Section: see *Guide to the manuscripts in the National Maritime Museum*, vol 2, 1980, pp79-80.

[1061] **E TIMMINS & SONS LTD**, engineers, ironfounders, pumping machinery mfrs and well borers, Runcorn, Cheshire

Well boring tender book 1886-1910, engineering drawings (76) 1891-1916.
Museum of Science and Industry in Manchester (EN 3). NRA 29451.

Engineering drawings (c90) 1886-1911.
In private possession. Enquiries to Museum of Science and Industry in Manchester. NRA 29451.

[1062] **TIMSONS LTD**, printing machinery mfrs and ironfounders, Kettering, Northants

Balance sheets 1899-1978, private ledgers (2) 1908-13, 1928-30, cash books (34) 1899-1954, day books (44) 1911-41, misc accounting records (5 vols) 1912-16, 1938-53, customer ledger 1897-8, sales ledgers, day books and return books (38) 1904-37, 1948, purchase ledgers, day books and analysis books (18) 1899-1958, order records (c14 vols) 1913-51, repair book 1922-6, pattern record book 1920, departmental journal 1901, misc production records (3 vols) 1934-50, staff and wages records (23 vols, bundles and items) 1900-53, leaflets, brochures, etc 1929-78, history of firm nd.
Northamptonshire RO (Accs 1978/201, 1978/402, 1979/231, 1979/326). NRA 22295.

Minutes from 1912, corresp from 1960s, technical drawings and plans from 1920s, photographs, press cuttings, scrapbooks, printed technical information, etc from c1910.
The Company. Enquiries to Northamptonshire RO. NRA 22295.

[1063] **JOHN WALLIS TITT & CO LTD**, agricultural engineers, windmill and pump mfrs, Warminster, Wilts

Ledgers and account books (20 vols) and plans c1885-c1950.
Wiltshire RO (WRO 2574).

[1064] **TROTH & HILLSON**, agricultural engineers, Langley, Warwicks

Nominal ledgers (3) 1876-82, 1900-48, day books (4) 1900-50, cash books (2) 1882-1945, bank book 1854-73, record of debts (1 vol) 1901-3, customer address books (2) nd, misc family and printed papers 1710-1950.
Warwickshire RO (CR 1186). NRA 26337.

[1065] **TURNER, ATHERTON & CO LTD** (formerly **GILES ATHERTON**), hatters' machinery mfrs, Stockport, Cheshire

Letter books (2) 1900-16, papers (1 bundle, 7 items) rel to inventions and patents 1880-98, misc engineers' drawings nd, misc papers (12 items) rel to premises, machinery and staff 1884-99.
Stockport Archive Service (B/AA/3/21-6). NRA 27964.

[1066] **GR TURNER LTD**, structural engineers and mfrs of railway rolling stock, Langley Mill, Derbys

Articles of association 1903, 1920, certificate of incorporation nd, directors' minutes (3 vols) 1903-53, management meeting minutes 1977-80, management, works committee and personnel records 1961-80, share ledger nd, dividend lists 1920-57, balance sheets 1904-63, revaluation of assets 1949, private journal 1902-48, accounting, sales and purchase records 1941-63, contracts (3 boxes) 1971-80, stock sheets 1973-80, salaries rate book 1904-52, workmen's rate book 1936-74, accident registers and reports (2 boxes) 1894-1977, staff and social club records (3 boxes) 1947-80, copies of conveyances, etc 1875-1920, insurance agreements, etc 1903-53, works development records 1961-78, photographs 20th cent.
British Steel East Midlands Regional Records Centre, Irthlingborough. NRA 35548.

[1067] **TURNER MACHINERY LTD**, tanning machinery mfrs, Leeds

Articles of association 1950, minutes (1 vol) 1901-36, register of members 1901-38 and other

share records (1 file) 1926-81, annual returns 1917-52, annual reports, etc 1950-66, register of seals 1926-52, day book 1876-81, private ledgers (5) 1918-41, ledger 1920-7, journals 1935-71, main cash books 1930-70 and balance book 1954-61, analysis, cost and foundry expenses books 1922-68, order book 1908-10, delivery note counterfoil book 1882-4, plans of premises 1888-1965 and valuations 1920-2, 1941-6, 1963, select personnel records 1901-69, wages books (3) 1915-44, brochures, drawings and price lists 1903-80, photographs to 1970, sports club minutes books 1935-74.
West Yorkshire Archive Service, Leeds (Acc 2482). NRA 24860.

Machine drawings and photograph albums.
Leeds Industrial Museum.

[1068] **TWEEDALES & SMALLEY LTD**, cotton machinery mfrs, Castleton, Lancs

Register of directors and share transfers 1938-54, capital asset record c1950, export account register c1950, home and foreign order books (44) 1891-1962, flat carding engines order books (11) 1895-1962, extracts from order books (1 vol) 1893-1935, specifications books (82) 1892-1962, service manuals (5 items) c1958-60, wages book 1945-8, catalogues, etc (15 items) 1925-c1955.
Lancashire RO (DDPSL/5). NRA 20296.

[1069] **TYNE DOCK ENGINEERING CO LTD**, engineers and ship repairers, South Shields, co Durham

Memorandum and articles of association 1889, 1920, share registers (3) 1905, 1914-20, nd and letter book 1900-20, annual returns 1900-3, annual reports and statements 1955-67, private ledger 1894-1906, personal ledgers (7) 1893-1950, nominal ledgers (3) 1905-50, cash books (13) 1907-57, journals (4) 1923-59, invoice books (16) 1881-5, 1889-1902, 1908-12, 1960-2, cost books (21) 1920-74, accident and other staff records (3 vols, 2 files) 1937-77.
Tyne and Wear Archives Service (Acc 1244). NRA 24218.

[1070] **UNITED ELECTRIC CAR CO LTD** (formerly **ELECTRIC RAILWAY & TRAMWAY CARRIAGE WORKS LTD**), tramcar and railway carriage mfrs, Preston, Lancs

Minutes (1 vol) 1905-17, agenda books (5) 1898-1917, directors' attendance book 1906-12, secretary's letter book 1916, registers of members, share transfers and mortgages (5 vols) 1898-1915, corresp and papers rel to Hadley Works (2 bundles) 1908, nd, misc corresp and papers (2 bundles) 1903-13; British Electric Car Co Ltd minutes (1 vol) 1905-17, register of members, etc (1 vol) 1905-18, summary of stock (2 vols) 1905, balance sheets, misc corresp and summary of inventory (1 bundle) 1904-15; English Electric Manufacturing Co Ltd board agendas (1 folder) 1902, management and works committee minutes (2 vols) 1900-5, 1908-9, share and debenture records (8 vols) 1899-1903, salaries book 1921-5.
Lancashire RO. NRA 31019.

Specifications for equipment required by tramway companies in Britain and overseas (c1,800 items) 1899-1939; card indexes (2) of customers and equipment ordered.
National Tramway Museum, Crich. NRA 33431.

[1071] **URQUHART, LINDSAY & CO LTD** (afterwards **URQUHART LINDSAY & ROBERTSON ORCHAR LTD**), textile machinery mfrs, Dundee

Minutes (4 vols) 1896-1953, register of shareholders and share transfers 1896-1918, other share records nd, balance sheets and accounts 1897-1964, papers rel to excess profits 1918-19, letter books (2) 1908-23, papers rel to joint working agreement with Robertson & Orchar Ltd 1899-1921, other legal papers 1917-44, other corresp and papers 1924-55, private ledgers (2) 1922-56, nd, order books (10) 1869-1903, loom details books (2) 1893-1904, specifications (10 vols, 2 files) 1880-1915, drawing office contract books (12) 1871-91, 1895-1900, progress books (7) 1858-1956, machinery drawings (2 folders) 1875-95 and engravings nd, salaries records 1941-58, misc corresp, papers, plans and photographs c1889-1953.
West Yorkshire Archive Service, Leeds (Acc 1323, 1325, 1341, 2371, 2710, 3514). NRA 14292.

[1072] **HERBERT P VACHER**, mechanical engineer, Kings Worthy, Hants

Letter books (2) 1888-9, 1893.
Hampshire RO (137M87). NRA 8807.

[1073] **VICKERS LTD**, steel, armaments and electrical machinery mfrs and ship and aircraft builders, London and Sheffield

Records from 1867 incl board minutes (21 vols) 1867-1970, general meeting minutes (5 vols) 1868-1943, register of directors (2 vols) 1900-47, letter books (9) 1904-12, documents circulated to stockholders (1 vol) 1886-1955, register of mortgages 1908-37, papers rel to share capital 1867-1969, annual reports and accounts (3 vols, 1 envelope) 1867-1955, accounts and schedules (134 vols) 1897-1968, corresp with Horse and Field Artillery Equipment Committee (1 envelope) 1902-4, tenders and contracts for guns (1 envelope) 1902-11, aviation contracts register (2 vols) 1915-18, armaments and aviation contracts index (2 vols) 1914-18, papers rel to gunboats for China (1 envelope) 1876-81 and guns sold to the United States (1 envelope) 1898-1917, patent specifications 1873-1917, testimonials (1 vol) 1903-20, reference book 1911-14, products brochures 1913, 1925, press cuttings 1860-1927, and photographs (28 vols, c500 items) 19th-20th cent; Barrow works and shipyard records incl lists of ships and submarines built 1873-1973, contracts book 1898-1906, register of quotations and contracts (2 vols) 1897-9, 1910, register of prices for naval armaments (2 vols) 1898-1921, arrangements with Armstrong Whitworth & Co Ltd rel to armaments orders (1 envelope) 1906-13, submarine costs and quotations (1 envelope) 1903-6 and patents held

(1 envelope) 1901-11, notes on launchings and fitting out (4 vols) 1903-32, papers rel to apprentices (1 envelope) 1891-1907, and brochures 1896-1954; Electric Boat Co letter book 1901-7 and misc papers 1902-46, nd; Naval Construction & Armaments Co Ltd directors' attendance books (2) 1888-98; Steel Manufacturers Nickel Syndicate Ltd minutes (1 vol) 1901-35; Thames Ammunition Works Ltd minutes (2 vols) 1902-42.
Cambridge University Library (Vickers Archives). NRA 27797.

Shipyard records from 1873 incl summary balance sheets 1889-1977, capital expenditure books 1906-22, works managers' report books 1903-14, ship, submarine and machinery contracts 1908-57, hull and engine specifications 1873-1949, other specifications and plans nd, industrial relations department records from 1905, property records 1874-1973 and photographs from c1873.
Vickers Shipbuilding & Engineering Ltd. NRA 23464; and see Ritchie.

List of orders for ships' gun mountings 1898-1938, misc contract and order books, etc nd, indexes to drawings issued and received (50 vols) 20th cent, drawings (15 rolls) nd, record tracings (several thousand items) 1898-1950, plans of docks and harbours, details of ship trials, publicity material, etc (4 boxes, 2 box files) c1900-1960, photographs of royal visit (3 vols) 1917.
Cumbria RO, Barrow (BDB/16). NRA 23464 (partial list); *Report of the County Archivist*, June 1985 p10, Oct 1985 p10 and Jan 1986 p11.

Barrow brass foundry manager's notebooks (3) c1900-1922.
Strathclyde Regional Archives (UCS 2/147). NRA 14659.

Records 19th-20th cent incl Sheffield local board of directors' minutes (1 vol) 1929, papers rel to directors' and shareholders' meetings (1 vol) 1902-11, register of corresp 1898-1926, balance sheets (1 box, c50 vols) from 1833, ledgers (2) nd, journal nd and foremen's mutual benefit society ledger 1907-17.
Sheffield Archives (MD 200). NRA 36163.

Analysis of crucible steel made (1 vol) 1903-21.
Sheffield Archives (LD 1878). NRA 23246.

Shipbuilding records incl Barrow order book 1873-96, design corresp c1910-88, particulars, specifications, calculations, plans and photographs.
National Maritime Museum Manuscripts Section: see Ritchie.

Brooklands aircraft works management, accountancy, design, technical and personnel records from c1915.
Brooklands Museum. NRA 34342.

[1074] **VIPAN & HEADLY** (formerly **HUNT & PICKERING**), dairy engineers and agricultural implement mfrs, Leicester

Cash book 1902-45, order and costing books (5) 1884-1902, nd, piece work price list 1862, catalogues, brochures and photographs 1896-1922, nd.
Leicestershire RO (5 D 64). NRA 21686.

[1075] **VULCAN FOUNDRY LTD**, locomotive builders and engineers, Newton-le-Willows, Lancs

Memorandum and articles of association 1864, 1909, directors' minutes (4 vols) 1864-1924 and vouchers (1 vol) 1875-86, shareholders' meeting minutes and annual reports (2 vols, etc) 1865-1960, share records (2 vols) 1864-84, letters of indemnity (1 vol) 1900-58, letter books (5) 1901-5, corresp (2 files) 1955-60, general ledger 1864-89, journals (2) 1864-1921, financial corresp 1909, cost books (3) 1844-1939, list of locomotives built 1833-1956, locomotive record books (5) 1863-98, specification 1859, boiler inspection reports 1887-1908, parts list and service manuals 1938-41, drawings mainly of locomotives 1825-1956, drawings mainly of other companies 1844-1952, nd, other technical drawings 1934-5, nd, apprenticeship indentures (21 items) 1873-90, wages book 1937-70 and other staff records 1950-64, deeds (copies) 1837-1908, insurance records 1939-40, plans of premises (13 items) 1927-60, nd, photographs mainly of locomotives and staff 1845-1963, visitors' book 1941-60, misc corresp, papers and photographs 1825-1978; letters to foreman c1828-68.
National Museums and Galleries on Merseyside, Merseyside Maritime Museum (B/VF, DX/603). NRA 29901.

Articles of association nd, balance sheets c1867-82, 1907-8, letter books c1864-93, general corresp 20th cent, ledger nd, record of sales c1890, boiler tent repair books (4) nd, specifications nd, workmen's registers c1865-1920s, company magazines (4 vols) 1848-59 and diaries 1927-63, photographs mainly 20th cent and misc papers.
Newton-le-Willows Community Library (NI/VU). NRA 36782.

Agreements, etc (3 items) 1902, 1930, preference stock certificates 1960, table of profits 1928, mortgage indentures (2 items) 1893, 1908, schedule of contracts 1833-1945, index of deeds 1833-1908, papers rel to company history 19th-20th cent.
St Helens Local History and Archives Library (VU). NRA 24416.

Memorandum and articles of association 1864, special resolutions 1889-1953, directors' and shareholders' attendance book 1900-31, notices of general meetings, etc (1 vol) 1889-1904, mortgage debenture book 1865-6 and register 1865-97.
The General Electric Company plc. Enquiries to the Company Secretary. NRA 34431.

Calculations books 1938-59, drawings 1934-62 and drawings registers 1934-69.
National Railway Museum, York.

Accounts (3 vols) 1837-49 of Charles Tayleur, Sons & Co.
National Museums and Galleries on Merseyside, Merseyside Maritime Museum (1993.298).

Copy tenders and estimates for locomotive engines, boilers and components (1 vol) 1920-1.
Untraced. Bloomsbury Book Auctions 14 May 1994, lot 180.

[1076] **WADDLE PATENT FAN & ENGINEERING CO LTD**, Llanelly, Carms

Records c1830-1970 incl corresp, ledgers, cost analyses, wage records and plans.
Dyfed Archives Service, Carmarthen (DB/102). *Quarterly Newsletter*, March 1981, p7.

Drawings (19 files) 1884-1964.
University College of Swansea Library. NRA 14358.

[1077] **J WADSWORTH & SON LTD**, smiths, machinists and wheelwrights, Ripponden, Yorks

Wages books (3) 1895-1938.
West Yorkshire Archive Service, Calderdale (MISC:662) NRA 21161.

[1078] **WILLIAM WADSWORTH & SONS LTD**, lift and hoist mfrs, Bolton, Lancs

Orders, specifications and instructions (4 vols) 1896-1914, maintenance handbook and publicity material (2 vols, 1 booklet) nd, photographs of plant and premises (1 album) 1941, notes rel to company history 1964.
Bolton Archive Service (ZZ/443). NRA 34859.

[1079] **WAGHORNE & MILES**, coachbuilders, Croydon, Surrey

Day book 1788-1800, 1826-8, album of crests, etc for carriage painting c1840-99.
Croydon Local Studies Library (AR 37, 40).

[1080] **GEORGE WAILES & CO LTD**, mechanical engineers and millwrights, iron and brass founders, London

Day books (67) 1889-1953, financial records (7 vols) 1941-55, purchase invoice books (7) 1944-53 and receipts (2 files) 1953-5, cost books (65) 1923-59, drawings 1878-1960, registers of drawings (3 vols) 1855-1960, and of tracings (5 vols) 1892-1960, tracing and pattern movement books (4) 1904-25, nd, wages books (9) 1911-42, plant book and inventory, etc (1 vol, 4 files) c1920-53; corresp and papers rel to engineering employers' associations 1897-9, nd.
Science Museum Library. NRA 28600.

[1081] **WALKER BROTHERS (WIGAN) LTD**, engineers and mining machinery mfrs, Wigan, Lancs

Records 19th-20th cent incl letter book 1907, order books 1905-11, 1942-53, production books (6) 1884-1960, progress book 1951, pipe books (6) 1896-1937, specification books (8) 1895-1948, diagram books (4) 1900-44, plan books (2) 1913-48, drawings 1929-59 and lists of drawings 1947-59, nd, plate sketch books (5) 1883-1921, drawing office sketch books (30) 1906-44.
Wigan Archives Service (Salford Mining Museum deposit). NRA 36424.

Private ledgers (3) 1875-86, 1902-8, general ledger 1875-88, contract books (4) 1867-73, 1891-1935, photographs of mining equipment produced (1 bundle) early 20th cent.
Wigan Archives Service (D/DY Pag). NRA 35103.

[1082] **C & W WALKER LTD**, gas engineers, Donnington, Salop

Quantities books (34) 1865-c1953, specifications and estimates (60 boxes) 1873-1940, registers (4) of drawings 1895-9, 1911-15, 1923-8, nd, plans (317 boxes, 28 rolls) from 1846, pamphlets and brochures (2 boxes).
Shropshire RO (SRO 3118). NRA 34475.

[1083] **WALKER & SMITH (BATLEY) LTD**, textile machinery mfrs, Batley, Yorks

Private ledger 1900-45, ledgers (20) 1870-1929, cash and stock book 1878-98, cash books (7) 1886-95, 1919-45, expenditure books (4) 1924-47, debts owing by firm (1 vol) 1890-6, bought ledgers (2) 1900-26, order books (35) 1900-30, letter book rel to orders nd, invoices received (14 binders) 1920-49, register of oiling machines 1929-41, wages books (7) 1886-90, 1913-45, unidentified index (1 vol) nd, photographs (1 parcel) nd, photographic negatives of machinery, etc (8 boxes) 20th cent; Morton, Son & Co ledgers (2) 1877-80, 1885-95.
West Yorkshire Archive Service, Leeds (Acc 1646). NRA 34673.

[1084] **WALLIS & LONGDEN**, lace making machinery mfrs, Long Eaton, Derbys

Letter books (36) 1902-44, machine order book 1901-11, quotations book 1905-39, time account 1888-94, pamphlet rel to lace manufacture 1948.
Nottingham University Library (Wa). NRA 14324.

[1085] **WALLIS & STEEVENS LTD**, mfrs of agricultural machinery, traction engines and road rollers, Basingstoke, Hants

Memorandum and articles of association, prospectuses and related papers (24 items) 1892-1953, board minutes (2 vols) 1893-1961, general meeting minutes (2 vols) 1893-1961, agenda book 1893-1908, register of directors (2 vols) 1901-70, register of mortgages 1893, share ledger 1897-1948, debenture registers (3) 1897-1964, dividend books (7) 1912-59 and other share and debenture records 1897-1977, annual reports and statements 1893-6, 1913-80, liquidation accounts (1 vol) 1897, general ledgers (8) 1897-1970, journals (4) 1897-1960, bill books (2) 1910-51, bank books (16) 1897, 1926-51, sales ledgers (50) 1856-1956 and misc sales records 1909-80, order number registers (2) 1919-74, prices records (4 vols, 1 file) 1902-80, pattern, gearing, boiler and production progress registers (10) 1862-1950s, production registers (11) 1866-1946, shop books (516) and indexes (3) c1900-1930s, other production records (12 vols and files) 1907, 1912, 1934-81, drawings and sketches 1850s-1963, nd, drawing registers (2) 1870s-1964, misc staff records (7 vols, 3 items) 1903, 1908, 1926-1970s, plant and machinery valuations, etc (4 vols, 1 file) 1881, 1892-6, 1947-73, photographs and printed papers 1906-1970s; Wallis & Steevens Auxiliary Ltd minutes 1929-48, register of directors from 1901, share ledger 1900-48, general ledger 1900-37.
Rural History Centre, Reading University. NRA 25547.

[1086] **WALLSEND SLIPWAY &
ENGINEERING CO LTD**, engineers,
boilermakers and ship repairers, Wallsend,
Northumb

Records 19th-20th cent incl trials book 1875-87,
graving dock registers (2) 1895-1968, and
notebooks, repair schedules, etc (3 vols, 5 files,
40 items) of William Clouston, foreman shipwright,
1876-88.
Tyne and Wear Archives Service (Acc 1471, 2271,
DX32). NRA 8919 and *Accessions to repositories 1988*,
p36.

[1087] **WANTAGE ENGINEERING CO LTD**,
agricultural and general engineers, Wantage, Berks

Minutes (1 vol) 1927-71, private ledgers (3)
1932-64, steam engine and thrashing machine
registers and indexes (10 vols) 1852-1902, materials
books (4) 1890s-1920s, prices book c1910-30,
suppliers' index (1 vol) c1920-40, photograph
albums (2) and misc printed papers (1 folder) nd.
The Company. Copies are in the Rural History
Centre, Reading University. NRA 20991.

Misc share records, agreements, patents, etc
c1880-c1920, transfer journals (2) 1908-10,
1922-59, cash books (10) 1930-68, sales, purchase
and bought ledgers, day books and journals (23 vols)
1900-68, advice, invoice, despatch and goods
received books (24) 1933-68, prices book 1920s,
cost books and registers (60) 1901-2, 1906-67,
pattern register 1930s, wages books (13) 1932-68.
Rural History Centre, Reading University. NRA 20991.

[1088] **THOS W WARD LTD**, mechanical and
constructional engineers, metal and coal merchants,
Sheffield

Memorandum and articles of association with
related corresp 1904-71, board and general meeting
minutes (11 vols, 1 folder) 1904-51, 1970-2,
management committee minutes and reports
1973-81, letter book 1895-1913, seal books (3)
1904-52, share records (4 vols) 1904-20, 1940-8,
annual accounts and directors' reports 1905-81,
trading and profit and loss accounts, balance sheets
and trial balances 1907-75, private ledgers (73)
1889-1953, general ledgers (2) 1894-5, 1936-48,
private journals and ledgers (2) 1903-24, 1954-8,
cash books (4) 1894-6, 1904-64, bank books (10)
1879-c1919, misc accounting records (16 vols, etc)
1930-76, purchase ledger 1887-90, sales journal
1899-1950, sales statistics (1 vol) 1903-51, foreign
sales records (18 vols, 2 bundles) 1919-80,
machinery department records (5 vols) 1897-8,
1934-68, scrap and dismantling department ledgers,
journals, etc (55 vols) 1897-1956, coal and coke
department records (5 vols) 1924-60, rail and
sidings department order, construction and stock
books (69) 1954-74, staff records (11 vols,
1 bundle) 1912-56, valuations, inventories, deeds
and other property records 1859-1979, misc
business and Ward family papers (17 vols and
bundles) 1912-60.
Sheffield Archives (TW 1-158). NRA 34879.

Purchase return journals (2) 1964-71.
Lincolnshire Archives (2 Marshall). NRA 35742.

[1089] **WILLIAM WATSON**, coachbuilder,
Guildford, Surrey

Sales ledger 1827-32.
Surrey RO, Guildford (BR/OC/4/14). NRA 24040.

[1090] **WEBLEY & SCOTT LTD**, gun and pistol
makers, Birmingham

Prospectus 1897, directors' and general meeting
minutes (6 vols) 1897-1956, directors' reports, profit
and loss accounts and balance sheets (1 box file)
1897-1957, private ledgers (3) 1897-1930, day
books (15) 1903-17, 1923, sales register of revolvers
1900-25, invoices (c35 files) 1930s-1960s, records of
pistols made (117 vols) 1898-1982, firearms
registers (13) from 1922.
The Company. Enquiries to the Managing Director.
NRA 33760.

Sales journal 1912-14, journal 1925-8 and misc
records 1948-70.
Holland & Holland Ltd. Enquiries to the Business
Archives Council. NRA 35073.

[1091] **WEBSTER & BENNETT LTD**, machine
tool mfrs, Coventry

Memorandum and articles of association, etc
1937-68, directors' minutes (3 vols) 1906-73,
committee minutes (3 vols) 1960-80, register of
probates 1956-80, share certificates (1 vol,
155 items) 1906-80, annual accounts 1936,
1941-61, company notes 1920-81, private ledgers
(5) 1899-1964, cash books (5) 1920-65, order books
(18) 1921-49, sales day books and ledgers (7 vols)
1908-39, purchase ledgers (5) 1911-39, credit
returns books (4) 1910-50, sundries book 1940-7,
specifications 1961, nd, patents 1939-66, wages and
personnel records 1947-83, plant, tools and fixtures
books 1911-20, inventories of vehicles 1951-3,
service and rental agreements 1943-79, insurance
policies 1923-55, building plans, estimates, etc
1906-84, catalogues and brochures 1887-1976, nd,
photographs (4 vols, 189 items) c1900-60, nd, press
cuttings books 1904-62, histories of the company
c1927-80, misc corresp and papers 1887-1983.
Coventry City RO (Acc 1050 and 1141). Access
restricted. NRA 28003.

[1092] **WILLIAM WEEKS & SON LTD**,
agricultural engineers, Maidstone, Kent

Certificate of incorporation and registration
counterfoil 1892, agenda and minute books (4)
1892-1971, directors' account book 1920-2, reports
and balance sheets, etc (25 items) 1893-1913,
1964-7, share transfers and related papers (c60 items)
1892-1961, lists of dividends, interest and cash
advanced, etc 1892-8, accounts and expenses rel to
the company's flotation, etc (3 items) 1893, mortgage
debentures (3 items) 1893, 1901, corresp and receipts
from accountants (20 items) 1893, journals (2)
1893-1961, expenses ledger 1893-1920, staff salaries
and holiday lists nd, misc papers.
Centre for Kentish Studies, Maidstone (U 2408). NRA
25251.

Letter book nd, engineering drawings and plans (23)
1861-1903, catalogues and price lists (c30 items)

20th cent, misc share certificates, reports, printed testimonials, photographs, etc 1890-1959.
Maidstone Museum and Art Gallery. NRA 25251.

[1093] **G & J WEIR LTD**, marine engineers and pump mfrs, Glasgow

Ledgers (16) 1891-1945, cash books (21) 1896-1950, orders records from *c*1900, contracts books (2) 1915-16, drawings (microfilms) from *c*1920, pay books (28) 1887-9, 1892-5, 1898-1940, time book 1950-2, employee service cards (1 filing cabinet) *c*1911-50, nd, register of machinery and plant 1886-1913, photographs of products and shop floor, operating manuals and publicity material from *c*1890.
Weir Pumps Ltd. Enquiries to NRA (Scotland) (survey 1035). NRA 19007.

Private ledgers (2) 1934-9, 1945-9, papers mainly rel to company organisation and technical developments (21 files) 1904-53, technical notebooks (24) of WD Weir and others 1893-1916, nd, technical reports, etc (13 files) 1961-2, nd, works council memoranda and minutes (2 files) 1920, job sheets (1 file) 1939-41, plant and toolroom records (2 files) 1932-9; Viscount Weir's personal and business corresp and papers.
Glasgow University Archives and Business Record Centre (Weir of Eastwood Papers). NRA 26835.

[1094] **WEST END ENGINE WORKS CO**, engineers and paper making machinery mfrs, Edinburgh

Minutes (1 vol) 1944-72, balance sheets 1933-72, letter books 1880-1973, financial records 1869-1970, order, job and sales records 1869-1972, estimate and cost records 1874-1972, specifications, etc 1902-11, drawings of products 1861-1973, wages records 1878-1961, trade catalogues 20th cent, photographs of machinery, etc *c*1890-1930.
Scottish Record Office (GD 341). NRA 18851.

[1095] **WESTERN WAGON & PROPERTY CO LTD**, railway wagon builders, Bristol

Memorandum and articles of association and certificate of incorporation 1881, prospectus nd, directors' and general meeting minutes (12 vols, etc) 1881-1935, agenda books (3) 1904-35, directors' attendance book 1905-35, reports of shareholders' meetings 1882-1935, debenture registers (2 vols) 1881-1929, share transfers 1924-35, dividend payments 1914-34, reports, accounts and balance sheets incl those of Western Wagon Co Ltd 1863-1935, annual returns and summaries 1900-8, registers of probates (1 vol) 1881-91, of seals (4 vols) 1906-35 and of mortgages (1 vol) 1895, registers of securities (3 vols) 1882-1934, of nominees (1 vol) 1900-35 and of investments (1 vol) 1926-35, secretary's corresp (3 files) 1899-1906 and financial diary 1904, general corresp (29 box files, 1 file, 85 folders) 1904-34, corresp rel to liquidation (1 folder) 1935, property and finance department letter books (16) 1887-1935 and letters received (37 folders) 1887-1905, wagon department letter

books (18) 1887-1935, letters received (33 folders) 1887-1905, agreements and other papers 1878-1934, transfer department letter book 1902-35, account books (2) 1873-1933, ledgers (4) 1876-1935, journals (4) 1879-1935, cash books (15) 1878-1935, cheque registers (3) 1910-35 and cheque book stubs 1923-32, employee addresses (1 vol) 1934, deeds, plans, corresp and papers rel to Filton Park estate 1863-1935, nd, misc deeds and papers 1878-1905, insurance policies 1903-17, press cuttings (2 vols, etc) 1907-31, misc corresp and papers 1881-1934.
Bristol RO (Acc 35810/WWP). NRA 32018.

[1096] **WHESSOE FOUNDRY CO LTD** (formerly **ALFRED KITCHING**), ironfounders, locomotive, engine and bridge builders, Darlington, co Durham

Legal papers rel to the dissolution of the Kitching partnership, etc (9 items) 1840-60, papers rel to sale of the firm (1 file, 4 items) 1891-4, share ledger 1866-80, stock, dividend and loans journals (3) 1867-82, letter books (7) 1834-42, 1885-91, London office memoranda book 1829-93, ledgers (13) 1831-91, day books (10) 1839-42, 1848-66, 1884-9, account books (6) 1833-82, cash books (5) 1833-62, 1867-82, 1888-91, estimate books (3) 1878-81, 1889, late 19th cent, invoice books (4) 1831-3, 1845-56, record of orders and tenders (1 vol) 1845-54, stock, costs and materials books (6) 1853-67, 1883-90, accounts for the building and repair of locomotives (11 vols) 1831-52, specifications, estimates, accounts, etc mainly rel to the Stockton and Darlington railway 1819-44, wages books (6) 1846-62, 1880, 1887-9; Whessoe Foundry Co Ltd letter books (2) 1903-21; diaries (3) 1843, 1845-8, nd and personal account books (4) 1845-76 of Alfred Kitching, with other Kitching family papers *c*1720-1957.
Durham County RO (D/Ki). NRA 27794.

Minutes (1 vol) 1915-18, corresp with London office (13 files) 1891-7, misc share records (4 files, 1 bundle, etc) 1911, 1919, 1949-55, private ledger 1920-32, general ledgers (5) 1891-1927, 1961-2, impersonal ledger 1927-9, accounts ledgers (8) 1891-1929, private journals (2) 1899-1932, general journals (2) 1919-29, cash books (53) 1920-67, order books (19) 1891-1939, general order books (19) 1925-61, other departmental order books (2) 1920-37, corresp with agents (2 files) 1901-19, sales journals (3) and purchase journals (5) 1919-29, analysis of orders received (1 file) 1831-62, 1882-91, estimates for gas plant (1 vol) 1905-7, specifications (1 vol) 1920-2 and other papers rel to estimates and orders (9 files, etc) 1853-1964, reports on business activity (8 files) 1949-55, patents and specifications (40 files, etc) 1880-1949, technical reports (1 vol, 16 files, etc) 1941-*c*1963, technical drawings (34 files and items) *c*1830-1934, nd and drawings registers (17) 1904-56, staff records (4 vols, 1 file, 3 items) 1916-19, 1941-3, deeds and papers rel to works site 1863-1951, works plans and photographs 1848-1978, photographs of staff, installations and products 19th-20th cent, sales and publicity material *c*1866-1960, scrapbooks and papers rel to history of firm 1793-1970.
Durham County RO (D/Whes). NRA 34911.

[1097] **JOHN WHITE & SON**, weighing machine mfrs and ironfounders, Auchtermuchty, Fife

Records 19th-20th cent incl ledgers (10) 1834-1940, day books (11) 1834-88, 1910-22, cash books (12) 1882-7, 1907-43, credit book 1921-4, sales ledger 1907-10, purchase and sales day books (6) 1922-39, sales books (2) 1879-90, minor jobbing ledger 1901-22, foundry ledgers (2) 1922-56, record of boxes sent out 1908-26, time and wages books (25) 1882-1932, building and foundry plans c1897-1965, factory inspector's report books (2) 1879-1900, notebooks (2) of Christian and John White c1840, 1880-1926; RD Simpson Ltd private ledger 1902-7. *John White & Son (Weighing Machines) Ltd.* Enquiries to NRA (Scotland) (survey 593). NRA 15223.

[1098] **J SAMUEL WHITE & CO LTD**, shipbuilders, ship repairers and marine engineers, Cowes, Isle of Wight

Directors' minutes 1898-1959, ledger 1878-93, bill book 1882-93, cost book 1899-1900, particulars of ships built 1784-1838, register of steam and life launches built 1864-78, 1888-1922, offset book nd, trial record book c1884-1906, misc corresp 1935-54, ship plans 1897-1960, engine plans 1900-27 (microfilm), plan of dock 1889, wages summary 1909-16, engine department wages record 1920-4, apprentices' book 1854-83, photographs 1886-1965, scrapbooks and publicity material 1911-67. *Cowes Maritime Museum*: see Ritchie.

Ship plans 1892-1968, but mainly rel to the Second World War. *National Maritime Museum Manuscripts Section.*

[1099] **TH WHITE LTD**, agricultural engineers, Devizes, Wilts

Memorandum and articles of association 1914-62, personal ledgers (2) 1911-43 and other accounting records (7 vols) 1914-64, sales ledger 1886-97 and other sales and purchase records (27 vols) 1918-71, invoice book 1876-7, schedules (2 vols) of engines, machinery and implements exhibited at Wiltshire agricultural shows 1900-24, catalogues, price lists, etc 1910-c1985, inventory and stock books (19) 1914-45, deeds (14) 1834-1960, notes on company history 1918-54, misc photographs c1900-60. *Wiltshire RO* (WRO 2440). NRA 33475.

[1100] **THOMAS WHITE & SONS LTD**, engineers, textile and woodworking machinery mfrs, Paisley, Renfrewshire

Minute books (2) from 1908, private ledgers and journals (3) from 1908, ledgers (6) 1907-24, 1929-51, sales ledgers for J & P Coats (2) 1927-51, testimonials 1894, order books (12) 1914-35, job books (22) 1899-1952, technical drawings (c130) 1886-1912, nd, pay and time books (21) 1897-1949, salaries book 1909-11, wages summary books (3) 1912-18, list of apprentices 1908-19, inventories of patterns, tools and machinery (2 vols) c1880, 1907-20, catalogues and price lists c1910, photographs of products (c1,000) from c1900. *The Company.* Enquiries to NRA (Scotland) (survey 721). NRA 16014.

[1101] **C WHITTAKER & CO LTD**, engineers and brick-making machinery mfrs, Accrington, Lancs

Papers rel to formation of company 1900, board and general meeting minutes incl reports and accounts (7 vols, etc) 1897-1950s, registers of shareholders and share transfers (3) 1897-1972, register of directors 1900-36, summaries of capital and shares 1901-15, dividend books 1901-4, balance sheets 1860-1971, investment interest journal 1931-63, annual reports and accounts 1901-71, annual returns 1918-53, statements of account 1948-70, letter books (7) 1879-1918, customer account books (2) 1854-7, summary account books (15) 1897-1964, ledgers c1870-1961, impersonal ledgers (5) 1897-1952, trade ledgers (10) 1897-1910, customer account ledgers (5) 1859-1902, day books (44) 1859-72, 1897-1970, cash books (17) 1890-1958, petty cash books 1897-1914, bank books 1862-1949, bills of exchange 1897-1946, invoices 1887-1917, credit books (2) 1899-1949, loan book 1901-5, order books 1872-96, shop order books (4) 1897-1914, purchase order books (36) 1897-1966, tenders book 1927-44, misc tenders and quotations early 20th cent, contract books 1873-88, 1909-29, record of small contracts 1910-14, other contract records to 1960s, sales corresp 1901-9, agency book early 20th cent, purchase journal 1859-65, purchase analysis records 1897-1910, other purchase records 1910-53, brick machines supplied and delivered 1872-83, 1897-1900, railway receiving books (2) 1935-72, stock records 1897-1971, cost analysis books (7) 1918-54, castings and other production records c1890-1969, wheel lists for pattern shop (4 vols) nd, list of steam engines 1907-12, index book of machine parts nd, patents and related papers (1 box) 1856-1960s, wages and related records (1 box) 1848, 1856-1969, time books 1902-34, insurance salaries books (10) 1912-66, registers of employees (3) 1868, 1880-1914, 1971, income tax details 1860s, unemployment insurance books early 20th cent, other staff records 1930-72, deeds 1855-1940, valuations 1865-85, 1941, 1964, boiler insurance policies c1912, catalogues c1880-1950s, glass plate negatives of products nd, address books nd, misc corresp and papers c1900-72; private ledgers (3) 1899-1904 and address book c1892 of CJ Whittaker; Bromley & Darbyshire account book 1850; Furnevall & Co Ltd minutes (1 vol) 1897-1900, debenture stocks nd, and purchase analysis record 1900; Patent Automatic Sewage Distributors Co Ltd letter books (2) 1902-11. *Lancashire RO* (DDX 1866). NRA 30813.

Plans and drawings of plant, machinery and customers' premises (8 folders, 160 items) 1870-1962. *Lancashire RO* (DDX 1219). NRA 3510.

[1102] **SIR JOSEPH WHITWORTH & CO LTD**, machine tool and armaments mfrs, Manchester

Stock book 1837, photographs of machine tools (2 vols) nd, press cuttings (2 vols) 1862-3. *Institution of Mechanical Engineers Library.* NRA 9515.

[1103] **WE WIGG & SON**, ironfounders, agricultural engineers and implement mfrs, Barnby, Suffolk

Customer accounts 1898-1915.
Suffolk RO, Lowestoft (Acc 495). *Accessions to repositories 1991*, p44.

[1104] **WIGRAMS & GREEN**, shipbuilders, London

Ledger 1810-30, journal day book 1810-65, Wigram family legal papers (13 items) 1765-1826.
National Maritime Museum Manuscripts Section (WIG). NRA 30121.

[1105] **JOHN WILDER LTD**, agricultural engineers, ironfounders and implement mfrs, Wallingford, Berks

Private ledger 1939-41, customer ledgers (4) 1859-64, 1885-6, 1891-6, 1901-7, journals (3) 1903-15, purchase day book 1907-13, wages books (3) 1890-4, 1921-35, further records 20th cent.
Berkshire RO (D/EWr). NRA 15941; *Accessions to repositories 1984*, p17.

[1106] **WILSON & LONGBOTTOM LTD**, textile machinery mfrs, Barnsley, Yorks

Sales ledgers (14) 1871-8, 1883-90, 1895-9, 1902-51, purchase ledger 1907-12, loom order books (41) 1871-1938, loom order and specifications books (5) 1906-53, general machine books and order books (30) 1863-5, 1875-1907, 1913-48.
Sheffield Archives (682/B). NRA 34844.

Cash books (2) 1933-44, 1953-8, order book 1875-6, order and specifications book 1928-36, sales and purchase records (17 vols) 1932-59, notes rel to machines, prices of parts, etc and drawings of machinery (4 vols, 162 items) c1954-74, nd, turning room foreman's book 1877-98, advertising literature and articles rel to firm's history nd, glass negatives (several boxes) nd.
Barnsley Archive Service (Wilson & Longbottom records). NRA 34104.

Letter books 1852-6.
In private possession. Enquiries to Barnsley Archive Service. NRA 4805.

[1107] **WOOD BROTHERS**, engineers and millwrights, Sowerby Bridge, Yorks

Register of apprentices 1861-1926.
West Yorkshire Archive Service, Calderdale (Sowerby Bridge Public Library Collection, box 41). NRA 19148.

[1108] **JOHN & EDWARD WOOD**, mechanical engineers and ironfounders, Bolton, Lancs

Registers of engines (5 vols) 1875-1913, list of firms supplied c1875-1930, registers of plans and drawings (2 vols) 1878-1920, plans and drawings nd.
Bolton Archive Service (ZWO). NRA 19836.

[1109] **JOHN WOOD & SONS LTD**, engineers, Wigan, Lancs

Job order books (28) 1900-60, foundry notebook 1875, 1892-3, list of winding engines made 1874-1953, lists of drawings (4 vols) 1906-54, misc corresp, papers and drawings 1933-62.
Wigan Archives Service. NRA 36424.

[1110] **WOODALL NICHOLSON LTD**, coachbuilders, Halifax

Ledgers/cash books (2) 1864-1915, bank books (5) 1889-1914, copy of partnership deed and misc accounts and receipts 1880-1944.
West Yorkshire Archive Service, Calderdale (MISC: 117). NRA 21161.

[1111] **WOOTTON BROS LTD**, engineers and iron and brass founders, Coalville, Leics

Specifications book 1921-31, sketch books (12) 1893-8, 1901-48 and index (1 vol) from 1904, advertisement and photographs (5 items) nd.
Leicestershire RO (DE 3843). NRA 6263.

[1112] **WORTHINGTON-SIMPSON LTD** (formerly **JAMES SIMPSON & CO LTD** and **WORTHINGTON PUMP CO LTD**), pump mfrs and hydraulic and general engineers, London and Newark, Notts

Drawings registers (10) 1865-1905, drawings c1880-1974, catalogues (7 binders and 29 items) 1895-c1935.
Nottinghamshire Archives (DD WO). NRA 35975.

Further records.
The Company. Enquiries to Nottinghamshire Archives. NRA 35975.

[1113] **YARROW & CO LTD**, engineers, shipbuilders and boilermakers, London and Glasgow

Directors' minutes (5 vols) 1897-1965, private ledgers (7) 1895-1919.
Glasgow University Archives and Business Record Centre (UGD 266). NRA 36358.

Records from 1869 incl shareholders' minutes 1922, contracts particulars 1872-1971, agreements (5 items) 1894-1931, extracts from testimonials (1 vol) 1899-1901, papers rel to firm's move to Scotstoun yard (2 files) 1905-12, visitors' books (6) 1907-69, employee regulations 1901-23, photographs of vessels, boilers, yards, staff, etc from 1869 and printed papers from 1896.
Yarrow Shipbuilders Ltd. Enquiries to NRA (Scotland) (survey 2190). NRA 24090.

[1114] **WJ YARWOOD & SONS LTD**, shipbuilders, ship repairers and marine engineers, Northwich, Cheshire

Records 1875-1965 incl directors' memoranda books 1896-1956, registers of ships built and repaired 1902-65, registered tonnage books 1906-25, offset book 1906-31, plans and diagrams

1875-1937, trials results 1890, 1919 and
apprenticeship indentures 1899-1914.
Cheshire RO (DDX 289): see Ritchie.

[1115] **YORKSHIRE ENGINE CO LTD**,
locomotive engineers, Sheffield

Memorandum and articles of association 1884,
1965, board and general meeting minutes (8 vols)
1865-1945, managing director's minutes 1910-13,
register of directors and secretaries 1948-54, register
of directors' holdings 1948, share records (9 vols)
1884-1965, misc corporate records (3 boxes)
1866-1965 incl directors' corresp (1 file) 1877-80,
annual reports, accounts and balance sheets (1 box)
1884-1964, accounting records (13 vols) 1922-65,
sales ledger cards 1962-5, purchase ledgers (2)
1962-5, stock book 1935-48, wages and salaries
records 1932-45, insurance schedule 1959-61,
agreements and legal papers rel to premises
1789-1869.
Sheffield Archives and *British Steel Northern Regional
Records Centre, Middlesbrough.* Enquiries to Sheffield
Archives. NRA 35687.

Order books (49) 1866-1956, quotation books (2)
1936-8, nd, specification book 1910-13, particulars
of order and dispatch of haulage engines (1 vol)
1918-22, engine parts weight books (8) 1867-1900,
1928-30, nd, plans of engines and parts nd,
photographs of engines (3 vols) 1865-1937, nd,
notebooks (2) nd, staff and wages records (18 vols,
1 item) 1888-93, 1902, 1910-48.
Sheffield Archives (YEC). NRA 34835.

[1116] **YORKSHIRE PATENT STEAM
WAGON CO**, Leeds

Order records (c13 vols, 4 files) 1903-44, sales
ledger 1920-41, notes rel to wagon construction
(1 vol) c1919-20, lists of drawings for steam wagons
(14 vols) 20th cent, registers (6) of drawings,
tracings and blueprints 1903-39, drawings,
catalogues and photographs of steam and motor
wagons, aircraft, etc 1901-53, nd.
West Yorkshire Archive Service, Leeds (Acc 1240).
NRA 34492.

[1117] **DANIEL YOUNG LTD**, mechanical
engineers, boilermakers and brassfounders, Witney,
Oxon

Letter books (51) 1893-1901, 1918-50, general
corresp (34 files) 1902-20, general ledgers (22)
1872-1957, monthly ledgers (9) 1920-56, Chubb
ledgers (6) 1904-65, bank books (23) 1886-1950,
cash books (4) 1924-59, price lists (2) 1890-1916,
contract records (150 files) 1896-1969, order books
(84) 1921-69, invoices and receipts (32 files)
1935-62, stock books (1 file) 1952-67, time made
ledgers (2) 1948-64, engineering drawings (11) nd.
Oxfordshire Archives (Daniel Young). NRA 35747.

INSTRUMENT AND
SCIENTIFIC ENGINEERING

[1118] **JAMES ANDERSON**, locksmiths and
window blind mfrs, Belfast

Time books (3) 1896-9, 1928.
Public Record Office of Northern Ireland (D 807).
Deputy Keeper's Report 1954-9, p36.

[1119] **ARON ELECTRICITY METER LTD**,
London

Minutes (4 vols) 1898-1930, directors' reports and
statements of accounts 1899-1911, letter books (2)
1896-1908, corresp between RE Crompton and
Hugo Hirst 1924, papers, press cuttings, etc rel to
firm's history (4 vols) 1898-1945, staff ledger
1893-1911, catalogues, leaflets, etc 1897-1932,
photographs of meters nd.
Ferranti International plc, Wythenshawe. Enquiries to
the Corporate Communications Manager. NRA
13215 (B24).

[1120] **SAMUEL BAKER**, lock mfrs, Willenhall,
Staffs

Sales ledger 1913-50, pattern book 1884-1927, lists
of employees 1898-9, misc vouchers and printed
catalogues nd.
Staffordshire RO (D 3043). NRA 3515.

[1121] **NATHAN BALL & SON**, clock and watch
makers and jewellers, Leicester

Ledgers (8) 1872-1972, cash books (38) 1921-74,
work books (4) 1904-29, watch repairs ledgers (9)
1887-1912, 1936-72, bead ledgers (2) 1960-2,
corresp, invoices, receipts, working papers, press
cuttings, etc (c700 items) 1863-1987, typescript
history of firm 1964.
Leicestershire RO (DE 3230). NRA 31379.

[1122] **WILLIAM JAMES BARNSDALE &
SON**, clock and watch makers, London

Cash books (6) 1935-59, expenditure analysis books
(4) 1935-57, order and repair books (2) 1881-1921,
repairs day books (12) 1923-60, pedigree of
Barnsdale family 18th-20th cent.
Guildhall Library, London (MSS 14784, 16841,
21335-7). NRA 35283.

[1123] **BARR & STROUD LTD**, engineers and
scientific instrument makers, Glasgow

Articles of association nd, share certificates from
1913, other share records (3 vols) 1923-54, balance
sheets and profit and loss accounts 1912-79, War
Office letter book 1888-98, Admiralty letter book
1892-5 and corresp 1892-1946, private letter book
1896-8, foreign letter book 1894-1901, general letter
books (2) 1889-94, other letter books (826)
1893-1984, general corresp 1939-72 and London
office letters 1936-75, agreements (60 items) nd,
misc corporate records 1918-88, ledgers (26)

1897-1970, journals (5) 1917-66, day book
1895-1901, cash books (7) 1913-56, petty cash
books (2) 1888-96, bank books (3) 1895-6, 1914,
1921-4, accounts with other firms 1912-15, other
financial records 1917-88, advice books (14)
1970-4, outward invoice books (45) 1925-74,
quotations nd, orders records 1900-88 and indexes
nd, patents 1860-1982, letters from Patrick Adie and
Lord Kelvin rel to rangefinders 1889, design
specifications nd and abridgements 1855-1904,
drawings of products 1901-76, tracings books (14)
nd, drawing office copy books (31) nd, indexes (38)
to drawings and misc drawings nd, other technical
records 1920-89, salary sheets 1914, unclaimed
wages book 1914-30, notes rel to premium system of
wage earning 1901, property records 1917-29, nd,
photographs of products, works and employees, etc
from late 19th cent, visitors' books (6) 1930-81,
press cuttings (5 vols) 1895-1954, pamphlets
(32 vols, etc) from 1912, publicity material
1899-1976, nd, published articles, reference works
and misc papers 1890-1980; corresp 1893-1906 of
William Stroud; corresp and papers 1898-1930 of
A Barr; collected papers 1892-1969 of W Strang rel
to company history.
Glasgow University Archives and Business Record Centre
(UGD/295). NRA 18741.

[1124] **FRANCIS BEDWELL**, locksmith, London

Account book 1771-6 incl notes of sums due for
work at royal residences.
British Library (Add MS 43679).

[1125] **BERRY & MACKAY**, opticians,
chronometer and nautical instrument makers,
Aberdeen

Ledgers, day and stock books, etc (2 vols) 1846-76
incl accounts 1866-70, other accounting records
(16 vols) 1928-63, purchase books (3) 1945-58.
Aberdeen Art Gallery and Museums. NRA (Scotland)
(survey 518). NRA 14565.

[1126] **BIRCH & GAYDON LTD**, watch, clock
and chronometer mfrs, silversmiths and jewellers,
London

Private ledgers (4) 1894-1923, journal 1905-24,
advertising account book 1916-20, petty cash book
1913-22, bought ledger 1881-4, sales book 1920-4,
watch books (5) 1840-1920, jobbing book 1839-48,
repair book 1920-4, register of rates of chronometers
in stock 1856-74, stock books (2) 1901-12,
scrapbooks (3) of advertisements, press cuttings, etc
c1930-40, 1959-60; William Turner jobbing book
1834-9, stock book 1834-8.
Guildhall Library, London (MSS 14469-70,
18446-59). NRA 30174.

[1127] **BRAMAH & CO**, lock makers, London

Corresp and papers incl bills and receipts
1825-1941, apprenticeship indentures (4 items)
1813-73, patents, etc 1783, 1813-14, 1934,

drawings (1 file) 1819-1904, nd, price lists,
catalogues and advertisements from 1799.
Science Museum Library (Bramah loan collection).
NRA 28467.

Drawings mainly of engines, machinery and locks
(17 vols) 1804-52, nd.
Science Museum Library (1991-349). NRA 28467.

[1128] **CAMBRIDGE INSTRUMENT CO LTD**,
scientific and medical instrument mfrs, Cambridge

Records 1877-1976 incl memorandum and articles
of association 1895, 1969, directors' agenda book
1895-1906, directors' reports, annual accounts, etc
1881-8, 1895-1966, letter books (4) 1881-3, 1899,
cash books (2) 1884-92, order books (3) 1880-7,
1898-1901, stock books (3) 1890, 1898, patents,
patent agreements and related corresp and papers
(9 boxes, etc) 1898-1969, reports on research and
experiments (3 files, 2 bundles) 1910-38, young
employees' and accident registers (6) 1915-38,
corresp and papers rel to property (1 bundle)
1904-29, visitors' book 1912-25, photographs of
staff, premises and instruments from c1877, printed
papers 19th-20th cent, and Sir Horace Darwin's
private letter books (2) 1877-83, misc corresp
1886-1925 and scientific notebook 1873-90.
Cambridge University Library. NRA 34867.

Journals (22) c1907-73, pamphlets (42 vols).
Whipple Museum of the History of Science, Cambridge.
NRA 34867.

Equipment instructions and photographs 1900-70,
notebooks of experiments 1922-74, circuit diagrams
1935-70, catalogues 1958-c1980, factory plan 1979.
*Cambridgeshire RO, Cambridge: see Annual Report
1983*, p16.

[1129] **CF CASELLA & CO LTD**, scientific
instrument makers, London

Order books (39) 1883-1962, stock books (9)
1862-1917, sales, patent and manufacturing
agreements and corresp 1910-30, drawings of
instruments (2 vols) 19th cent, test readings (1 vol)
at Royal Observatory, Edinburgh 1873, staff time
book 1914-15, publicity material, press cuttings,
photographs, etc 19th-20th cent.
Hackney Archives Department (D/B/CAS). NRA
29015.

[1130] **CHATWOOD SAFE CO LTD**, safe mfrs,
Bolton, Lancs

Certificates of incorporation 1864, 1909, works
progress books (8) 1898-1929, safe registers (9)
c1864-c1958 and indexes (2 vols) nd, lock registers
(16) 1875-9, 1883-1900, 1907-11, 1922-56, patents
(photocopies) 1876-96, catalogues, sales leaflets,
price lists, drawings and photographs of products,
press cuttings, etc 1872-1979; Chatwood-Milner Ltd
misc sales, production and staff records c1940-75.
*Chubb Historical Information and Resources Centre,
Leatherhead.* Enquiries to the Archivist. NRA 28631;
BAC *Company Archives* no 198.

Corporate, sales and production records 1920-63,
catalogues, photographs, etc 20th cent, manuscript

history of firm nd; Chatwood-Milner Ltd corporate, sales and production records 1956-65, nd.
In private possession. NRA 28631; BAC *Company Archives* no 198.

[1131] **CHUBB & SON LTD**, lock and safe mfrs, London and Wolverhampton, Staffs

Records from 1814 incl minutes from *c*1945 and other misc corporate records from 1882, ledgers (4) 1859-83 and misc accounting records from 1840, order book 1881-2, misc corresp and diagrams (1 vol) rel to orders, etc 1877-*c*1904, price lists, catalogues and related papers from *c*1852, London and Wolverhampton factory minutes and corresp (1 vol, 3 files) 1860-1930, production day book 1827-30, lock number registers (13) 1819-28, 1834-9, 1844-50, 1854-81, safe number registers (12) 1847-60, 1865-6, 1951-3, safe deposit register 1900-40, patent and trade mark records (*c*10 files and envelopes, *c*55 items) 1820-1976, legal case papers (3 envelopes, 1 bundle, 1 item) 1876-93, photographs of safes, strongrooms, staff, etc from *c*1860, salaries book 1877-89, deeds and related papers from 1814, corresp, press cuttings, advertisements and other collected papers rel to firm's history, etc 1796-1980s; Chubb family papers from 1837.
Chubb Historical Information and Resources Centre, Leatherhead. Enquiries to the Archivist. NRA 28631; BAC *Company Archives* no 422.

[1132] **THOMAS COOKE & SONS** (afterwards **COOKE, TROUGHTON & SIMMS LTD**), optical and scientific instrument mfrs, York

Memorandum and articles of association (incl other companies) 1916-62, board minutes (5 vols) 1897-1963, other corporate and share records (18 boxes, vols, envelopes, etc) 1918-69, corresp 1860-90, customer record books (19) 1905-71, papers rel to foreign trips (1 box) 1913-60, order book 1856-68, order and repairs book 1898-9, stores dockets and specifications (1 box) *c*1900, patents and technical specifications (1 box) nd, records of work for the government (1 box) 1940s, stock book 1919-27, rough stock figures 1913-16, index cards (1 box) 1882-1954, wages book 1879-1920, social club rule books and minutes (1 box) nd, deeds, plans and related papers (1 box, 4 bundles) 1783-1956, corresp and papers rel to the history of the orrery 1930-60, scrapbooks (15) rel to company history 1876-1969, catalogues 1862-1970 and other printed material 18th-20th cent, photographs (13 vols, etc) 1880-1980; Troughton & Simms Ltd balance sheets, income tax papers, etc 1905-19, patents (2) 1788, technical and other notes (5 vols, etc) 1823-1901, misc letters, bills, etc 1736-1948, misc indentures, wills and other legal papers 1761-1843, catalogues early 20th cent-1925, photographs (4 vols) 1874-1909, nd; C Baker Instruments Ltd articles of partnership 1897, notebook 1886-9, misc letters, accounts, deeds, etc 1861-1961.
Borthwick Institute of Historical Research, York University (Vickers Instruments Archives). NRA 34851.

[1133] **COVENTRY MOVEMENT CO LTD**, watch makers, Coventry

Memorandum and articles of association 1887, 1889, 1973, minute books (4) 1889-1985, management committee minutes (1 vol) 1897-1905, agenda book 1944-74, meeting papers 1911-30, registers of members (3) 1889-1985 and related papers 1917-86, papers rel to liquidation of the company (133 items) 1974, accounts, trading accounts and balance sheets (1 file, 3 bundles, 224 items) 1889-1983, private ledger 1918-34, cash book 1896-9, building society and bank books (10) 1933-75, misc financial, staff and legal records 1889-1972, factory notices 1916-55, deeds of premises (2 bundles) 1691-1925, account of the early development of the company by its accountant, EJ Pierson 1891.
Coventry City RO (Acc 540, 542, 1246). NRA 32959.

[1134] **JH DALLMEYER LTD**, mfrs of lenses, telescopes and photographic apparatus, London

Register of members, etc (1 vol) 1892-1973, register of debentures (1 vol) 1892-1919, cash book 1899-1900, sales ledgers (4) 1870-84, 1900-6, purchase ledger 1942-5, prices day books (3) 1898-1902, 1905-6, patents and specifications and related corresp (1 envelope, 37 items, etc) 1864-1927, nd, lens books (33) 1866-1911, 1920-44, rough stock books (8) 1863-74, 1883-1906, photographic lens stock books (2) 1867-84, camera stock book 1899-1909, lantern slides 19th cent, press cuttings, advertisements, etc 20th cent.
Brent Community History Library and Archive. NRA 22228.

[1135] **JOHN ROY DAVIDSON**, watch maker, Leadhills, Lanarkshire

Notebooks (3) with details of work done 1884-5.
The Marquess of Linlithgow. Enquiries to NRA (Scotland) (survey 888, bundle 3423). NRA 17684.

[1136] **E DENT & CO LTD**, clock and watch makers, London

Partnership bond 1872, agreement for purchase of MF Dent 1920, corresp (1 file) rel to shares 1922, letter books (2) 1838-43, misc corresp, notes, accounts, etc (6 bundles) 1828-1908, balance sheets (1 envelope) 1860-4, private ledger 1884-91, royal warrants (3) 1884, 1934, 1938, watch and chronometer manufacturing books (8) 1858-1931, register of items made (1 vol) *c*1890-*c*1920, record of watches tested 1898-1924, estimates (1 bundle) for clock cases 1954-66, stock books (12) 1842-69, 1878-84, 1889-1928, patent records (14 bundles and items) 1840-1940, foreign trade mark certificates (*c*20 items) 1887-1930, drawings, photographs and related papers (25 vols, bundles, rolls, etc) *c*1840-*c*1964, property records (10 bundles) 1850-1932, scrapbooks (3) rel to firm's history *c*1823-1947, misc printed papers 1844-1955; MF Dent balance sheets 1902-7, misc business

papers (1 bundle) 1864-1922 and manufacturing books (2) 1858-1901; Dent family papers 18th-20th cent.
Guildhall Library, London (MSS 18005-76, 23814-24). NRA 33248.

[1137] **DANIEL DESBOIS & SONS**, clock and watch makers, London

Ledgers (14) 1853-1958, day books (12) 1855-1916, 1943-58.
Guildhall Library, London (MSS 14284-5). NRA 33363.

[1138] **CW DIXEY & SON LTD**, opticians and mathematical and scientific instrument mfrs, London

Deeds of partnership 1921, 1928, minutes, share register and legal papers from 1930, trading and profit and loss accounts and balance sheets 1902-66, letters from clients, receipts, trade cards, etc (1 vol) 1807-1979, royal warrants (11) 1824-1940, patents (4) 1856, 1919-47, premises records 20th cent, misc papers rel to history of firm and Dixey family 1812-1977.
Dixey Instruments Ltd. Enquiries to the Business Archives Council. NRA 23697.

[1139] **DOBBIE McINNES LTD**, scientific, marine and industrial instrument mfrs, Glasgow

Memorandum and articles of association 1962, minutes (6 vols) 1903-64, corresp and papers rel to share transfers (197 items) 1934-5, photographs of premises, machine shops and personnel (16 items) 1920s-1960s; TS McInnes & Co Ltd minutes (1 vol) 1893-1905 incl memorandum and articles of association; Alexander Dobbie & Son Ltd certificate of incorporation 1967, minutes (1 vol) 1896-1903; Dobbie, Hutton & Gebbie Ltd minutes (1 vol) 1899-1907 incl memorandum and articles of association.
Scottish Record Office (GD1/780). NRA 34391.

[1140] **DRING & FAGE**, scientific and measuring instrument makers, London

Balance sheets, accounts and income tax and legal papers (11 folders) 1831-1900, journeyman rule maker's ledger 1797-1818, lists of prices and work done (2 vols) 1862, 1865-76, corresp and papers rel to patents and products (14 folders) 1790-1937, papers rel to customers, employees and premises (7 folders) 1854-1913, printed and misc items (9 folders) 1860-c1930.
Science Museum Library (D&F). NRA 35278.

[1141] **JOHN DYSON & SONS LTD**, watch makers and jewellers, Leeds

Sales ledgers (20) 1881-4, 1903-23, 1940-81, customer ledgers (2) 1914-20, 1949-64, stock books (70) 1884-1979, Wakefield branch sales ledgers (8) 1898-1946 and stock books (13) 1897-1945.
West Yorkshire Archive Service, Leeds (LCO 3399). NRA 35091.

[1142] **ELLIOTT BROTHERS**, nautical and electrical instrument mfrs, London

Minutes of factory committee (1 binder) 1905, annual reports and accounts 1956-66, sales ledgers (4) 1855-68 and journals (2) 1913-32, order books (c24) 1816, 1840-99, 1924-52, prices record (1 vol) 1892-1907, royalties and commission accounts c1941-9, commission book c1956-63, cost books (2) 1858-86, 1893-c1902, registers of resistance coils (2 vols) 1863-1905, ammeter record book 1898-9, voltmeter record book 1898-9, instruction manuals 1900-79, notebook rel to electrical discoveries c1833, patent specification ledger 1857-1909, test records (2 vols) c1862-1915, artwork (1 box file) 1912-54, diagrams, sketches and drawings, etc (3 bundles, 2 folders) c1890-1910, c1950-79, registers of building drawings (2 vols) 1898-1954, research papers, etc 1878-89, c1915-58, nd, wages book 1860-2, wage rate book 1911-13, alarm control log books (5) 1941-4, price lists and catalogues from c1855, photographs of products (15 vols, 11 folders, 1 binder, etc) c1890-1969, press cuttings (9 vols, etc) c1820-89, nd, house magazines 1912-c1965, misc corresp and papers from c1817.
Fisher Controls Ltd. Enquiries to the Archivist, Institution of Electrical Engineers. NRA 25546.

Photographs and publicity material c1900-90.
Lewisham Local History Centre (A93/3).

[1143] **CHARLES FRODSHAM & CO LTD**, chronometer, clock and watch makers, London

Directors' and general meeting minutes (1 vol) 1893-1939, private ledger 1939-55, watch manufacturing books (15) 1876-1910.
Guildhall Library, London (MSS 19904-7). NRA 30179.

[1144] **GAS METER CO LTD**, gas meter mfrs, London

Share ledgers (2) 1880-1963 incl misc legal documents and lists of shareholders, private ledger 1867-71.
Thorn EMI plc. NRA 28631; BAC *Company Archives* no 27.

[1145] **JOSEPH GRAY & SON**, surgical instrument mfrs, Sheffield

Private ledger and balance sheets 1906-62, note of profit and loss 1905-34, valuation and letter rel to war damage 1942, 1961, catalogue of dental instruments 1936.
Sheffield Archives (233/B). NRA 22735.

[1146] **ADAM HILGER LTD**, manufacturing opticians and scientific instrument makers, London

Private ledgers (3) 1913-22, nd, journal 1919-40, cash books (3) 1913-16, 1919-25, expenses books (2) 1907-10, 1917-19, bought, purchase and customer ledgers (7) 1903-39, factory charges (1 vol) 1913-18, order books (19) 1900-32, schedule of plant and fixtures at firm's works 1910-13.
Camden Leisure Services, Holborn Library (D/99). NRA 35204.

Lists (17) of customers 1875-1949, sales invoices, etc 1881, 1912-13, research and product development reports (9 vols) 1916-41, papers rel to history of firm (3 bundles).
Science Museum Library (HILG). NRA 35277.

[1147] **HOBBS HART & CO LTD**, lock and safe mfrs, London

Records from 1857 incl partnership agreements, etc 1860-88, memorandum and articles of association 1887-1953, board minutes (13 vols) 1887-1973, general meeting minutes (2 vols) 1897-1973, directors' attendance books (5) 1898-1955, share records from 1877, annual returns, reports, balance sheets and accounts 1888-1961, ledgers (5) 1887-1959 and other accounting records 1887-1973, price lists from *c*1885, list and cost price ledgers (18) *c*1883-1959, factory order books (12) 1880-1959, customer order books (30) 1894-1958, patent specifications 1865-1915, salaries and wages books (17) 1872-1961 and other staff records 1881-1960, valuations, leases and other plant and property records 1857-1958.
Chubb Historical Information and Resources Centre, Leatherhead. Enquiries to the Archivist. NRA 28631; BAC *Company Archives* no 422.

[1148] **KELVIN & JAMES WHITE LTD** (afterwards **KELVIN & HUGHES LTD**), marine and scientific instrument mfrs, Glasgow

Account book 1879-1900, private ledger 1880-90, ledger 1891-1900, cash books (17) 1949-61, Lord Kelvin's patent compass books (4) 1876-1918, employees' friendly society subscription register 1902-56, inventories and valuations (4 items) 1919, 1928, papers partly rel to proposed Canadian company (1 envelope) 1922.
Glasgow University Archives and Business Record Centre (UGD/33). NRA 13691.

[1149] **VICTOR KULLBERG**, watch and chronometer makers, London

Out-letter books (8) 1871-96, 1903-27, register of in-letters 1873-94, ledgers (4) 1857-92, journal 1931-40, order books (8) 1870-1943, address books (2) late 19th-early 20th cent, shop day books (3) 1890-1946, stock records (3 vols) 1885-7, 1897-1930, manufacturing books (8) 1868-1904, 1912-43, notes (1 vol) about watches made 1865-9, shop and workshop repair instruction books (14) 1896-1909, 1915-47, copies of instructions to outside repairers (24 vols) 1920-47, outside repairers' and suppliers' order and running account books (18) 1904-35, rating books (5) late 19th-early 20th cent; E Sills job order books (2) 1901-43.
Guildhall Library, London (MSS 14537-54). NRA 33366.

[1150] **LANCASHIRE WATCH CO**, Prescot, Lancs

Sales ledgers (5) *c*1889-1910.
Prescot Museum of Clock and Watch Making.

[1151] **THOMAS MERCER**, chronometer and scientific instrument mfrs, St Albans, Herts

Records from *c*1864 incl statements of account, day books of chronometers made and repaired, sales records, workshop assembly records, manufacturing agreements and wages books.
Prescot Museum of Clock and Watch Making: see Tony Mercer, *Mercer chronometers: Radical Tom Mercer and the house he founded,* 1978.

[1152] **MILNERS' SAFE CO LTD**, safe mfrs, London and Liverpool

Board meeting minutes (17 vols) 1874-1956 with indexes (2 vols) nd, finance committee minutes (3 vols) 1913-21, share records (83 vols and bundles) 1874-1958, report and accounts 1955, general ledgers (7) 1911-56, returns book 1940-9; Chatwood-Milner Ltd corporate, sales and production records 1956-65, nd; Milners' Safety Cycle Co Ltd minutes 1896-8.
In private possession. NRA 28631; BAC *Company Archives* no 198.

Certificates of incorporation and memorandum and articles of association 1874-1951, directors' reports and accounts 1875-1955, misc corporate records (1 vol) 1899-1938, day book 1859-61, order book 1857-61, sales and depot ledgers (4) 1929-41, lock register 1870-83, key registers (3) 1887-1954, patents 1857, 1865, 1910, corresp, plans, drawings, specifications and photographs *c*1930-60, catalogues, sales leaflets, price lists, etc *c*1870-1956, papers rel to firm's history 20th cent; Chatwood-Milner Ltd misc sales, production and staff records *c*1940-75; Milners' Safe Co (South Africa) Ltd memorandum and articles of association 1900, minutes (2 vols) 1901-58; Whitfields' Safe & Door Co Ltd order book 1871-4, specifications (1 file) 1857-74, catalogues and misc papers 1868-1960.
Chubb Historical Information and Resources Centre, Leatherhead. Enquiries to the Archivist. NRA 28631; BAC *Company Archives* no 198.

[1153] **RW MORTON**, chronometer mfr, Liverpool

Day book listing customers and work undertaken 1881-1921.
National Maritime Museum Manuscripts Section (REC/50). NRA 30121.

[1154] **RW MUNRO LTD**, instrument makers, London

Records 1873-1970 incl cash books from 1916, sales ledgers from 1926, purchase books from 1935, invoice books from 1924, works order books from 1881, particulars and parts lists from 1905, sketch and calculations books from 1896 and wages books from 1873.
Haringey Community Information. NRA 22597.

[1155] **L OERTLING LTD**, mfrs of balances and hydrometers, London

Account book 1867-75, day book 1919-20, order books (2) 1849-59, 1895-1937.
Birmingham Central Library Archives Division (MS 1588). NRA 36399.

[1156] **PALATINE ENGINEERING CO LTD** (formerly **WASTE WATER METER CO LTD**), water meter mfrs, Liverpool

Minutes 1877-1978, patents (2) and specification 1876-7, results record 1898-1901, drawings nd, misc printed papers 1882-1913.
Merseyside RO. NRA 28631; BAC *Company Archives* no 259.

[1157] **JAMES PARKES & SON**, mfrs of optical and mathematical instruments, Birmingham

Card book of items and customers 1833-7.
Birmingham Central Library Archives Division (MS 335). NRA 29847.

[1158] **PARKINSON & FRODSHAM**, chronometer, clock and watch makers, London

Lists of customers and manufacturers (5 vols) c1900-41, customers' accounts (1 vol, 1 envelope) 1923-45, sales book 1911-14, register of clocks, watches and jewellery supplied 1866-1914, watch manufacturing book 1872-1925, repair and cleaning books (2) 1937-45.
Guildhall Library, London (MSS 19908-14). NRA 30180.

[1159] **JOSEPH PRESTON & SONS**, clock, watch and chronometer movement mfrs, Prescot, Lancs

Jobbing ledgers (2) 1895-1923, day book 1901-5.
Merseyside RO (DX 73/1-3). NRA 21591.

Cash book 1893-1904, bank book 1907-12, parts and prices book c1890-5, parts supplied (1 vol) 1892-1914.
Guildhall Library, London (MSS 14545, 14558-60). NRA 33366.

[1160] **NATHANIEL RANDALL**, clock and watch maker, Ixworth, Suffolk

Sales register c1869-91.
Suffolk RO, Bury St Edmunds (Acc 2891). *Report of County Archivist 1973.*

[1161] **JAMES RITCHIE & SON**, clock and watch makers, Edinburgh

Watch book 1809-1920, repairs book 1809-12.
James Ritchie & Son (Clockmakers) Ltd. Enquiries to NRA (Scotland) (survey 248). NRA 10798.

[1162] **ROTHERHAM & SONS LTD**, precision engineers and watch mfrs, Coventry

Memorandum and articles of association 1912-58, share certificates, etc for other companies 1864-78, other investment records 1911-58, agreements and other legal papers 1777, 1842, 1918-91, corresp 1892, 1928-77, ledger 1795-1809, other financial records 1938-87, bills (2 items) 1823, 1838, certificates of manufacture and code book nd, register of patents in force 1897-1957, employees' club minutes 1904-9, plans of works (4) 1851-1964, nd, inventory of premises 1917-20, photographs of premises, products, staff and Rotherham family c1863-1973, price lists and publicity material 1906-73, nd, misc certificates 1885-1957, papers rel to history of company and watchmaking industry 19th-20th cent.
Coventry City RO (Acc 1467). NRA 34151.

[1163] **JESSE SIMMONS & SONS**, lock mfrs, Willenhall, Staffs

Ledger 1902-42, day books (13) 1883-1950, account books (6) 1900-28, 1933-9, cash books (6) 1905-20, bank books (4) 1904-14, 1920-8, corresp and orders (1 bundle) 1912-29, order counterfoils (6 vols) 1903-28, record of patterns sent and prices quoted 1865-74, wages books (2) 1906-17, misc legal and other papers (13 items) 1871-1946; Simmons family financial papers (5 vols, 1 bundle) 1914-43.
Walsall Archives Service (Acc 186, 201). NRA 21625.

[1164] **WILLIAM SKIDMORE & CO LTD**, surgical instrument mfrs, Sheffield

Sales and purchase ledger c1890-1930s, sales ledgers (2) 1905-1930s, price list 20th cent, pattern book c1882-1909, cost books (6) 1850s-1938, copy lease 1853.
The Company. Enquiries to the Company Secretary. NRA 8805.

[1165] **HENRY SQUIRE & SONS**, lock mfrs, New Invention, Staffs

Agreement for Henry Squire to buy out family interests in forge and iron warehouse 1853, directors' minutes (1 vol) 1906-43, general meeting minutes (1 vol) 1907-43, draft company accounts (1 envelope) 1949, bank books (10) 1907-21 and other accounting records (8 vols, 1 box, 1 bundle) 1930-70, nd, sales ledger c1931-50 and purchase journals (2) 1940-7, corresp with customers (1 drawer) from 1937, misc production records (4 vols) c1935-51, lock patents and related papers (2 envelopes) 1892-3, salaries book, etc (1 vol, 1 bundle) 1944-9, records rel to new office block (1 bundle) 1958-9 and photographs of original premises (1 bundle, 1 item) 1980s, price lists, publicity material, etc 20th cent; Squire family papers early 19th-mid 20th cent incl misc business papers of James Squire (1779-1853) and Henry Squire (1823-1892).
The Company and *GPJ Squire Esq.* Enquiries to the Chairman. NRA 35486.

[1166] **JH STEWARD LTD**, scientific instrument mfrs and opticians, London

Corresp, notebooks and papers mainly rel to product development (7 vols, c55 items) 1887-1939, nd,

patent specifications (11 items) 1876-1913, drawings
and photographs mainly rel to tests (12 items)
1914-24, nd, corresp rel to sale of premises
(53 items) 1937, product catalogues incl some of
other firms 1873-1939, nd, printed material rel to
export duty (13 items) 1907-32 and to research on
scientific instruments (37 items) 1888-1948.
Science Museum Library (STEWD). NRA 28458.

[1167] **TAYLOR, TAYLOR & HOBSON LTD**,
manufacturing opticians and measuring instrument
mfrs, Leicester

Committee minutes (2 vols) 1901-14, 1920, private
ledgers (10) 1886-1935, general ledger 1899-1903,
invoice purchase books (32) 1927-60; Allan &
Stallybrass minutes (1 vol) 1907-11; Talykron Ltd
minutes (2 vols) 1912-15.
Leicestershire RO (DE 3095). NRA 30291.

[1168] **THWAITES & REED** (formerly
AINSWORTH, THWAITES & CO), clock
makers, London

Letter books (4) 1919-20, private ledger 1902-21,
ledgers (9) 1788-1913 and index 1827-59, bank
ledger 1902-7, day books (30) 1780-1955, journal
and day book 1809-25, journals (3) 1872-6, 1890-9,
cash books (26) 1812-75, 1881-1907, 1911-51,
bank books (14) 1886-93, 1896-1907, 1911-54,
order books (50) 1843-81, 1895-6, 1907-45,
estimate book 1802-49, invoice books (4) 1917-20,
stock book 1814-55, stock accounts (4 vols)
1904-54, jobbing and order books (6) 1867-88,
1898-1900, shop ledgers (2) 1821-76, small-shop
book 1874-80, work, maintenance and repair
accounts (3 vols) 1822-47, 1866-72, watch repair
book 1825-42, spare parts issue books (2)
1842-1912, workmen's time and material books (6)
1812-53, 1882-1919, 1951-8, wages books (10)
1828-84, 1925-31.
Guildhall Library, London (MSS 6788-6808,
9194-8). NRA 35284.

[1169] **GEORGE & THOMAS TURNER**, lock
mfrs, Wolverhampton, Staffs

Business and personal bills and receipts (36 bundles)
1802-48, nd.
Wolverhampton Borough Archives (DB/2). NRA
22581.

[1170] **VULLIAMY & SON**, clock and watch
makers, London

Letter books (3) 1807-14, ledger 1802-23, day
books (4) 1799-1815, journals (5) 1798-1808,
1811-14, cash book c1793-c1803, account book with
Devaynes Dawes Noble & Co 1801-6, bill books (8)
1803-11, ornament books (4) 1801-15, record of
silver work done (1 vol) 1810-15.
Public Record Office (C 104/57-8). NRA 35828.

[1171] **THOMAS WALKER & SON LTD**, ship
log, sounding machine and steam gauge mfrs,
Birmingham

Letter books (22) 1877-1901, order books (28)
1888-90, 1894-1929, stock book of gauges 1868-
early 20th cent, graph book of sales, wages, etc late
19th-early 20th cent.
Birmingham Central Library Archives Division
(MS 1233). NRA 32222.

[1172] **WALSALL LOCKS & CART GEAR
LTD**, Walsall, Staffs

Records (19 boxes, 21 vols) 19th-20th cent incl
minute book 1930-40, balance book nd, day book
1941-2, order books (2) 1901-26 and from 1903,
sales ledger 1960s and wages books; Albert Minors
order book 1851-1924.
Walsall Archives Service (Acc 459).

[1173] **JOHN WEISS & SON**, surgical instrument
and razor mfrs, London

Sample book 1870-92.
Science Museum Library (MS 213).

[1174] **SAMUEL WILKES & SONS LTD**, lock
and metal fittings mfrs, Bloxwich, Staffs

Ledgers (2) 1909-11, 1915-22, day book 1909, cash
books (8) 1909-38, 1945-71, bank books (4)
1910-19, analysis of expenditure 1968-75, order
books (6) 1905-71, sales ledgers (4) 1917-24,
1933-6, 1964-71, sales analysis 1920-74, purchase
ledgers (3) 1949, 1955, 1967-72, and day books (5)
1907-34, prices books (2) 1921-5, c1930-40, invoice
books incl orders completed (15) 1927-8, 1934-7,
requisitions of supplies sampled 1969, invoices,
corresp, designs, plans and patterns (4 vols, 6 files,
1 bundle) 1920-46, records rel to staff, wages and
health and safety (27 vols and bundles) 1902-79,
trade catalogues (2) 1938, c1950.
Walsall Archives Service (Acc 251). NRA 23478.

ELECTRICAL ENGINEERING

[1175] **ANCHOR CABLE CO LTD**, electrical
cable mfrs, Leigh, Lancs

Directors' minutes (5 vols) 1901-3, 1909-47, works
joint committee minutes (1 vol) 1935-41.
*National Museums and Galleries on Merseyside,
Merseyside Maritime Museum* (BICC Collection).
NRA 35537.

[1176] **ANDERSON, BOYES & CO LTD**,
electrical and mining machinery mfrs, Motherwell,
Lanarkshire

Memoranda and articles of association 1904-60,
minutes (2 vols) 1904-70, agenda books (2)
1904-63, registers (4) of documents 1903-30 and
members 1917-60, share ledger 1904, misc
corporate corresp and papers (c7 files, etc) 1904-66,

balance sheets 1927-39, 1951-9, private ledger
1909-33, journal 1904-48, income tax papers
(9 files) 1918-66, papers and plans rel to property
(3 files) 1904-12, 1920-c1948.
Anderson Mavor Ltd. Enquiries to NRA (Scotland)
(survey 2601). NRA 27341.

[1177] ANDREWS & CAMERON LTD,
engineers, valve and evaporating machinery mfrs,
Kirkintilloch, Dunbarton

Order books (5) 1903-22, 1932-65, cost books (3)
1921-56, job and job specification books (9)
1917-59, chief engineer's notebook 1933-4, valve
register nd, shop print and tracing books (4)
1903-65, steam indicator cards for marine engines
(2 drawers) 1900-50, list of ships with tracing
numbers nd, nightshift work book 1967-70.
Hutsons Ltd. Enquiries to NRA (Scotland)
(survey 932). NRA 18283.

Enquiries record (1 file) 1962, drawings 20th cent,
photographs of pumps (7 boxes) from 1903,
publicity material and product catalogues of other
firms (2 boxes, etc) 20th cent.
Strathclyde Regional Archives (TD 1002). NRA
33979.

[1178] BEST & LLOYD LTD, mfrs of steam, gas
and electric light fittings, Birmingham

Ledgers (2) 1905-62.
Birmingham Central Library Archives Division
(MS 1299). NRA 29847.

[1179] BRITISH ELECTRIC PLANT CO LTD
(afterwards **HARLAND ENGINEERING CO
LTD**), power engineers and contractors, Alloa,
Clackmannanshire

Private journal 1904-28 and accounts before 1904.
Weir Group plc. Enquiries to NRA (Scotland)
(survey 759). NRA 17526.

**[1180] BRITISH INSULATED & HELSBY
CABLES LTD,** electrical cable mfrs, Prescot,
Lancs and Helsby, Cheshire

Directors' minutes (15 vols) 1908-45, finance
committee minutes (6 vols) 1907-36 and works
committee minutes (13 vols) 1902-45.
*National Museums and Galleries on Merseyside,
Merseyside Maritime Museum* (BICC Collection).
NRA 35537.

[1181] BRITISH INSULATED WIRE CO LTD,
electrical cable mfrs, Prescot, Lancs

Directors' minutes (5 vols) 1890-1906, finance
committee minutes (1 vol) 1902.
*National Museums and Galleries on Merseyside,
Merseyside Maritime Museum* (BICC Collection).
NRA 35537.

See also British Insulated & Helsby Cables Ltd.

**[1182] BRITISH THOMSON-HOUSTON CO
LTD,** mfrs of electrical machinery and components,
London

Corporate records from 1895 incl directors' minutes
(3 vols) 1896-1922 and index (1 vol), executive
committee minutes (2 vols) 1901-17, general
meeting minutes (1 vol) 1895-1920, seal register
1903-26 and annual reports (1 vol) 1897-1931.
The General Electric Company plc. Enquiries to the
Company Secretary. NRA 34431.

Financial, technical and production records from
1897, incl financial report on company 1901,
financial and other company information (5 vols)
1908-44, order books from 1910, specifications from
1898, job files from 1902, serial number books from
1905, drawing registers from 1904, design sheets
from 1910 and test records from 1902.
GEC Alsthom Ltd, Rugby. Enquiries to the Archivist,
Institution of Electrical Engineers. NRA 35712.

**[1183] BRITISH VACUUM CLEANER &
ENGINEERING CO,** Ashtead, Surrey

Share certificate books (2) 1953-61, testimonial
letters and accounts paid (3 vols) 1902-9, printed
proceedings of legal case against London & South
Western Railway Co 1910, papers rel to accounting,
trade marks, advertising, etc (49 boxes) 1930s-1982.
Surrey RO, Kingston upon Thames (3164, 3202,
3838). NRA 28361.

**[1184] BRITISH WESTINGHOUSE
ELECTRIC & MANUFACTURING CO LTD**
(afterwards **METROPOLITAN-VICKERS
ELECTRICAL CO LTD** and **ASSOCIATED
ELECTRICAL INDUSTRIES LTD**), electrical
and mechanical engineers and mfrs of domestic
appliances and electric lights, London

Corporate records from 1899 incl directors' minutes
(5 vols) 1899-1925, general meeting minutes (1 vol)
1899-1920, seal registers (2) 1899-1920 and annual
reports (1 vol) 1900-28; Westinghouse Electric Co
Ltd memorandum and articles of association 1889,
directors' minutes (2 vols) 1889-1919, general
meeting minutes (1 vol) 1889-1921.
The General Electric Company plc. Enquiries to the
Company Secretary. NRA 34431.

Technical and production records from 1901, incl
order books from 1909, electrical specifications from
1901, design sheets and pattern books from 1907,
tool numbers and drawings registers from 1913 and
test records from 1910.
GEC Alsthom Ltd, Rugby. Enquiries to the Archivist,
Institution of Electrical Engineers. NRA 35712.

Trafford Park factory research notes and property
plans 1900-80.
Ironbridge Gorge Museum (Acc 1992.14945).

Costings of railway electrification schemes
1920s-1950s.
National Railway Museum, York.

[1185] **TW BROADBENT LTD**, electrical engineers, Huddersfield, Yorks

Records 1874-1984 incl articles of association 1907-70, financial records 1894-1983, sales literature 1896-1917, machinery testing books 1913-47, plan of works 1898, and inventory and valuation 1945.
West Yorkshire Archive Service, Kirklees: see *Annual Report 1988-89*.

[1186] **BRUSH ELECTRICAL ENGINEERING CO LTD**, Loughborough, Leics

Experiment book 1891-3, test books (10) 1894-1903, 1911-39, dynamo test index (8 vols) 1889-1901, c1918-43, numbers for locomotive engine parts (1 vol) 1906, photographs of vehicles and parts (17 files and 9,997 items) 1885-1940.
Leicestershire RO (13 D 71, DE 2857). NRA 33013.

Papers 1896-1903 of AJ Lawson, general manager, incl confidential reports on electric light and tramway undertakings, draft memoranda, and specifications.
Institution of Electrical Engineers Archives Department (NAEST 11). NRA 20573.

[1187] **CALLENDER'S CABLE & CONSTRUCTION CO LTD**, electrical engineers and cable mfrs, London, Erith, Kent and Leigh, Lancs

Directors' minutes (18 vols) 1882-1945, debenture stockholders' minutes (1 vol) 1902, Erith Works joint committee minutes (3 vols) 1933-45, agenda book 1882-3.
National Museums and Galleries on Merseyside, Merseyside Maritime Museum (BICC Collection). NRA 35537.

[1188] **CAMPBELL & ISHERWOOD LTD**, electrical and mechanical engineers, Bootle, Lancs

Minutes (3 vols) 1908-64, register of directors 1908-51, directors' attendance books (2) 1954-71, register of mortgages and charges 1912-43, preference share register nd, private ledgers (6) 1902-43, winding specifications books (27) nd, output books (151) 1947-67, corresp, instructions sheets, technical data, drawings and negatives (c758 boxes, c200 files, several thousand items) 1924-66, nd, salaries books (3) 1915-18, 1940-2, inventory and valuation 1952.
The Company. Enquiries to the Business Archives Council. NRA 23349.

[1189] **CROMPTON & CO LTD**, electrical engineers, London and Chelmsford, Essex

Prospectus 1888, patents 1878-1945, patent specifications for switchgear (1 vol) 1884-1907, machine numbers and calculations (6 vols) 1892-6, 1904, nd, misc corresp, technical notes, etc (2 files) c1924-34, catalogues, brochures, price lists, etc (7 files, c415 items) 1886-1966, photographs of staff, premises and products (3 boxes, 1 vol, 29 files and bundles, etc) 1882-1969, nd, press cuttings,

offprints of articles, etc 1879-1967, nd, corresp and papers rel to firm's history 1877-1966; Colonel REB Crompton's letter books (4) 1870-1, 1883-1921, diaries (33) 1872-7, 1898-9, 1910-33, technical notebooks (c7) and other papers 1853-1939.
Science Museum Library (CRO). NRA 35481.

Serial numbers books from c1900, drawings registers from 1907, drawings from 1928, personnel records from 1970, sales records from 1974.
Crompton Instruments Ltd, Witham, Essex. Enquiries to the Company Secretary.

Misc corresp, plans, drawings and photographs c1913-41.
Essex RO, Chelmsford (D/F107). *Update* 6, Winter 1984/5.

[1190] **HA DAVIE LTD**, electrical engineers, Sunderland, co Durham

Directors' and general meeting minutes (1 vol) 1902-23, ledger 1901-10, journal 1916-59.
Tyne and Wear Archives Service (DX70). NRA 22785.

[1191] **EDISON SWAN ELECTRIC CO LTD**, mfrs of electric lamps and fittings London

Directors' minutes (12 vols) 1883-1957, rough and committee minutes (1 vol) 1888-9, 1895, 1901, annual reports and accounts 1904-55; Manchester Edison & Swan Co Ltd directors' minutes (1 vol) 1893-6; Swans Electric Appliances Ltd minutes, annual reports and accounts (1 vol) 1902-7.
GEC-Henley Ltd. NRA 28631; BAC *Company Archives* no 317.

See also Swan United Electric Lighting Co Ltd.

[1192] **ELECTRICAL POWER ENGINEERING CO (B'HAM) LTD**, electric motor mfrs, Birmingham

Memorandum and articles of association 1914, order books (2) 1899-1910, record of stock, etc (1 vol) 1897-1909, technical data rel to motors (2 vols) nd, test records (1 folder) 1920s, technical drawings (1 roll) nd, misc leaflets, instruction manuals, etc 20th cent.
Institution of Electrical Engineers Archives Department (NAEST 63). NRA 35715.

[1193] **EVERSHED & VIGNOLES LTD**, electrical engineers, London

Board and general meeting minutes (5 vols) 1895-1946, register of members (1 vol) 1895-1929, register of debentures (1 vol) 1902-33, share certificate books (4) 1895-1954, share receipts (1 folder) 1899, register of mortgages (1 vol) 1902-11, trust deeds (2 items) 1902, 1904, annual returns (1 folder) 1902-41, letter books (10) 1893-1909, 1917-29, papers rel to capital, debentures, etc (1 box file) 1928-33, valuers' reports (2) 1904, 1907, ledger 1895-8, invoice book 1895-6, list of customers (1 vol) 1895, agency agreements, etc (1 vol, 2 binders, 1 folder) 1909-1970s,

assignments, licences, etc (1 bundle) 1894-5, patents, patent specifications and related papers (c17 box files and c70 items) c1892-c1972, papers rel to research, development and specifications of products from 1904, general work notebooks (2) 1892-4, 1908, plans and drawings (several hundred rolls) nd, salaries books (3) 1895-1936, wages books (2) 1894-1900, sick club cash book 1892-1912, papers rel to profit sharing, employee bonuses, tax, etc (2 folders) 1914-30, visitors' book c1934-54, catalogues (3 boxes) 20th cent, press cuttings (7 vols) from c1912, photographs of products, etc from 1910, printed history of firm 1932 and misc printed papers 20th cent.
Institution of Electrical Engineers Archives Department (NAEST 102). NRA 35716.

[1194] **FERRANTI LTD**, electrical engineers, Hollinwood, Lancs

Records from c1875 incl misc corresp and papers mainly rel to formation and reconstructions of the company 1883-1920, annual reports and accounts, balance sheets, prospectuses, notices, etc 1901-31, general corresp 1881-1931, corresp and papers rel to shares, income tax, etc 1884-1924, corresp with institutions and organisations 1905-28, manufacturing and agency agreements, licences and related corresp and papers 1882-1918, lists of orders and contracts 1913-27, technical corresp, notes, reports, drawings, etc 1880-1933, patents specifications and related corresp and papers 1882-1933, employee agreements 1888-1904, catalogues, scrapbooks and press cuttings c1875-1930, photographs of products, premises and staff 1881-1930; SZ de Ferranti's letter books (21) 1902-27, technical notes 1882-1929 and diaries 1883, 1915, 1917-26, and papers and collections of CP Sparks, general manager, mainly 1884-99.
Ferranti International plc, Wythenshawe. Enquiries to the Corporate Communications Manager. NRA 13215.

[1195] **GENERAL ELECTRIC CO LTD**, mfrs of electric plant, light fittings, bells, motors, telephones and other electrical equipment, London

Corporate records from 1893 incl memorandum and articles of association 1900, general meeting minutes (1 vol) 1901-58 and annual reports, etc 1893-1901.
The General Electric Company plc. Enquiries to the Company Secretary. NRA 34431.

Records rel to GEC and Hugo Hirst, Baron Hirst incl corresp 1885-1910, ledgers (9) 1881-1900, 1911, nd, capital expenditure record 1901-12, catalogues from 1890, photographs from 1893 and press cuttings from 1899.
GEC-Marconi Research Centre, Great Baddow. Enquiries to Mr AJ Walkden. NRA 22872.

[1196] **GLOBE ELECTRIC CO LTD**, electrical engineers, Leeds

Ledger and stock book 1891-4.
West Yorkshire Archive Service, Leeds (Vavasour 1282-3). *Sources of business and industrial history in Leeds Archives Department*, 1977, p38.

[1197] **WT GLOVER & CO LTD**, electrical wire and cable mfrs, Manchester

Directors' minutes (11 vols) 1898-1977.
National Museums and Galleries on Merseyside, Merseyside Maritime Museum (BICC Collection). NRA 35537.

[1198] **GRAMOPHONE CO LTD** (afterwards **ELECTRIC & MUSICAL INDUSTRIES LTD**), mfrs of gramophones, gramophone records and accessories, radios and electrical appliances, Hayes, Middx

Records from 1897 incl board, committee, managing director's and general meeting minutes and related papers (c60 boxes) 1898-c1975, general meeting minutes (1 vol) 1899-1901, board meeting index books (4) 1912-30, directors' attendance book 1899-1904, register of members (1 vol) from 1900, share allotment book c1900, dividend warrants book 1899-1900, prospectuses, share certificates, letters of allotment, notices and other share records from 1899, annual reports and accounts from 1898, corresp, telegrams, agreements, orders, litigation papers, etc rel to formation and early years of the firm (2 filing cabinet drawers) 1897-c1911, corresp, minutes, memoranda, etc rel to formation of EMI (1 drawer) 1929-31, private and nominal ledger (1 vol) 1900-2, investment ledger 1905-29, trade reports (2 box files) 1924-30, corresp and papers from 1898 rel to statistics, patents, trade marks and copyright, relations with British and overseas subsidiaries, associates and competitors, the First and Second World Wars, development of radio and television, etc, artists' and contracts' files from 1898, recording ledgers and related papers from early 20th cent, papers of and rel to former members of staff from 1897, corresp, memoranda, agreements, plans and photographs rel to British and overseas property from c1906, and catalogues of the Gramophone Co, EMI and other firms from 1898.
EMI Music Archives, Hayes. Enquiries to the Manager, Archives Department. NRA 35644.

[1199] **J & E HALL LTD**, boilermakers and refrigeration machinery mfrs, Dartford, Kent

Memorandum and articles of association 1891, 1900, debenture holders' minutes (1 vol) 1898, general meeting minutes (1 vol) 1907-9, inventions and improvements committee minutes (1 vol) 1918-20, letter books (2) 1881-6, 1924-7, share and debenture corresp, certificates, etc (c150 items) 1888-1902, 1976, annual reports and related papers 1913-82, misc corporate records (1 bundle, c300 items) 1889-1924, annual accounts, audit books, accounting summaries and statistics, etc (65 vols) 1912-82, private ledgers (7) 1892-1901, 1907-48, ledgers, journals, account books and cash books (22) 1910-70, sales book 1864-6, sales records for cooling machines (2 vols) 1893-1954, machine record books (13) 1888-1944, specifications books (2) 1907-10, 1919-24, other sales and order records (17 vols, 1 folder, 7 items) 1820-2, 1912-74, patents, assignments and related papers (c410 items) 1877-1912, 1944, testing

department records (307 files) 1895-1954, machine report books (13) 1895-1948, technical notebooks (181) 1880, 1894, 1911-57, nd, other research and technical records (c33 vols, c34 items) 1882-1979, machinery plans (59 items) 1942-60, wages and salaries books (13) 1910-69, benefit trust fund and welfare committee minutes (14 vols) 1912-70, misc staff records (c13 vols and files, c35 items) 1836-1975, valuations, plans, drawings and photographs of works 1897-1969, deeds (108 items) 1886-1947, photographs of installed equipment (54 folders) and indexes (2 vols) nd, catalogues, house magazines, photographs, press cuttings, etc rel to advertising and the firm's history c1885-1985; HJ West & Co (1908) Ltd directors' minutes (2 vols) 1908-40.
Centre for Kentish Studies, Maidstone (U1570, U2835). NRA 14719.

Patent 1855, papers rel to machinery for making paper 1841 and polishing glass 1864, Hall family testamentary papers 1836-70, deeds (90 items) 1662-1870.
Centre for Kentish Studies, Maidstone (U302). *Guide to Kent County Archives Office*, 1958, p196.

[1200] **HASLAM FOUNDRY & ENGINEERING CO LTD**, electrical and refrigeration machinery mfrs, Derby and London

Estimates books (11) 1912-34, sales books (4) for ammonia compressor refrigerating machines c1905-29, instruction manuals and trade catalogues for refrigerating machines (5 items) 1923, nd.
Derbyshire RO (D1522). NRA 34309.

[1201] **WT HENLEY'S TELEGRAPH WORKS CO LTD**, mfrs of telegraph and telephone cables, magnetic machinery and batteries, London

Directors' and general meeting minutes (23 vols) 1880-1901, 1905-66, annual reports and returns, etc 1886-1966, agreement for sale of company 1880, letter book 1880-1, misc sales and production records 1897-1953, staff benefit fund records, etc 1916-77, notes and papers rel to history of firm and photographs 1880-1959; Henley's (South Africa) Telegraph Works Co Ltd minutes 1903-30 and annual reports from 1933.
GEC-Henley Ltd. NRA 28631; BAC *Company Archives* no 317.

[1202] **A HIRST & SON LTD**, electrical engineers, Dewsbury, Yorks

Agreement for sale of business 1898, debentures and share transfers (48 items) 1898-9, 1910, balance sheets (6) 1911-20, corresp and papers (over 70 items) rel to patents 1907-49, misc papers (31 items) 1897-1910.
West Yorkshire Archive Service, Kirklees (B/H). NRA 34069.

[1203] **HOLLAND HOUSE ELECTRICAL CO LTD**, electrical equipment mfrs and suppliers, Glasgow

Directors', shareholders' and extraordinary meeting minutes and reports (3 vols) from 1906, balance sheets from 1927.
The Company. Enquiries to NRA (Scotland) (survey 2777). NRA 30004.

[1204] **INDIA RUBBER, GUTTA PERCHA & TELEGRAPH WORKS CO LTD**, mfrs of electrical machinery and instruments, cables and rubber goods, London

Records from 1864 incl board minutes (16 vols) 1864-1937, directors' private minutes (1 vol) 1868-71, general meeting minutes (1 vol) 1864-1917, committee minutes (3 vols) 1864-6, 1875, 1887-1902, share registers c1917-38, balance sheets and accounts 1920-36, ledgers and other accounting records 1926-64 and overseas agency accounts 1889-1954.
Greater London RO. NRA 24145.

Indenture 1848, deeds of dissolution of partnership (2) 1852-3, agreement 1869, corresp (7 bundles) 1857-1926, record of manufacture of insulated core (4 vols) 1850-1931, stock books (2) 1910-18, experimental joints diary (2 vols) 1917-23, 1931-7.
National Maritime Museum Manuscripts Section (TCM/21/1-19). NRA 36131.

[1205] **JONES, BURTON & CO LTD**, electrical engineers and machine tool mfrs, Liverpool

Ledger 1890-7, financial papers 1916-63, order books (6) 1911-14, sales and service corresp and papers 1923-63, drawings and photographs of machinery c1910-63, price lists and catalogues incl some of other firms 1892-1967, press cuttings and misc papers 1933-69.
National Museums and Galleries on Merseyside, Merseyside Maritime Museum (D/B 157). NRA 35599.

[1206] **KING & CO LTD**, plane makers, manufacturing ironmongers, heating and electrical engineers, Hull, Yorks

Memorandum and articles of association 1881-1949, directors' meeting minutes 1881-4 and from 1950, annual reports and balance sheets 1882-1968, schedule of deeds 1797, catalogues, press cuttings and other printed papers 1899-1980.
The Company. NRA 28631; BAC *Company Archives* no 361.

Partnership deeds, assignments, etc (1 bundle) 1807-47, nd, contract, invoice and cost books, general corresp, etc (22 vols, c104 files, c150 items) 1915-71, drawings (c700) of heating systems 1910-64, deeds mainly 18th cent.
Kingston upon Hull City RO (DBKC). NRA 24720.

[1207] **LAURENCE, SCOTT & CO LTD**, electric machinery and apparatus mfrs, Norwich, Norfolk

Technical drawings (144 bundles) 1894-1936.
Institution of Electrical Engineers Archives Department (NAEST 27). NRA 20573.

[1208] **MACFARLANE ENGINEERING CO LTD**, electric motor and generator mfrs, Glasgow

Minute book 1911-62, order book 1911-12, JW MacFarlane's letter book mainly rel to pumps and centrifuges 1907-9, photographs (7) of employees and publicity material, etc 20th cent; Walter MacFarlane & Co product catalogues (2 vols) 1883.
Strathclyde Regional Archives (TD 289, 299). NRA 12501.

[1209] **WILLIAM McGEOCH & CO LTD**, electrical engineers and brassfounders, Glasgow and Birmingham

Copartnery contracts 1867, 1874, summary of turnover 1867, balance sheet 1900, brass foundry price lists (2) c1900, sales list 1913-53, manufacturing account (Birmingham) 1891, misc corresp and papers 1865-1910, brochure of head office and warehouse 1906.
McGeoch Distribution Ltd. Enquiries to NRA (Scotland) (survey 1462). NRA 20584.

[1210] **MACKENZIE & MONCUR LTD**, heating, ventilation and electrical engineers and iron founders, Edinburgh

Records 19th-20th cent incl minute books (3) from 1894, agenda book 1894-1926, letter books from 1886, corresp rel to incorporation and purchase of the company 1894-1904, private ledgers (3) 1895-1949, ledgers (15) 1898-1939, credit ledgers (16) 1876-80, 1890-1915, journals (3) 1894-1950, cash book 1934-6, bank account 1894-1949, order books 1882-1941, order letter books 1913-50, oncost and working expenses books (3) 1907-24, specification books 1896-1930, plans of customers' property from 1883, wages and salaries books 1888-1955.
In private possession. Enquiries to NRA (Scotland) (survey 262). NRA 10787.

[1211] **MARCONI'S WIRELESS TELEGRAPH CO LTD** (formerly **WIRELESS TELEGRAPH & SIGNAL CO LTD**), mfrs of wireless, broadcasting and marine communications equipment, London and Chelmsford, Essex

Memorandum and articles of association and special resolutions from 1897, board minutes (24 vols) from 1897, general meeting minutes (2 vols) from 1897, finance committee minutes (9 vols) 1908-29, annual reports and accounts from 1898, general meeting papers (9 files) from 1898, share dividend details (2 vols) from 1911, unclaimed dividend books 1911-65, cancelled share certificates and warrants 20th cent, registers of agreements 1897-1976,

summaries and sundries (1 file) from 1919; Marconi International Marine Communication Co Ltd memorandum and articles of association and special resolutions from 1900, board minutes (7 vols) from 1900, general meeting minutes (2 vols) from 1900, committee minutes (7 vols) 1900-42, registers and attendance books of directors from 1900, general meeting reports, accounts, chairman's addresses, etc from 1900, seal books (11) from 1900, registers of agreements, documents signed, mortgages and debentures from 1900, unclaimed dividends book 1911-71, summaries and sundries (1 file) from 1921.
GEC-Marconi Ltd, Stanmore. Enquiries to the Secretary. NRA 35463.

Selected records for the history of the companies (c260 files) from 1896 incl papers rel to Guglielmo Marconi (35 files) 1890s-1930s, formation and administration of the companies (19 files) from 1896, early demonstrations and tests of equipment (15 files) 1896-1902, development of international communications (25 files) from c1900, patents (6 files) from 1891 and litigation (20 files) 1899-1922; drawing registers and indexes and performance specifications (c35 vols) from 1901, messages, reports, etc rel to the *Titanic* disaster (2 boxes) 1912, engineers' final reports, obsolete job records, etc (c28 box files) 1930s, diaries of GS Kemp as Marconi's chief assistant (21 vols) 1897-1920, company catalogues from 1905, photographs from c1896, press cuttings from 1897.
GEC-Marconi Ltd, Chelmsford. Enquiries to the Company Archivist. NRA 35463.

[1212] **FRANCIS J MUDFORD LTD** (formerly **EIDSFORTH & MUDFORD**), electrical engineers and mfrs of electric alarms, bells and instruments, London

Letter book 1914-38, cash book 1883, bank books (2) 1883-91, invoice books (3) 1883-6, 1889-90, sales ledger 1883-8, purchase ledger 1923-31, costing book 1884-91, job books (2) 1910-20, attendance and wages books (2) 1887-1936, iron and steel catalogue 1932.
Institution of Electrical Engineers Archives Department. NRA 22568.

[1213] **MUIRHEAD & CO LTD**, mfrs of electrical measuring and control instruments, Beckenham, Kent

Records 1870s-1970s incl memorandum and articles of association 1904-60, board minutes (2 vols) from 1904, share allotment book 1904, register of seals 1912-51, letter books (3) 1910-30, accounts from 1905, works orders (2 vols) 1892-1902, 1927-30, stock sheets (3 binders) 1904-6, engraving books (6) 1892-1916, test room connection book 1890s-1920s, printed patents (4 vols) 1874-1912, drawings and related papers from 1900, papers rel to building of factory, etc (1 folder) 1896-8, catalogues, leaflets, etc from c1882, and private letter books (5) of John Muirhead junior 1880-2.
Science Museum Library (MURHD). NRA 35707.

[1214] NEW GUTTA PERCHA CO LTD (later **CROYDON CABLE WORKS LTD**), electrical cable mfrs, London

Directors' minutes (3 vols) 1902-28.
National Museums and Galleries on Merseyside, Merseyside Maritime Museum (BICC collection). NRA 35537.

[1215] THOMAS PARKER LTD, electrical engineers, Wolverhampton

Minute book 1894-1909, registers (2) of members and share transfers 1894-1908, annual lists of shareholders and summaries of capital 1904-7.
Wolverhampton Borough Archives (DX/147/1-4). NRA 21915.

[1216] CA PARSONS & CO LTD, turbine mfrs, Newcastle upon Tyne

Records incl directors' minutes 1913-46, management and committee minutes 1903-14, production records from *c*1903 incl turbine registers and machine files, patent registers and photographs 1878-1950.
Tyne and Wear Archives Service (Acc 2402).

Records incl agreements and corresp with Westinghouse Machine Co 1898-1917 and other overseas firms, technical notebooks of CA Parsons (*c*25 vols) 1881-1914 and other technical records.
Science Museum Library (PAR). NRA 28456.

Machine construction log books (2) 1904-5, 1908, lading book 1919-46.
Tyne and Wear Archives Service (Acc 1321, 2323). NRA 8919.

Instruction files *c*1930, works plans 1942-56.
Tyne and Wear Archives Service (Acc 2553).

[1217] BRUCE PEEBLES & CO LTD (afterwards **PARSONS PEEBLES LTD**), engineers and electrical machinery mfrs, Edinburgh

Prospectus 1903, list of shareholders 1903, annual reports and accounts, etc 1903-37, corresp rel to liquidation and reconstruction (7 files, 54 items) 1901-18, corresp and papers rel to other firms (5 files, 90 items) 1903-9, misc corresp and accounts (5 files) 1907-8, corresp and papers rel to contracts (3 files) 1904-11, patent and specification 1902, creditors' meeting minutes (4 items) 1908, misc papers (48 items) 1903-39.
Scottish Record Office (GD 282/13/68-105). NRA 20359.

Machine number books (5) 20th cent, electric motor test sheets (219 items) 1905-65, staff newsletters (16 vols, etc) 1947-79, press cuttings 1903, 1910-15, 1933-67, catalogues and publicity material partly rel to plant machinery (317 items) 1901-*c*1980, photographs of products, employees and works (7 albums, *c*20,000 items) 1875-1975, misc papers 1821-1979.
Scottish Record Office (GD 349). NRA 21847.

Order files from *c*1937, customers' specification files nd, machine number files from 1970, works

instruction records (69 vols, etc) 1905-47, operating instructions from 1945, machine test book from 1898, test records 20th cent, design office calculations from 1940, drawing office registers from 1898 and drawings from 1906.
Peebles Electrical Machines. Enquiries to NRA (Scotland) (survey 1731). NRA 21847.

[1218] RADENITE BATTERIES LTD, accumulator mfrs, Coventry

Directors' minutes (1 vol) 1903-65, registers of directors 1903-43, members 1903-29 and returns of allotments 1903-7, share certificates 1903-24, summary of shares and directors 1930-6, balance sheets, summaries of accounts, etc 1919-77, other accounting records (5 vols) 1919-68, orders (1 file) 1918-19, sales day book 1950-2, prices of lead and antimony 1934-55, patents and legal papers (1 file, 5 items) 1906, 1919-45, technical notebooks, battery record cards and related papers *c*1910-81, staff notices, etc (1 file, 27 items) 1925-66, corresp and plans rel to premises (1 file, 7 items) 1912-74, corresp and papers mainly rel to firm's history (1 file, 27 items) *c*1934-78, nd, catalogues, price lists and other advertising material 1903-81, photographs (1 vol, *c*68 items) 1905-81.
Coventry City RO (Acc 1562). NRA 35455.

[1219] RAILWAY SIGNAL CO LTD, signal and electrical appliance mfrs, Liverpool

Directors' and shareholders' minutes (7 vols) 1881-1975, attendance book 1881-1974, registers of directors and directors' holdings (2 vols) 1948-73, share ledger 1924-74 and transfer registers and certificates (2 vols, etc) 1892-1974, pension fund minutes (1 vol) 1949-65.
Westinghouse Brake & Signal Co Ltd. Enquiries to Wiltshire RO. NRA 35708.

Orders schedule and index 1912, shipments book 1902-3, record of components despatched 1902-5, locking books (3) 1885-6, 1890-1, 1900-3, foreman's specifications 1909, patent specifications of signalling equipment 1892-1909, signal diagrams (45 items) nd, index of drawings 1914-17, plans of works (41 items) 1902-16, nd, photographs (2 albums, 1 file, etc), catalogues and misc papers *c*1890-1950.
National Museums and Galleries on Merseyside, Merseyside Maritime Museum (D/RS). NRA 35597.

[1220] ROYCE LTD, electrical and mechanical engineers, Manchester

Order books (10) 1897-1939, cost books (4) 1898-1907, 1927-35, summaries of crane installations (9 vols) 1907-32, estimates (2 vols) 1915-16, 1929, specifications (5 vols) 1915-24, crane parts pattern registers (11) 1901-69, calculation and experiment books (11) 1887-1932; drawing office order books (2) 1903-5, record books (13) 1901-33, print books (3) 1920-32 and misc records (4 vols) *c*1900, 1925-32; electrical department order book 1900-3, registers (28) of motor starters and other electrical equipment

supplied 1902-36, dynamo and motor specification books (20) 1898-1936, work books (7) 1890-9, connector diagrams (7 files) 1909-31 with index c1917-19, and calculations, etc (8 vols) 1891-1932; glass negatives (18 boxes) c1900.
Leicestershire RO (28D69/125-67). NRA 32956.

Production and technical corresp rel to cranes (2 files and loose items) 1927-30.
Rolls-Royce Enthusiasts Club. Enquiries to the Warden, The Hunt House, Paulerspury, Northants. NRA 35052.

[1221] **SHIRRAS, LAING & CO LTD**, electrical and heating engineers, sheet metal workers and oil merchants, Aberdeen

Directors' minutes (2 vols) 1903-48, expenses account book 1933-4, day books (3) 1943-6, order and sales books (2) 1932-62, oil contracts, stock inventories and price lists (1 vol, 9 bundles) c1886-1950, wages books (11) 1913-48, bonus receipts (1 bundle) 1924-5, corresp and papers incl discharged bills and employment contracts (5 bundles) 1888-1943.
The Company. Enquiries to NRA (Scotland) (survey 1434). NRA 20364.

[1222] **SIEMENS BROTHERS & CO LTD**, telegraph and electrical engineers, London

Memorandum and articles of association from 1880, directors' general meeting and committee minutes incl reports and accounts (36 vols) 1880-1965, directors' agenda and attendance books (8) 1955-65, registers of directors, members and mortgages, share records, annual returns, etc (17 vols) 1880-1977, registers of seals (10 vols) 1909-80, corresp and papers rel to integration with Edison Swan Electric Co Ltd 1957, agreements 1918-1960s, ledgers (3) 1913-55, memoranda mainly rel to staff (2 vols) 1881-1908, staff magazine 1930-49; Siemens Brothers Dynamo Works Ltd minutes and other corporate records (6 vols) 1906-39.
GEC-Henley Ltd. NRA 28631; BAC *Company Archives* no 317.

[1223] **RP STAFFORD & SON**, heating, electrical and sanitary engineers, Halifax, Yorks

Letter books (5) 1889-1903, 1913-33, corresp (4 bundles) 1885-91, 1896-9, ledgers (3) 1864-6, 1903-15, day books (14) 1861-4, 1900-4, 1929-60, cash books (5) 1891-4, 1916-23, 1935-47, estimates book 1924-6, contract ledger 1878-1900, purchase ledger 1919-49, invoice books (3) 1881-6, 1892-7, bills, invoices, delivery notes, etc (2 bundles) 1870-1967, petty stock book 1898-1919, staff job books (13) 1965-7, nd, insurance and salaries books (2) 1913-55.
West Yorkshire Archive Service, Calderdale (ST). NRA 24678.

Account book 1954-8.
West Yorkshire Archive Service, Calderdale (Misc 254). NRA 21161.

[1224] **LOUIS STERNE & CO LTD**, engineers and refrigeration machinery mfrs, Glasgow

Register of members 1874-82, share records (3 vols) 1874-1909, directors' and private letter books (4) 1876-1908, corresp and misc papers (1 file, 1 bundle) 1886-1908, agreements 1874-1900, account books (2) 1875-1953, private ledgers (6) 1871-1935, ledgers (6) 1882-1950, journals (4) 1875-1920, cash books (6) 1897-1953, photographs of refrigeration units, etc (4 box files) 1950s.
In private possession. Enquiries to NRA (Scotland) (survey 625). NRA 15345.

Order books (14) 1908-39, contracts (4 vols) nd, specifications, drawings and sketch books (38 vols) 1916-36, nd, indexes (12) to sketch books, drawings and names from c1890.
Glasgow University Archives and Business Record Centre (UGD/15). NRA 15345.

[1225] **J STONE & CO LTD**, electrical and mechanical engineers, London

Memorandum and articles of association, etc (7 items) 1904-68, share letter books (7) 1916-28 and copy annual returns (1 file) 1909-14, letter books (31) 1905-39, company and departmental corresp and papers 1937-65, account of directors' fees 1925-33, draft accounts and annual summaries of sales and commissions (1 vol, 1 bundle) 1960-6, private ledger and journal (2 vols) 1904-17, general ledgers and journals (16) 1918-59, transfer journals (6) 1943-65, expenses ledger 1948-50, supplies accounts (2 vols) 1936-40, cash books (7) 1917-18, 1940-62 and summaries (4 vols) 1943-67, bank book 1917-18 and vouchers (3 bundles) 1967-8, customers' journals (10 vols) c1940-59, commissions and royalties account c1912-21, further records rel to sales and customers 1919-68, patents and related papers c1907-48 (3 boxes, 1 vol, 1 bundle, etc), staff and salaries records 1913-62, deeds and premises records 19th cent-1941, catalogues and publicity material 19th cent-1967; Stone family corresp, papers and photographs 1848-67.
Lewisham Local History Centre (A69/10). Access restricted. NRA 29318.

Share registers (18 vols) 1915-62 and related corresp and papers 1905, 1922, 1949-62.
Lancashire RO (DDPSL/16). NRA 20296.

[1226] **SWAN UNITED ELECTRIC LIGHTING CO LTD**, electric lamp mfrs, London

Directors' minutes (2 vols) 1881-90, register of members 1881-2, share ledger 1881-2, register of transfers 1881-2, private ledger 1881-2, cheque counterfoils, etc (3 vols, 1 bundle, 1 item) 1882-9, reports, agreements, publicity material, press cuttings, etc (2 vols) 1880-96, corresp and receipt (9 items) 1884-98; papers of Sir Joseph Swan rel to experiments with electric lighting, patents, legal cases, amalgamation with the Edison Co, etc (c260 items) 1876-1905 and other personal and Swan family papers 19th-20th cent.
Tyne and Wear Archives Service (Acc 1101). NRA 24634.

Directors' and general meeting minutes (2 vols) 1882-94, annual reports and accounts from 1883. *GEC-Henley Ltd.* NRA 28631, no 317.

See also Edison Swan Electric Co Ltd.

[1227] **TELEGRAPH CONSTRUCTION & MAINTENANCE CO LTD**, submarine telegraph cable mfrs, London

Board minutes (18 vols) 1864-1967 and general meeting minutes (2 vols) 1865-1957.
National Museums and Galleries on Merseyside, Merseyside Maritime Museum (BICC Collection). NRA 35537.

Memorandum and articles of association incl resolutions 1864-1920, general meeting minutes 1871 and indexes (2 vols) 1930-60, signatures of shareholders (1 vol) 1867-1936 and share notices (1 vol) nd, annual report 1860, balance sheet 1864, legal papers 1867-73, general corresp 1859-1951, contract records 1858-1956, works order book 1876-96, records of cable loading (2 vols) 1879-1925, registers and other records of cables 1850-1957, nd, cable engineers' log books (413) 1869-1940, diaries (4) rel to cable laid 1874, 1889, 1926, test diaries (7) 1866-1918, engine room log book 1888 and ships' log books (17) 1866-1932, message diary 1874, papers rel to the first transatlantic cables (4 vols, etc) 1857-74, 1936, reports rel to laying and testing of cables 1860-1954, cable ships' statistics (15 vols) 1877-1962, papers rel to CS *Ocean Layer* 1953-60, other production records 1900-64, patents 1864, 1881-5, pattern book 1901-23, data rel to cables (5 vols) 1868-1934, other technical records 1883-1956, nd, misc staff records 1876-1966, records rel to Ocean Works 1953-68, nd, visitors' books (2) 1950-78, publicity material 1850-1969, papers rel to company history and centenary celebrations 1903-59, books and pamphlets 1836-1968.
National Maritime Museum Manuscripts Section (TCM). NRA 36131.

Reports and accounts 1865-1928, agreements 1868-1926, cable section sheets, etc *c*1915-37, misc papers (6 items) 1876-1950, nd.
Cable & Wireless plc. Enquiries to the Curator. NRA 21652.

Copies of contracts and specifications (*c*45 items) 1869-1929, log books, reports, corresp, papers and photographs *c*1901-30 of cable engineer CAO Berner.
Science Museum Library (BERN, MURHD). NRA 28631; BAC *Company Archives* no 52.

[1228] **H TINSLEY & CO LTD**, scientific equipment and electric measuring instrument mfrs, London

Order books (2) 1913-20, invoices (2 bundles) 1918, corresp and papers mainly rel to orders (11 bundles and folders) 1910-33, catalogues (1 file) 1920s-1930s.
Science Museum Library (TINS). NRA 28460.

[1229] **WESTINGHOUSE BRAKE & SIGNAL CO LTD**, mfrs of railway brakes and signalling systems, pumps and air compressors, London and Chippenham, Wilts

Records from 1881 incl board minutes from 1881, general meeting minutes, reports and accounts 1882-1955, share summary 1881-1935, private ledgers from 1921 and production specifications from 1932.
The Company. Enquiries to Wiltshire RO. NRA 35708.

Records *c*1900-80 incl account books, patent files and glass plate negatives.
Wiltshire RO. NRA 35708 and *Accessions to repositories 1989*, p38.

[1230] **YORKSHIRE SWITCHGEAR & ENGINEERING CO LTD** (formerly **TRAMWAY SUPPLIES LTD**), electrical engineers, Leeds

Inwards order books (14) 1909-45, purchase, sales and cost records (8 vols) 1927-66, labour and materials account book 1907-15, wages books (2) 1935-43, Marconi international code books (2) 1919.
West Yorkshire Archive Service, Leeds (Acc 2450). NRA 34522.

Index of Businesses

The references are to entry numbers

Belliss & Morcom Ltd 624
Bennie, David, & Sons Ltd 43
Bentall, EH, & Co Ltd 625
Bentham, FH, Ltd 626
Bergius Co Ltd 627
Berry & Mackay 1125
Bertram, James, & Son Ltd 628
Bertrams Ltd 629
Bessemer, Henry, & Co Ltd 612
Best & Lloyd Ltd 1178
Bettridge, John, & Son 630
Betts & Co Ltd 44
Beyer, Peacock & Co Ltd 631
Bingham & Hall 538
Birch & Gaydon Ltd 1126
Birkett, Samuel, & Sons (Cleckheaton) Ltd 632
Birmingham Battery & Metal Co Ltd 45
Birmingham Metal & Munitions Co Ltd 46
Birmingham Railway Carriage & Wagon Co Ltd 633
Birmingham Small Arms Co Ltd 634
Bischof White Lead Corporation (1900) Ltd 78
Bishop Bros 635
Bissoe Mining & Smelting Co 47
Bissoe Tin Smelting & Arsenic Co Ltd 48
Blaenavon Co Ltd 49
Blair, Campbell & McLean Ltd 636
Blakemore, D, & Sons Ltd 50
Blezard, R, & Sons 637
Bligh Bros 638
Blochairn Iron Co 51
Bluemel Bros Ltd 639
Blundell, Thomas 52
Boardman, Glossop & Co 53
Boby, Robert, Ltd 640
Bodley Bros & Co Ltd 54
Bolckow, Vaughan & Co Ltd 55
Bolitho, Thomas, & Sons 56
Bolton, Thomas, & Sons Ltd 57
Bomford & Evershed Ltd 641
Bond, JW, & Co 58
Booth & Brookes Ltd 59
Borough Steam Wheel Works 642
Botfield family 60
Boulton & Fothergill 643
Boulton, Watt & Co 643
Bower, Original 644
Bowerbank, Joseph, & Son 61
Bowesfield Steel Co Ltd 62
Bowling Iron Co Ltd 63
Bowling, John, & Co Ltd 64
Boyd, J & T, Ltd 645
Braby, Frederick, & Co Ltd 65
Bradbury, Thomas, & Sons Ltd 66
Braddell, Joseph, & Son Ltd 646
Bradley & Co Ltd 67
Bradley, John, & Co (Stourbridge) Ltd 68
Bradley & Turner Ltd 69
Braithwaite, Isaac, & Son Engineers Ltd 647
Bramah & Co 1127
Bramall, Henry, & Sons 70
Bramham & Henderson 626
Bramley Engineering Co Ltd 648
Brampton Brothers Ltd 71
Brandauer, C, & Co Ltd 72
Brass Battery Wire & Copper Co 73
Bray, George, & Co Ltd 74

Brett's Stamping Co Ltd 75
Bridge Iron Foundry 76
Bridgeness Iron Works 77
Brigham & Cowan Ltd 649
Brimsdown Lead Co Ltd 78
Bristol Aeroplane Co Ltd 650
British Electric Car Co Ltd 1070
British Electric Plant Co Ltd 1179
British Insulated & Helsby Cables Ltd 1180
British Insulated Wire Co Ltd 1181
British Machine Co Ltd 768
British Machine Made Cable Co Ltd 79
British Mannesman Tube Co Ltd 80
British Pens Ltd 81
British Piston Ring Co Ltd 651
British Screw Co Ltd 82
British Structural Steel Co Ltd 83
British Thomson-Houston Co Ltd 1182
British Vacuum Cleaner & Engineering Co 1183
British Welding Co Ltd 84
British Westinghouse Electric & Manufacturing Co Ltd 1184
Brittain, SS, & Co 85
Broadbent, TW, Ltd 1185
Bromley & Darbyshire 1101
Brookfield Foundry Co 86
Broughton Copper Co Ltd 87
Brown, Archibald, & Co Ltd 88
Brown Bayley's Steel Works Ltd 89
Brown Brothers & Co Ltd 652
Brown, David 653
Brown & Englefield 90
Brown, George, & Co (Marine) Ltd 654
Brown, John, & Co Ltd 91, 655
Brown, Lenox & Co Ltd 92
Brownlie & Murray Ltd 656
Brush Electrical Engineering Co Ltd 1186
Brymbo Steel Co Ltd 93
Bryn Works Ltd 94
Buck & Hickman Ltd 657
Buckley, Samuel, & Co Ltd 658
Bullivant & Co Ltd 95
Bullock, William, & Co 96
Bullows, Alfred, & Sons Ltd 97
Burgon & Ball Ltd 98
Burman & Sons Ltd 659
Burnell & Co Ltd 99
Burys & Co Ltd 100
Butler, Spragg & Co Ltd 101
Butlin, Thomas, & Co Ltd 102
Butterley Co Ltd 660
Butters Brothers & Co Ltd 661
Byass, Robert B, & Co Ltd 23

Caerleon Tin Plate Works 103
Caird, David, Ltd 104
Calder Iron Co 105
Calder Ironworks 106
Caledon Shipbuilding & Engineering Co Ltd 662
Callender's Cable & Construction Co Ltd 1187
Cambridge Instrument Co Ltd 1128
Cameron & Roberton Ltd 107
Cammell Laird & Co Ltd 663
Campbell & Calderwood Ltd 884
Campbell & Isherwood Ltd 1188
Campbeltown Shipbuilding Co Ltd 664

Galton, Samuel 758
Gardiner, Sons & Co Ltd 211
Gardner, L, & Sons Ltd 759
Garnock, Bibby & Co Ltd 212
Garrard & Co Ltd 213
Garrett, Richard, Engineering Ltd 760
Garton & King Ltd 214
Gas Meter Co Ltd 1144
Gateside Mills Co Ltd 761
Gee, R, & Son 156
General Electric Co Ltd 1195
Gentle, Alfred J 762
Gibbins, RC, & Co 763
Gibbons family 215
Gibbons, James, Ltd 216
Gibbs, George, Ltd 764
Gibson Brothers 217
Gilbertson, William, & Co Ltd 218
Gilkes, Gilbert, & Gordon, Ltd 765
Gillett & Johnston Ltd 219
Gimson & Co (Leicester) Ltd 766
Glaholm & Robson Ltd 220
Glasgow Railway Engineering Co Ltd 767
Gledhill, GH, & Sons Ltd 768
Glenbuck Iron Works 221
Glenfield & Kennedy Ltd 769
Globe Electric Co Ltd 1196
Gloucester Railway Carriage & Wagon Co Ltd 770
Glover, WT, & Co Ltd 1197
Glynbeudy Tinplate Co Ltd 222
Goldenhill Cobalt Co 223
Goodfellow, B 771
Goodman, George, Ltd 224
Goodwin Barsby & Co Ltd 772
Gorrie, David, & Son 773
Gosling & Gatenbury Ltd 774
Gould, William 253
Gourlay Brothers & Co (Dundee) Ltd 775
Grafton Cranes Ltd 776
Grahamston Iron Co Ltd 225
Gramophone Co Ltd 1198
Grangemouth Dockyard Co Ltd 777
Grant, Lewis C, Ltd 714
Grapho Ltd 81
Gray, James, & Son Ltd 226
Gray, Joseph, & Son 1145
Gray, William, & Co Ltd 778
Grazebrook, M & W, Ltd 779
Green, R & H, & Silley Weir Ltd 780
Green, Thomas, & Son Ltd 781
Green's Patent Tube Co Ltd 227
Greener, WW, Ltd 782
Greenwell, TW, & Co Ltd 783
Greenwood & Batley Ltd 784
Greenwood, JT, & Sons 785
Grenfell, Pascoe, & Sons 228
Grice, Grice & Son Ltd 229
Griffiths, Wilfred C 155
Grimmer, AE, & Co 745
Grindrod, Alfred, & Co Ltd 786
Grose Ltd 787
Groveland Iron Works 230
Grover & Co Ltd 788
Grovesend Steel & Tinplate Co Ltd 231
Guest & Chrimes 232
Guest, Keen & Nettlefolds Ltd 233

Guest, Whitehouse & Wilkinson 234

Habershon, JJ, & Sons Ltd 235
Haden, GN, & Sons Ltd 789
Hadfields Ltd 236
Hadley Engineering Co Ltd 449
Haggie, R Hood, & Son Ltd 237
Haigh, John, & Sons Ltd 790
Hall, Alexander, & Co Ltd 791
Hall, J & E, Ltd 1199
Hall, Robert, & Sons (Bury) Ltd 792
Hall, Russell & Co Ltd 793
Hallamshire Steel & File Co Ltd 238
Halls Patent Anchor Co Ltd 239
Halsted, CT 240
Hamilton & Purvis 241
Hamilton, William, & Co Ltd 794
Hammond, James 795
Hampton Loade Ironworks 242
Hamshaw, HA, Ltd 796
Hanson, Dale & Co Ltd 243
Harding (Leeds) Ltd 797
Hardman, John, & Co Ltd 244
Hardy & Padmore Ltd 245
Harland Engineering Co Ltd 1179
Harland & Wolff Ltd 798
Harper, John, & Co Ltd 246
Harrington Iron & Coal Co Ltd 247
Harrison, Ainslie & Co Ltd 248
Harrison, McGregor & Guest Ltd 799
Harrison, William, & Sons (Falkirk) Ltd 249
Harts Hill Iron Co Ltd 250
Harvey & Co Ltd 800
Harvey Engineering Co Ltd 801
Harvey, Matthew, & Co Ltd 251
Haslam Foundry & Engineering Co Ltd 1200
Hastie, John, & Co Ltd 802
Hathorn, Davey & Co Ltd 803
Hattersley, George, & Sons Ltd 804
Hawthorn, R & W, Leslie & Co Ltd 805
Hayward-Tyler & Co Ltd 806
Head, Wrightson & Co Ltd 807
Heap, Joshua, & Co Ltd 808
Heaton, Ralph, & Sons 252
Hedges & Son 809
Hemming, Richard, & Son 253
Henderson, David & William, & Co Ltd 810
Henley's, WT, Telegraph Works Co Ltd 1201
Herbert, Alfred, Ltd 811
Hetherington, John, & Sons Ltd 812
Hewetson, Robert 254
Hexham Foundry 255
Heywood & Porteous Ltd 256
Hibbert, Joseph, & Co Ltd 813
Hick Hargreaves & Co Ltd 814
Hickman, Alfred, Ltd 257
Higgins, Francis 258
Hilger, Adam, Ltd 1146
Hill, Charles, & Sons Ltd 815
Hill family 259
Hill & Robinson 816
Hind, John, & Sons Ltd 817
Hingley, N, & Sons Ltd 260
Hirst, A, & Son Ltd 1202
Hoad & Sons 818
Hobbs Hart & Co Ltd 1147

Hodgson, George, Ltd 819
Hoffmann Manufacturing Co Ltd 820
Holcroft, Thomas, & Sons Ltd 261
Holden & Brooke Ltd 821
Holland & Holland Ltd 822
Holland House Electrical Co Ltd 1203
Holman Bros Ltd 823
Holmes, Thomas, & John Pyke 824
Holmes, WC, & Co Ltd 825
Holroyd, John, & Co Ltd 826
Holtzapffel & Co 827
Homfray, Jeremiah, & Co 262
Hooper & Co (Coachbuilders) Ltd 828
Hope, Henry, & Sons Ltd 263
Hopper, F, & Co Ltd 729
Hopper, John I, Ltd 264
Hornsby, Richard, & Sons Ltd 829
Horrax (Ambleside) Ltd 1043
Horsehay Co Ltd 265
Horseley Bridge & Engineering Co Ltd 830
Hoskins & Sewell Ltd 266
Howard & Bullough Ltd 831
Howard, Henry, & Co 316
Hoyland, J 267
Hudson, Thomas, Ltd 832
Hudswell Clarke & Co Ltd 833
Hughes-Stubbs Metal Co Ltd 195
Humber Graving Dock & Engineering Co Ltd 834
Humber Ltd 835
Hume, William, & Co 268
Humphries, Edward, Ltd 836
Hunslet Engine Co Ltd 837
Hunt & Pickering 1074
Hunt, R, & Co Ltd 838
Hunt, William, & Sons, Brades, Ltd 269
Hunts 839
Huntsman, B, Ltd 270
Hutchinson, Hollingworth & Co Ltd 840
Hutton, T & J, & Co Ltd 271
Hutton, William, & Sons Ltd 272
Hydraulic Engineering Co Ltd 841

Ibbotson Bros & Co Ltd 273
Ibis Engineers Ltd 647
Illidge & Sons 274
Imperial Typewriter Co Ltd 842
India Rubber, Gutta Percha & Telegraph Works Co Ltd 1204
Inglis, A & J, Ltd 843
Inshaw Seamless Iron & Steel Tubes Ltd 275
International Harvester Co of Great Britain Ltd 844
Inverness Foundry Co 276
Islip Iron Co Ltd 277

Jackson & Brother Ltd 845
Jackson, Elphick & Co Ltd 278
Jackson, W & T, & Co Ltd 279
Jahncke Ltd 280
Jaquin, GJ 281
Jeffery, WJ, & Co Ltd 846
Jenks Brothers Ltd 282
Johnson, Christopher, (Cutlers) Ltd 283
Johnson, Thomas, & Co 284
Johnson, WW & R, & Sons 318
Johnsons of Hendon Ltd 285
Joice, J, & Son 847

Jointless Rim Ltd 848
Jones, Burton & Co Ltd 1205
Jones, Burton Parry & Kyrke 286
Jones, Evan, & Son 849
Jones & Lloyd Ltd 287
Jones & Willis Ltd 288
Jopling, E, & Sons Ltd 289
Jordan, JA, & Sons Ltd 424
Jowett, John 290

Kay & Backhouse Ltd 850
Kearns, HW, & Co Ltd 851
Keats & Bexon Ltd 852
Kelly, Robert, & Sons Ltd 291
Kelvin & James White Ltd 1148
Kennedy, H, & Sons 292
Kennedy's Patent Water Meter Co Ltd 769
Kenrick, Archibald, & Sons Ltd 293
Kenyon, John, & Co 294
Kerr, Stuart, & Co Ltd 853
Keswick School of Industrial Arts 295
Kettering Iron & Coal Co Ltd 296
Kilner, Joseph, & Son 854
Kincaid, John G, & Co Ltd 855
King & Co Ltd 1206
King, HJH, & Co Ltd 856
Kings Norton Metal Co Ltd 297
Kingsmead Motor Co Ltd 754
Kirkstall Forge Ltd 298
Kirkwood, Alexander, & Son 299
Kitching, Alfred 1096
Knight family 300
Knowles, John, (Wednesbury) Ltd 301
Kullberg, Victor 1149
Kynoch Ltd 302

Lack, Charles, & Sons Ltd 857
Laing, Sir James, & Sons Ltd 858
Lake & Elliot Ltd 303
Lamberton & Co Ltd 859
Lanarkshire Steel Co Ltd 304
Lancashire Watch Co 1150
Lanceleys Ltd 860
Lane, Charles, & Sons Ltd 305
Lane, JJ, Ltd 861
Lang, John, & Sons Ltd 862
Lanston Monotype Corporation Ltd 863
Latch & Batchelor Ltd 547
Laurence, Scott & Co Ltd 1207
Lawrence, Thomas, & Co Ltd 238
Leach, Flower & Co 345
Leclere & Bray 306
Lees, Asa, & Co Ltd 864
Lees, H, & Sons Ltd 307
Leng, Alfred 865
Lewis, Samuel, & Co Ltd 308
Leys Iron Works 309
Lilleshall Co Ltd 866
Lincoln File, Steel & Cutlery Co Ltd 310
Linkleters Patent Ship Fittings Co Ltd 867
Lion Foundry Co Ltd 311
Lister, RA, & Co Ltd 868
Lister & Wright Ltd 312
Lithgows Ltd 869
Llandovery Weighing Machine Co 870
Llanelly Copper Smelting Co 313

Tyzack, Samuel, & Co Ltd 526

Union Iron Co 527
United Electric Car Co Ltd 1070
United Wire Ltd 528
Ure, George, & Co Ltd 529
Urquhart, Lindsay & Co Ltd 1071

Vacher, Herbert P 1072
Vale family 530
Vessey, John, & Sons Ltd 531
Vickers Ltd 1073
Victoria Tube Co Ltd 532
Villiers Tin Plate Co Ltd 345
Vipan & Headly 1074
Vivian & Sons 533
Vulcan Foundry Ltd 1075
Vulliamy & Son 1170

Waddle Patent Fan & Engineering Co Ltd 1076
Wadsworth, J, & Son Ltd 1077
Wadsworth, William, & Sons Ltd 1078
Waghorne & Miles 1079
Wailes, George, & Co Ltd 1080
Waine, John, & Sons 534
Waite, John Newman 535
Waldron, TN, Ltd 536
Walker Brothers Ltd 537
Walker Brothers (Wigan) Ltd 1081
Walker, C & W, Ltd 1082
Walker & Hall 538
Walker, Samuel, & Co 539
Walker & Smith (Batley) Ltd 1083
Walker, Thomas, & Son Ltd 1171
Walkers, Parker & Co Ltd 540
Wallis & Longden 1084
Wallis & Stevens Ltd 1085
Wallsend Slipway & Engineering Co Ltd 1086
Walmsley, Thomas, & Sons Ltd 541
Walsall Locks & Cart Gear Ltd 1172
Walton, John, & Co 542
Wantage Engineering Co Ltd 1087
Ward, Thos W, Ltd 1088
Wardrobe & Smith Ltd 543
Warner & Co Ltd 544
Wassell's, John, Union Engine Factory 816
Waste Water Meter Co Ltd 1156
Watson & Bradbury 66
Watson, William 1089
Watt, James, & Co 643
Waverley Iron & Steel Co Ltd 545
Webley & Scott Ltd 1090
Webster & Bennett Ltd 1091
Webster & Co Ltd 546
Webster & Horsfall Ltd 547
Weeks, William, & Son Ltd 1092
Weir, G & J, Ltd 1093
Weiss, John, & Son 1173
Wellfield Galvanising Co Ltd 231
Wellington Tube Works Ltd 548
Welsh Cycle Co Ltd 849
West End Engine Works Co 1094
West, HJ, & Co (1908) Ltd 1199
Western Wagon & Property Co Ltd 1095
Westinghouse Brake & Signal Co Ltd 1229
Westinghouse Electric Co Ltd 1184

Wheatley, WT, Bros 371
Whessoe Foundry Co Ltd 1096
White, Henry, & Co Ltd 549
White, John, & Son 1097
White, J Samuel, & Co Ltd 1098
White, TH, Ltd 1099
White, Thomas, & Sons Ltd 1100
Whitechapel Bell Foundry 343
Whitecross Co Ltd 550
Whitehaven Hematite Iron & Steel Co Ltd 551
Whitehead & Haynes 552
Whitehouse family 553
Whitfields' Safe & Door Co Ltd 1152
Whitford Steel Sheet & Galvanising Co Ltd 231
Whittaker, C, & Co Ltd 1101
Whitworth, Sir Joseph, & Co Ltd 1102
Wick Iron Co 554
Wickman Lang Ltd 862
Wigan Coal & Iron Co Ltd 555
Wigg, WE, & Son 1103
Wigrams & Green 1104
Wilder, John, Ltd 1105
Wilkes, Ernest, Ltd 556
Wilkes, Samuel, & Sons Ltd 1174
Wilkinson, Joshua 557
Wilkinson Sword Co Ltd 558
Willenhall Furnaces Ltd 559
Williams, Edward 560
Williams, Harvey & Co Ltd 561
Williams, John, (Wishaw) Ltd 562
Wilmot, WH, Ltd 563
Wilson family 564
Wilson & Longbottom Ltd 1106
Wilson & Southern 485
Winfields Rolling Mills Ltd 565
Winkles, T, & Co 566
Winter & Co 567
Wireless Telegraph & Signal Co Ltd 1211
Witham, Stephen 568
Wolverhampton Corrugated Iron Co Ltd 569
Wood Brothers 1107
Wood, John & Edward 1108
Wood, John, & Sons Ltd 1109
Woodall, Isaiah, & Sons Ltd 570
Woodall Nicholson Ltd 1110
Woodhouse & Co 571
Wooton Bros Ltd 1111
Workington Foundry 572
Workington Iron & Steel Co Ltd 573
Worrall, Hallam & Co 574
Worsley Mesnes Ironworks Ltd 575
Worthington-Simpson Ltd 1112
Wostenholm, George, & Son Ltd 576
Wright, George, (Rotherham) Ltd 577
Wright, Joseph, & Co Ltd 578
Wrights' Ropes Ltd 579

Yarrow & Co Ltd 1113
Yarwood, WJ, & Sons Ltd 1114
Yniscedwyn Iron, Steel & Coal Co Ltd 580
Yorkshire Engine Co Ltd 1115
Yorkshire Patent Steam Wagon Co 1116
Yorkshire Switchgear & Engineering Co Ltd 1230
Youle, J, & Co Ltd 581
Young, Daniel, Ltd 1117
Ystalyfera Iron Co 582

Gazetteer

Business locations given at the head of each entry in the guide are here grouped alphabetically under the pre-1974 counties, in accordance with the ninth edition of Bartholomew's *Gazetteer of the British Isles*. The references are to entry numbers.

ENGLAND

BEDFORDSHIRE
Ampthill 745
Bedford 776, 924
Dunstable 608
Luton 356, 806

BERKSHIRE
Bucklebury 809
Challow 919
Newbury 952
Reading 964
Wallingford 1105
Wantage 1087

CAMBRIDGESHIRE
Cambridge 757, 1128
Cottenham 857
Hildersham 429
Soham 839

CHESHIRE
Alderley Edge 702
Altrincham 879
Birkenhead 589, 663, 680
Bromborough 738
Chester 841, 860, 937
Dukinfield 584
Ellesmere Port 99, 569
Hyde 771
Macclesfield 327
Newton 584
Northwich 34, 1114
Runcorn 1061
Sandbach 746
Stockport 1065
Winsford 35

CORNWALL
Bissoe 47, 48
Camborne 689, 823
Charlestown 117
Falmouth 695, 736
Hayle 800
Penzance 56
Perranarworthal 412
Redruth 678
Truro 523
Wadebridge 385

CUMBERLAND
Carlisle 120, 692, 959
Cleator 125
Cleator Moor 551
Cockermouth 254
Harrington 20, 247
Keswick 295, 694
Millom 350
Penrith 8, 61
Whitehaven 744
Workington 363, 572, 573

DERBYSHIRE
Alfreton 384
Belper 1024
Butterley 660
Chesterfield 27, 185, 462, 479, 712, 894
Derby 150, 743, 989, 1003, 1200
Dronfield 322
Ilkeston 447
Langley Mill 414, 1066
Long Eaton 1084
Ridgeway 271
Staveley 491

DEVON
Brixham 709
Exeter 54, 214, 399

DORSET
Blandford 955
Weymouth 690

DURHAM
Barnard Castle 1028
Castleside 542
Consett 137
Darlington 163, 164, 676, 704, 1038, 1096
Felling 925
Gateshead 1, 152, 174, 329, 671, 880
Hartlepool 455
Hebburn 934, 978, 1038
Jarrow 934
Port Clarence 10
Seaham 453
Shields, South 649, 975, 1029, 1069
Stockton-on-Tees 62, 110, 183, 483
Sunderland 220, 289, 438, 526, 546, 590, 602, 621, 670, 699, 716, 783, 858, 928, 1015, 1059, 1190
Swalwell 423
West Hartlepool 778

DOWN
Ballyroney 25
Newry 886

LONDONDERRY
Coleraine 292

Printed in the United Kingdom for HMSO
Dd297906 9/94 C10 G3396 10170